MW01629028

How to

How to use gra
to sell things, e
make things lo
make people la
people cry, an
in a while) cha

Michael Bierut

phic design
plain things,
k better,
ugh, make
(every once
ge the world

Revised
and expanded
edition

Also published in the United Kingdom in 2015
and 2021 by Thames & Hudson Ltd.

Typeset in NeueHelvetica DOT
Used by special arrangement with Monotype and
the New York City Department of Transportation

Written and designed by Michael Bierut
Production management by Sonsoles Alvarez
with Chloe Scheffe
Production supervision by Julia Lindpaintner
Design supervision by Hamish Smyth
Editorial consulting by Andrea Monfried
Copy editing by Rebecca McNamara

Revised and expanded edition
Production management by Lauren Fox
with Camila Pérez
Design supervision by Britt Cobb
Copy editing by Rebecca McNamara

First published in the United States in 2021 by
Harper Design
An Imprint of HarperCollins*Publishers*

195 Broadway
New York, NY 10007
Tel: (212) 207-7000
Fax: (855) 746-6023
harperdesign@harpercollins.com
www.hc.com

Distributed throughout North America by
HarperCollins*Publishers*
195 Broadway
New York, NY 10007

ISBN 978-0-06-314157-5
Library of Congress number has been applied for.

Printed in China

First Printing, 2021

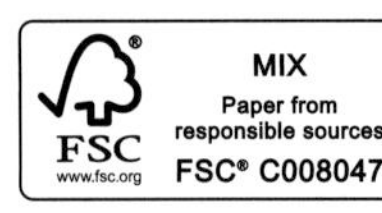

Contents

You harmonize, then you customize.

Wilson Pickett

NORMANDY HIGH SCHOOL

WAIT UNTIL DARK

FRI. & SAT: NOV. 17 & 18, 1972

$1.00
8:00 PM

How to be a graphic designer in the middle of nowhere
An introduction

Opposite
My first mass-produced piece of graphic design was a poster for our high school production of *Wait Until Dark*, a tense drama about a blind woman threatened by a criminal gang (hence the eyes). I can still remember the thrill of seeing it hanging in every hallway of my high school.

As far back as I can remember, I always wanted to be a graphic designer.

I must have been no more than five or six years old. I was in the car with my father on a Saturday on my way to get a haircut. We were stopped at a light, and my dad pointed at a forklift truck parked in a nearby lot. "Isn't that neat?" he asked. What, I said. "Look at the way they wrote 'Clark.'" Clark was the logo on the side of the truck. I didn't get it. "See how the letter L is lifting up the letter A?" explained my father. "It's doing what the truck does."

It was as if an amazing secret had been revealed, right there in plain sight. I was dumbfounded and thrilled. How long had this been going on? Were these small miracles hidden all over the place? And who was responsible for creating them?

I was in the first grade at St. Theresa's School in Garfield Heights, Ohio, when my teachers first noticed that I was good at drawing. This was no small thing. I was a good student, but among my peers in 1960s suburban Cleveland, academic diligence was viewed with suspicion, if not outright contempt. Artistic ability, on the other hand, was like a kind of magic. Inept at sports and generally withdrawn, I suddenly had a way to distinguish myself in the schoolyard. The nuns called it a "God-given talent," and I milked it for all it was worth. Luckily, I received nothing but encouragement from my parents. They bought me a succession of ever-more esoteric implements (charcoal sticks! pastels! kneaded erasers!) and signed me up for Saturday morning art classes at one of the world's great cultural institutions, the Cleveland Museum of Art. By the time I reached junior high school, I could render anything realistically. Everyone assumed I would be an artist when I grew up.

Art was something I used to make friends (and, occasionally, to keep from getting beaten up). At the request of one of the school's more frightening bullies, I painstakingly replicated the Budweiser logo on the cover of his civics notebook. Having acquired a Speedball pen set and having mastered a convincing Fraktur, I generated heavy metal insignia upon request.

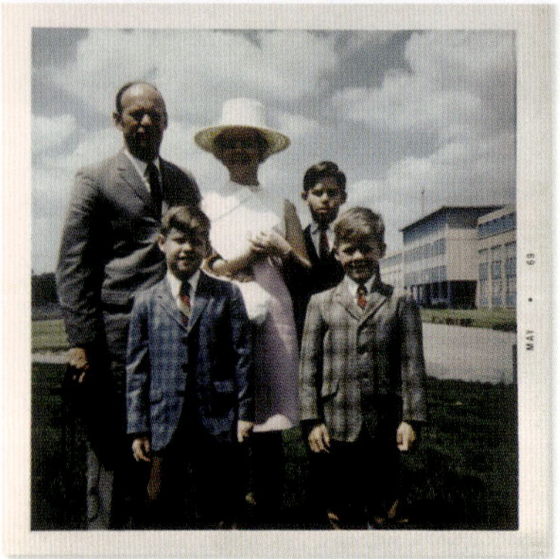

Above
Easter Sunday, 1969, in Parma, Ohio. I'm standing with my parents, Leonard and Anne Marie, and behind my twin brothers, Ronald and Donald.

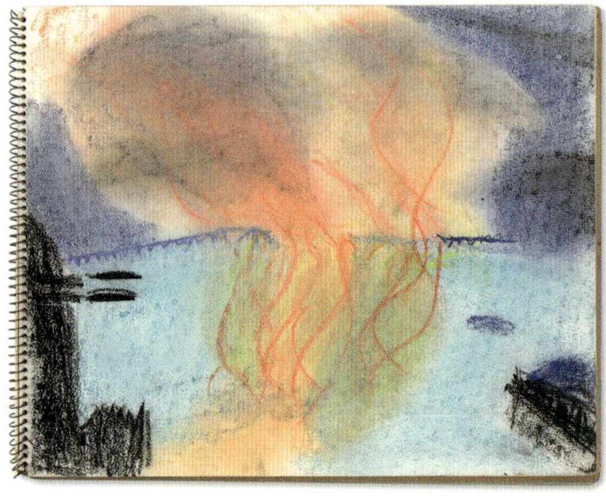

Above
My parents enrolled me in Saturday morning art classes at the Cleveland Museum of Art. Here is my rendition of a masterpiece in their collection, J. M. W. Turner's *The Burning of the Houses of Lords and Commons*. I was seven years old.

A turning point came in the ninth grade when I was asked to do a poster for the school play. I handed in the artwork on a Friday morning, it was printed that afternoon, and by Monday morning my poster was hanging all over the school. This was my first experience with the miracle of mass production. More people would see my poster than would see the play. I realized then I didn't want to settle for just doing a single painting to be stuck on the wall at someplace like the Cleveland Museum of Art. I wanted to create things with a purpose, things that people would see all over the place, things that were about something other than themselves. It was hard to explain.

I had no idea how posters and logos came into the world. I didn't know any working artists, and didn't know anyone else to ask. If pressed, I would have guessed that things like album covers were designed by real artists like Franz Kline and Robert Rauschenberg who had decided to take a day off and make some extra money. One day, I was in our school library, idly browsing the Career Resource Center. This was a grandiose name for what was no more than a shelf bearing a matched set of books called the Aim High Vocational Series. The titles included *Aim for a Job in Baking*, *Aim for a Job in the Dry Cleaning Industry*, and *Aim for a Job in Domestic Help Occupations*. One caught my eye: *Aim for a Job in Graphic Design/Art* by someone named S. Neil Fujita. I opened it and realized with a start that I was staring at my future.

Here were page after page of men and women who were doing what I wanted to do, with examples of work from ad man George Lois, magazine designer Ruth Ansel, and television art director Lou Dorfsman. I now realized this activity that fascinated me had a name: graphic design. Newly armed and wanting more, I went to my local public library and looked up those two words in the card catalog. There was exactly one book listed. It was *Graphic Design Manual: Principles and Practice* by Armin Hofmann.

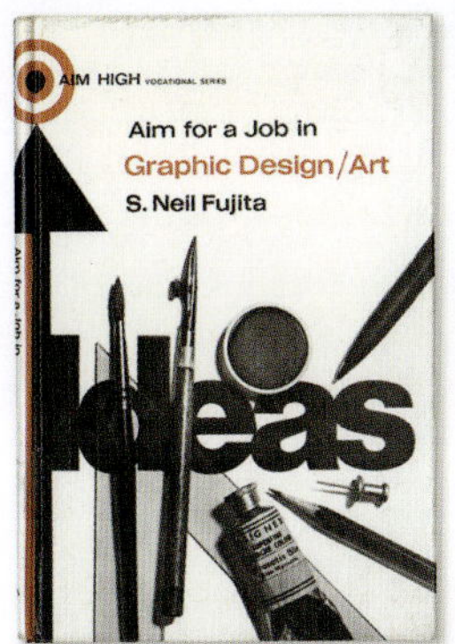

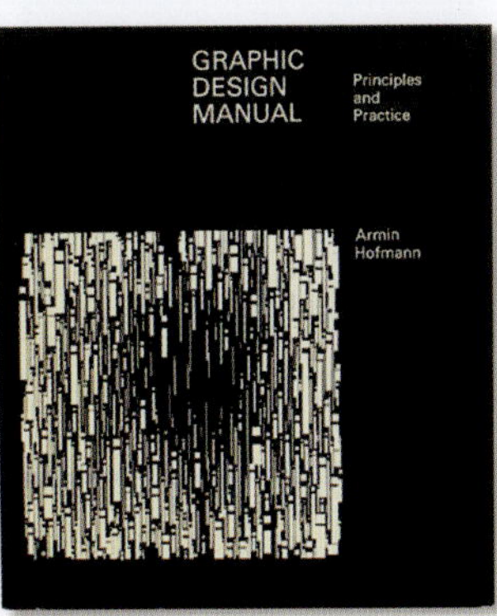

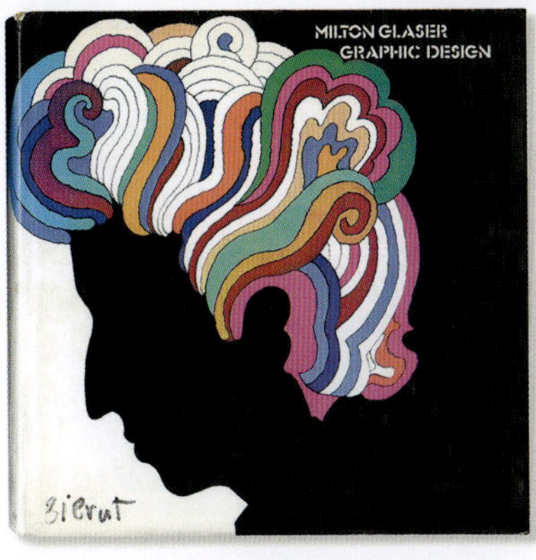

Above
These are the three books that changed my life: *Aim for a Job in Graphic Design/Art* by S. Neil Fujita, *Graphic Design Manual: Principles and Practice* by Armin Hofmann, and *Graphic Design* by Milton Glaser. Today, everyone knows Hofmann and Glaser, but Fujita is an unsung hero: he designed the Columbia Records logo and the cover of Mario Puzo's *The Godfather*.

Looking back, I am utterly mystified that this obscure book, a dry account of the coursework at the Kunstgewerbeschule in Basel, Switzerland, ended up on the shelves of a small suburban library in Parma, Ohio. At the time, I was electrified. From the black-and-white studies of dots and squares to the exercises involving the redesign of European lightbulb packages, I devoured it all. After checking it out repeatedly—as far as I knew, I was the only one who ever did—I told my parents that the only thing I wanted for Christmas was my very own copy.

My mother, God bless her, called every store in town, miraculously finding someone who had just gotten it in stock. I opened it on Christmas morning to discover my poor mother's mistake. She had accidentally bought me *Graphic Design* by Milton Glaser, 240 glorious pages of unfettered eclecticism from the cofounder of Push Pin Studios, without a trace of dogma in sight.

My career was set in motion by these three books: a pragmatic guide by an East Coast journeyman, a rigorous manifesto by a Swiss theoretician, and a dazzling tour de force by a brilliant virtuoso. I was barely 18 years old, and without ever having met a graphic designer in person, I knew what I wanted to do for the rest of my life.

Somehow, my high school guidance counselor found just the right college for me at the opposite end of the state, where the University of Cincinnati's College of Design, Architecture, and Art offered a five-year program in graphic design. There I was plunged into a milieu that owed more to the minimalism of the Swiss Kunstgewerbeschule and less to the vibrant worldview of Push Pin Studios. Submitting myself to a boot camp's worth of punishing visual exercises, I unlearned my bad habits and replaced them with the basics of design, typography, color, and layout. Imagination and energy may be innate traits, but precision and craftsmanship are skills that can only be mastered through hard practice. Our professors were determined that no one graduate without them. It was telling that the degree I received was a bachelor of science, for in Cincinnati I mastered a kind of design that was as logical, self-contained, and elegant as the laws of physics. It was later in New York that I would discover the power of passion.

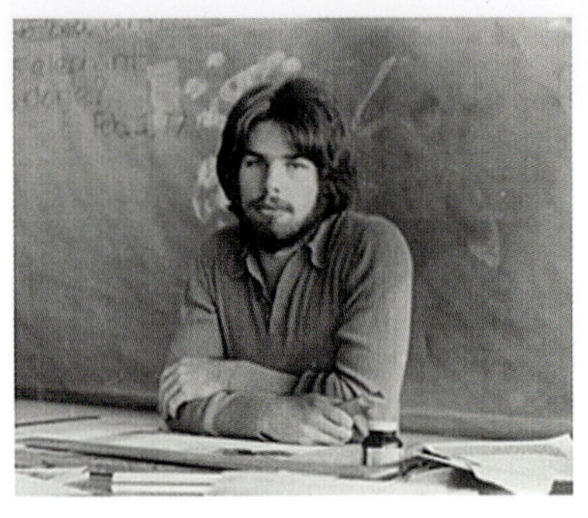

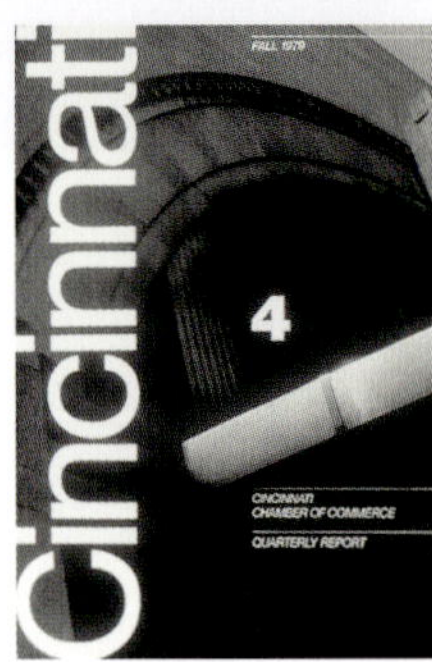

Above left
Here I am looking pensive in the studios at the University of Cincinnati's College of Design, Architecture, and Art, circa 1976.

Above right
By the time I left Cincinnati, I had mastered the use of Helvetica and modular grid systems. I was never any good at photography; I didn't tell my teachers that my girlfriend Dorothy actually took this picture. (I married Dorothy in 1980.)

In retrospect, it wasn't a surprise that Massimo Vignelli loved my portfolio: sans serif typefaces on every page, modular grids underpinning every layout. After all, this was the acclaimed designer who had introduced Helvetica to the United States, created a relentlessly geometric map for the New York subway system, and devised a system to ensure that every national park from Acadia to Yosemite would have a matching brochure. With his wife, Lella, Massimo ran a Manhattan office from which issued a mind-boggling stream of logos, posters, books, interiors, and products. In the summer of 1980, I married my high school sweetheart, Dorothy, and moved to New York to become Vignelli Associates' newest and most junior employee. I was in awe of Massimo and couldn't believe my luck. But I also knew that my new boss had a strong point of view, and that his designers worked within clearly prescribed aesthetic limits. My plan was to spend 18 months there and move on.

I ended up staying ten years. Despite the firm's reputation for modernist austerity, Lella and Massimo presided over a workplace of extraordinary warmth, filled with noise and laughter and varied, exciting projects. Design there was a sacred calling, and in joining the profession you were committing to a fight against stupidity and ugliness. The clients who came to us were enlisting in the same battle. It helped that I was a good, even compulsive, mimic. Having learned my earliest lessons about graphic design by copying from library books, I found it impossible not to imitate Massimo's unmistakable style. He came to trust me, and continued to encourage me even when my ideas began to diverge from his. After ten years, I was managing the firm's graphic design operations. But more and more I wondered: what kind of work would I do if I were on my own?

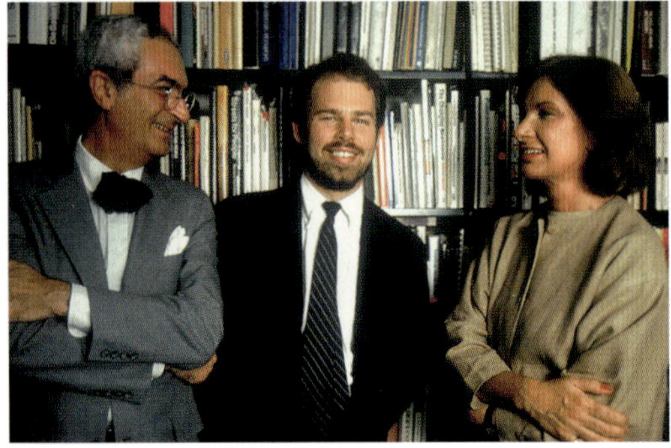

Above
I worked for Massimo and Lella Vignelli for ten years. They were my surrogate parents, and their studio was my adoptive family.

The answer came in the form of a dinner invitation from a colleague, Woody Pirtle. Woody was a partner in the New York office of a firm called Pentagram, legendary for its unique structure. Its partners worked in a hierarchy-free collective, each managing a small design team, each sharing the resources of an international organization.

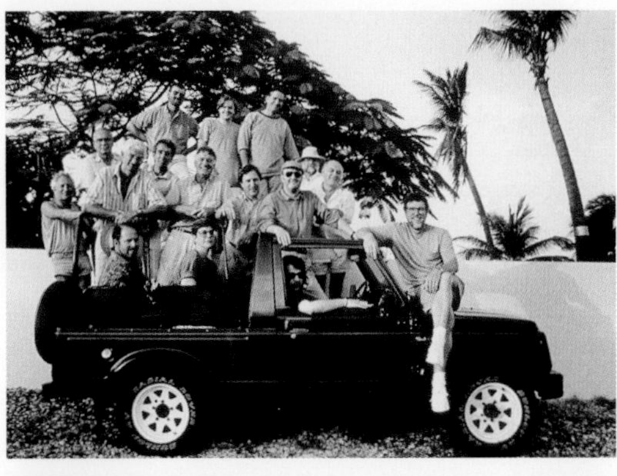

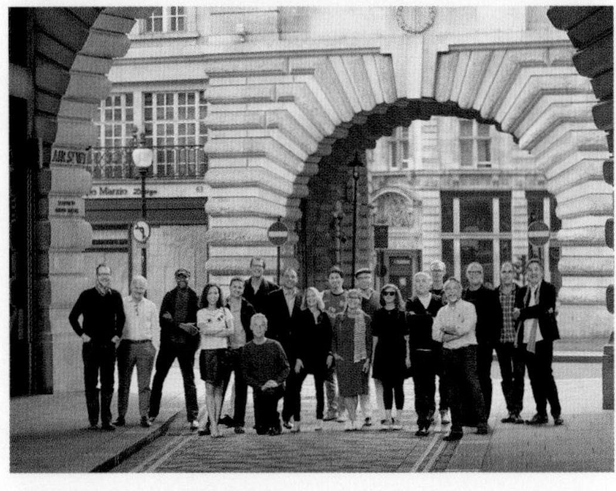

Top
A new family: my first international meeting in Antigua, 1990, as the newest partner in the firm's New York office. I'm seated in the back of the truck, surrounded by Mervyn Kurlansky, Colin Forbes, Theo Crosby, David Hillman, Neil Shakery, John Rushworth, Kenneth Grange, Linda Hinrichs, Etan Manasse, Woody Pirtle, John McConnell, Kit Hinrichs, Alan Fletcher, and Peter Harrison. Peter Saville is at the wheel.

Bottom
A more recent partners' meeting in London, 2014. From left to right: Abbott Miller, John Rushworth, Eddie Opara, Natasha Jen, Luke Hayman, Harry Pearce, Michael Gericke, Lorenzo Apicella, Paula Scher, Angus Hyland, Marina Willer, me, Emily Oberman, Domenic Lippa, William Russell, Daniel Weil, DJ Stout, Naresh Ramchandani, and Justus Oehler.

A casual conversation about my future turned into something else. Over coffee, he asked if I might be interested in becoming Pentagram's newest partner. His timing was perfect. I loved the bustle of a big office. The loneliness of a sole proprietorship held little appeal. Combining autonomy and community, Pentagram offered the best of both worlds. I thought about it overnight, talked it over with Dorothy, and said yes. In the fall of 1990, I started my second job.

My second job may be my last job. I've been at Pentagram for nearly 25 years. And, to a remarkable extent, I am doing exactly what I always wanted to do. I still recall the seismic jolt of seeing that forklift truck logo, or opening that book in my school library. What I couldn't figure out then was how people came to make these kinds of things. Where did the ideas come from? What happened between an idea and its realization? How could you tell if the ideas worked? How were people talked into accepting them? Was it magic? Or was there a limit to what graphic design could do? And, finally, how could I get to do it, too?

Since my first poster in the ninth grade, I've discovered that my questions have many possible answers. Although none of them are final, all of them are interesting. No one can tell you what to do. But once you decide, the real fun is figuring out how to do it.

How to think with your hands

Four decades of notebooks

On August 12, 1982, I opened up a standard 7½" by 9¾" composition book and began taking notes on a phone conversation. I forget where the book came from. I may have found it in the supply cabinet of Vignelli Associates, where I had been working for a little over two years.

This was the beginning of a habit—or a compulsion—that has continued to this day. I cannot walk into a meeting or start a phone call without my notebook. Other designers have amazing sketchbooks. Not me. A few pages look like they belong to a real designer: drawings, type studies, visual ideas being worked out. But most are filled with to-do lists, phone calls to be returned, budget calculations, meeting notes. In college, I discovered that writing down something helped me remember it later. Paradoxically, that means that a lot of these notes, taken once, are never referred to again.

Although I am (or I used to be) a good draughtsman, drawing may no longer be a relevant skill in the digital world. (Knowing how to read is more important than knowing how to draw.) But looking back through the years, I'm surprised by the occasional visual notes in these books, and how often they anticipated the design work to come. Often, in the midst of a dense list of bullet points, there will sit a quick diagram, an embryonic sketch that represented the first step of what would be months of work.

When the idea of a personal digital assistant was first described to me, I thought, oh, sort of like my notebook, except a computer. (It's no accident that the iPad is nearly the same size.) Like most designers, I'm dependent on my digital devices. But my notebook is still with me: diary, sketchbook, security blanket, friend. On August 26, 2013, 31 years after the first, I started notebook number 100. How I would love to fill 100 more.

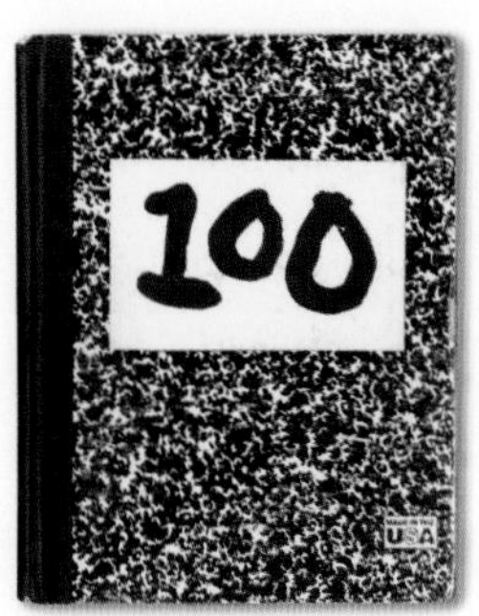

Opposite and above
For more than 30 years, I've seldom gone anywhere without a composition book. As a result, they take a beating.

Right
It took me a while to find my favorite notebook. Early ones have lined or gridded paper, which I came to dislike. Much of my time over the last few decades was consumed by a quest for notebooks with unlined pages. These pages from 1995 show the sketches for what would become our design for the Brooklyn Academy of Music's Next Wave Festival (see page 44).

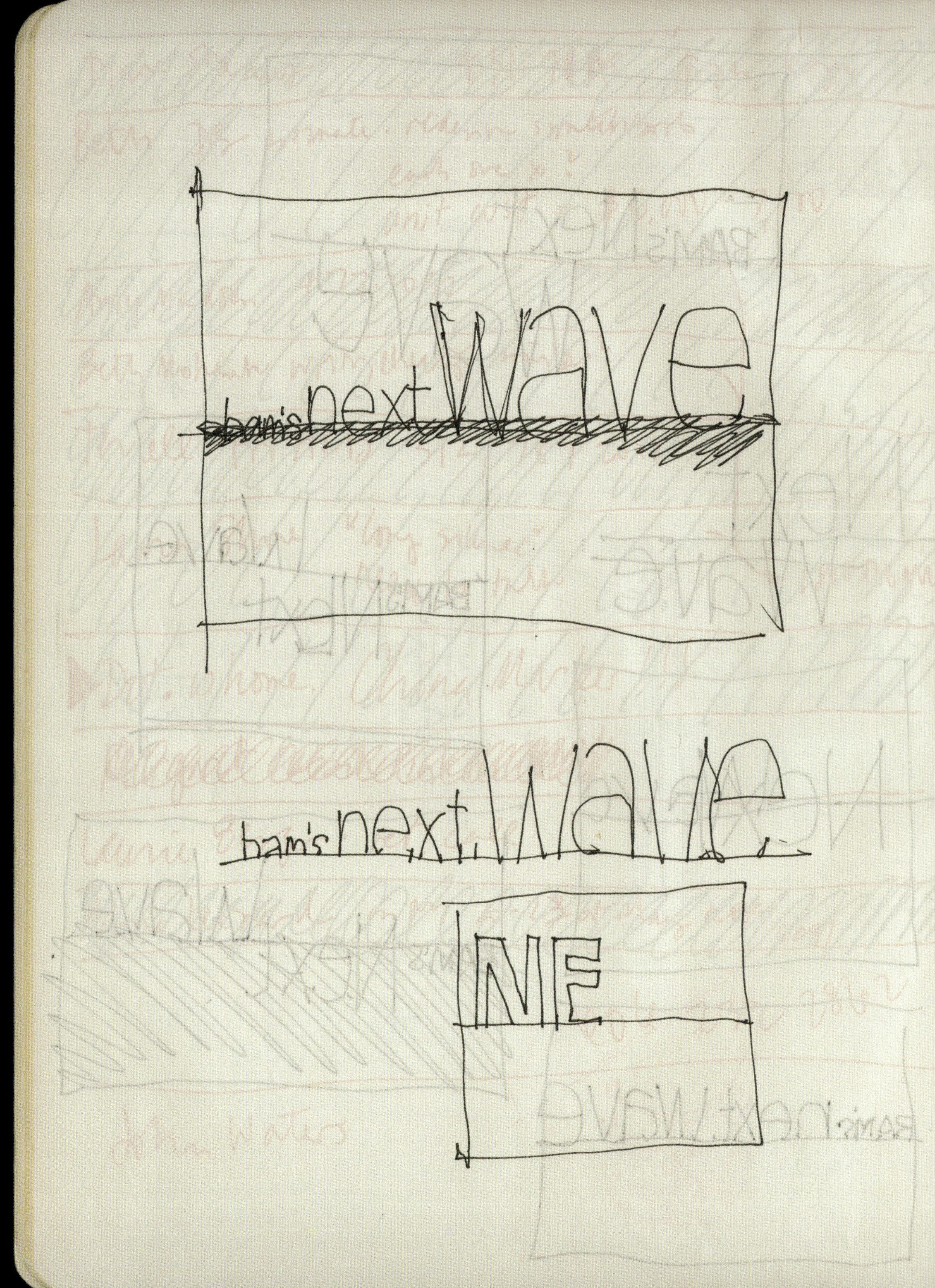

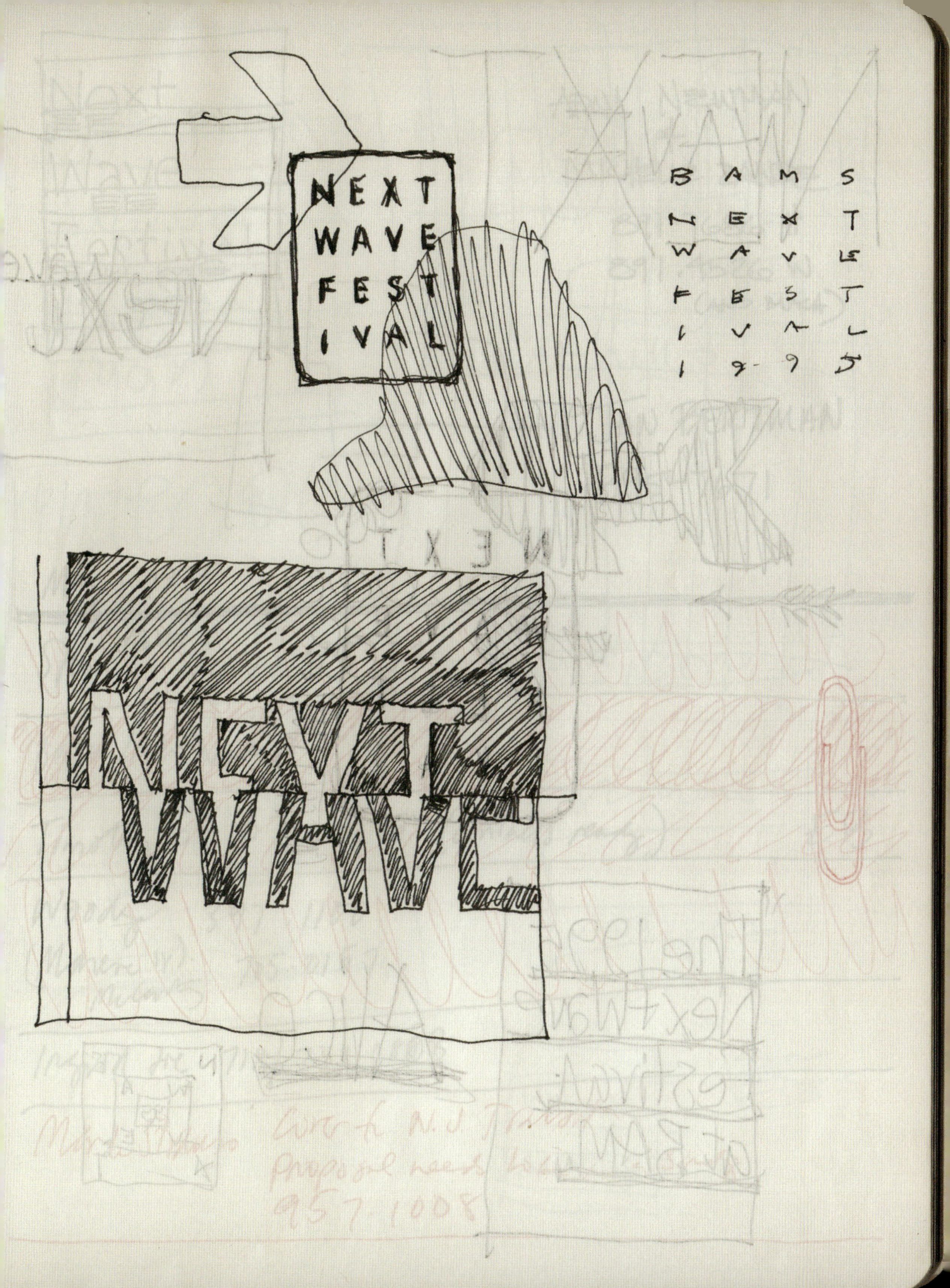
NEXT
WAVE
FEST
IVAL
B A M S
N E X T
W A V E
F E S T
I V A L
1 9 9 5
NEXT
WAVE

Right
Usually the pages are filled with meeting notes, phone numbers, and columns of numbers. In this case I must have been bored during a meeting. The final poster (see page 63) looked like none of these.

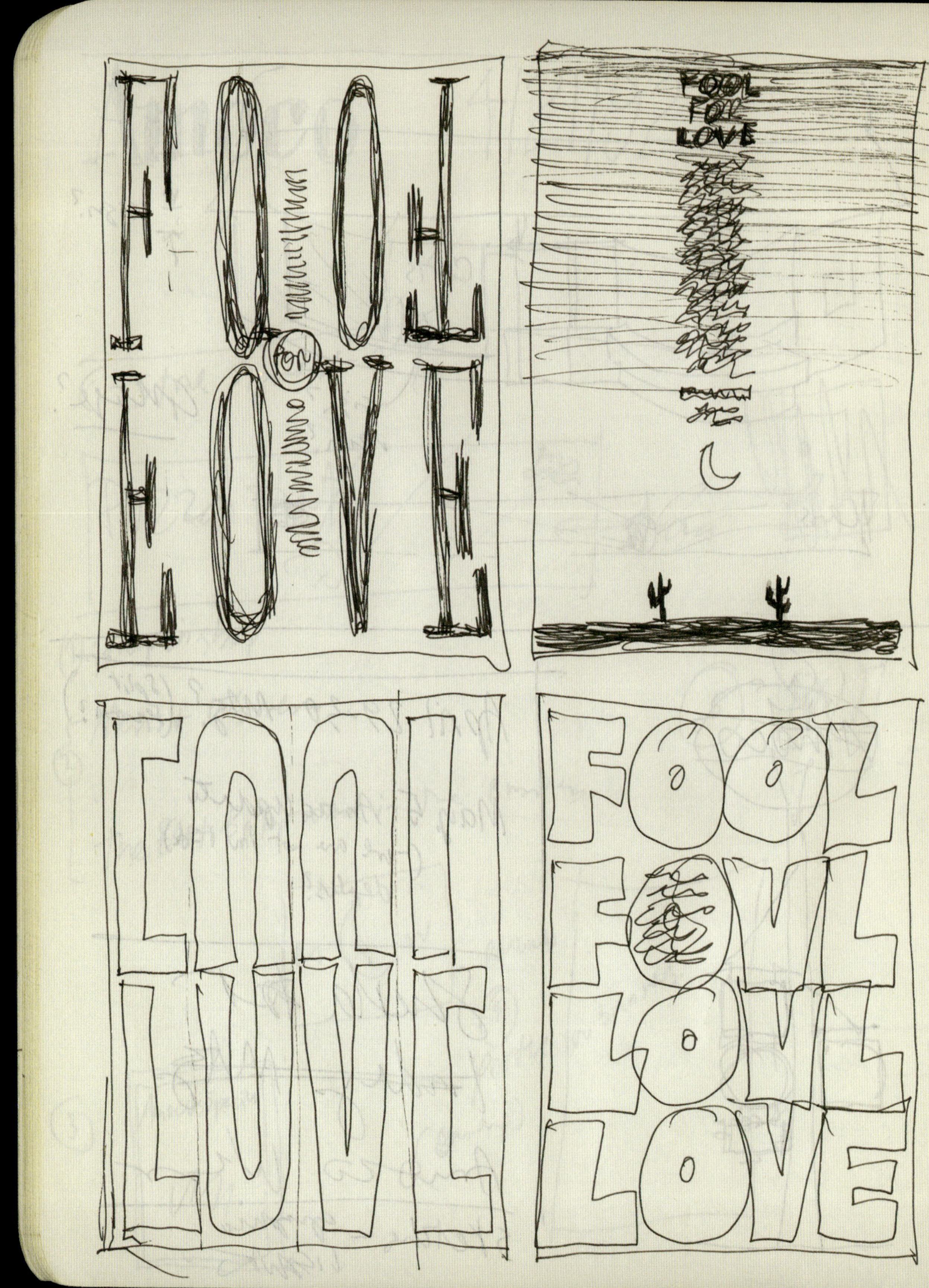

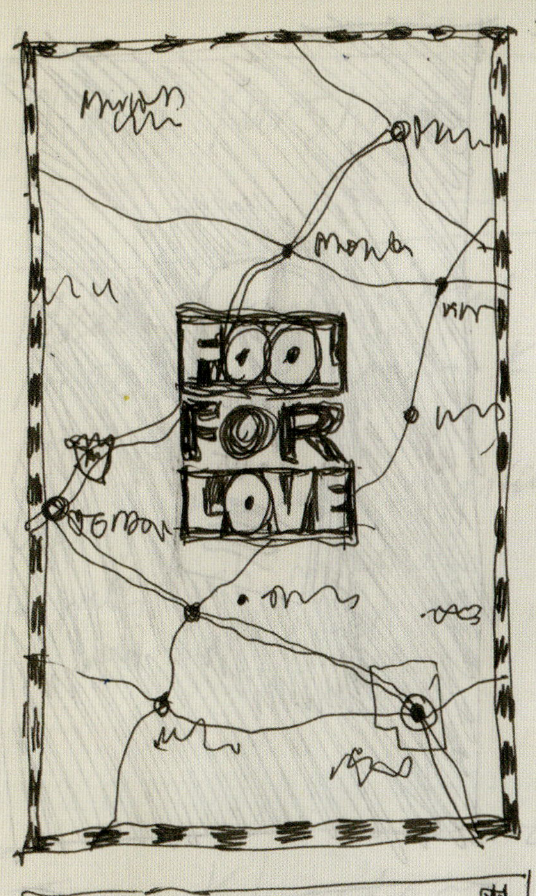
FOOL
FOR
LOVE

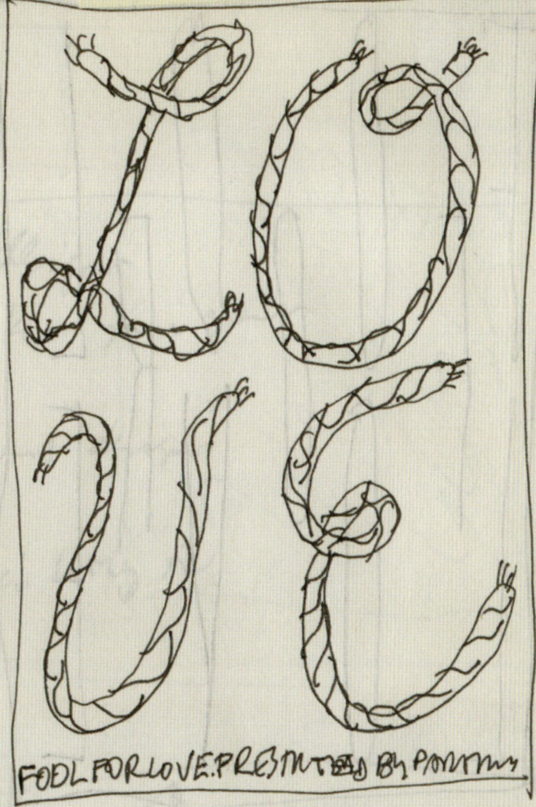
LO
VE

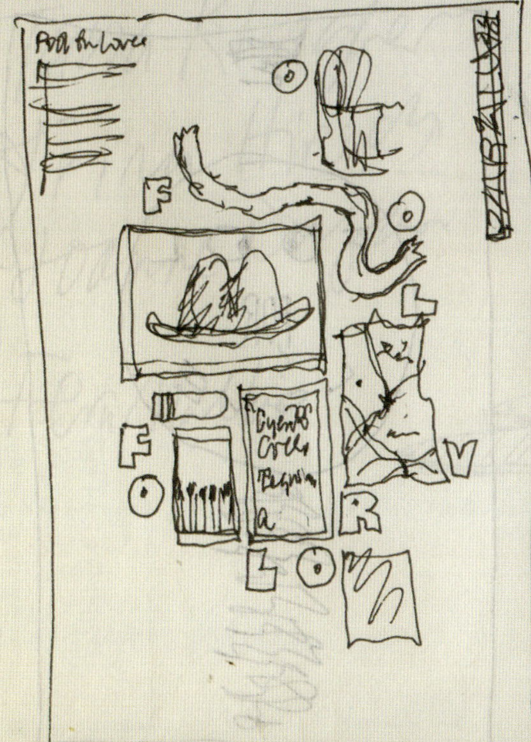
Fool for Love

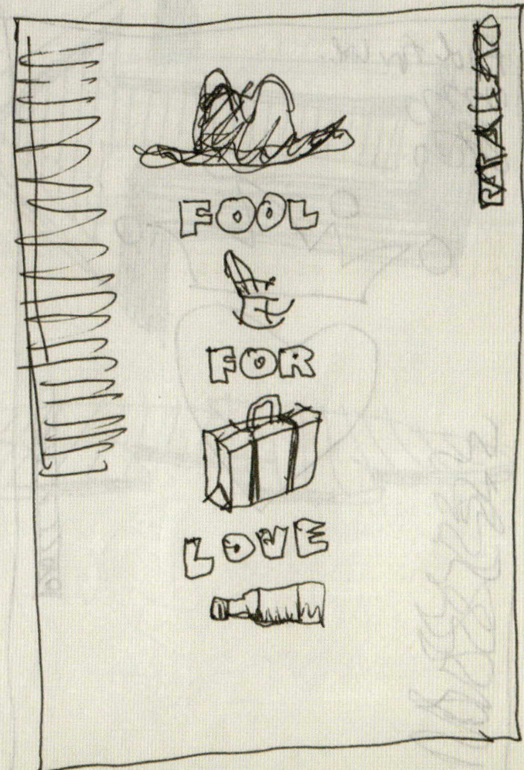
FOOL
FOR
LOVE

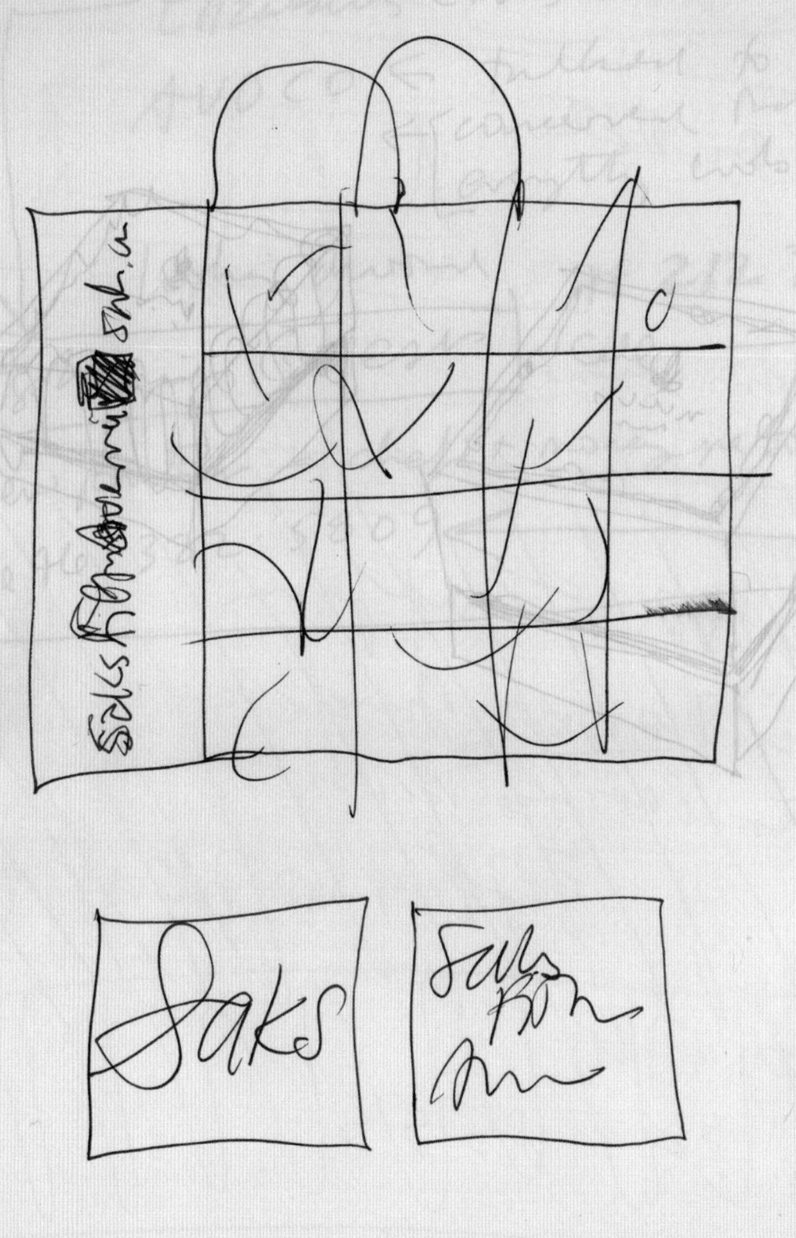
Saks

Saks Fifth Avenue

Right
Sometimes a detailed sketch is enough to get an idea out of my system. For this poster for a Yale symposium on the architect Charles Moore, we went with the simpler approach (see page 144, bottom left).

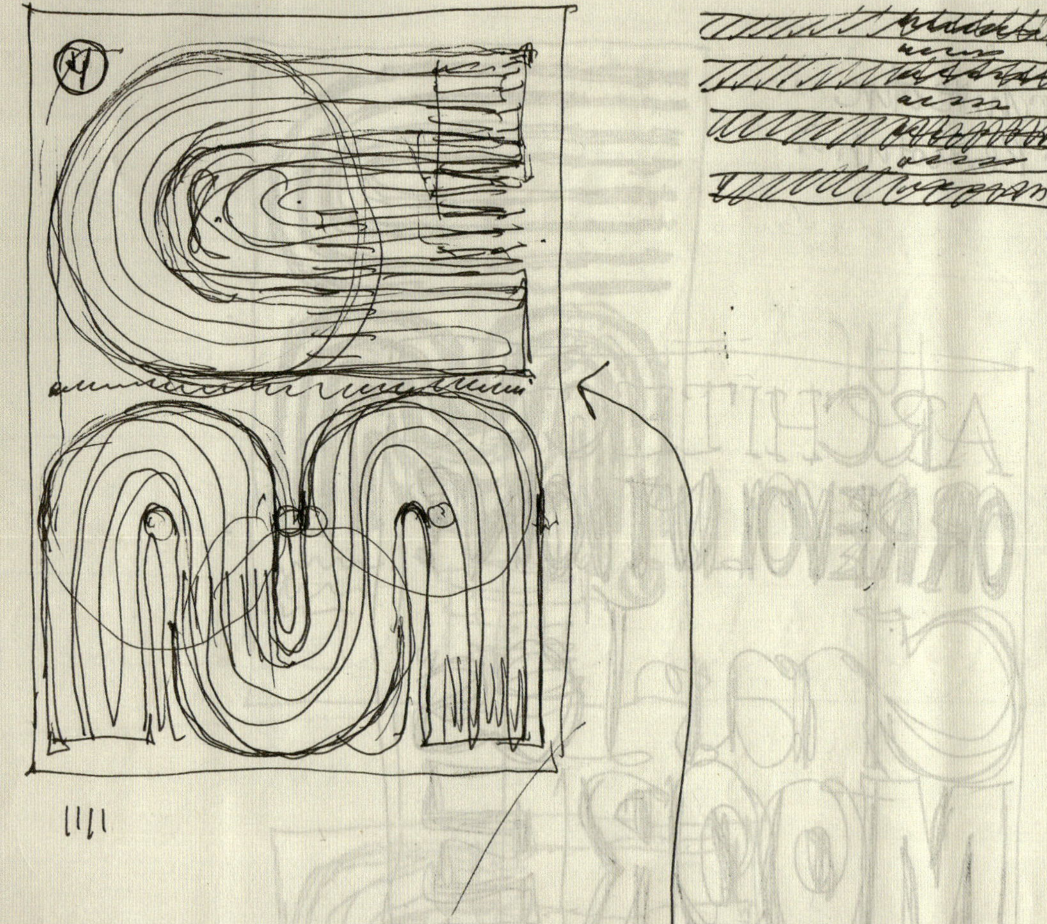

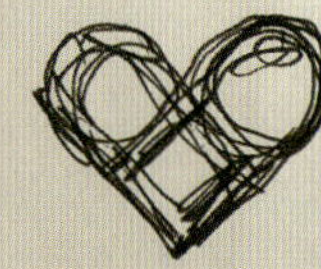

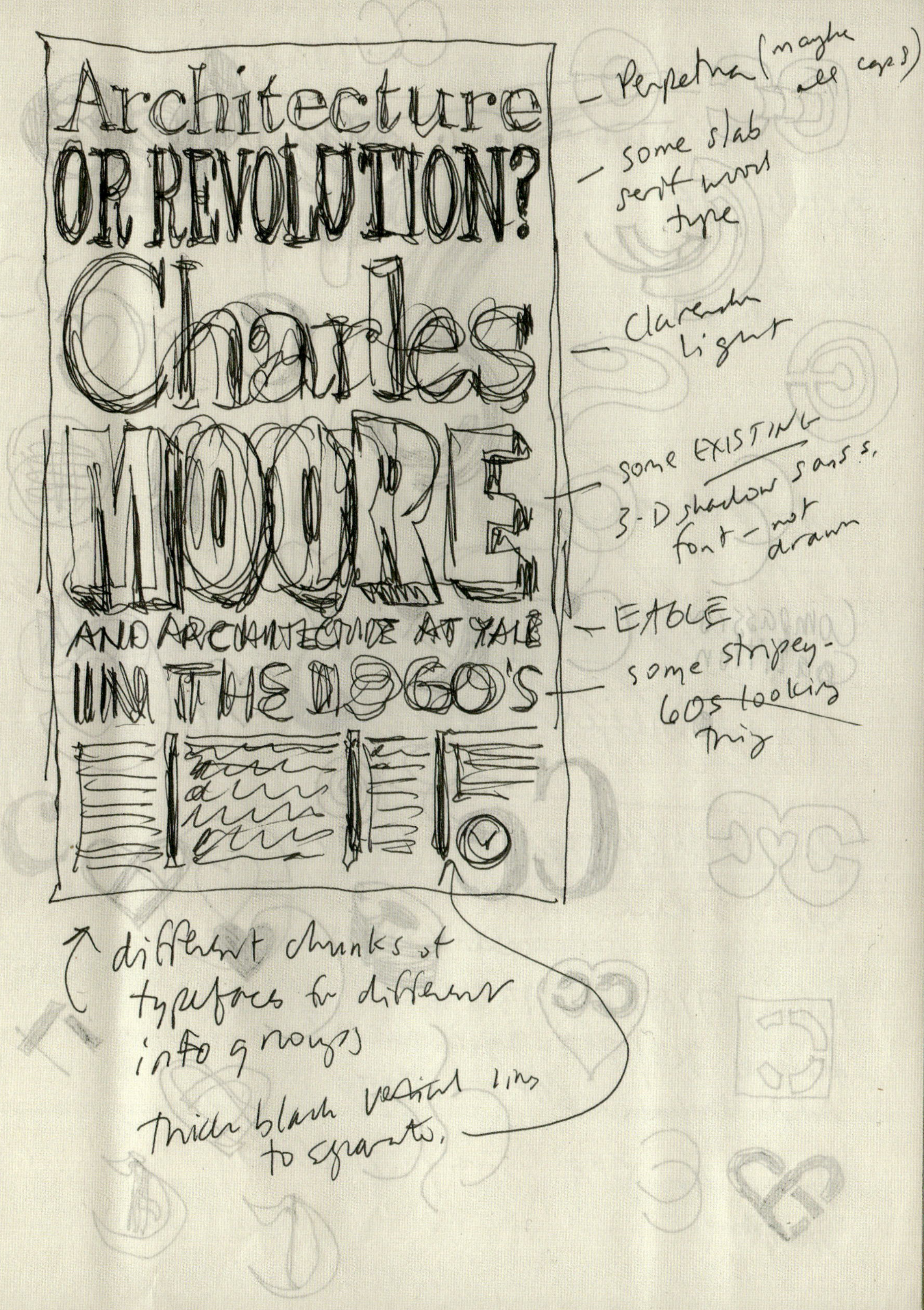
Architecture
OR REVOLUTION?
Charles
MOORE
AND ARCHITECTURE AT YALE
IN THE 1960's
— Perpetua (maybe all caps)
— some slab serif wood type
— Clarendon Light
some EXISTING 3-D shadow sans s. font — not drawn
— EAGLE
some stripey-60s looking thing
different chunks of typefaces for different info groups
Thick black vertical lines to separate.

David Cundy
2031
914 234
· 1912
→ MOA Nat'l Bd.
Jeanne Nathan
Jan Abrams
Christine
N.B.B.J.

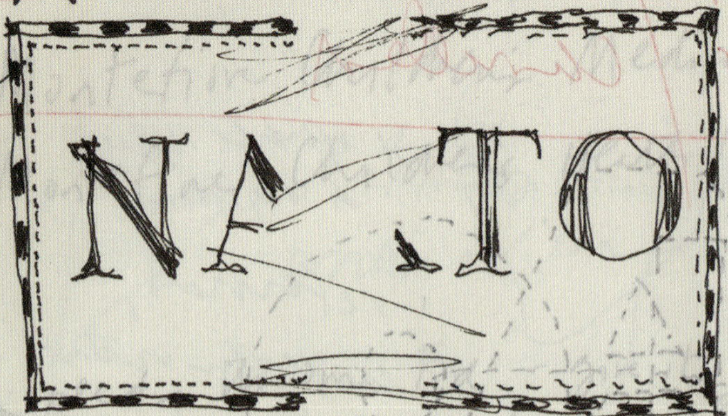

NATO

Brad Powell
CMS
Kathy Levine
875.

NATO

Barbara

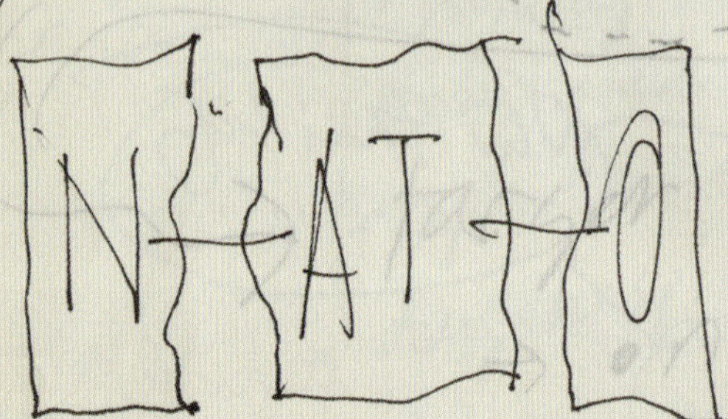

✓ ARB checklist
is site plan
Key thing on agenda for ZL to mail?

Sign looks attractive

914/332

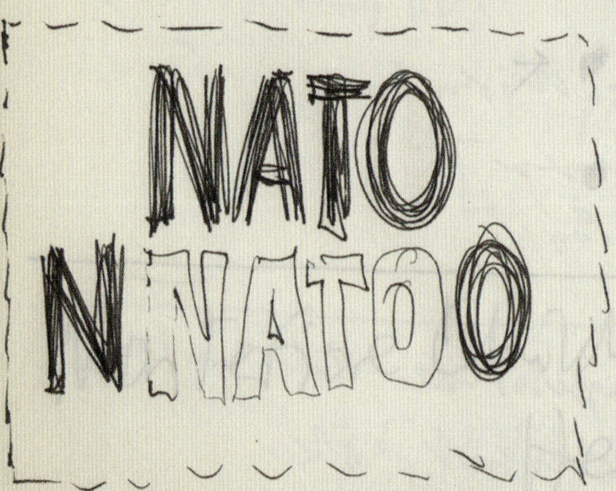

Mastine Chalm. 2

415/537

NATO
NNATOO

NNATOO

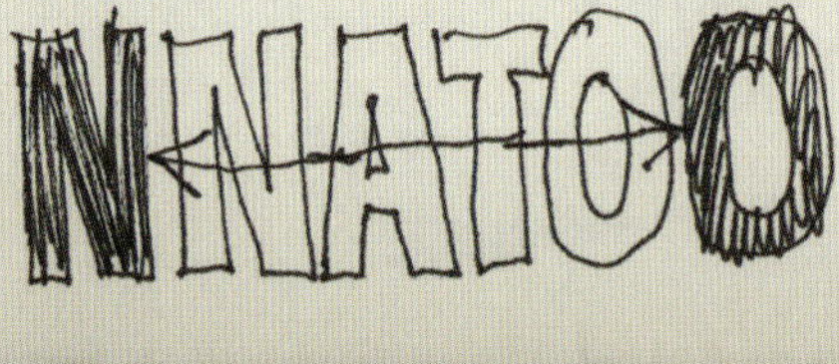

Rethinking Design #9
Deliver Oct 4 M
) — Sked

Jackie to → at work till 2/14
on vacation 2/15 - 2/23
starts 2/26

United mtg w/ 2/4/97
John Rubado

Civics
Cargo -
Scott to send cargo

Shuttle 737 | 300 + 500's

Richmond Childrens
Museum.

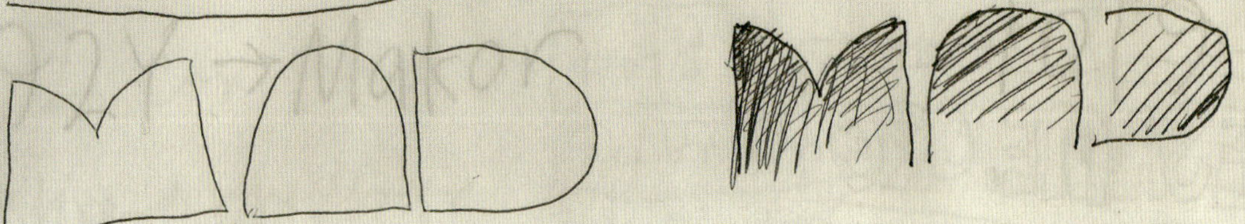

MAD MAD

process, materials, presentations

Original
differentiates
Creative

Alex Kroll
Y+R writer

MAD

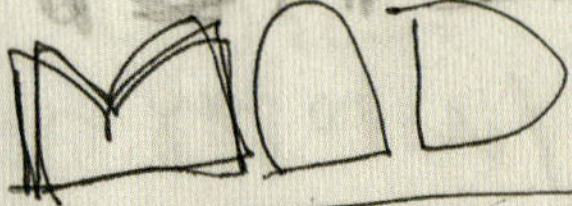

Sven, Creative Director

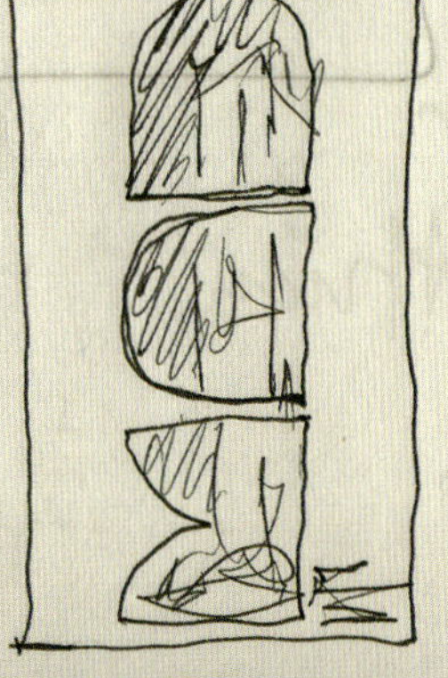

MAD

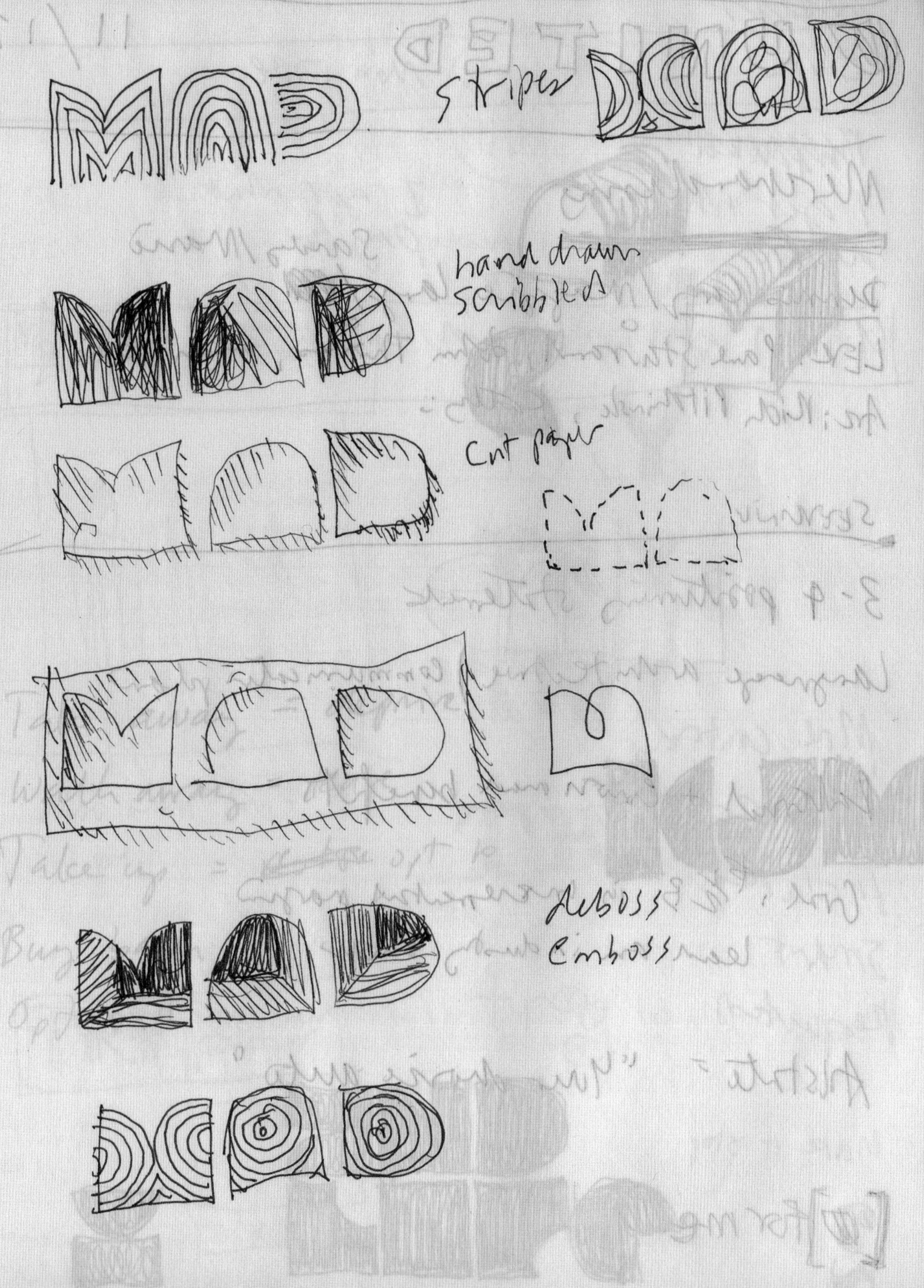
stripes
hand drawn
scribbled
Cut paper
deboss
emboss

Right
There is nothing glamorous about working out a layout grid, as I am reminded by my sketches for *Billboard*'s chart pages (see page 220).

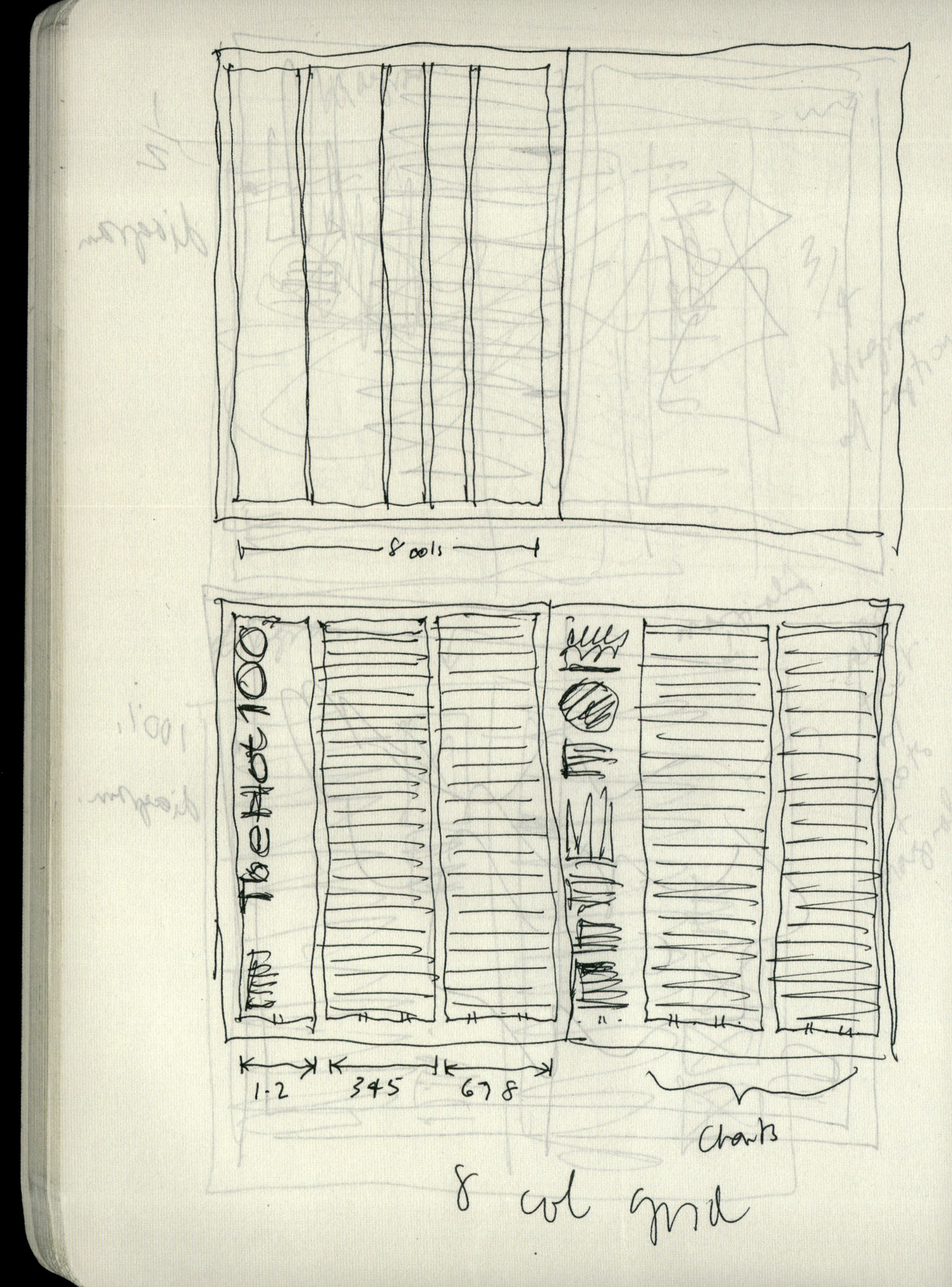

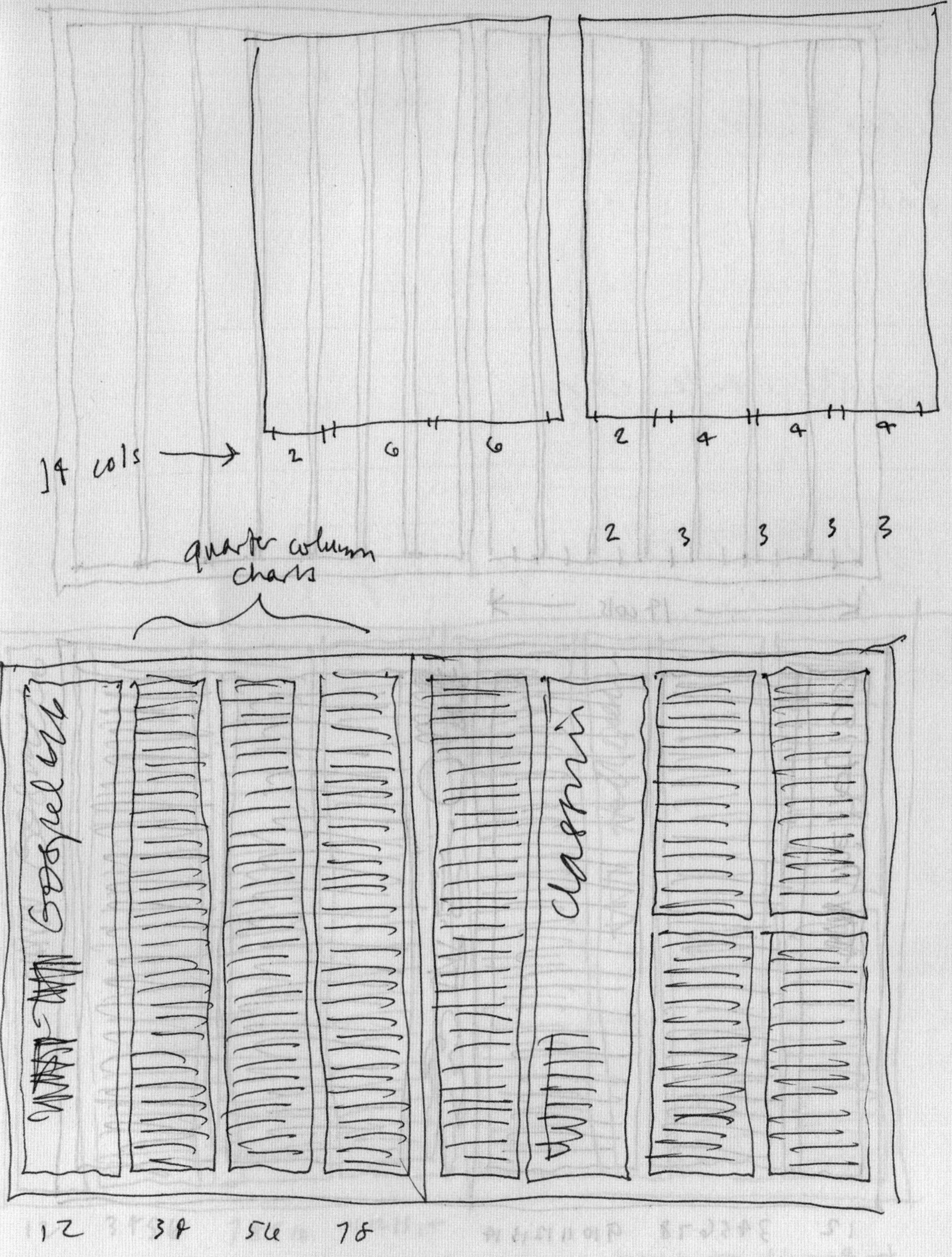
14 cols
2
6
6
2
4
4
4
2
3
3
3
3
quarter column charts
Goospel
classnis
12
34
56
78

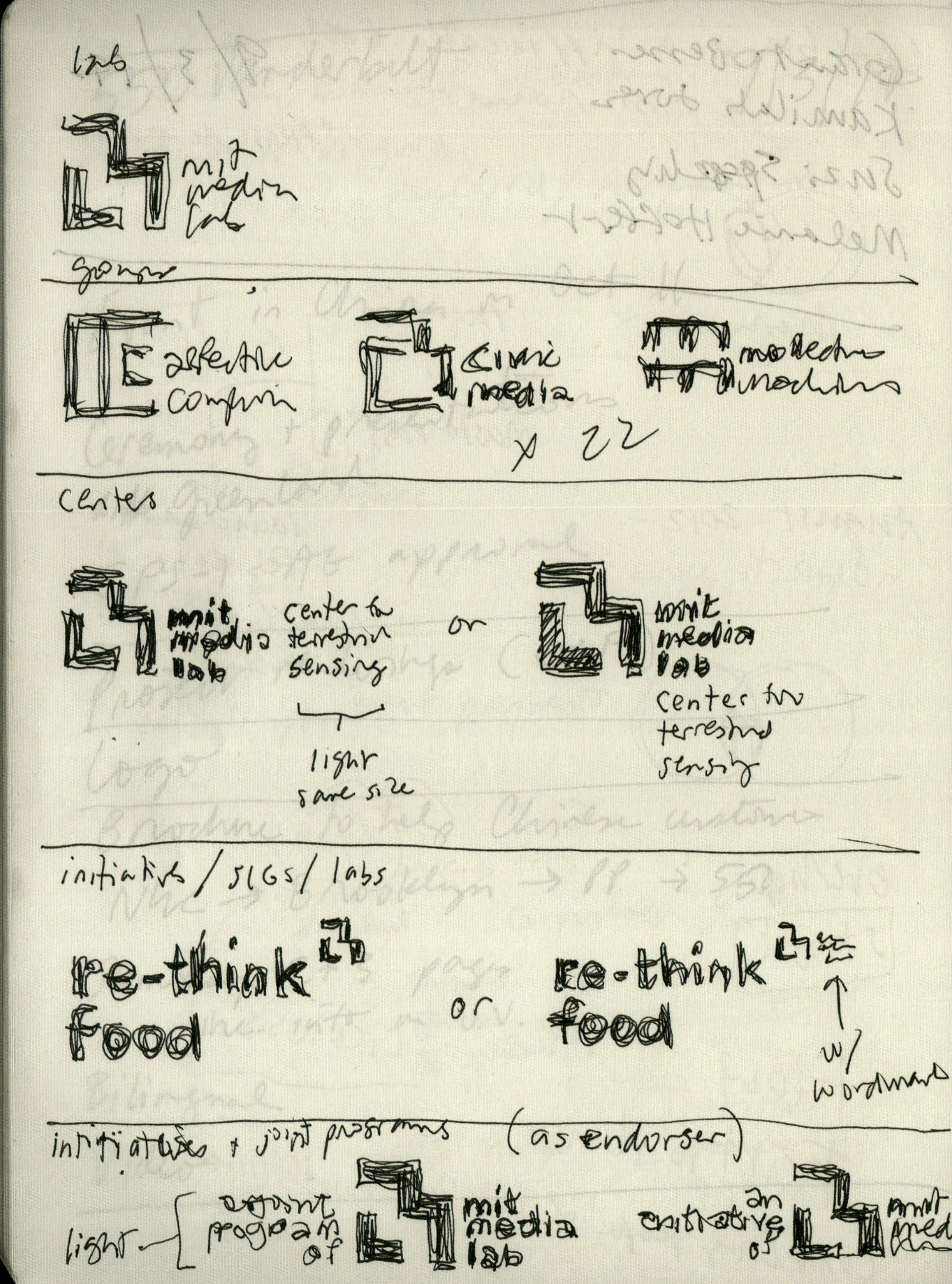

Right
I filled two pages with notes on the relationship between the various components that make up the MIT Media Lab (see page 310).

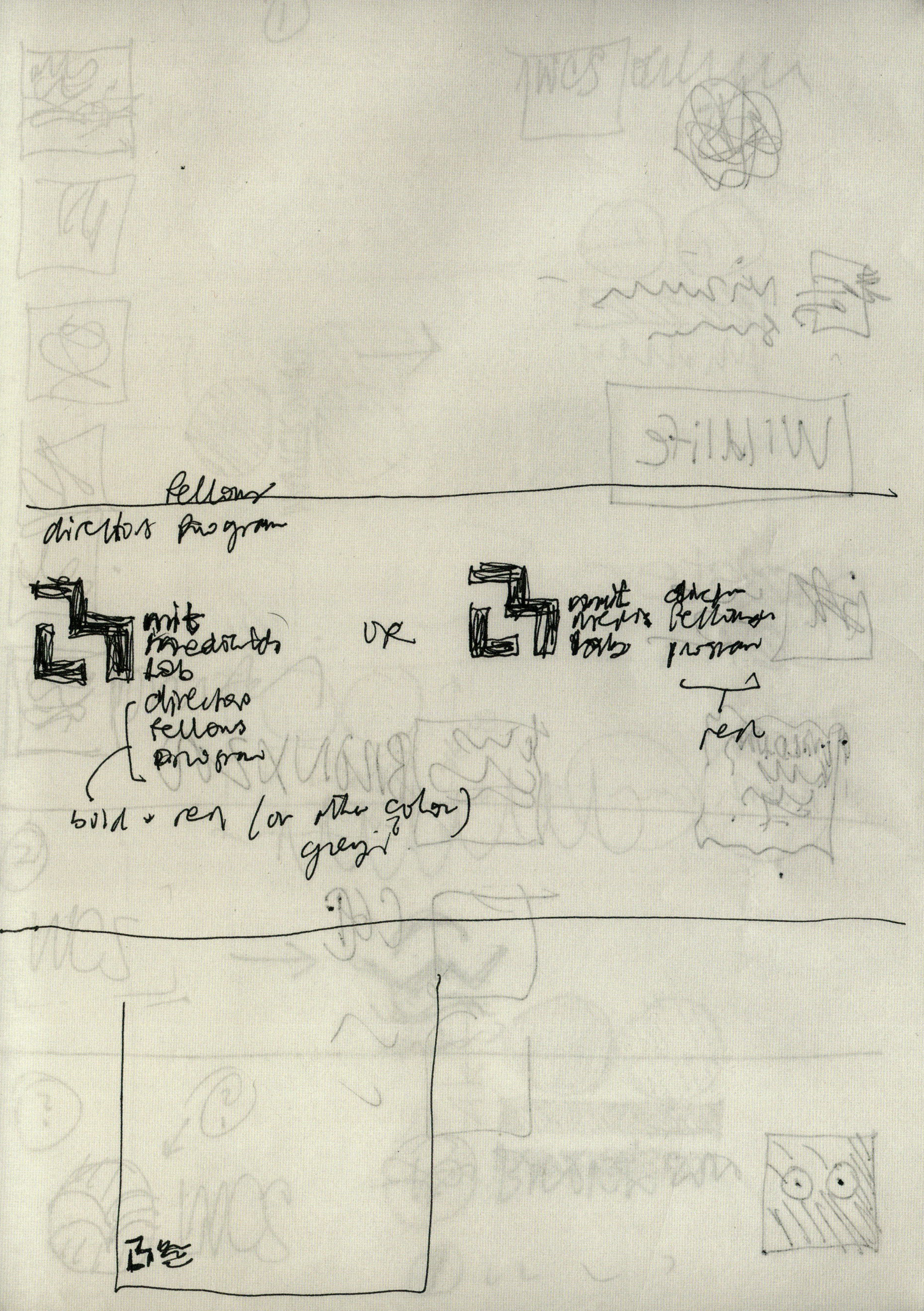

fellows

directors program

MIT Media Lab directors fellows program

OR

MIT Media Lab directors fellows program

red

bold + red (or other color) grey?

Right
After a number of false starts, I hit on a simple concept for a logo for the Robin Hood Foundation's Library Initiative (see page 338). Generating more ideas than we would ever actually need reassured me that we were on the right track.

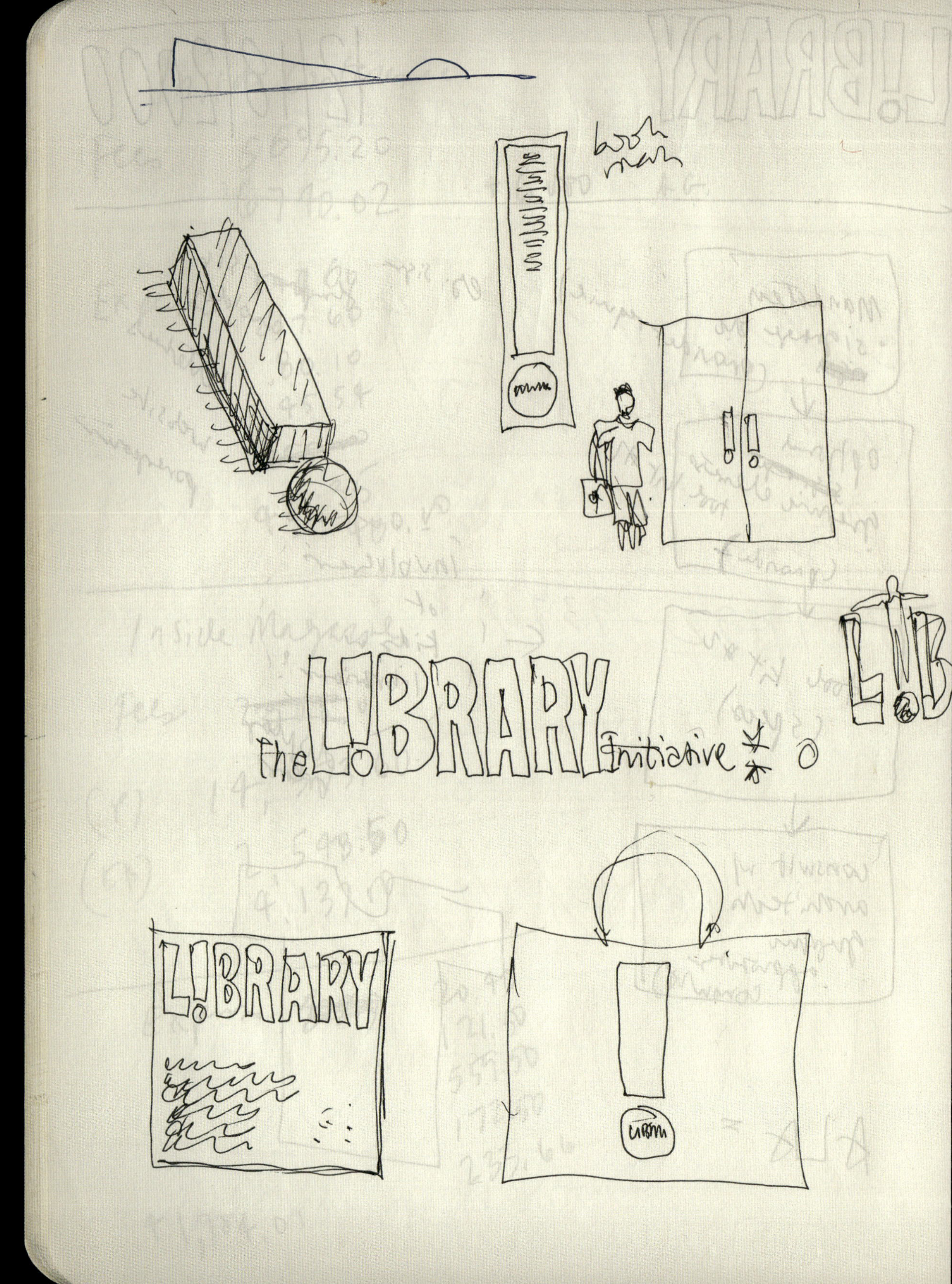

Reinventing the ~~elementary~~ public school library for New York City's ~~public~~ children

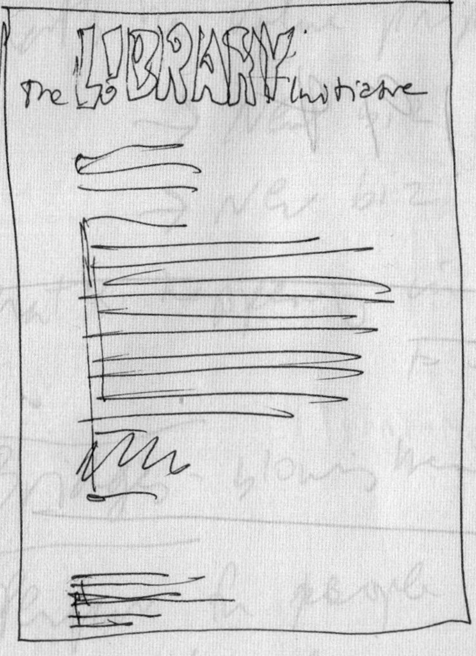

The L!BRARY Initiative

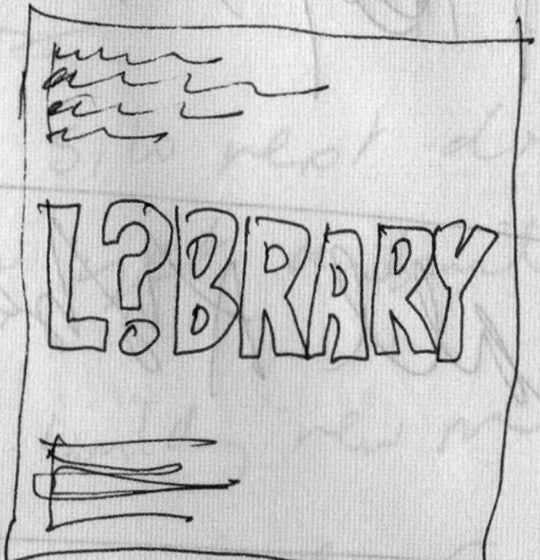

L?BRARY

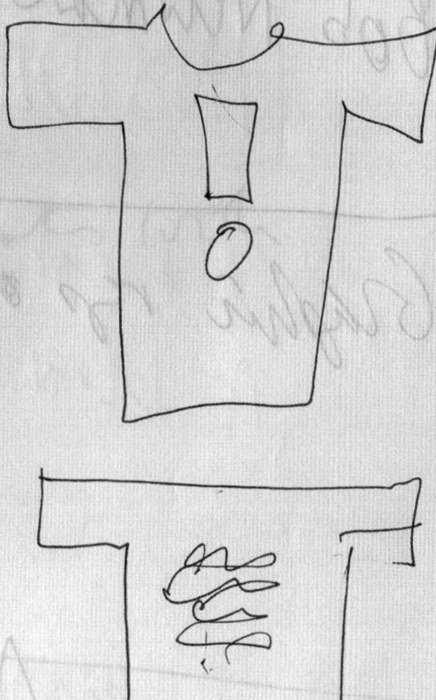

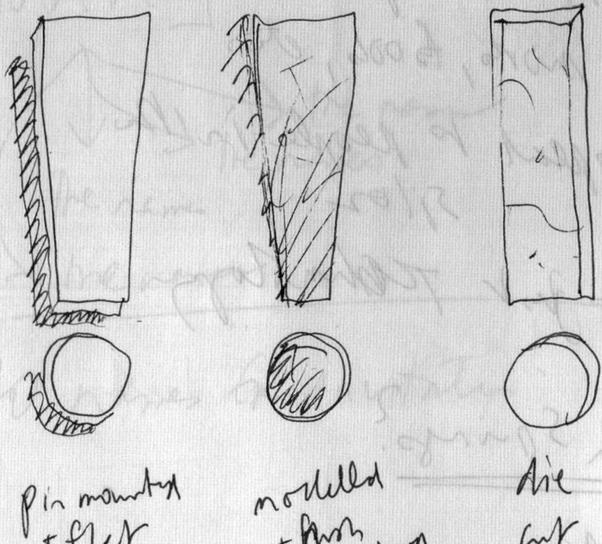

pin mounted + flat

modelled + flush mounted

die cut

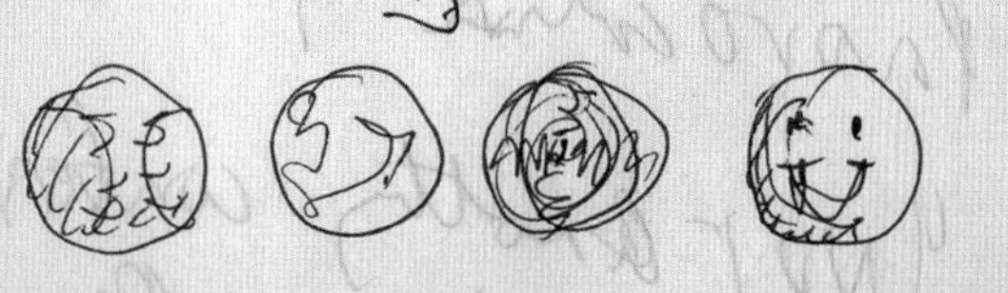

7:30 Balthazaar. Friday

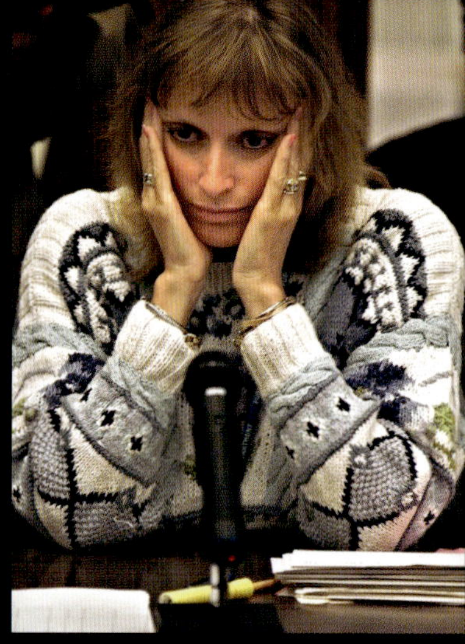

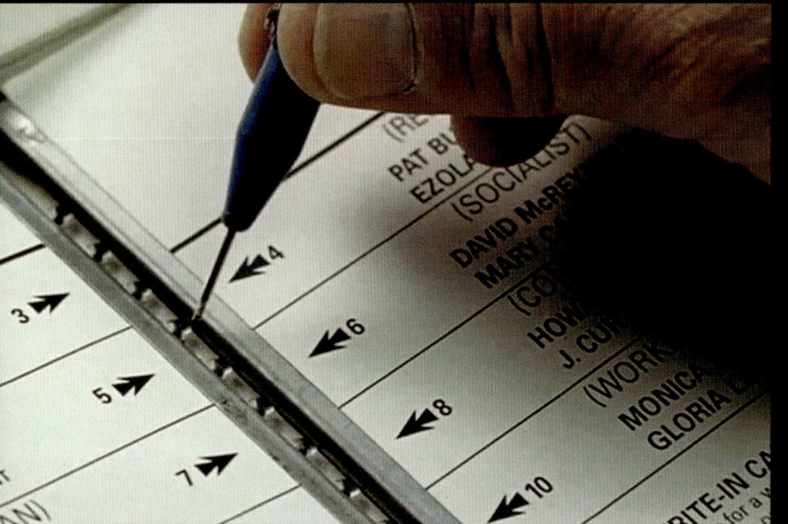

Left
The butterfly ballot was not a new invention, but its flaws threw the 2000 election into chaos.

Above
Theresa LePore, the 21st century's most influential graphic designer.

Below
It took more than a month to determine the election's outcome, still disputed 15 years later.

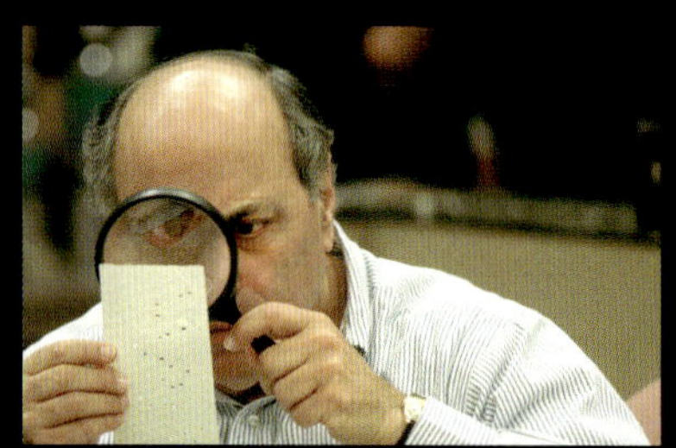

How to destroy the world with graphic design

American Institute of Graphic Arts

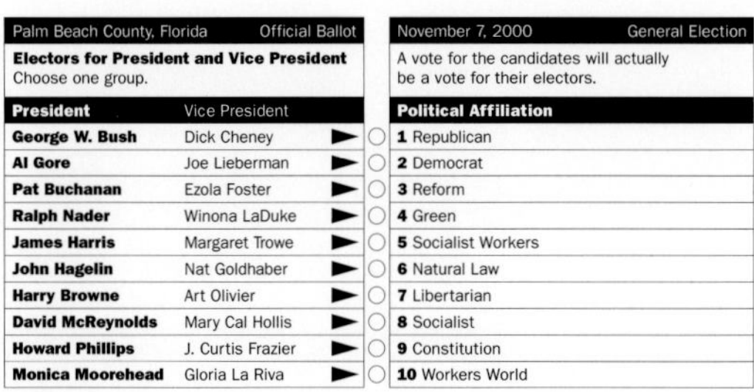

Palm Beach County, Florida | Official Ballot | November 7, 2000 | General Election

Electors for President and Vice President
Choose one group.

A vote for the candidates will actually be a vote for their electors.

President	Vice President		Political Affiliation
George W. Bush	Dick Cheney	► ○	**1** Republican
Al Gore	Joe Lieberman	► ○	**2** Democrat
Pat Buchanan	Ezola Foster	► ○	**3** Reform
Ralph Nader	Winona LaDuke	► ○	**4** Green
James Harris	Margaret Trowe	► ○	**5** Socialist Workers
John Hagelin	Nat Goldhaber	► ○	**6** Natural Law
Harry Browne	Art Olivier	► ○	**7** Libertarian
David McReynolds	Mary Cal Hollis	► ○	**8** Socialist
Howard Phillips	J. Curtis Frazier	► ○	**9** Constitution
Monica Moorehead	Gloria La Riva	► ○	**10** Workers World

Above
An alternate design, using the same format, demonstrates how confusion could have been avoided.

It was the fall of the year 2000, and Theresa LePore had a problem. As supervisor of elections in Palm Beach County, Florida, she was not a trained graphic designer, but her challenge was one that every graphic designer in the world has faced: too much text, not enough space. In this case, the text couldn't be edited. It was the list of candidates for president and vice president in the upcoming national election. The format couldn't be changed. It was the ballot for the Palm Beach County voting machines, on which voters would register their choice by punching out a hole adjacent to the name of their preferred candidate.

But this year, there were too many candidates to fit in a single column. So LePore came up with a new layout. She alternated the names on either side of the holes, first on the left, second on the right, third on the left, and so on. This turned out to be a problem on election day. The first name on the left side of the ballot was George W. Bush. If you wanted to vote for him, you punched the first hole. Right under Bush's name was Al Gore's. But if you punched the second hole, you wouldn't be voting for Gore, but for archconservative Pat Buchanan, the first name on the right side of the holes.

Confused? You aren't alone. The *Palm Beach Post* later estimated that over 2,800 Gore voters accidentally voted for Buchanan. As it turned out, Florida's votes, counted and recounted over a month, decided the election's outcome. And Palm Beach County decided Florida's. Bush won the state by a margin of 537 votes. By this count, Theresa LePore's design gave the presidency to George W. Bush.

Compared with architecture and product design, graphic design seems ephemeral and harmless. Bad typesetting, as they say, never killed anybody. But in this case, the execution of a trivial, aggravating job—laying out a humble government form—ended up affecting the fate of millions around the world. It was such a dramatic demonstration that I made it into a poster for the American Institute of Graphic Arts.

Human beings communicate with words and images. Good graphic designers know how to make those elements effective. And every once in a while that really matters.

(REPUBLICAN)

ORGE W. BUSH - PRESIDENT

CK CHENEY - VICE PRESIDENT

(DEMOCRATIC)

GORE - PRESIDENT

Desig

LIVIER - VICE PRESIDENT

(GREEN)

NONA LaDUKE - VICE PRESIDENT

(SOCIALIST WORK

MES HARRIS - PRESIDENT

ARGARET TROWE - VICE PRESIDEN

(NATURAL LAW

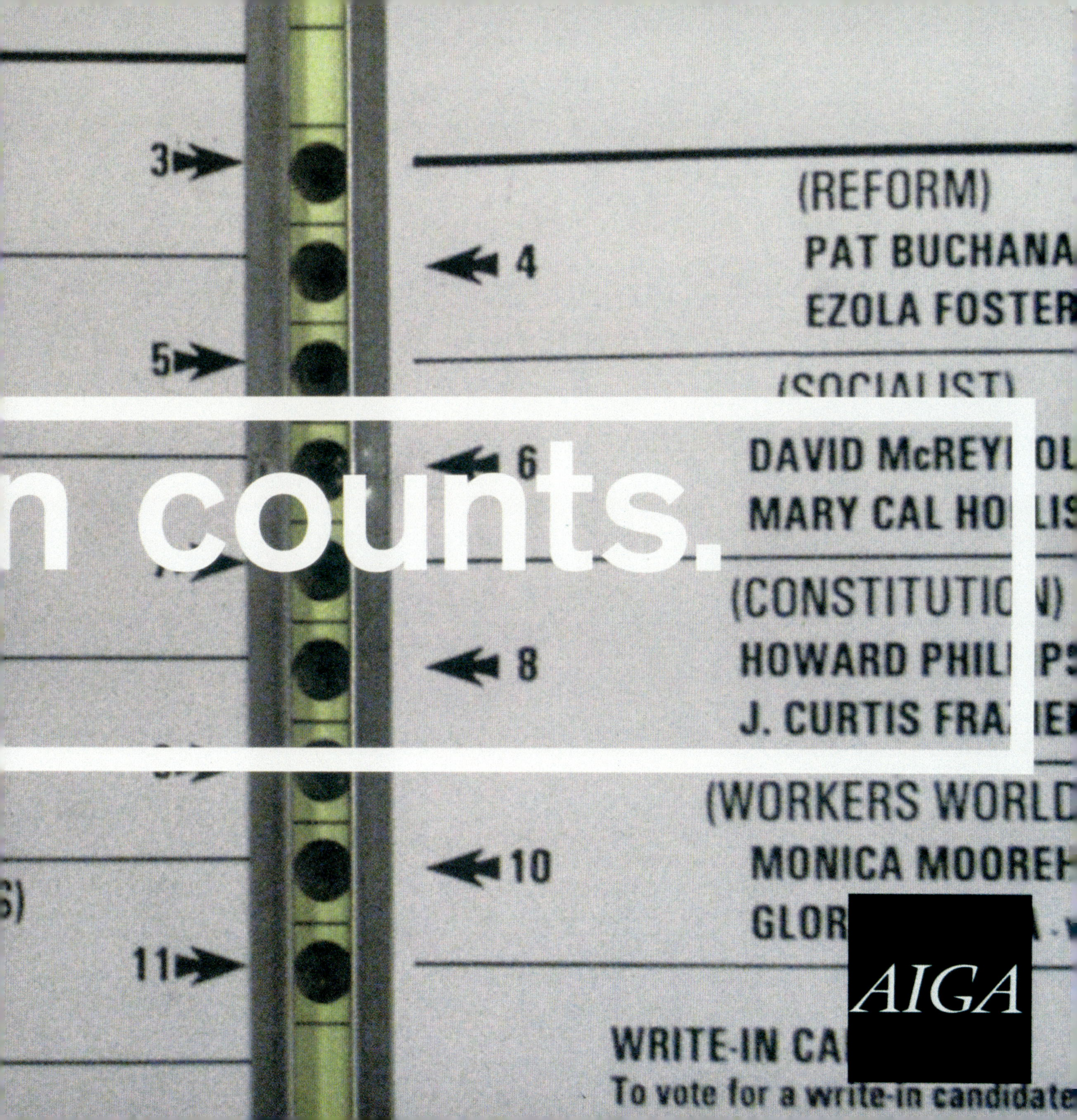
n counts.
3
(REFORM)
4
PAT BUCHANA
EZOLA FOSTER
5
DAVID McREY
MARY CAL HO
6
(CONSTITUTIO
HOWARD PHIL
8
J. CURTIS FRA
(WORKERS WORLD
10
MONICA MOOREH
GLOR
11
AIGA
WRITE-IN CA
To vote for a write-in candidate

Progressive Architecture
International
Furniture Awards
May 14

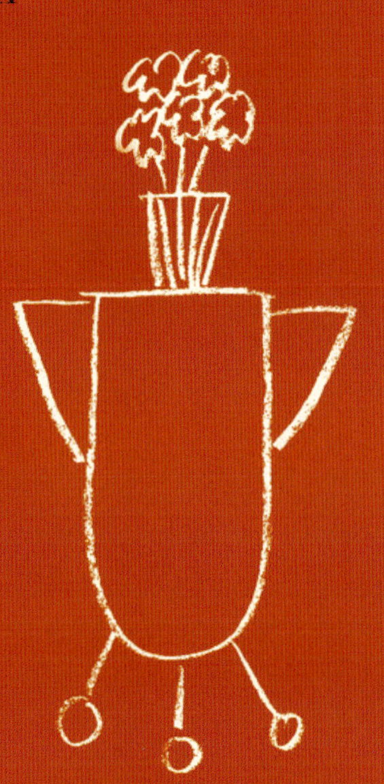

NASA News for Now:
Space Planning
in Outer Space
June 4

NASA News for Now:
Space Planning
in Outer Space
June 4

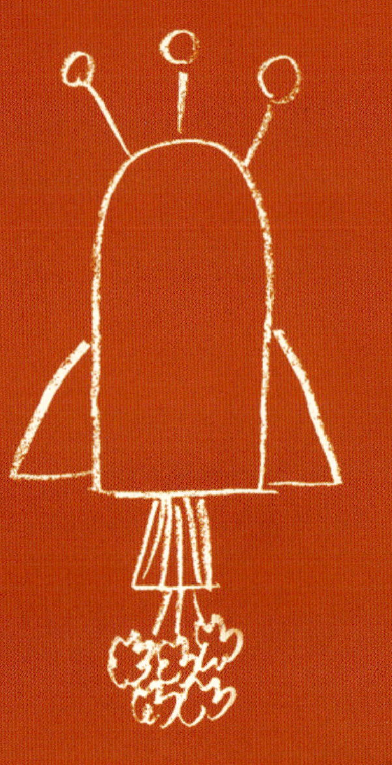

Progressive Architecture
International
Furniture Awards
May 14

How to have an idea

The International Design Center, New York

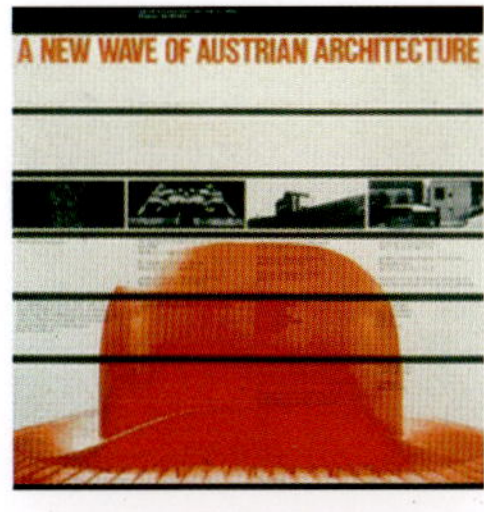

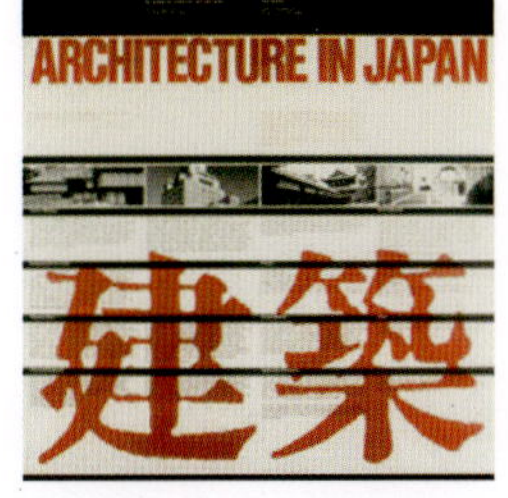

Opposite
I was so pleased with this design that I hurried home to show it to my wife, Dorothy. "Who did this drawing?" she asked. Me, I said. "Well," she said, "who are you going to get to do it?" With no budget, I stuck with my naive doodle and the conviction that the idea was good enough to surmount the crudeness of the execution. To this day, it is my favorite piece from the first ten years of my career.

Above
I mastered Massimo Vignelli's trademark approach to the point where I fancied people couldn't tell our work apart: his poster above, mine below.

I had been working for Massimo Vignelli for four years, devoting my days to mastering what I thought of as "the Vignelli style": a few preapproved typefaces, two or three bright colors, and structural elements like lines and stripes, all deployed on a modular grid. I enjoyed mimicry and flattered myself with the delusion that Massimo couldn't tell the difference between my designs and his. Now he had entrusted me with a big client, a complex of furniture showrooms called the International Design Center, New York. We set the ground rules at the outset: the typeface, Bodoni; the color, PMS Warm Red. As long as I stuck to those ingredients, I was on my own.

I worked with the brilliant young marketing manager Fern Mallis, a quick-talking New Yorker who was my favorite client. She asked me to design invitations for two upcoming events: an exhibition of experimental furniture and a lecture by NASA scientists on designing spacecraft interiors. I was excitedly completing designs for both invitations (Bodoni, PMS Warm Red) when my phone rang.

It was Fern. "I'm afraid we just got our budget cut, and we can only afford one invitation. Can you combine them?" "No, of course not," I sputtered. The two subjects were completely different: end tables and outer space. No one will come to either event. Plus, I liked the designs I had already done.

Fern didn't budge. I hung up the phone in frustration. Clients! Would it never get easier? How was one supposed to work under these conditions? What were they expecting, something like this? Almost without thinking, intending to do nothing more than demonstrate the impossibility of the problem, I did a drawing. Viewed one way, it was a table and a vase of flowers. Upside down, a rocket ship. I was smart enough to realize this drawing was the answer.

Like everything else I did for this client, it was in Bodoni and PMS Warm Red. But people don't care about typefaces and colors. They are merely the delivery mechanisms for something else: ideas. And my drawing, crude as it was, was an idea, something with the capacity to surprise, engage, and amuse people. It was at that moment of scribbling I realized content is more important than form.

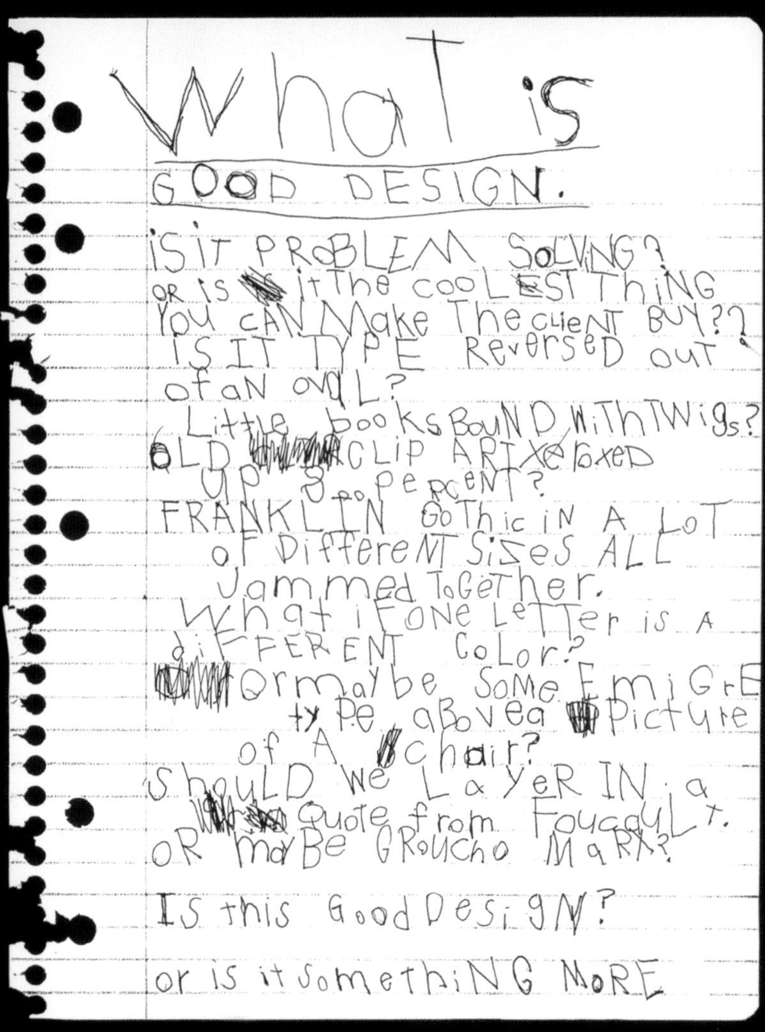

Call for Entries
The Fifteenth Annual American Center for Design
One Hundred Show

Alexander Isley, Jilly Simons, Erik Spiekermann, Judges
Michael Bierut, Chair

Entry Deadline: May 1, 1992

Design: Michael Bierut / Pentagram
Lettering: Elizabeth Ann Kresz Bierut / Transfiguration School

How to transcend style

American Center for Design

When style is referred to in design circles, it's usually disparagingly. Most designers claim to "have no style," inventing new approaches for each assignment. Original design work is said to be reduced to "mere style" by those who imitate it. Shallow cosmeticians are dismissed by their critics as trafficking in "nothing but style."

Yet in any artistic activity style is inescapable. This is particularly true in graphic design, where the functional requirements of most projects are minimal. A business card has to bear legible type and fit in a wallet. After that, all the decisions—typeface, color, layout, material, production technique—are bafflingly arbitrary, what regular people call "a matter of taste." But ask a designer about the last time a meeting degenerated into a taste discussion. It was probably yesterday, and the memory will not be pleasant.

In the early 1990s, still fresh from my ten years at Vignelli Associates, I was desperate to find my own voice, and at a total loss as to how to do it. With the design world roiled by change, from the typographic daring of *Emigre* to the experimental invention of Cranbrook and CalArts, I brooded about the seeming impossibility of moving beyond style. Consumed as I was with soul searching, it was ironic to be asked to chair the world's most progressive (and stylish) design competition, the American Center for Design's 100 Show, and create the poster that would invite my fellow designers to participate. Predictably, weeks of paralysis followed. An increasingly panicked ACD staff wondered if I was up to the task. Finally, I was asked to at least write the statement that would appear on the announcement's reverse side. I responded with a stream of consciousness that would have been better suited to an analyst's couch. They liked it, and suggested I simply run the text on the front of the poster. Ah, an all-type solution.

But what typeface? The decision was now reduced to its toughest core. Should I pander to the trendsetters with a newly designed grunge font? Hold strong with the modernists with Helvetica? Or play it safe with Garamond No. 3? At the last possible moment, the solution hit me. I dictated the text, letter by letter, to my four-year-old daughter Elizabeth. The innocence of the form vanquished the weary cynicism of the content, and I was free at last.

Opposite
Adults think they can imitate children's handwriting. Don't bother. Today, the American Center for Design is long gone, but my daughter Elizabeth is still with us, an attorney practicing in Manhattan. She has no memory of lettering this poster.

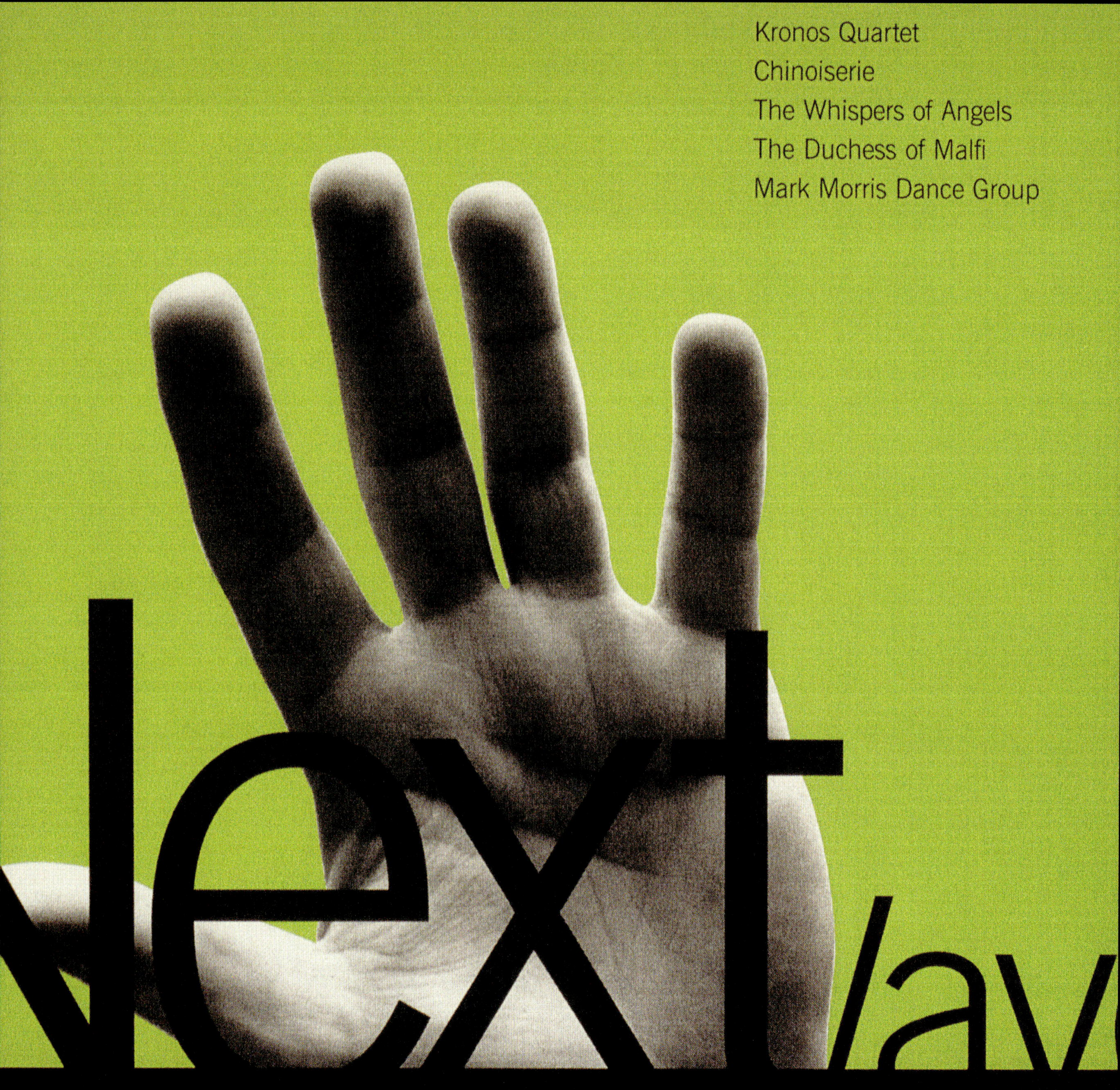
Kronos Quartet
Chinoiserie
The Whispers of Angels
The Duchess of Malfi
Mark Morris Dance Group
Next Wav

How to create identity without a logo

Brooklyn Academy of Music

Opposite
Founded in 1861, BAM's early decades saw performances by Enrico Caruso, Sarah Bernhardt, and Isadora Duncan. Over 100 years later, Harvey Lichtenstein gave alternative performers like Robert Wilson, Philip Glass, Pina Bausch, and Peter Brook their first large-scale American venue there.

Next spread
By treating the bland sans serif News Gothic typeface in a distinctive way, we created a look that says "BAM" even if the logo is nowhere in sight. Coincidentally, the typeface was designed by Morris Fuller Benton in 1908, the same year that the BAM Opera House opened.

When the Brooklyn Academy of Music, the oldest continuously operating performing arts center in the United States, fell on hard times in the 1960s, it was saved by a young visionary, Harvey Lichtenstein, who remade it as a destination for the global avant-garde. Lichtenstein's Next Wave Festival stole the standard of progressive performance from Manhattan, and launched an unstoppable revival of Brooklyn that continues to this day.

In 1995, after years of experimenting with different graphic approaches for the Next Wave, BAM asked us to create something permanent. ("You don't keep changing the Marlboro Man," said board member Bill Campbell, longtime head of marketing for Philip Morris.) From now on, they wanted everything—from a poster to a 36-page subscription mailer to a small-space ad—to simply look like BAM. What they didn't want was a logo.

I was inspired by the legendary midcentury advertising art director Helmut Krone. "I've spent my whole life fighting logos," he once said. "A logo says, 'I am an ad. Turn the page.'" Instead, he created indelible identities for his clients by making distinctive choices and deploying them relentlessly, most famously on behalf of Volkswagen, still using the combination of Futura and white space that he introduced in his "Think small" ad in 1959.

So I hit on the idea of using one typeface, workhorse News Gothic, but with a twist: we would cut the type off, as if it couldn't fit in the frame. As I explained to Harvey and his colleagues Karen Brooks Hopkins and Joe Melillo, this suggested that BAM crossed borders and couldn't be contained on a single stage. But it was economical, too, allowing us to use four-inch-tall letters in two inches' worth of space. It was like seeing King Kong's eye in your bedroom window, I explained. Even if you couldn't see the whole beast, you knew it was big.

The new look for the Next Wave launched in 1995. The idiosyncratic headline treatment (dubbed "Cuisinart typography" by BAM's longtime architectural consultant Hugh Hardy) was disorienting at first. Twenty years later, it is inextricably linked to BAM.

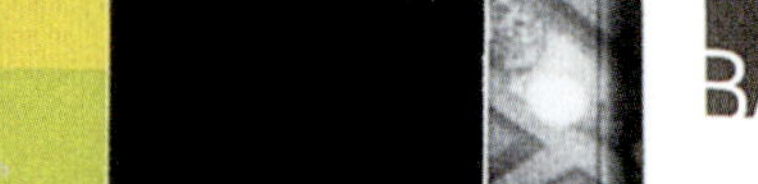
BAMbill
The Brooklyn Academy of Music
Light
Brooklyn Academy of Music
BAM
ee
tickets
to the 15th
Anniversary of
the BAM Next
Wave Festival
BAM's 1995
Next Wave Festival
Robert Wilson
Tom Waits
Vito Acconci
Kristin Jones & Andrew Ginzel
Ilya Kabakov
Don Byron
Bill Frisell
Vernon Reid
Steven Berkoff
Cloud Gate Dance Theatre
Carl Dreyer
Richard Einhorn
The Camerata Chorale
Brooklyn Philharmonic
Kronos Quartet
Ping Chong
David Rousseve / REALITY
Cheek by Jowl
Mark Morris Dance Group
Wav
Brooklyn
Academy
of
Music
BAM
95
guid
Mark Morris
Dance Group
Brooklyn Academy of Music
1995 Next Wave Festival
is sponsored by
Philip Morris Companies Inc.
For tickets call TicketMaster
212.307.4100
For information call BAM
718.636.4100
BAM Prefers VISA
Brooklyn
Academy
of
Music
30 Lafayette Avenue
Brooklyn NY 11217
Telephone: 718.636.4122
Fax: 718.857.2021
Stephen P. Millikin
Audience Development Manager
BAM
Brooklyn
Academy
of
Music
30 Lafayette Avenue
Brooklyn NY 11217
Telephone: 718.636.4100
Fax: 718.857.2021
BAM

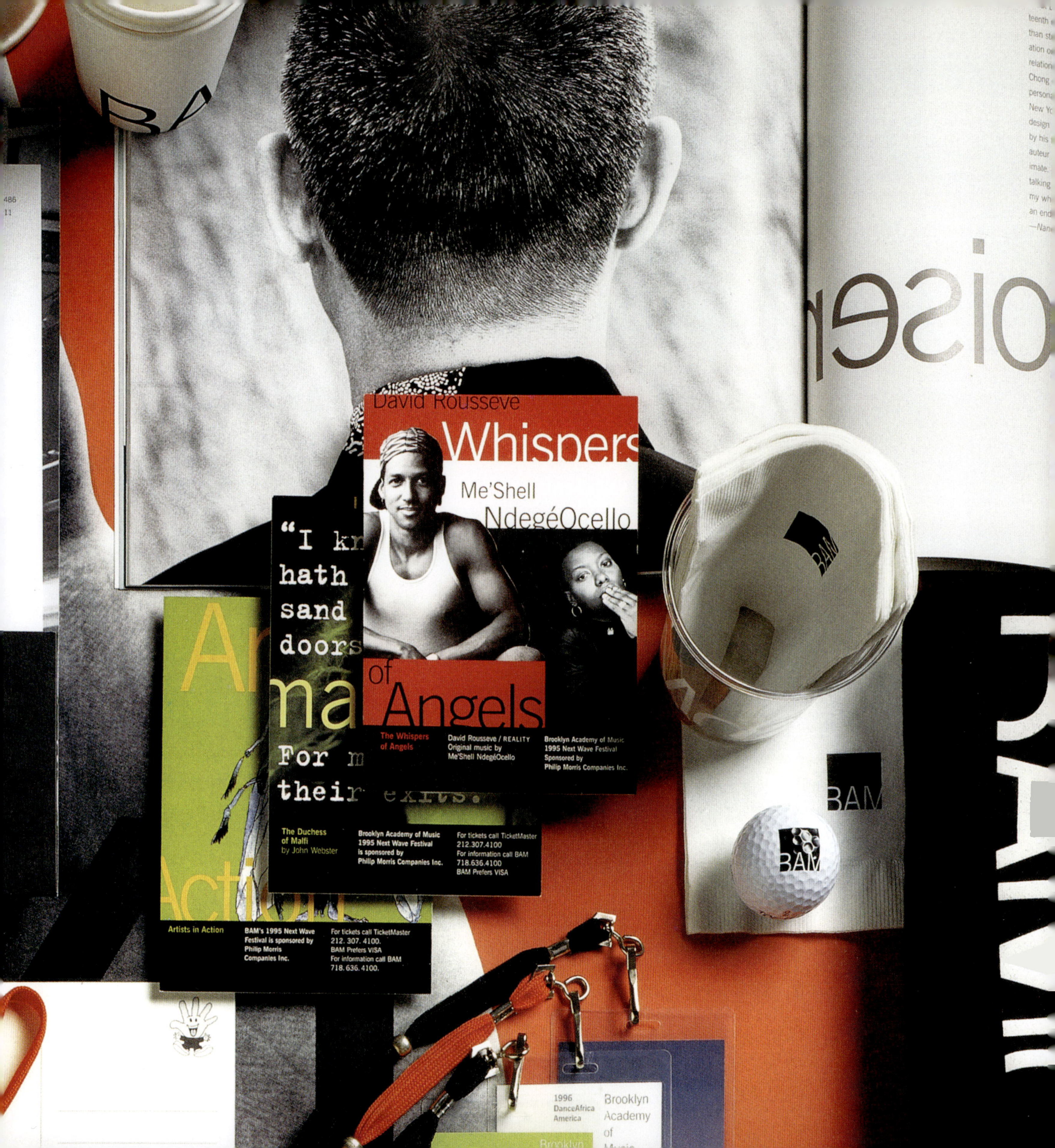
David Rousseve
Whispers
Me'Shell
NdegéOcello
of
Angels
The Whispers of Angels
David Rousseve / REALITY
Original music by
Me'Shell NdegéOcello
Brooklyn Academy of Music
1995 Next Wave Festival
Sponsored by
Philip Morris Companies Inc.
The Duchess of Malfi
by John Webster
Brooklyn Academy of Music
1995 Next Wave Festival
is sponsored by
Philip Morris Companies Inc.
For tickets call TicketMaster
212.307.4100
For information call BAM
718.636.4100
BAM Prefers VISA
Artists in Action
BAM's 1995 Next Wave
Festival is sponsored by
Philip Morris
Companies Inc.
For tickets call TicketMaster
212. 307. 4100.
BAM Prefers VISA
For information call BAM
718. 636. 4100.
BAM
BAM
1996
DanceAfrica
America
Brooklyn
Academy
of

Below left
Getting printers to manufacture cups with the type going off the bottom is harder than you'd think: they can't believe you want to print them "wrong."

Below right
By mounting the hand on a metronome motor, we made the Next "Wave" pun a bit more obvious.

The late design genius Tibor Kalman was once asked to design a brand identity for a museum. Rather than designing a logo, he handed the client a book of typefaces and said to simply pick one and use it over and over again: if they did that long enough, they'd have an identity. He was right. I'm convinced the most important characteristic for a great brand is consistency. This is different from sameness. Sameness is static and lifeless. Consistency is responsive and vibrant. Working with, yes, just one typeface, BAM is a model of consistency.

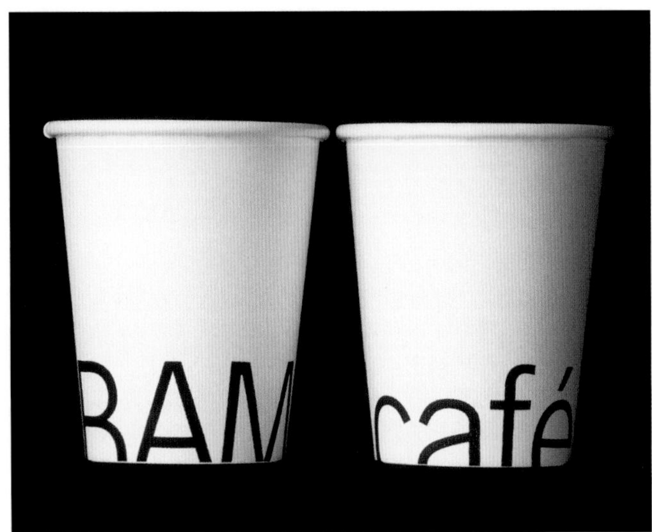

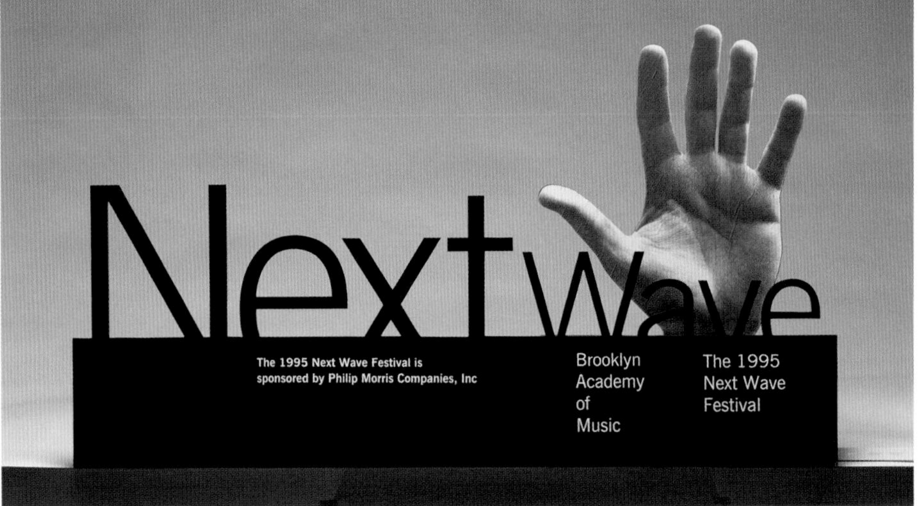

Left top
The Majestic Theatre was renamed the BAM Harvey Theater when Lichtenstein retired in 1999.

Left bottom
Even the BAM bathroom icons are subject to chopping.

Below
After resisting creating a logo for several years, we finally made one using BAM's signature typography. The guidelines for use, created by designer Emily Hayes Campbell and only six pages long, are still faithfully followed.

Next spread
Contemporary lettering collides with the BAM Opera House's century-old Beaux-Arts details.

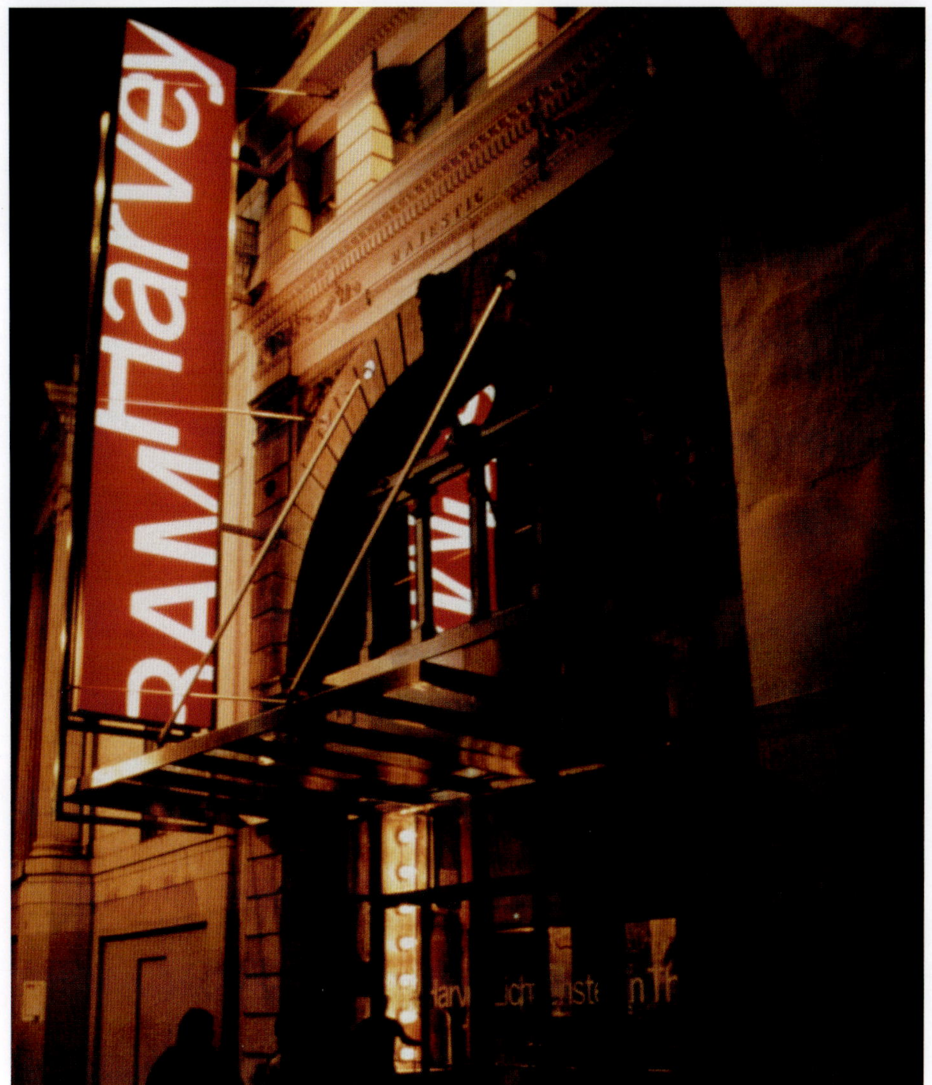

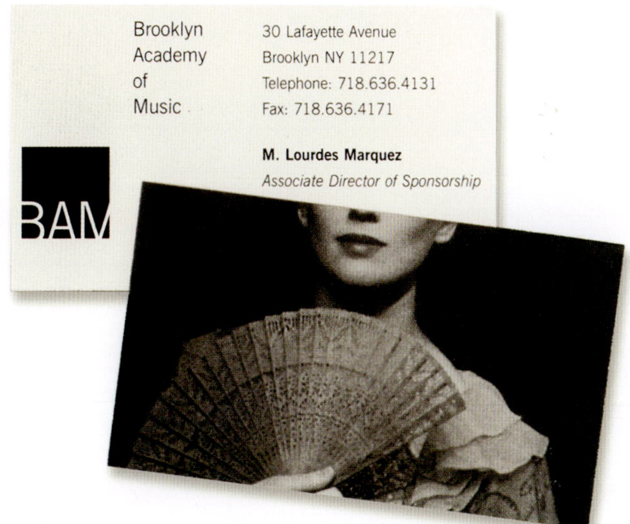

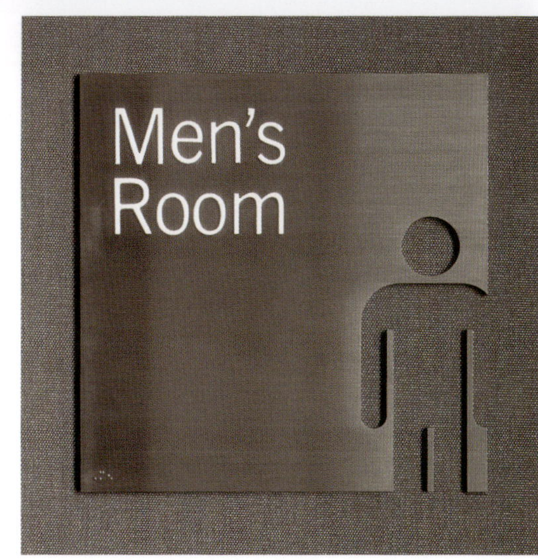

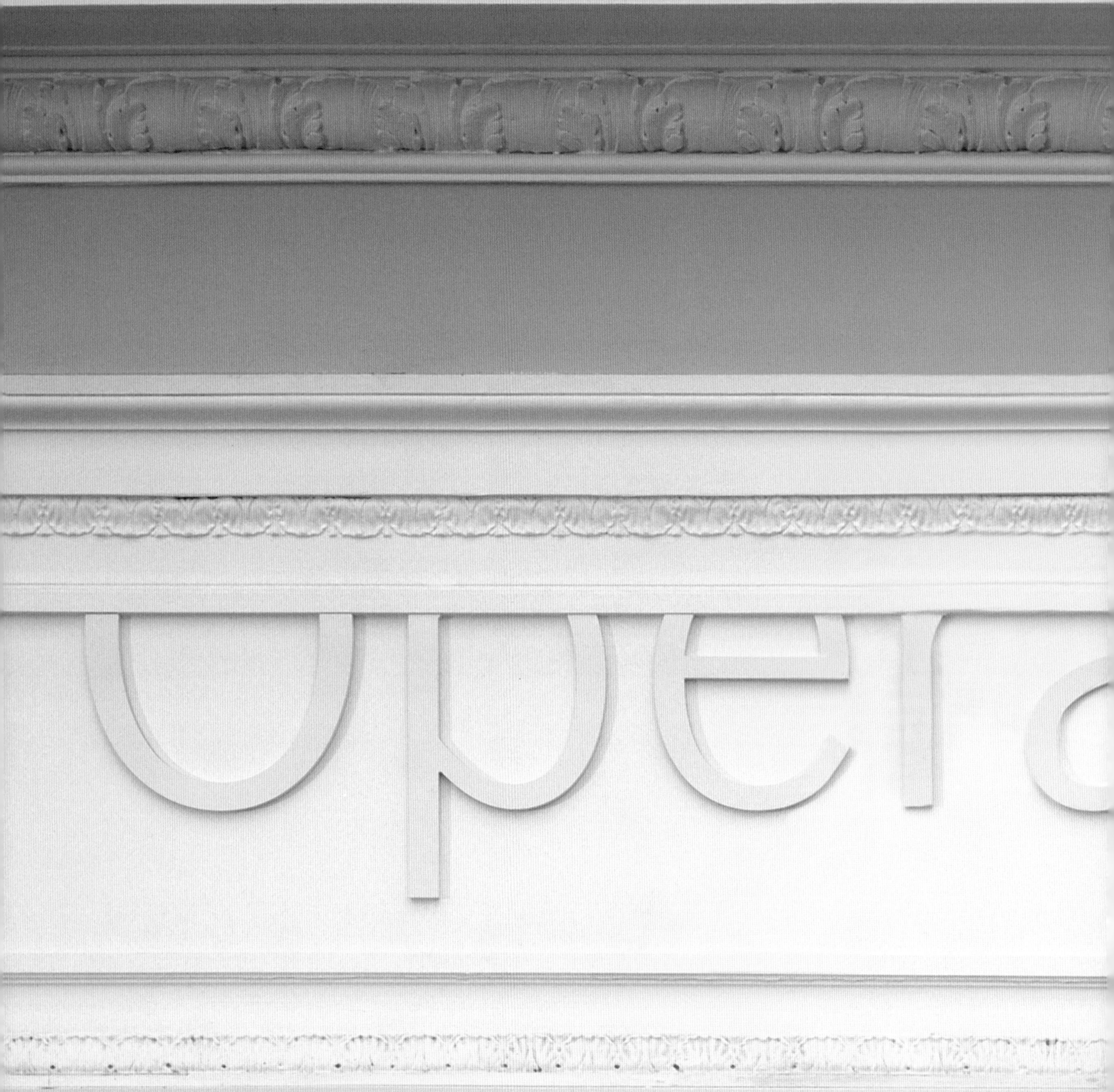

Oper

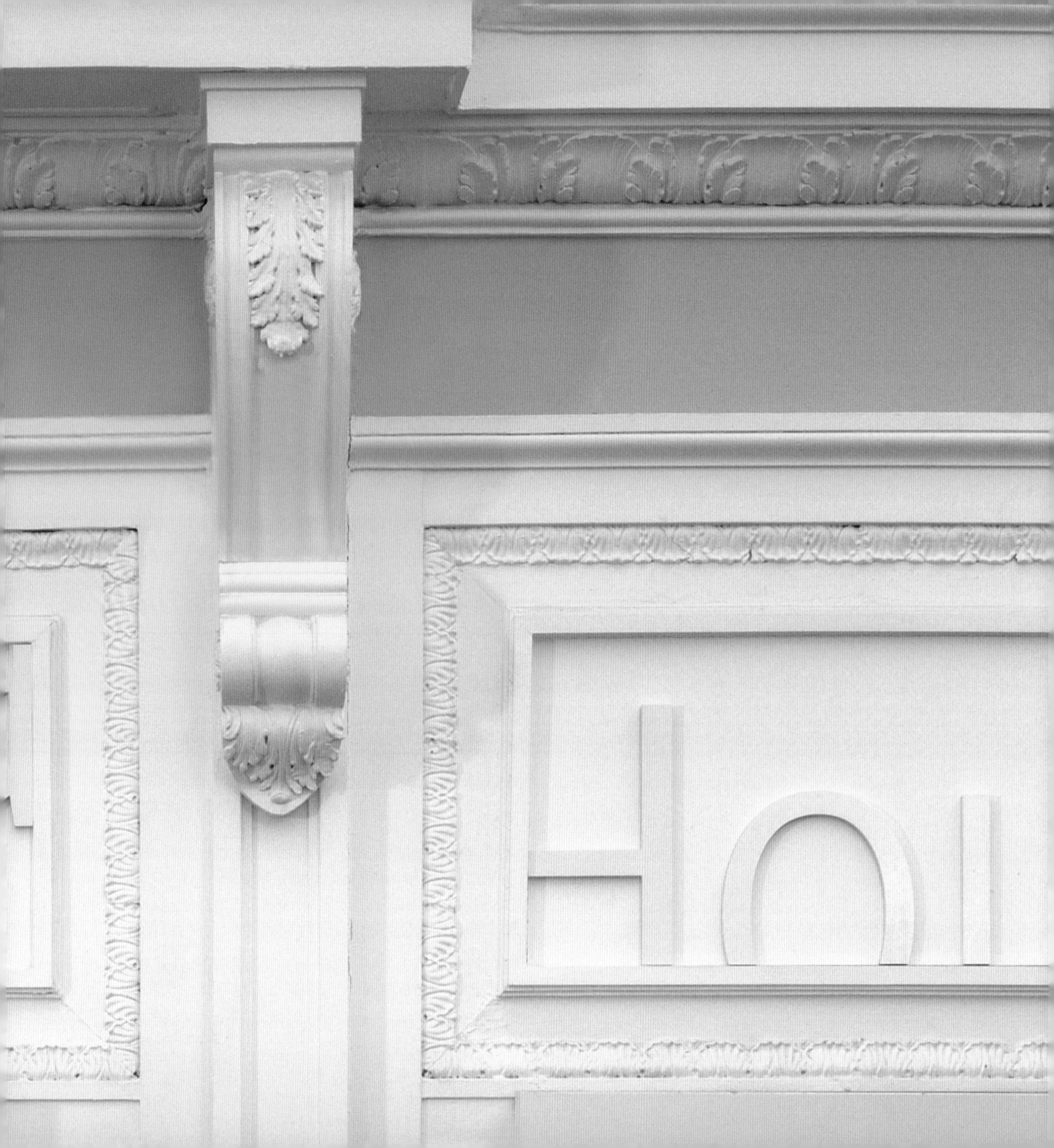

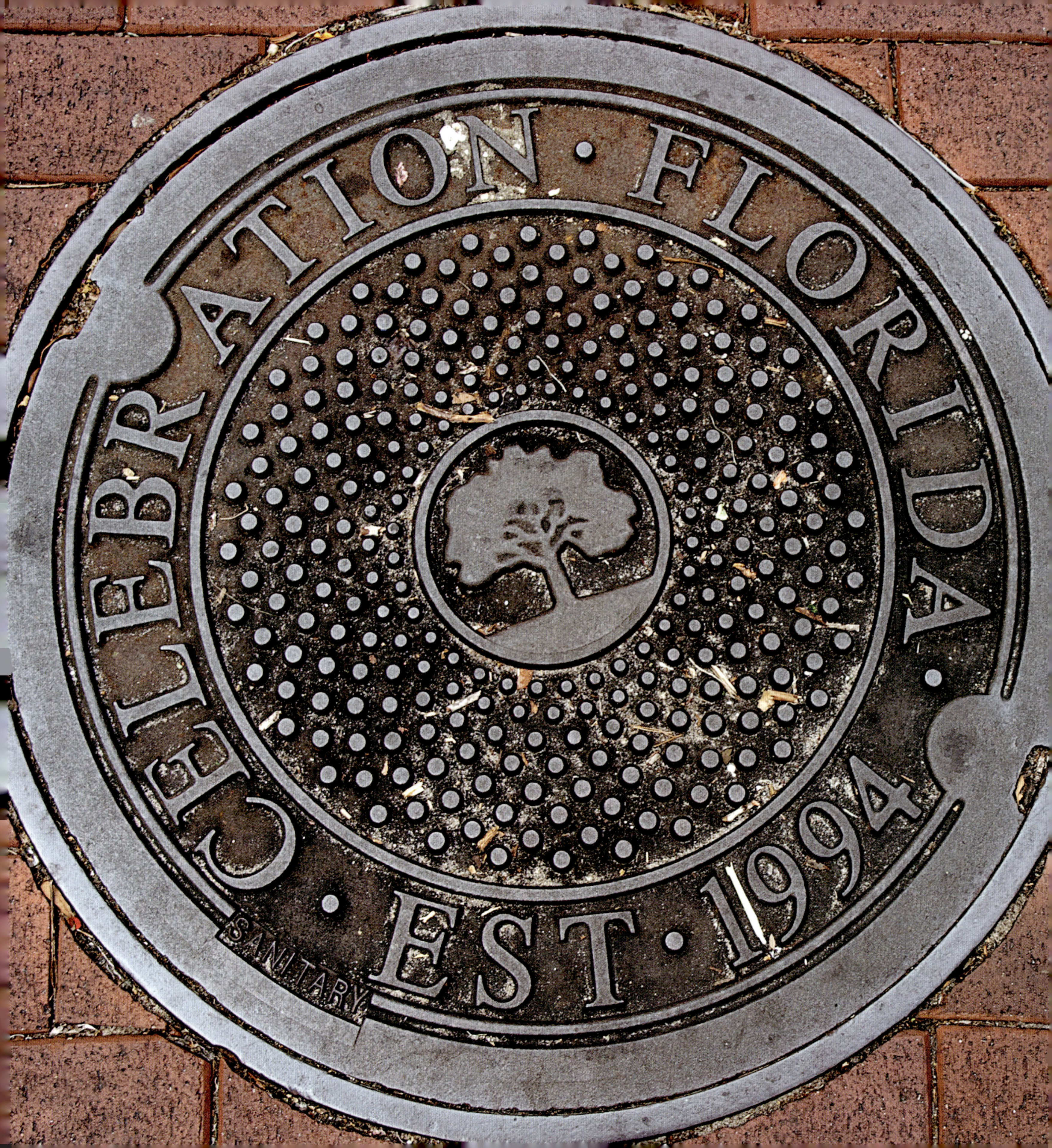
CELEBRATION · FLORIDA ·
· EST · 1994
SANITARY

How to invent a town that was always there

Celebration, Florida

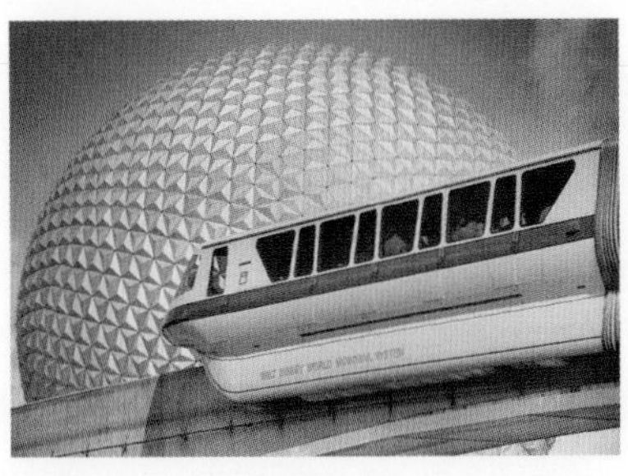

Opposite
Our designs in Celebration, Florida, are ubiquitous, including places that usually escape notice, like manhole covers.

Above
Walt Disney's original dream to create a futuristic utopia in central Florida morphed into a theme park, the Experimental Prototype Community of Tomorrow (EPCOT), which opened in 1982. A dozen years later, Celebration, built on considerably different theories, broke ground.

If you drive down Interstate 4 in central Florida, exit on Route 192, and make a right turn at a long white fence, you will enter another world. Traditional houses with front porches on small lots set close to the street. A town center with the scale of a classic Main Street, small shops lining the sidewalks. Parks and schools within an easy walk. It is utterly unlike the world of parking lots and warehouse stores that surrounds it, and it is all about twenty years old. This is Celebration, Florida.

In the early 1990s, the Walt Disney Company decided to take 5,000 acres of land it had acquired around its theme park properties and try something new: residential development. CEO Michael Eisner was passionate about design, and he enlisted architects Robert A. M. Stern and Jaquelin Robertson to plan the project. They proposed a large-scale experiment in New Urbanism, design principles that call for planning small-scale, mixed-use communities similar to towns familiar from a century ago. Among the traditional homes are public buildings by some of the most famous architects in the world: a town hall by Philip Johnson, a post office by Michael Graves, and a bank by Robert Venturi and Denise Scott Brown.

It was our job to create all the graphics: the street signs, the names over the shops, the markings at the holes at the public golf course, even the manhole covers. Authenticity is a tricky thing, especially for a graphic designer. We are not just creators of form but communicators of ideas. This requires fluency in a common language, an ability to manipulate elements that are widely, if subconsciously, understood—typefaces, colors, images. There is a reason a sign in an airport looks different from a sign on a small town street corner. To create graphics that 7,500 people would have to live with, day in and day out, was a challenge. Our goal in Celebration was to become part of the scenery.

I have worked with many idealistic clients, but none more so than the team that created Celebration. We were inventing a new world, and it was thrilling. Today the town is not so new anymore. And the older it gets, the more I like it.

Below
Towns don't have logos, but they do have seals. The Celebration seal created by Pentagram Associate Tracey Cameron was meant to invoke the quintessential American small town. It was also made into a wristwatch on which, once a minute, the dog overtakes the girl cyclist (see opposite, bottom right).

Right and opposite
Our graphics were designed to be approved by some of the world's best architects, including Robert A. M. Stern, Robert Venturi and Denise Scott Brown, Cesar Pelli, Michael Graves, and Philip Johnson. It was a bit of luck that our recommendation for the town's official typeface was created by an architect: Cheltenham, designed by Bertram Goodhue in 1896. Classic without being fussy, available in multiple weights and versions, it was used on everything from painted signs to cut metal details to a fence that enclosed a 40-foot live oak at the community's entrance.

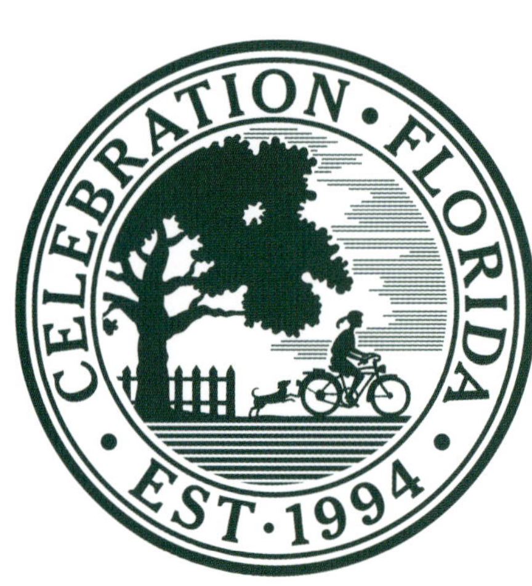

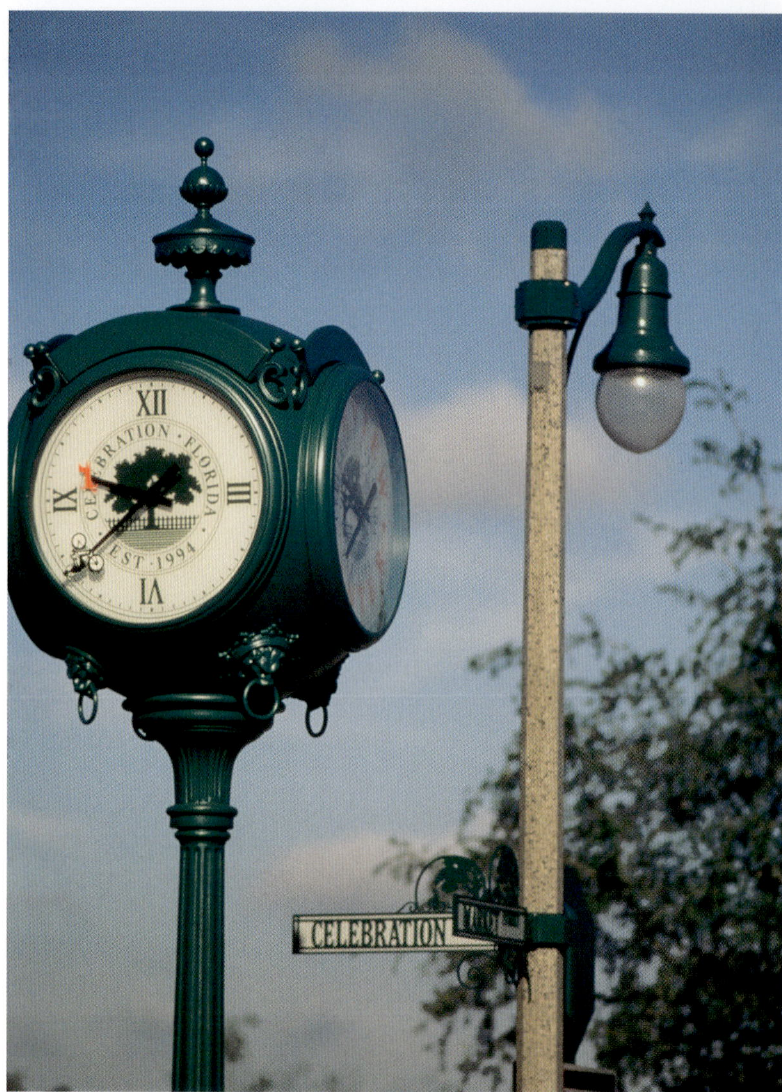

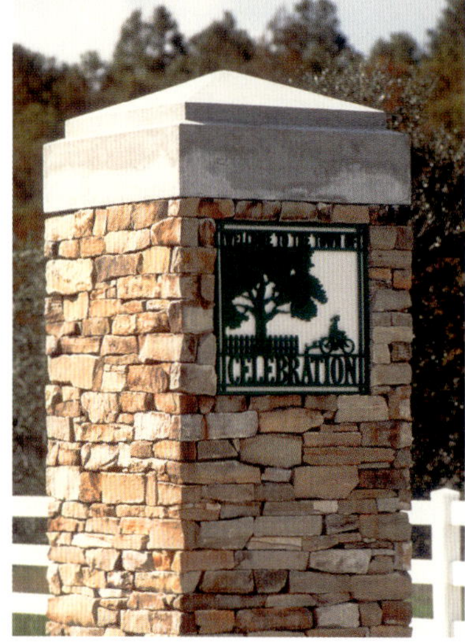

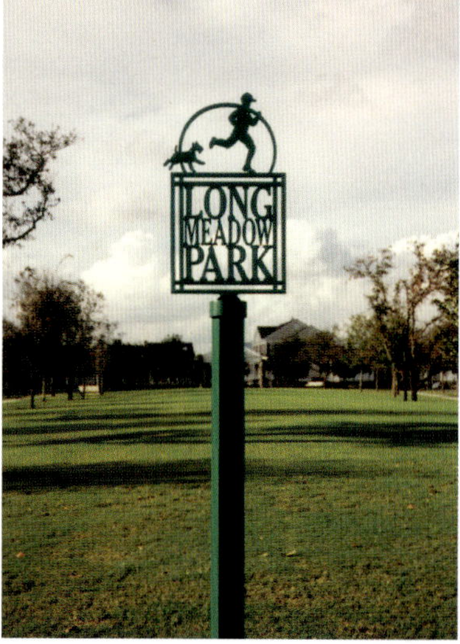

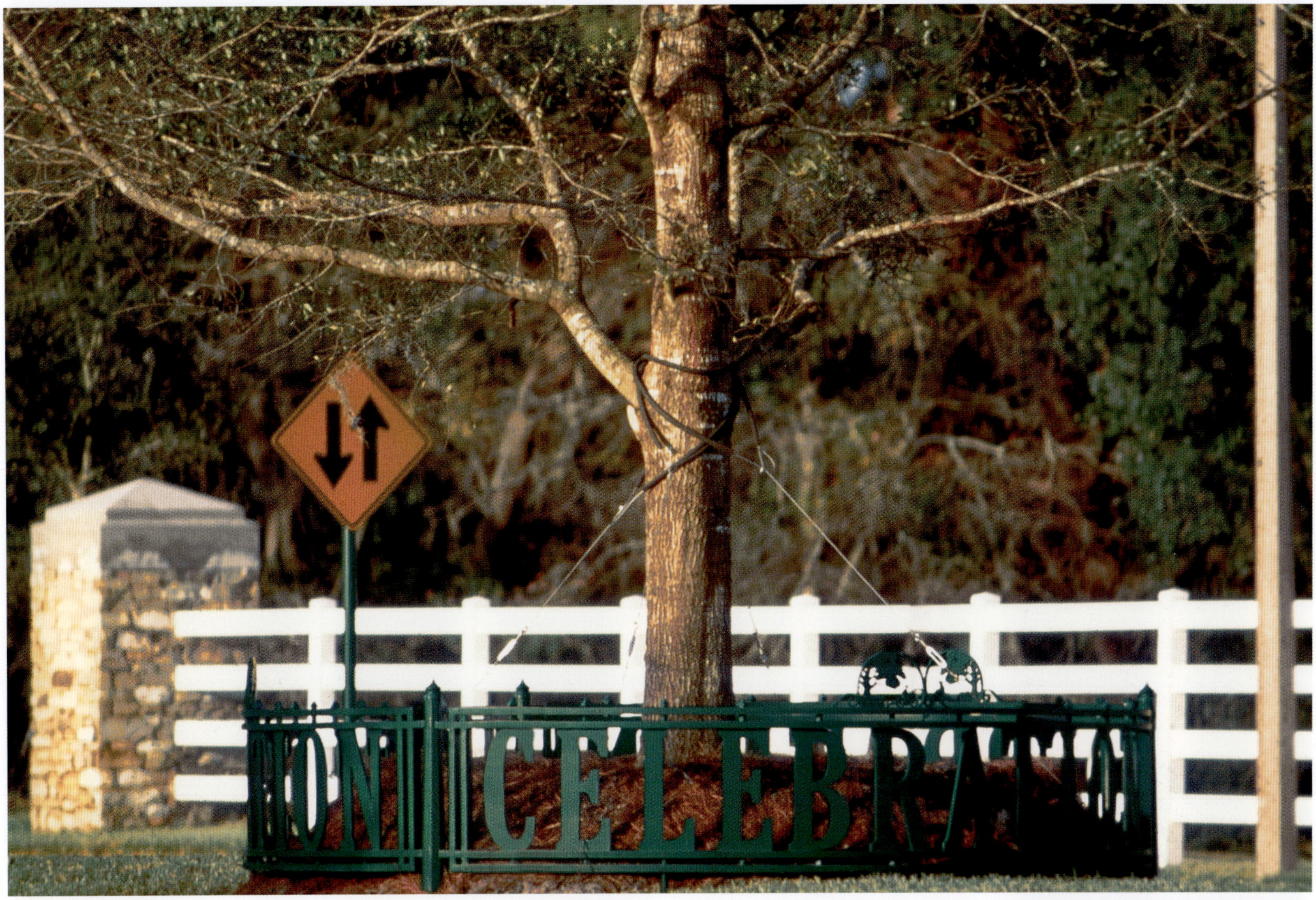

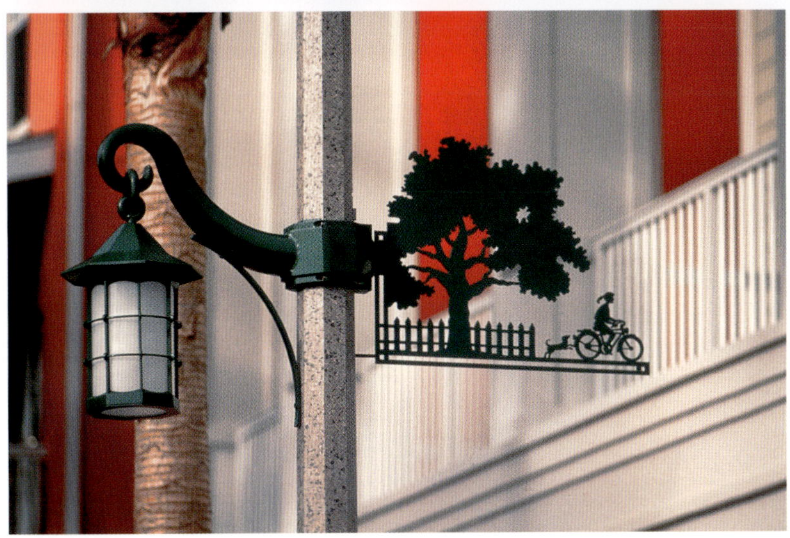

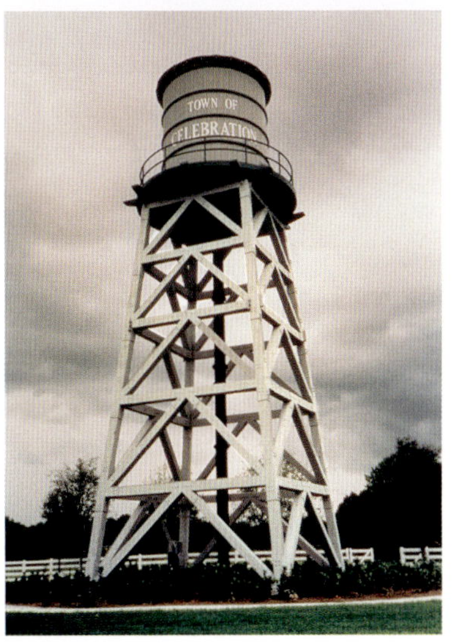
TOWN OF

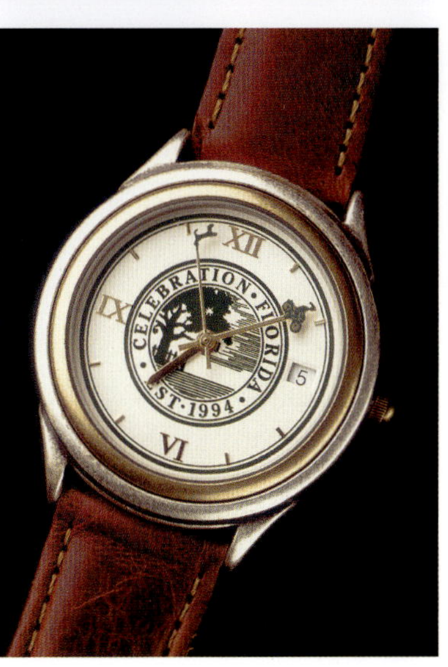
CELEBRATION·FLORIDA
EST·1994

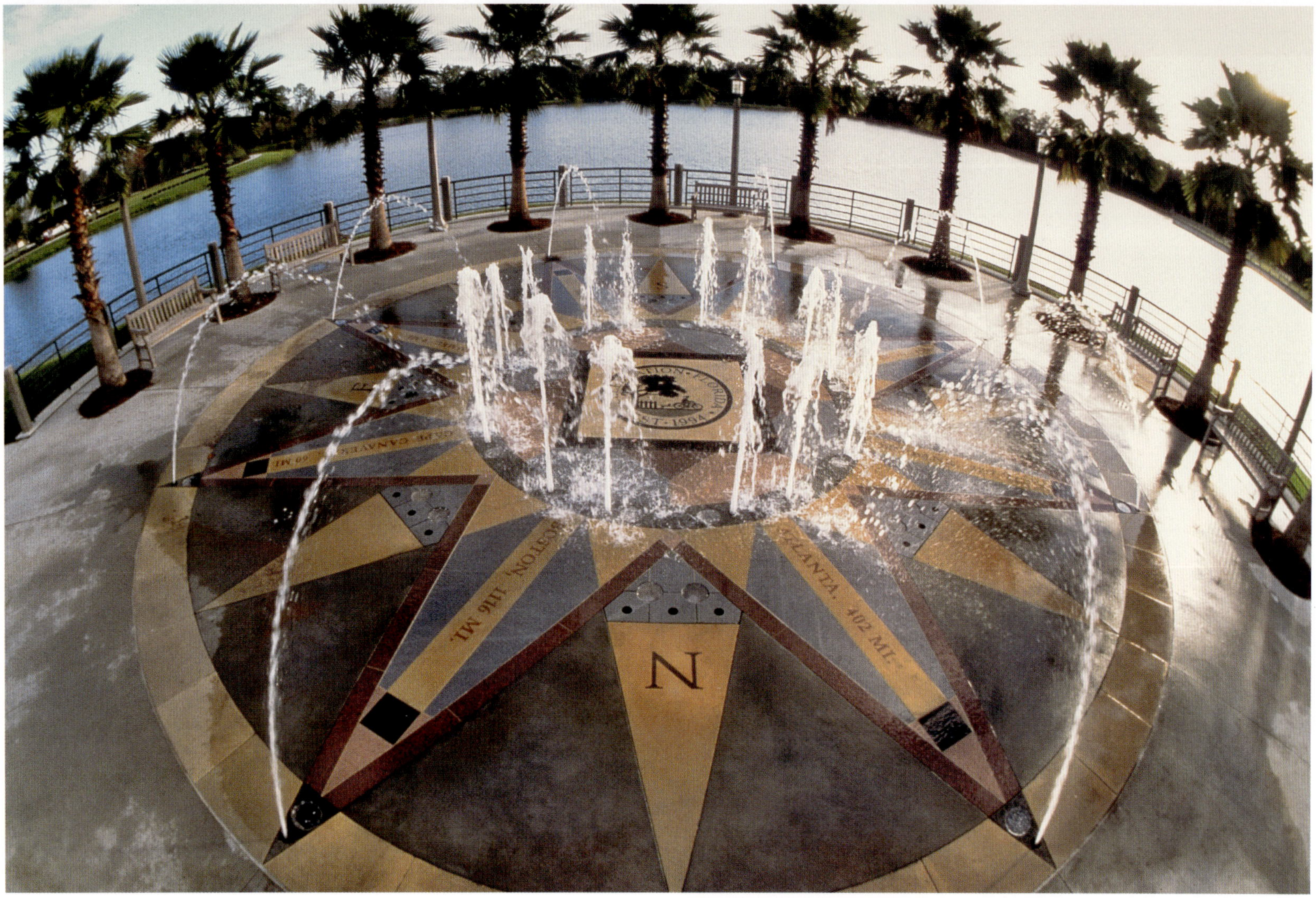

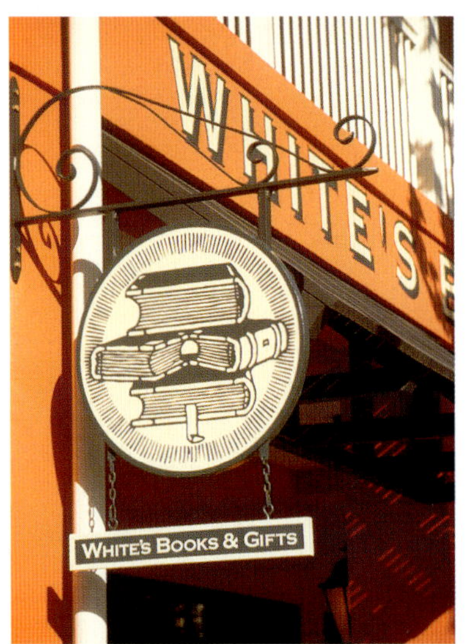
WHITE'S BOOKS & GIFTS

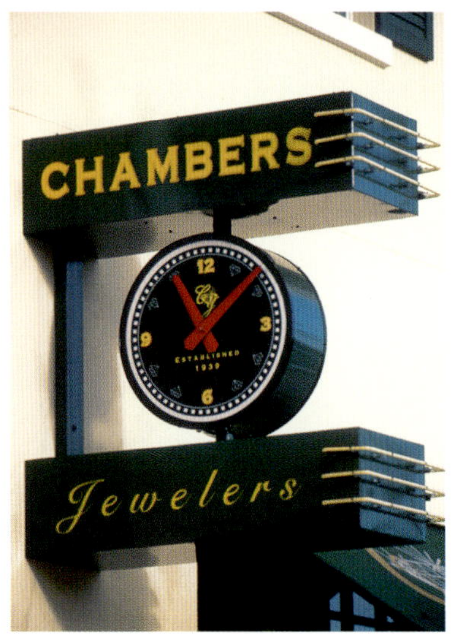
CHAMBERS
Jewelers

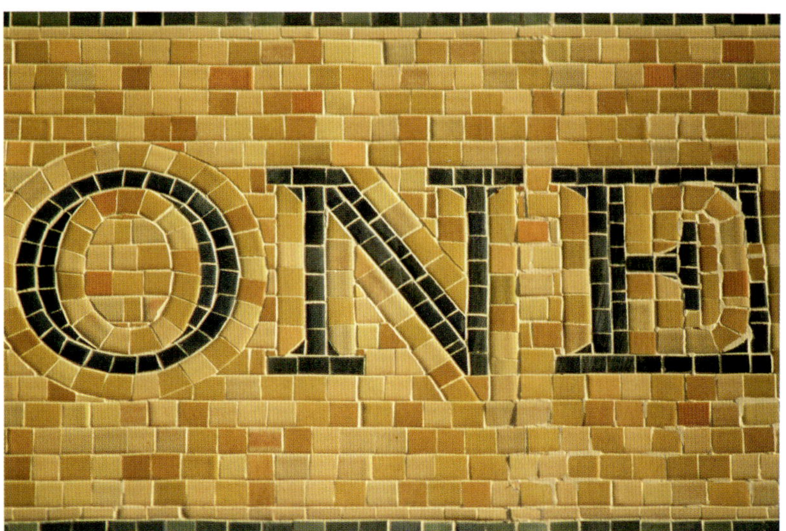
ONE

Opposite top
Our graphics included the design of a fountain in the heart of Celebration's shopping district, with compass points connecting the community to the rest of the world.

Opposite bottom
Overlaying the consistency of the town's infrastructure were the signs for the town's retailers. Whereas street signs and manhole covers used a consistent visual language, store signs explored the history of American vernacular signage, from neon to woodcarving to mosaic tile.

Right top
The town's movie theater, a stylish contemporary take on American Moderne by Cesar Pelli, is a landmark that bears the town's name on its twin masts.

Right bottom
Designing the graphics for Celebration's public golf club was much harder than designing the town seal. It took me some time to realize why: none of our clients were Schwinn-riding, ponytailed girls, but most of them were enthusiastic golfers. The silhouette on the golf club sign was refined endlessly as various executives demonstrated their swings in client meetings.

Next spread
Ironically, the town that celebrates Main Street values has no Main Street itself. (There was already another street with that name in Osceola County.) Instead, the central thoroughfare is called Celebration Avenue.

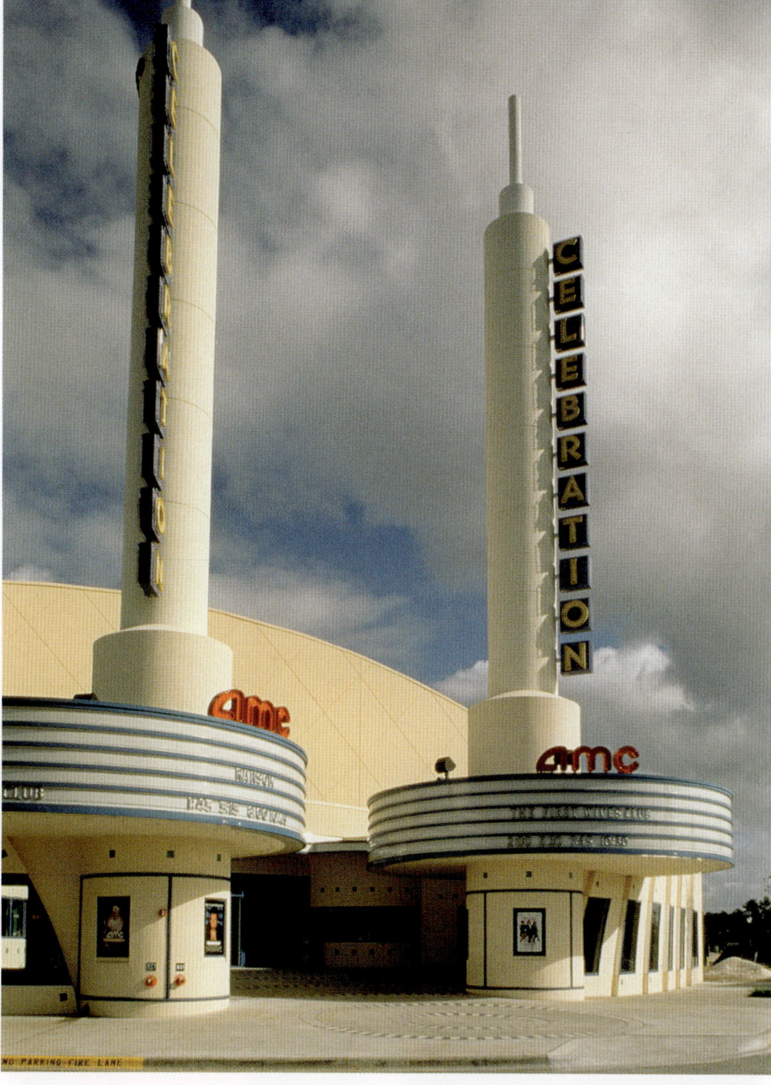

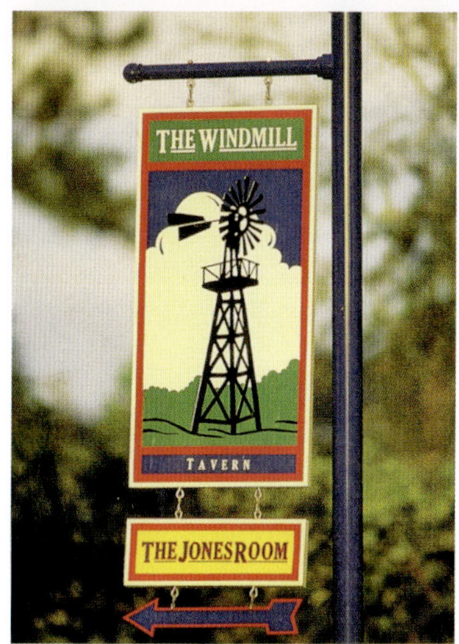

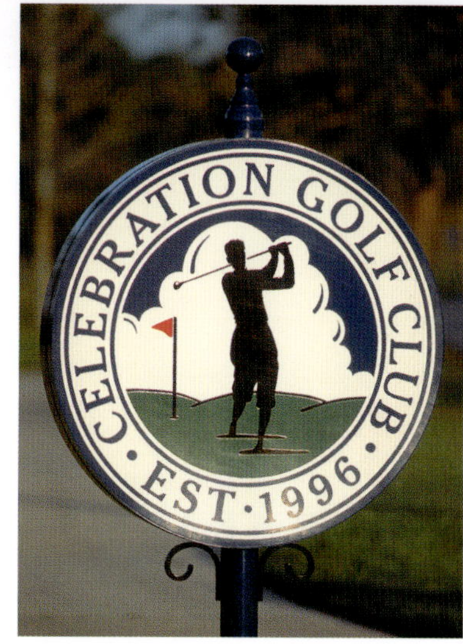

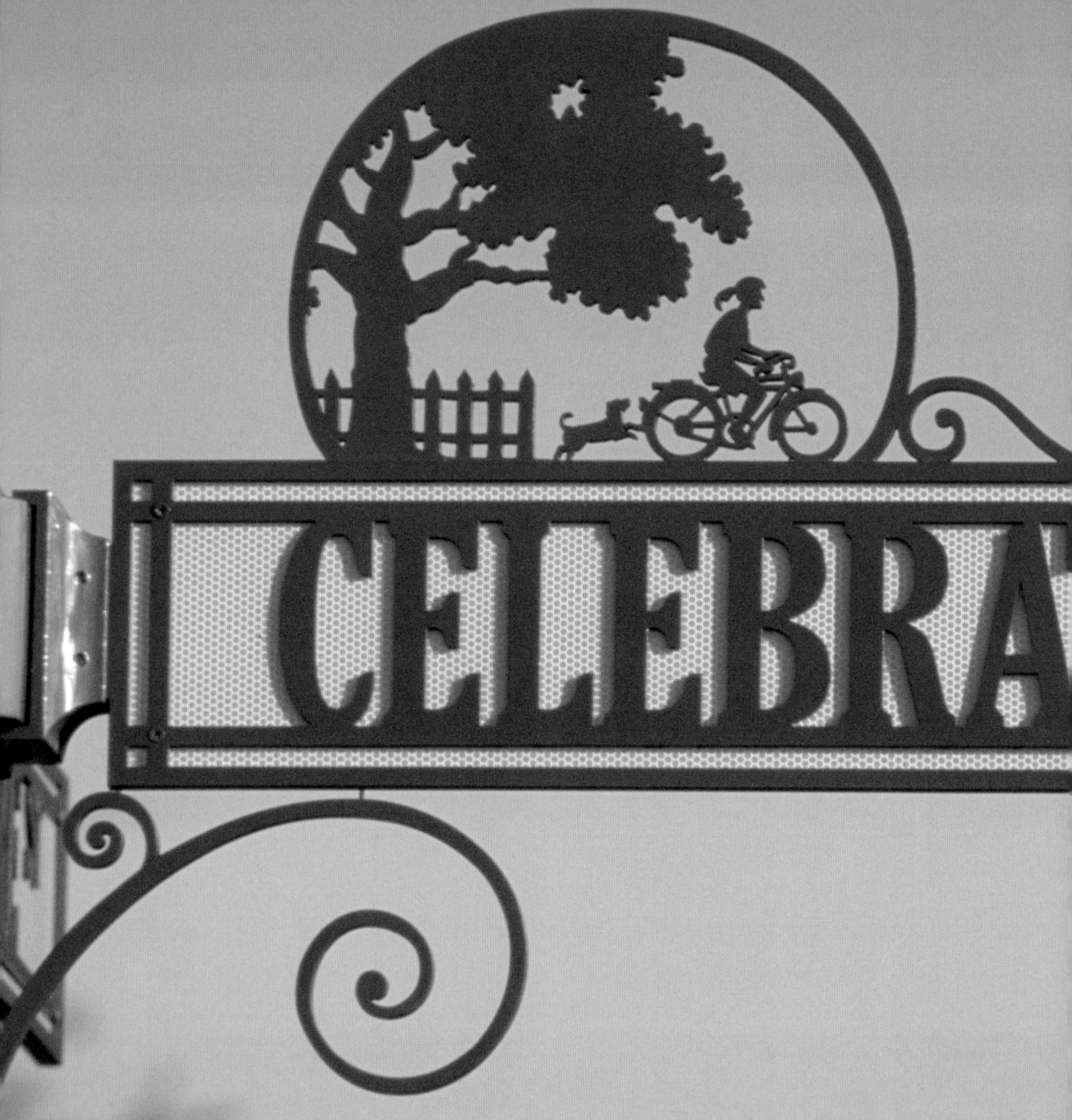
CELEBRA

TION AVE

PARALLAX.

How to work for free

Parallax Theater

Opposite
Victor D'Altorio's theater company was called Parallax. I never asked him what the name meant, and he never asked me why the logo looked the way it did.

Victor D'Altorio was the best actor in my high school. He was in every play our school mounted, and if not in the starring role, at least in the hammiest one: Captain Hook in *Peter Pan*, Boris Kolenkhov in *You Can't Take It with You*, Malvolio in *Twelfth Night*. I did the posters.

After college, he arrived in New York to look for work as an actor as I was just starting out as a designer. Before long, I got a call. "Hey, Mike?" he asked. (Only my family and oldest friends still call me Mike.) "We're putting on a show. Could you do the poster?" I said, sure. He told me they didn't have much money. I said, don't worry about that.

Victor would never hit the big time as an actor. But he became a beloved teacher and a sometime director, first in New York, then Chicago, and ultimately Los Angeles. And I designed every one of his posters for free. The Internet is filled with designer rants about the corrosive evils of free work. I love working for free, especially under the unspoken terms that governed the relationship I had with Victor.

First, the work was fun. Victor would explain what the play was about in two sentences, and would send me the text that had to go on the poster. The explanation was always vivid and inspiring, and the text was always complete and free of typographical errors. Second, after receiving my design, Victor would permit himself a single question: "How can I thank you?" Finally, he never promised me exposure to movie stars on opening night or high-paying jobs down the road. I think as an actor, he understood what so many clients don't: that for a creative person, the real reward is to simply do the work. Getting a "Hey, Mike?" call from Victor meant I'd have one more chance to do my best.

Sadly, I won't get that call again. Victor died, too young, in 2009.

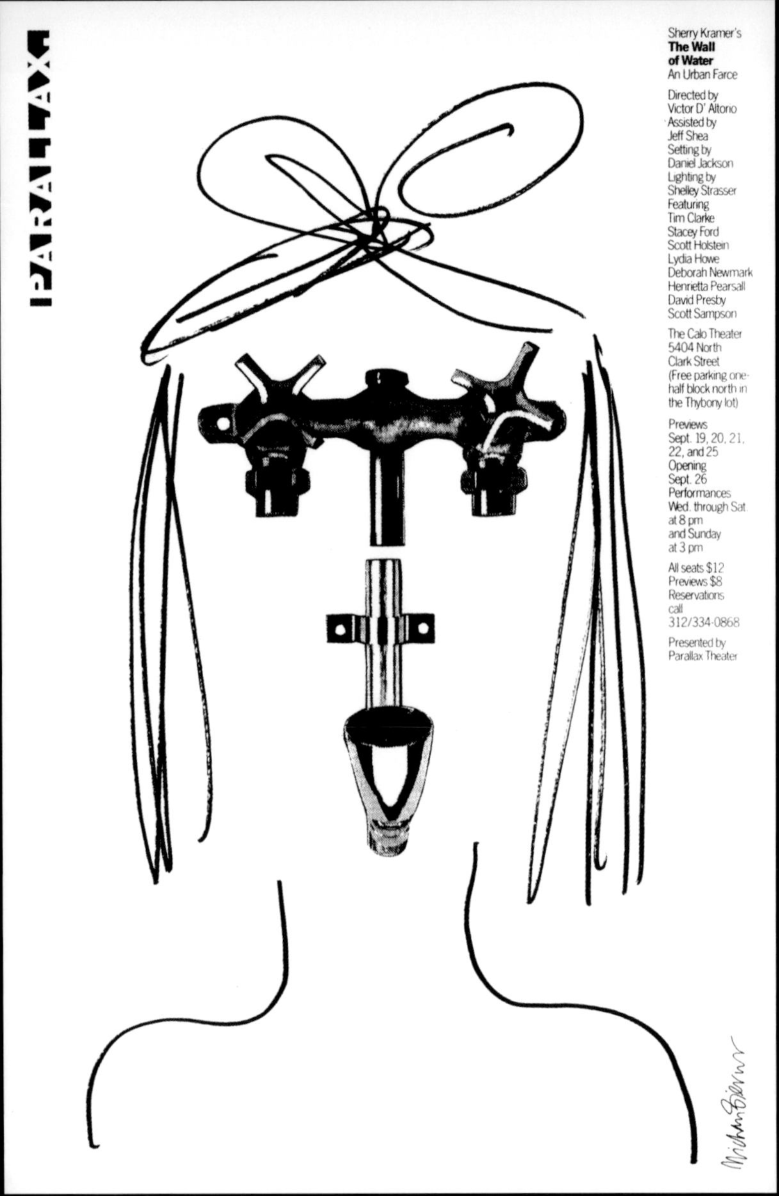

PARALLAX

Sherry Kramer's
The Wall of Water
An Urban Farce

Directed by
Victor D' Altorio
Assisted by
Jeff Shea
Setting by
Daniel Jackson
Lighting by
Shelley Strasser
Featuring
Tim Clarke
Stacey Ford
Scott Holstein
Lydia Howe
Deborah Newmark
Henrietta Pearsall
David Presby
Scott Sampson

The Calo Theater
5404 North
Clark Street
(Free parking one-half block north in the Thybony lot)

Previews
Sept. 19, 20, 21, 22, and 25
Opening
Sept. 26
Performances
Wed. through Sat at 8 pm
and Sunday at 3 pm

All seats $12
Previews $8
Reservations call
312/334-0868

Presented by
Parallax Theater

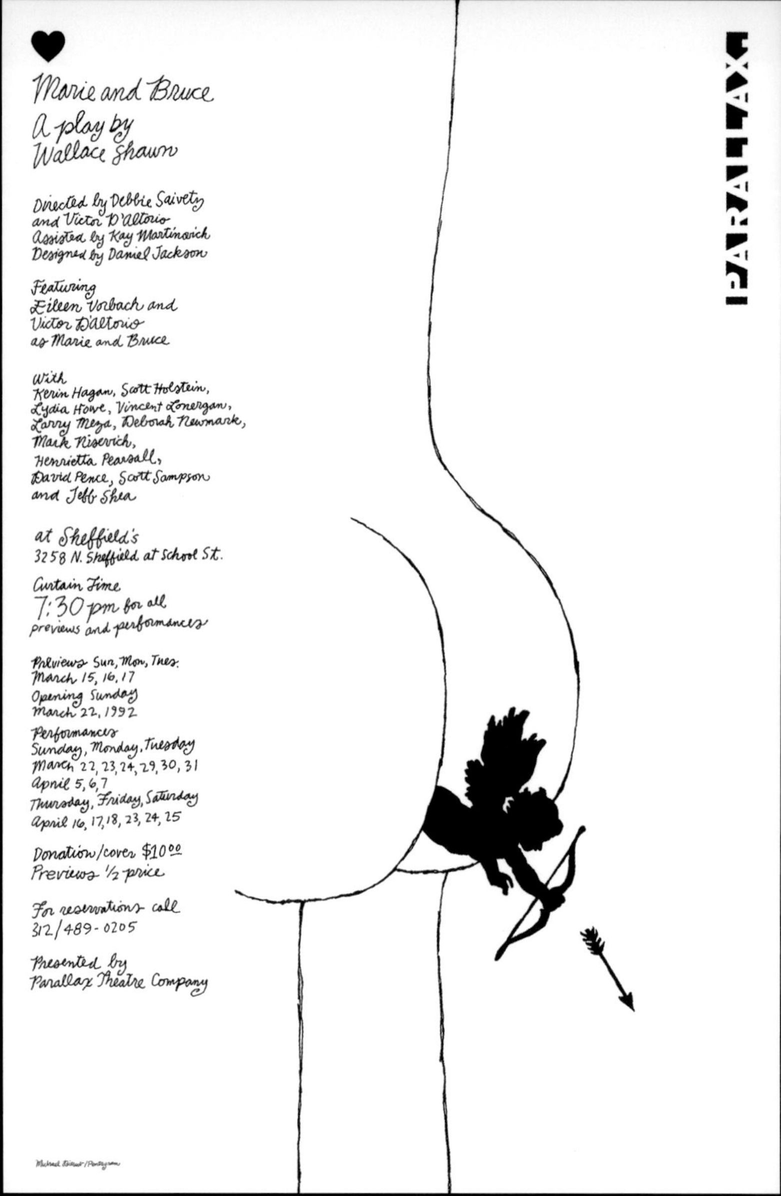

Marie and Bruce
A play by
Wallace Shawn

Directed by Debbie Saivetz
and Victor D'Altorio
Assisted by Kay Martinovich
Designed by Daniel Jackson

Featuring
Eileen Vorbach and
Victor D'Altorio
as Marie and Bruce

With
Kevin Hagan, Scott Holstein,
Lydia Howe, Vincent Lonergan,
Larry Meza, Deborah Newmark,
Mark Niseviich,
Henrietta Pearsall,
David Pence, Scott Sampson
and Jeff Shea

at Sheffield's
3258 N. Sheffield at School St.

Curtain Time
7:30 pm for all
previews and performances

Previews Sun, Mon, Tues.
March 15, 16, 17
Opening Sunday
March 22, 1992

Performances
Sunday, Monday, Tuesday
March 22, 23, 24, 29, 30, 31
April 5, 6, 7
Thursday, Friday, Saturday
April 16, 17, 18, 23, 24, 25

Donation/cover $10.00
Previews ½ price

For reservations call
312/489-0205

Presented by
Parallax Theatre Company

PARALLAX

Above
The Wall of Water is a farce about four female roommates living in a small apartment with a single bathroom who gradually drive each other crazy. The challenge was to make the visual connection between

Above
Wallace Shawn's play *Marie and Bruce* is one of the funniest, darkest, and most scatological portraits of a dysfunctional relationship ever put on stage. For many years, this poster hung in one of

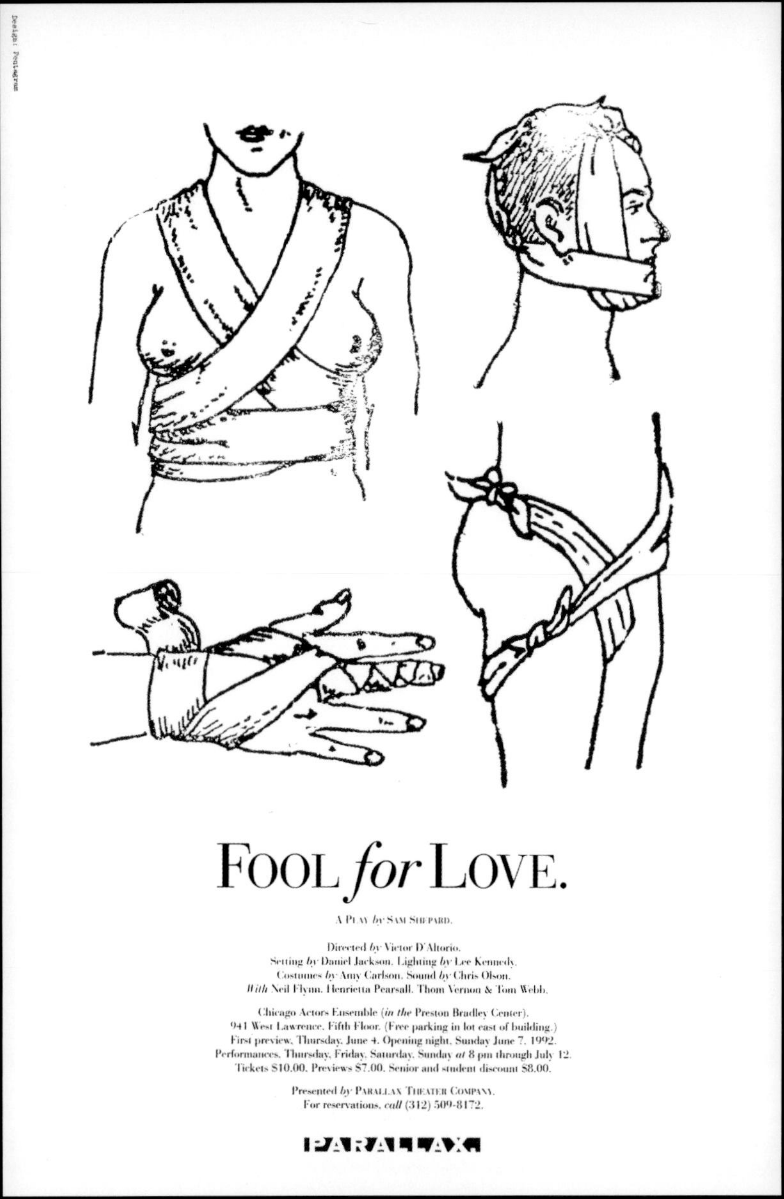

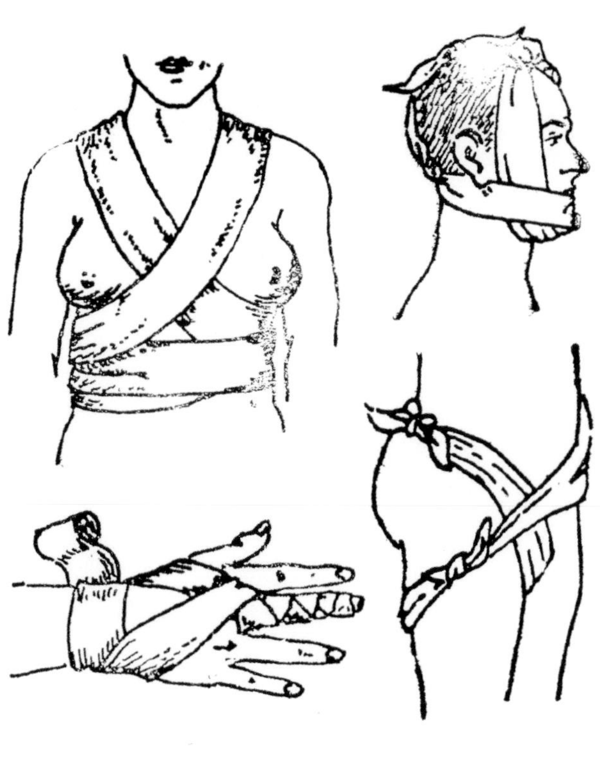

FOOL *for* LOVE.

A PLAY *by* SAM SHEPARD.

Directed *by* Victor D'Altorio.
Setting *by* Daniel Jackson. Lighting *by* Lee Kennedy.
Costumes *by* Amy Carlson. Sound *by* Chris Olson.
With Neil Flynn, Henrietta Pearsall, Thom Vernon & Tom Webb.

Chicago Actors Ensemble (*in the* Preston Bradley Center).
941 West Lawrence, Fifth Floor. (Free parking in lot east of building.)
First preview, Thursday, June 4. Opening night, Sunday June 7, 1992.
Performances, Thursday, Friday, Saturday, Sunday *at* 8 pm through July 12.
Tickets $10.00. Previews $7.00. Senior and student discount $8.00.

Presented *by* PARALLAX THEATER COMPANY.
For reservations, *call* (312) 509-8172.

PARALLAX.

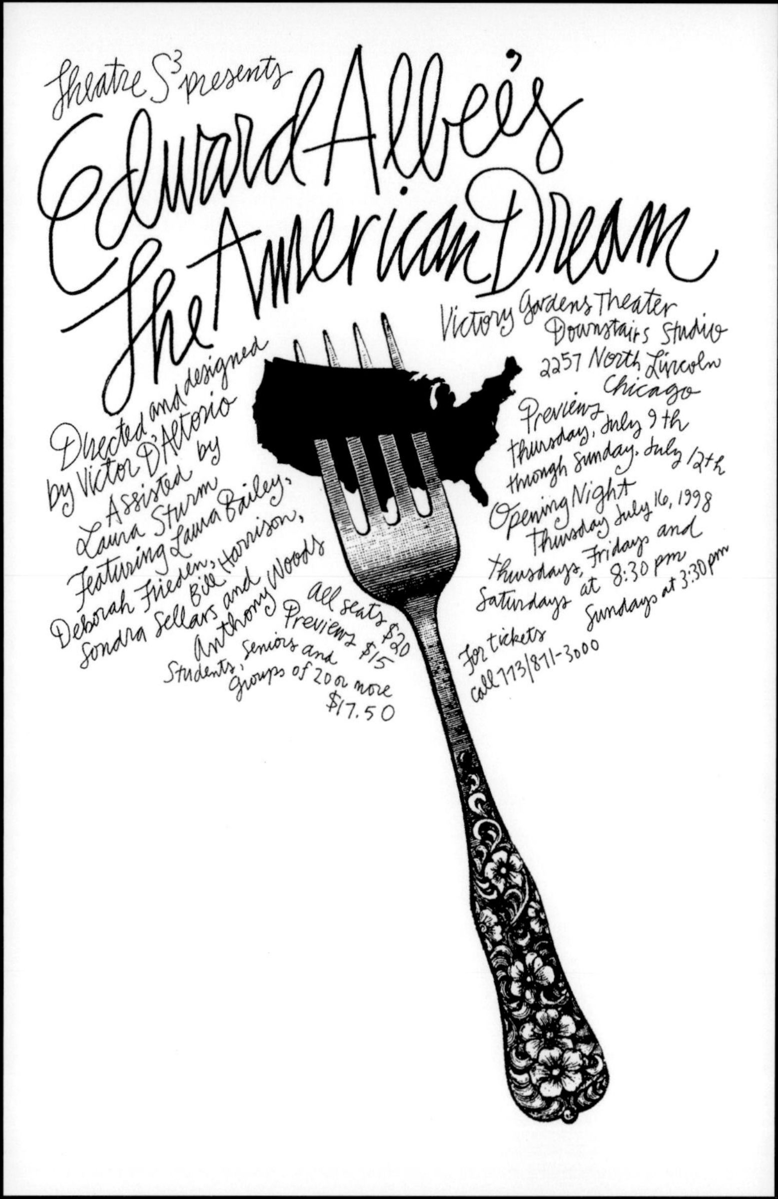

Above
For some reason, many of Victor's productions seemed to revolve around broken or mutually abusive relationships, including Sam Shepard's *Fool for Love*. As with most Parallax productions, I took pleasure in contrasting the name of the play with the grim brutality suggested by the illustrations.

Theatre S[3] presents
Edward Albee's
The American Dream

Victory Gardens Theater
Downstairs Studio
2257 North Lincoln
Chicago

Directed and designed
by Victor D'Altorio
Assisted by
Laura Sturm
Featuring Laura Bailey,
Deborah Frieden, Harrison,
Bill
Sondra Sellars and
Anthony Woods

Previews
Thursday, July 9th
through Sunday, July 12th
Opening Night
Thursday July 16, 1998
Thursdays, Fridays and
Saturdays at 8:30 pm
Sundays at 3:30 pm

All seats $20
Previews $15
Students, Seniors and
Groups of 20 or more
$17.50

For tickets
call 773/871-3000

Above
America's obsession with consumption meets a delicate whisper of mutilation in Edward Albee's classic, and ironically titled, play *The American Dream*.

Design by Pentagram

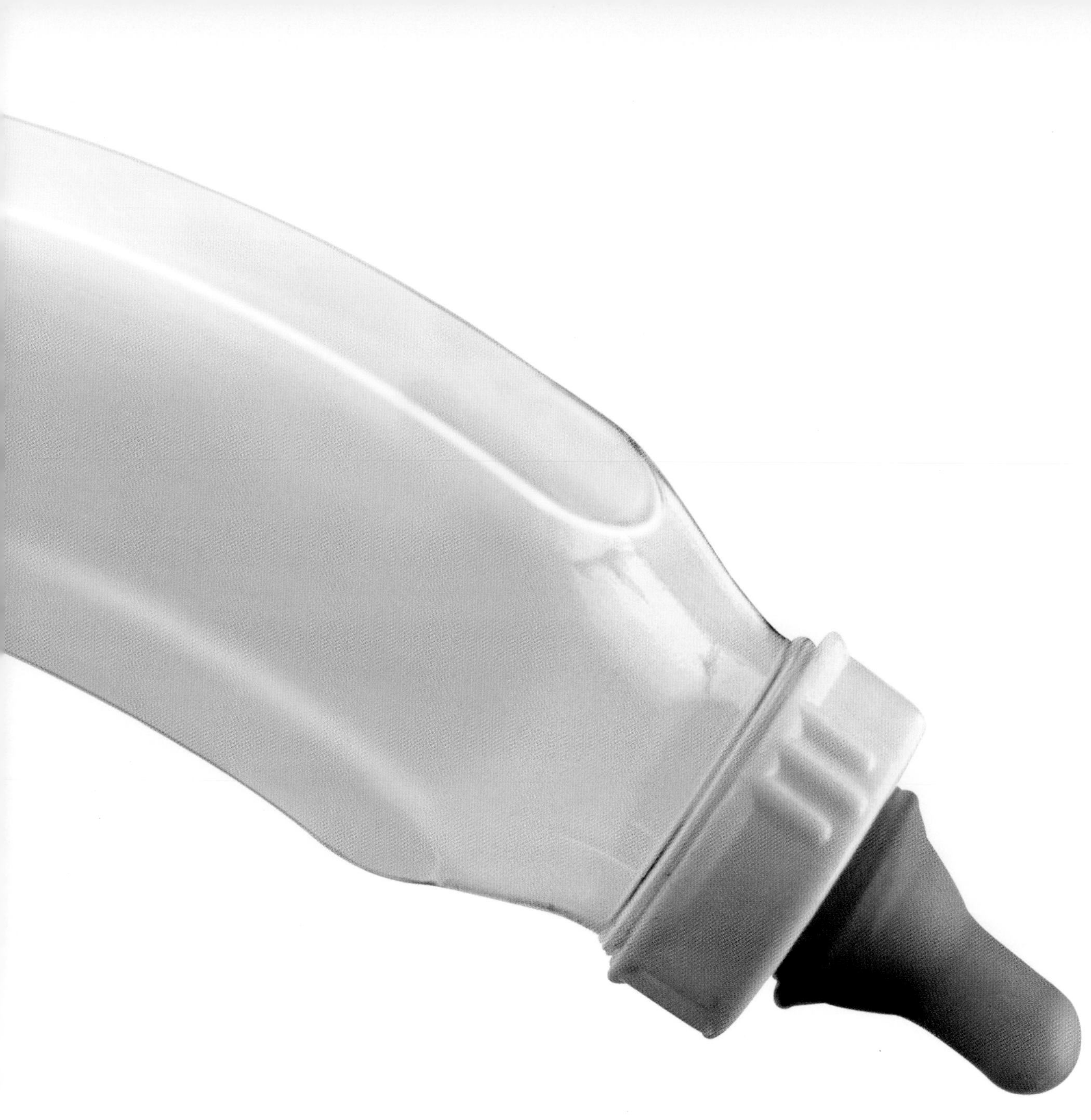

Parallax Theater presents

TheBabysitter

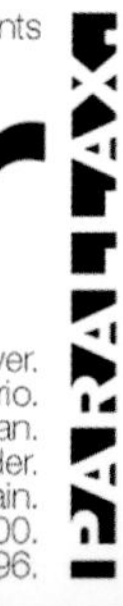

A short story by Robert Coover.
Designed and directed by Victor D'Altorio.
Adapted by Victor D'Altorio and Henrietta Pearsall. Lighting by Rand Ryan.
Performed by Keith Bogart, T. L. Brooke, Winifred Freedman, James C. Leary, John Eric Montana, Rhonda Patterson, Henrietta Pearsall & Darin Toonder.
McCadden Place Theater at 1157 North McCadden Place, one block east of Highland between Santa Monica and Fountain.
Thursdays, Fridays & Saturdays at 8pm. Previews Thursday, January 6,7,8,13. Opening night Friday, January 14, 2000.
All seats $20, previews $14. For tickets 323/960-7896.

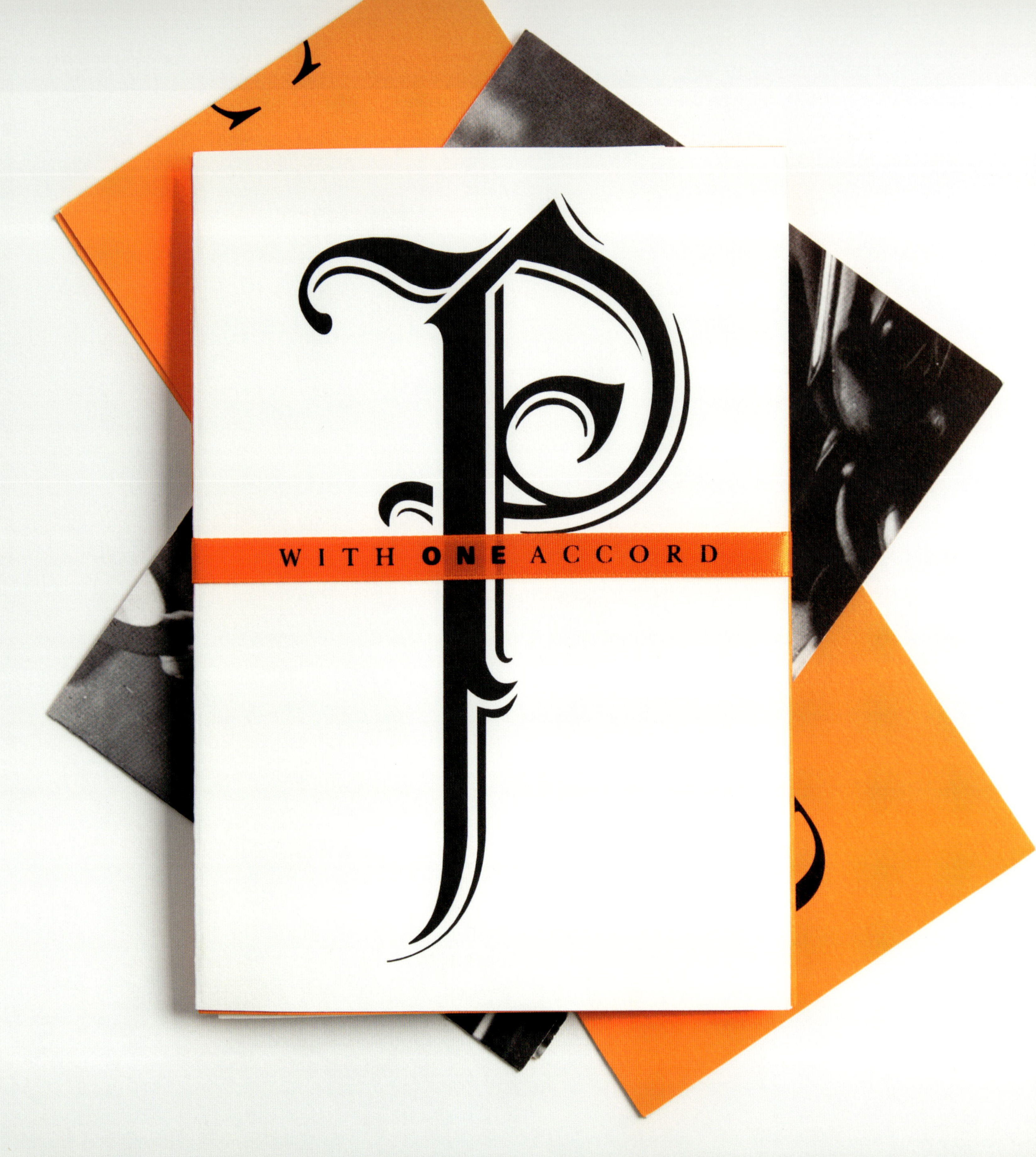
WITH ONE ACCORD

How to raise a billion dollars

Princeton University

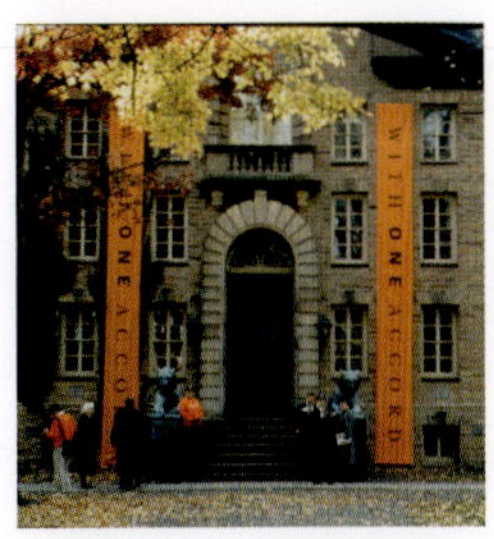

Opposite For the theme of its biggest fundraising effort to date, Princeton looked to the words of its alma mater. "With One Accord" was the result.

Above At the campaign launch, **giant** banners in the school colors of orange and black flanked the doors to Nassau Hall, the oldest building on campus and the song's subject.

One day, after I had been at Pentagram a few years, I got a call from a former client, Jody Friedman. She had just gotten a new job doing something called "development communications" at her alma mater, Princeton. She said they were about to launch a capital campaign and asked if I could help.

I didn't know what development communications were, I didn't know what a capital campaign was, and I had never set foot on the campus of Princeton University. Jody patiently explained to me that this was all basically about fundraising. I got uneasier. As someone who had spent his career working like a plumber (my customer needed something done, I figured out how much it would cost, the customer agreed, I did the work, the customer paid), the idea of making money by simply asking for it was absolutely foreign.

Secretly, I was scared of venturing into unknown territory, and preemptively intimidated by the very smart, very well-educated people I was sure to encounter. I tried to back out, but Jody was persistent. I agreed, and learned an obvious lesson: your best chance to grow is to do something you don't know how to do. My clients at Princeton were wonderful guides, and initiated me in the mysterious world of university fundraising. We devised a theme and a graphic treatment. I created some innovative pieces of communication not because I was daring or imaginative, but simply because I didn't actually know how such things were usually done. Not being familiar with the ritualized ways of asking for money, I simply portrayed the university in a way that its alumni would recognize as authentic, and asked for their support. They responded. It helped that the economy was booming. The campaign's goal was $750,000; it raised $1.2 billion.

Graphic design, where form is so dependent on content, is a perfect way to learn about the world. My projects have put me at laboratory benches with microbiologists and in locker rooms with professional football players. I design best when I'm interested in the subject matter. As a result, I've learned to be as interested in as many things as possible.

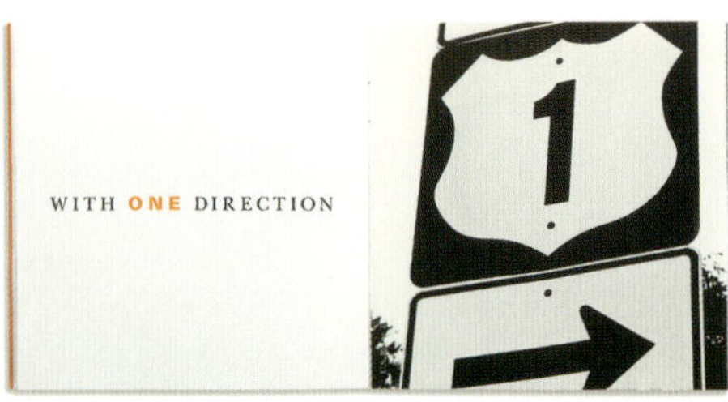

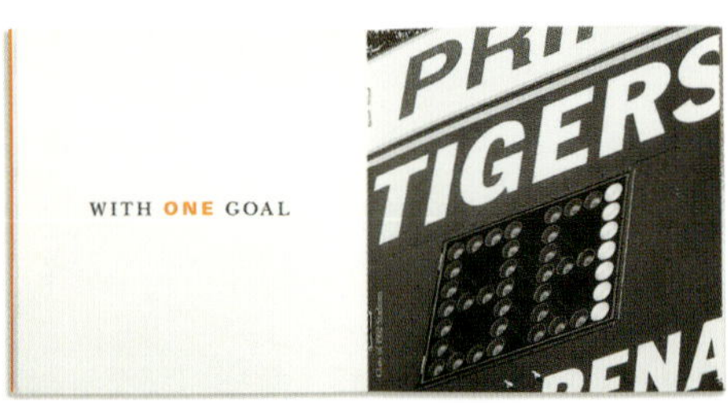

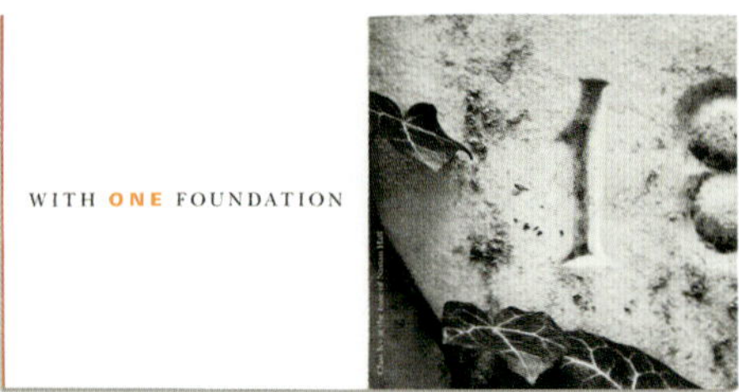

Above
A small book designed by Pentagram's Lisa Cerveny hinted at the campaign to come by finding number ones on and around campus, from cornerstones to street signs.

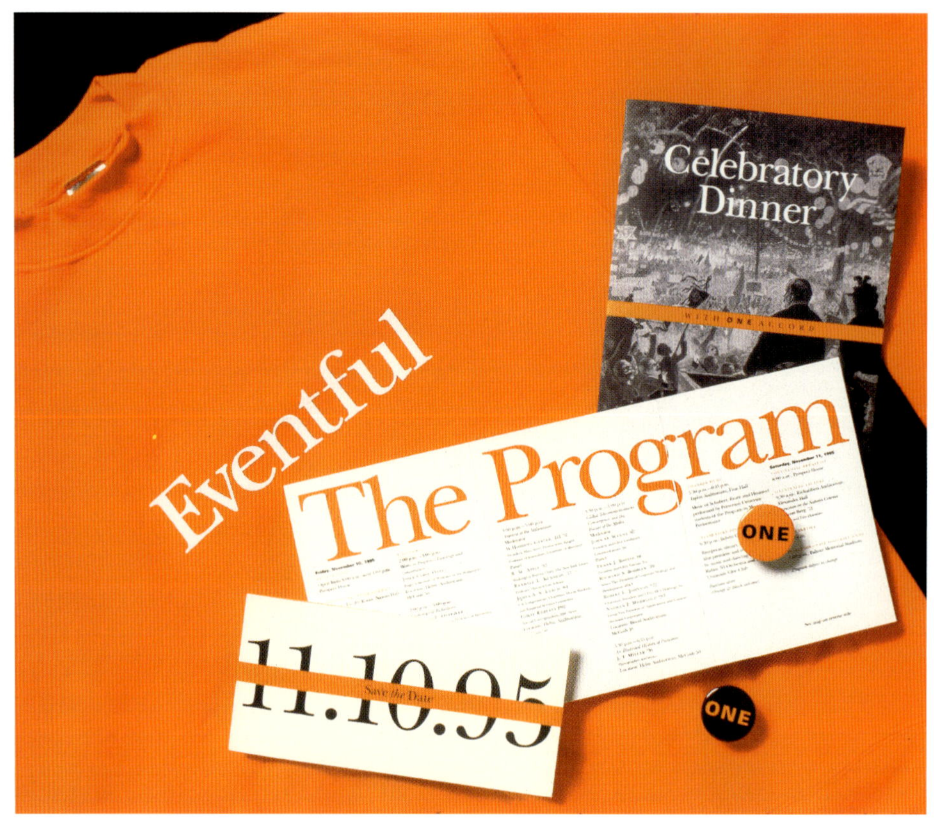

Above
A graphic program devised by Princeton-educated designer Bill Drenttel with his partner Stephen Doyle had designated Baskerville as the school's typeface.

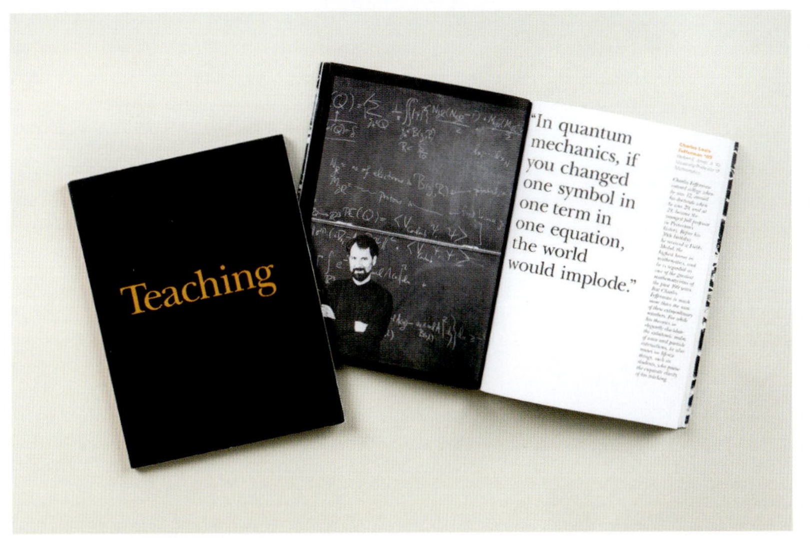

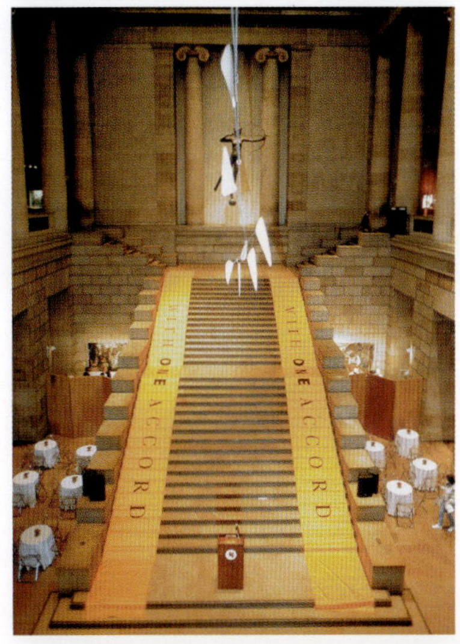

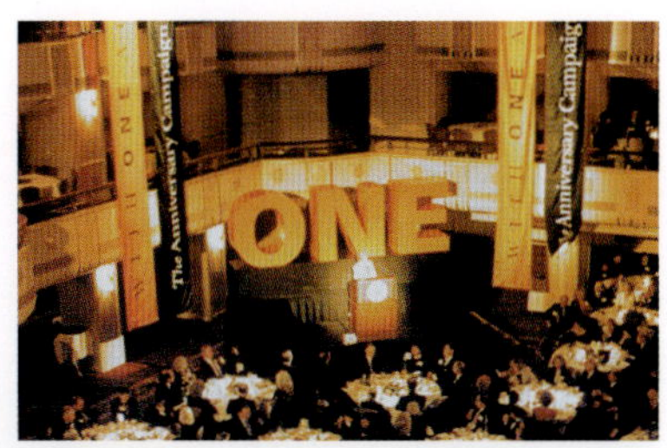

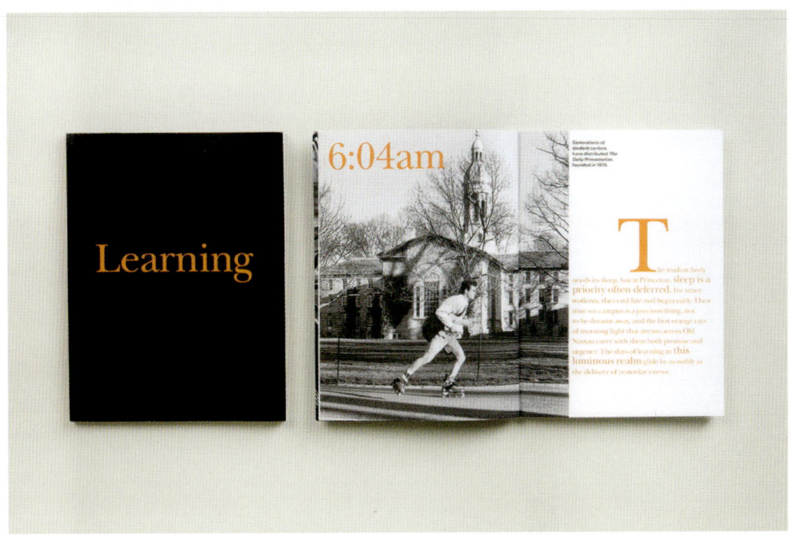

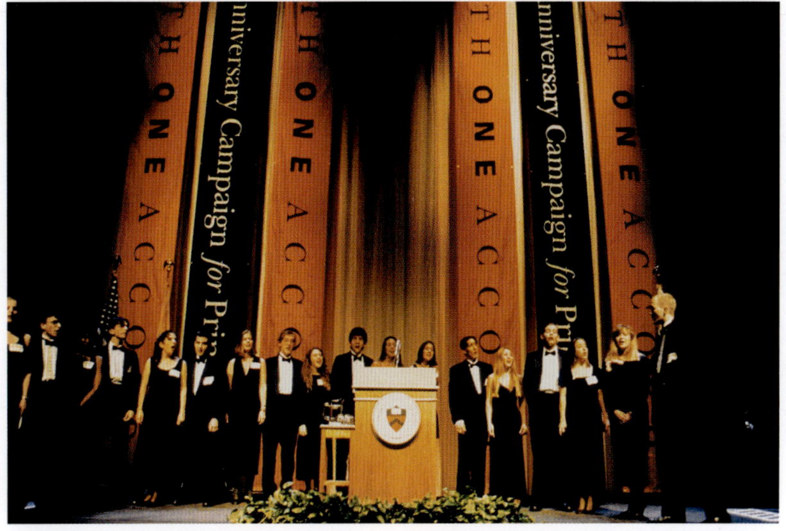

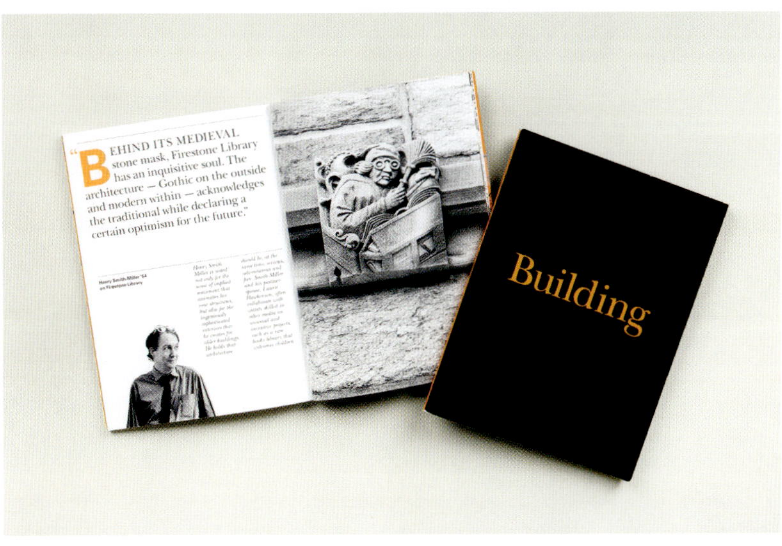

Left top, middle, and bottom
Three small paperbacks, modestly printed in black and white, replaced the ponderous tomes that were then the default way to raise money for schools in the early 1990s. *Teaching* focused on beloved professors on campus and raised money to support the faculty. *Learning* traced a day in the life of five students and made the case for scholarships. *Building* interviewed the distinguished architects who were working on campus and built support for new facilities.

Above
Launch events for the campaign around the country turned the graphic identity into celebratory pageantry. A huge, three-dimensional "ONE" traveled with the school's vocal groups and served as instant photo opportunities for proud alumni.

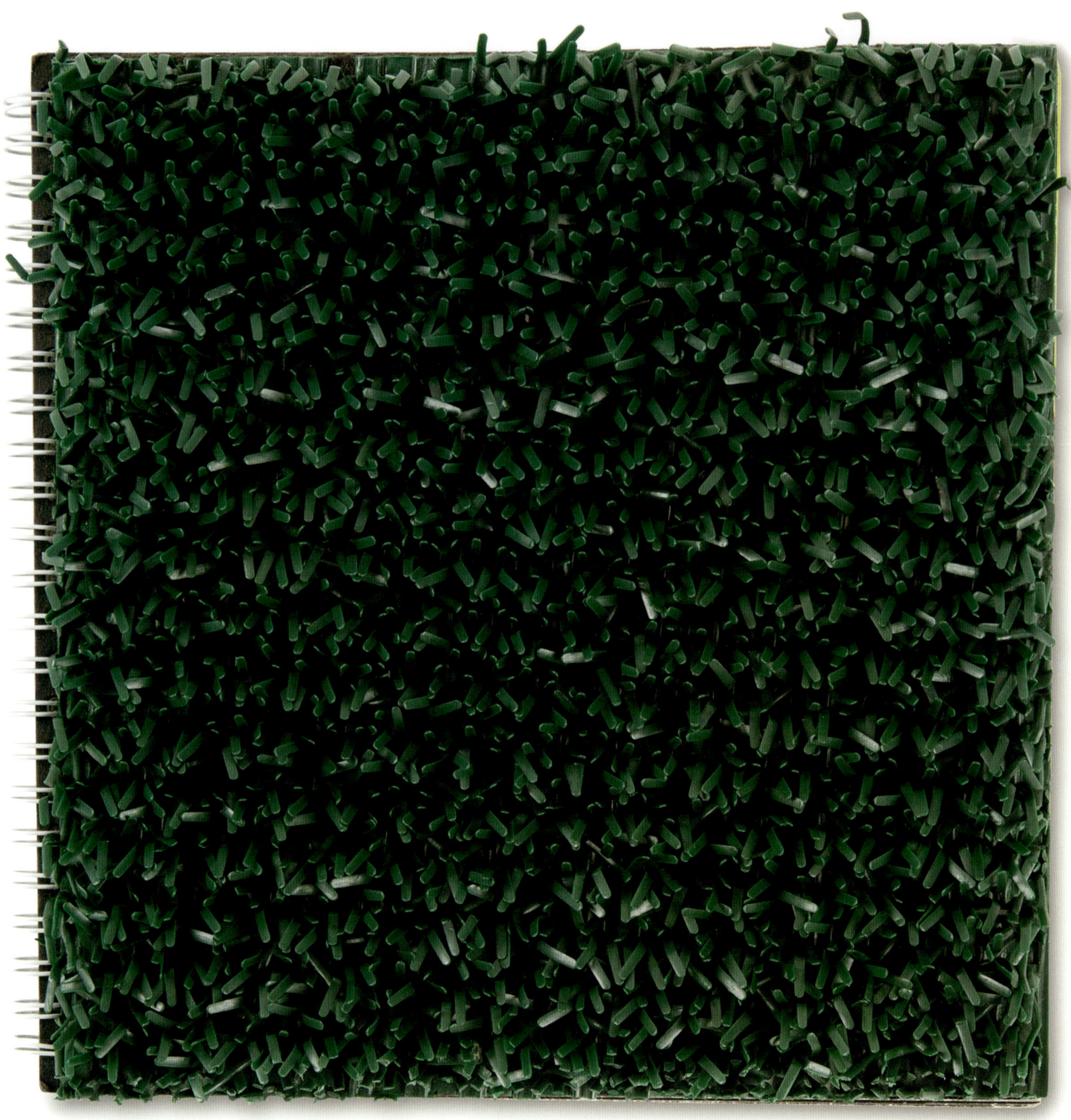

How to win a close game
New York Jets

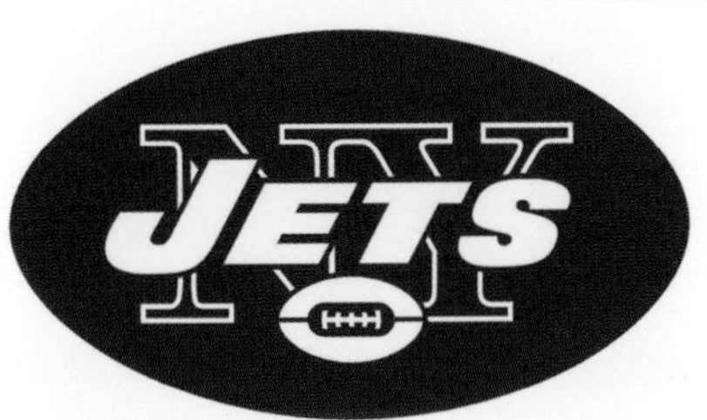

Opposite
The New York Jets are the only organization in the world with graphic guidelines bound in Astroturf.

Above
The original logo is a not-very-good piece of commercial art from the early 1960s. Could it be transformed while remaining unchanged?

In 2001, we got a call from Jay Cross, then president of the New York Jets. Probably the only person in sports management with degrees in both architecture and nuclear engineering, Cross had an assignment with a catch. The assignment was to rebrand the team. The catch? We couldn't touch the logo.

The New York Jets are a media-age invention. Founded in 1959 as the New York Titans, the team changed its name and logo in 1963. The Jets had one indelible moment of glory six years later when the glamorous quarterback Joe Namath led them to an upset victory in Super Bowl III. Since then, the team has been a reliable source of heartbreak to its loyal fans, with a rotating cast of colorful players and outspoken coaches who could never quite regain the heights attained in 1969.

Probably no genre of graphic design is more fraught with emotion than the design of identities for sports teams. If you change a logo for a bank, no one will notice. If you change a logo for a football team, you will get hate mail. The logo that Namath and his teammates wore to the Super Bowl was thought to have totemic power. (Identity design is one of the few professions in which magical thinking qualifies as a business strategy.) As we undertook our work, it was this original logo, now sacrosanct, drawn by an anonymous artist four decades ago, that we were stuck with. This is what designers call a "cat's breakfast": the name of the team in one typeface, superimposed upon the initials NY in another typeface, a tiny football underneath, all placed on another football shape. We made it our starting point.

It turned out that for all its messiness, the logo was a source of endless inspiration. The four letters in the team name could be extrapolated into a proprietary alphabet. The letters NY, superimposed on the football shape, became an immediately identifiable alternate logo. Even the tiny football turned out to be a character we could bring to life. Combined with an expanded color range and a few other graphic devices, the logo provided the Jets with a whole new identity, one that is still in use more than a dozen years later.

Printed standards manuals, once ubiquitous, have been largely replaced by online tools. Yet a physical document can convey a level of authority that a website cannot, particularly if it's made simple and memorable. The book that introduced the new graphic identity for the Jets, bound with hard-to-ignore artificial turf, was meant to provide both instruction and inspiration.

Below The Jets had already updated their logo once before, introducing an aerodynamic version, not shown here, in 1978. The fans viewed it with suspicion if not outright distaste. Twenty years later, in an attempt to evoke the glory of the Namath years, coach Bill Parcells reinstated the original logo. It was the unlikely source of the whole brand system.

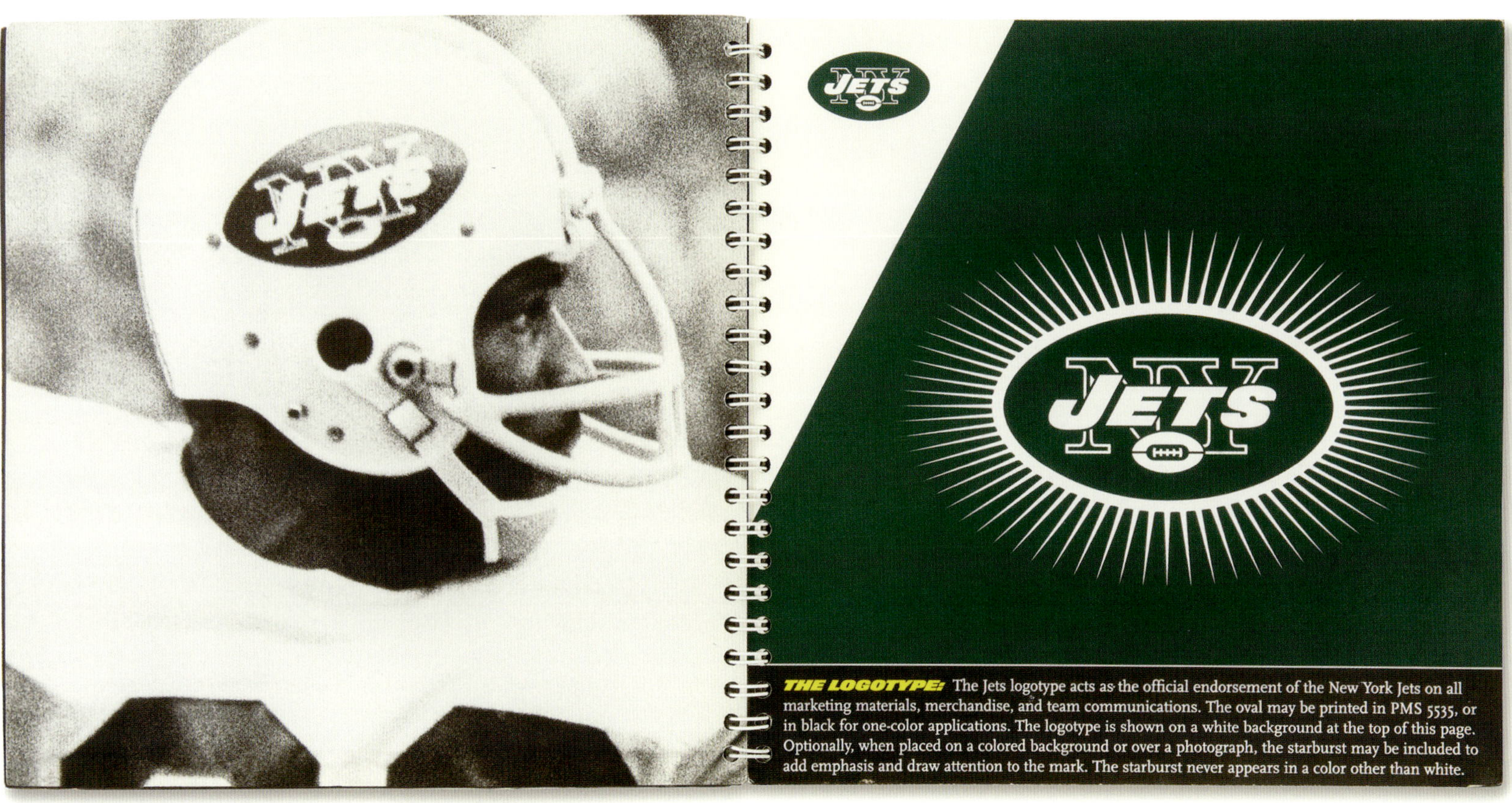

Below
Working with the letters J, E, T, and S, type designers Jonathan Hoefler and Tobias Frere-Jones created a complete typeface. It exists in only one form: extra heavy super italic.

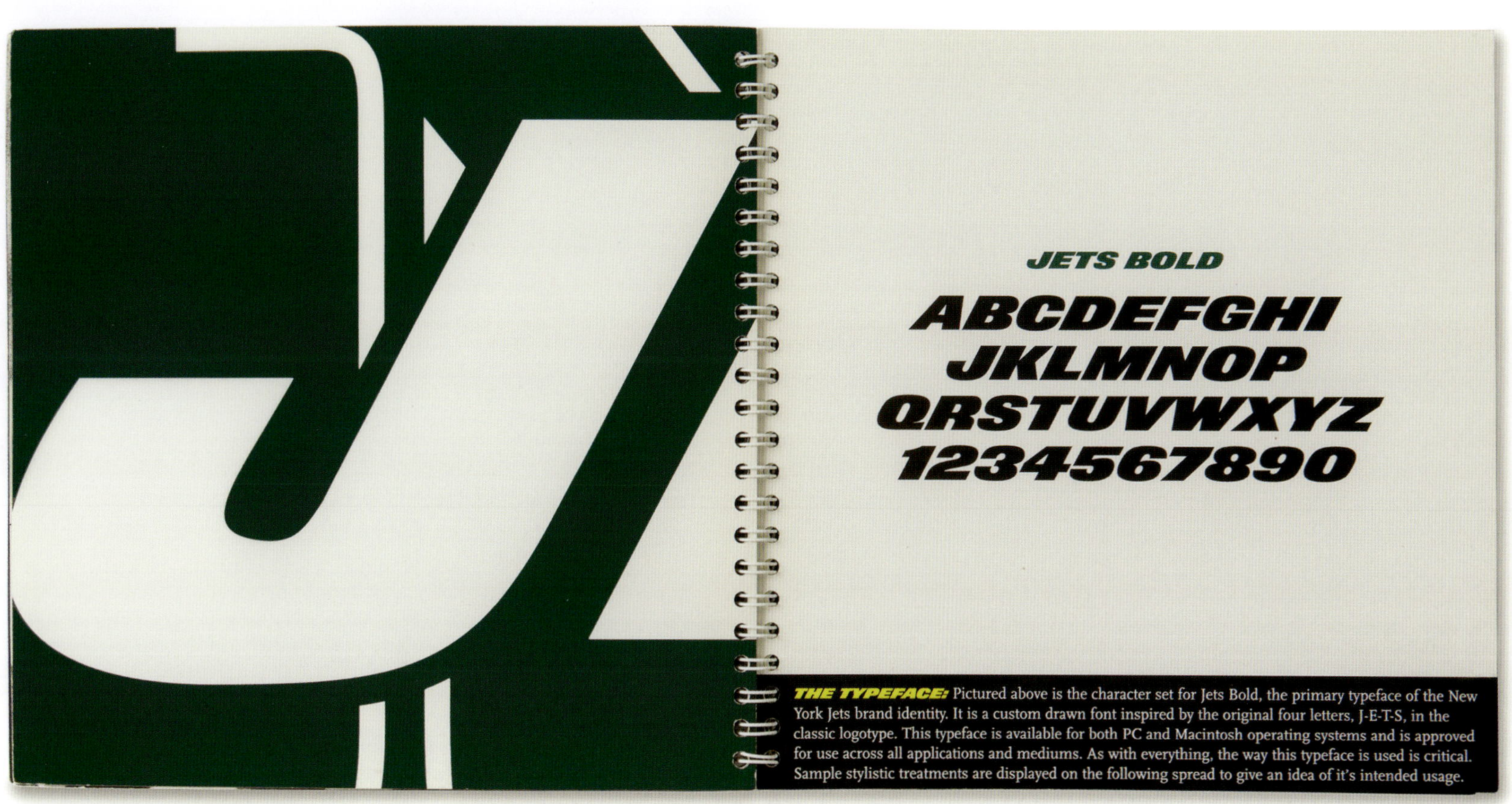

Right
The new typeface, Jets Bold, made any word look intimidating. Jonathan and Tobias used to joke that it would be perfect for Michael Bay movie posters.

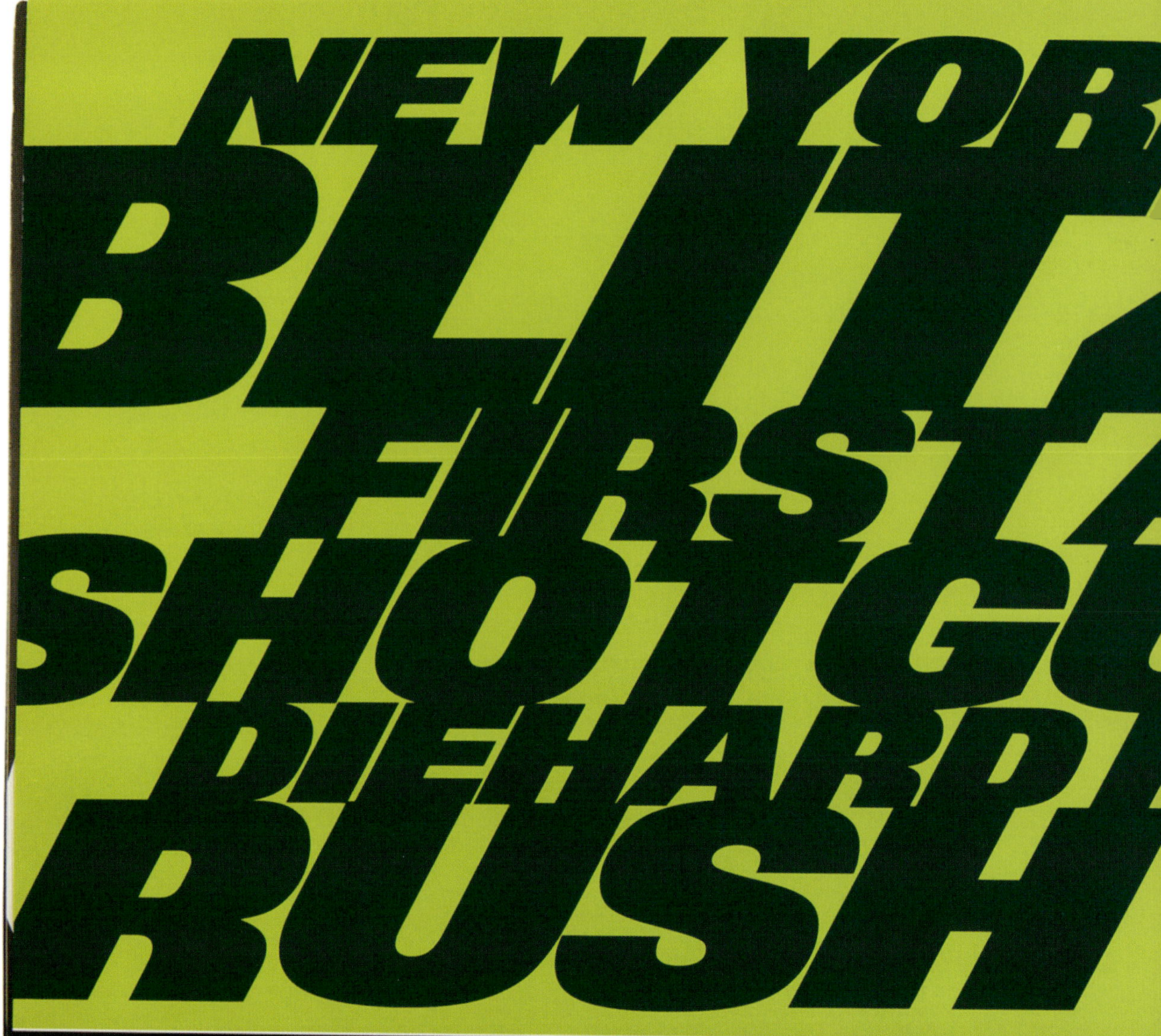

TYPOGRAPHIC STYLE: The vocabulary of football is rich with hard-hitting, descriptive terms such as those displayed above. Whether it be for a promotional flyer for a Jr. Jets event, or the design of stadium graphics, it's use instantly adds an unmistakable New York Jets flavor. It is intended primarily as a display typeface for headlines and titles, but works well at both small and large sizes. It is also extremely legible for a typeface of such angle and weight. Do not stretch, or otherwise manipulate the letterforms.

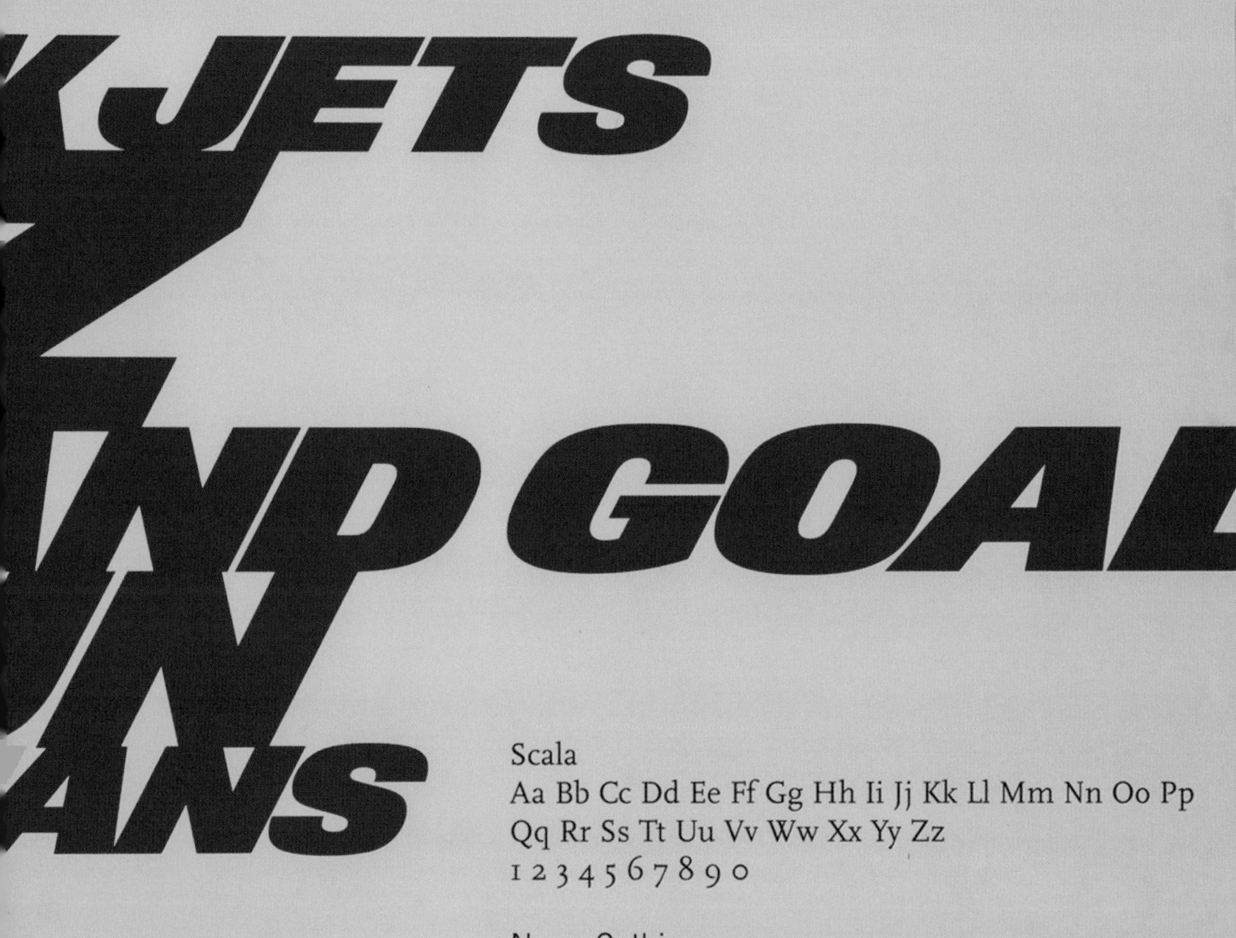

Next spread, top left
Fans are as obsessed with color as they are with logos. We very carefully introduced several complementary colors to the green-and-white Jets palette.

Next spread, top right
Designer Brett Traylor discovered a fierce linesman hidden in the tiny football within the logo, and a new mascot, "Gameface," was born.

Next spread, bottom left
Unlike that of their crosstown rivals, the New York Giants, the Jets logo failed to highlight the team's highly marketable hometown. We remedied this with an alternate logo that put the initials NY, set in Jets Bold, inside the football shape created by the logo.

Next spread, bottom right
The brand system, derived as it is from a common source, is designed to permit maximum variety while remaining close to the team.

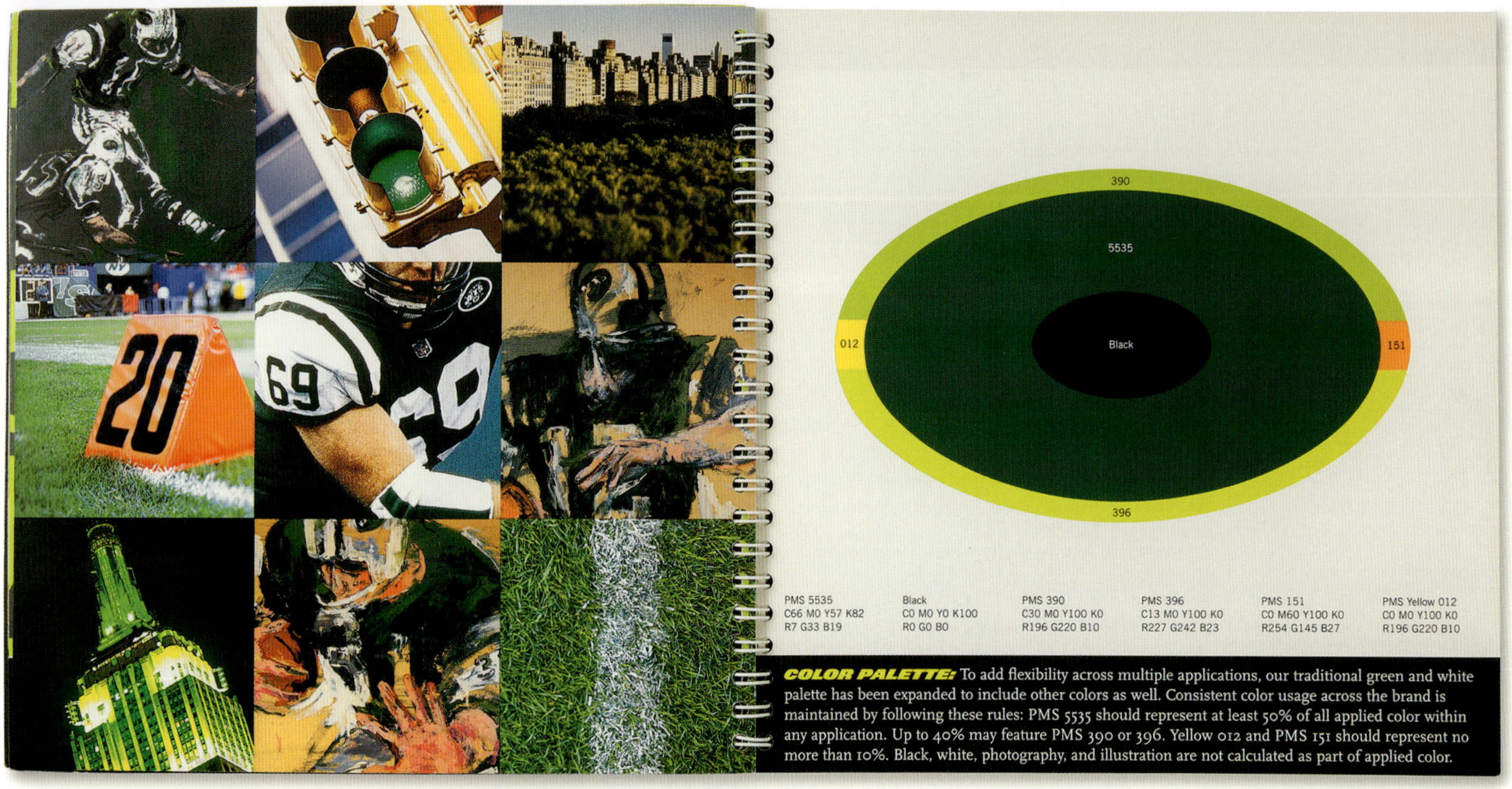

390

5535

012

Black

151

396

PMS 5535	Black	PMS 390	PMS 396	PMS 151	PMS Yellow 012
C66 M0 Y57 K82	C0 M0 Y0 K100	C30 M0 Y100 K0	C13 M0 Y100 K0	C0 M60 Y100 K0	C0 M0 Y100 K0
R7 G33 B19	R0 G0 B0	R196 G220 B10	R227 G242 B23	R254 G145 B27	R196 G220 B10

COLOR PALETTE: To add flexibility across multiple applications, our traditional green and white palette has been expanded to include other colors as well. Consistent color usage across the brand is maintained by following these rules: PMS 5535 should represent at least 50% of all applied color within any application. Up to 40% may feature PMS 390 or 396. Yellow 012 and PMS 151 should represent no more than 10%. Black, white, photography, and illustration are not calculated as part of applied color.

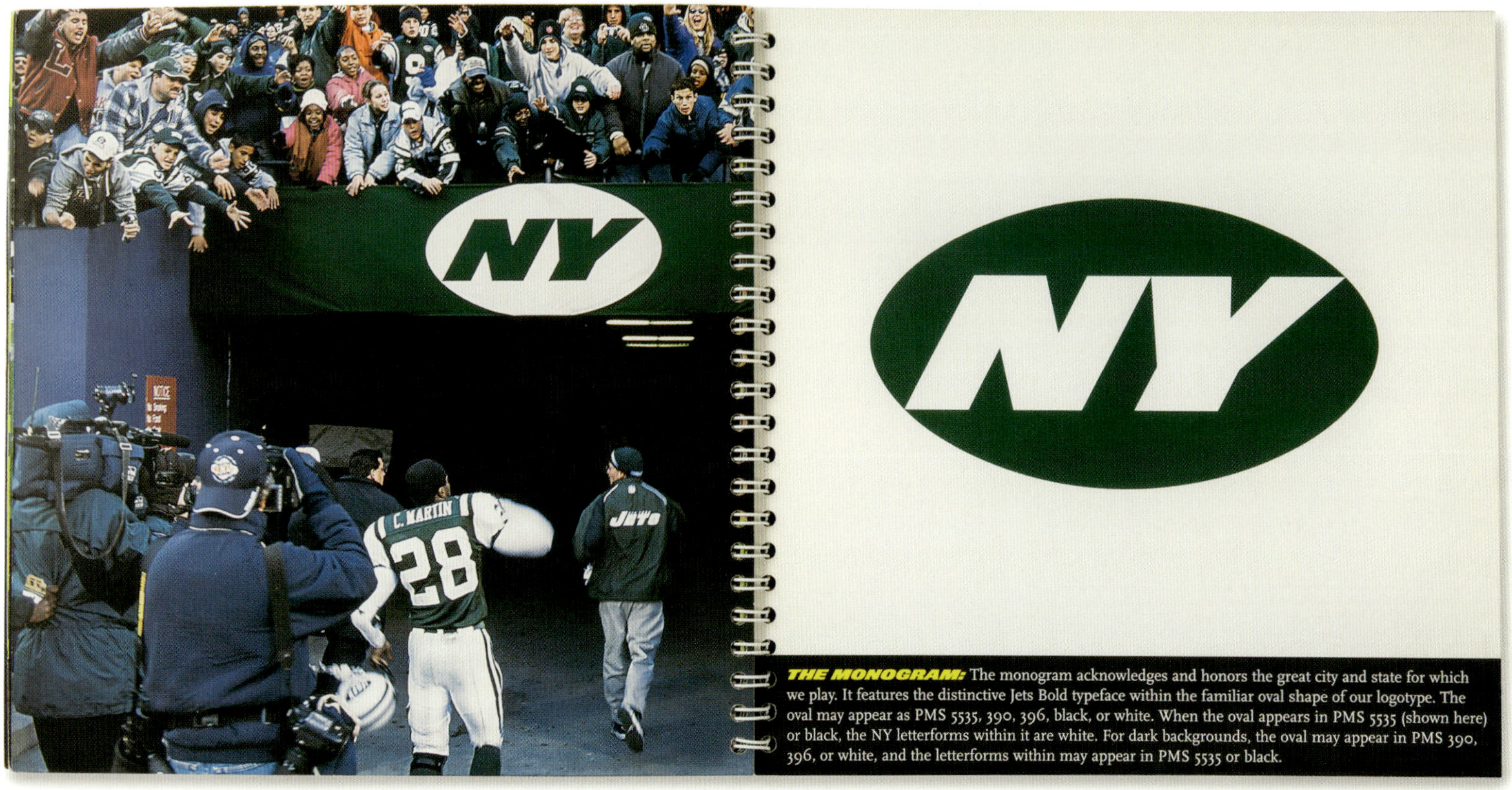

NY

THE MONOGRAM: The monogram acknowledges and honors the great city and state for which we play. It features the distinctive Jets Bold typeface within the familiar oval shape of our logotype. The oval may appear as PMS 5535, 390, 396, black, or white. When the oval appears in PMS 5535 (shown here) or black, the NY letterforms within it are white. For dark backgrounds, the oval may appear in PMS 390, 396, or white, and the letterforms within may appear in PMS 5535 or black.

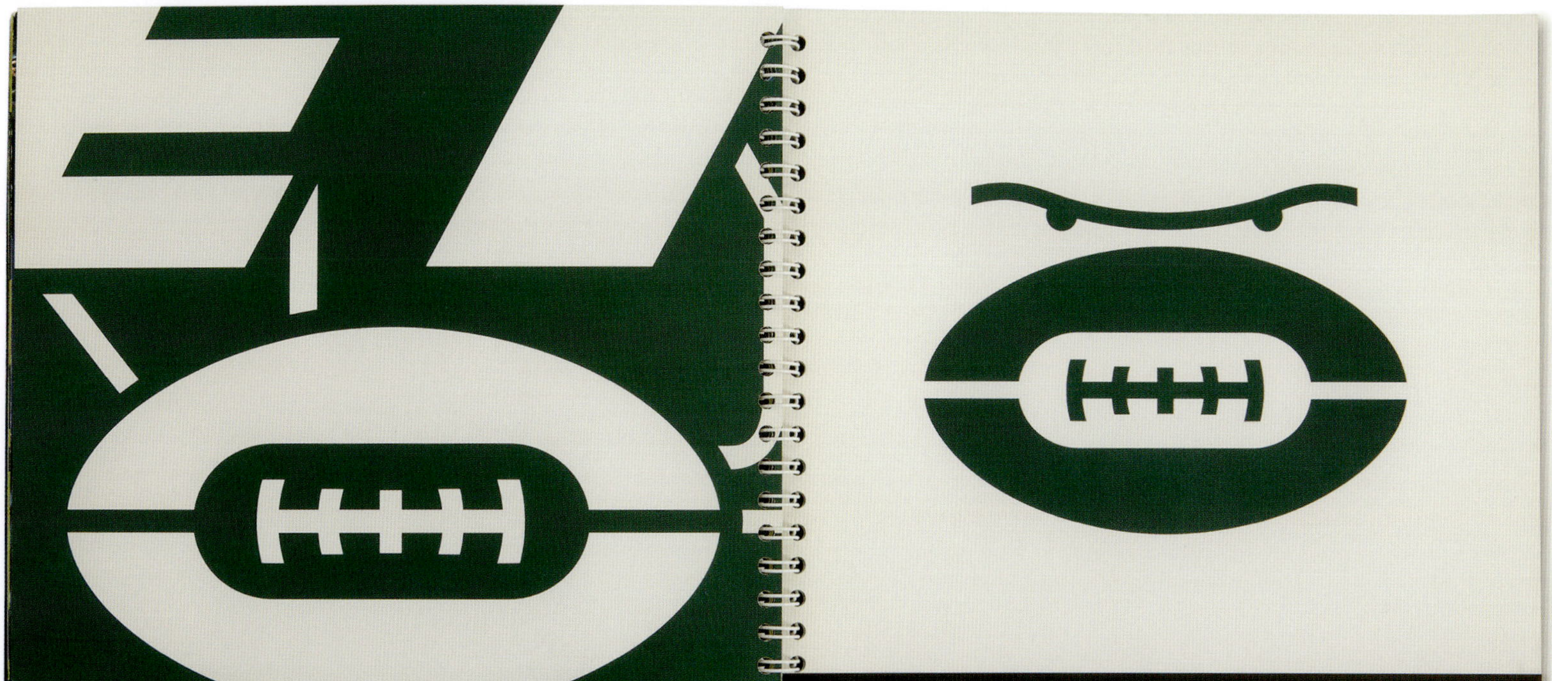

THE GAMEFACE: The closest thing to a Jets mascot, the "Gameface" mark represents the passion and fervor of our fans, players and coaches. It is derived from the little football shape that has long been anchored at the base of the New York Jets logotype. It may appear in PMS 5535, 390, 396, or black, but is most effective when the background is lighter in color than the mark itself. Showing the Gameface mark in white on dark backgrounds is not recommended.

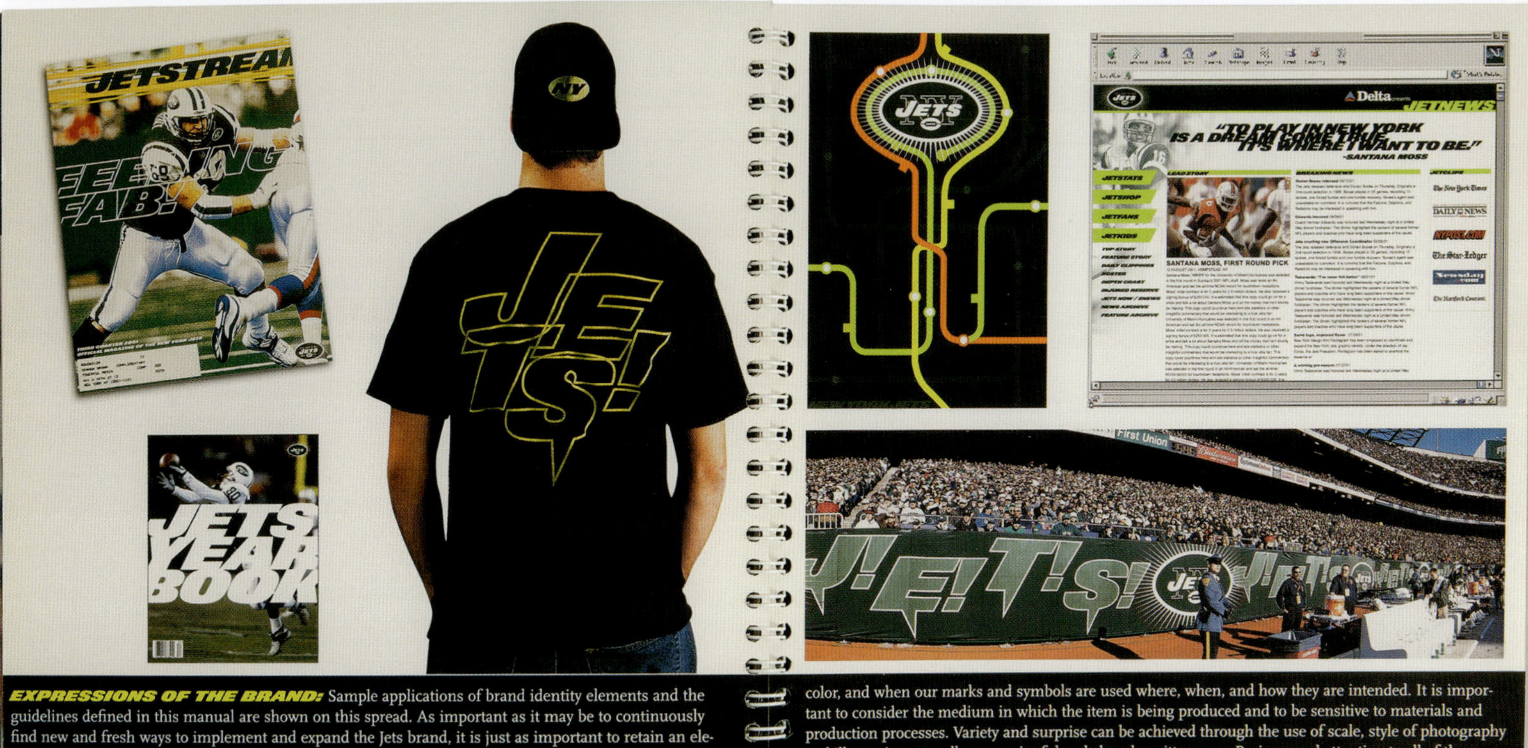

EXPRESSIONS OF THE BRAND: Sample applications of brand identity elements and the guidelines defined in this manual are shown on this spread. As important as it may be to continuously find new and fresh ways to implement and expand the Jets brand, it is just as important to retain an element of continuity across everything produced, even when these items are made by different people in different parts of the world. Consistency is ensured when we work within the specifications of type and color, and when our marks and symbols are used where, when, and how they are intended. It is important to consider the medium in which the item is being produced and to be sensitive to materials and production processes. Variety and surprise can be achieved through the use of scale, style of photography and illustration, as well as meaningful and cleverly written copy. Paying equal attention to all of these should result in a consistent, but unique application of brand identity. This is how we build the Jets brand.

Right
A signature part of the Jets brand is aural: the chant "J! E! T! S! JETS! JETS! JETS!" that is heard as a rallying cry at every game. Its graphic interpretation became still another element in the Jets brand identity.

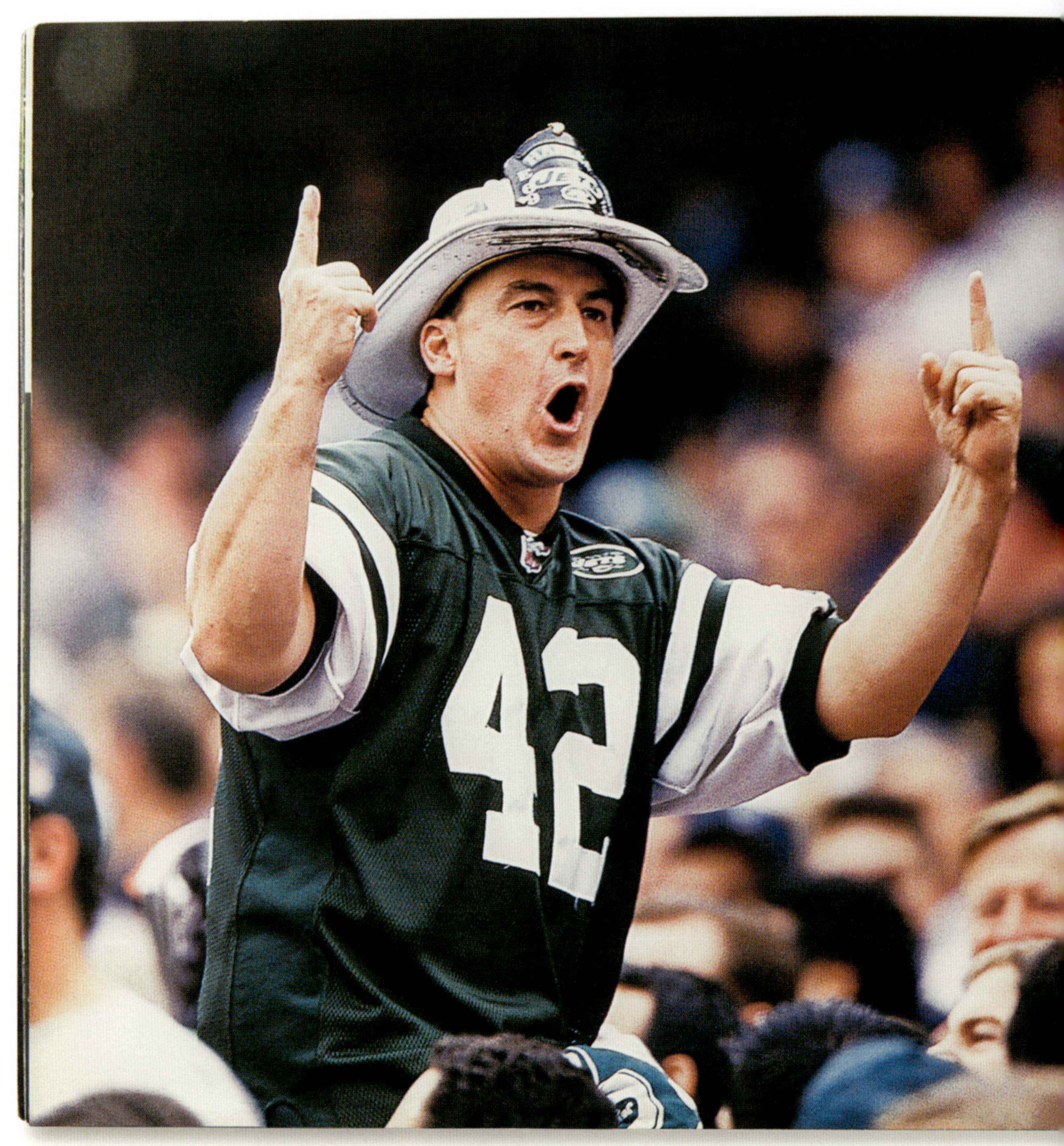

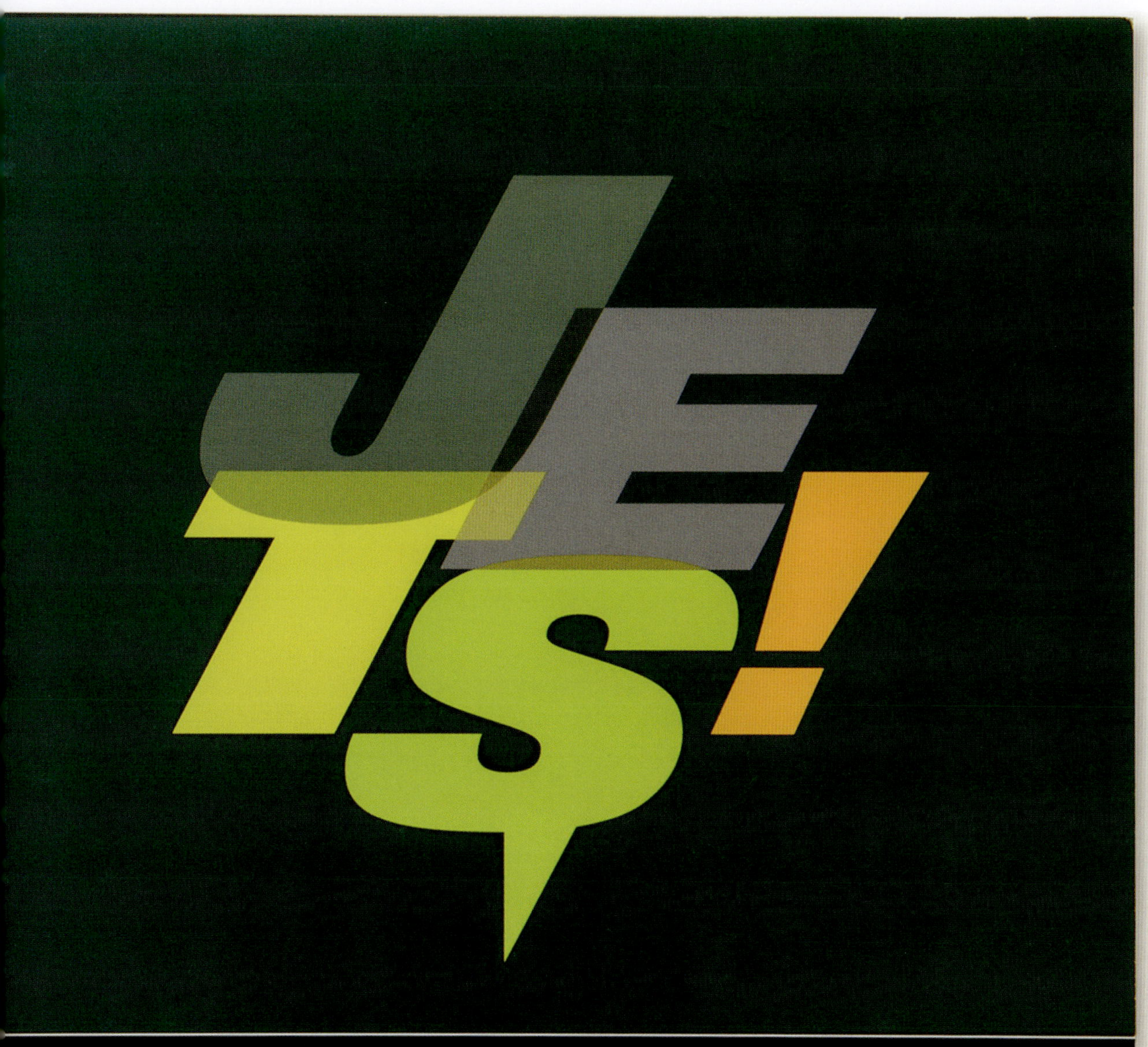

THE CHANT: Perhaps the most dynamic and inspiring element of the Jets personality is the Chant: J! E! T! S! JETS! JETS! JETS!... as shouted by thousands of Jets fans at our games throughout the country. So simple and authentic, the Chant unites entire stadiums in support for their team. A graphic treatment of the chant, in multiple colors and configurations, has been adopted as an official part of the Jets brand identity. Options and variations for Chant graphics are illustrated on the next spread.

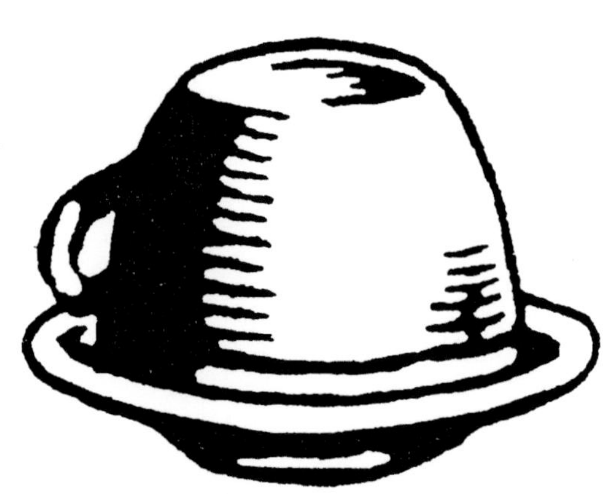

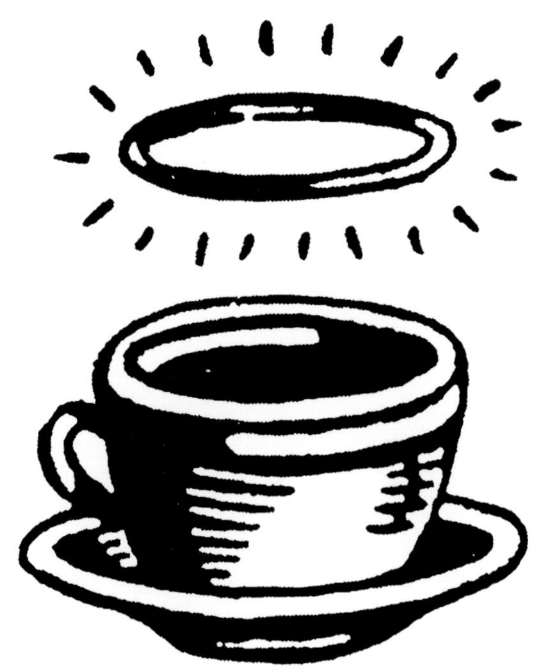

(BAD) (GOOD)

How to be good
The Good Diner

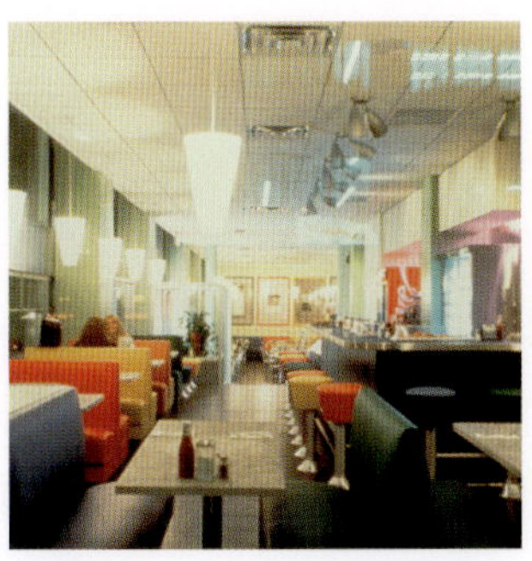

Opposite
The Good Diner's name and logo delineated the restaurant's caffeine-fueled value system.

Above
Thanks to a photogenic design, this restaurant was briefly one of the most widely published greasy spoon joints in the world. When visitors would call our office asking if tours were available, Jim Biber would respond, "It's open 24 hours and takes no reservations. It's a diner."

Sheldon Werdiger and Evan Carzis were smart architects. The recession of the late 1980s had brought building in New York to a halt. So they decided to open a diner. They didn't want it to be fancy, they explained to us. Not a retro, Fabulous Fifties place. Not a hip, reverse chic place. Just a plain diner where you could get two eggs, bacon, and toast for $4.99. The location was the corner of Eleventh Avenue and 42nd Street. Sheldon and Evan wanted to cast a wide net: "We'll get tourists on their way to the Circle Line, UPS drivers on their way to the morning shift, club kids on their way home after last call." This place had to appeal to all of them.

Our challenge was to deliver populist design, short-order style on a no-design budget, starting with the name. I suggested Jersey Luncheonette, and a logo with the state's silhouette on a plate like a piece of veal scaloppine. That didn't fly. Nor did they like Wild West Diner, or Sunset Café, or The Last Stop. Too clever. Finally I suggested The Good Diner. Not great, not fantastic, just...good. For the logo, our partner Woody Pirtle put a halo on a coffee cup.

We installed the logo in hand-cut linoleum at the front door. My partner Jim Biber, who had created some of Manhattan's best restaurants, explained that diners weren't really designed as much as ordered from catalogs. So he ordered one of everything, upholstering the booths and the counter seats with every color available. With no art budget, we decorated the walls with photocopied images of kitchen implements. Light shades shaped like milkshake containers and a single bespoke railing were the only concessions to custom manufacturing.

As is often the case, we took part of our design fees in trade for food. Eating our third helping of $4.99 bacon and eggs in a week, Jim and I realized we would be dead from cholesterol poisoning before we ever made our money back.

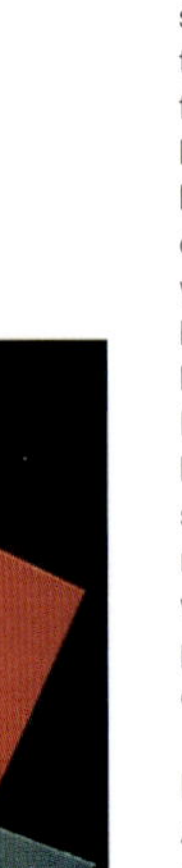

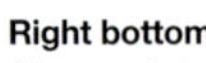

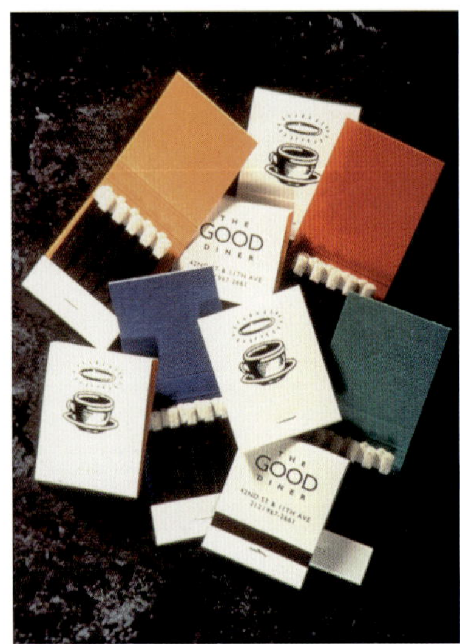

Above
For a diner, matchbooks serve as the annual report, corporate image campaign, and 60-second Super Bowl ad, all in one.

Right top
The Good Diner was an experiment in vernacular design processes. No drawing was made for the neon sign; I simply dictated the words to the fabricator over the phone and said to make the second line the biggest, the first and third lines the next biggest, and so on, and to use whatever colors he thought looked nice. It was a tense but ultimately satisfying moment when the final product was delivered.

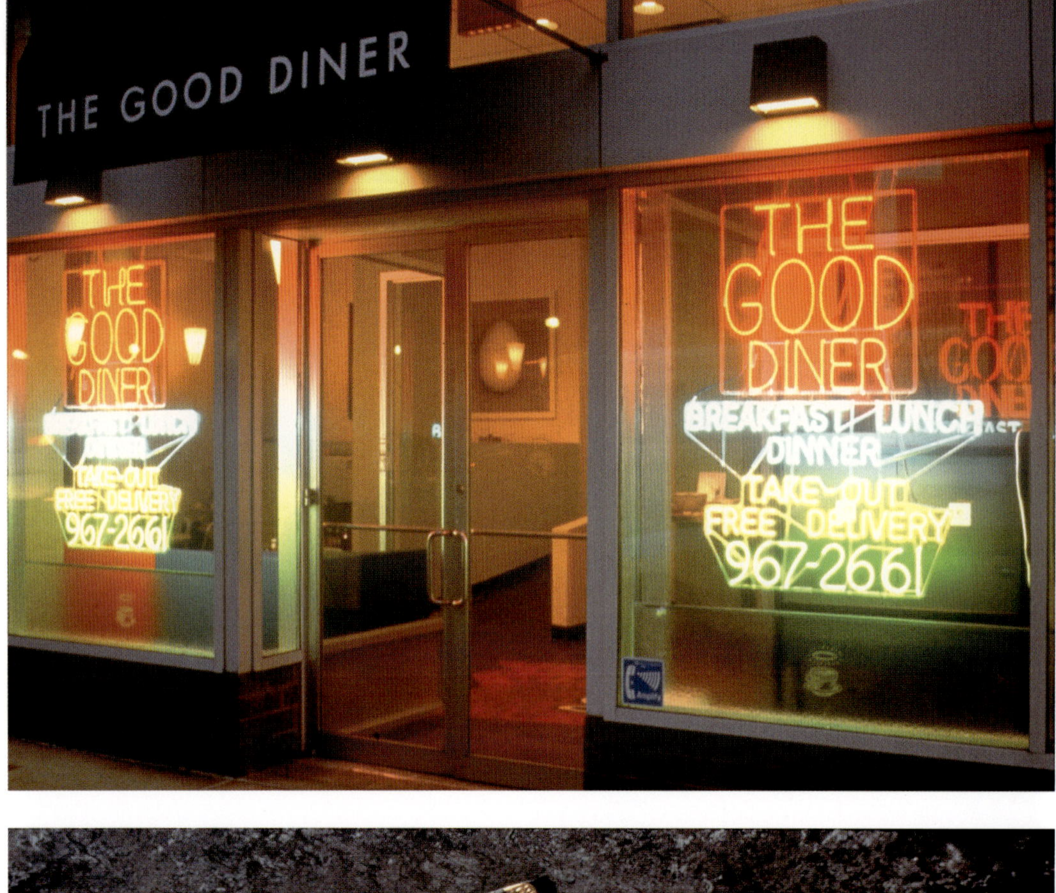

Right bottom
At one point, our clients hesitated about the name, fearing that the equivocal adjective might be too wimpy for their truck-driving clientele. “Okay, how about The Fuckin’ Good Diner?” I suggested. We kept the original name.

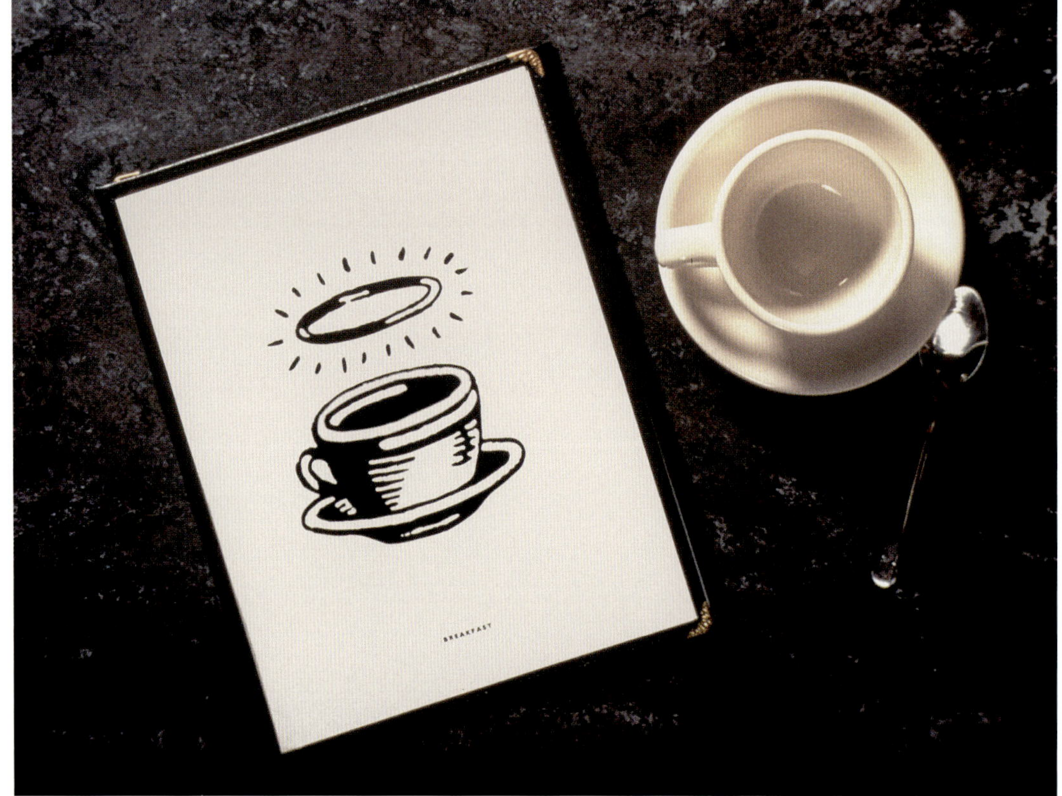

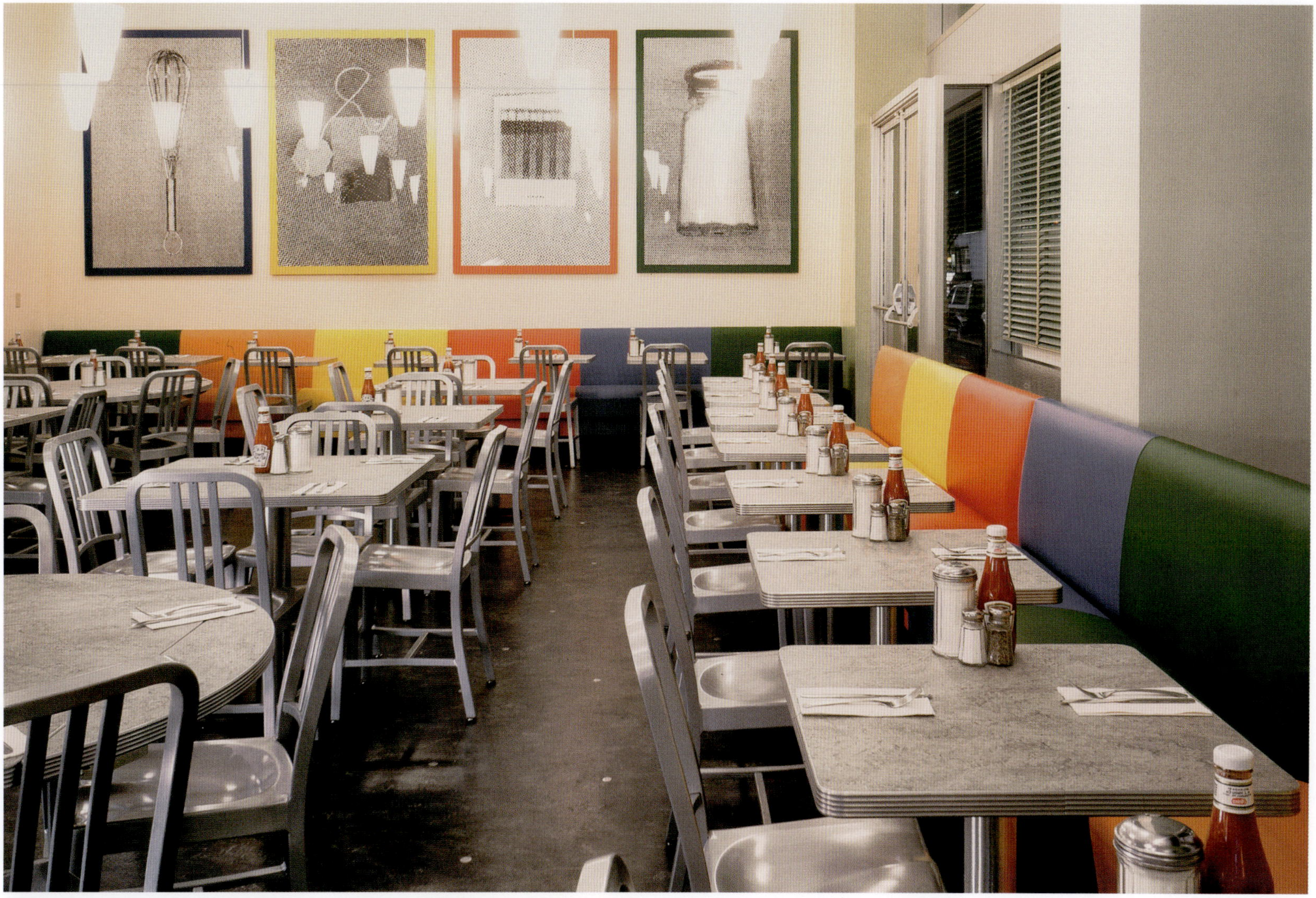

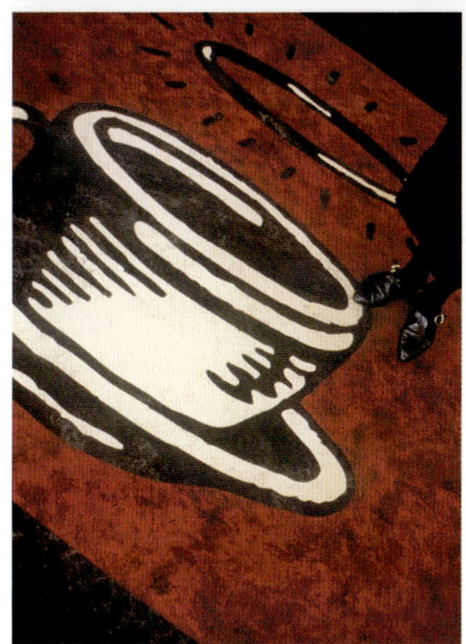

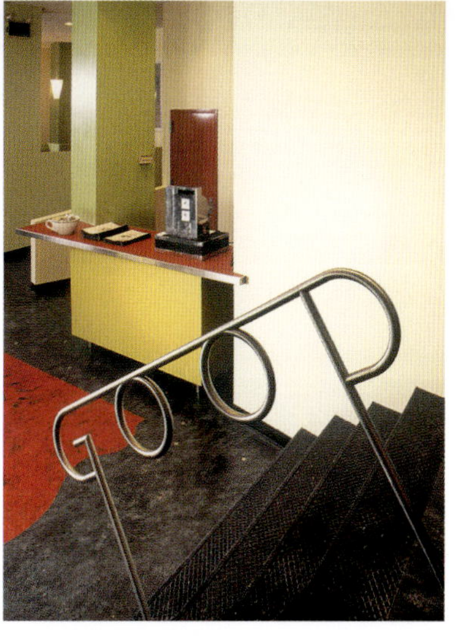

Far left
In a luxurious gesture, Woody Pirtle's logo was installed in hand-cut linoleum at the entrance.

Left
The railing connecting the counter area to the main dining room could be read alternately as "Good" or "Goop" depending on your reaction to the food.

Above
With no budget for art but lots of walls to fill, we simply put objects on a photocopier and blew them up. The framed images represent the four primal elements: wind, water, fire, and earth. We're not sure anyone noticed.

Next spread
Why settle for one color of Naugahyde when you can have them all? The installers determined the order of colors at the counter.

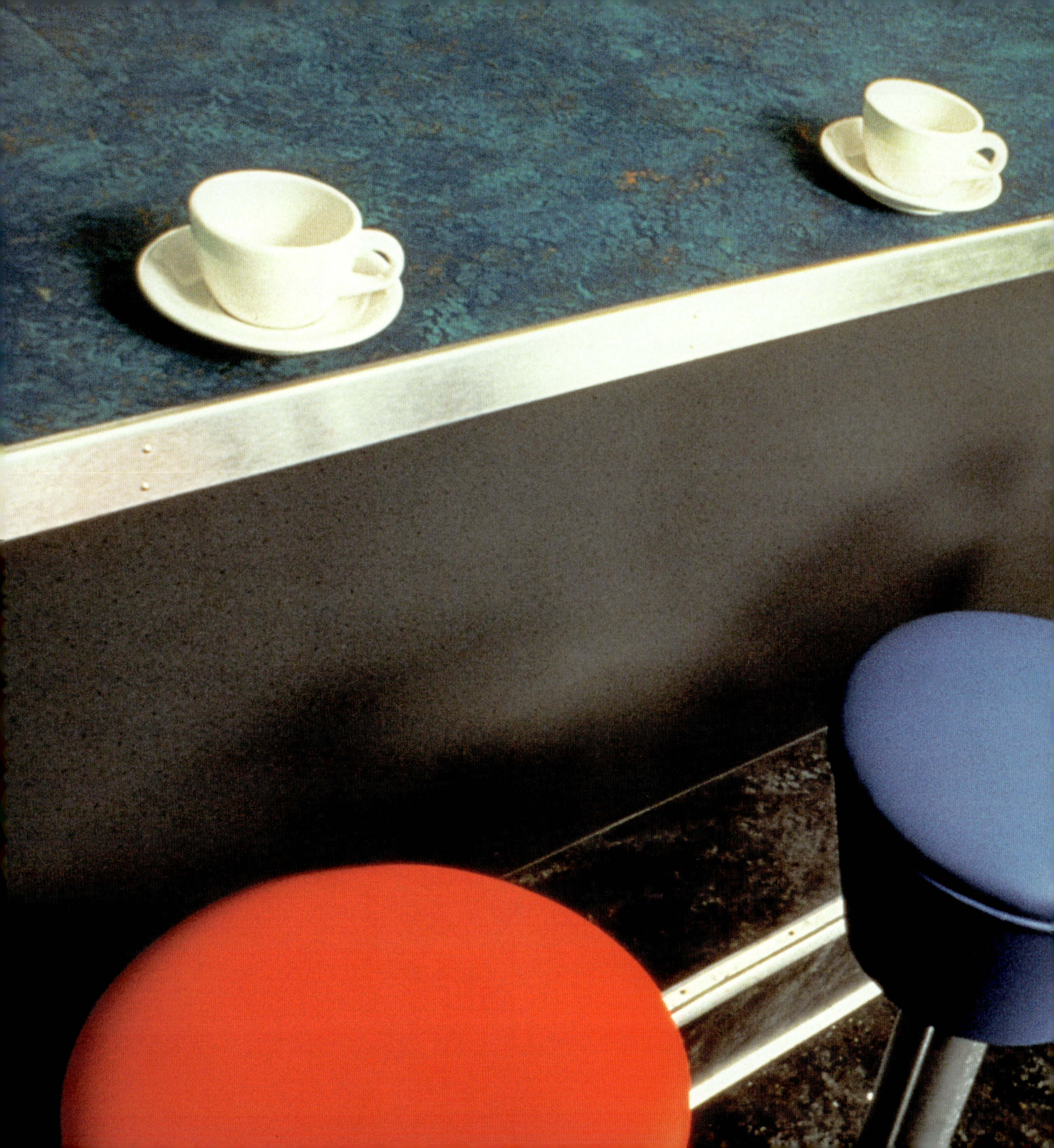

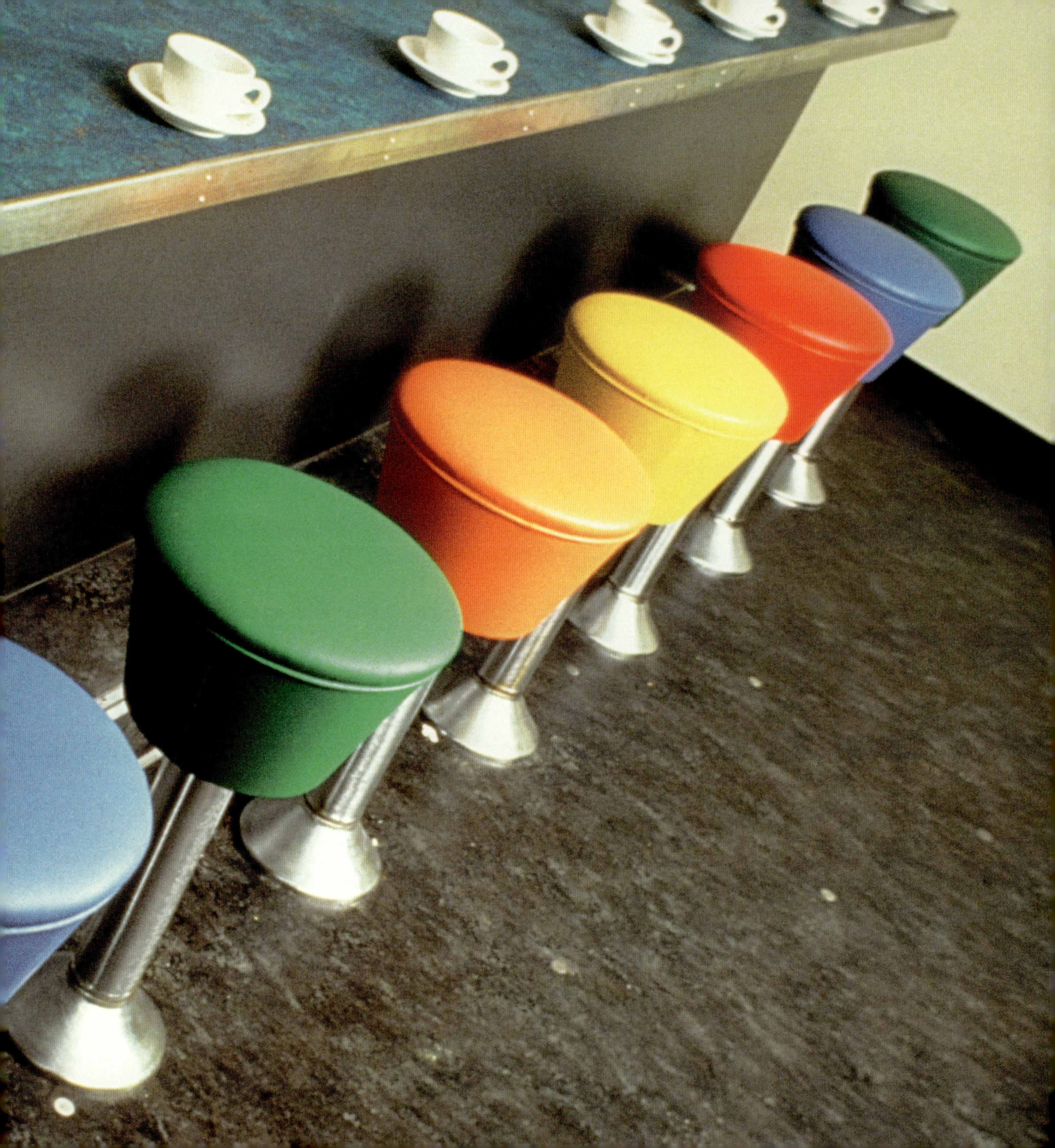

THE ASSOCIATION YEARBOOK
1999
THEARCHI
TECTURAL
LEAGUENY
THE STORY OF
PITNEY-BO
Max Huber
Paul Rand Thoughts on Design
design: Vignelli
-ism
LOOKING CLOSER
CRITICAL WRITINGS ON GRAPHIC DESIGN
Fifty Very Short Essays on Michael Bierut
D.J.R. BRUCKNER
Encyclopedia of Comparative Letterforms
tagram

How to run a marathon
The Architectural League of New York

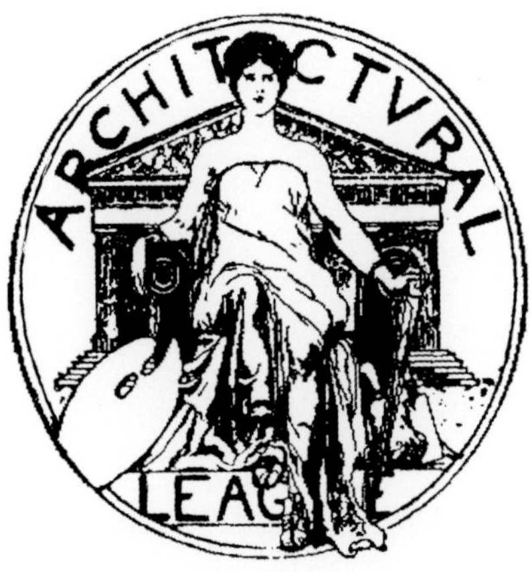

Opposite
The Architectural League hosts the Beaux Arts Ball, the architectural community's party of the year, with a new theme every time. In 2013, we responded to the somewhat esoteric concept of "ism" with pure typography.

Above
The original seal of the Architectural League, which I avoided changing for over 20 years.

A few weeks into my first job, my boss Massimo Vignelli summoned me into his office. I was a naive kid from Ohio and I barely knew what I was doing. Massimo and his wife and partner, Lella, were going to Italy for a month, and he told me to follow up on a project he was doing for an organization called the Architectural League of New York. I liked architecture but my knowledge didn't extend much beyond Frank Lloyd Wright and Howard Roark. Suddenly I was on the phone with Richard Meier, Michael Graves, and Frank Gehry, chasing down material for the organization's centennial exhibition. My education was about to begin. My postgraduate academy was the Architectural League.

Founded in 1881 to bring together architects with other creative practitioners, the League has always included artists and designers of all disciplines in its leadership. As a board member, Massimo Vignelli served as the organization's pro bono graphic design consultant. As Massimo's assistant, I took over the (free) work we were doing on their behalf. Ten years later I was appointed to the board myself. Twenty-plus years after that I am still working for them. This marathon run is the longest sustained relationship I've enjoyed in my professional life.

Designers are often asked to create images for organizations. We come in from the outside, get our bearings, and give the best advice we can. Working as an external consultant like this, I design systems for others to implement and hope and pray they get it right after I'm gone. Working for the League year after year, I learned the pleasures of working from the inside. There are no formal graphic standards, but there is an evolving portrait of an organization where the paint never quite dries. For years, I resisted designing a logo, viewing each new assignment as an open brief, a chance to extend the League's visual profile. Over time, certain patterns began to emerge—we finally did create a logo, for instance—but still each assignment offers the very best (and scariest) kind of challenge: if you could do anything you wanted, what would you do?

Right
Early in my time working for the Architectural League, I designed several lecture invitations that also functioned as miniature posters. These were the first instances that Massimo Vignelli encouraged me to sign my own work.

Opposite
Working for the League's ongoing programs has been a special pleasure. Its Emerging Voices series, which mounts lectures by up-and-coming architects from around the world, began in 1981 and continues today. Its poster series is a not-so-subtle homage to my childhood obsession with the album covers designed by John Berg and Nick Fasciano for the band Chicago.

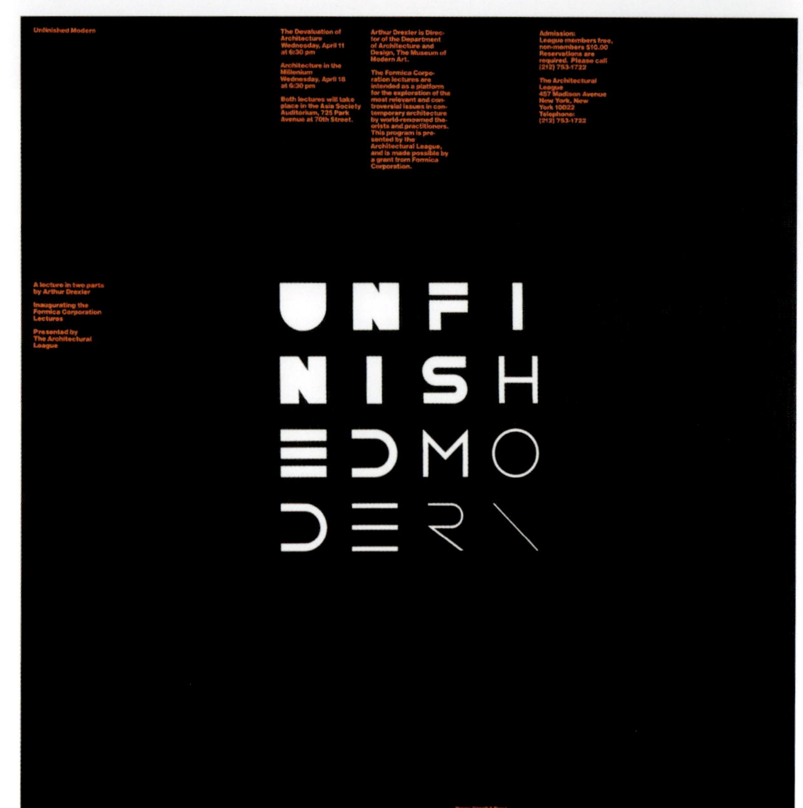

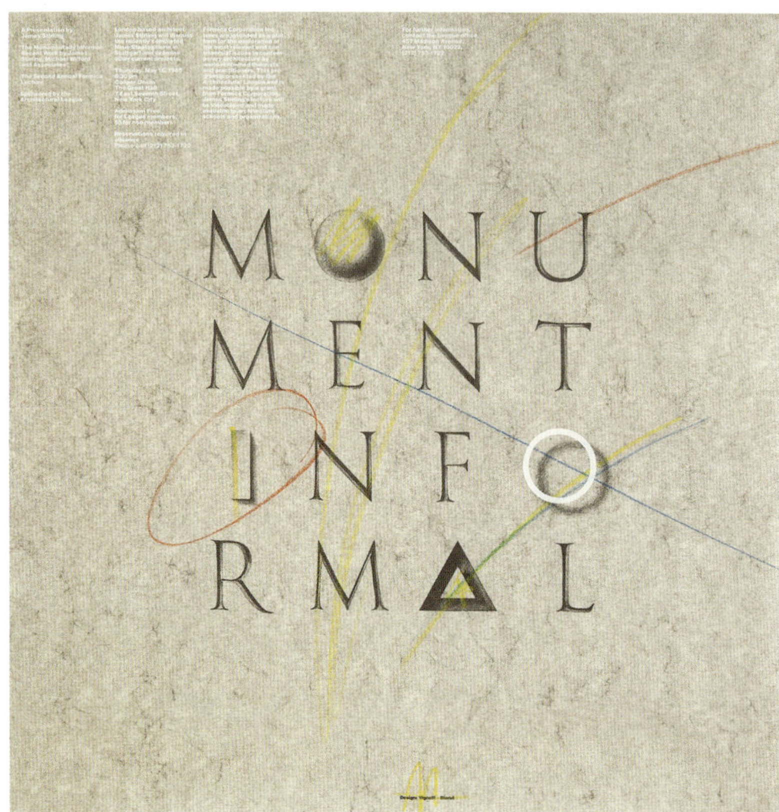

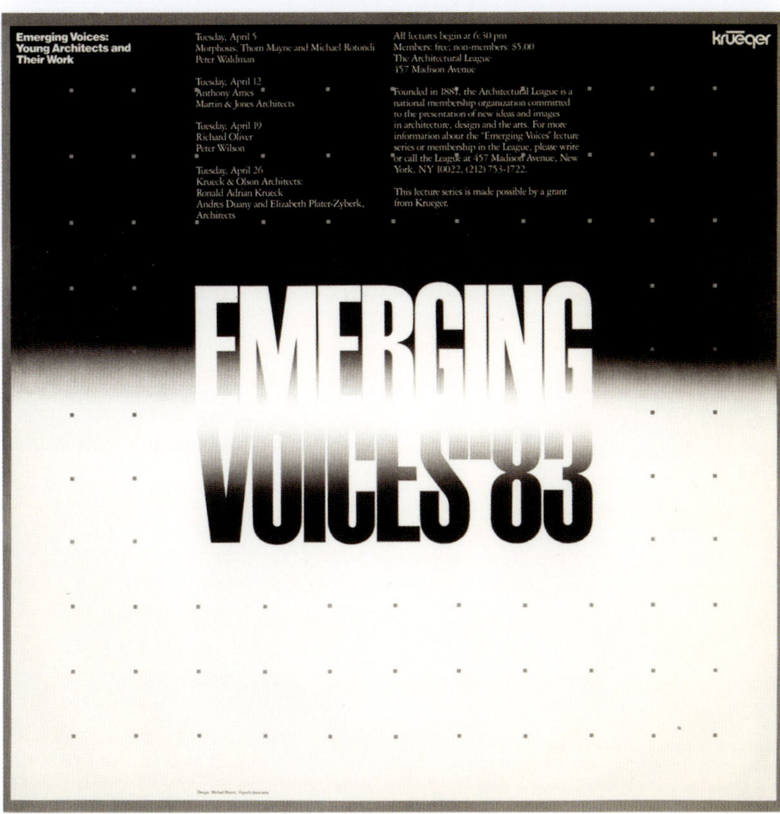
Emerging Voices:
Young Architects and
Their Work
Tuesday, April 5
Morphosis: Thom Mayne and Michael Rotondi
Peter Waldman
Tuesday, April 12
Anthony Ames
Martin & Jones Architects
Tuesday, April 19
Richard Oliver
Peter Wilson
Tuesday, April 26
Krueck & Olson Architects:
Ronald Adrian Krueck
Andres Duany and Elizabeth Plater-Zyberk, Architects
All lectures begin at 6:30 pm
Members: free; non-members: $5.00
The Architectural League
457 Madison Avenue
Founded in 1881, the Architectural League is a national membership organization committed to the presentation of new ideas and images in architecture, design and the arts. For more information about the "Emerging Voices" lecture series or membership in the League, please write or call the League at 457 Madison Avenue, New York, NY 10022, (212) 753-1722.
This lecture series is made possible by a grant from Krueger.
krueger
EMERGING
VOICES '83

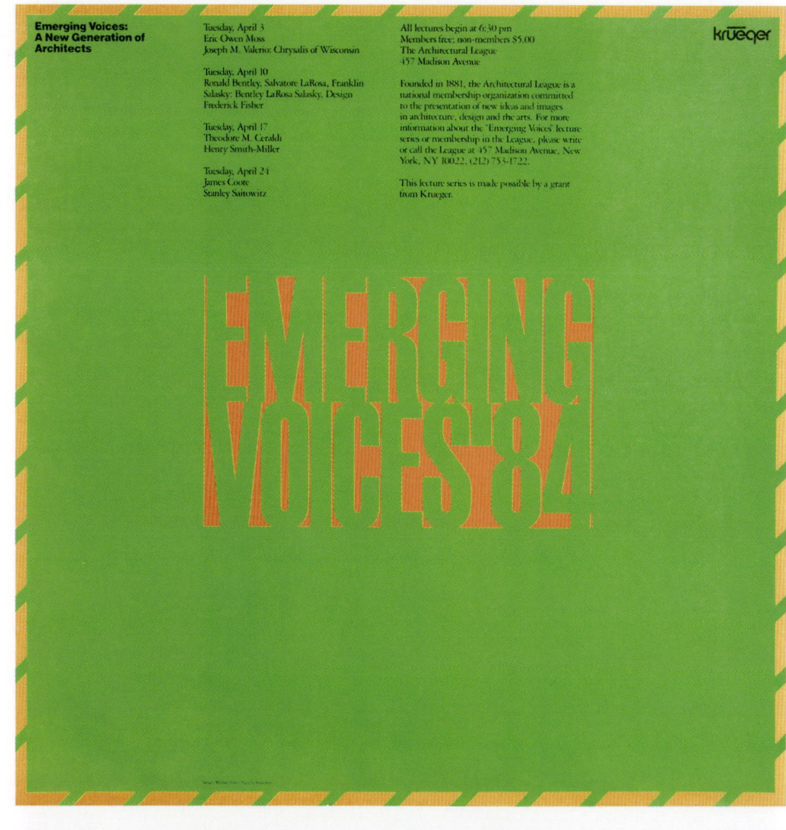
Emerging Voices:
A New Generation of
Architects
Tuesday, April 3
Eric Owen Moss
Joseph M. Valerio: Chrysalis of Wisconsin
Tuesday, April 10
Ronald Bentley, Salvatore LaRosa, Franklin Salasky: Bentley LaRosa Salasky, Design
Frederick Fisher
Tuesday, April 17
Theodore M. Ceraldi
Henry Smith-Miller
Tuesday, April 24
James Coote
Stanley Saitowitz
All lectures begin at 6:30 pm
Members free; non-members $5.00
The Architectural League
457 Madison Avenue
Founded in 1881, the Architectural League is a national membership organization committed to the presentation of new ideas and images in architecture, design and the arts. For more information about the "Emerging Voices" lecture series or membership in the League, please write or call the League at 457 Madison Avenue, New York, NY 10022, (212) 753-1722.
This lecture series is made possible by a grant from Krueger.
krueger
EMERGING
VOICES '84

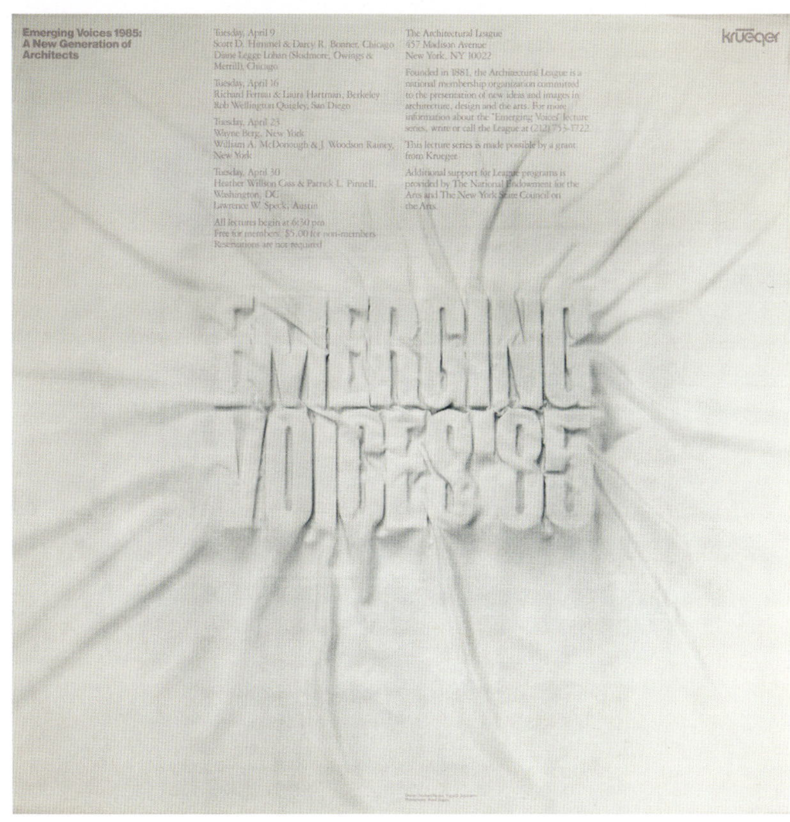
Emerging Voices 1985:
A New Generation of
Architects
Tuesday, April 9
Scott D. Himmel & Darcy R. Bonner, Chicago
Diane Legge Lohan (Skidmore, Owings & Merrill), Chicago
Tuesday, April 16
Richard Fernau & Laura Hartman, Berkeley
Rob Wellington Quigley, San Diego
Tuesday, April 23
Wayne Berg, New York
William A. McDonough & J. Woodson Rainey, New York
Tuesday, April 30
Heather Willson Cass & Patrick L. Pinnell, Washington, DC
Lawrence W. Speck, Austin
All lectures begin at 6:30 pm
Free for members; $5.00 for non-members
Reservations are not required
The Architectural League
457 Madison Avenue
New York, NY 10022
Founded in 1881, the Architectural League is a national membership organization committed to the presentation of new ideas and images in architecture, design and the arts. For more information about the "Emerging Voices" lecture series, write or call the League at (212) 753-1722.
This lecture series is made possible by a grant from Krueger.
Additional support for League programs is provided by The National Endowment for the Arts and The New York State Council on the Arts.
krueger
EMERGING
VOICES '85

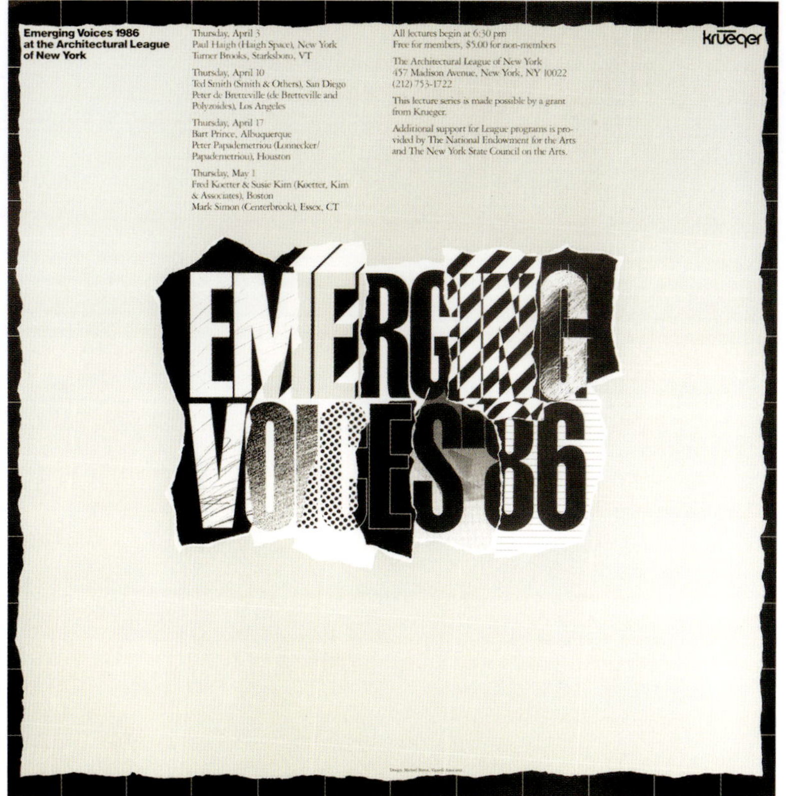
Emerging Voices 1986
at the Architectural League
of New York
Thursday, April 3
Paul Haigh (Haigh Space), New York
Turner Brooks, Starksboro, VT
Thursday, April 10
Ted Smith (Smith & Others), San Diego
Peter de Bretteville (de Bretteville and Polyzoides), Los Angeles
Thursday, April 17
Bart Prince, Albuquerque
Peter Papademetriou (Lonnecker/Papademetriou), Houston
Thursday, May 1
Fred Koetter & Susie Kim (Koetter, Kim & Associates), Boston
Mark Simon (Centerbrook), Essex, CT
All lectures begin at 6:30 pm
Free for members, $5.00 for non-members
The Architectural League of New York
457 Madison Avenue, New York, NY 10022
(212) 753-1722
This lecture series is made possible by a grant from Krueger.
Additional support for League programs is provided by The National Endowment for the Arts and The New York State Council on the Arts.
krueger
EMERGING
VOICES '86

Below
The remarkable 30-year legacy of the Emerging Voices series culminated with our design for *Idea, Form, Resonance*, a 300-page book documenting the League's remarkable ability to identify mid-career architects destined for worldwide influence. These have included Brad Cloepfil, James Corner, Marion Weiss and Michael Manfredi, Teddy Cruz, SHoP, and Jeanne Gang.

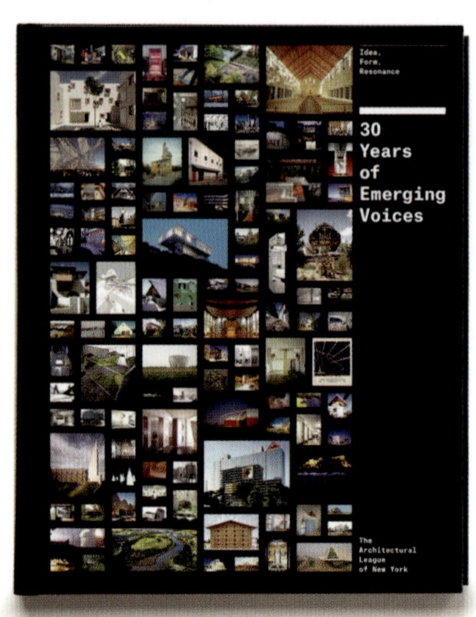

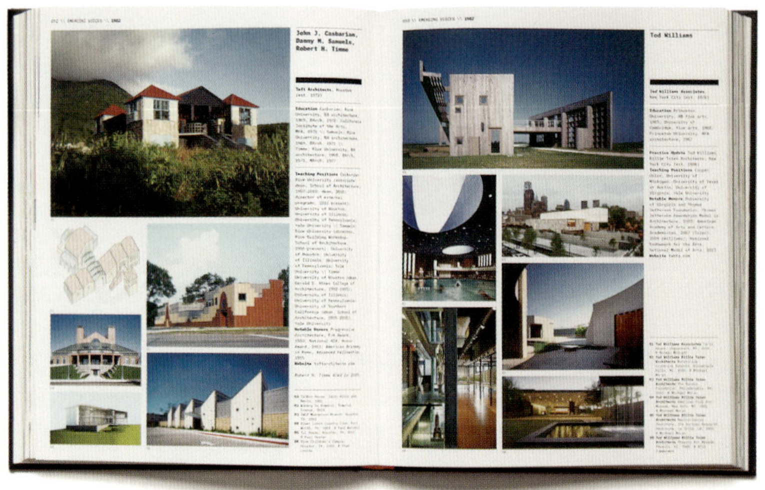

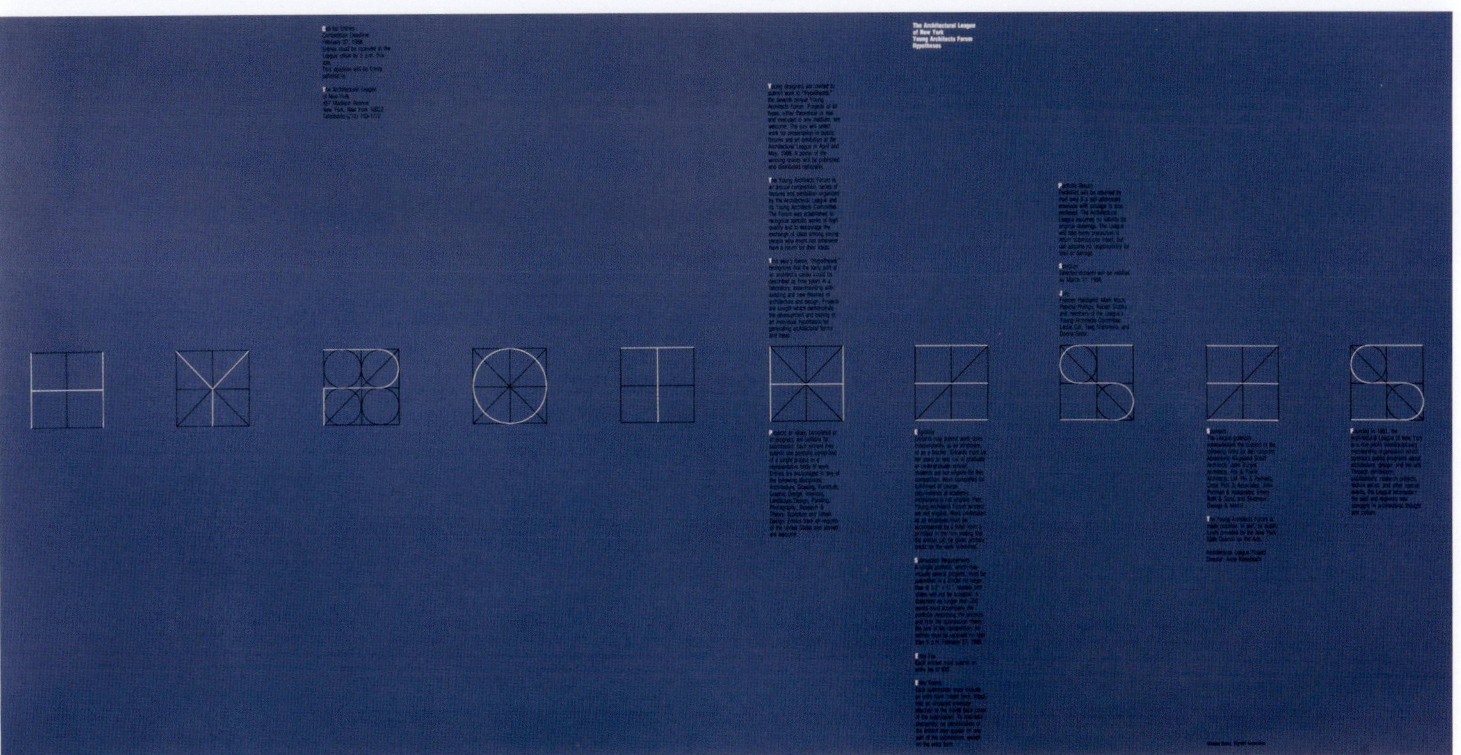

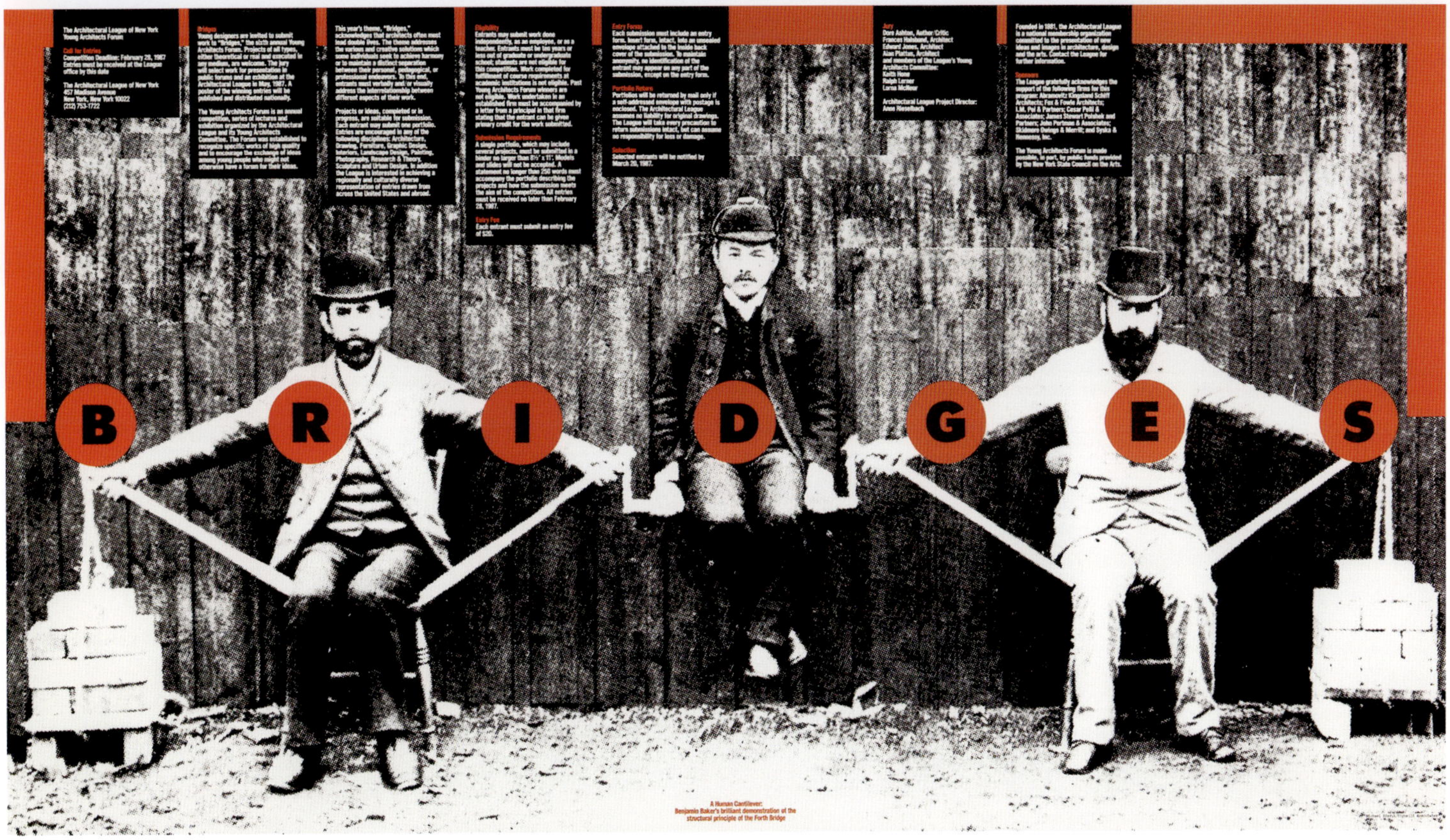

Left
Since the early 1980s, my clients at the League have been executive director Rosalie Genevro and program director Anne Rieselbach. By now, our communication is nearly telepathic. Nonetheless, they still reject as many of my ideas as they accept. The Architectural League's competition for young designers has a different theme every year, and my feigned exasperation with it is a cherished part of our relationship. I recall that 1987's Bridges theme was particularly vexing.

Right
The poster for the 1999 competition responded directly to the theme, Scale, with an oversized poster that would be unlikely in today's sustainability-conscious digital age.

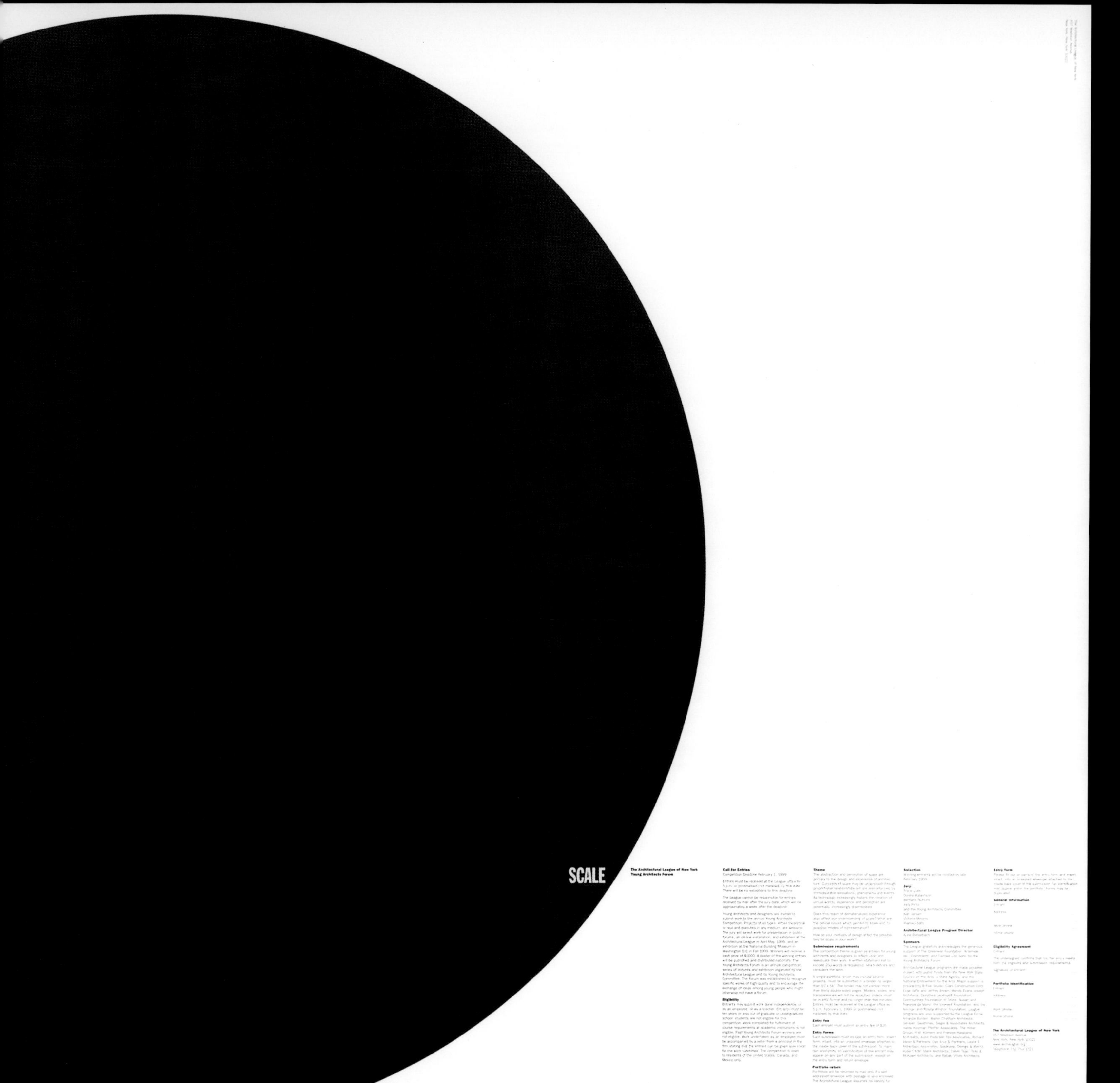

SCALE

The Architectural League of New York
Young Architects Forum

Call for Entries

Competition Deadline February 1, 1999

Eligibility

Theme

Submission requirements

Entry fee

Entry forms

Portfolio return

Selection

Jury

Architectural League Program Director

Sponsors

Entry form

General information

Eligibility Agreement

Portfolio identification

The Architectural League of New York

Below
When the League moved to new offices in Soho, we created this homage to the cover of Paolo Soleri's *Visionary Cities*.

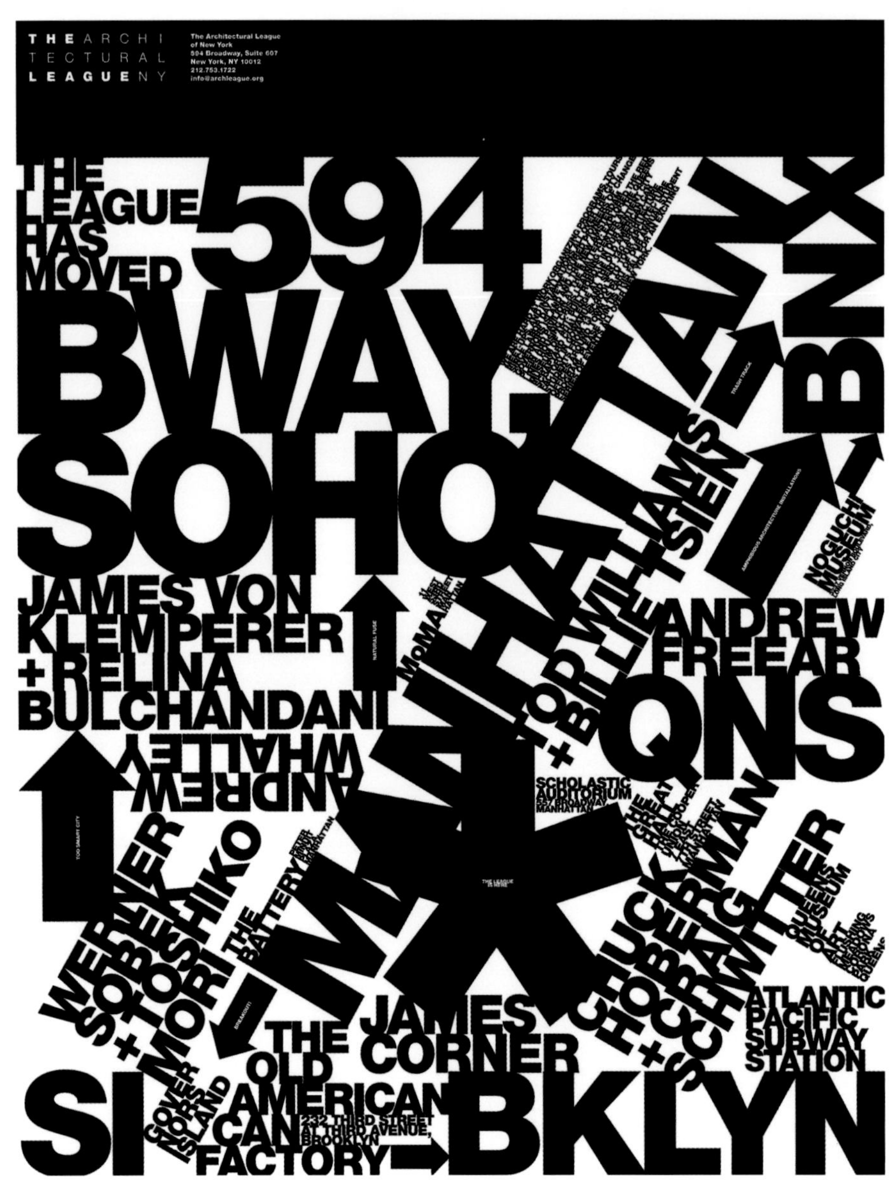

Below
The Beaux Arts Ball is the high point of the social calendar for any trendy New York architect. In 2006, the theme was Dot Dot Dot, with appropriately customized typography.

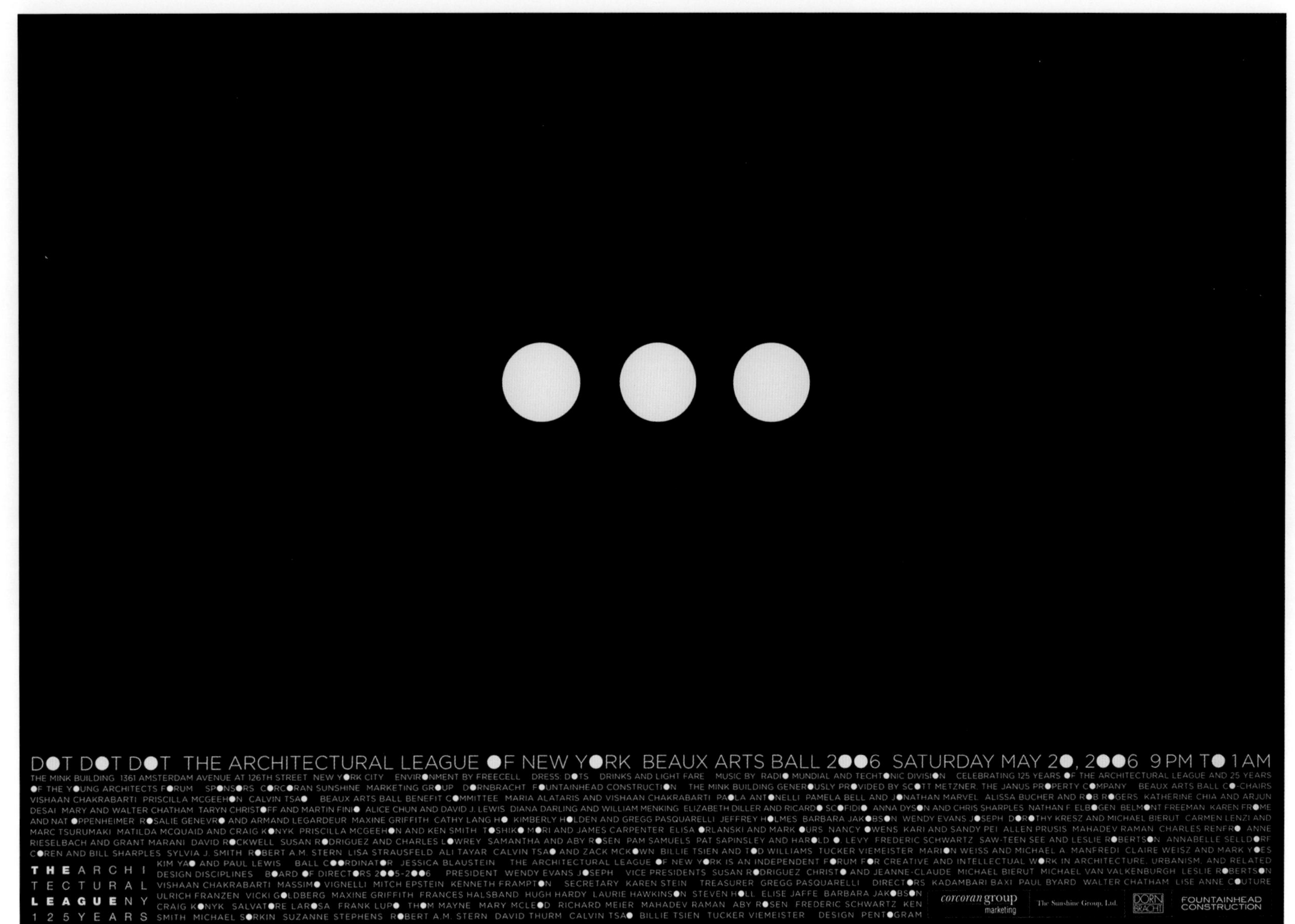

Right
The poster for the 1999 Beaux Arts Ball became one of the League's most enduring images.

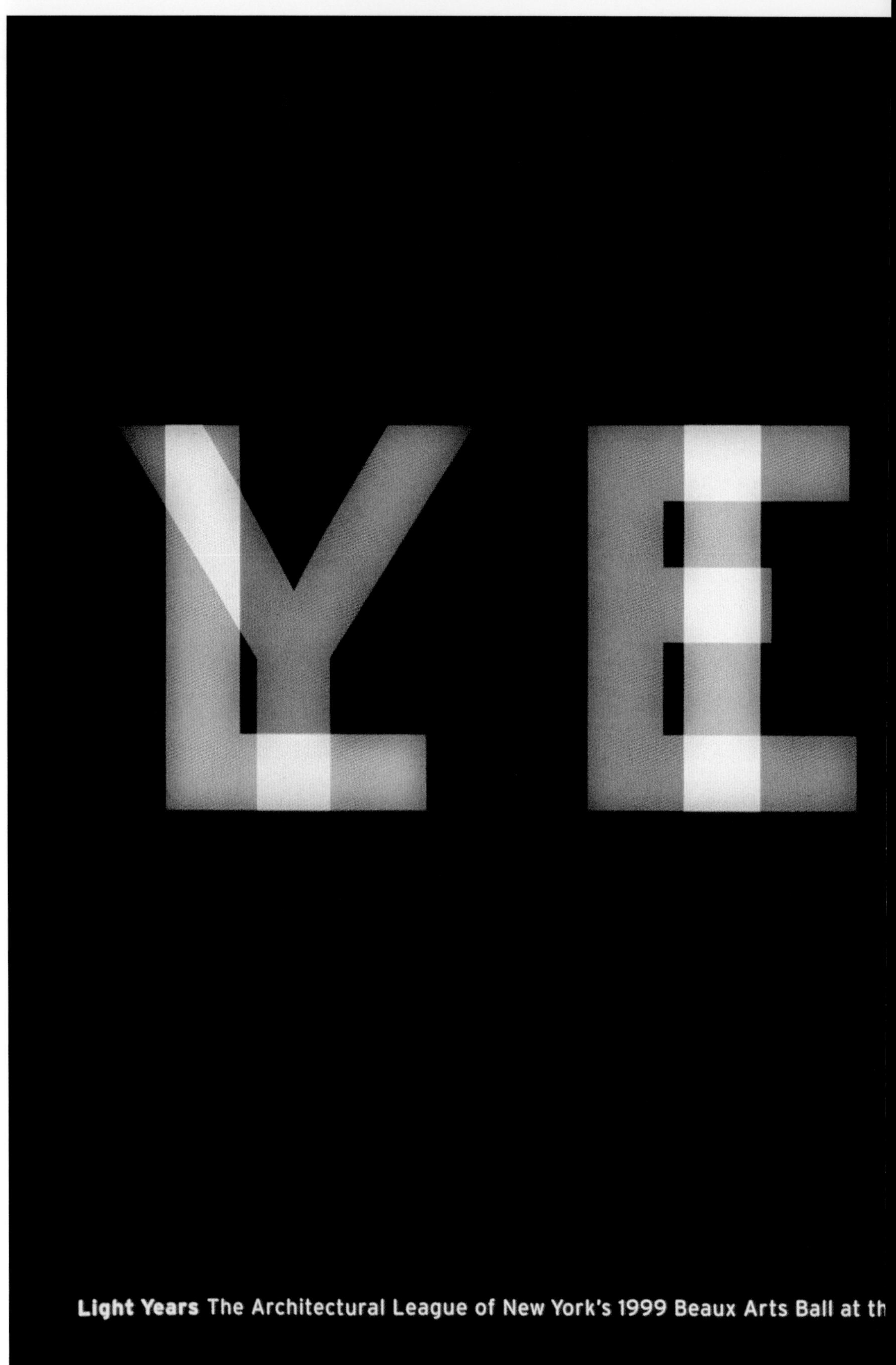

ett-Lehigh Building, Saturday March 13, 1999. For tickets please call (212) 753 1722. Corporate Sponsor Artemide

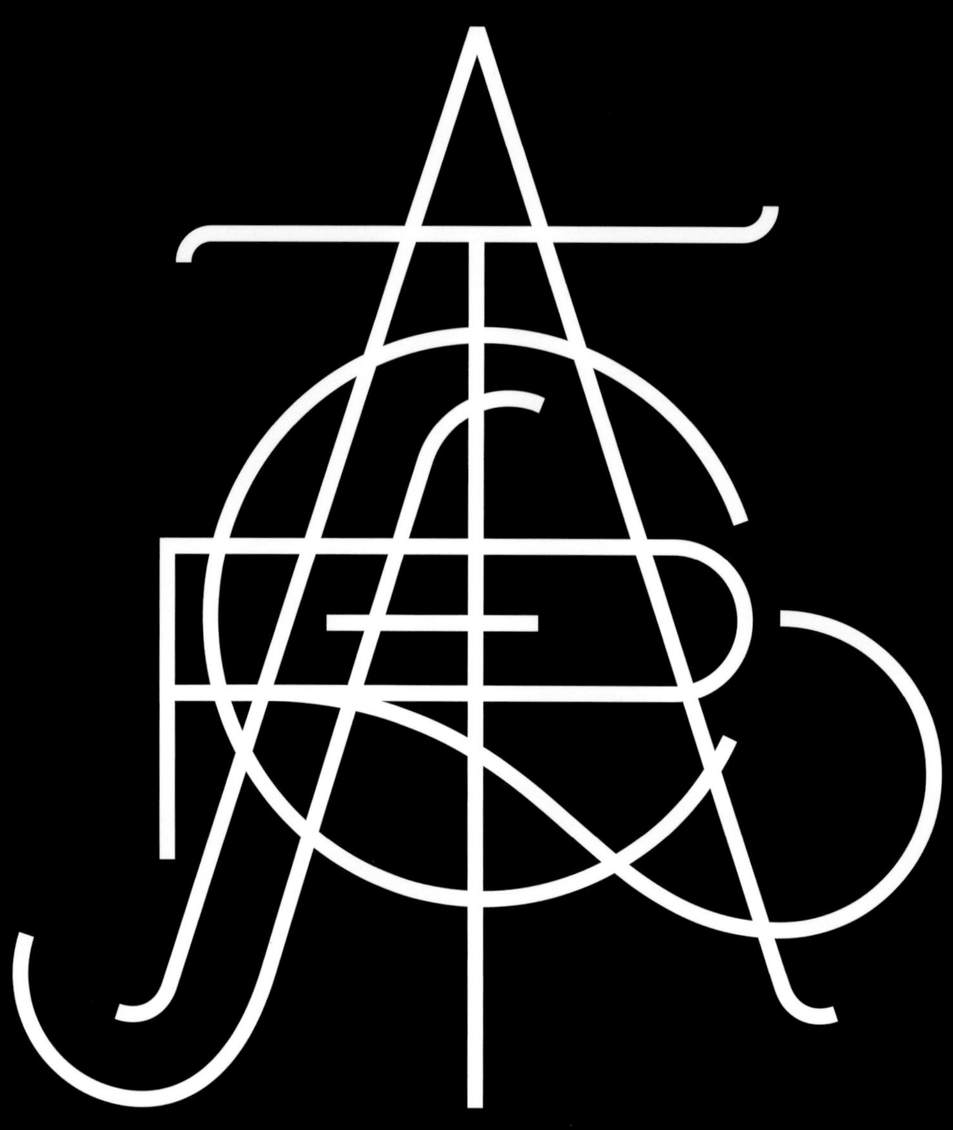

Opposite
The 2014 Beaux Arts Ball was held at the staggeringly ornate Williamsburgh Savings Bank in Brooklyn. The theme, Craft, was memorialized with an illegibly baroque insignia.

Right
For years, I felt the Architectural League's logo wasn't important, that dramatic posters communicated more powerfully than any symbol could. This changed with the rise of digital communications and social media. In response, we created a wordmark that imbeds their colloquial name within their formal one.

THE ARCHI
TECTURAL
LEAGUE NY

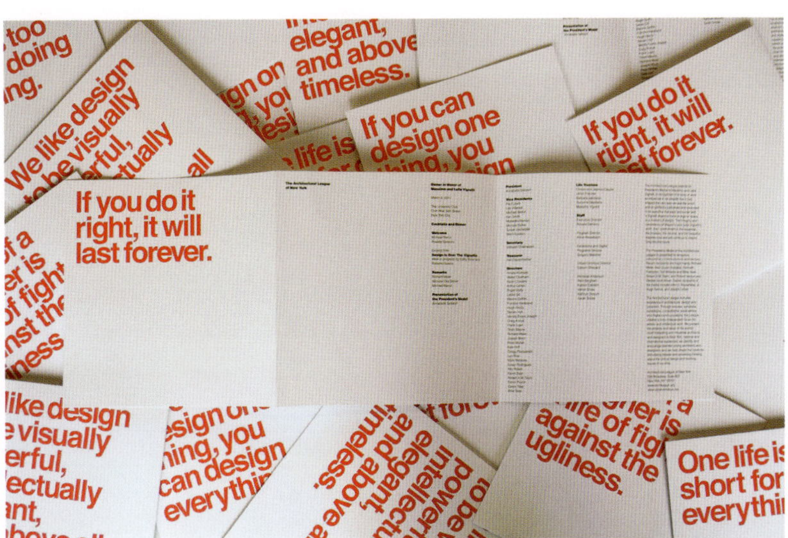

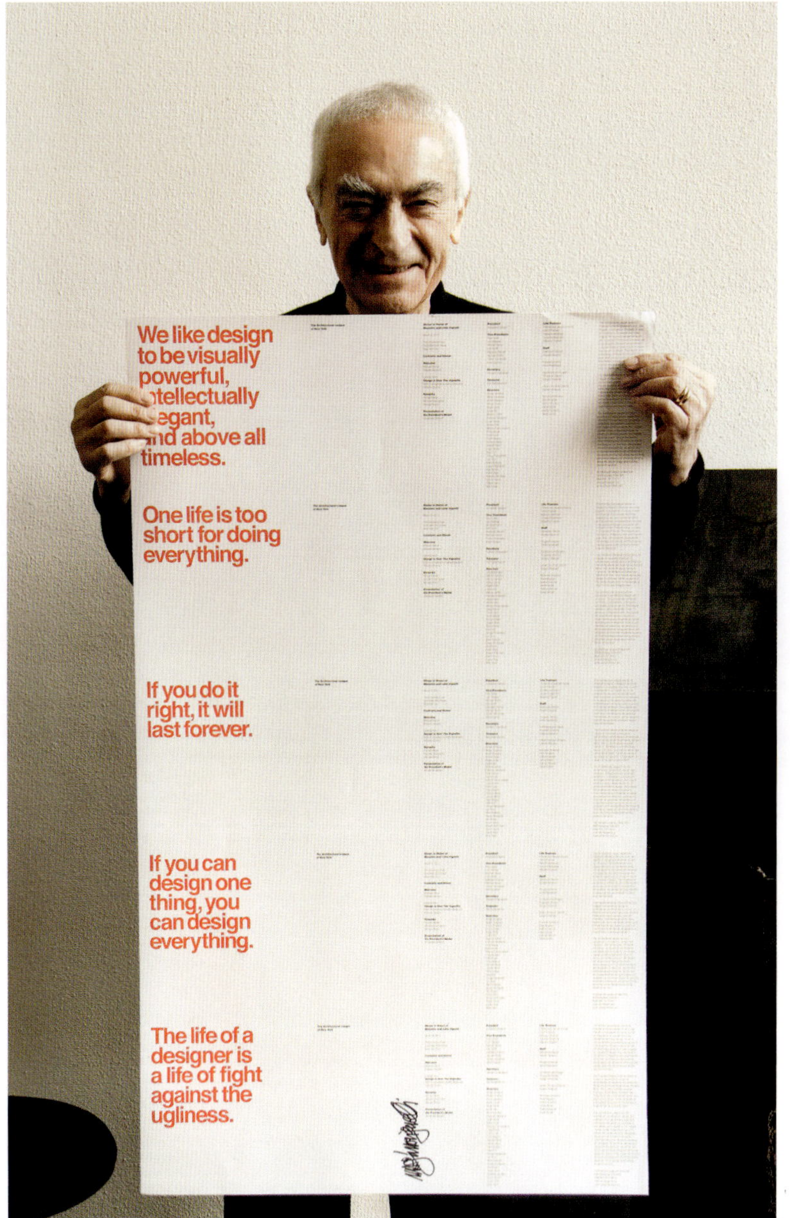

Above and right
In 2011, Massimo and Lella Vignelli were the recipients of the League's prestigious President's Medal. The programs we designed featured five different Vignelli quotes—in Helvetica, of course. The untrimmed press sheet became an informal poster, and a way for me to honor the man whose generosity transformed my life.

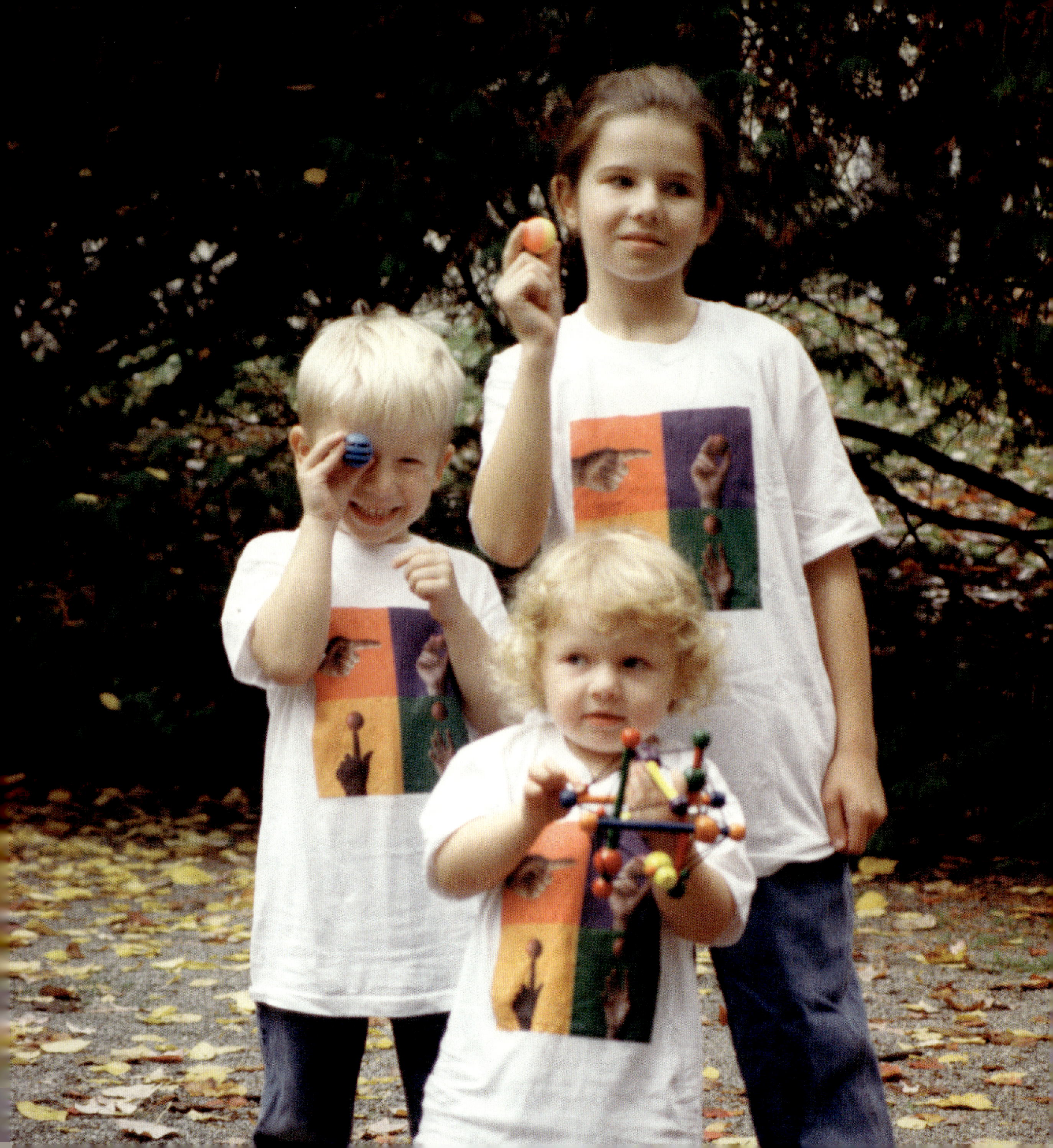

How to avoid the obvious
Minnesota Children's Museum

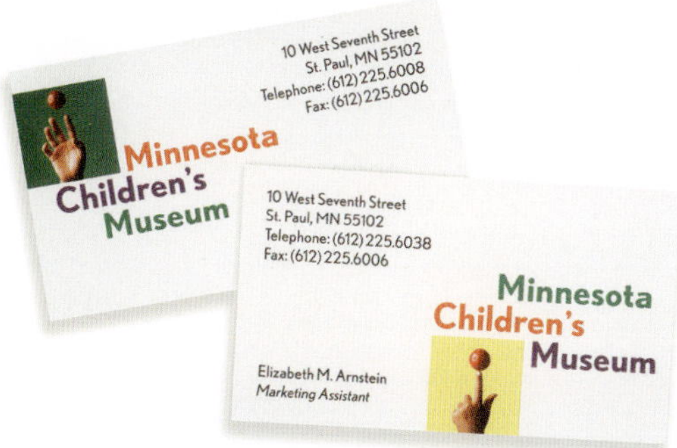

Opposite
Drew, Liz, and Martha Bierut model the Minnesota Children's Museum's graphic identity. Having kids of my own helped me understand how to design for them.

Above
Business cards remind staff members that theirs is truly a hands-on destination. Photographer Judy Olausen used local kids as hand models.

Graphic designers have a love/hate relationship with clichés ("love/hate relationship" being itself a cliché). In design school, we're taught that the goal of design is to create something new. But not entirely new. A jar of spaghetti sauce should stand out from its competitors. But if it looks too different, say, like a can of motor oil, it will disorient shoppers and scare them away. Every graphic design solution, then, must navigate between comfort and cliché. Pentagram founder Alan Fletcher admired this "ability to stroke a cliché until it purrs like a metaphor."

In 1995, the Minnesota Children's Museum was moving from a cramped but cozy space in a shopping mall to a beautiful new building in downtown St. Paul designed by up-and-coming architects Julie Snow and Vincent James. We were asked to do the signage and graphics. Inevitably, the clichés poured out. Crayon markings. Bright primary colors. Building blocks, balloons, smiley faces.

In design, as in life, the antidote to stereotype is experience. Forget about the abstract idea of "children's museums." What makes this particular children's museum special? Ann Bitter, the museum's dynamic director, described her ambitions and confessed her fears. The new building was beautiful, she said, but she worried about losing the intimacy that visitors were accustomed to in the museum's old home. Like most children's museums, this one provided "hands-on experiences" (another cliché). Would kids feel as comfortable amid the big, beautiful, brand-new architecture?

Sometimes avoiding the obvious means embracing it—and wrestling it to the ground. Children's hands, with their invitation to touch and their inherent sense of scale, provided the key. Instead of trying to draw them (silhouettes? crayon scribbles?) we recruited local kids to serve as hand models and photographed them pointing, counting, playing. Today, at the Minnesota Children's Museum, these hands—of children that are now in their twenties—continue to point the way, and pick out that delicate path between what's expected and what surprises.

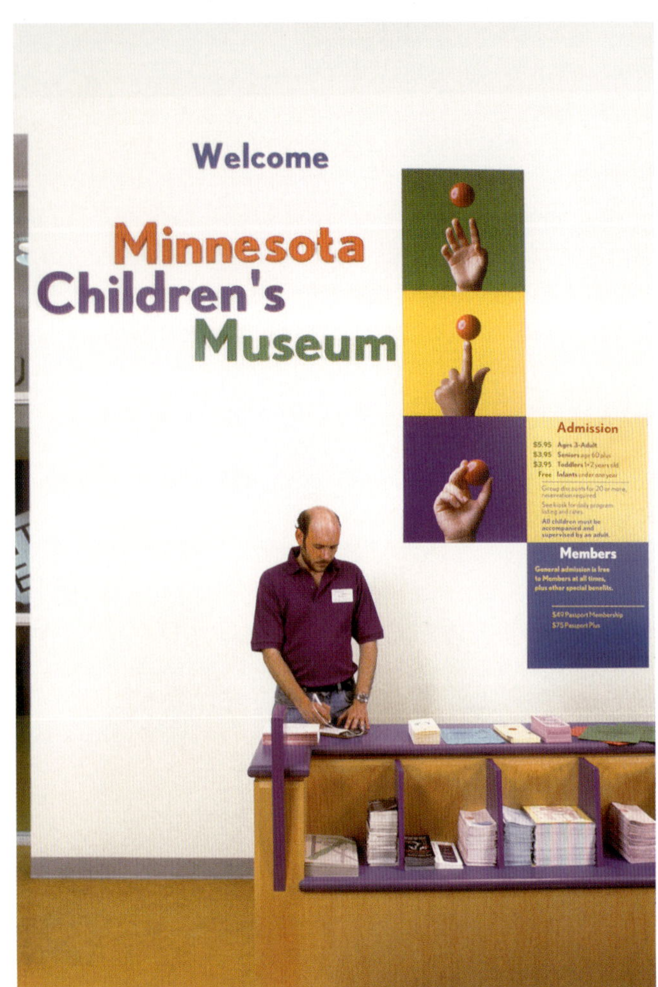

Left
Instead of a logo, the museum combines two dozen photographs of children's hands in various ways.

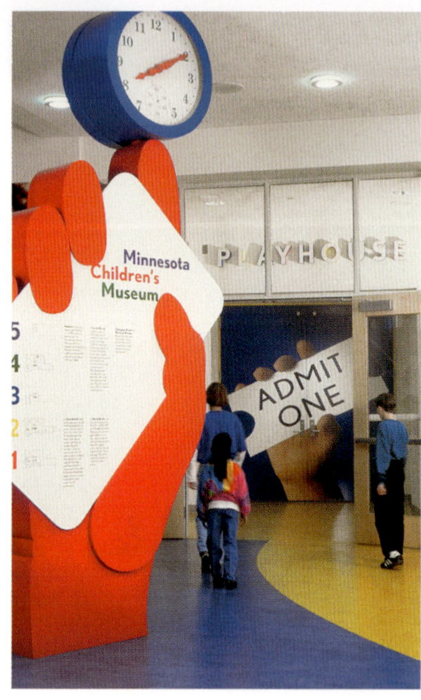

Right
A sculptural hand balancing a clock serves as a central meeting place and reinforces the graphic theme.

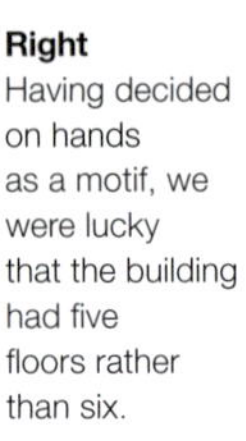

Right
Having decided on hands as a motif, we were lucky that the building had five floors rather than six.

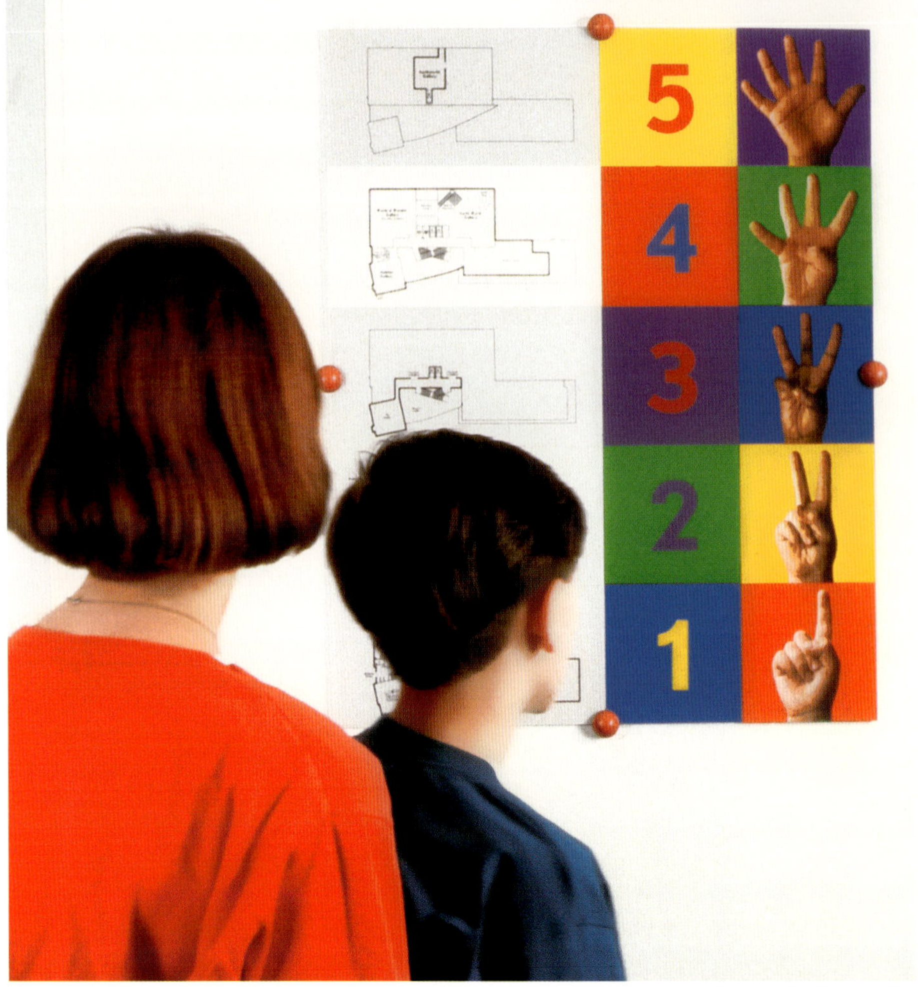

Below
Children's hands point the way throughout the building, providing a sense of scale and, in the case of the bathroom signs, a bit of wit.

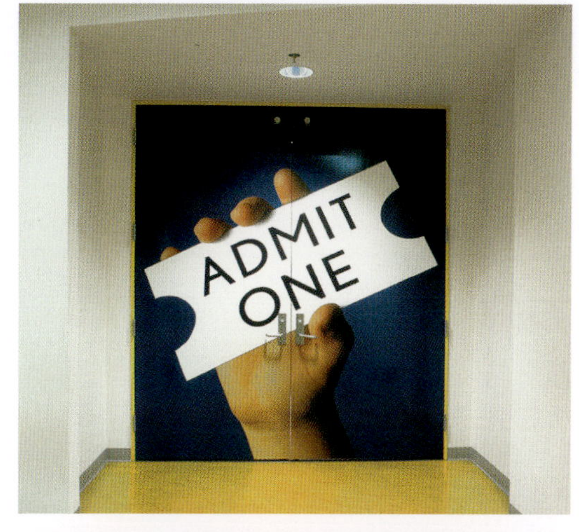

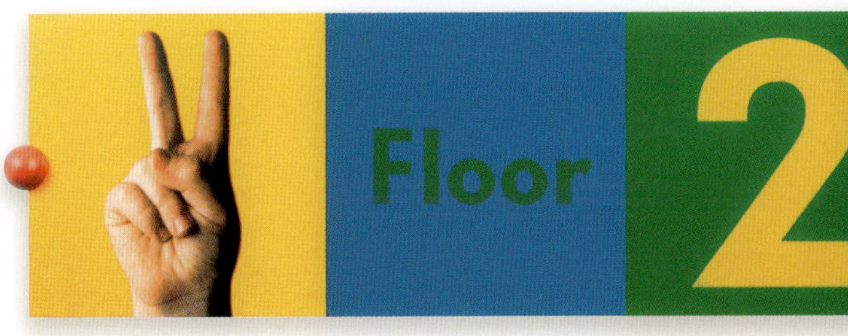

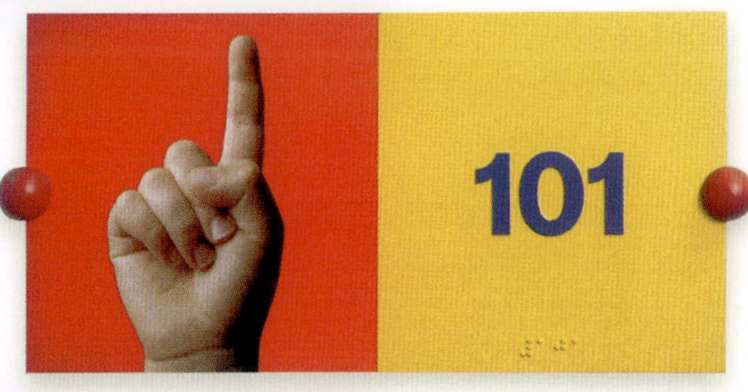

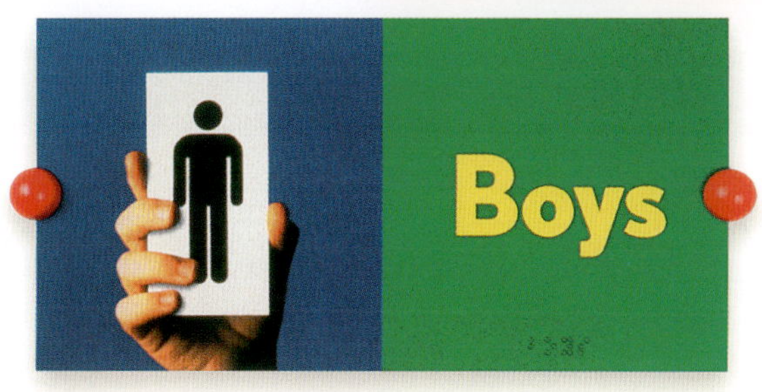

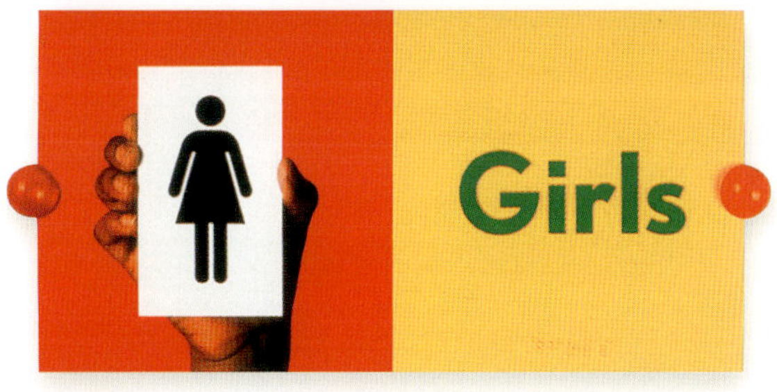

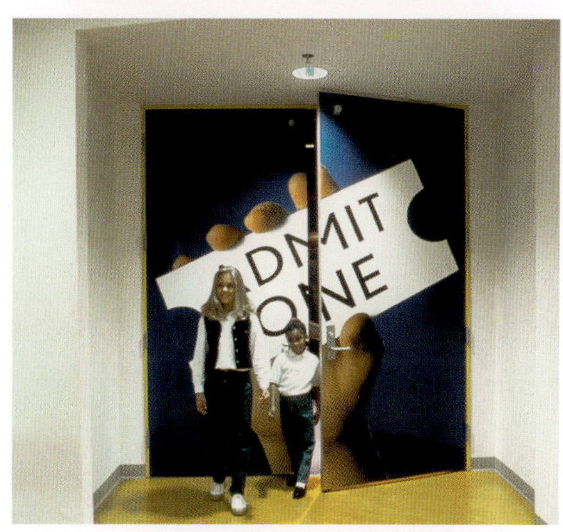

Above
A giant ticket on the auditorium door is torn in half each time the door opens.

Next spread
For the museum's grand opening, it celebrated its audience by merging identity and architecture.

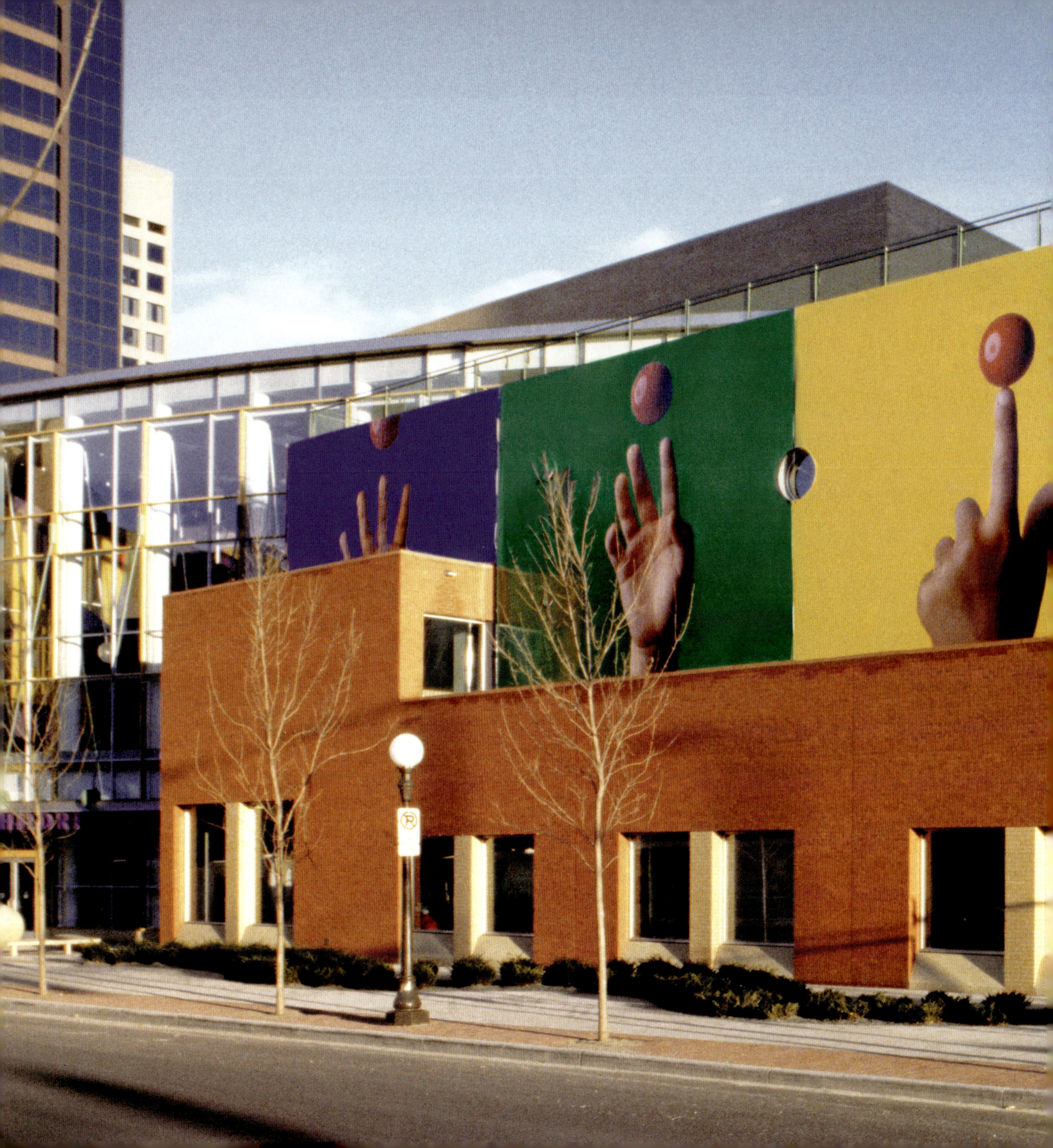

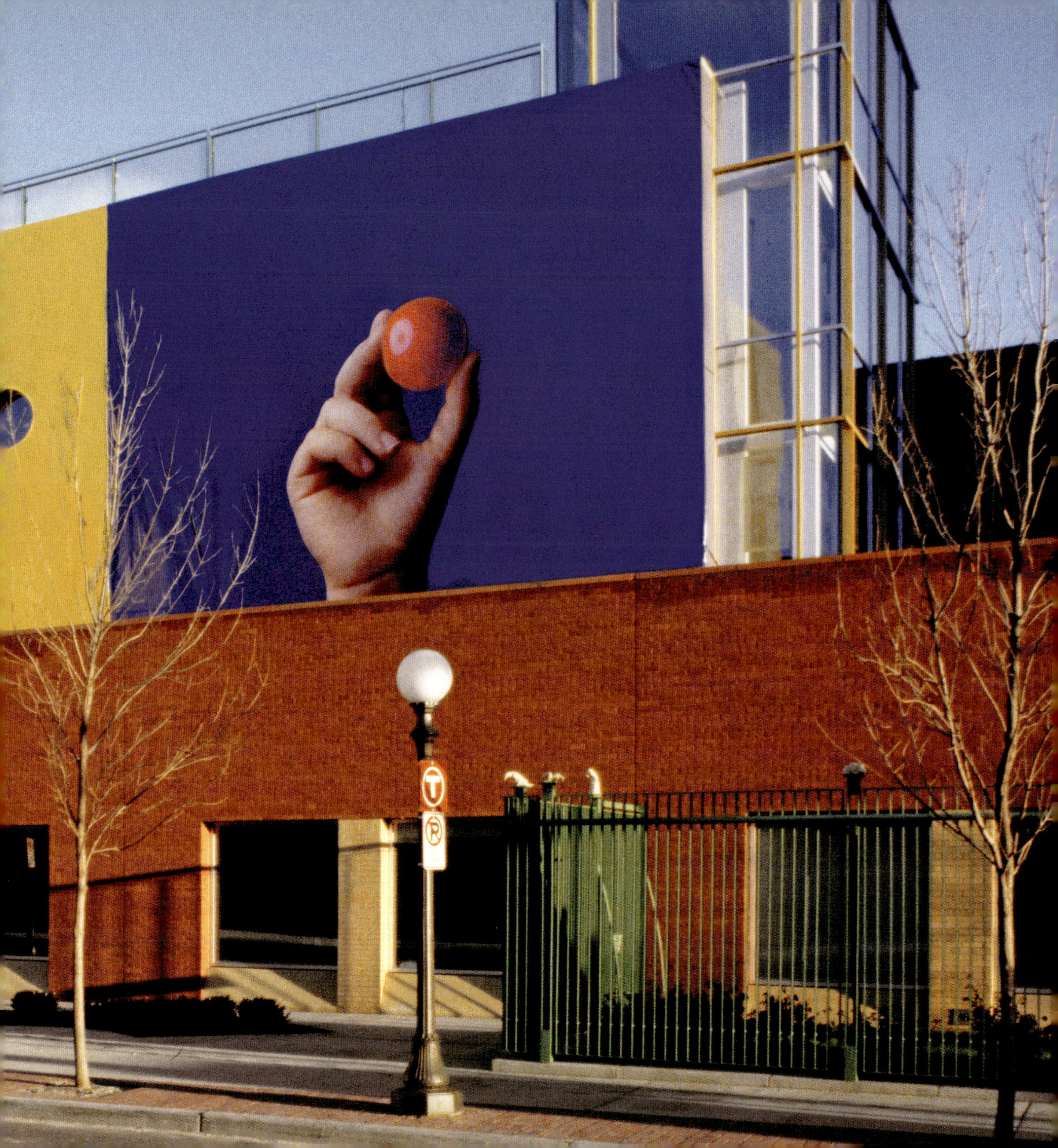

It is five minutes to midnight.

How to avoid doomsday
Bulletin of the Atomic Scientists

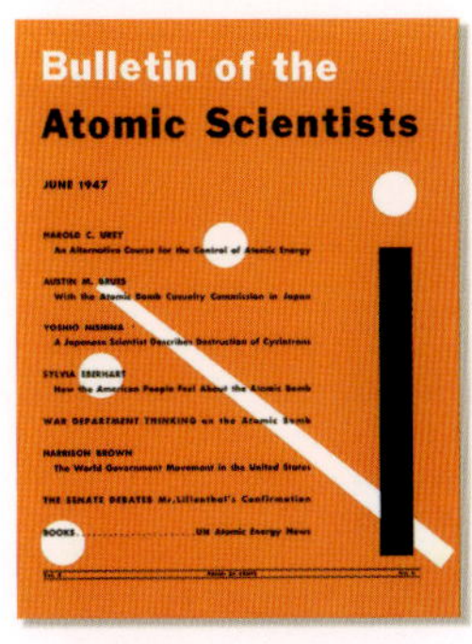

Opposite
Our design for the annual report of the *Bulletin of the Atomic Scientists* announces the current position of the Doomsday Clock, summarizing the assessment of dozens of experts.

Above
The original clock was the creation of artist Martyl Langsdorf. Called to provide an illustration for the *Bulletin*'s first magazine cover in 1947, she created a universally compelling image of rare power.

The most powerful piece of information design of the 20th century was designed by a landscape painter. In 1943, nuclear physicist Alexander Langsdorf Jr. was called to Chicago to join hundreds of scientists in a secret wartime project: the race to develop an atomic bomb. Their work on the Manhattan Project made possible the bombs that were dropped on Hiroshima and Nagasaki and ended World War II. But Langsdorf, like many of his colleagues, greeted the subsequent peace with profound unease. What were the implications of the fact that the human race had invented the means to render itself extinct?

To bring this question to a broader audience, Langsdorf and his fellow scientists began circulating a mimeographed newsletter called the *Bulletin of the Atomic Scientists*. In June 1947, the newsletter became a magazine. Langsdorf's wife, Martyl, was an artist whose landscapes were exhibited in Chicago galleries. She volunteered to create the first cover. There wasn't much room for an illustration, and the budget permitted only two colors. But she found a solution. The Doomsday Clock was born.

Arguments about nuclear proliferation have been complicated and contentious. The Doomsday Clock translates them into a brutally simple visual analogy, merging the looming approach of midnight with the drama of a ticking time bomb. Appropriately for an organization led by scientists, the Clock sidesteps overwrought imagery of mushroom clouds in favor of an instrument of measurement. Martyl set the minute hand at seven to midnight on that first cover "simply because it looked good." Two years later, the Soviets tested their own nuclear device. The arms race was officially on. To emphasize the seriousness of these circumstances, the clock was moved to three minutes to midnight. It has been moved 20 times since. What a remarkable, clear, concise piece of communication!

Several years ago, the organization was looking for a logo. We told them they already had one. That began a relationship with the *Bulletin of the Atomic Scientists* that still continues. Each year, we publish the report that accompanies the announcement of the Clock's position. And each year, we hope we turn back time.

Right and next spread
Designer Armin Vit and I suggested that the Doomsday Clock be adopted as the organization's logo. Its non-specific neutrality has permitted the *Bulletin* to integrate data on bioterrorism and climate change into the yearly scientific assessment, which has led to more than 20 changes to the position of the clock's hands over the past 70 years.

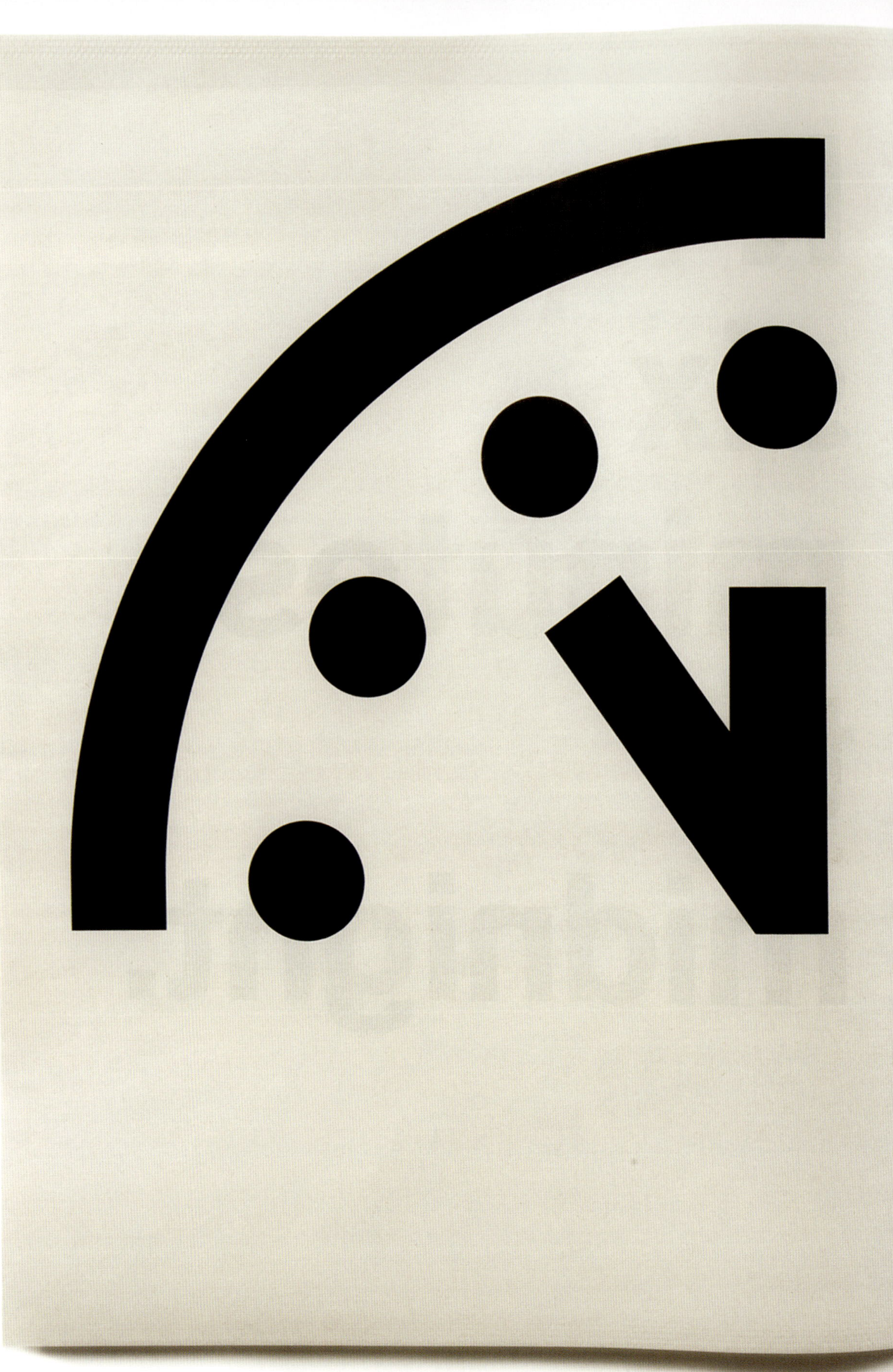

How close are we to catastrophic destruction? The Doomsday Clock monitors "minutes to midnight," calling on humanity to control the means by which it could obliterate itself. First and foremost, these include nuclear weapons, but they also encompass climate-changing technologies and new developments in the life sciences that could inflict irrevocable harm.

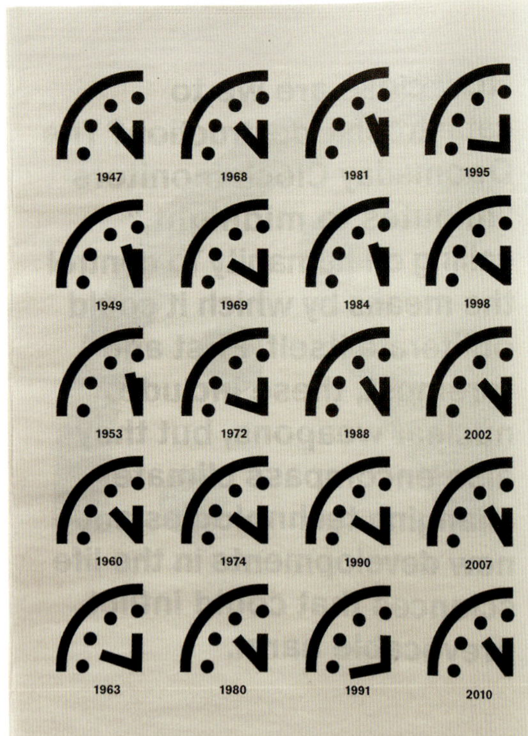

In 1947, the Bulletin first displayed the Doomsday Clock on the cover of the print magazine to convey, through a simple design, a sense of urgency and peril posed by nuclear weapons. The minute hand of the Clock has moved 19 times since, based on a global risk assessment by the Bulletin's Science and Security Board in consultation with other experts, and the Board of Sponsors, which currently includes 19 Nobel Laureates.

1947 As the Bulletin evolves from a newsletter into a magazine, the Clock appears on the cover for the first time. It symbolizes the urgency of the nuclear dangers that the magazine's founders – and the broader scientific community – are trying to convey to the public and political leaders around the world.
It is seven minutes to midnight.

1949 The Soviet Union denies it, but in the fall, President Harry Truman tells the American public that the Soviets tested their first nuclear device, officially starting the arms race. "We do not advise Americans that doomsday is near and that they can expect atomic bombs to start falling on their heads a month or year from now," the Bulletin explains. "But we think they have reason to be deeply alarmed and to be prepared for grave decisions."
It is three minutes to midnight.

1953 After much debate, the United States decides to pursue the hydrogen bomb, a weapon far more powerful than any atomic bomb. In October 1952, the United States tests its first thermonuclear device, obliterating a Pacific Ocean islet in the process; nine months later, the Soviets test an H-bomb of their own. "The hands of the Clock of Doom have moved again," the Bulletin announces. "Only a few more swings of the pendulum, and, from Moscow to Chicago, atomic explosions will strike midnight for Western civilization."
It is two minutes to midnight.

1960 Political actions belie the tough talk of "massive retaliation." For the first time, the United States and Soviet Union appear eager to avoid direct confrontation in regional conflicts such as the 1956 Egyptian-Israeli dispute. Joint projects that build trust and constructive dialogue between third parties also quell diplomatic hostilities. Scientists initiate many of these measures, helping establish the International Geophysical Year, a series of coordinated, worldwide scientific observations, and the Pugwash Conferences, which allow Soviet and American scientists to interact.
It is seven minutes to midnight.

1963 After a decade of almost non-stop nuclear tests, the United States and Soviet Union sign the Partial Test Ban Treaty, which ends all atmospheric nuclear testing. While it does not out law underground testing, the treaty represents progress in at least slowing the arms race. It also signals awareness among the Soviets and Americans that they need to work together to prevent nuclear annihilation.
It is twelve minutes to midnight.

1968 Regional wars rage. U.S. involvement in Vietnam intensifies, India and Pakistan battle in 1965, and Israel and its Arab neighbors renew hostilities in 1967. Worse yet, France and China develop nuclear weapons to assert themselves as global players. "There is little reason to feel sanguine about the future of our society on the world scale," the Bulletin laments. "There is a mass revulsion against war, yes; but no sign of conscious intellectual leadership in a rebellion against the deadly heritage of international anarchy."
It is seven minutes to midnight.

1969 Nearly all of the world's nations come together to sign the Nuclear Non-Proliferation Treaty. The deal is simple – the nuclear weapon states vow to help the treaty's non-nuclear weapon signatories develop nuclear power if they promise to forego producing nuclear weapons. The nuclear weapon states also pledge to abolish their own arsenals when political conditions allow for it. Although Israel, India, and Pakistan refuse to sign the treaty, the Bulletin is cautiously optimistic: "The great powers have made the first step. They must proceed without delay to the next one – the dismantling, gradually, of their own oversized military establishments."
It is ten minutes to midnight.

1972 The United States and Soviet Union attempt to curb the race for nuclear superiority by signing the Strategic Arms Limitation Treaty (SALT) and the Anti-Ballistic Missile (ABM) Treaty. The two treaties force a nuclear parity of sorts. SALT limits the number of ballistic missile launchers either country can possess, and the ABM Treaty stops an arms race in defensive weaponry from developing.
It is twelve minutes to midnight.

1974 South Asia gets the Bomb, as India tests its first nuclear device. And any gains in previous arms control agreements seem like a mirage. The United States and Soviet Union appear to be modernizing their nuclear forces, not reducing them. Thanks to the deployment of multiple independently targetable reentry vehicles (MIRV), both countries can now load their intercontinental ballistic missiles with more nuclear warheads than before.
It is nine minutes to midnight.

1980 Thirty-five years after the start of the nuclear age and after some promising disarmament gains, the United States and the Soviet Union still view nuclear weapons as an integral component of their national security. This stalled progress discourages the Bulletin: "[The Soviet Union and United States have] been behaving like what may best be described as 'nucleoholics' – drunks who continue to insist that the drink being consumed is positively 'the last one,' but who can always find a good excuse for 'just one more round.'"
It is seven minutes to midnight.

1981 The Soviet invasion of Afghanistan hardens the U.S. nuclear posture. Before he leaves office, President Jimmy Carter pulls the United States from the Olympics Games in Moscow and considers ways in which the United States could win a nuclear war. The rhetoric only intensifies with the election of Ronald Reagan as president. Reagan scraps any talk of arms control and proposes that the best way to end the Cold War is for the United States to win it.
It is four minutes to midnight.

1984 U.S.-Soviet relations reach their iciest point in decades. Dialogue between the two superpowers virtually stops. "Every channel of communications has been constricted or shut down; every form of contact has been attenuated or cut off. And arms control negotiations have been reduced to a species of propaganda," a concerned Bulletin informs readers. The United States seems to flout the few arms control agreements in place by seeking an expansive, space-based anti-ballistic missile capability, raising worries that a new arms race will begin.
It is three minutes to midnight.

1988 The United States and Soviet Union sign the historic Intermediate-Range Nuclear Forces Treaty, the first agreement to actually ban a whole category of nuclear weapons. The leadership shown by President Ronald Reagan and Soviet Premier Mikhail Gorbachev makes the treaty a reality, but public opposition to U.S. nuclear weapons in Western Europe inspires it. For years, such intermediate-range missiles had kept Western Europe in the crosshairs of the two superpowers.
It is six minutes to midnight.

1990 As one Eastern European country after another (Poland, Czechoslovakia, Hungary, Romania) frees itself from Soviet control, Soviet General Secretary Mikhail Gorbachev refuses to intervene, halting the ideological battle for Europe and significantly diminishing the risk of all-out nuclear war. In late 1989, the Berlin Wall falls, symbolically ending the Cold War. "Forty-four years after Winston Churchill's 'Iron Curtain' speech, the myth of monolithic communism has been shattered for all to see," the Bulletin proclaims.
It is ten minutes to midnight.

1991 With the Cold War officially over, the United States and Russia begin making deep cuts to their nuclear arsenals. The Strategic Arms Reduction Treaty greatly reduces the number of strategic nuclear weapons deployed by the two former adversaries. Better still, a series of unilateral initiatives remove most of the intercontinental ballistic missiles and bombers in both countries from hair-trigger alert. "The illusion that tens of thousands of nuclear weapons are a guarantor of national security has been stripped away," the Bulletin declares.
It is seventeen minutes to midnight.

1995 Hopes for a large post-Cold War peace dividend and a renouncing of nuclear weapons fade. Particularly in the United States, hard-liners seem reluctant to soften their rhetoric or actions, as they claim that a resurgent Russia could provide as much of a threat as the Soviet Union. Such talk slows the rollback in global nuclear forces; more than 40,000 nuclear weapons remain worldwide. There is also concern that terrorists could exploit poorly secured nuclear facilities in the former Soviet Union.
It is fourteen minutes to midnight.

1998 India and Pakistan stage nuclear weapons tests only three weeks apart. "The tests are a symptom of the failure of the international community to fully commit itself to control the spread of nuclear weapons – and to work toward substantial reductions in the numbers of these weapons," a dismayed Bulletin reports. Russia and the United States continue to serve as poor examples to the rest of the world. Together, they still maintain 7,000 warheads ready to fire at each other within 15 minutes.
It is nine minutes to midnight.

2002 Concerns regarding a nuclear terrorist attack underscore the enormous amount of unsecured – and sometimes unaccounted for – weapon-grade nuclear materials located throughout the world. Meanwhile, the United States expresses a desire to design new nuclear weapons, with an emphasis on those able to destroy hardened and deeply buried targets. It also rejects a series of arms control treaties and announces it will withdraw from the Anti-Ballistic Missile Treaty.
It is seven minutes to midnight.

2007 The world stands at the brink of a second nuclear age. The United States and Russia remain ready to stage a nuclear attack within minutes, North Korea conducts a nuclear test, and many in the international community worry that Iran plans to acquire the Bomb. Climate change also presents a dire challenge to humanity. Damage to ecosystems is already taking place; flooding, destructive storms, increased drought, and polar ice melt are causing loss of life and property.
It is five minutes to midnight.

2010 A new spirit of international cooperation and negotiation gives hope that our leaders will act to rid the world of nuclear weapons. Governments are also proposing collaborative action on global warming. By shifting the hand back by only one minute, we emphasize how much needs to be accomplished as we affirm the new initiative that the United States, Russia, the European Union, India, China, Brazil, and others are displaying on nuclear security and on climate change. With 23,000 nuclear weapons in the world, the potential for use, inadvertent launches, accidents, and proliferation remains high. Scientists also believe that humanity has less than a decade to arrest greenhouse gas emissions before Earth cascades into irreversible climate disaster. History shows that progress toward disarmament and environmental protection occurs when citizens are engaged and express their concerns to policy makers.
It is six minutes to midnight.

Turn back the Clock.

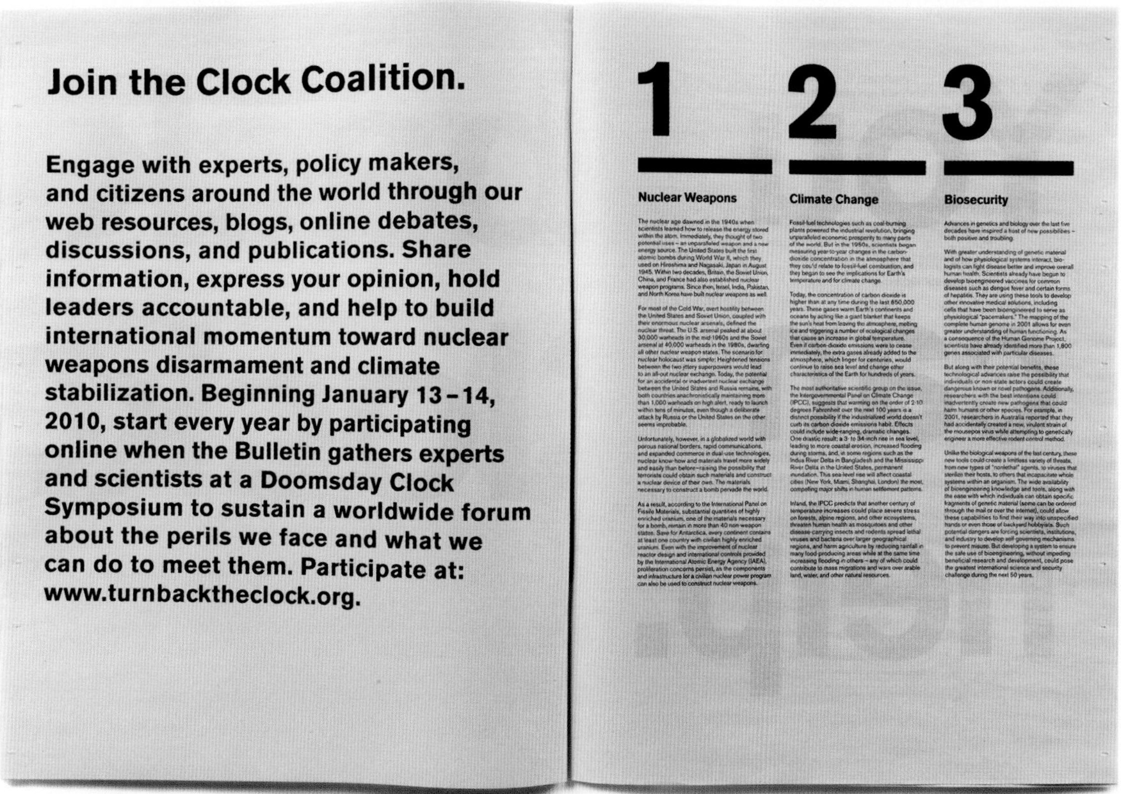

Join the Clock Coalition.

Engage with experts, policy makers, and citizens around the world through our web resources, blogs, online debates, discussions, and publications. Share information, express your opinion, hold leaders accountable, and help to build international momentum toward nuclear weapons disarmament and climate stabilization. Beginning January 13–14, 2010, start every year by participating online when the Bulletin gathers experts and scientists at a Doomsday Clock Symposium to sustain a worldwide forum about the perils we face and what we can do to meet them. Participate at: www.turnbacktheclock.org.

1

Nuclear Weapons

The nuclear age dawned in the 1940s when scientists learned how to release the energy stored within the atom. Immediately, they thought of two potential uses – an unparalleled weapon and a new energy source. The United States built the first atomic bombs during World War II, which they used on Hiroshima and Nagasaki, Japan in August 1945. Within two decades, Britain, the Soviet Union, China, and France had also established nuclear weapon programs. Since then, Israel, India, Pakistan, and North Korea have built nuclear weapons as well.

For most of the Cold War, overt hostility between the United States and Soviet Union, coupled with their enormous nuclear arsenals, defined the nuclear threat. The U.S. arsenal peaked at about 30,000 warheads in the mid-1960s and the Soviet arsenal at 40,000 warheads in the 1980s, dwarfing all other nuclear weapon states. The scenario for nuclear holocaust was simple: Heightened tensions between the two jittery superpowers would lead to an all-out nuclear exchange. Today, the potential for an accidental or inadvertent nuclear exchange between the United States and Russia remains, with both countries anachronistically maintaining more than 1,000 warheads on high alert, ready to launch within tens of minutes, even though a deliberate attack by Russia or the United States on the other seems improbable.

Unfortunately, however, in a globalized world with porous national borders, rapid communications, and expanded commerce in dual-use technologies, nuclear know-how and materials travel more widely and easily than before–raising the possibility that terrorists could obtain such materials and construct a nuclear device of their own. The materials necessary to construct a bomb pervade the world.

As a result, according to the International Panel on Fissile Materials, substantial quantities of highly enriched uranium, one of the materials necessary for a bomb, remain in more than 40 non-weapon states. Save for Antarctica, every continent contains at least one country with civilian highly enriched uranium. Even with the improvement of nuclear reactor design and international controls provided by the International Atomic Energy Agency (IAEA), proliferation concerns persist, as the components and infrastructure for a civilian nuclear power program can also be used to construct nuclear weapons.

2

Climate Change

Fossil-fuel technologies such as coal-burning plants powered the industrial revolution, bringing unparalleled economic prosperity to many parts of the world. But in the 1950s, scientists began measuring year-to-year changes in the carbon-dioxide concentration in the atmosphere that they could relate to fossil-fuel combustion, and they began to see the implications for Earth's temperature and for climate change.

Today, the concentration of carbon dioxide is higher than at any time during the last 650,000 years. These gases warm Earth's continents and oceans by acting like a giant blanket that keeps the sun's heat from leaving the atmosphere, melting ice and triggering a number of ecological changes that cause an increase in global temperature. Even if carbon-dioxide emissions were to cease immediately, the extra gases already added to the atmosphere, which linger for centuries, would continue to raise sea level and change other characteristics of the Earth for hundreds of years.

The most authoritative scientific group on the issue, the Intergovernmental Panel on Climate Change (IPCC), suggests that warming on the order of 2-10 degrees Fahrenheit over the next 100 years is a distinct possibility if the industrialized world doesn't curb its carbon dioxide emissions habit. Effects could include wide-ranging, dramatic changes. One drastic result: a 3- to 34-inch rise in sea level, leading to more coastal erosion, increased flooding during storms, and, in some regions such as the Indus River Delta in Bangladesh and the Mississippi River Delta in the United States, permanent inundation. This sea-level rise will affect coastal cities (New York, Miami, Shanghai, London) the most, compelling major shifts in human settlement patterns.

Inland, the IPCC predicts that another century of temperature increases could place severe stress on forests, alpine regions, and other ecosystems, threaten human health as mosquitoes and other disease-carrying insects and rodents spread lethal viruses and bacteria over larger geographical regions, and harm agriculture by reducing rainfall in many food-producing areas while at the same time increasing flooding in others – any of which could contribute to mass migrations and wars over arable land, water, and other natural resources.

3

Biosecurity

Advances in genetics and biology over the last five decades have inspired a host of new possibilities – both positive and troubling.

With greater understanding of genetic material and of how physiological systems interact, biologists can fight disease better and improve overall human health. Scientists already have begun to develop bioengineered vaccines for common diseases such as dengue fever and certain forms of hepatitis. They are using these tools to develop other innovative medical solutions, including cells that have been bioengineered to serve as physiological "pacemakers." The mapping of the complete human genome in 2001 allows for even greater understanding of human functioning. As a consequence of the Human Genome Project, scientists have already identified more than 1,800 genes associated with particular diseases.

But along with their potential benefits, these technological advances raise the possibility that individuals or non-state actors could create dangerous known or novel pathogens. Additionally, researchers with the best intentions could inadvertently create new pathogens that could harm humans or other species. For example, in 2001, researchers in Australia reported that they had accidentally created a new, virulent strain of the mousepox virus while attempting to genetically engineer a more effective rodent control method.

Unlike the biological weapons of the last century, these new tools could create a limitless variety of threats, from new types of "nonlethal" agents, to viruses that sterilize their hosts, to others that incapacitate whole systems within an organism. The wide availability of bioengineering knowledge and tools, along with the ease with which individuals can obtain specific fragments of genetic material (some can be ordered through the mail or over the internet), could allow these capabilities to find their way into unspecified hands or even those of backyard hobbyists. Such potential dangers are forcing scientists, institutions, and industry to develop self-governing mechanisms to prevent misuse. But developing a system to ensure the safe use of bioengineering, without impeding beneficial research and development, could pose the greatest international science and security challenge during the next 50 years.

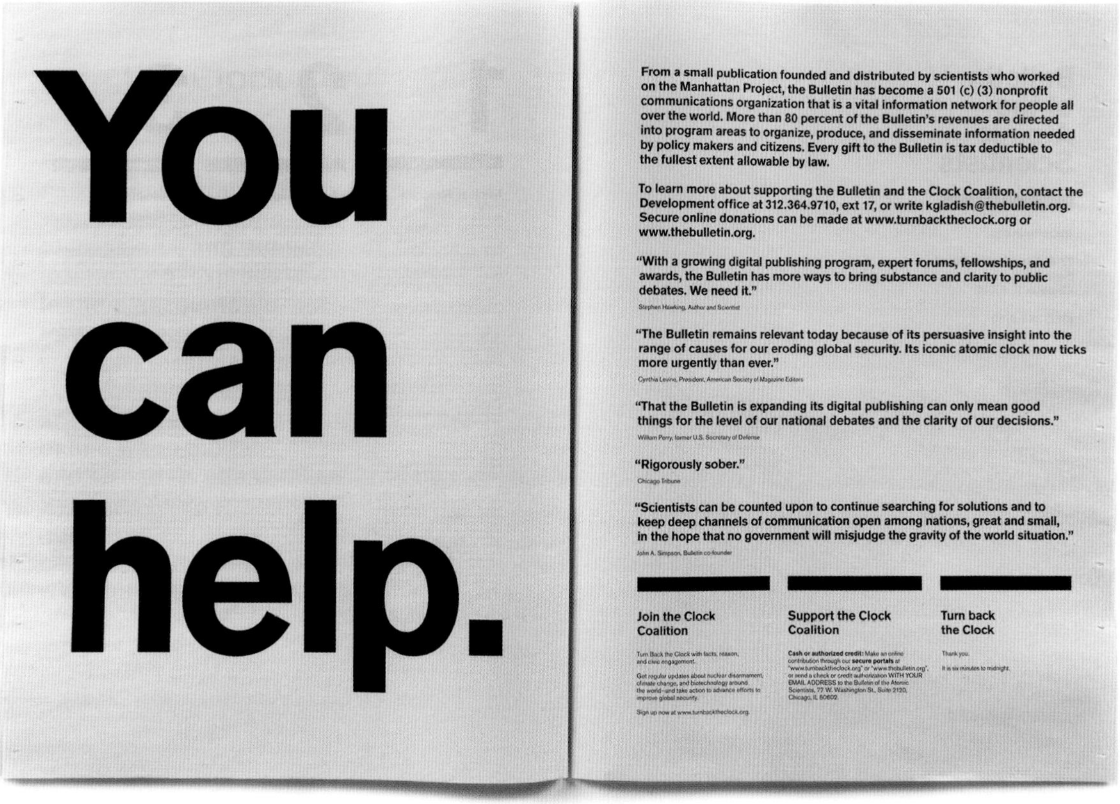

You can help.

From a small publication founded and distributed by scientists who worked on the Manhattan Project, the Bulletin has become a 501 (c) (3) nonprofit communications organization that is a vital information network for people all over the world. More than 80 percent of the Bulletin's revenues are directed into program areas to organize, produce, and disseminate information needed by policy makers and citizens. Every gift to the Bulletin is tax deductible to the fullest extent allowable by law.

To learn more about supporting the Bulletin and the Clock Coalition, contact the Development office at 312.364.9710, ext 17, or write kgladish@thebulletin.org. Secure online donations can be made at www.turnbacktheclock.org or www.thebulletin.org.

"With a growing digital publishing program, expert forums, fellowships, and awards, the Bulletin has more ways to bring substance and clarity to public debates. We need it."

Stephen Hawking, Author and Scientist

"The Bulletin remains relevant today because of its persuasive insight into the range of causes for our eroding global security. Its iconic atomic clock now ticks more urgently than ever."

Cynthia Levine, President, American Society of Magazine Editors

"That the Bulletin is expanding its digital publishing can only mean good things for the level of our national debates and the clarity of our decisions."

William Perry, former U.S. Secretary of Defense

"Rigorously sober."

Chicago Tribune

"Scientists can be counted upon to continue searching for solutions and to keep deep channels of communication open among nations, great and small, in the hope that no government will misjudge the gravity of the world situation."

John A. Simpson, Bulletin co-founder

Join the Clock Coalition

Turn Back the Clock with facts, reason, and civic engagement.

Get regular updates about nuclear disarmament, climate change, and biotechnology around the world–and take action to advance efforts to improve global security.

Sign up now at www.turnbacktheclock.org.

Support the Clock Coalition

Cash or authorized credit: Make an online contribution through our **secure portals** at "www.turnbacktheclock.org" or "www.thebulletin.org", or send a check or credit authorization WITH YOUR EMAIL ADDRESS to the Bulletin of the Atomic Scientists, 77 W. Washington St., Suite 2120, Chicago, IL 60602.

Turn back the Clock

Thank you.

It is six minutes to midnight.

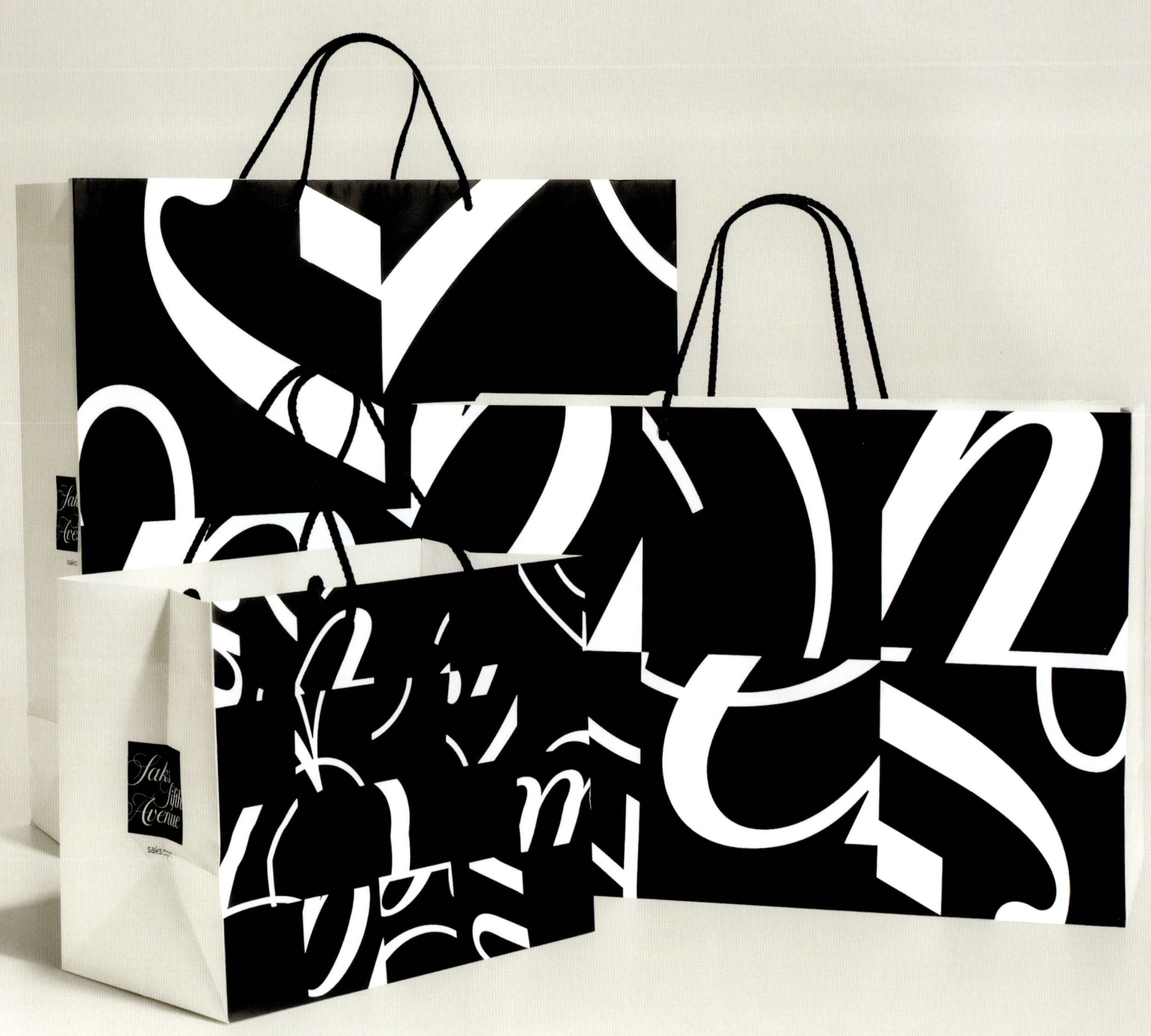
Saks Fifth Avenue

How to be fashionably timeless

Saks Fifth Avenue

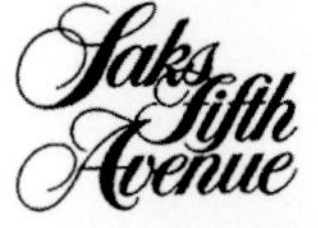

Opposite
Saks uses nearly 60 different bags and boxes. Thanks to the variations made possible by the modular logo system, no two are alike.

Above
The store has been represented by over 40 logos across the years. Most memorable was a calligraphic logo, first introduced in the 1940s and refined in the 1970s.

Terron Schaefer told me I could do anything I wanted. As head of marketing at Saks Fifth Avenue, the New York retail mecca founded in 1924, he had decided the store was ready for a new graphic program. He offered me a blank slate.

There is nothing I like less than a blank slate. Where other designers yearn for assignments without constraints, I do best when straining against thorny problems, baggage-burdened histories, and impossible-to-reconcile demands. Luckily, buried in Terron's assignment was a tantalizing challenge. The store was proud of its heritage and the authority it conferred. Yet it also offered up-to-the-minute fashions. And in merging opposites—timelessness and trendiness—they wanted a brand as immediately recognizable as Tiffany with its blue boxes or Burberry with its signature plaid.

We tried everything. We set the name in dozens of different typefaces: they looked inauthentic. We tried images of their flagship building: too old. We invented patterns: frustratingly arbitrary. Finally, sensing our exhaustion, Terron made a suggestion: a lot of people, he said, still liked a cursive logo from the 1970s by lettering artist Tom Carnase. A florid bit of stylized Spencerian script, it looked dated to me, but I asked our designer Kerrie Powell to see if it could be refined. Later that afternoon, I glanced at Kerrie's computer screen from across the room. On it was a small fragment of that dated 1970s logo. The enlarged detail looked as fresh and dramatic as the Nike swoosh. I realized this was it.

Solving a design problem happens like so many other things: slowly, then all at once. We divided the cursive logo into 64 squares. Each square was a dramatic abstract composition. Together, they generated a nearly infinite number of combinations, perfect for boxes and bags. The new graphic language at once evoked the history of the store and the promise of perpetual newness. For Saks Fifth Avenue, the answer was there all along.

When seeking the new, the question is: compared to what? Deconstructing the vintage Saks logo signaled change more effectively than inventing a new one. The jumbled puzzle was solved on each package by the inclusion of the whole logo in the bag gusset or on the underside of the box lid.

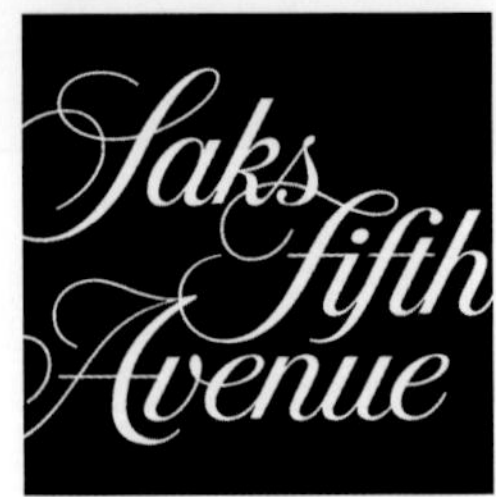

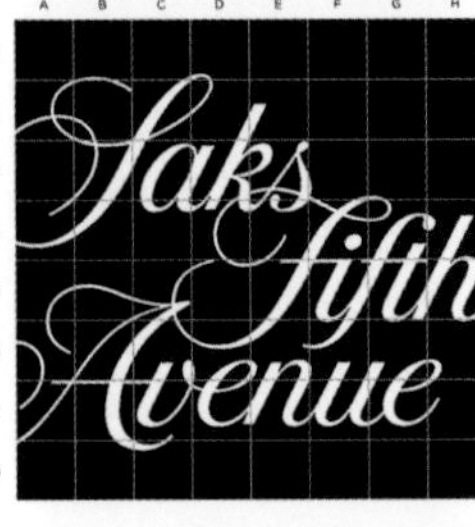

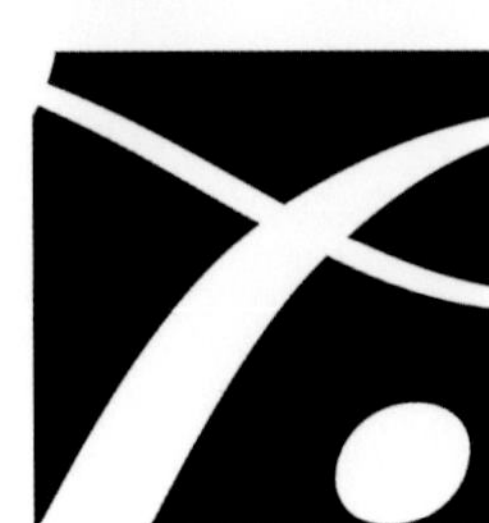

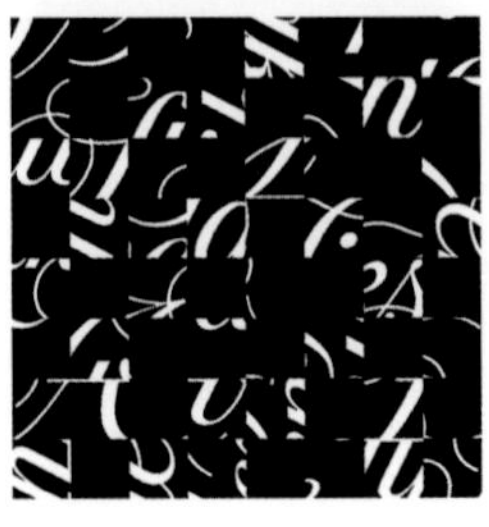

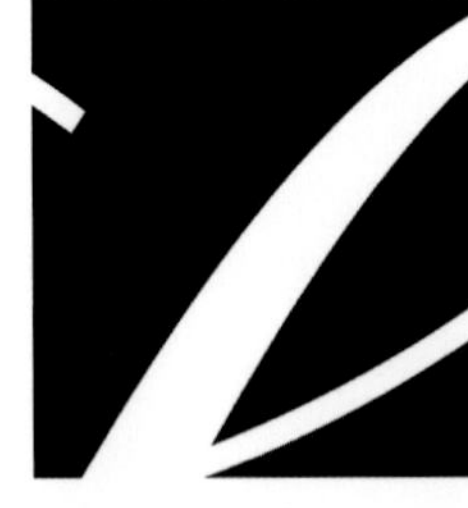

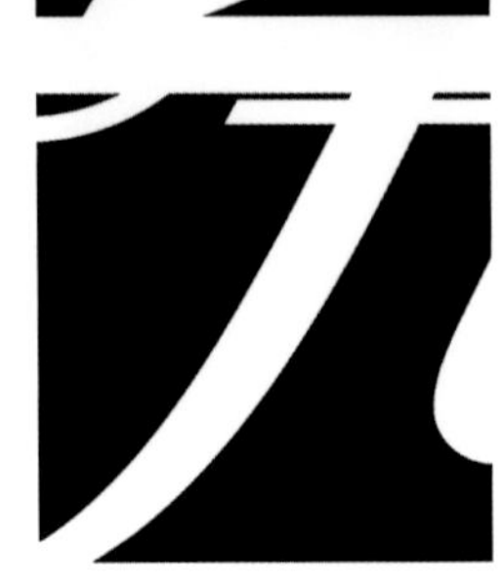

Above and right
A lighter and more graceful logo was redrawn by artist Joe Finocchiaro. Saks was looking for flexibility, so we divided the logo into 64 squares. Our designer Jena Sher's fiancé was a physics PhD at Yale. He calculated that the squares could be arranged in more configurations than there are particles in the known universe.

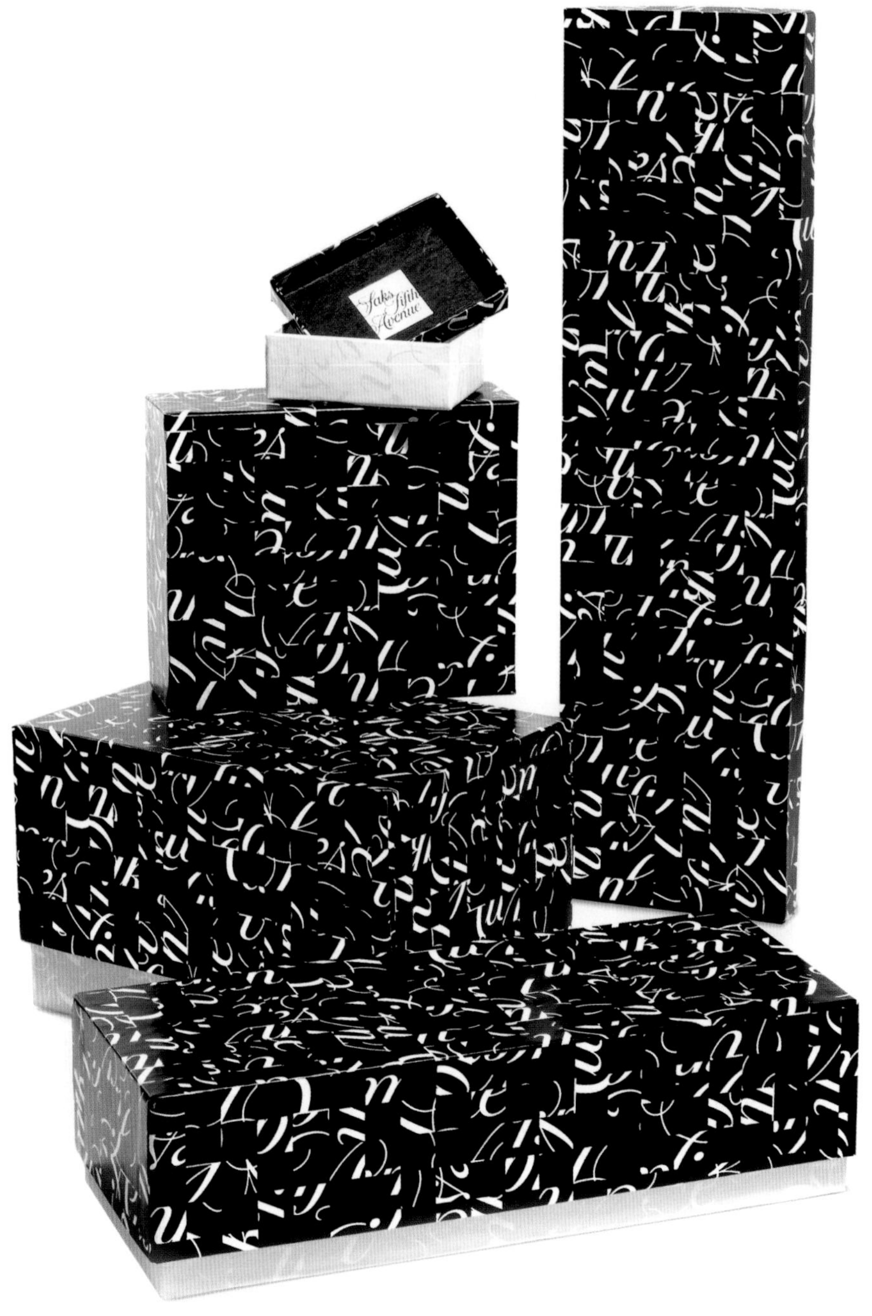

The logo pattern, wrapped around premade boxes at small scale, resembles houndstooth.

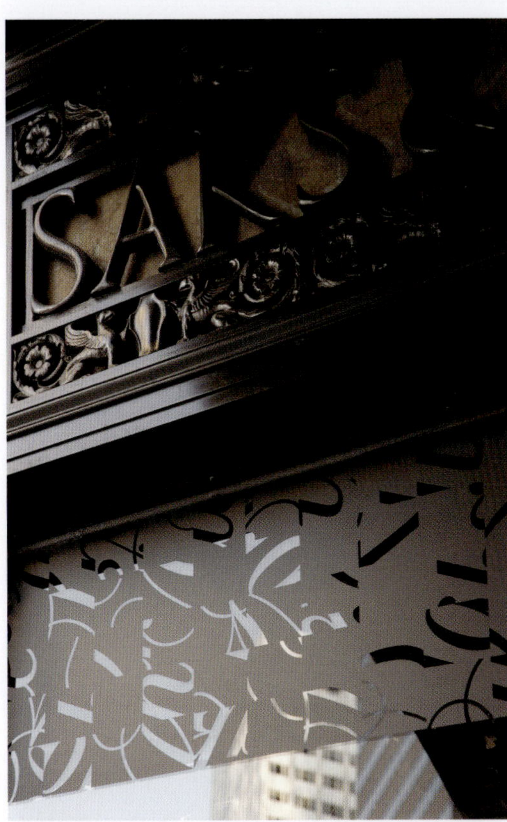

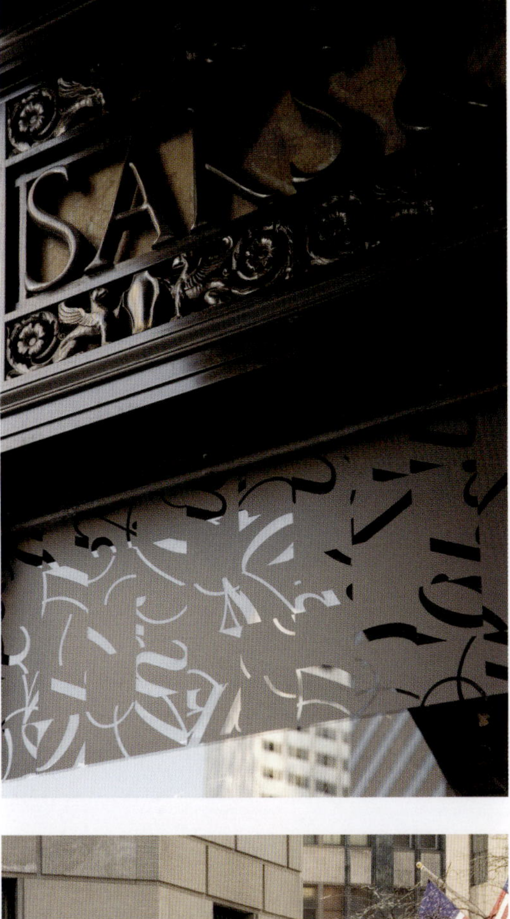

Left top
The new pattern complements the filigree of the flagship store's classic architecture.

Left bottom
When the packaging was launched in 2007, Saks store windows diagrammed the new graphic program. Even without this help, shoppers quickly came to associate the new look with Saks.

Below
Some felt the dramatic collision of details, always in black and white, echoed the work of New York School artists like Franz Kline, Barnett Newman, and Ellsworth Kelly. My real inspiration was the typographic collages of Yale School of Art professor Norman Ives.

Next spread
The logo pattern unifies the store's block-long presence in midtown Manhattan.

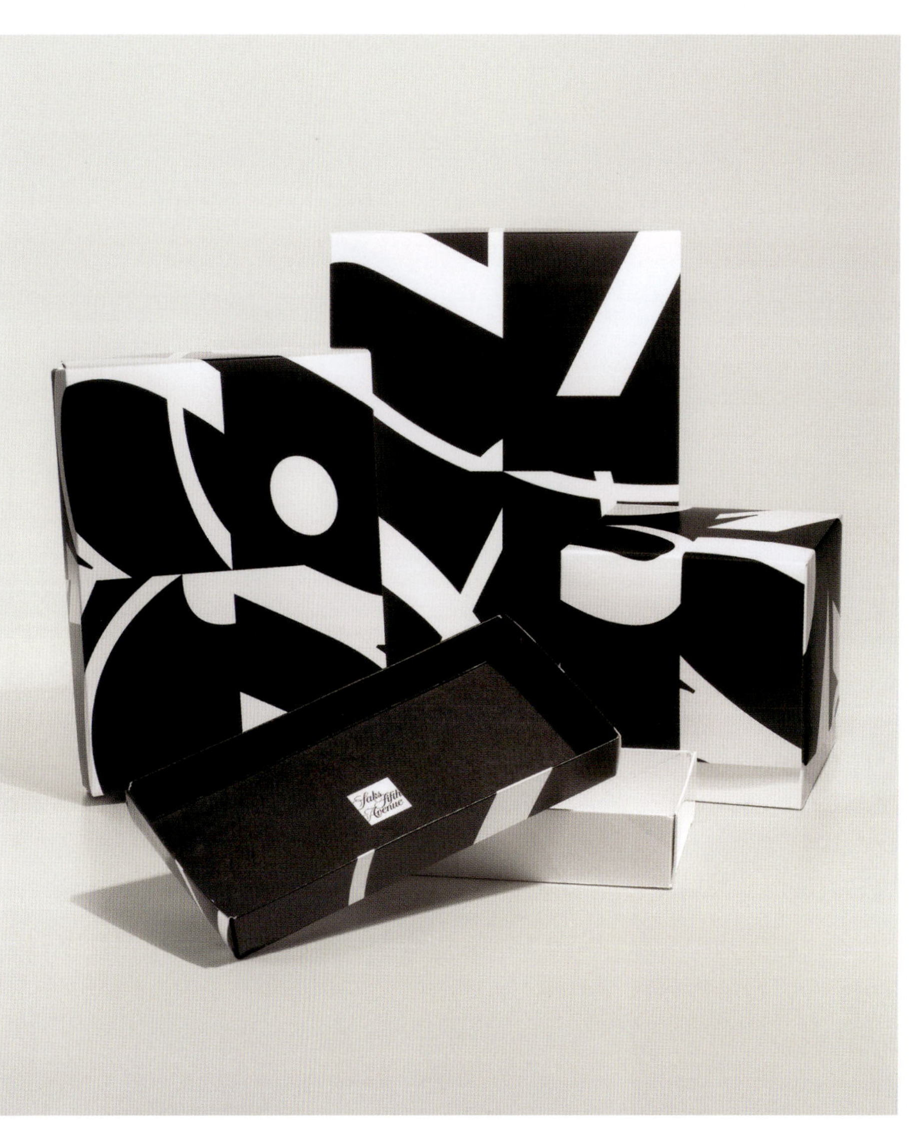

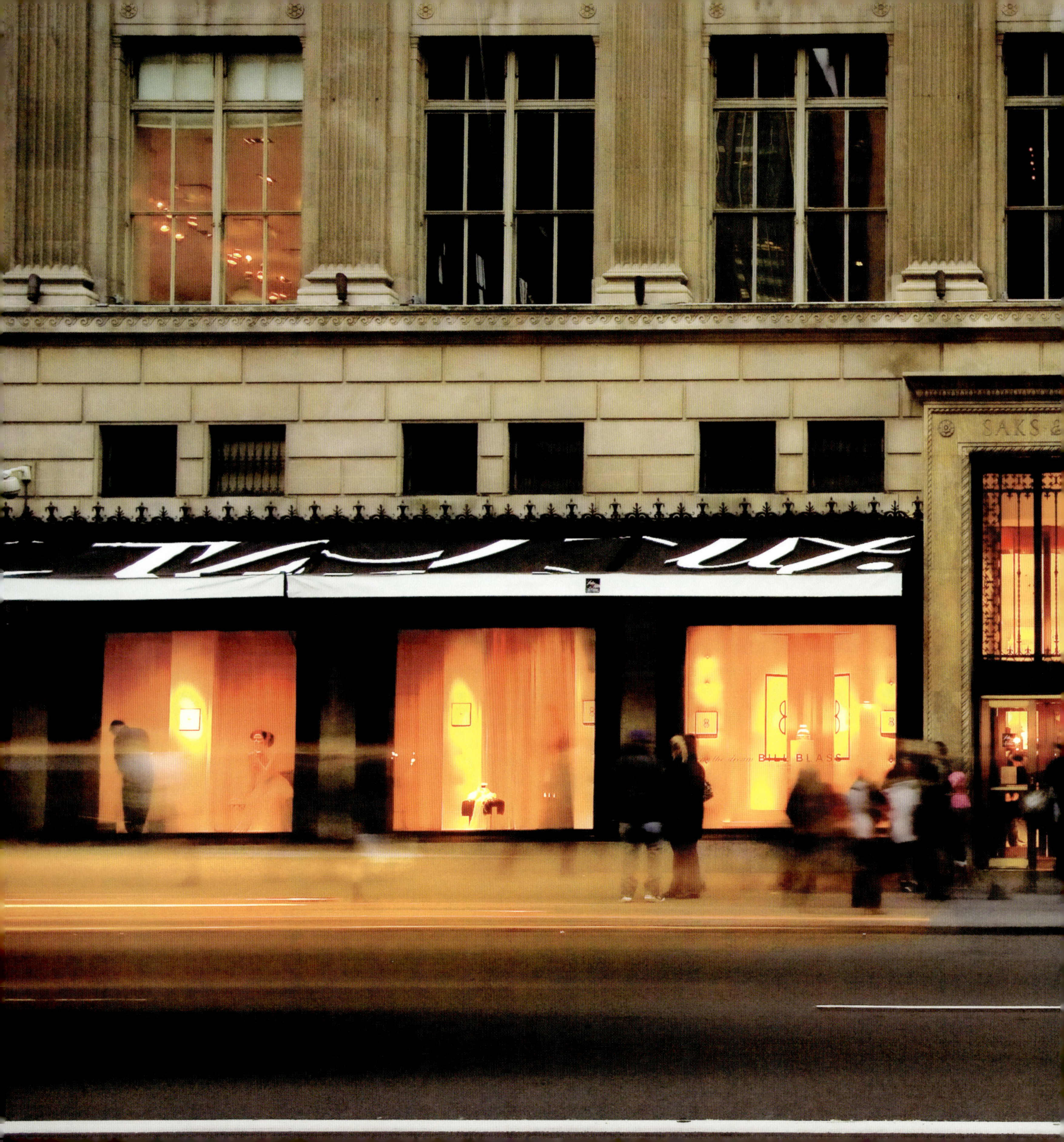
SAKS
BILL BLASS

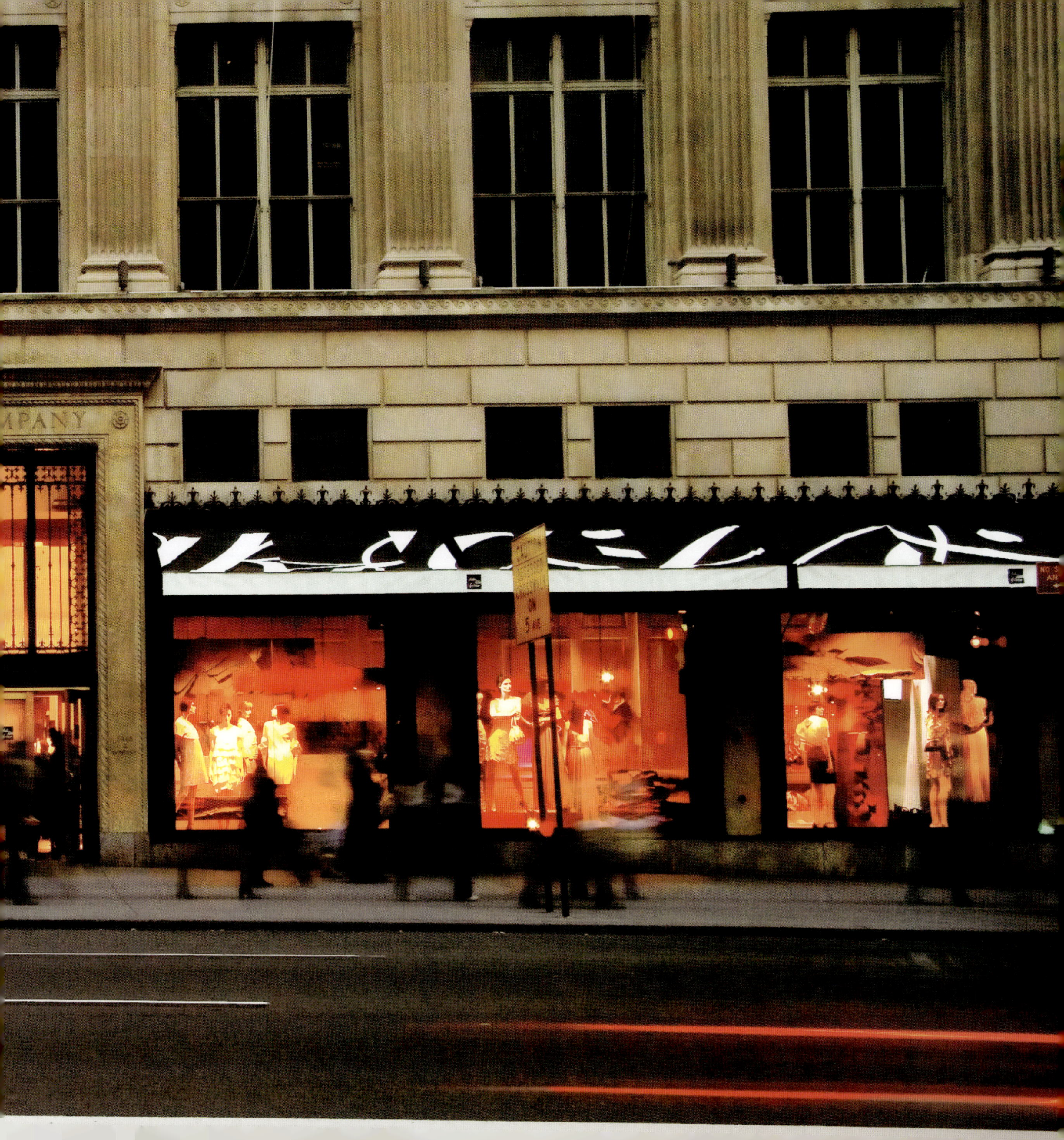
MPANY

With the new look firmly established, Terron Schaefer commissioned a series of seasonal campaigns, each based on a different theme. We used this as an opportunity to stretch the brand's basic premises, keeping certain elements constant (a black-and-white color scheme, the use of a square layout grid) while varying others. This provided a way to simultaneously refresh and reinforce the basic identity.

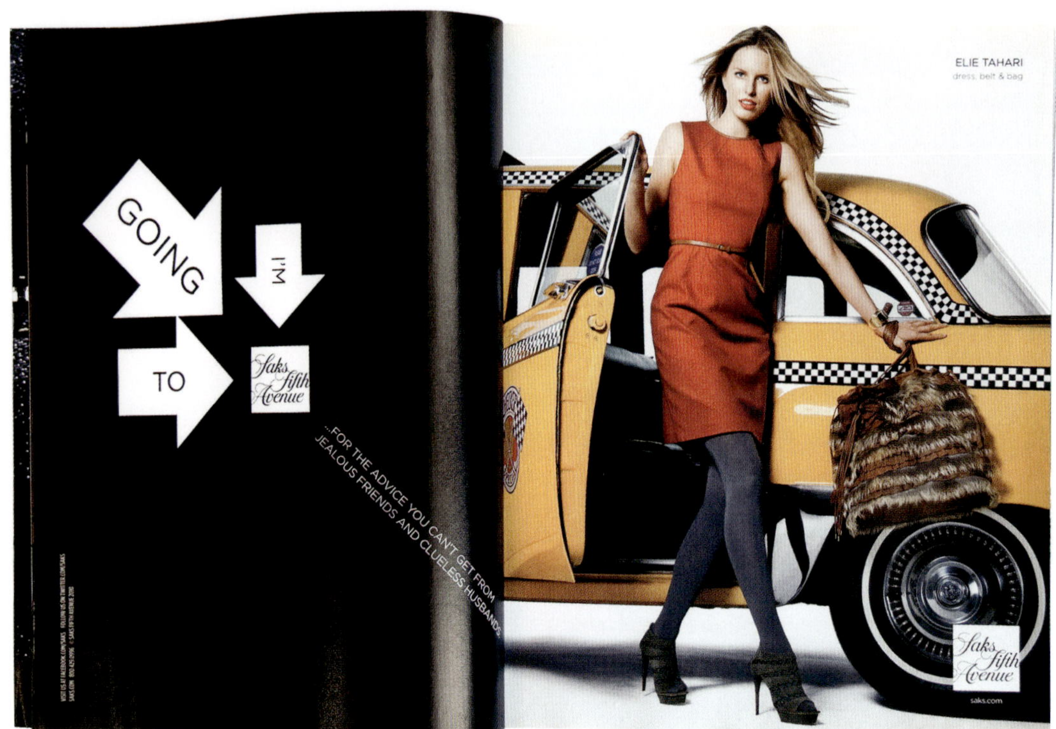

Left
Anders Overgaard's photography for the fall 2010 "I'm going to Saks" campaign paired models with modes of transportation, from taxis to skateboards.

Opposite
The campaign was literally directional, with arrows guiding shoppers to the store. Designer Jennifer Kinon worked out the intricate patterns.

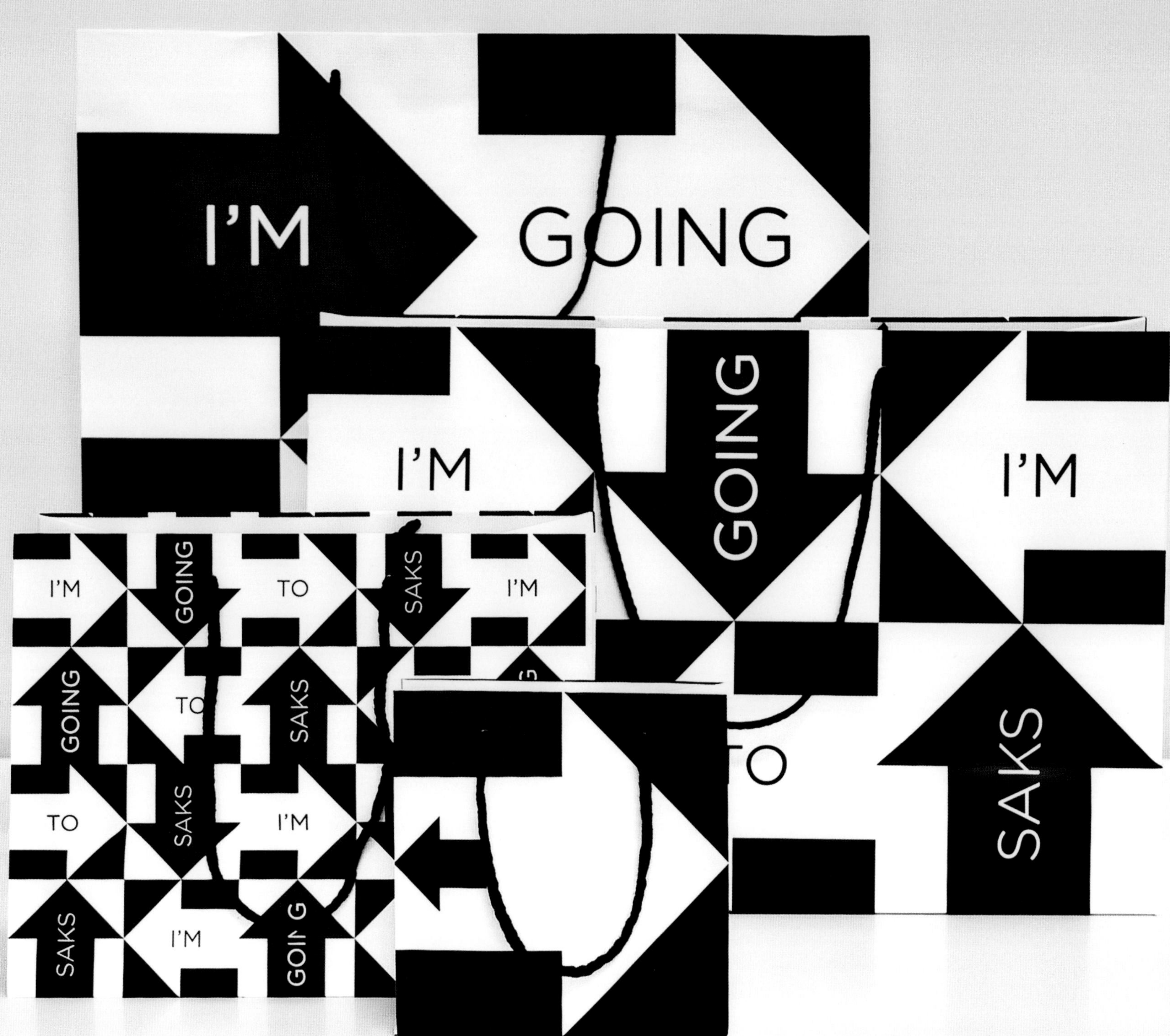

I'M
GOING
I'M
GOING
I'M
TO
SAKS
I'M
GOING
TO
SAKS
I'M
GOING
TO
SAKS
TO
SAKS
I'M
SAKS
I'M

Below
"Think about…," the spring 2010 campaign, was inspired by Diana Vreeland's longtime *Harper's Bazaar* column, "Why don't you…" Each of the ten letters in the theme was associated with one of the ten catalogs Saks publishes each year.

Right
Pentagram's Jennifer Kinon and Jesse Reed used tiny silhouettes to render the theme's typography and tie each catalog back to its subject: animal prints, shoes, jewelry, men's accessories, and so on.

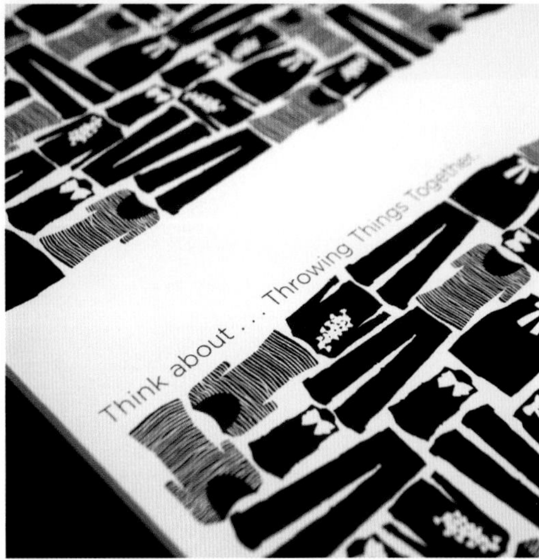

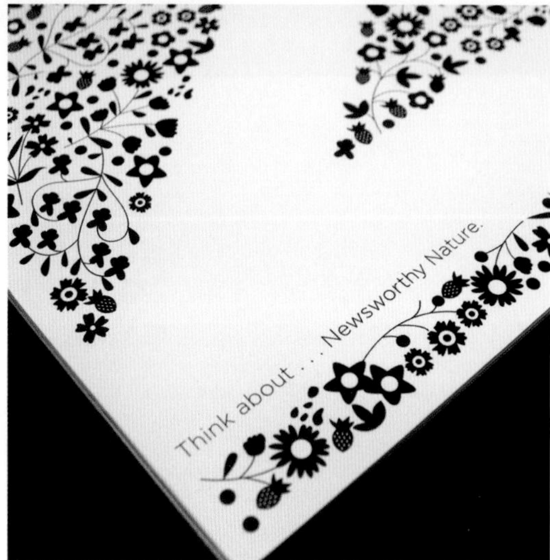

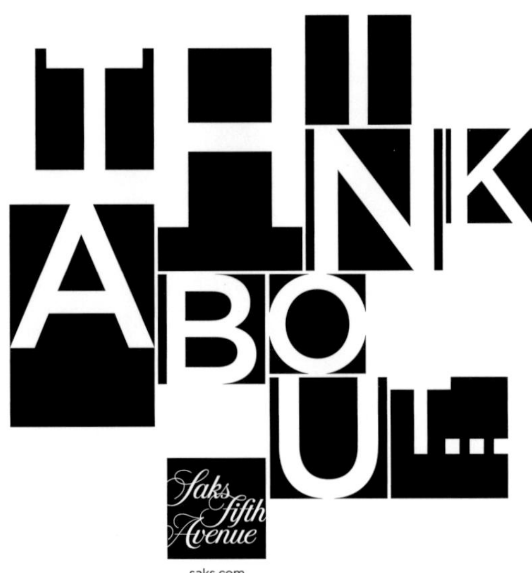

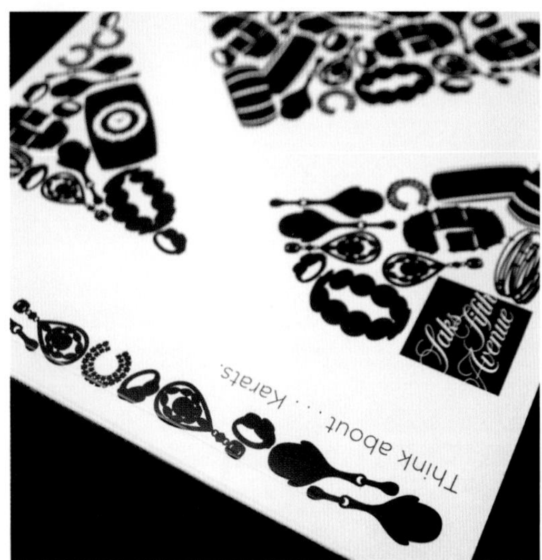

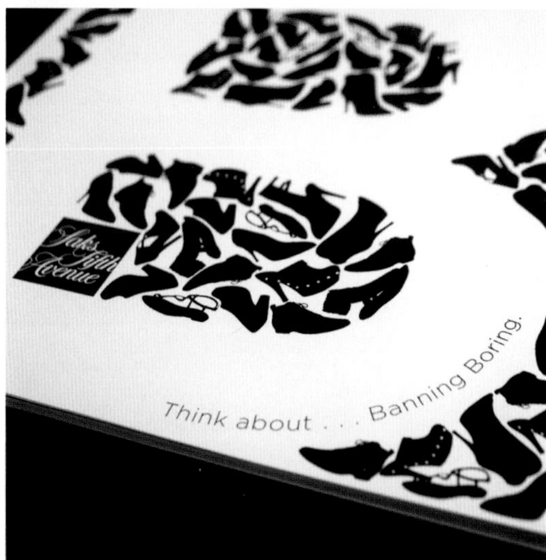

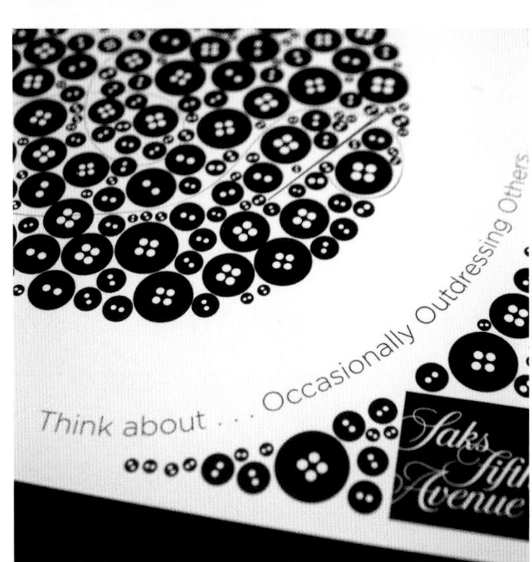

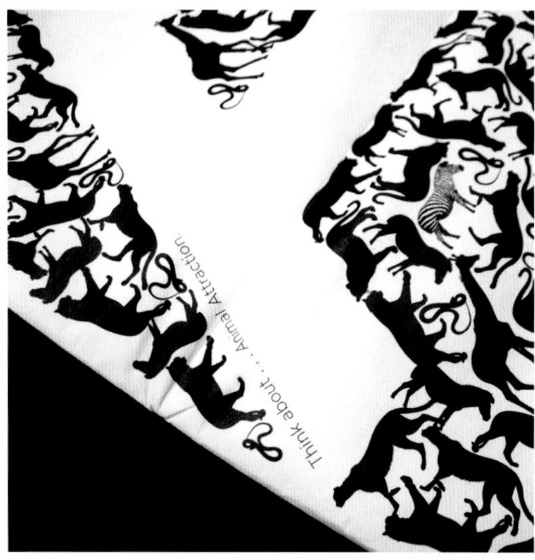

Below and right
"At Saks," the store's campaign for fall 2011, reflected the rise of social media. Joe Finocchiaro created a custom @ symbol to match the Saks calligraphy.

Pentagram's Katie Barcelona deployed the symbol in a range of hypnotic patterns.

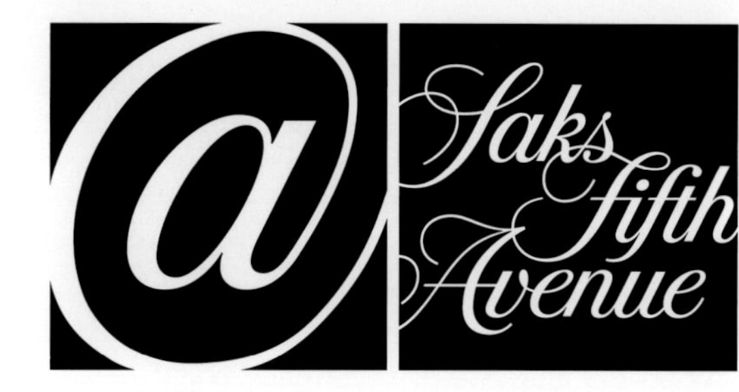

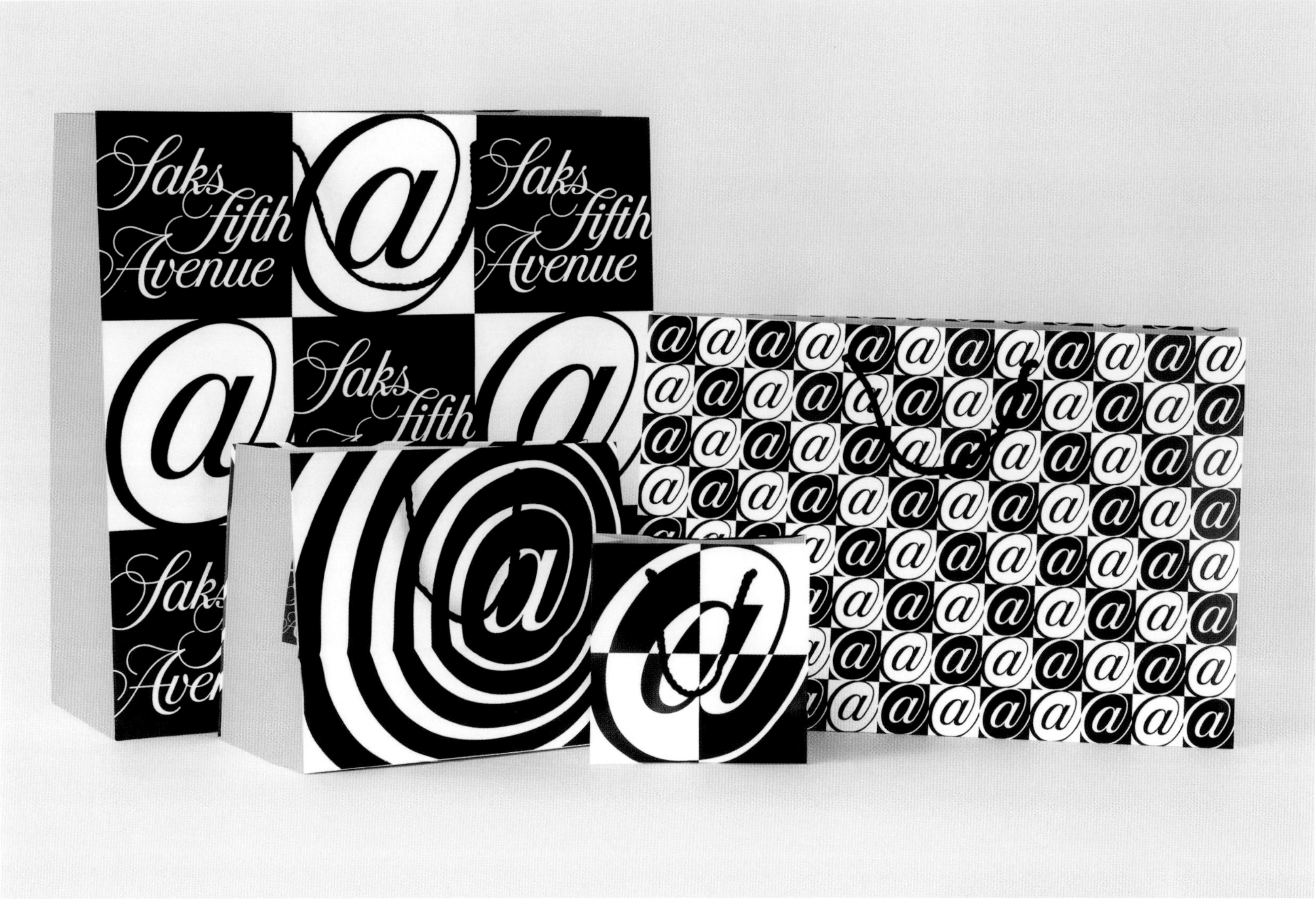

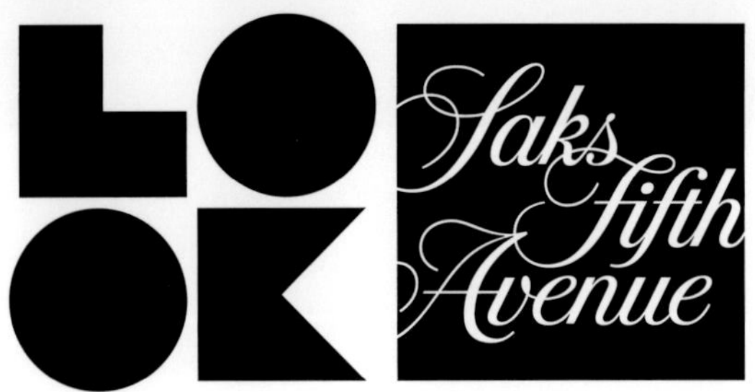

Above, right, and opposite
Our last project for Saks, 2013's "Look" campaign, was based on geometric letterforms that could be stacked, repeated, and used as windows. Designer Jesse Reed created a wide range of patterns that, as in each of our campaigns for this client, both extended the basic identity and demonstrated the identity's capacity to surprise.

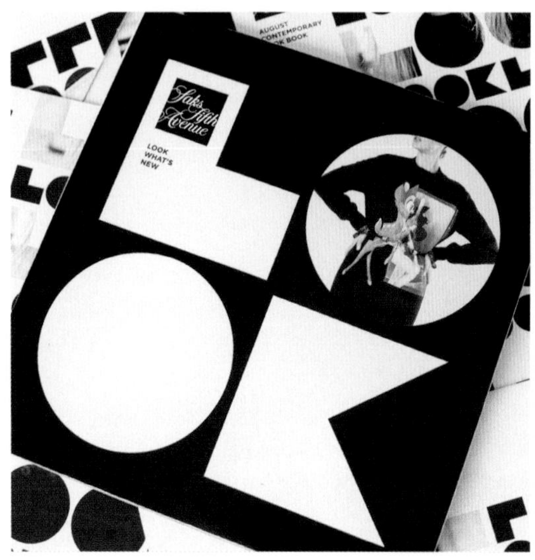

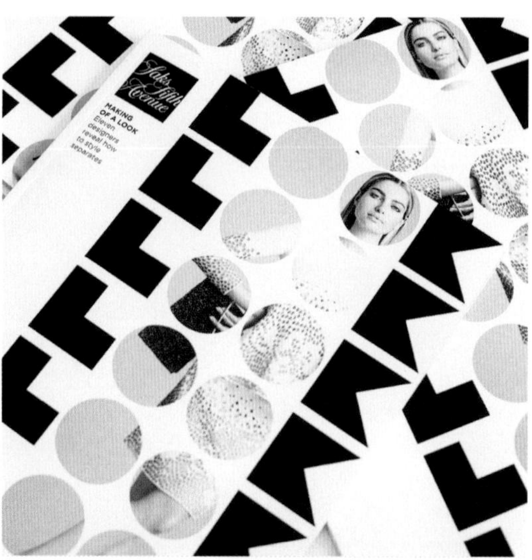

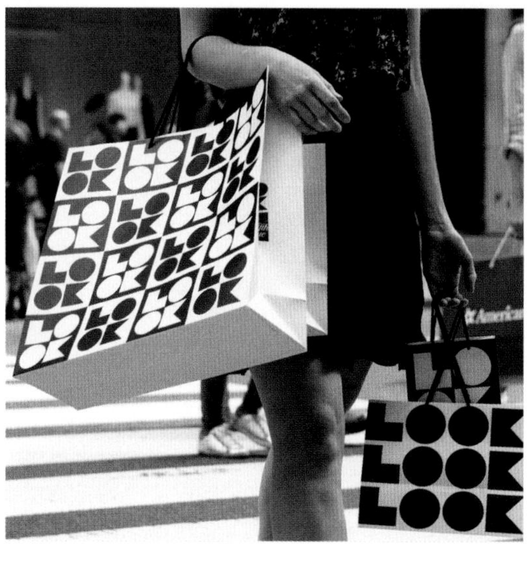

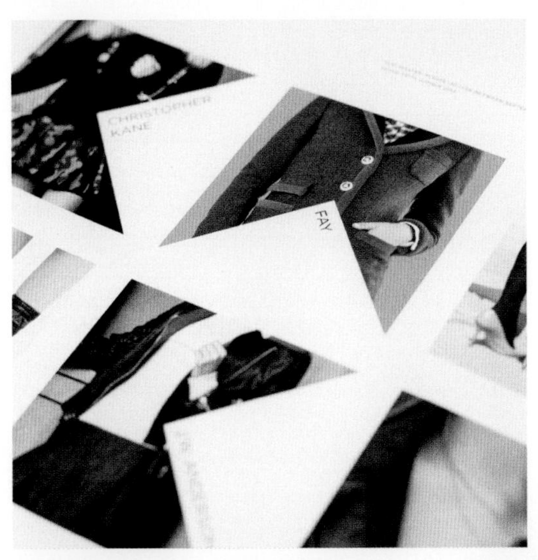
CHRISTOPHER
KANE
FAY

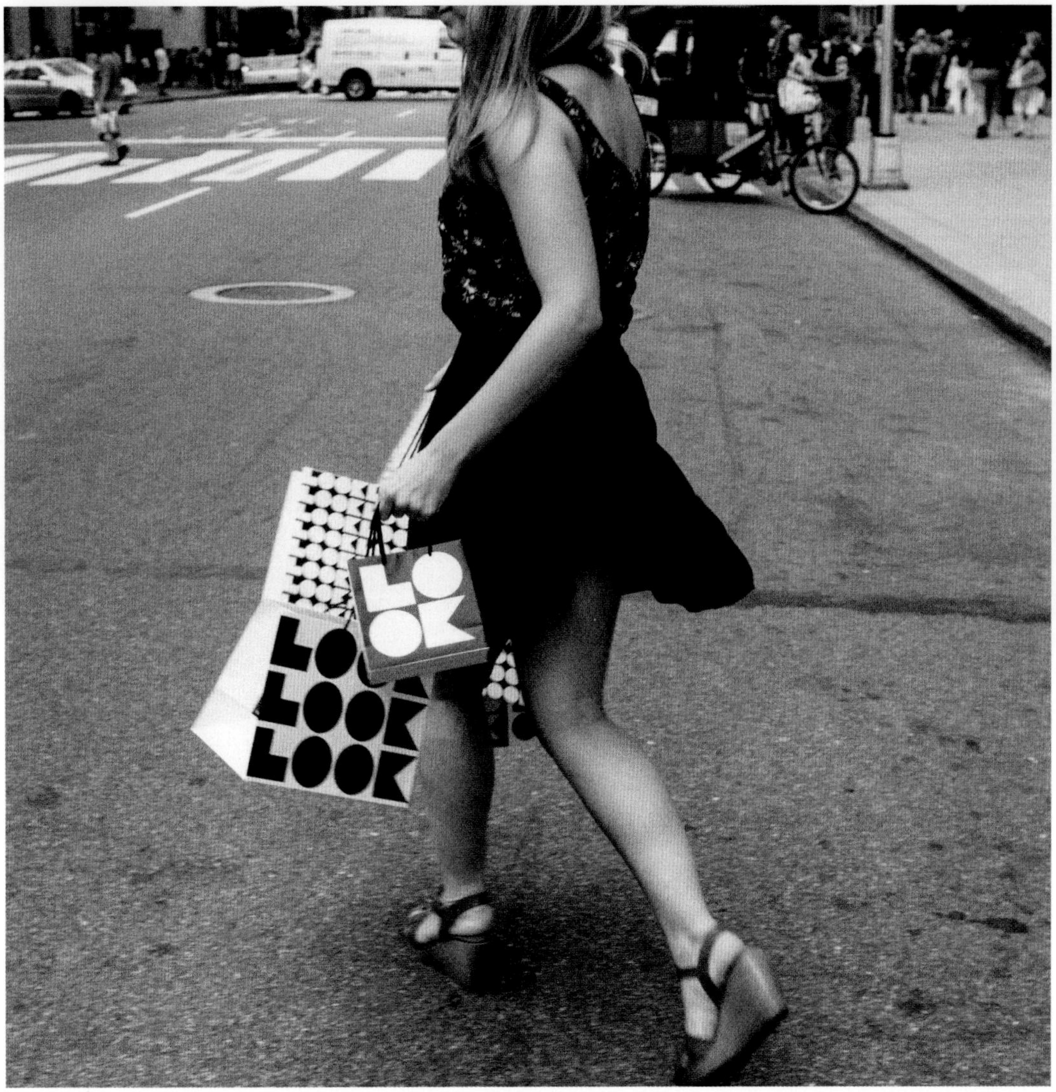

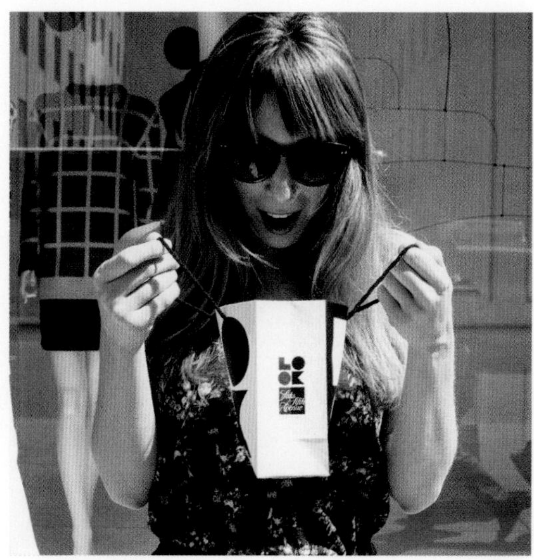

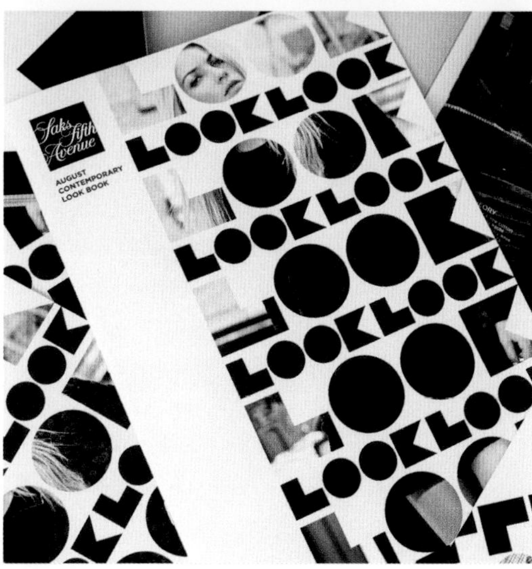
Saks Fifth Avenue
AUGUST
CONTEMPORARY
LOOK BOOK
LOOK LOOK

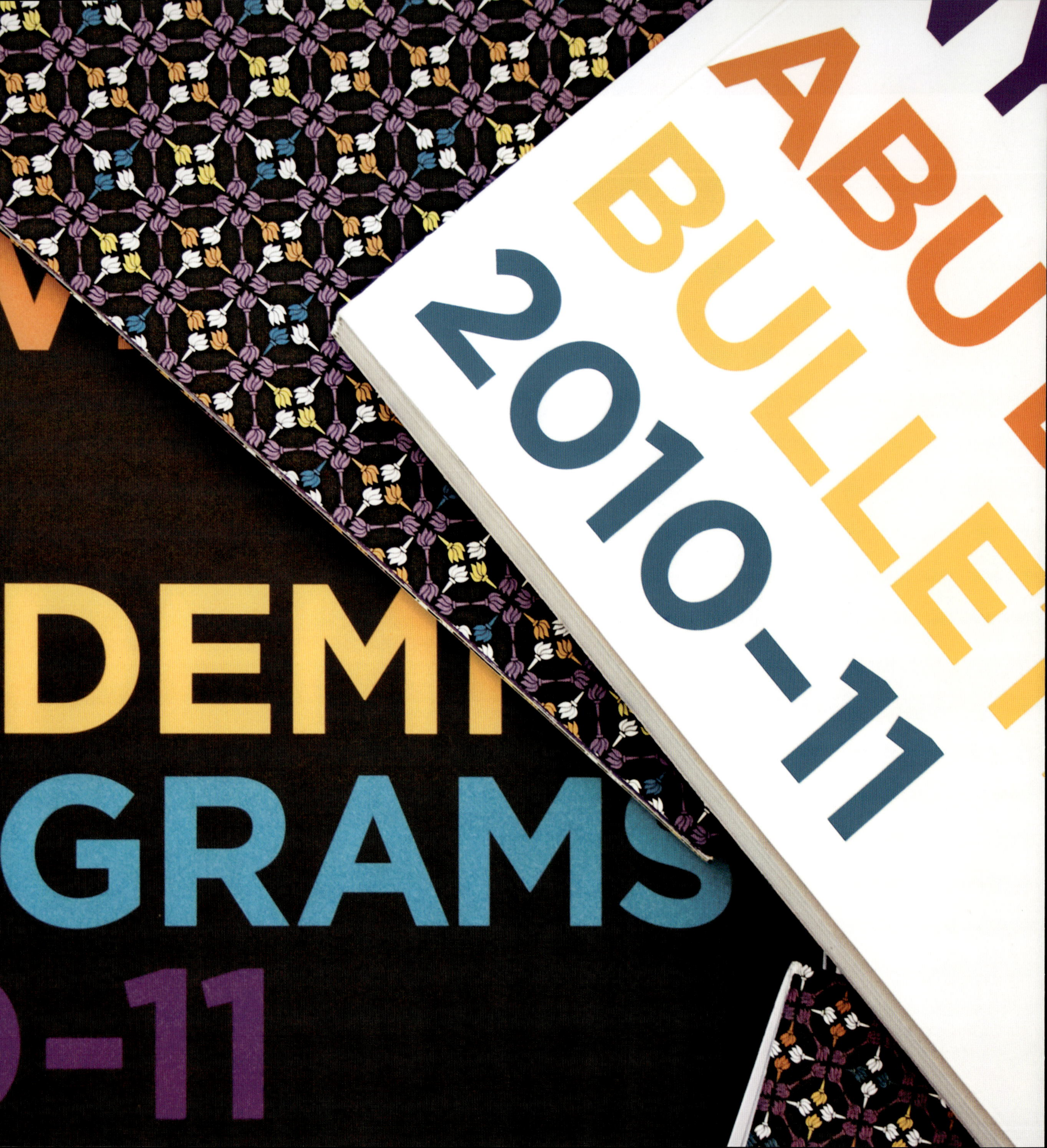
ABU
BULLE
2010–11
DEMI
GRAMS
-11

How to cross cultures

New York University Abu Dhabi

Opposite and above
An unprecedented challenge, a new global campus for NYU in the Middle East, demanded an unprecedented response. By radically deconstructing the NYU torch, we merged the urban and the arabesque.

In 2007, New York University's dynamic and outspoken president, John Sexton, announced the next step in his vision to create what he called "the world's first global university in the world's first truly global city." NYU Abu Dhabi would be much more than a typical study-abroad program. A complete campus, 40 acres of academic facilities and dormitories built from the ground up in Abu Dhabi's cultural district on Saadiyat Island, it is designed to serve a projected 2,000 students and faculty members, bringing Western-style liberal arts education to this emerging world capital.

Scattered among nearly 100 buildings in New York's Greenwich Village and beyond, NYU is the quintessential urban university. Instead of a leafy quad ringed with stately neo-Georgian halls is a celebration of the messy vitality of the city. As a result, the university's most important, if not only, means of coherence is its graphic design. We have worked with NYU for years, doing projects for its School of Law, Stern School of Business, and Wagner School of Public Service, and had come to appreciate the unifying power of its symbol, a simplified torch on a purple background. Now the power of this graphic identity would be put to a new test in Abu Dhabi. How could NYU use design to assert its global presence while celebrating this new local context?

An institution's graphic assets are usually inviolable. But in this case the most effective way to signal both continuity and change was to demonstrate what the NYU torch could do. Inspired by the dazzling chromatics and hypnotic repetition so typical of Islamic art, we created an arabesque pattern by expanding the university color palette and rotating and repeating the torch. This new signature motif, applied in print, online, and on campus, confirms that the new campus is at once part of New York University, of Abu Dhabi, and of the world.

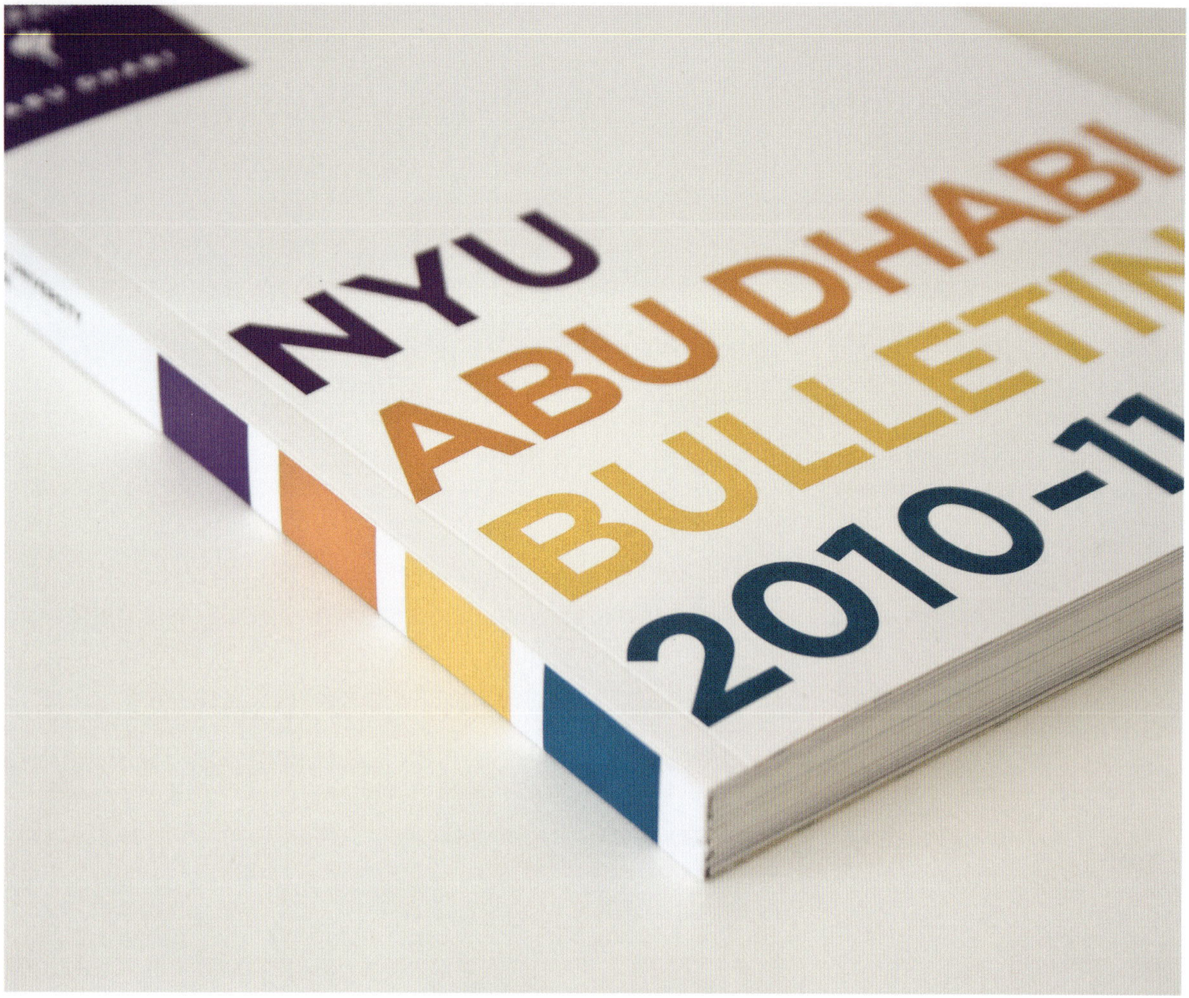

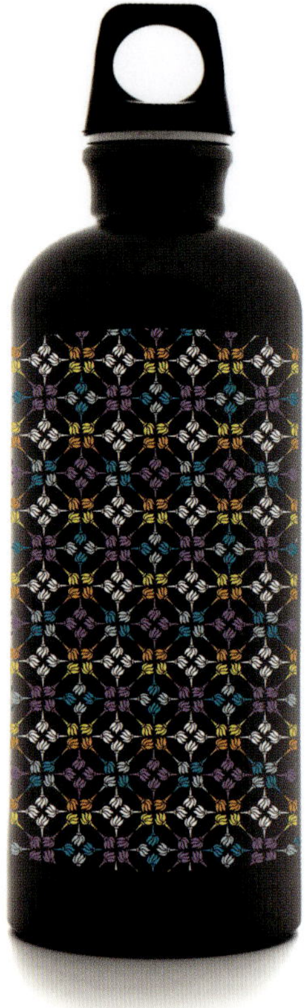

Above left
New colors, complementing NYU's purple, were meant to evoke (but not copy) the rich decorative traditions of Islamic art.

Above right
The NYU Abu Dhabi pattern is a familiar sight in the campus bookstore. The school has been overwhelmed with applications, and has an acceptance rate nearly as low as Harvard's.

Right
The brochure that introduced the new campus to potential students paired images from the two cultures.

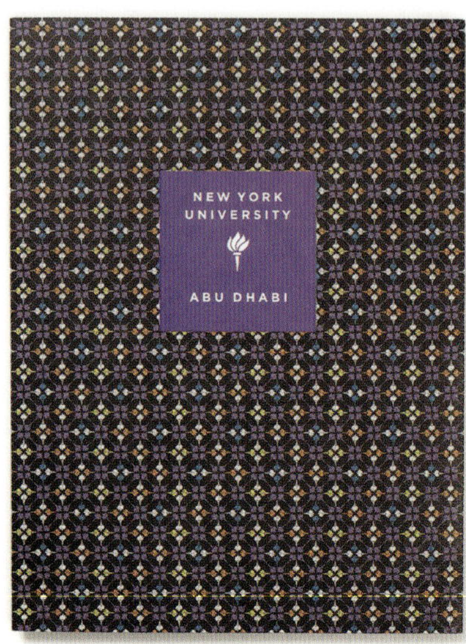

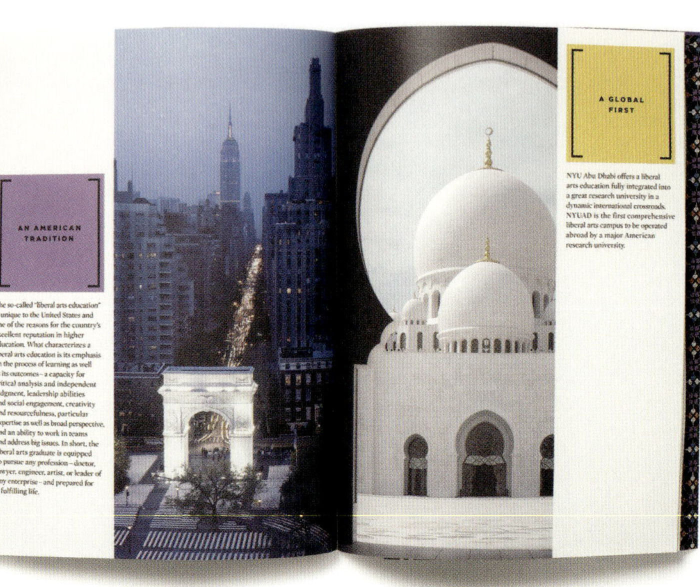

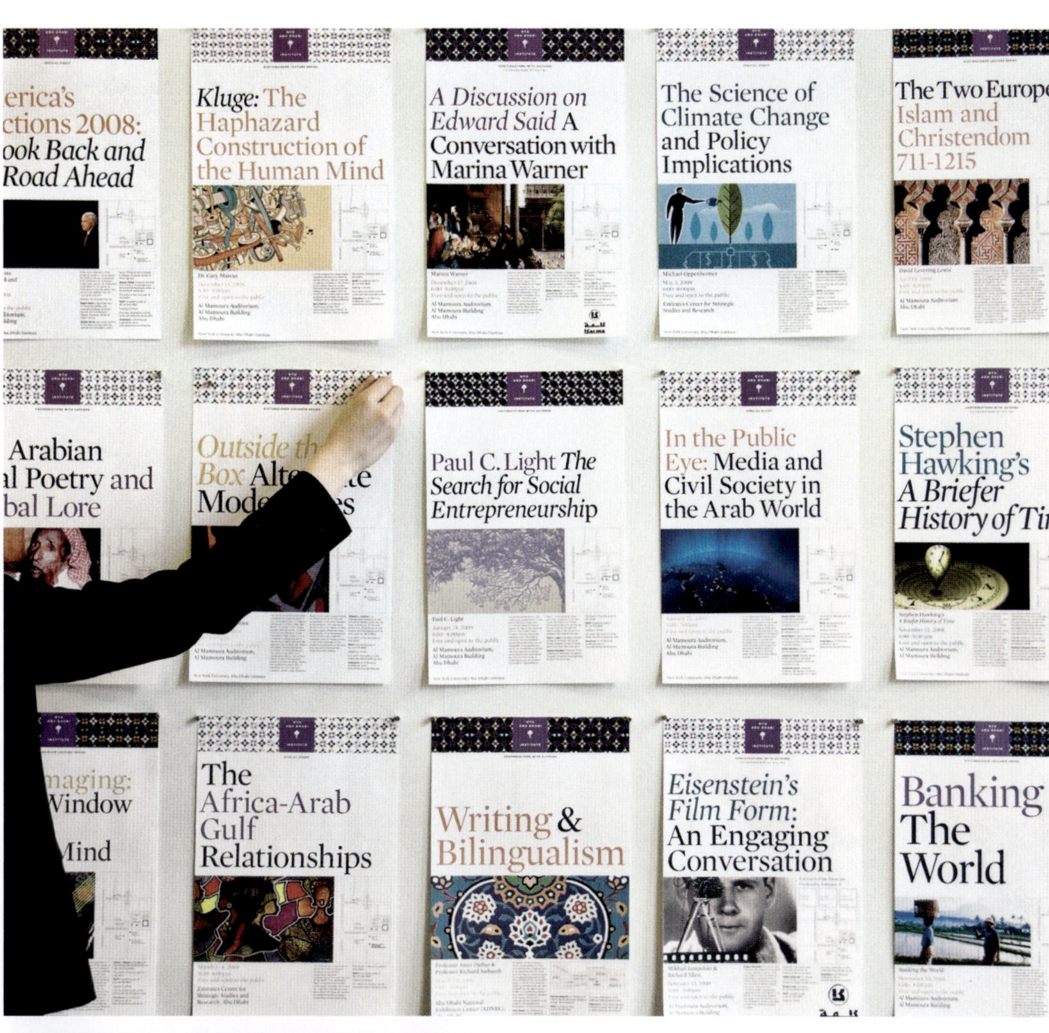

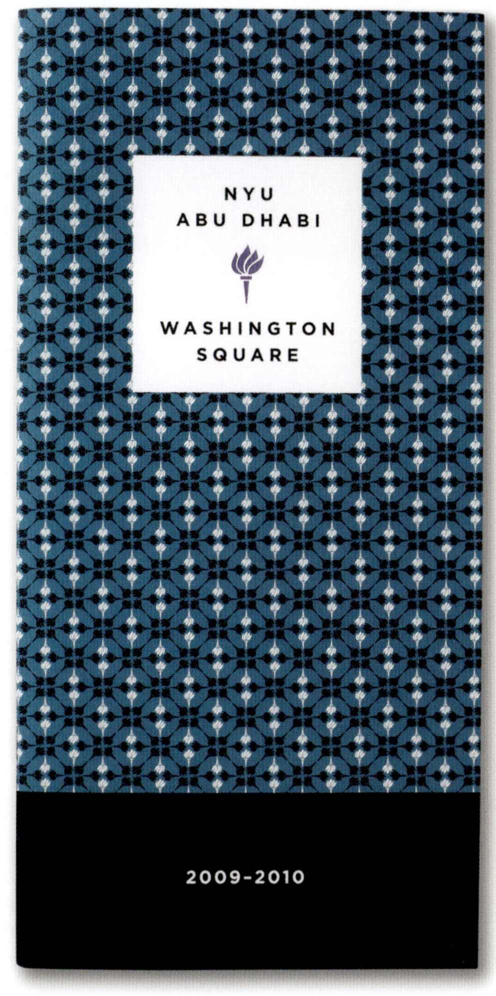

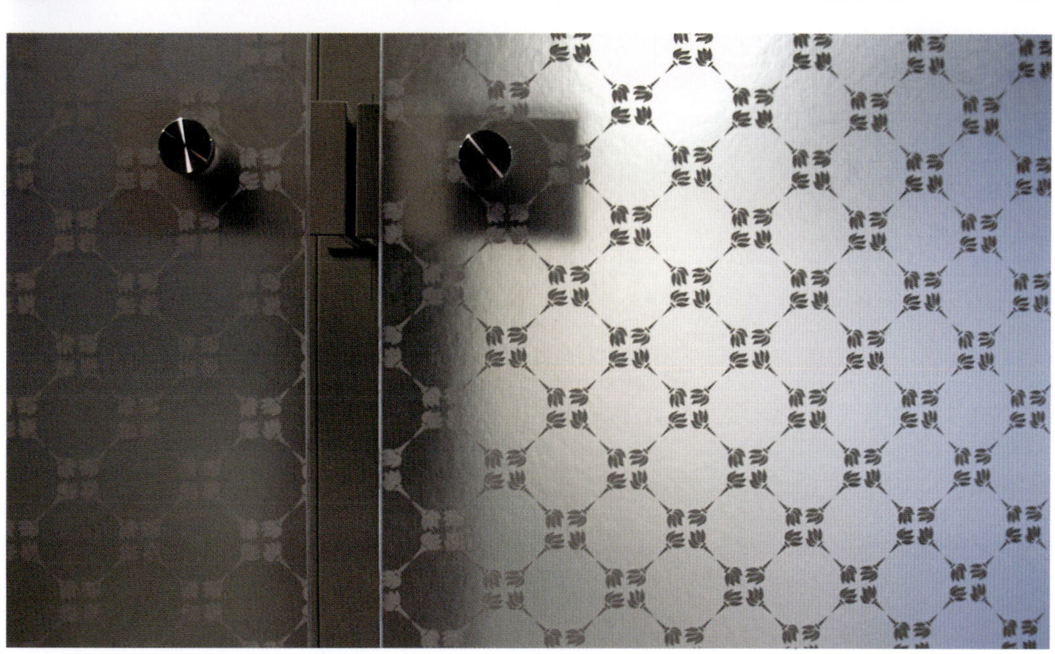

Above left
Even before a single student was accepted, NYU Abu Dhabi had inaugurated a robust program of lectures, presentations, and symposia.

Left
The arabesque pattern provides decorative relief in campus architecture.

Above right
Supporting John Sexton's vision of a worldwide network, NYU Abu Dhabi maintains an active presence in Washington Square, the heart of the school's New York campus.

Next spread
Pentagram designer Katie Barcelona worked out an intricate set of formats for NYU Abu Dhabi's broad suite of materials, using color, pattern, and typography to create a complex but coherent graphic program.

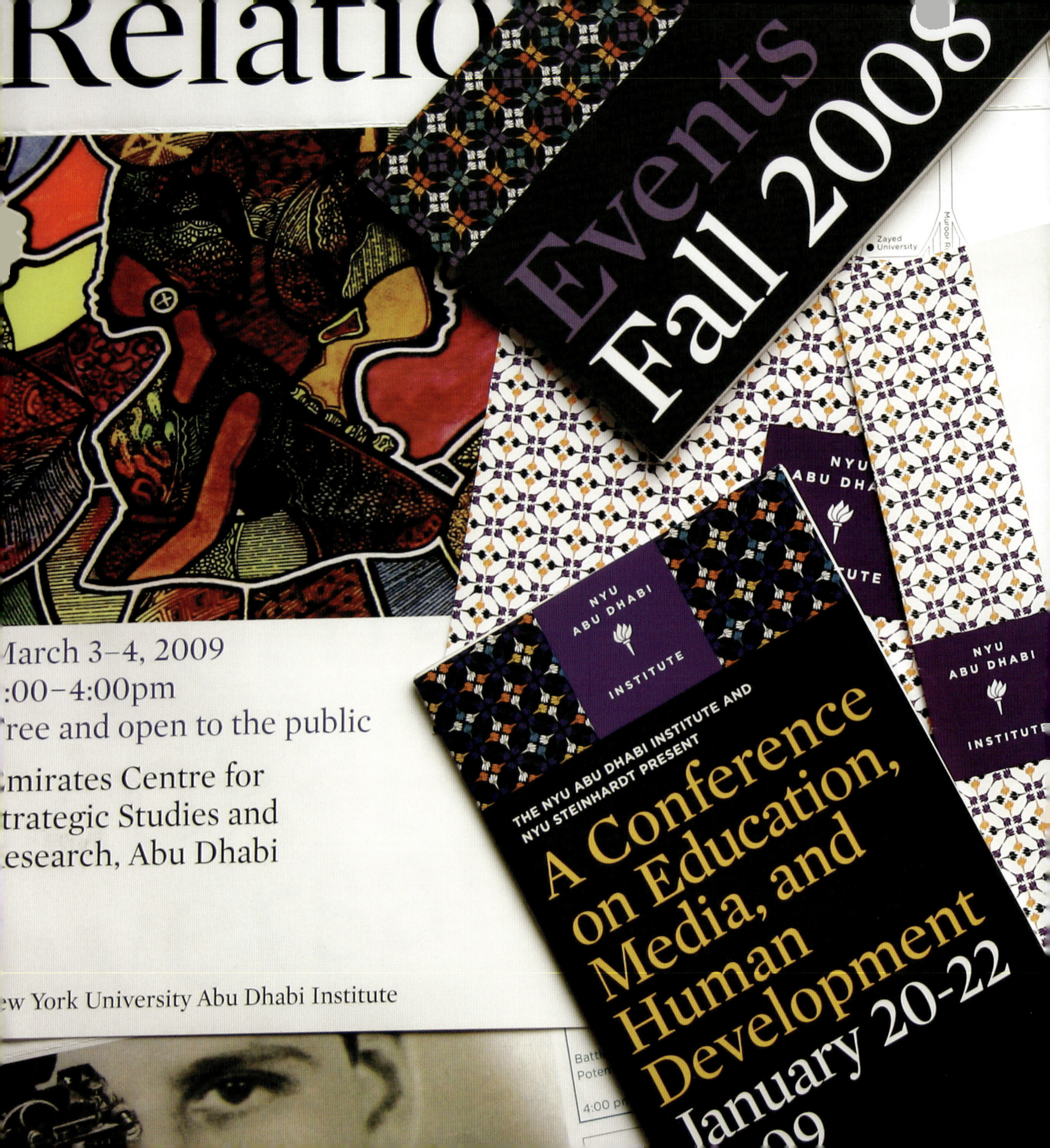

Relatio
Events
Fall 2008
arch 3–4, 2009
:00–4:00pm
ree and open to the public
mirates Centre for
trategic Studies and
esearch, Abu Dhabi
w York University Abu Dhabi Institute
NYU
ABU DHABI
INSTITUTE
THE NYU ABU DHABI INSTITUTE AND
NYU STEINHARDT PRESENT
A Conference
on Education,
Media, and
Human
Development
January 20-22
Zayed
University

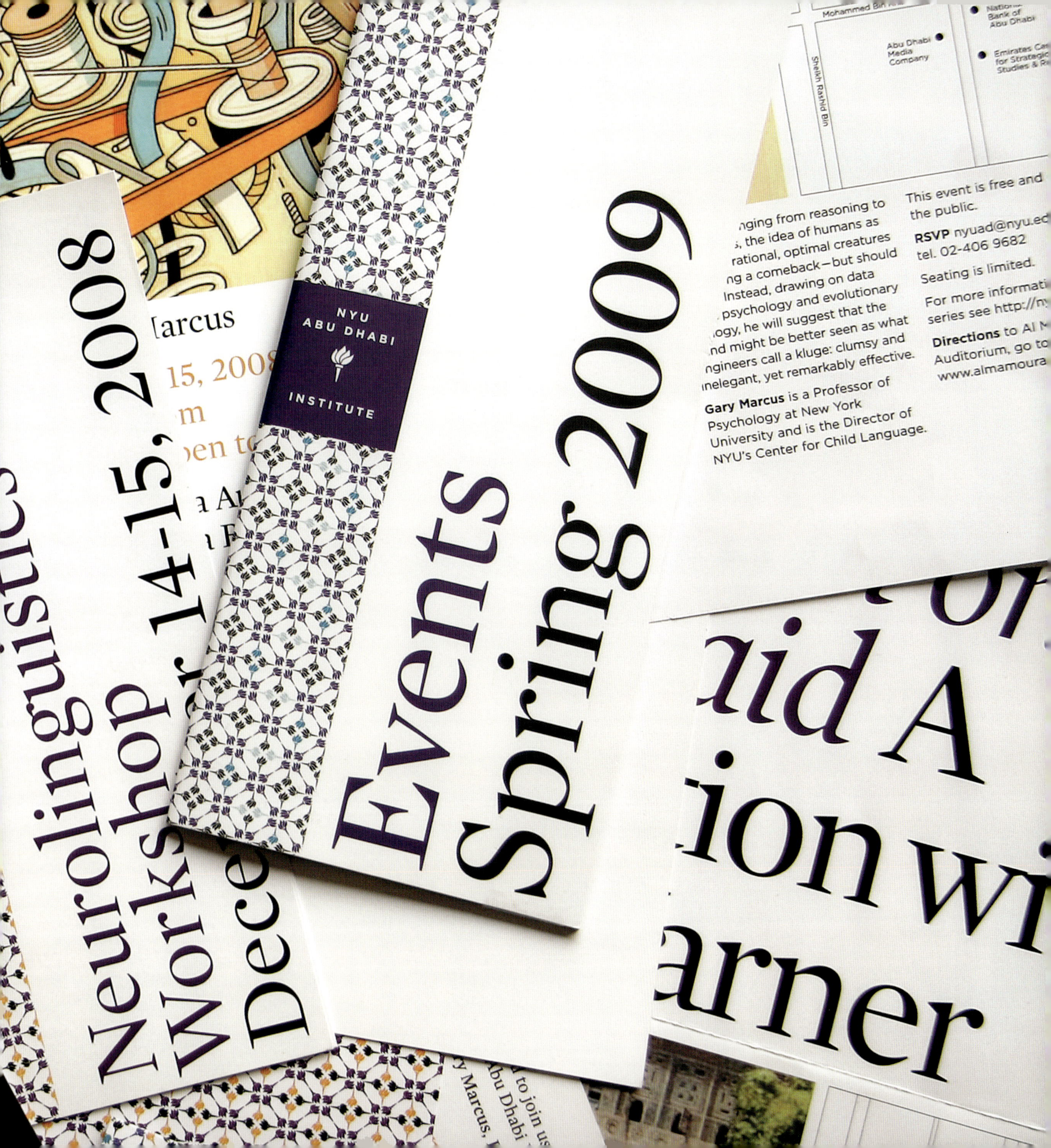

Workshop
14-15, 2008
NYU
ABU DHABI
INSTITUTE
Events
Spring 2009
Abu Dhabi Media Company
Sheikh Rashid Bin
the public.
tel. 02-406 9682
Seating is limited.
Gary Marcus is a Professor of Psychology at New York University and is the Director of NYU's Center for Child Language.

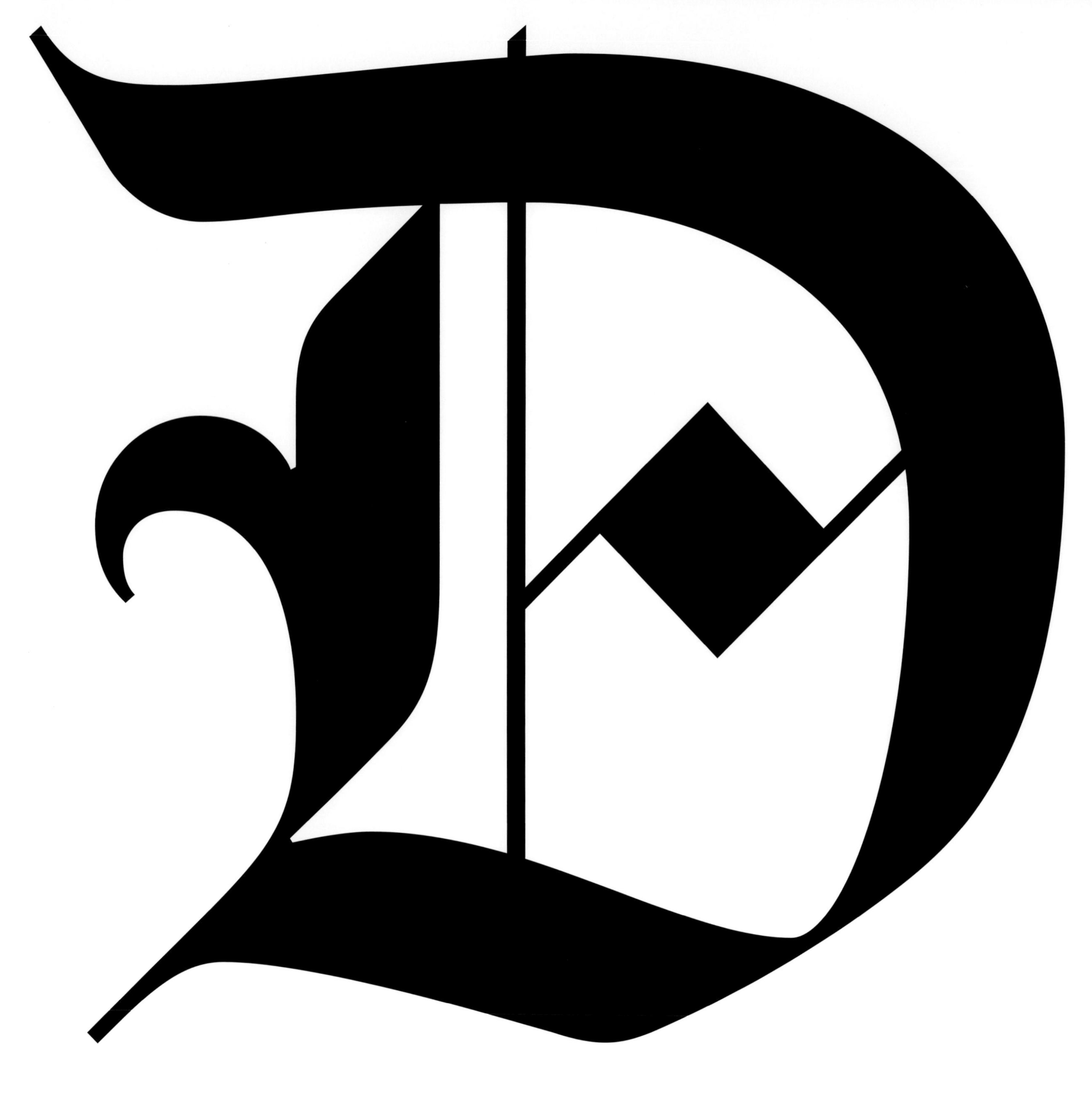

How to behave in church

The Cathedral Church of St. John the Divine

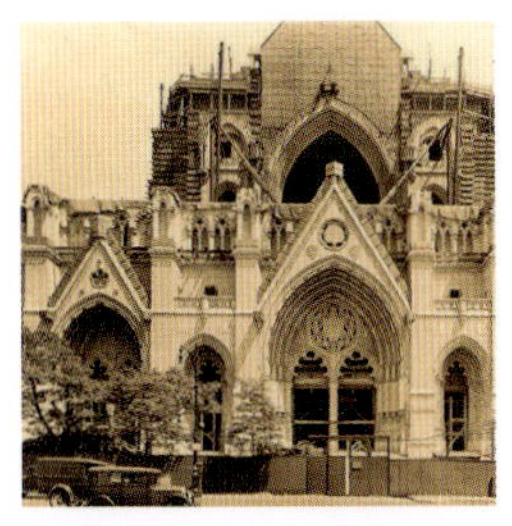

Opposite
To unify the voice of the Cathedral Church of St. John the Divine and to create a distinctive personality that no other institution could match, we asked typeface designer Joe Finocchiaro to redraw 1928's Goudy Text, creating a proprietary font that we named "Divine."

Above
The cathedral, located on Manhattan's Upper West Side, has been under intermittent construction for over 100 years, and is still unfinished. It is one of New York's most popular destinations.

Organizations seeking an identity often think what they want is a logo. But this is like acquiring a personality by buying a hat. The way you look can be an important signal of who you are, but it's not the only signal. More important is what you say and how you say it. And most important of all, of course, is what you do.

The Cathedral Church of St. John the Divine does remarkable things. It is the fourth largest Christian church building in the world, begun in 1892 and never finished, with a 124-foot-high nave that is a mandatory destination for tourists visiting New York. But more than a beautiful Gothic structure, St. John's hosts concerts, art exhibits, and idiosyncratic events. Its soup kitchen serves 25,000 meals a year. And people from a wide range of faiths worship together in 30 services a week. What is the best way to signal that a stone monument over 120 years old is a vibrant, indispensable part of 21st-century life?

We were mesmerized by this combination of old stones and modern life, and sought a way to replicate the surprise that visitors experience when they step through its great west doors. We started with a frankly contemporary, even humorous, tone of voice. But then we took that voice and set it in a new version of an old typeface: Divine, a redrawn, digitized version of a 1928 blackletter by Frederic Goudy, who in turn had based his designs on the type in Gutenberg's 42-line Bible. This contrast between historical form and contemporary content became our way to echo the contrasting but symbiotic relationship of the container and the thing it contains.

My boss Massimo Vignelli used to quote an old Italian saying, "Qui lo dico, e qui lo nego" ("Here I say it, here I deny it"). People are complex. So are organizations. The ability of graphic design to synthesize multiple, and sometimes contradictory, codes never fails to surprise me.

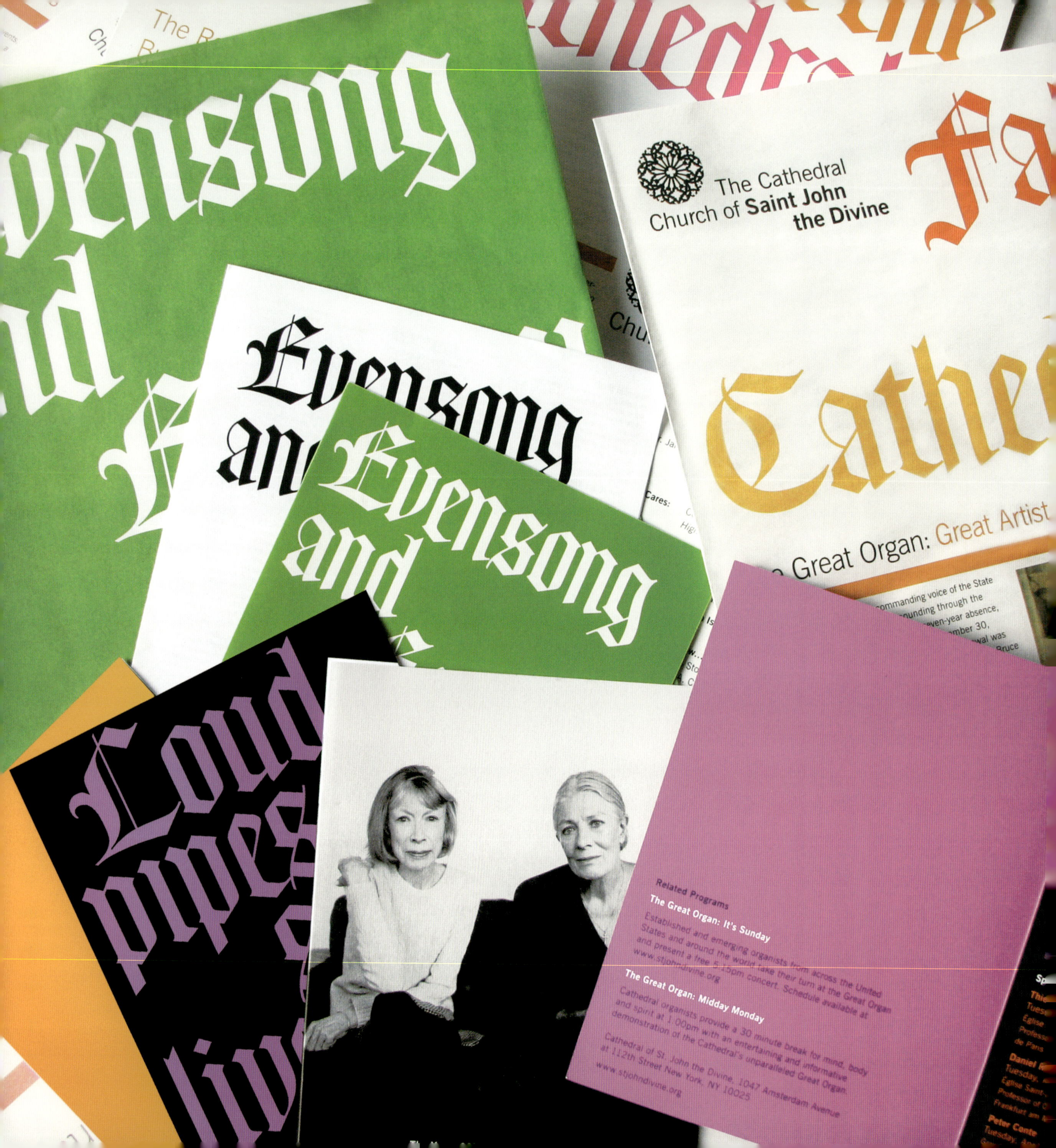

Evensong and
The Cathedral Church of Saint John the Divine
Great Organ: Great Artist
Evensong and
Evensong and
Loud pipes
Related Programs
The Great Organ: It's Sunday
Established and emerging organists from across the United States and around the world take their turn at the Great Organ and present a free 5:15pm concert. Schedule available at www.stjohndivine.org
The Great Organ: Midday Monday
Cathedral organists provide a 30 minute break for mind, body and spirit at 1:00pm with an entertaining and informative demonstration of the Cathedral's unparalleled Great Organ.
Cathedral of St. John the Divine, 1047 Amsterdam Avenue at 112th Street New York, NY 10025
www.stjohndivine.org

Opposite
St. John's communications program combines contemporary language, lively layouts, bright colors, and its century-old typeface.

Below
The cathedral's symbol is based on its stunning rose window, the largest in the United States. The wordmark, in contrast, is set in a simple sans serif typeface that subtly emphasizes its colloquial name.

The Cathedral
Church of **Saint John**
the Divine

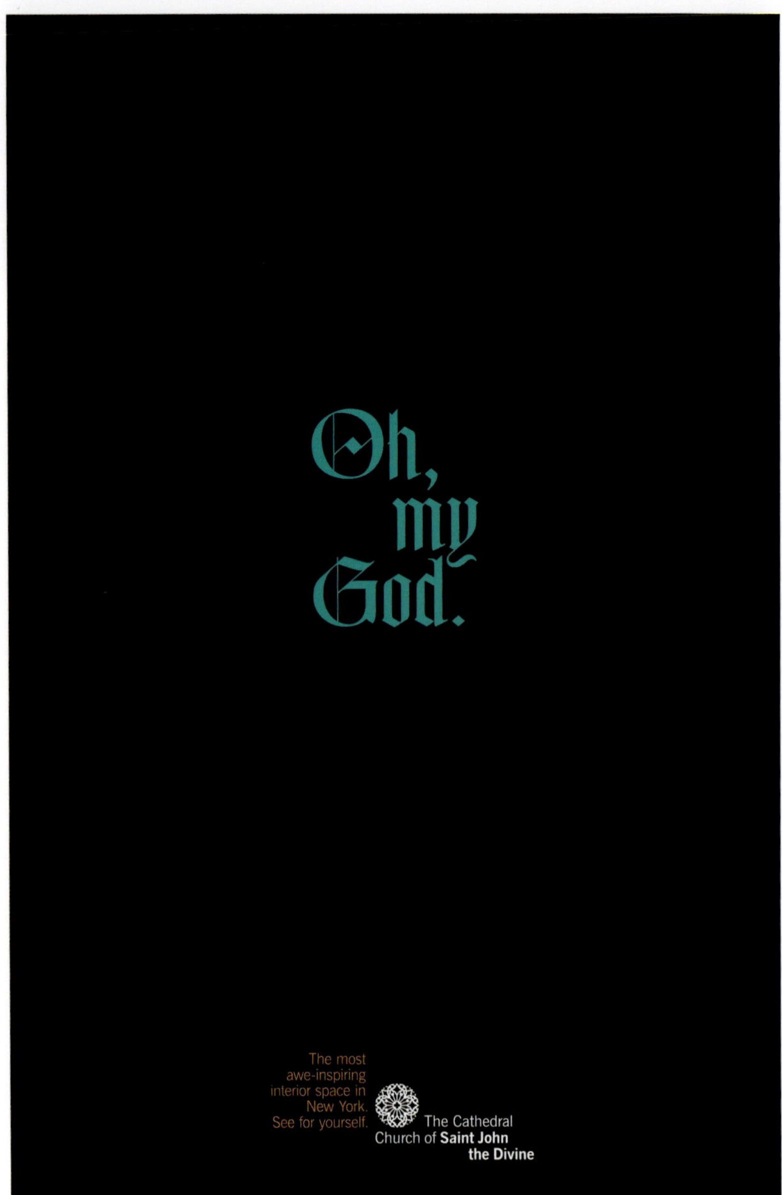

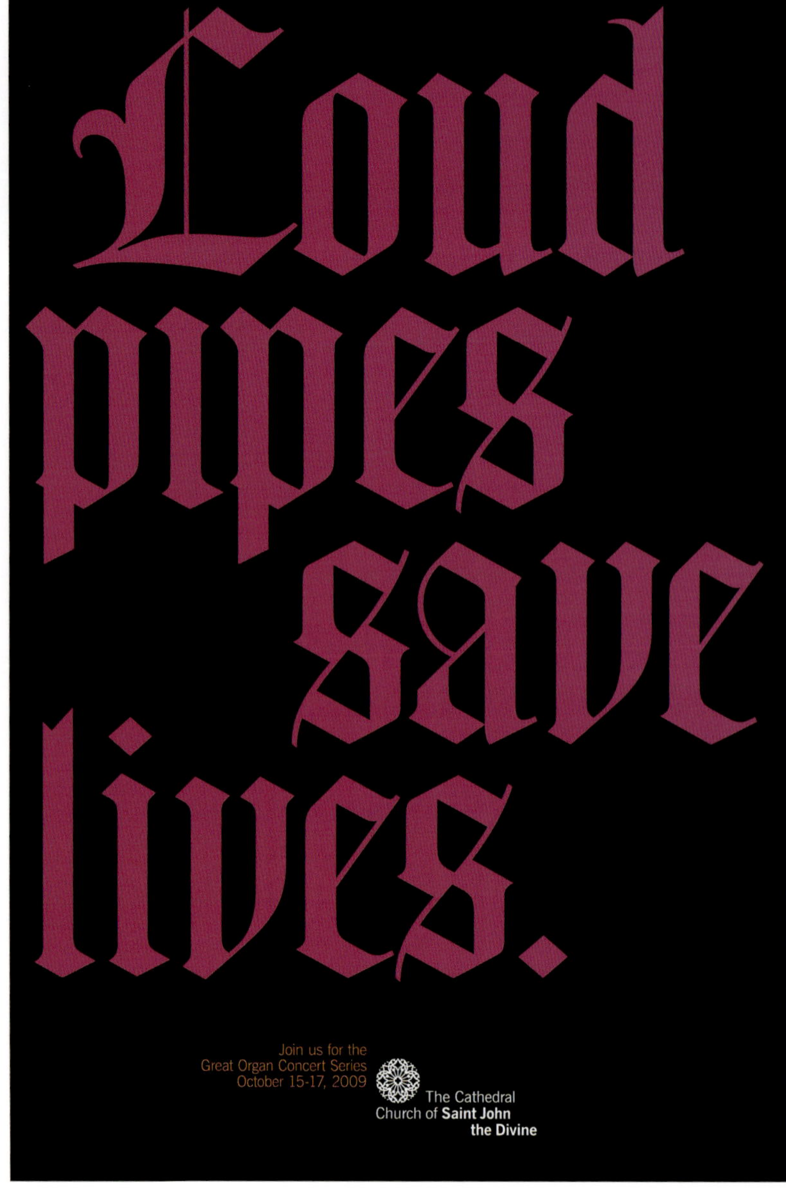

Above
In late 2001, a fire that covered much of the cathedral's interior with soot led to its first cleaning in 100 years. When it reopened, its grandeur newly restored, expressions of awe were common.

Above
The Great Organ series is just one example of the many music programs held at this venue. This poster appropriates a slogan usually associated with Harley-Davidson riders.

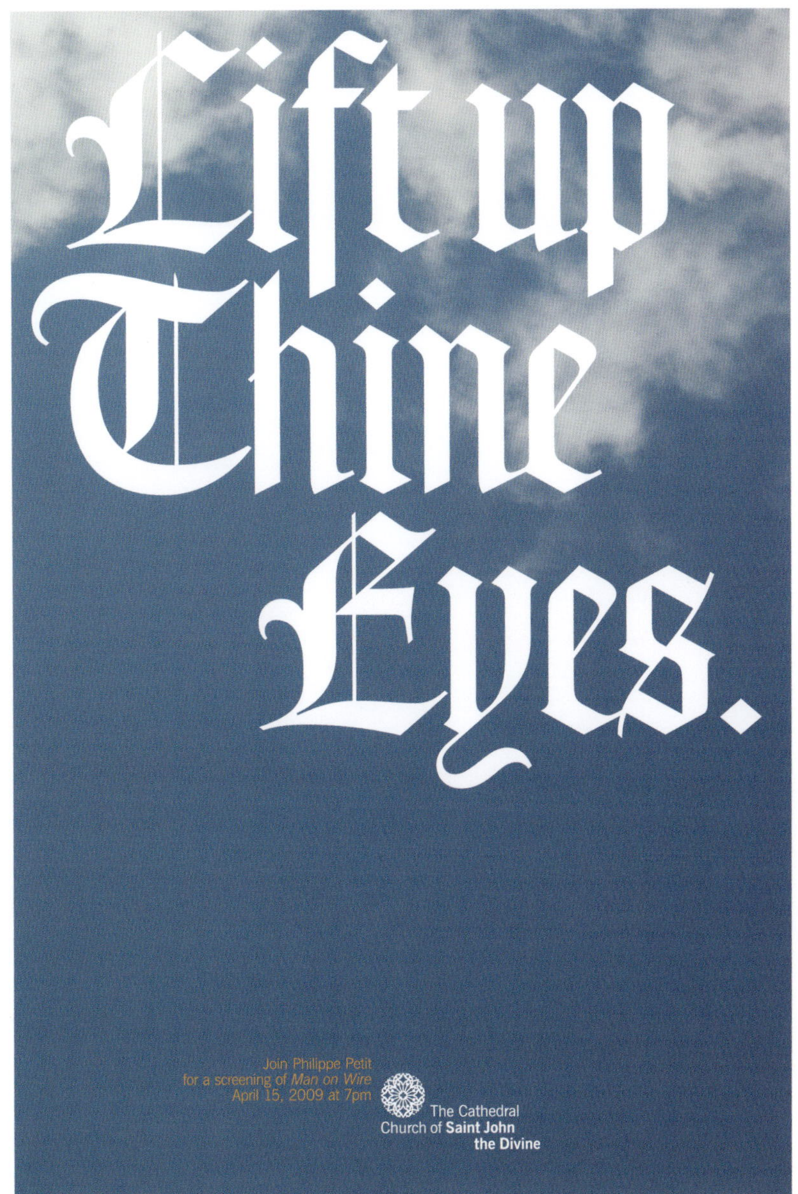

Above
Tightrope artist Philippe Petit has been the cathedral's artist in residence since 1982. This poster promoted a benefit showing of the biographical movie *Man on Wire*.

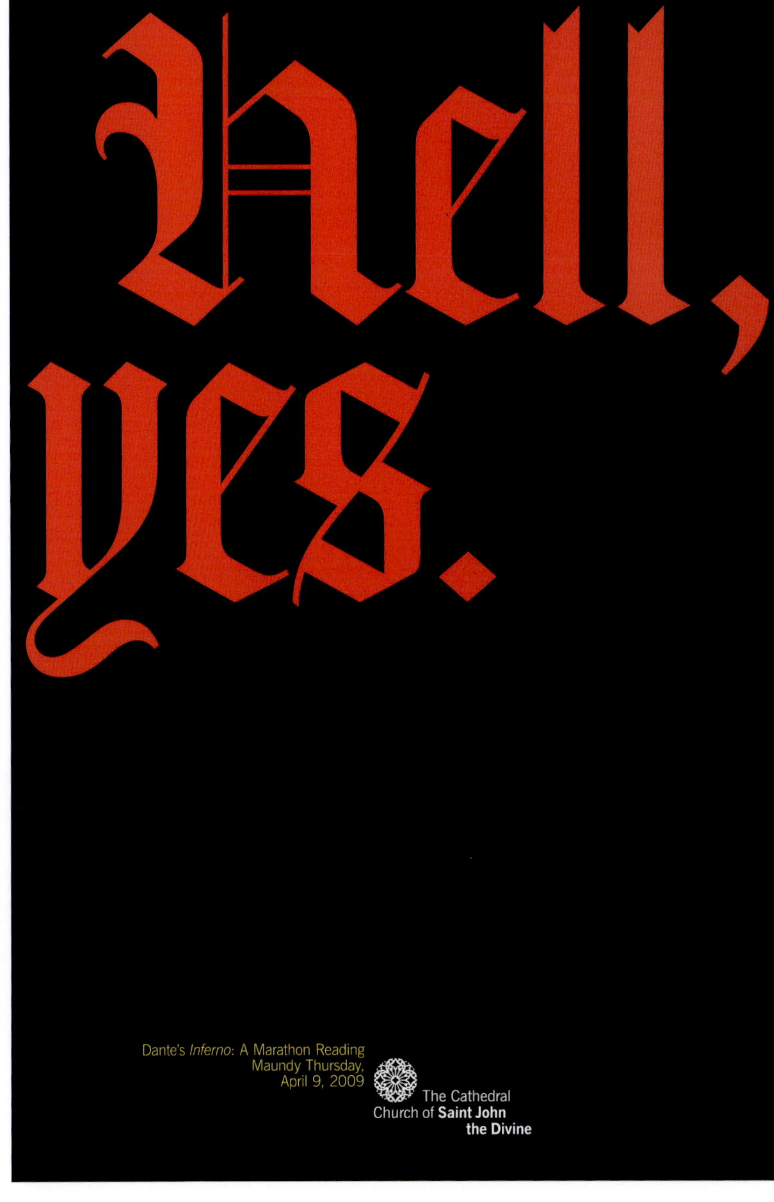

Above
A poster to promote the annual marathon reading of Dante's *Inferno* held on Holy Week's Maundy Thursday.

Right
For the cathedral's 2012 exhibition *The Value of Water*, we rendered Goudy's blackletter in liquid form.

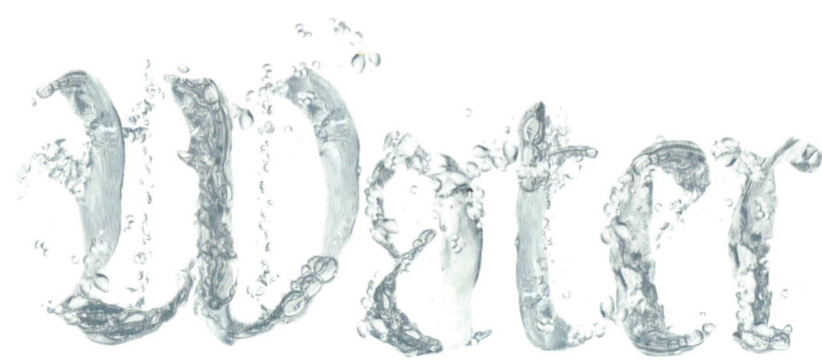

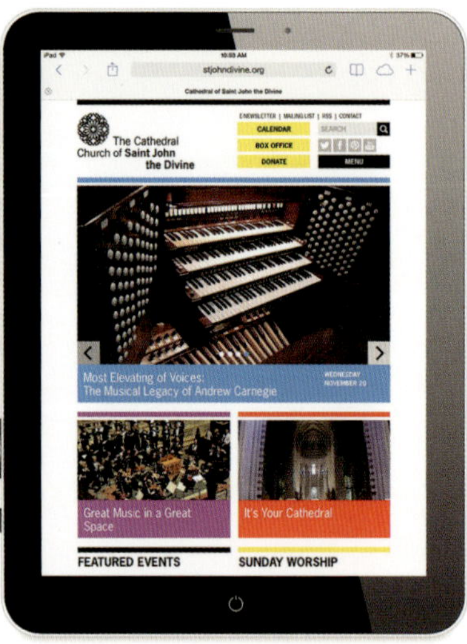

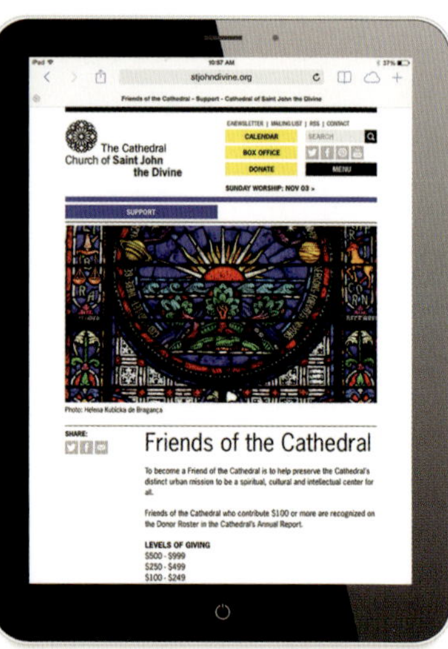

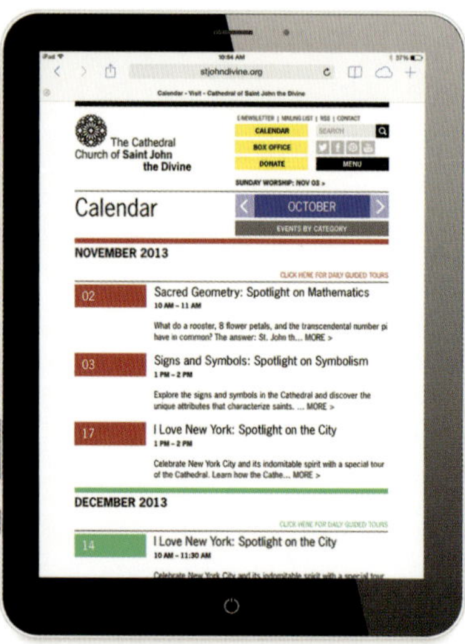

Left
The identity carries through to digital applications, from desktop to mobile.

Right
St. John's communications director Lisa Schubert always seeks opportunities to surprise visitors. Each year, on the Feast of St. Francis of Assisi, the cathedral convenes its traditional Blessing of the Animals. We created T-shirts to mark the event.

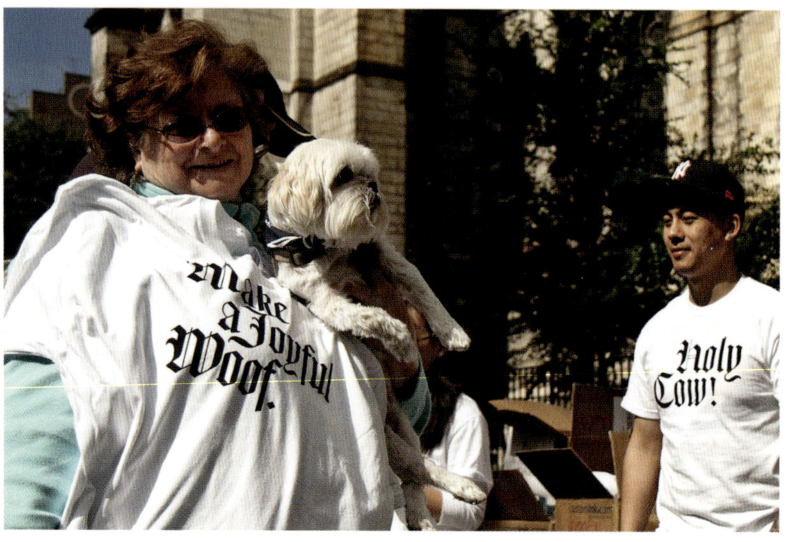

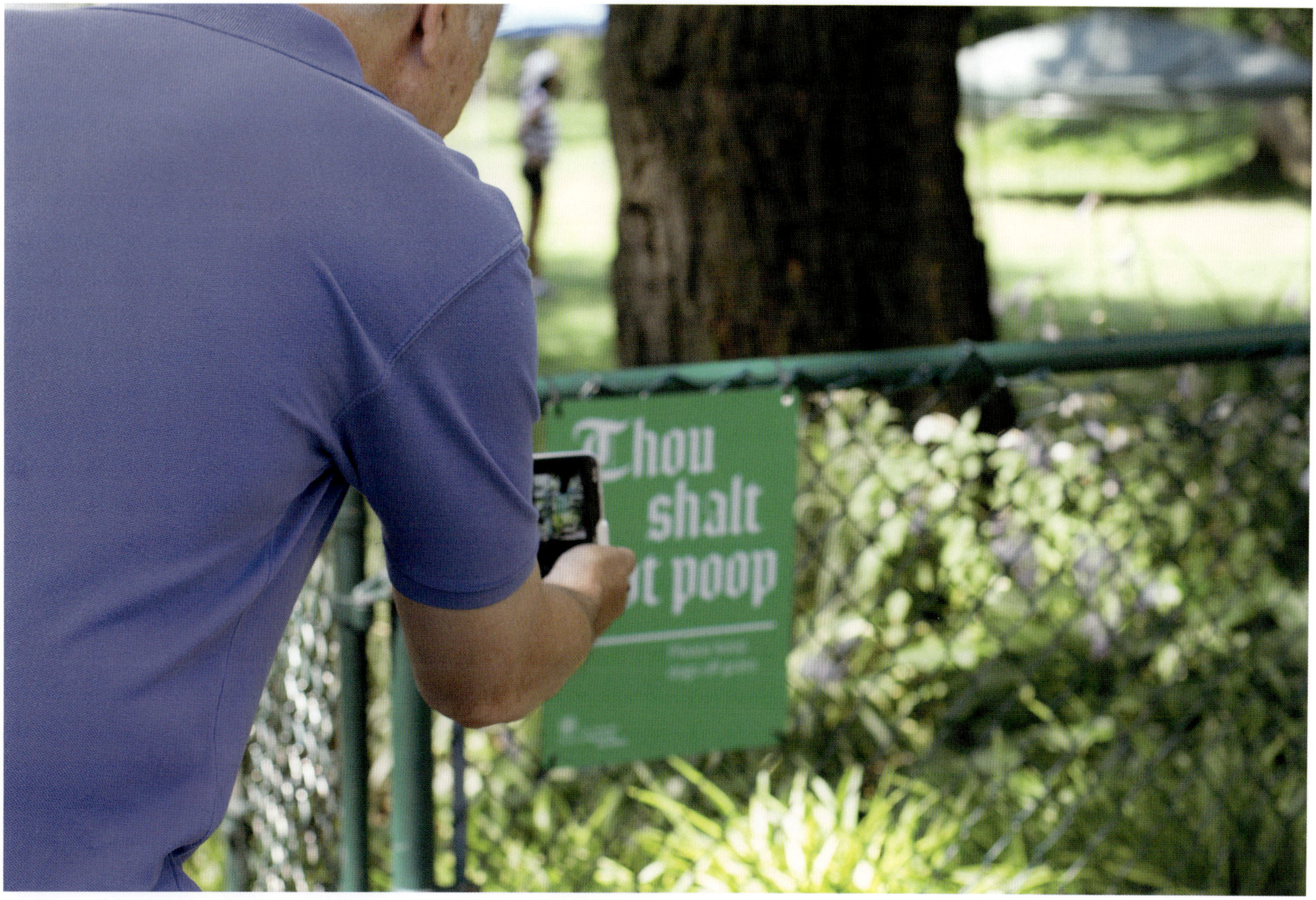

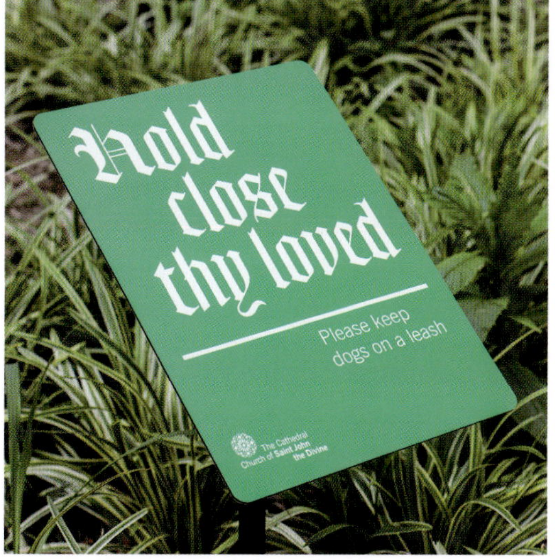

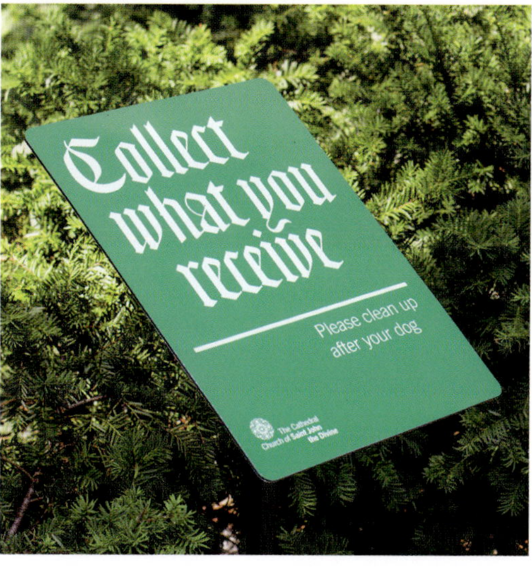

Above and left
Canine commandments? The signs I created with Pentagram's Jesse Reed to encourage visitors to respect the cathedral grounds have become attractions in their own right.

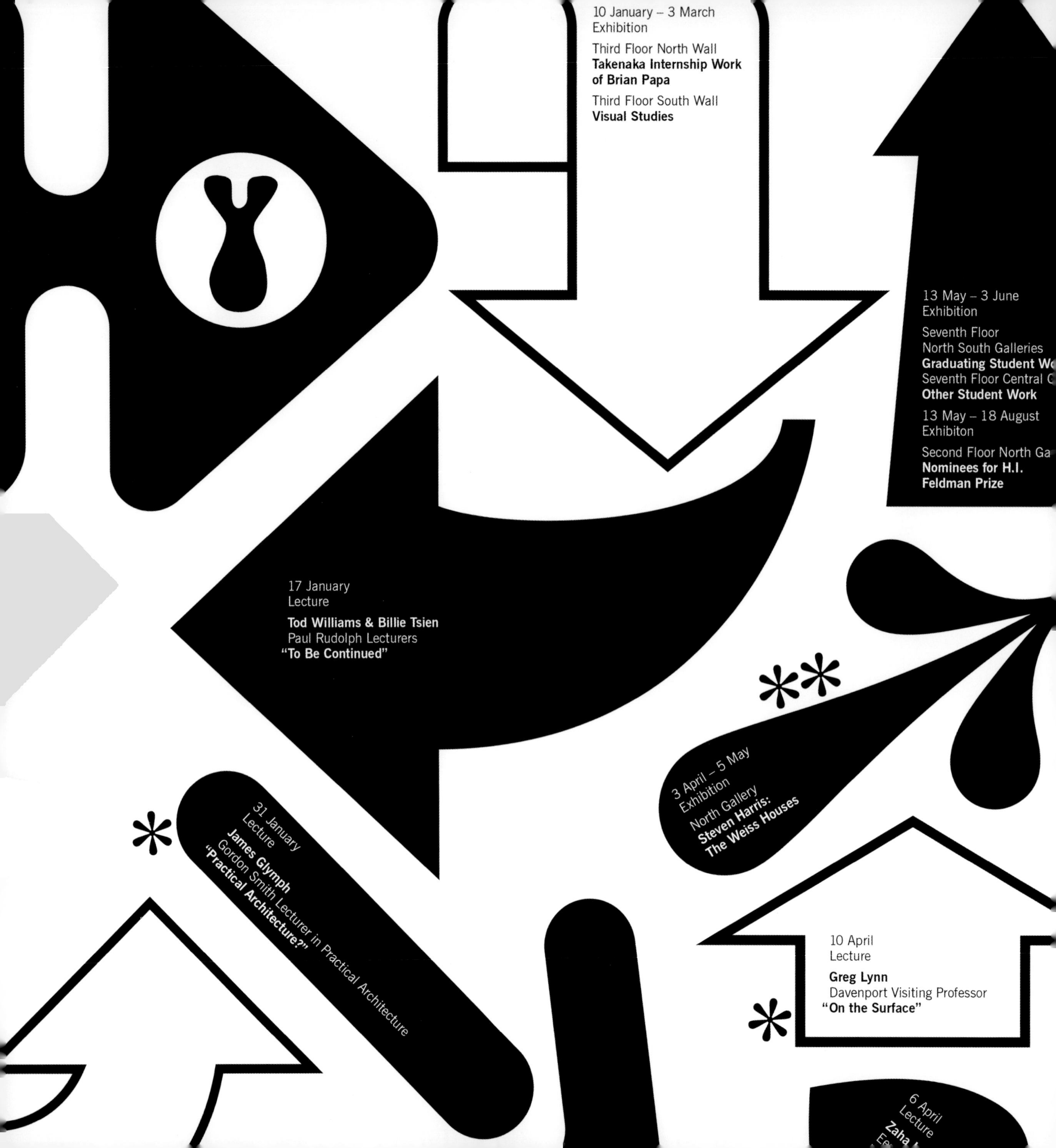

10 January – 3 March
Exhibition
Third Floor North Wall
Takenaka Internship Work of Brian Papa
Third Floor South Wall
Visual Studies
13 May – 3 June
Exhibition
Seventh Floor
North South Galleries
Graduating Student W
Seventh Floor Central
Other Student Work
13 May – 18 August
Exhibiton
Second Floor North Ga
Nominees for H.I. Feldman Prize
17 January
Lecture
Tod Williams & Billie Tsien
Paul Rudolph Lecturers
"To Be Continued"
3 April – 5 May
Exhibition
North Gallery
Steven Harris:
The Weiss Houses
31 January
Lecture
James Glymph
Gordon Smith Lecturer in Practical Architecture
"Practical Architecture?"
10 April
Lecture
Greg Lynn
Davenport Visiting Professor
"On the Surface"
6 April
Lecture

How to disorient an architect

Yale University School of Architecture

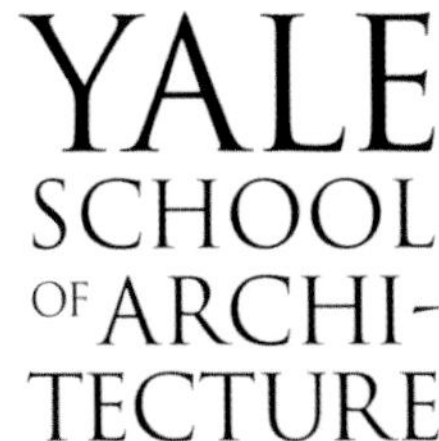

Opposite
The posters for Yale use hundreds of typefaces but only one color: black.

Above
My original presentation to Robert A. M. Stern contrasted what was expected (classicism) with what we delivered (eclecticism).

"I want to surprise people."

Robert A. M. Stern was being watched, and he knew it. He was the newly appointed dean of the Yale University School of Architecture, from where he had graduated in 1965. Expectations were running high, and so were suspicions. As editor of *Perspecta*, the school's student magazine, he had been an early promoter of the then-radical postmodernist theories of Robert Venturi and Denise Scott Brown. He took up the practice himself as an idealistic young designer in New York City.

35 years later, he was one of the most successful architects in the world, effortlessly moving between Shingle Style vacation homes for millionaires and impeccably detailed dormitories for Georgian Revival college campuses. But Stern's mastery of the language of architectural history was a red flag for some of his modernist colleagues, one of whom had already dismissed him as a "suede-loafered sultan of suburban retrotecture." Would he remake Yale into a 21st-century Beaux-Arts finishing school?

Stern relished the prospect of overturning expectations. The school had been dormant too long, predictable and easy to ignore, he told me in 1999. He laid out an aggressive program of lectures, exhibitions, and symposia, filled with complexity and contradiction, and asked me to create a graphic program to broadcast it to the world. It was an intimidating challenge. Stern's previous appointment was at Columbia University, in a program famous for a long-running series of posters designed by Swiss-born Willi Kunz, which used only a single typeface family, Univers. They were immediately identifiable and impossible to compete with. What single typeface could possibly sum up Stern's agile eclecticism?

The answer seems obvious in retrospect. Instead of using a single typeface, I proposed never using the same typeface twice: a graphic system that would achieve consistency through diversity. Fifteen years in and counting, including encounters with a few fonts I may never use again (cf. Brush Script, Robert E. Smith, 1942), our posters for Yale Architecture still surprise even me.

Right and opposite
Stern has turned Yale's architecture program into a hothouse of activity, with an overstuffed calendar of events emphasizing contrasting points of view.

Next spread
Each year, posters announce the school's fall and spring program of events. How many different ways can we find to present the same information?

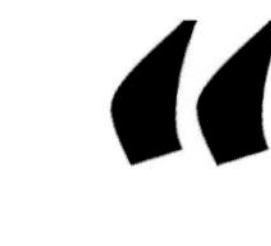

Yale School of Architecture

Lectures and Exhibitions
Fall 2000

A&A Building
180 York Street
New Haven, CT
Phone: 203.432.2889
Email: architecture.pr@yale.edu

Lectures begin at 6:30 PM in Hastings Hall–located on the basement floor. Doors Open to the General Public at 6:15 PM

Exhibition hours are Monday through Saturday, 10:00 AM to 5:00 PM. Main, North, and South Galleries are located on the second floor.

Cesar Pelli: Building Designs 1965-2000
Exhibition: Main, North and South Galleries
September 5–November 3

Bernard Cache[2]
September 7
"Current Work"

Marion Weiss and Michael Manfredi
Paul Rudolph Lecture
September 11
"Site Specific"

Steven Holl[2]
September 14
"Parallax"

Dietrich Neumann
September 18
"Architecture of the Night"

Douglas Garofalo
Bishop Visiting Professor
September 25
"Materials, Technologies, Projects"

Elizabeth Diller[2]
September 28
"Blur–Babble"

Herman D. J. Spiegel
Myriam Bellazoug Lecture
October 2
"Gaudi's Structural Expression and Its Implications for Architectural Education"

William McDonough[1,2]
October 5
"Future Work"

Hon. Anthony Williams[3]
Mayor, Washington, D.C.
Eero Saarinen Lecture
October 6
"Recasting the Shadows: The District in the Twenty-First Century"

Richard Sennett[3]
Roth-Symonds Lecture
October 7
"Urbanism and the New Capitalism"

Aaron Betsky
October 9
"Architecture Must Burn"

Julie Bargmann[1]
October 12
"Toxic Beauty: Regenerating the Industrial Landscape"

Beatriz Colomina[2]
October 23
"Secrets of Modern Architecture"

Ken Yeang[1]
October 26
"The Ecological Design of Large Buildings and Sites: Theory and Experiments"

Charles Jencks
Brendan Gill Lecture
October 30
"The New Paradigm in Architecture"

Craig Hodgetts and Ming Fung[2]
Saarinen Visiting Professors
November 2
"By-products: Form Follows Means"

Kathryn Gustafson
Timothy Lenahan Memorial Lecture
November 6
"European and American Landscape Projects 1984-2000"

Jacques Herzog[2]
November 9
"Architecture by Herzog & de Meuron"

Ignacio Dahl Rocha
November 13
"Learning From Practice: the Architecture of Richter and Dahl Rocha"

The British Library
Colin St. John Wilson & M. J. Long
Exhibition: Main Gallery
November 13–December 15

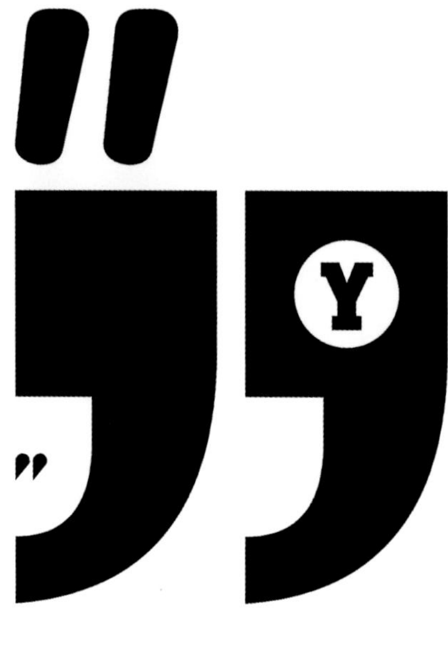

(a)way station
a project by KW:a
Paul Kariouk & Mabel Wilson
Exhibition: North Gallery
November 13–December 15

in.formant.system
Douglas Garofalo
Exhibition: South Gallery
November 13–December 15

Max Fordham and Patrick Bellew[1]
November 16
"Labyrinths and Things"

Barry Bergdoll
November 20
"Siting Mies: Nature and Consciousness in the Modern House"

Richard Foreman[1]
November 30
"Landscape, Ecology and Road System Ecology: Foundation for Meshing Nature and People So They Both Thrive"

1 These lectures are part of **"Issues in Environment and Design"** seminar given in collaboration with Yale School of Forestry and Environmental Studies.

2 These lectures are part of **"The Millennium House"** seminar.

3 These lectures are part of **"Next Cities"** symposium.

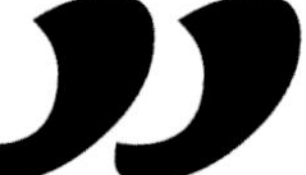

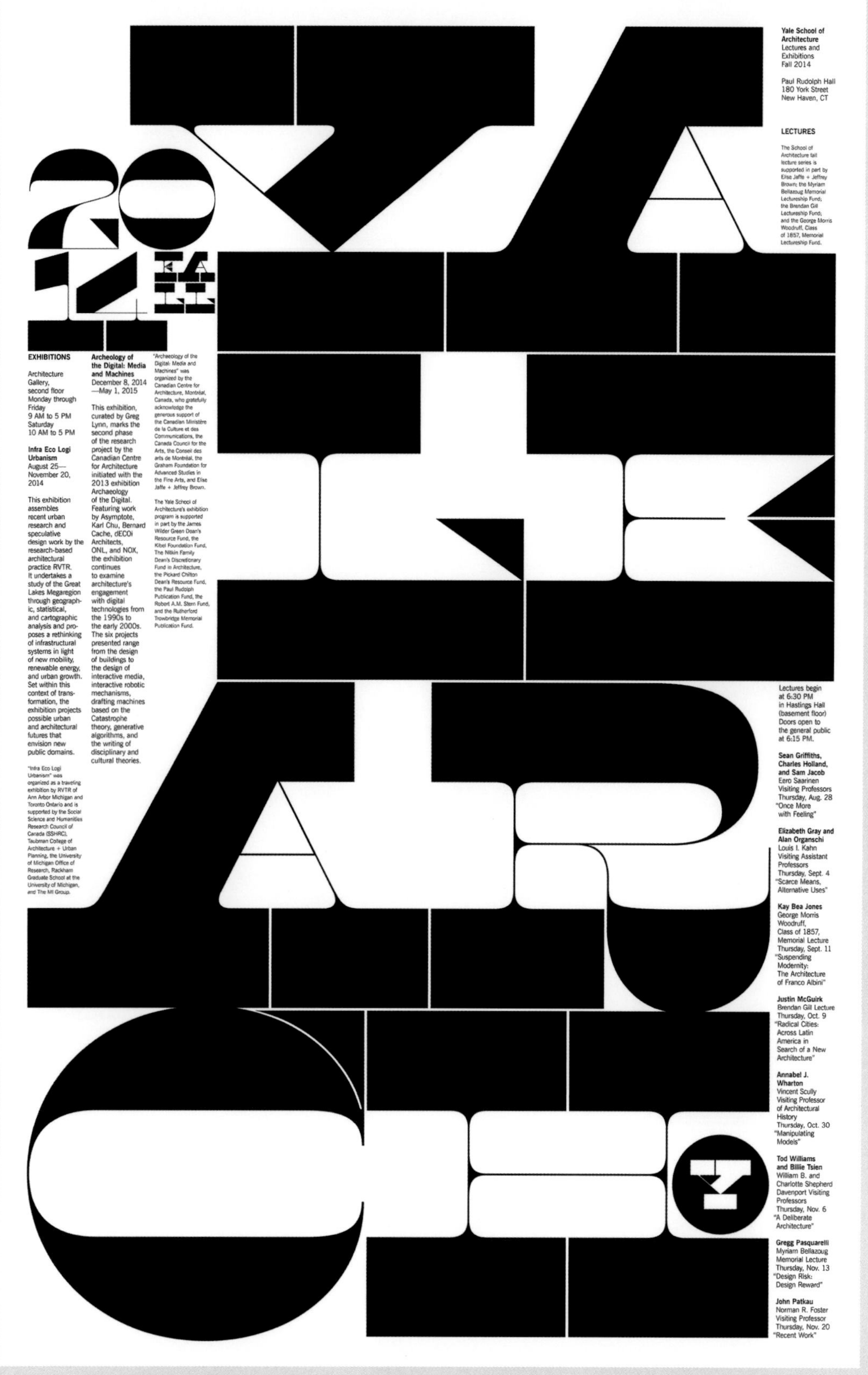
Yale School of Architecture
Lectures and Exhibitions
Fall 2014
Paul Rudolph Hall
180 York Street
New Haven, CT
LECTURES
The School of Architecture fall lecture series is supported in part by Elise Jaffe + Jeffrey Brown; the Myriam Bellazoug Memorial Lectureship Fund; the Brendan Gill Lectureship Fund; and the George Morris Woodruff, Class of 1857, Memorial Lectureship Fund.
EXHIBITIONS
Architecture Gallery, second floor
Monday through Friday
9 AM to 5 PM
Saturday
10 AM to 5 PM
Infra Eco Logi Urbanism
August 25—November 20, 2014
This exhibition assembles recent urban research and speculative design work by the research-based architectural practice RVTR. It undertakes a study of the Great Lakes Megaregion through geographic, statistical, and cartographic analysis and proposes a rethinking of infrastructural systems in light of new mobility, renewable energy, and urban growth. Set within this context of transformation, the exhibition projects possible urban and architectural futures that envision new public domains.
"Infra Eco Logi Urbanism" was organized as a traveling exhibition by RVTR of Ann Arbor Michigan and Toronto Ontario and is supported by the Social Science and Humanities Research Council of Canada (SSHRC), Taubman College of Architecture + Urban Planning, the University of Michigan Office of Research, Rackham Graduate School at the University of Michigan, and The MI Group.
Archeology of the Digital: Media and Machines
December 8, 2014—May 1, 2015
This exhibition, curated by Greg Lynn, marks the second phase of the research project by the Canadian Centre for Architecture initiated with the 2013 exhibition Archaeology of the Digital. Featuring work by Asymptote, Karl Chu, Bernard Cache, dECOi Architects, ONL, and NOX, the exhibition continues to examine architecture's engagement with digital technologies from the 1990s to the early 2000s. The six projects presented range from the design of buildings to the design of interactive media, interactive robotic mechanisms, drafting machines based on the Catastrophe theory, generative algorithms, and the writing of disciplinary and cultural theories.
"Archaeology of the Digital: Media and Machines" was organized by the Canadian Centre for Architecture, Montréal, Canada, who gratefully acknowledge the generous support of the Canadian Ministère de la Culture et des Communications, the Canada Council for the Arts, the Conseil des arts de Montréal, the Graham Foundation for Advanced Studies in the Fine Arts, and Elise Jaffe + Jeffrey Brown.
The Yale School of Architecture's exhibition program is supported in part by the James Wilder Green Dean's Resource Fund, the Kibel Foundation Fund, The Nitkin Family Dean's Discretionary Fund in Architecture, the Pickard Chilton Dean's Resource Fund, the Paul Rudolph Publication Fund, the Robert A.M. Stern Fund, and the Rutherford Trowbridge Memorial Publication Fund.
Lectures begin at 6:30 PM in Hastings Hall (basement floor) Doors open to the general public at 6:15 PM.
Sean Griffiths, Charles Holland, and Sam Jacob
Eero Saarinen Visiting Professors
Thursday, Aug. 28
"Once More with Feeling"
Elizabeth Gray and Alan Organschi
Louis I. Kahn Visiting Assistant Professors
Thursday, Sept. 4
"Scarce Means, Alternative Uses"
Kay Bea Jones
George Morris Woodruff, Class of 1857, Memorial Lecture
Thursday, Sept. 11
"Suspending Modernity: The Architecture of Franco Albini"
Justin McGuirk
Brendan Gill Lecture
Thursday, Oct. 9
"Radical Cities: Across Latin America in Search of a New Architecture"
Annabel J. Wharton
Vincent Scully Visiting Professor of Architectural History
Thursday, Oct. 30
"Manipulating Models"
Tod Williams and Billie Tsien
William B. and Charlotte Shepherd Davenport Visiting Professors
Thursday, Nov. 6
"A Deliberate Architecture"
Gregg Pasquarelli
Myriam Bellazoug Memorial Lecture
Thursday, Nov. 13
"Design Risk: Design Reward"
John Patkau
Norman R. Foster Visiting Professor
Thursday, Nov. 20
"Recent Work"

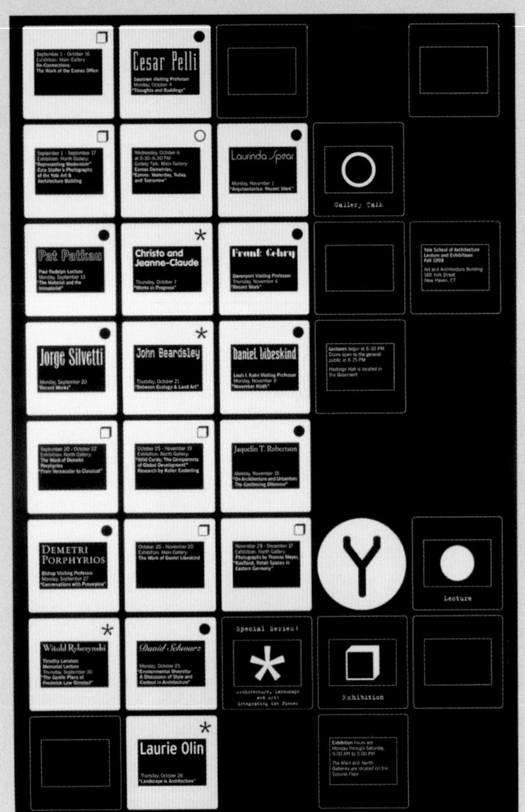

Cesar Pelli
Pat Pathan
Christo and Jeanne-Claude
Frank Gehry
Jorge Silvetti
John Beardsley
Daniel Libeskind
Demetri Porphyrios
Witold Rybczynski
David Schwarz
Laurie Olin
Gallery Talk
Lecture
Exhibition

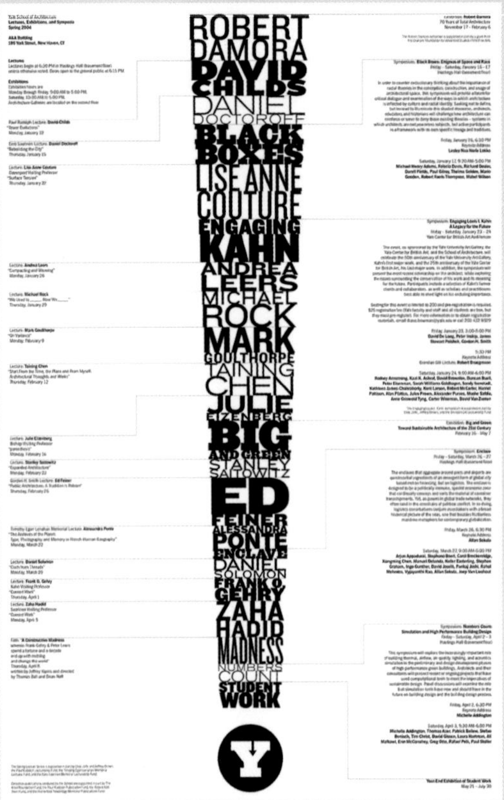

ROBERT
DAMORA
DAVID
CHILDS
DANIEL
DOCTOROFF
BLACK
BOXES
LISE ANNE
COUTURE
ENGAGING
KAHN
ANDREA
LEERS
MICHAEL
ROCK
MARK
GOULTHORPE
TAINING
CHEN
JULIE
EIZENBERG
BIG
AND GREEN
STANLEY
SAITOWITZ
ED
FEINER
ALEXANDRA
PONTE
ENCLAVE
DANIEL
SOLOMON
FRANK O.
GEHRY
ZAHA
HADID
MADNESS
NUMBERS
COUNT
STUDENT
WORK

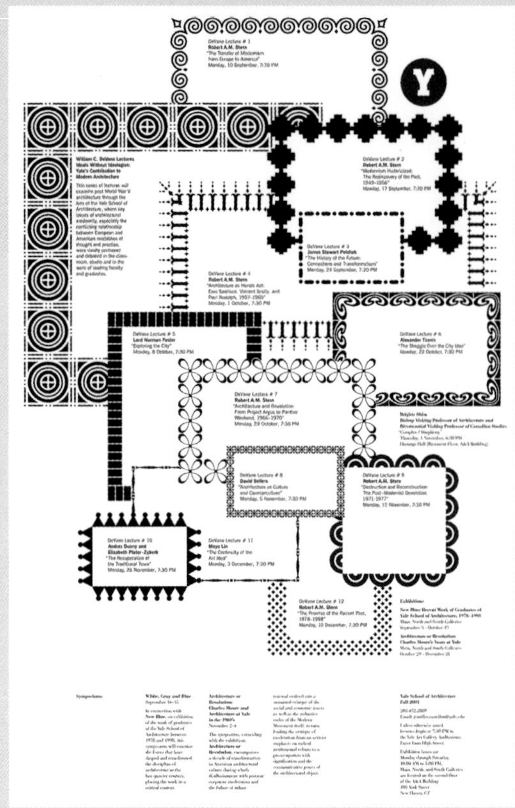

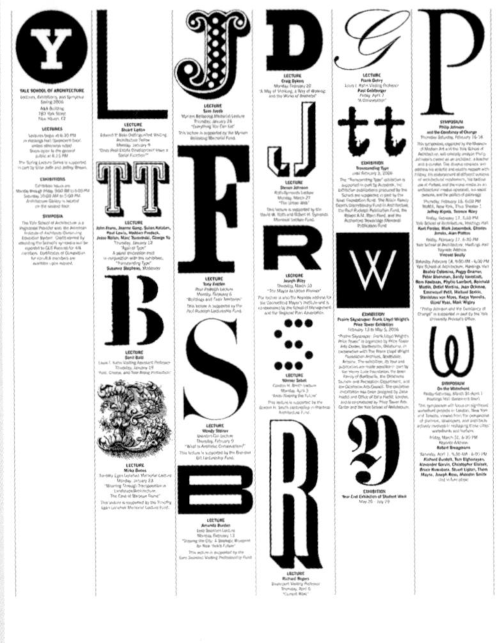

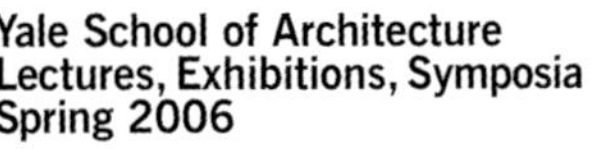

Yale School of Architecture
Lectures, Exhibitions, Symposia
Spring 2006

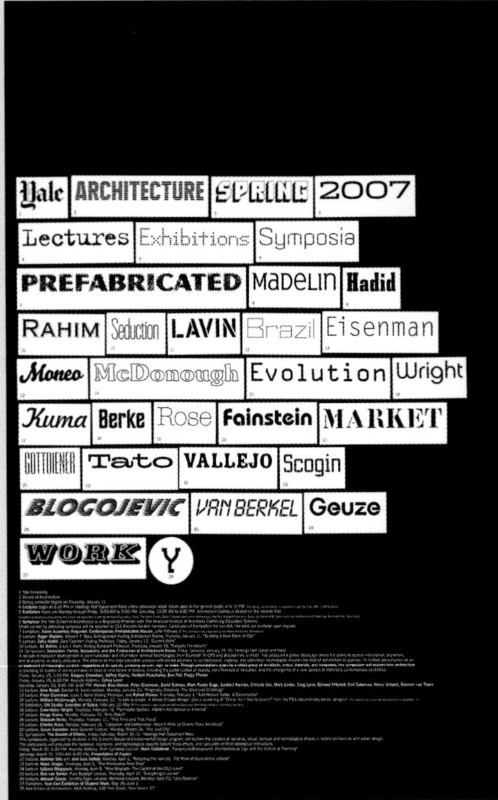

Yale ARCHITECTURE SPRING 2007
Lectures Exhibitions Symposia
PREFABRICATED MADeLIN Hadid
RAHIM Seduction LAVIN Brazil Eisenman
Moneo McDonough Evolution Wright
Kuma Berke Rose Fainstein MARKET
GOTTDIENER Tato VALLEJO Scogin
BLOGOJEVIC VAN BERKEL Geuze
WORK

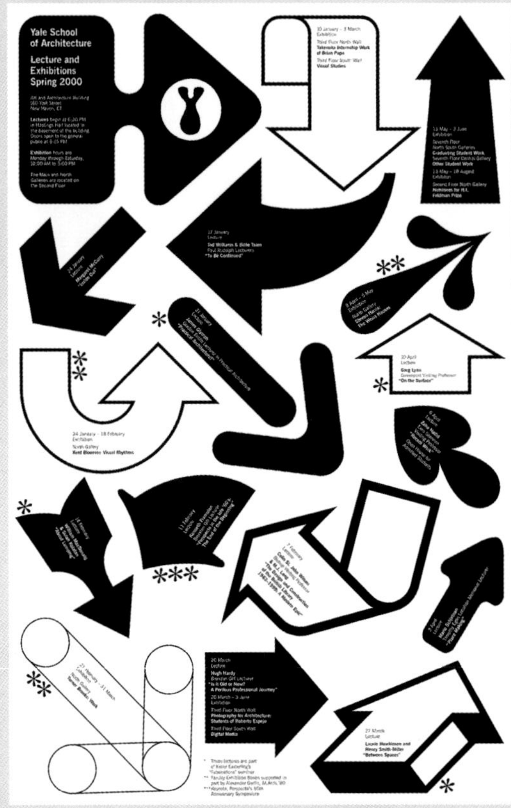

Yale School of Architecture
Lectures and Exhibitions
Spring 2000

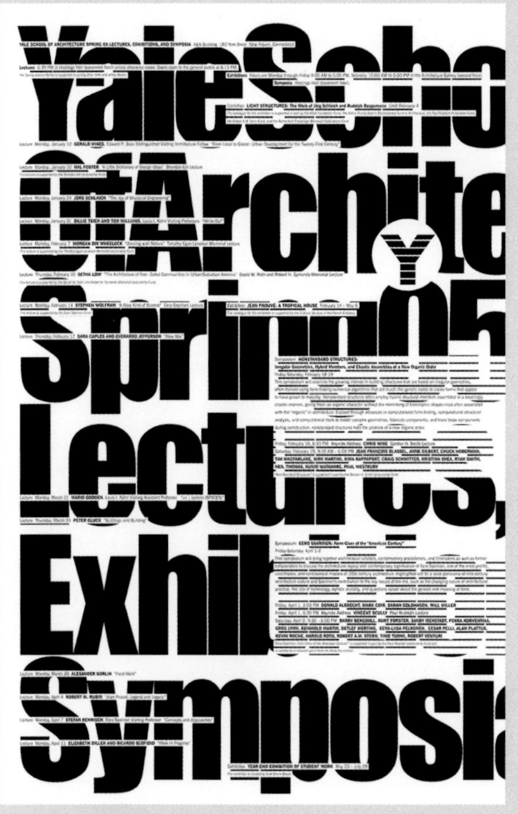
YALE SCHOOL OF ARCHITECTURE SPRING 05 LECTURES, EXHIBITIONS, AND SYMPOSIA
Symposia
Lectures,

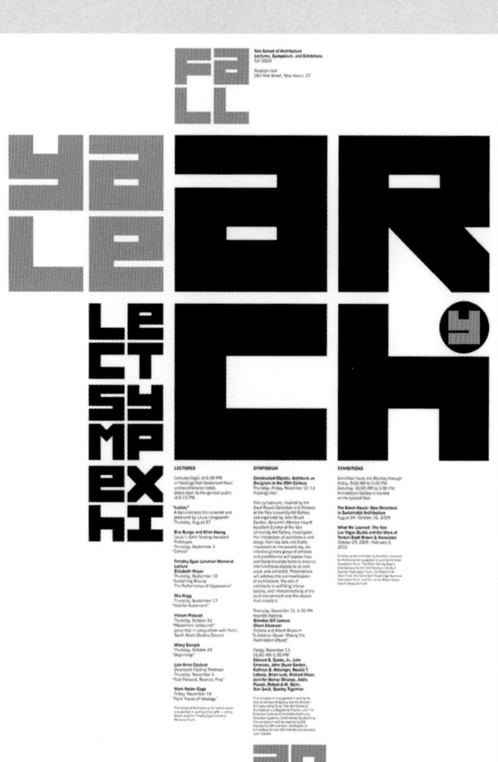
FALL
YALE
ARCH
LECTURES
SYMPOSIUM
EXHIBITIONS
2009

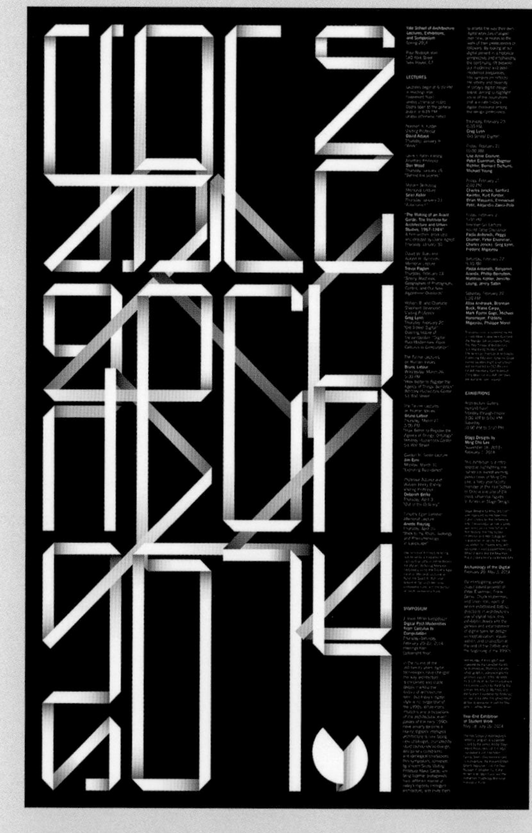

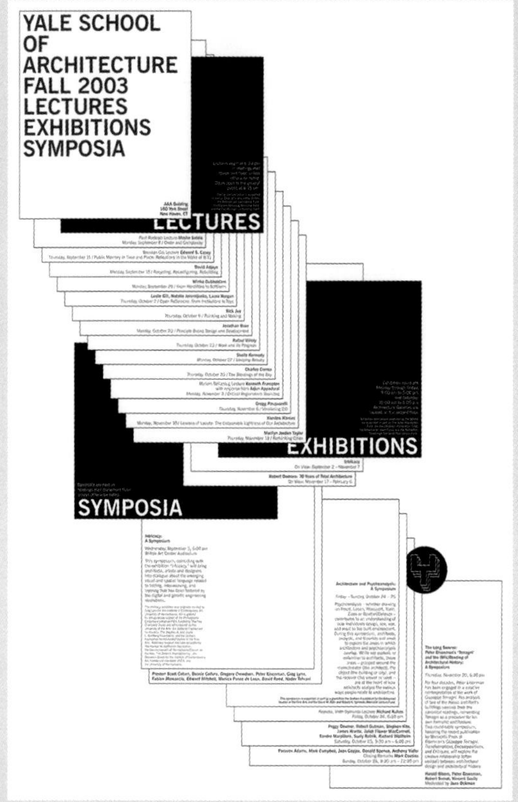
YALE SCHOOL
OF
ARCHITECTURE
FALL 2003
LECTURES
EXHIBITIONS
SYMPOSIA
LECTURES
EXHIBITIONS
SYMPOSIA

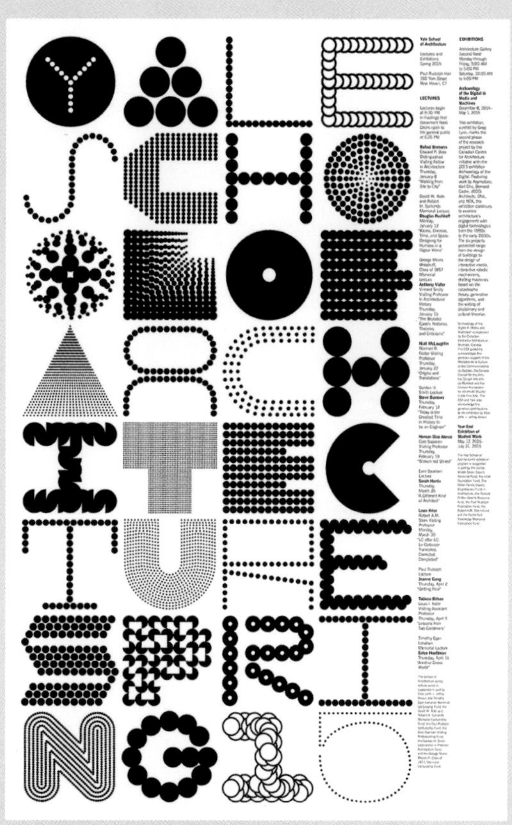

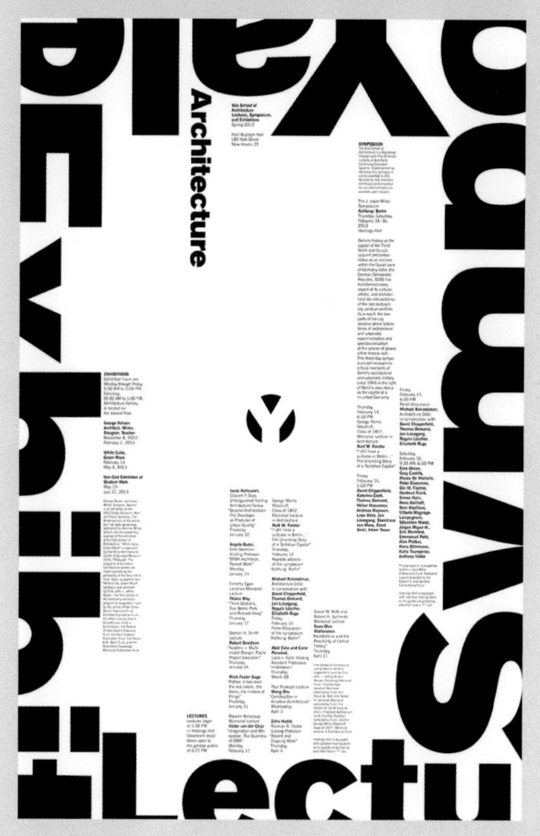
Architecture

Right and opposite
Designing posters for symposia is an opportunity to make direct references to specific subject matter, including the density of urban life, the architecture of Charles Moore, the signage of the Las Vegas strip, the lost art of drawing, or the legacy of George Nelson.

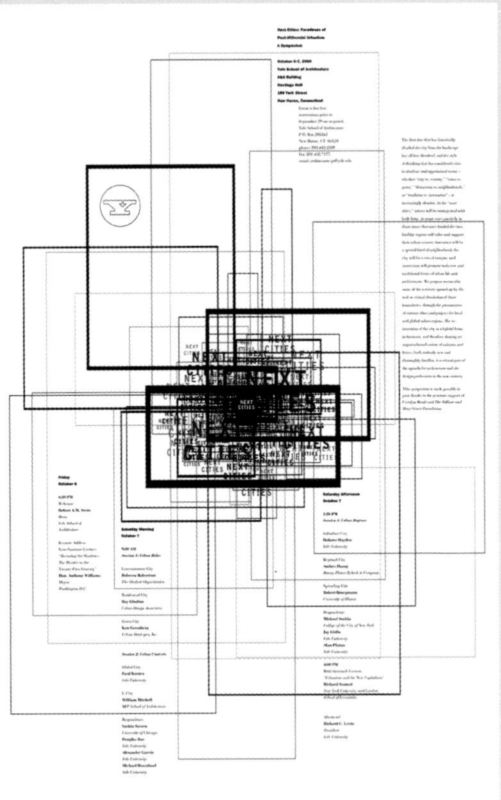

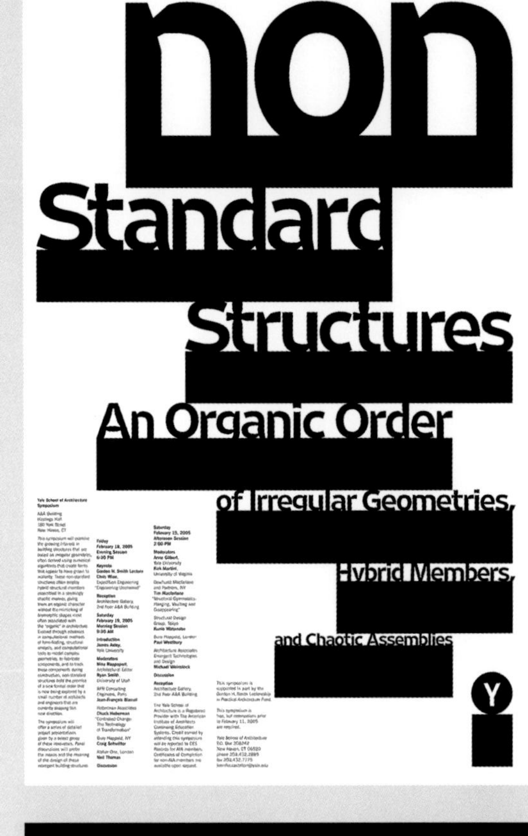

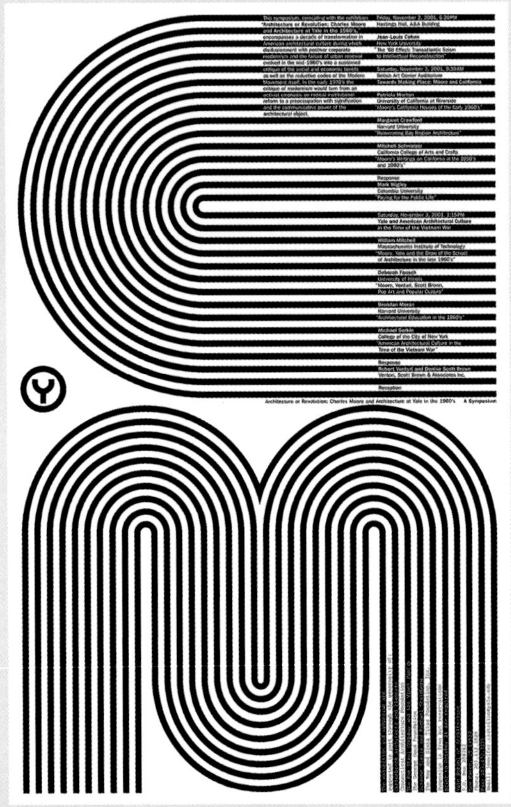

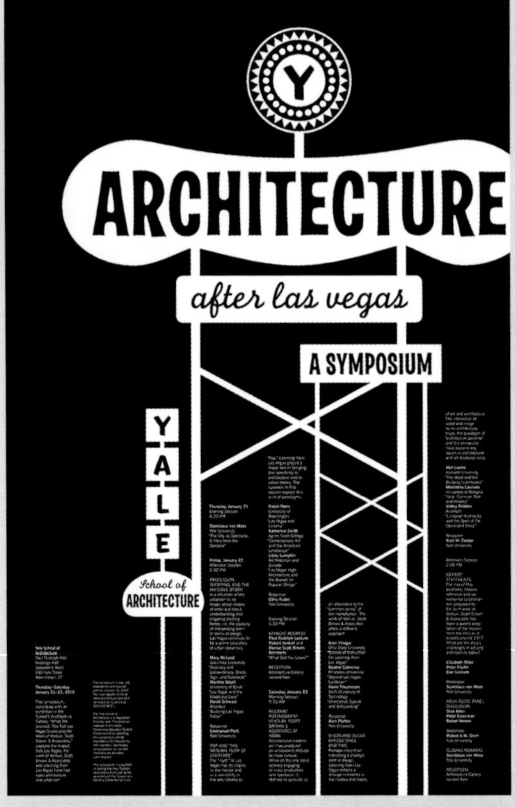

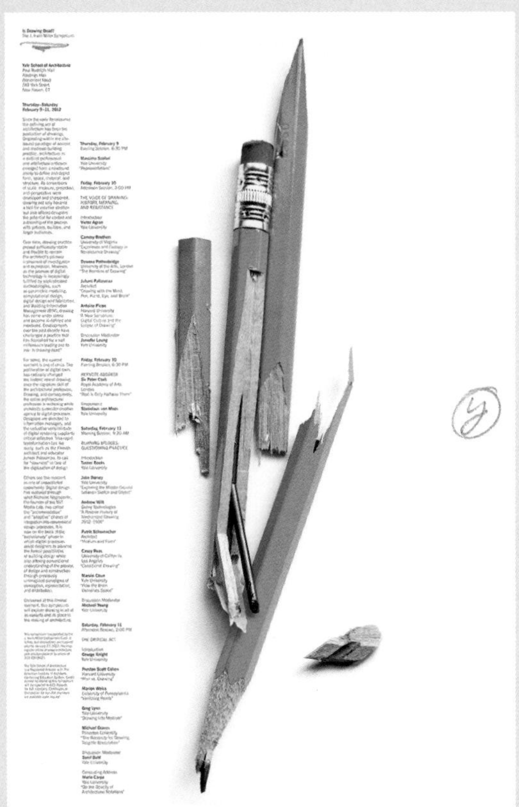

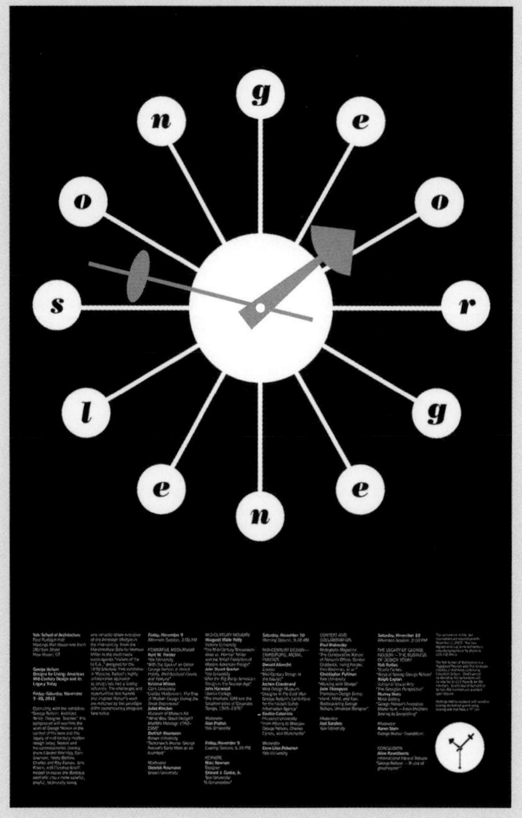

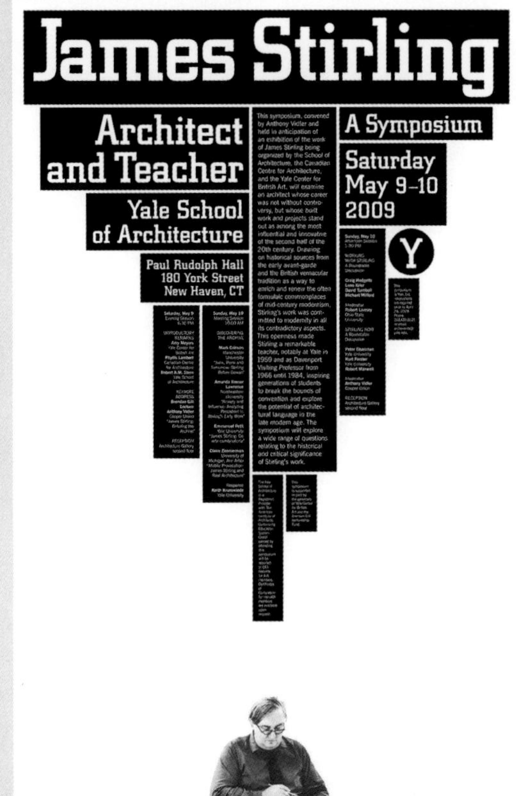
James Stirling
Architect and Teacher
Yale School of Architecture
Paul Rudolph Hall
180 York Street
New Haven, CT
This symposium, convened by Anthony Vidler and held in anticipation of an exhibition of the work of James Stirling being organized by the School of Architecture, the Canadian Centre for Architecture, and the Yale Center for British Art, will examine an architect whose career was not without controversy, but whose built work and projects stand out as among the most influential and innovative of the second half of the 20th century. Drawing on historical sources from the early avant-garde and the British vernacular tradition as a way to enrich and extend the often formulaic commonplaces of mid-century modernism, Stirling's work was committed to modernity in all its contradictory aspects. This openness made Stirling a remarkable teacher, notably at Yale in 1959 and as Davenport Visiting Professor from 1966 until 1984, inspiring generations of students to break the bounds of convention and explore the potential of architectural language in the late modern age. The symposium will explore a wide range of questions relating to the historical and critical significance of Stirling's work.
A Symposium
Saturday May 9–10 2009
Y

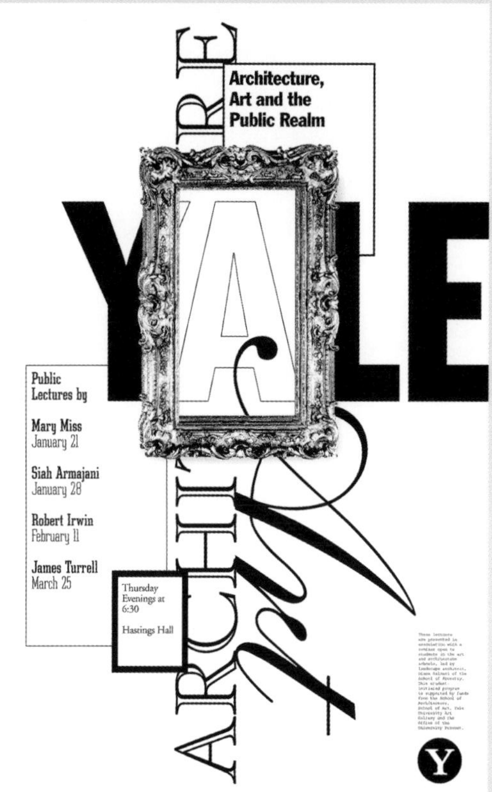
ARCHITECTURE
Architecture, Art and the Public Realm
YALE
Public Lectures by
Mary Miss
January 21
Siah Armajani
January 28
Robert Irwin
February 11
James Turrell
March 25
Thursday Evenings at 6:30
Hastings Hall
Y

Right and opposite
Each year, Yale holds an open house for prospective architecture students. Many of the accompanying posters have exploited the geometry of the letter Y or the implied invitation of the letter O.

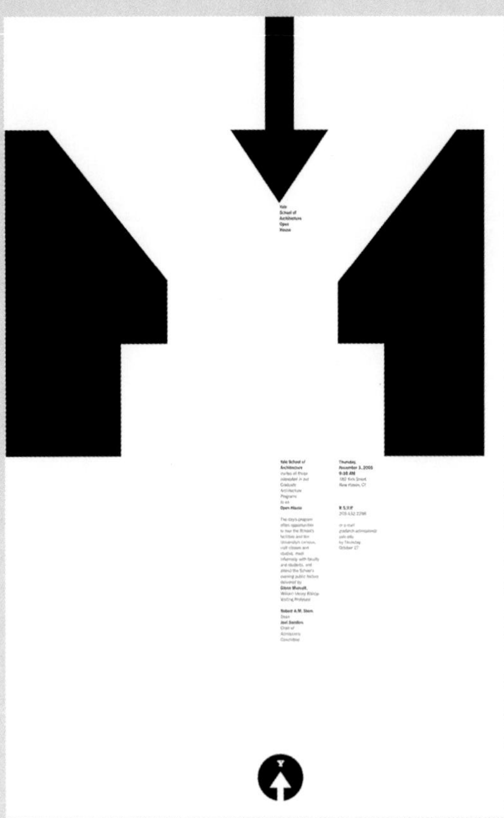

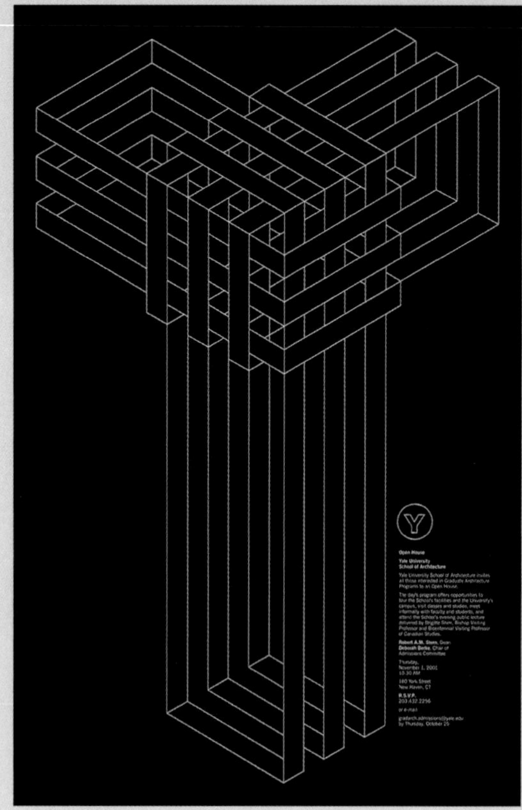

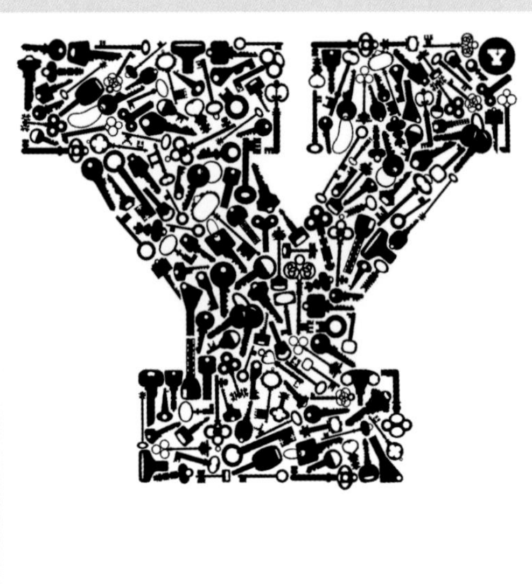

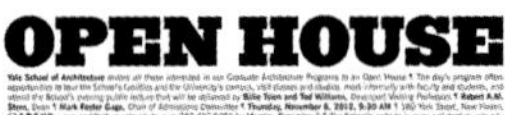

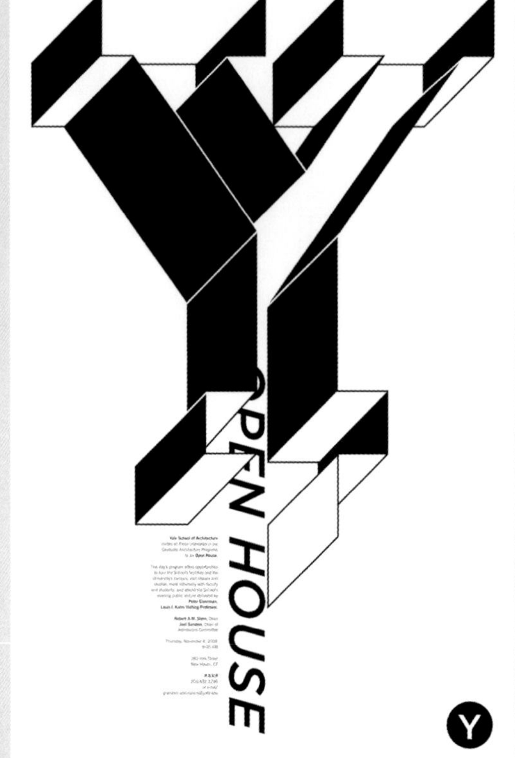

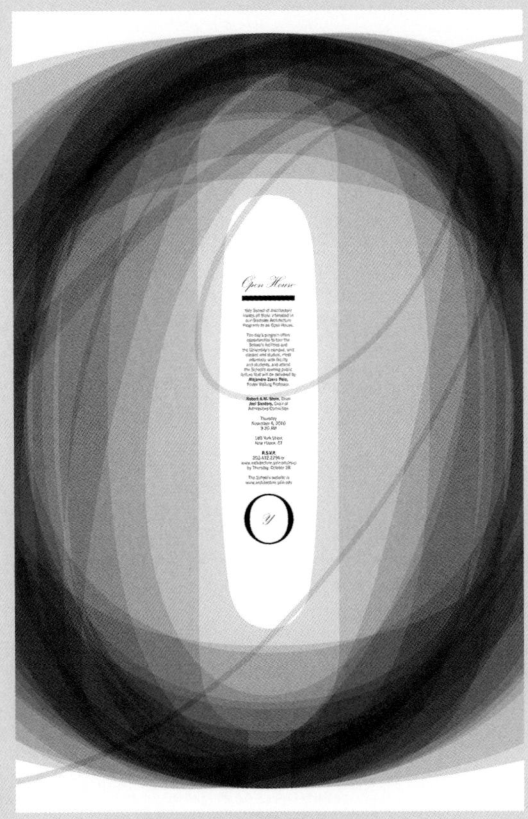

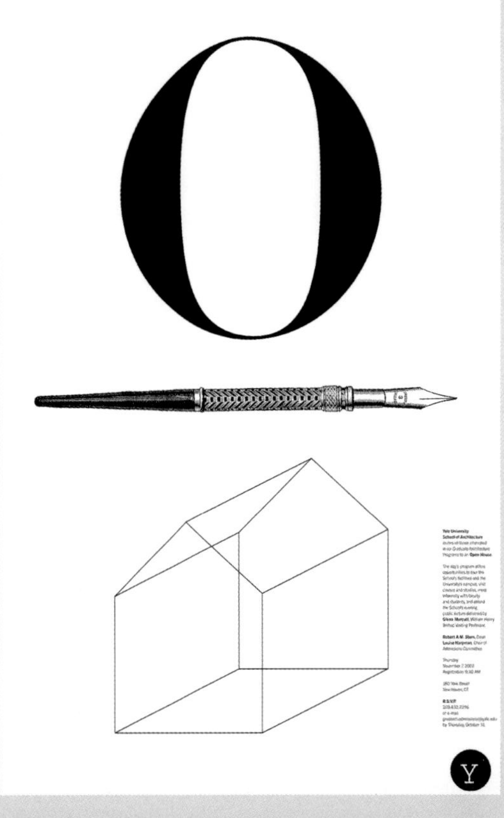

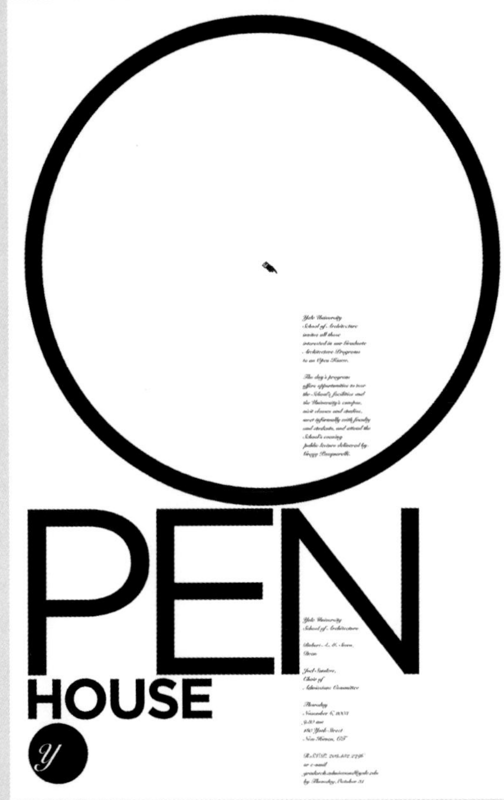
PEN
HOUSE

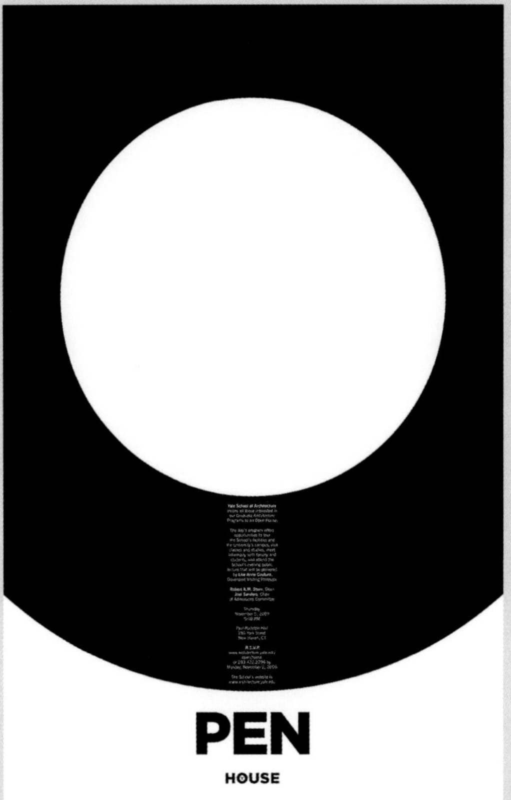
PEN
HOUSE

Right
Our clients at Yale have been remarkably tolerant. When we proposed a poster using only one size of type (the smallest), and indicating emphasis with cues like bold weight and underlines, they acquiesced, and politely asked us not to do it again.

YALE SCHOOL OF ARCHITECTURE

Lectures, Symposia, Special Events, and Exhibitions • Fall 2012

Paul Rudolph Hall, 180 York Street, New Haven, CT

LECTURES

Lectures begin at 6:30 PM in Hastings Hall (basement floor). Doors open to the general public at 6:15 PM.

Thursday, August 30 • **Peter Eisenman** • "Palladio Virtuel: Inventing the Palladian Project"

Thursday, September 6 • **Amale Andraos and Dan Wood** • "Nature-City"

Thursday, September 13 • **Tom Wiscombe**, Louis I. Kahn Visiting Assistant Professor • "Composite Thinking"

Thursday, September 20 • **Diana Balmori**, William Henry Bishop Visiting Professor, **and Joel Sanders** • "Between Landscape and Architecture"

Thursday, October 4 • **Paul Rudolph Lecture** • **Brigitte Shim** • "Ways of Seeing Sound: The Integral House" • Opening lecture of the symposium "The Sound of Architecture"

Friday, October 5 • **Elizabeth Diller** • "B+/A-" • Keynote to the symposium "The Sound of Architecture"

Thursday, October 11 • **Keller Easterling** • "The Action is Form"

Thursday, November 1 • **Brendan Gill Lecture** • Panel Discussion • **Mary Ann Caws, Jean-Louis Cohen, Beatriz Colomina, Peter Eisenman, Mark Jarzombek, Kevin Repp** • "The Eisenman Collection: An Analysis"

Thursday, November 8 • **Billie Tsien and Tod Williams**, William B. and Charlotte Shepherd Davenport Visiting Professors • "The Still Place"

Friday, November 9 • **Marc Newson with Edward S. Cooke, Jr.** • "A Conversation" • Keynote to the symposium • "George Nelson: Design for Living, American Mid-Century Design and Its Legacy Today"

Thursday, November 15 • **Eero Saarinen Lecture** • **Dr. Richard Jackson** • "We Shape Our Buildings: They Shape Our Bodies"

The School of Architecture fall lecture series is supported in part by Elise Jaffe + Jeffrey Brown, the Brendan Gill Lectureship Fund, the Paul Rudolph Lectureship Fund, and the Eero Saarinen Visiting Professorship Fund.

SYMPOSIA

Thursday–Saturday, October 4–6, 2012 • The J. Irwin Miller Symposium • **THE SOUND OF ARCHITECTURE** • Hastings Hall (basement floor) unless otherwise noted

Architecture is not tone deaf: It can create silent places and eddies of noise, deeply affecting our experience and facilitating or frustrating communication. Buildings have long been thought of in visual and practical terms, leaving their aural dimension largely unconsidered. Today, the ways we listen in built spaces have been transformed by developments in media, music, and art. New design tools are helping architects shape the soundscapes of their buildings, while new audio technologies afford access to previously undetected sonic environments. This symposium will draw on a variety of disciplinary expertise in its quest for an understanding of architecture as an auditory environment. Leading scholars from fields as diverse as archeology, media studies, musicology, philosophy, and the history of technology will converge to discuss critical questions alongside major architects, acoustical engineers, composers, and artists. This symposium aims to stake out a new set of questions for ongoing scholarly inquiry and to reaffirm architecture as a place of convergence among old and emerging disciplines.

Thursday, October 4, 6:30 PM • **Brigitte Shim** • "Ways of Seeing Sound: The Integral House"

Friday, October 5, 9:00 AM–6:00 PM • **Dorothea Baumann, Barry Blesser, Mario Carpo, Carlotta Darò, Ariane Lourie Harrison, Craig Hodgetts, Mark Jarzombek, Randolph Jordan, Brian Kane, Graeme Lawson, Ingram Marshall, Raj Patel, John Durham Peters, Linda-Ruth Salter, Joel Sanders, Jonathan Sterne, Peter Szendy, Jack Vees, Beat Wyss**

Friday, October 5, 6:30 PM • Keynote Address • **Elizabeth Diller** • "B+/A-"

Saturday, October 6, 9:30 AM–3:30 PM • Whitney Humanities Center • 53 Wall Street • **Michelle Addington, Niall Atkinson, Timothy Barringer, Joseph Clarke, J.D. Connor, Veit Erlmann, Brandon LaBelle, Alexander Nemerov, John Picker, William Rankin, Karen Van Lengen, Sabine von Fischer**

Friday–Saturday, November 9–10, 2012 • **GEORGE NELSON: DESIGN FOR LIVING, AMERICAN MID-CENTURY DESIGN AND ITS LEGACY TODAY** • Hastings Hall (basement floor)

Coinciding with the exhibition "George Nelson: Architect, Writer, Designer, Teacher" at the School, this symposium will examine the work of the designer George Nelson in the context of his time and the legacy of mid-century modern design today. Nelson and his contemporaries (among them Edward Wormley, Eero Saarinen, Harry Bertoia, Charles and Ray Eames, Jens Risom, and Florence Knoll) helped to evolve the Bauhaus aesthetic into a more colorful, playful, technically savvy, and versatile idiom evocative of the American lifestyle in the mid-century. From the Marshmallow Sofa for Herman Miller to the multimedia extravaganza "Visions of the U.S.A.," designed for the 1959 Sokolniki Park exhibition in Moscow, Nelson's highly collaborative approach to design has had a lasting influence. The challenges and opportunities that framed and inspired Nelson's work are matched by the paradigm shifts contemporary designers face today.

Friday, November 9, 2:00 PM–6:00 PM • **Kurt W. Forster, John Stuart Gordon, John Harwood, Juliet Kinchin, Murray Moss, Dietrich Neumann, Margaret Maile Petty, Kristina Wilson**

Friday, November 9, 6:30 PM • Keynote Address • **Marc Newson with Edward S. Cooke, Jr** • "A Conversation"

Saturday, November 10, 9:30 AM–4:00 PM • **Donald Albrecht, Ralph Caplan, Beatriz Colomina, Jochen Eisenbrand, Rob Forbes, Paul Makovsky, Christopher Pullman, Alice Rawsthorne, Jane Thompson**

"The Sound of Architecture" is supported by the J. Irwin Miller Endowment Fund. "George Nelson: Design for Living, American Mid-Century Design and Its Legacy Today" is supported in part by the generosity of the Edward and Dorothy Clarke Kempf Fund. The Yale School of Architecture is a Registered Provider with The American Institute of Architects Continuing Education Systems. Credit earned by attending these symposia will be reported to CES Records for AIA members. Certificates of Completion for non-AIA members are available upon request.

SPECIAL EVENT

Friday–Saturday, November 30–December 1, 2012 • **YALE WOMEN IN ARCHITECTURE: A REUNION AND CELEBRATION OF THE 30TH ANNIVERSARY OF THE SONIA SCHIMBERG AWARD**

This first-ever gathering of the alumnae of the Yale School of Architecture will celebrate the accomplishments of women architects across the years and mark the 30th anniversary of the Sonia Albert Schimberg Award. Sonia Albert (M.Arch. 1950) was one of two women architecture graduates that year and her daughters created the award in her memory to recognize the most promising woman graduate each year. The gathering will present and discuss the legacy of women graduates of Yale and take stock of the current conditions in architecture and related fields. Topics include the roles of client and architect, social change, shifting and enlarging the definition of practicing and teaching architecture. Alumnae spanning over 30 years of graduating classes as well as current students and experts from other disciplines, will participate in the program. Come and take part in helping to shape the future for Yale women in architecture.

EXHIBITIONS

Architecture Gallery, second floor • Monday through Friday, 9:00 AM to 5:00 PM • Saturday, 10:00 AM to 5:00 PM

August 20–October 27, 2012 • **PALLADIO VIRTUEL**

November 8, 2012–February 2, 2013 • **GEORGE NELSON: ARCHITECT, WRITER, DESIGNER, TEACHER**

"Palladio Virtuel" is supported in part by the Graham Foundation for Advanced Studies in the Fine Arts and by Elise Jaffe + Jeffrey Brown. "George Nelson: Architect, Writer, Designer, Teacher" is an exhibition of the Vitra Design Museum, Weil am Rhein, Germany. The American tour of the exhibition has been generously sponsored by HermanMiller, who is also the presenting sponsor of the exhibition at the Yale School of Architecture. The Yale School of Architecture's exhibition program is supported in part by the James Wilder Green Dean's Resource Fund, the Kibel Foundation Fund, The Nitkin Family Dean's Discretionary Fund in Architecture, the Pickard Chilton Dean's Resource Fund, the Paul Rudolph Publication Fund, the Robert A.M. Stern Fund, and the Rutherford Trowbridge Memorial Publication Fund.

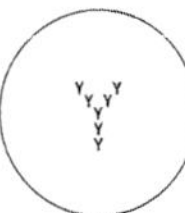

Yale University School of Architecture

Right
I asked Marian Bantjes to hand-letter a poster on seduction in architecture, specifying a treatment that was "sick with lust." She delivered. In a bizarre turn of events, the design was stolen by P. Diddy's fashion label; with a few deft changes, they changed "Seduction" to "Sean John." How strange and wonderful to live in a world with such porous borders.

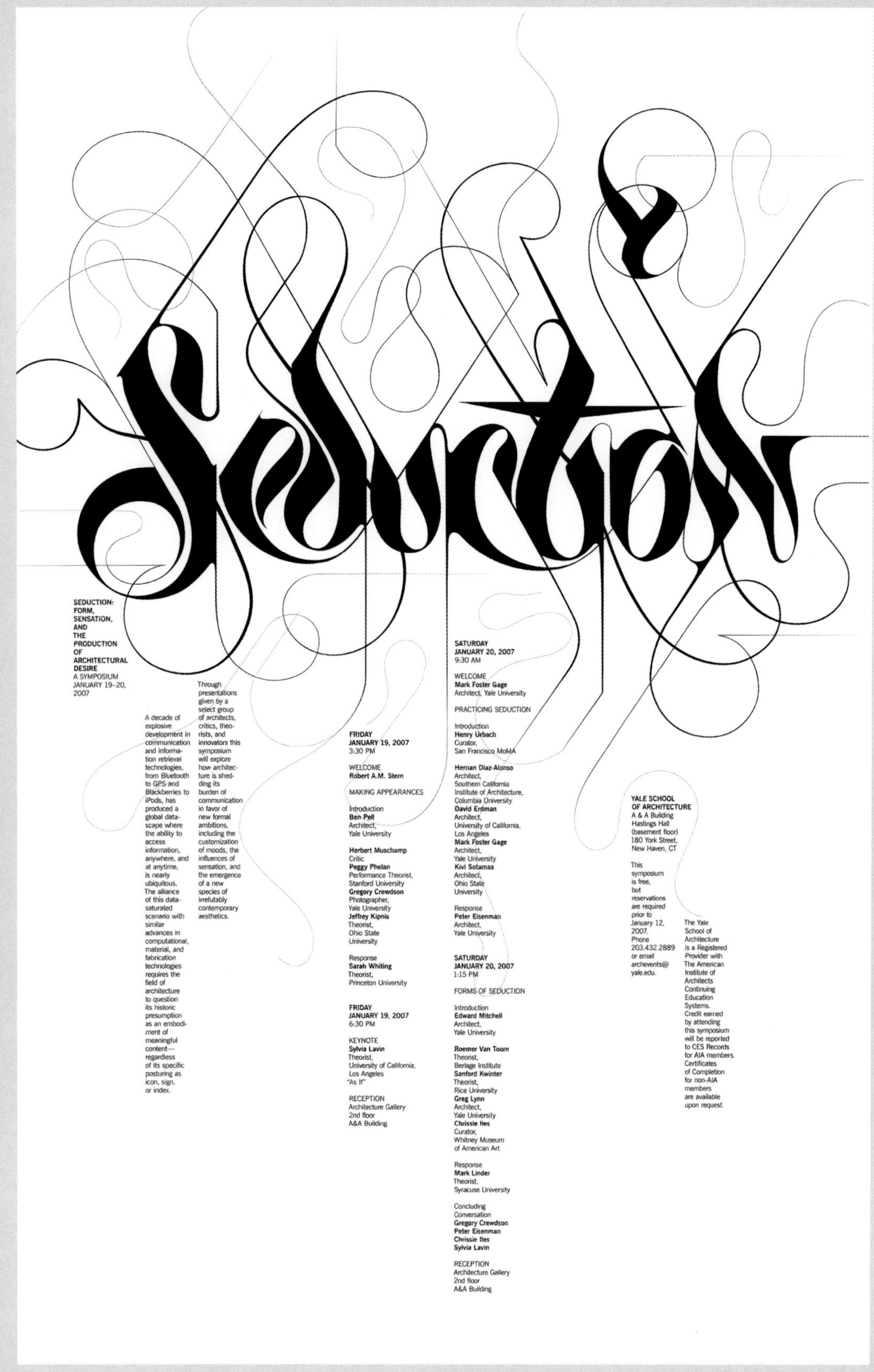

Yale School of Architecture
Symposium

A&A Building, Hastings Hall
180 York Street, New Haven, CT

This symposium is partially funded by a grant from the Graham Foundation for the Advanced Studies in the Fine Arts and the David W. Roth and Robert H. Symonds Memorial Lecture Fund.

This symposium is free but reservations prior to Oct 10, 2003 are required.

Yale School of Architecture
P.O.Box 208242
New Haven, CT 06520

Phone: 203.432.2889
Fax: 203.432.7175
email: jennifer.castellon@yale.edu

Architecture and Psychoanalysis

Friday
October 24, 2003
Evening Session
6:30 pm

KEYNOTE
Roth-Symonds Lecture
Richard Kuhns, Professor of Philosophy, Columbia University
"Constructive and Destructive Passion: Architecture and Psychoanalytic Thought"

RECEPTION
Architecture Gallery, 2nd floor A&A Building

Saturday
October 25, 2003
Morning Session
9:30 am

THE CREATIVE SUBJECT: ARCHITECTS / ARCHITECTURE

IDENTITY
Juliet Flower MacCannell, Professor Emeritus, English and Comparative Literature, U.C. Berkeley
"Breaking Out"
Suely Rolnik, Professor, Dept. of Social Psychology, Catholic University of Sao Pãulo
"Beyond the Pumping of Creation"

ORGANIZATION
Robert Gutman, Lecturer in Architecture, Princeton University
James Krantz, Organizational Consultant
"The Psychodynamics of Architectural Practice"

Saturday
October 25, 2003
Afternoon Session
1:15 pm

THE OBJECT: BUILDING / CITY

THE BUILDING
Stephen Kite, Architect and Professor, University of Newcastle
"Adrian Stokes and the 'Aesthetic Position': Psycho-analysis and the Spaces In-Between"
Peggy Deamer, Associate Professor, Yale University
"Form and (Dis)Content"

THE CITY
Sandro Marpillero, Adjunct Associate Professor of Architecture, Columbia University
"Urban Operations: Unconscious Effects"
Richard Wollheim, Professor in Residence, Dept. of Philosophy, U.C. Berkeley; faculty, San Francisco Psychoanalytic Institute
"Why We Hate the Modern City"

Sunday
October 26, 2003
Morning Session

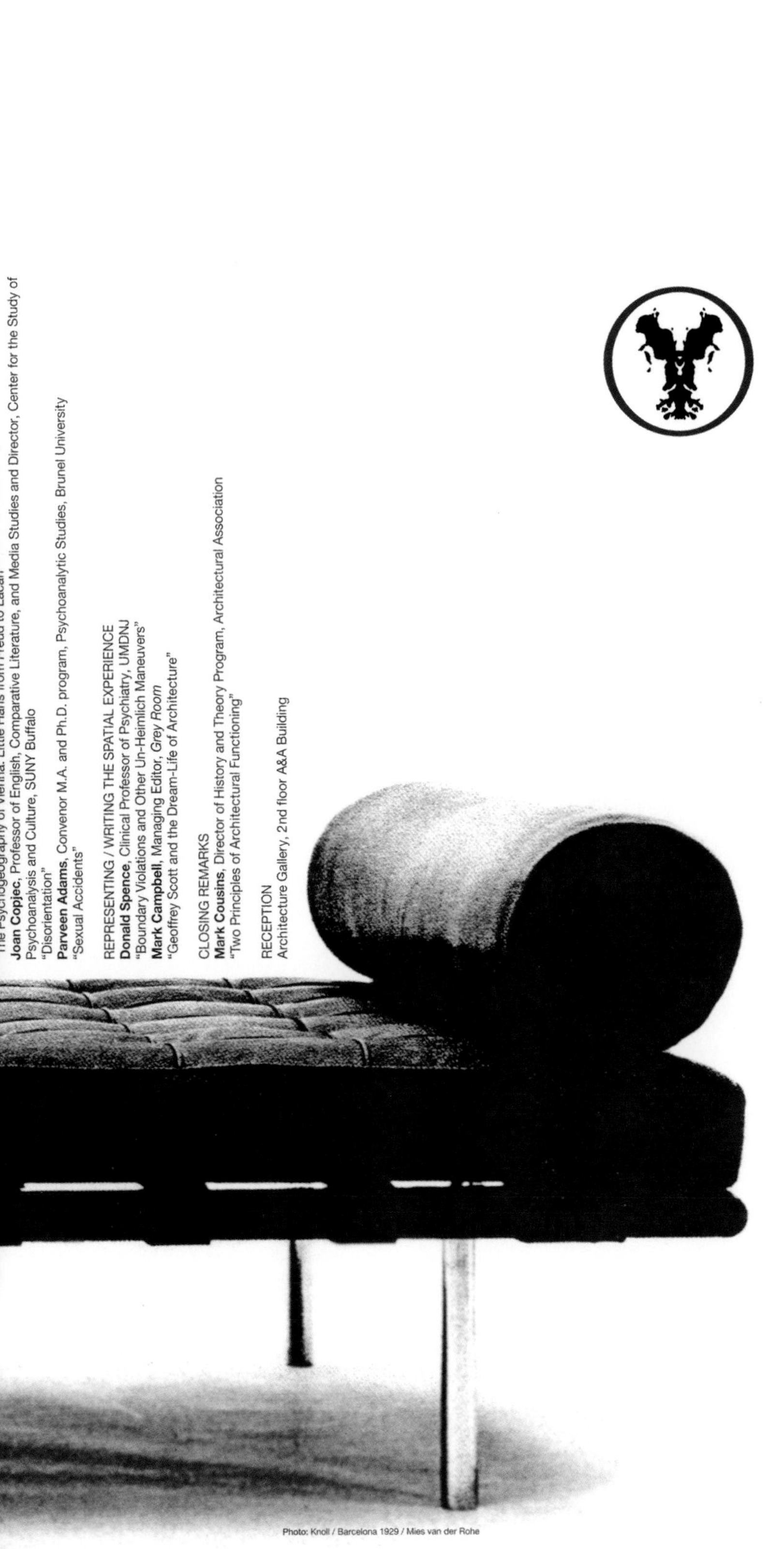

Left
To reinforce the theme of constant variation, the logo for the school is a Y in a circle, but a different Y each time. Here it appears as a Rorschach blot.

Next spread
The posters for Yale are a favorite project in the studio, and countless designers and interns on my team have contributed to them over the past 15 years, most notably Kerrie Powell, Michelle Leong, Yve Ludwig, Laitsz Ho, and Jessica Svendsen. John Jacobson at Yale has supervised the work from the start. And, of course, my greatest thanks go to Robert A. M. Stern, whose support has been continuous and inspiring throughout my career.

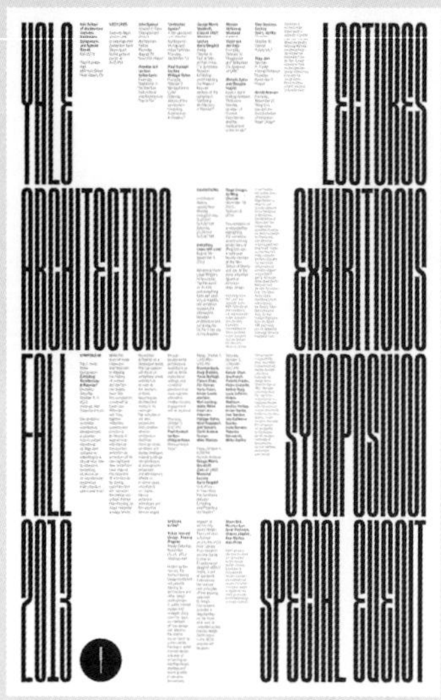
YALE
ARCHITECTURE
FALL
2013
LECTURES
EXHIBITIONS
SYMPOSIUM
SPECIAL EVENT

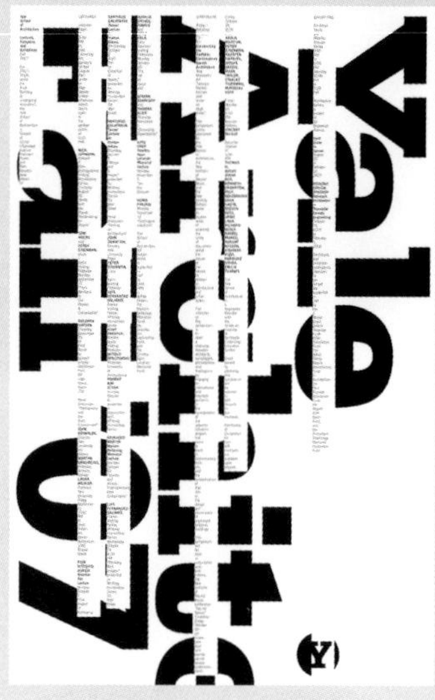
Yale

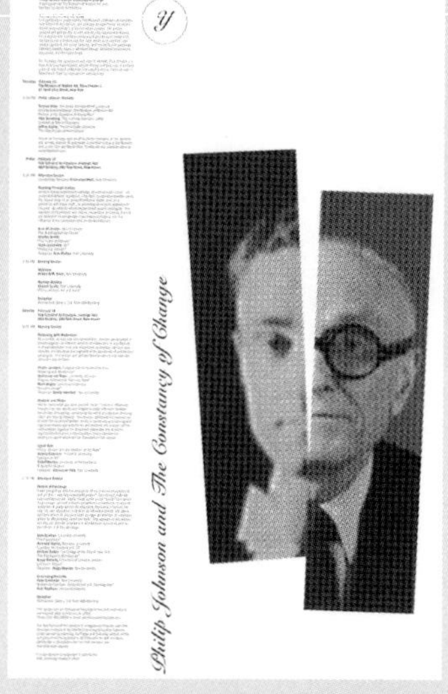
Philip Johnson and The Constancy of Change

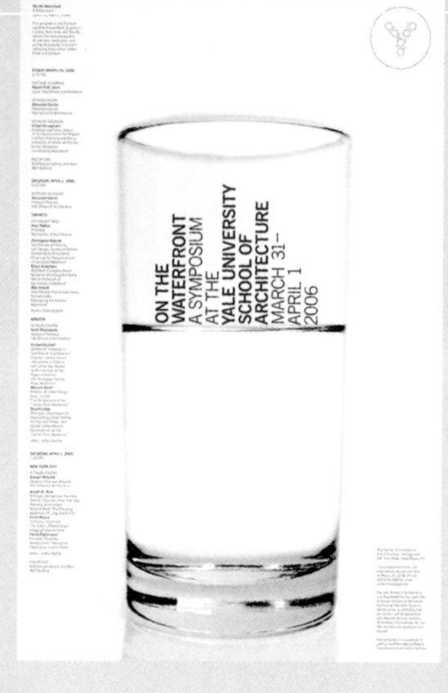
ON THE
WATERFRONT
A SYMPOSIUM
AT THE
YALE UNIVERSITY
SCHOOL OF
ARCHITECTURE
MARCH 31–
APRIL 1
2006

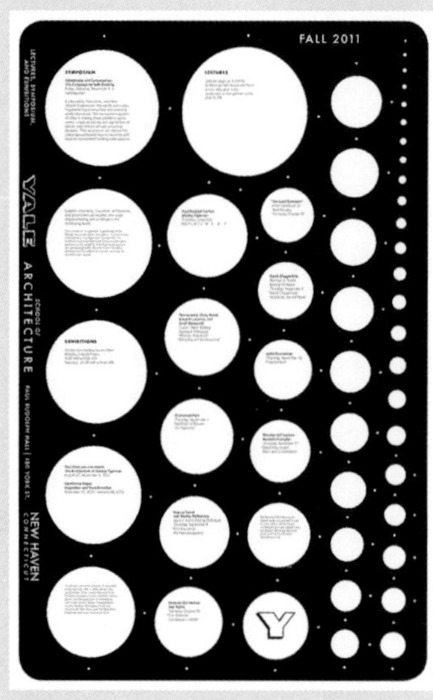
FALL 2011
YALE
ARCHITECTURE

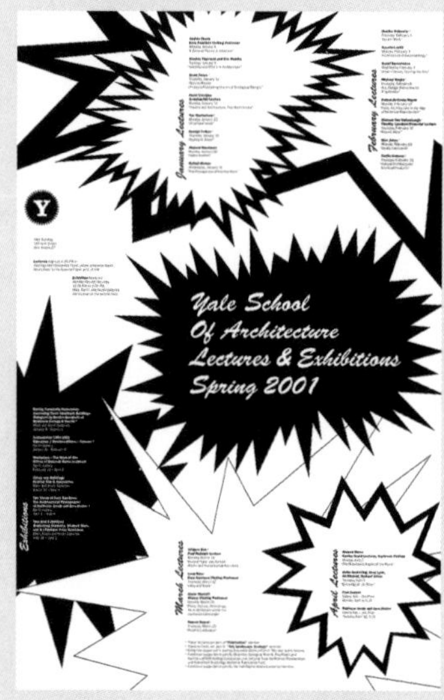
Yale School
Of Architecture
Lectures & Exhibitions
Spring 2001

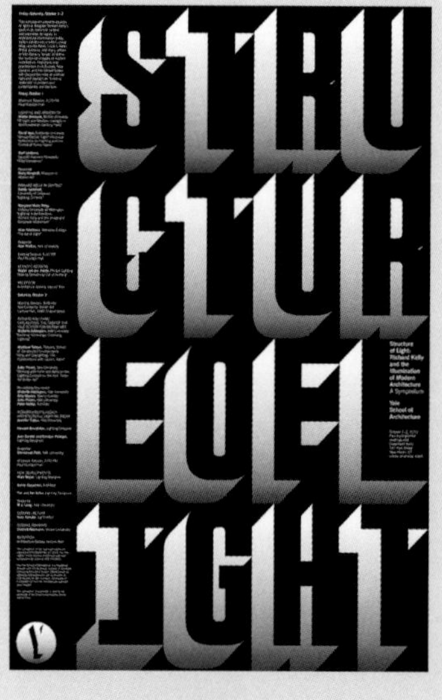

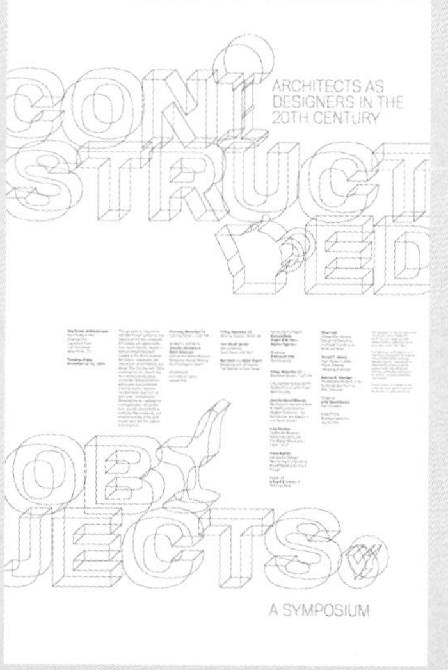
CONSTRUCTED
ARCHITECTS AS
DESIGNERS IN THE
20TH CENTURY
OBJECTS
A SYMPOSIUM

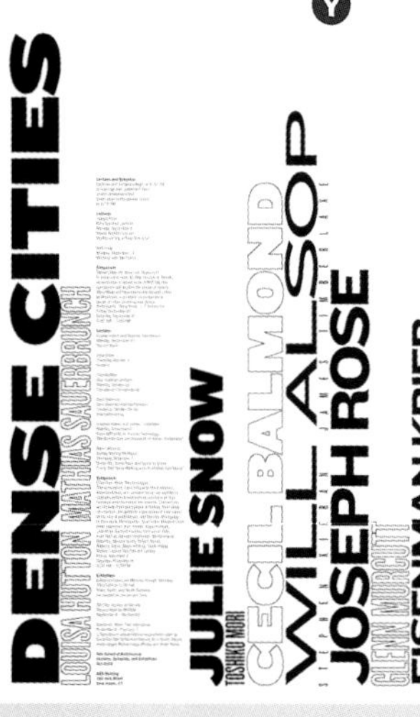
DENSE CITIES
JULIE SNOW
CECIL BALMOND
WILL ALSOP
JOSEPH ROSE
EISENMAN KRIER

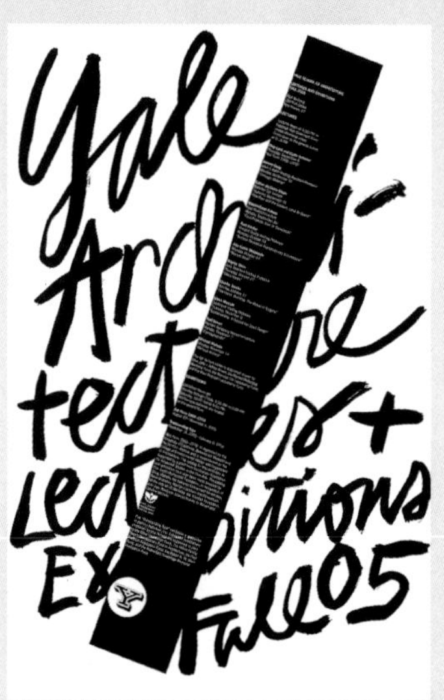
Yale
Architecture
Lectures +
Exhibitions
Fall 05

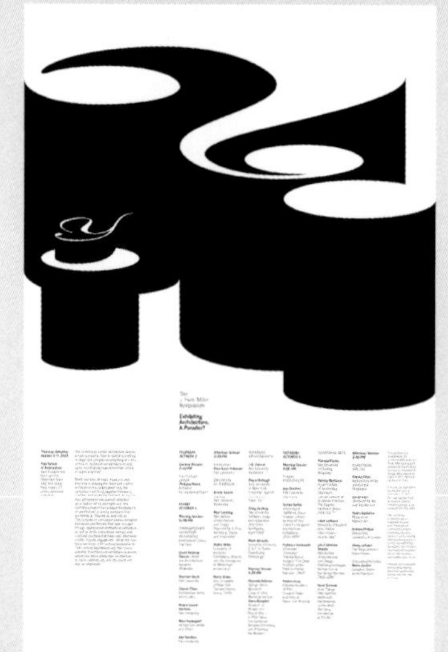

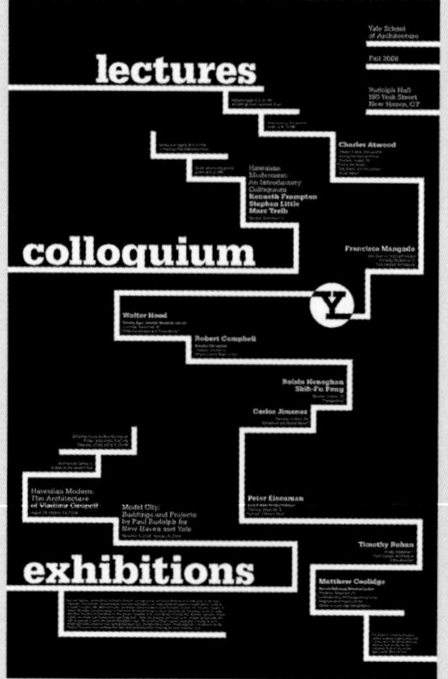
lectures
colloquium
exhibitions

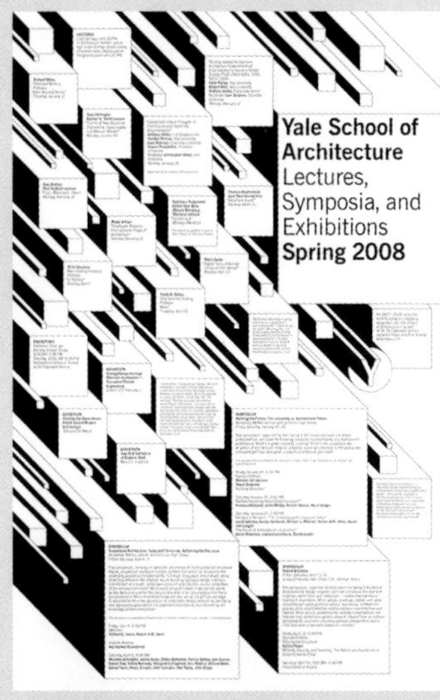
Yale School of Architecture
Lectures, Symposia, and Exhibitions
Spring 2008

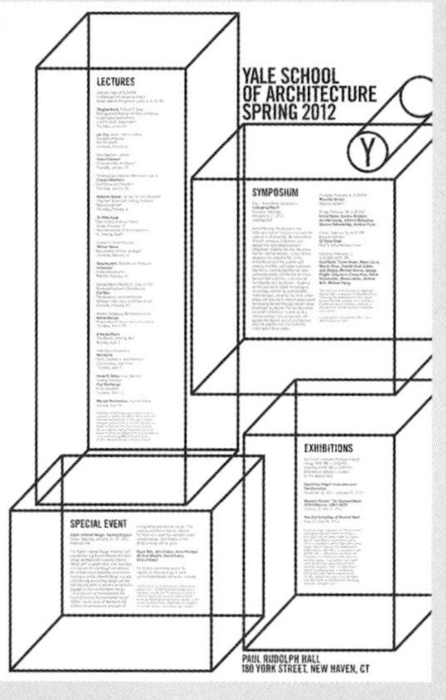
YALE SCHOOL OF ARCHITECTURE SPRING 2012
LECTURES
SYMPOSIUM
EXHIBITIONS
SPECIAL EVENT
PAUL RUDOLPH HALL
180 YORK STREET, NEW HAVEN, CT

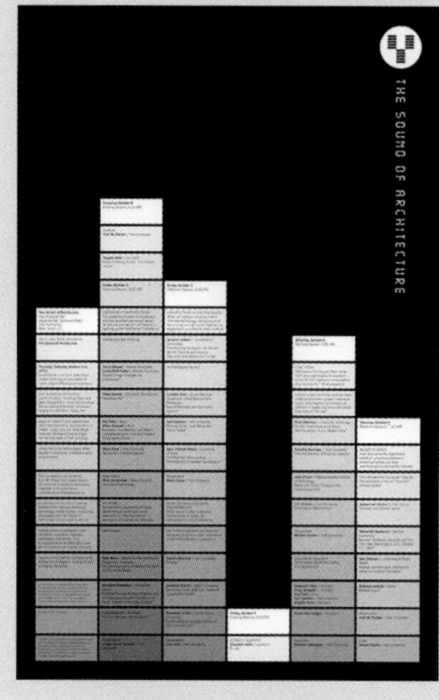
THE SOUND OF ARCHITECTURE

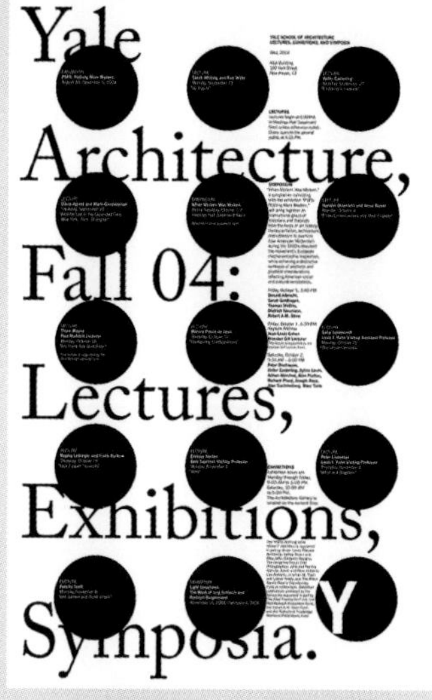
Yale
Architecture,
Fall 04:
Lectures,
Exhibitions,
Symposia.

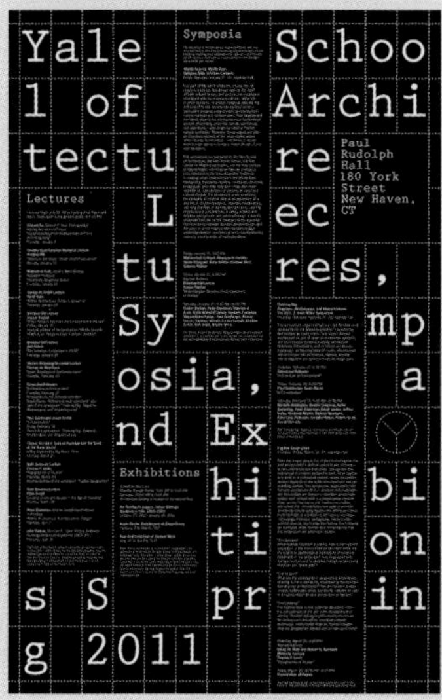
Symposia
Lectures
Exhibitions
Paul Rudolph Hall
180 York Street
New Haven, CT
g 2011

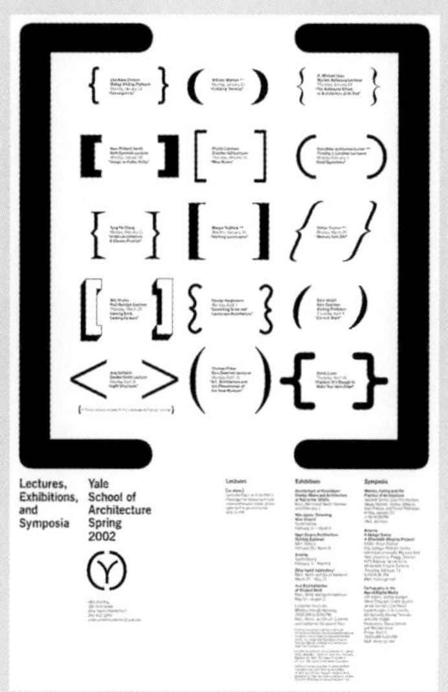
Lectures, Exhibitions, and Symposia
Yale School of Architecture Spring 2002

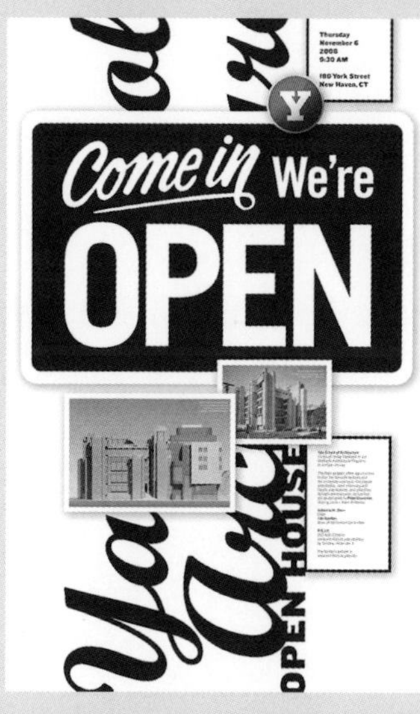
Come in We're
OPEN
Thursday November 6 2008 9:30 AM
180 York Street New Haven, CT
OPEN HOUSE

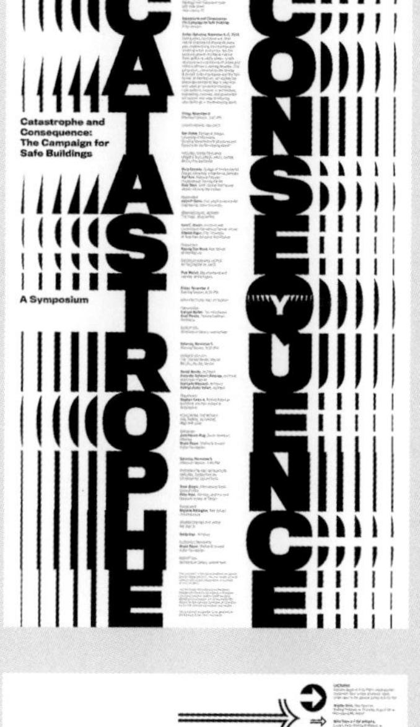
CATASTROPHE
CONSEQUENCE
Catastrophe and Consequence: The Campaign for Safe Buildings
A Symposium

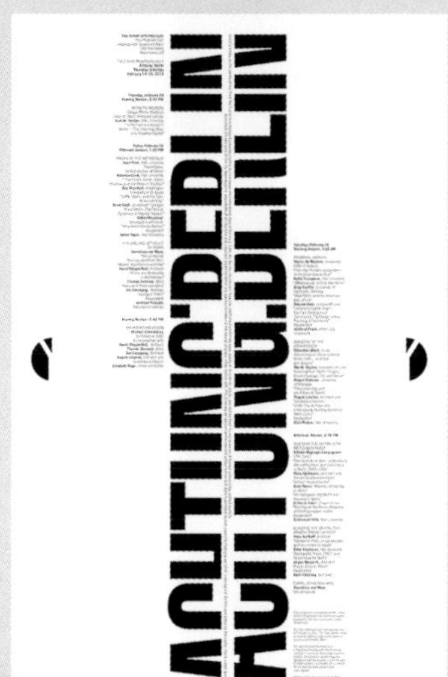

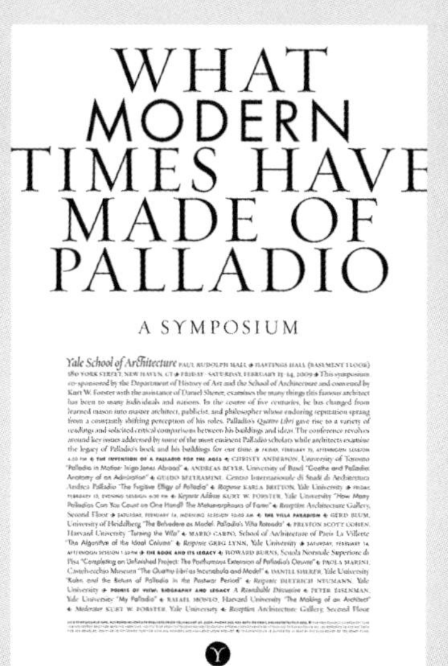
WHAT MODERN TIMES HAVE MADE OF PALLADIO
A SYMPOSIUM

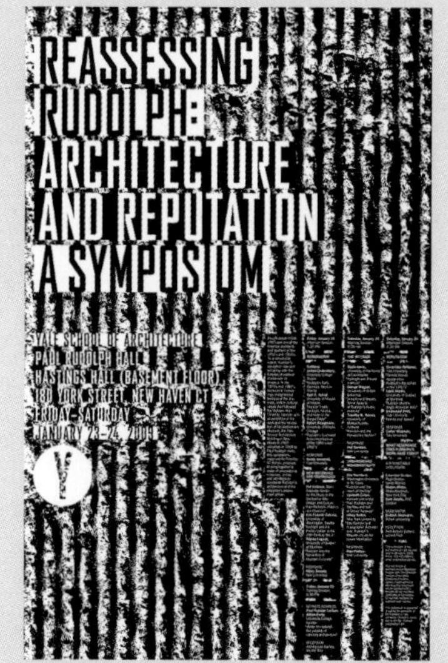
REASSESSING RUDOLPH: ARCHITECTURE AND REPUTATION A SYMPOSIUM

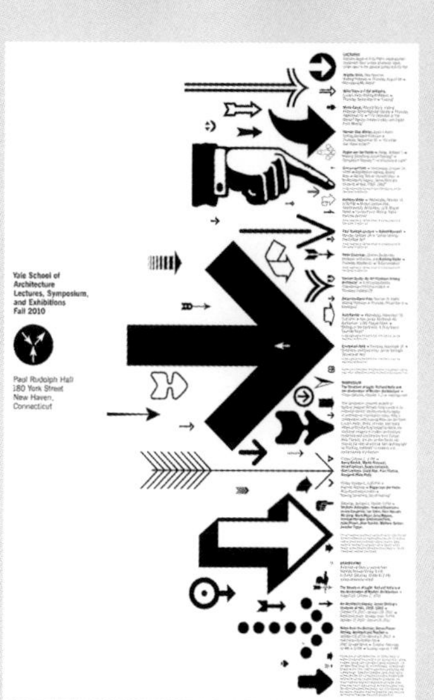
Yale School of Architecture
Lectures, Symposium, and Exhibitions
Fall 2010
Paul Rudolph Hall
180 York Street
New Haven, Connecticut

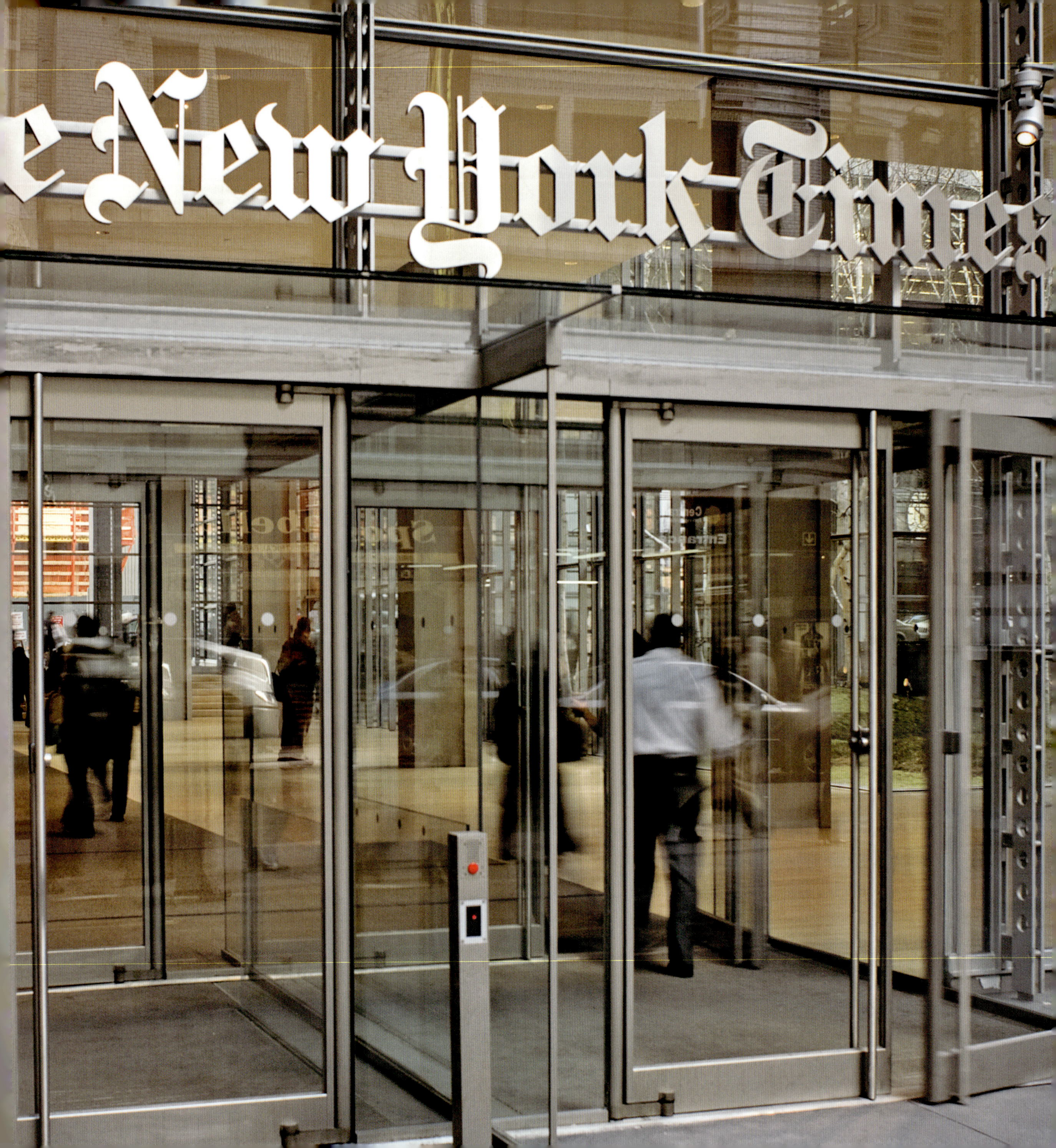
e New York Times

How to put a big sign on a glass building without blocking the view

The New York Times Building

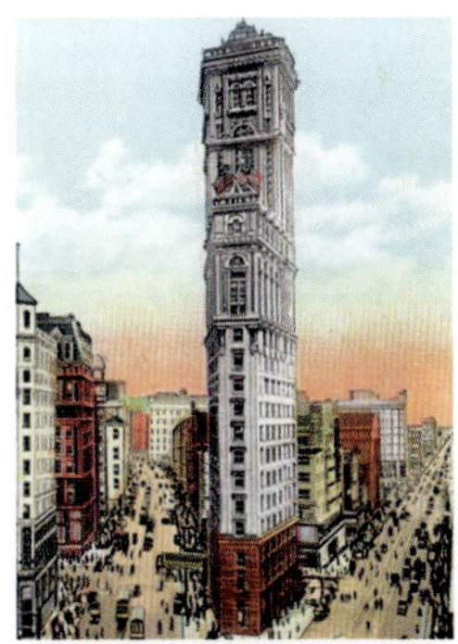

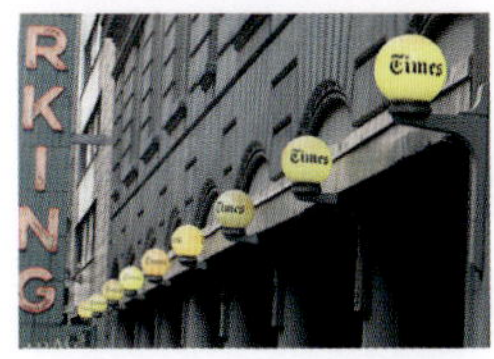

Opposite
Visitors to the *Times* pass beneath the ornate Fraktur of the paper's nameplate, a contrast to the minimalist architecture.

Above top
Times Square is named after the paper's turn-of-the-century headquarters at 42nd and Broadway.

Above bottom
Glass globes marked the truck docks at the *Times*' former 43rd Street facility.

In 2001, the *New York Times* hired the Pritzker Prize-winning architect Renzo Piano to design its new headquarters. For nearly 90 years, the *Times* had operated out of a drab masonry heap on West 43rd Street. It looked like a factory because that's what it was. The newspapers were printed in its basement and loaded on trucks that departed each morning before dawn to deliver the news to the world.

Piano's design, located three blocks south, was radically different: clad in glass from top to bottom, veiled with a sunscreen of horizontal ceramic rods that evoke the lines of type on the paper's front page, it is a hymn to digital immateriality and journalistic transparency.

But there was a problem. The new building sits within a district that is governed by signage restrictions that are unlike any in the nation. Created to preserve the cacophonous character of Times Square, instead of minimizing the size and quantity of signs, they mandate more, bigger, and flashier signs, signs that by law must be attached to buildings rather than integrated into their facades. But where could a sign go on a building that was glass from top to bottom? As the project's sign designers, this was our problem to solve.

Our solution was to install the paper's iconic nameplate, 110 feet long, on the building's Eighth Avenue facade. The sign is made of 959 small teardrop-shaped pieces, each applied precisely to the grid of ceramic rods. The two-inch projections that form the tail of the drops make the sign seem opaque when viewed from below. Viewed straight on—from inside the building—they are nearly invisible.

The building is beautiful, but some feared the staff might miss the decades-old patina of their previous home. In response, we made each sign inside the building—all 800 of them from conference rooms to bathrooms—unique. Each features a different image from the *Times*' vast photo archive, rendered in an exaggerated dot pattern as an homage to the presses that once rumbled each night beneath the reporters' offices.

Like many other designers, my earliest assignments from the *New York Times* were illustrations for their opinion pages: reductive, telegraphic images meant to tempt readers to engage with complex and sometimes dense ideas. This is high-pressure design at its most exciting: you get the job a few days before presentation, your design must be submitted and approved within 24 hours, and it runs in the paper a day later. This immediate gratification is refreshing compared with the months- (or years-) long process associated with most design projects.

Right
George Kennan argues against the expansion of NATO. Extending the acronym negates it.

Below
Invading an oil-rich region as the odometer turns.

THE NEW YORK TIMES **OP-ED** WEDNESDAY, FEBRUARY 5, 1997

NNATOO

Michael Bierut

A Fateful Error

Foreig

THOMAS L

The Neutr

DAVOS, Switzerland

In virtually every article about the dispute between Swiss bankers and Jewish groups over the bank accounts of Holocaust victims, there is a historical reference that is blandly repeated over and over: "Switzerland was neutral during World War II." Every time I read that reference I can't help thinking: What does it mean to be neutral between the perpetrators of the worst crimes against humanity in modern history and their victims? What does it mean to say that the same rules should apply to the money of both? What does it mean to put yourself outside history?

The reason this Nazi banking issue continues to fester is because too many Swiss still insist on being morally neutral, on trying to live off the international system without being fully part of it. As one senior Swiss official remarked to me: "The Swiss people are shocked by this banking affair, because they are not used to seeing themselves on CNN." In their view, they are the victims of a plot to take their quiet little country away, to drag them back into history.

THE NEW YORK TIMES **OP-ED** WEDNESDAY, APRIL 23, 2003

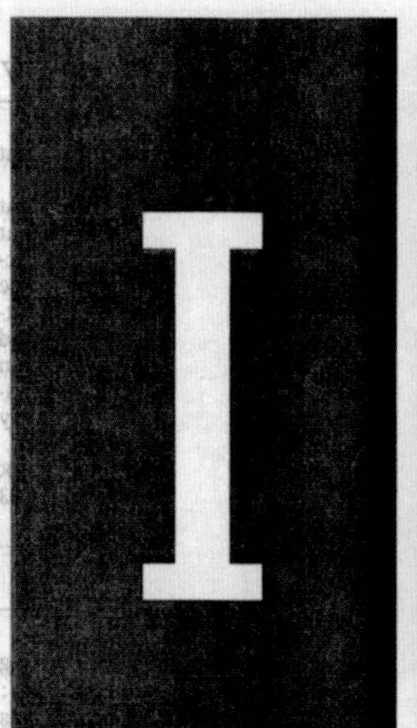

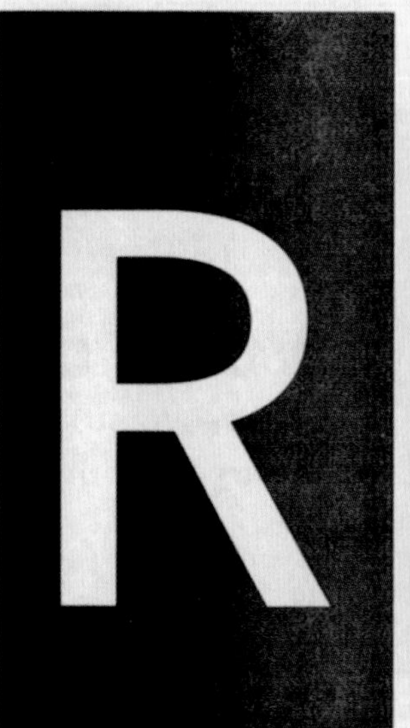

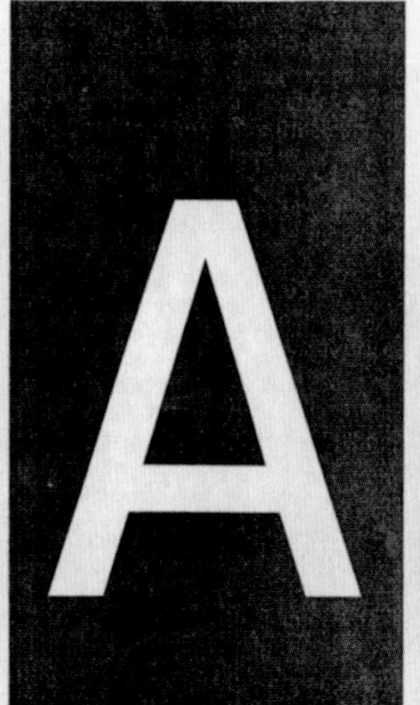

Michael Bierut

Why the Mullahs Love a Revolution

By Dilip Hiro

LONDON

The Bush team's vision for a postwar Iraq was founded on the dreams of exiles and defectors, who promised that Iraqis would shower American troops with flowers. Now, with the crowds shouting, "No to America; no to Saddam," and most Iraqis already referring to the American "occupation," the Bush administration seems puzzled

ity south and the Shiite neighborhoods of Baghdad. Over the centuries, as members of a community that was discriminated against and repressed, the Shiites learned to find comfort in religion and piety to a much greater extent than the ruling Sunnis. In recent decades, Shiite clerics devised clandestine networks of communication that even Saddam Hussein's spies failed to infiltrate. Eschewing written messages or telephones, they used personal envoys who spoke in code. In the wake of Iraq's collapse, this messenger system has proved remarkably efficient.

solid: although he is a Shiite, he lacks any constituency inside Iraq. Nor is he likely to inspire new followers. Had he joined the hundreds of thousands of Shiites who made the pilgrimage to Karbala this week he might have enhanced his standing. But apparently he couldn't be bothered.

Compare this luxury-loving, highly Westernized banker (who was convicted by Jordan in absentia of embezzlement and fraud) with Ayatollah Khomeini, the ascetic Iranian Shiite cleric who shunned worldly goods and and led a popular revolution that over-

nial government had to call in troops from the Indian Army to quell it. By the time they restored order, 6,500 people were dead, all but 500 Iraqi civilians. The 1920 revolt is the crucible in which Iraqi nationalism was formed. That unity showed its durability during Iraq's armed conflict with the predominantly Shiite Iran in the 1980's. To the complete surprise of the Iranians, Saddam Hussein managed to retain the loyalty of the Iraqi Army, where Shiite conscripts formed a majority.

Thus the only viable solution for

THOMAS L.

Regime Ch

While the war in Iraq has rightly grabbed all the attention in the Middle East, another effort at regime change has also been going on in the neighborhood, and it's been quite a drama. It's the silent coup that Palestinian moderates, led by Mahmoud Abbas, have been trying to undertake against Yasir Arafat.

Mr. Arafat was forced by the Palestinian legislature to designate Mr. Abbas (a k a Abu Mazen) as his first prime minister. The move was openly designed to diminish Mr. Arafat's power and to ease him upstairs, if not out the door. Mr. Abbas has been trying to assemble a cabinet, and Mr. Arafat has been fighting him at every turn — trying to stuff the cabinet with his cronies and deny Mr. Abbas the key security portfolios. Mr. Arafat "fears he will not be the strongman in the coming phase," a Palestinian legislator, Hassan Khraisheh, told The Associated Press in Jerusalem.

He's right, but Mr. Arafat is no pushover, and if Mr. Abbas and his allies in the Palestinian legislature are to prevail, they will need help. America, Europe, Israel and the Arab states should all pitch in.

The Bush team has a huge strategic stake in the outcome of this Palestinian struggle, because it will affect America's room for maneuvering in Iraq. Let me explain. What does America want in Iraq? It wants the emergence of an Iraqi political center, of both parties and politicians, who are authentically Iraqi, authentically nationalist and respectful of Islam — but with a progressive, modernizing agenda and a willingness to

Left top
Joyce Carol Oates on the passive-aggressive ironies of anonymity.

Left bottom
The formerly pacifist left supports armed intervention in Kosovo.

Below top
The consequences of split decisions from the Supreme Court. Lucky for me, their building has eight columns.

Below bottom
Readers react to the abrupt finale to *The Sopranos*.

The Art Of Being No One

By Joyce Carol Oates

PRINCETON, N.J.

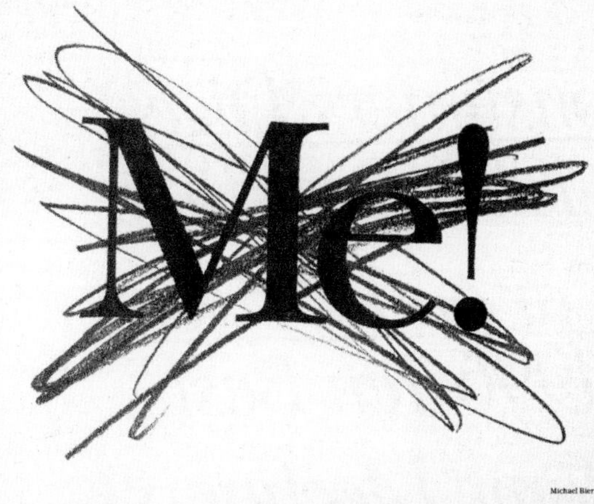

Michael Bierut

Joe Klein has literary history

Welfare b… let kids s…

THE NEW YORK TIMES **OP-ED** FRIDAY, APRIL 2, 1999

Give War a Chance

Michael Bierut

not believe that Russia will rush to the aid of its Serb-Orthodox brethren. Unlike the czar's divisions in 1914, the

"will not allow itself to be drawn into military conflict." It is always easier to heed the call of obligation when the risks are low

The Supreme Court

The Night We Watched as Tony Went . . .

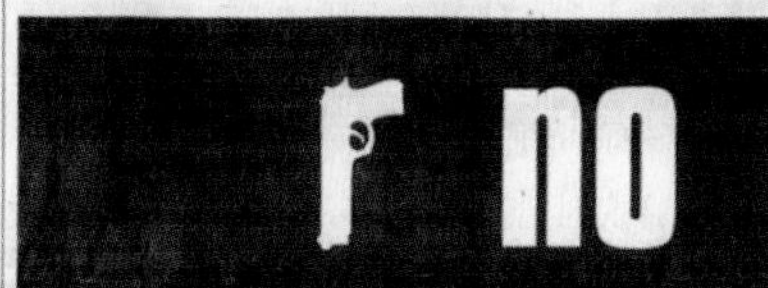

Michael Bierut

To the Editor:
Re "One Last Family Gathering: You Eat, You Talk, It's Over," by Alessandra Stanley (The TV Watch, front page, June 11):
I'm not mad at David Chase, creator of "The Sopranos," for leaving Tony in a diner at the end, alive, and eating onion rings with Carmela and the kids (let's believe that Meadow makes it to her seat).
Where else could the story have closed more compassionately than at a small Formica table?

To the Editor:
The last episode of "The Sopranos" is neither a prank nor a joke.
I believe that David Chase's brilliant ending is in the mind of Tony Soprano, whose world goes dark at that moment.
ELIZABETH SEYDEL MORGAN
Richmond, Va., June 11, 2007

Cut the Nuclear Arsenal

To the Editor:
Re "Nasty, Unfinished Cold War Business" (editorial, June 9): Ever since August 1945, mankind has known how to destroy itself with atomic bombs. How to avoid doing so must be at the top of every country's agenda, and our children and grandchildren must be kept aware of the danger.
When the Soviet Union had 100 bombs and seemed close to using them, I was scared. Now, 15,000 bombs do not scare me anymore. But the sooner we reduce the number to 100, the better.
Better still, but more difficult, will be a comprehensive treaty that keeps these weapons out of international disagreements. What is holding us back?
RICHARD WILSON
Cambridge, Mass., June 10, 2007
The writer is emeritus professor of physics at Harvard University.

Orthopedic Surgery

To the Editor:
Re "Health Care as if Costs Didn't Matter," by David Leonhardt (Economix column, June 6):

To create the main sign on the *Times*' building, each letter in its logo was divided into narrow horizontal strips, ranging in number from 26 (the i in "Times") to 161 (the Y in "York"). Pentagram designer Tracey Cameron labored for months with the designers at Renzo Piano Building Workshop and their associated architects, FXFowle, working and reworking the exact pattern. Despite tests, we were never sure it would work. Riding an uptown Eighth Avenue bus, I startled my fellow passengers by clapping when I saw the first letters installed.

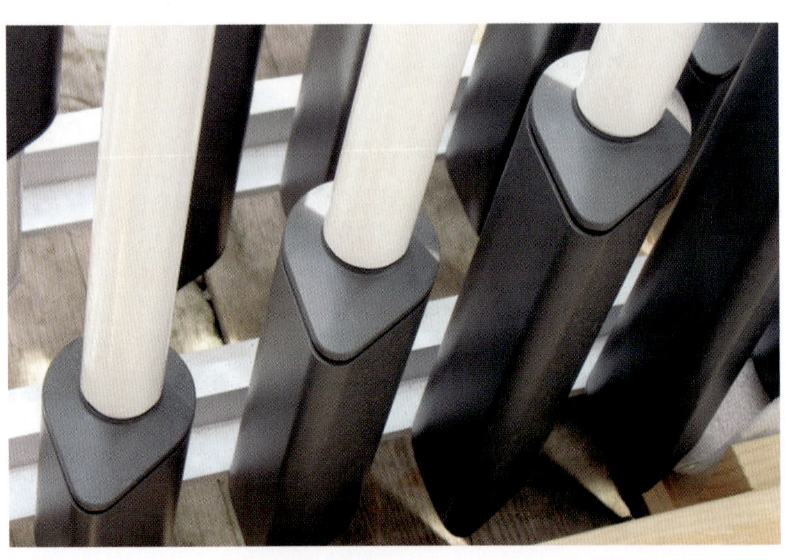

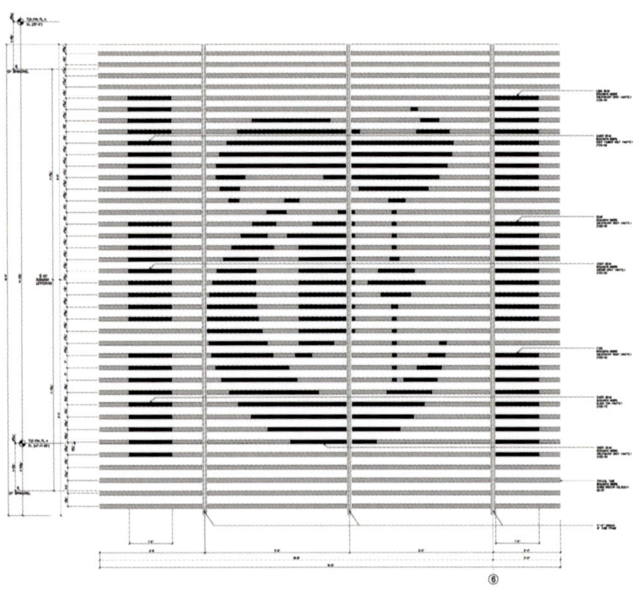

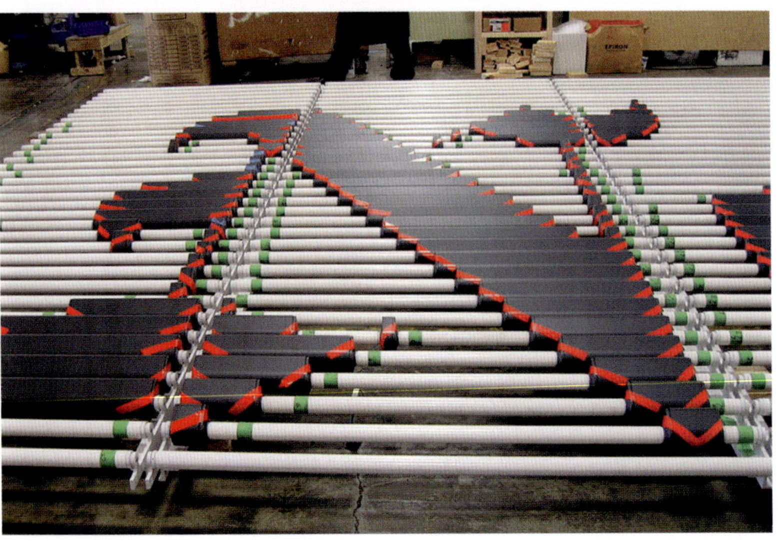

Left top
Each precisely located element has a projecting "beak."

Left below
When viewed from below the projections overlap, creating the illusion of opacity.

Above
The horizontal rods that hold the sign were designed to mediate heat gain and loss in the glass-clad skyscraper.

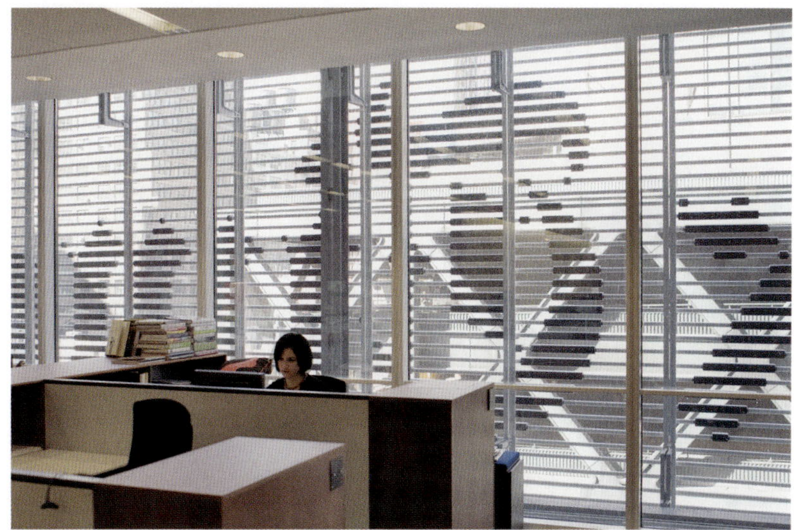

Left
Viewed from inside, the logo barely blocks the view (of, alas, the Port Authority Bus Terminal).

Below
The *Times*' signature Fraktur is a custom version by master type designer Matthew Carter, rendered here at 10,116 point.

Next spread
At one point, I suggested that we consider a subtle white-on-white sign that would disappear at certain times. The paper's CEO, Arthur Sulzberger Jr., looked at me as if I were crazy and said, "Well, the logo is black on the front page, isn't it?"

Following spread
The project manager for the *Times*, the irrepressible David Thurm, asked for ways to bring the paper's history to the new location. The result was 800-plus different room and door signs.

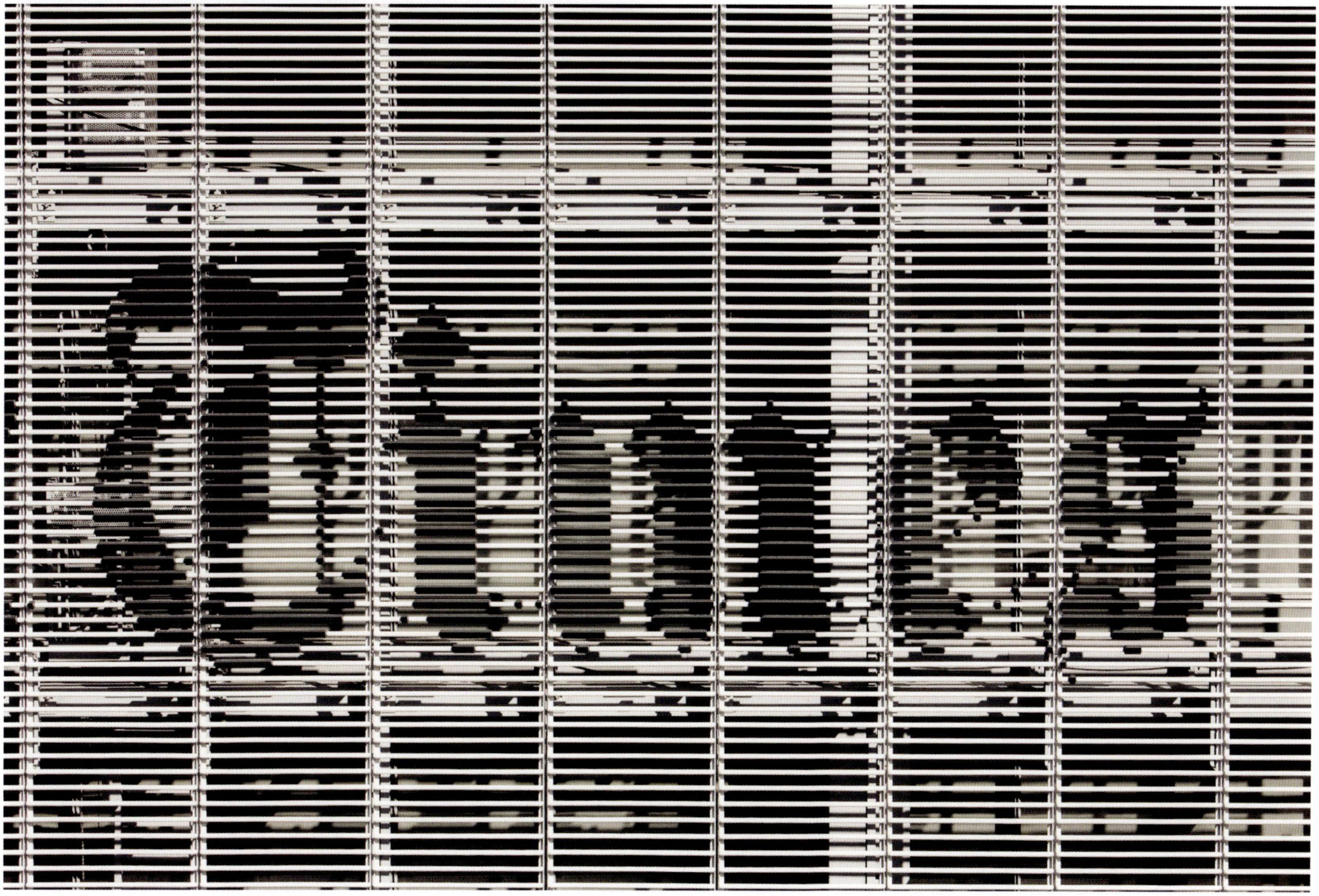

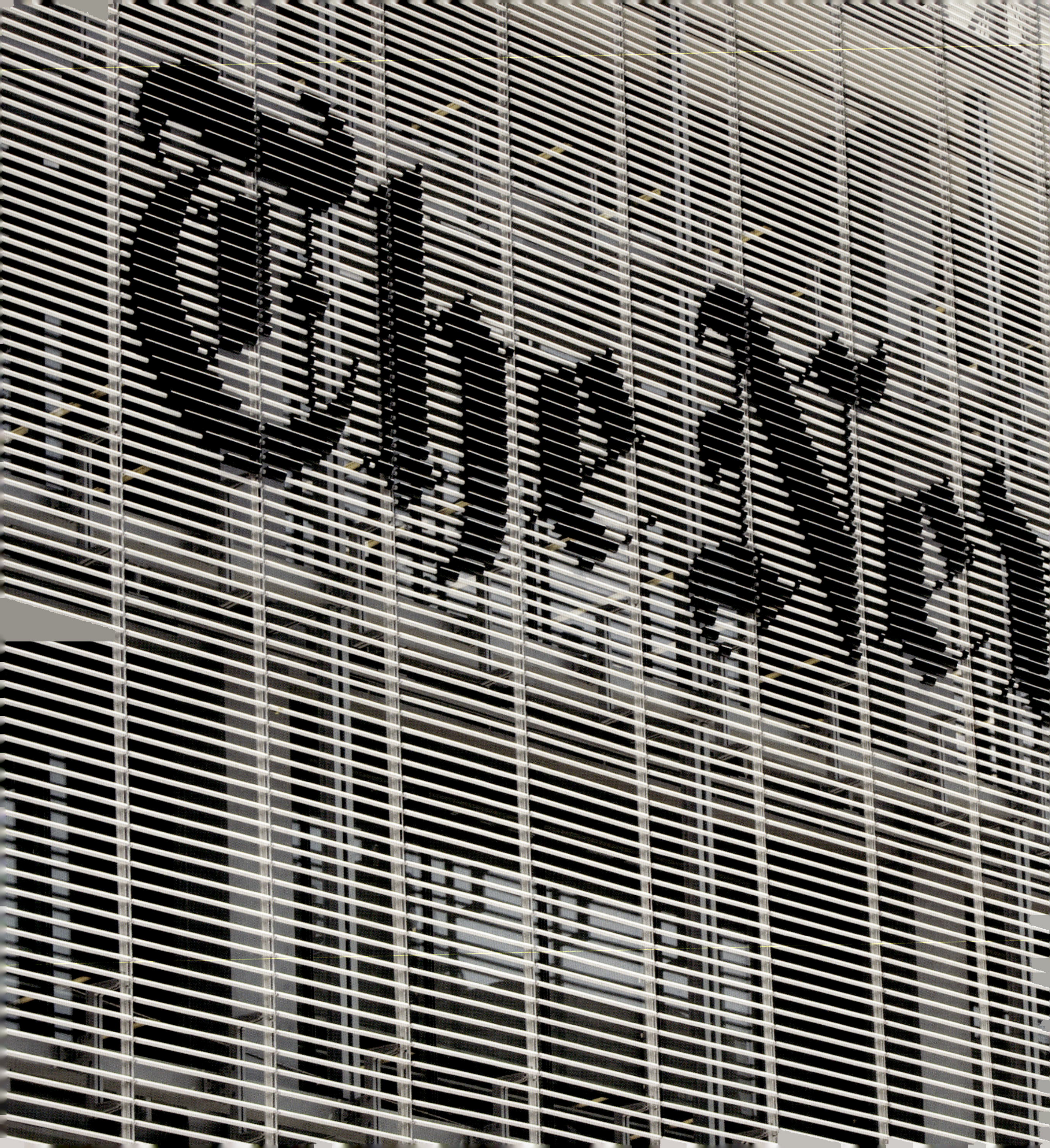
The

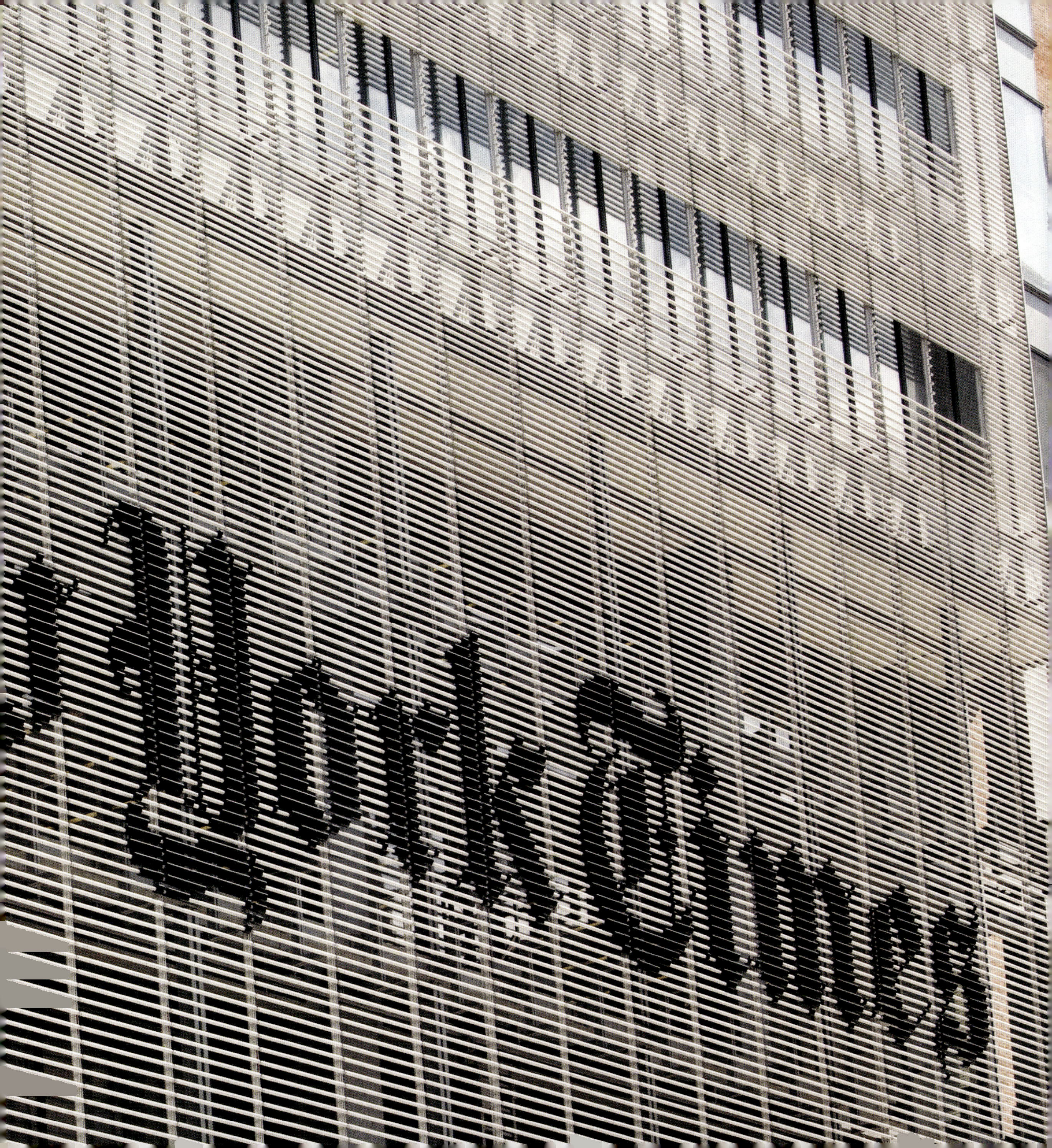
York Times

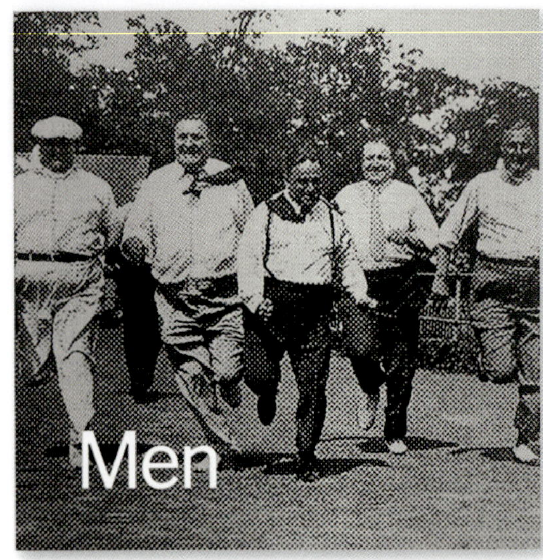
Men

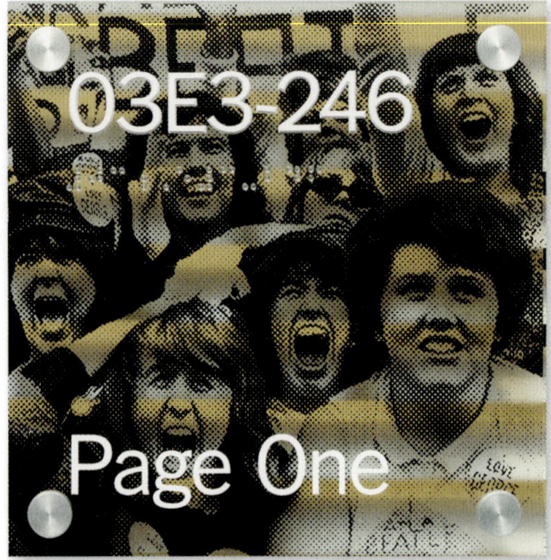
03E3-246
Page One

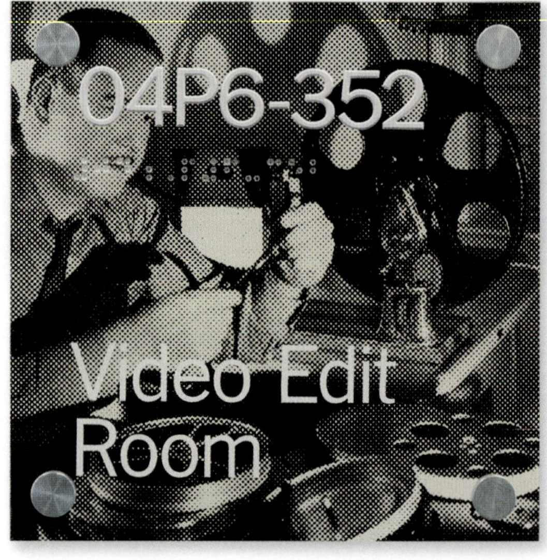
04P6-352
Video Edit
Room

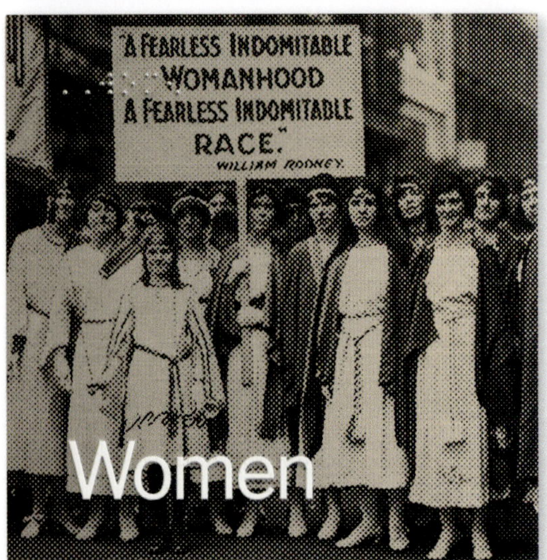
"A FEARLESS INDOMITABLE
WOMANHOOD
A FEARLESS INDOMITABLE
RACE."
WILLIAM RODNEY
Women

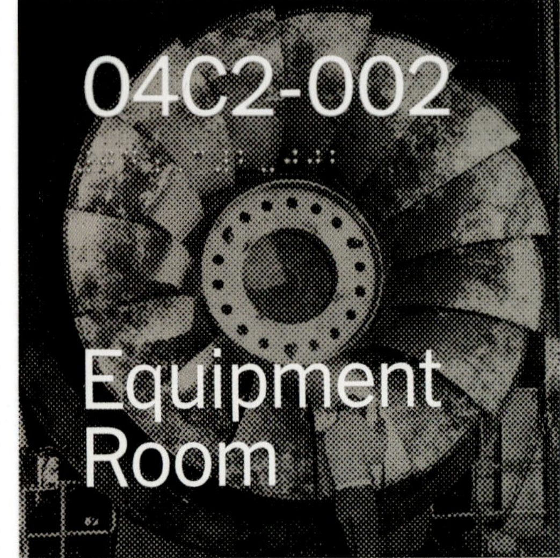
04C2-002
Equipment
Room

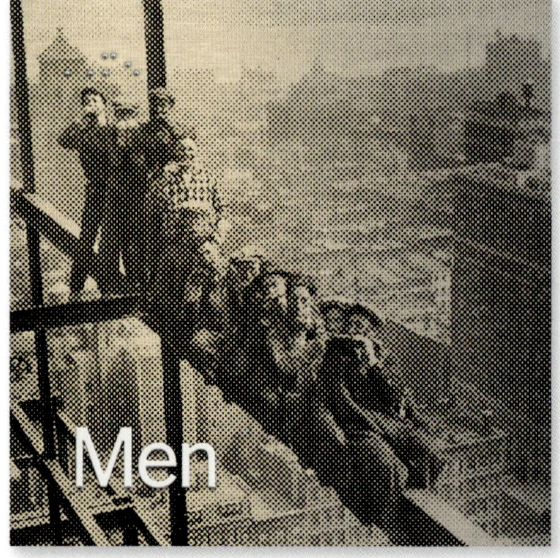
Men

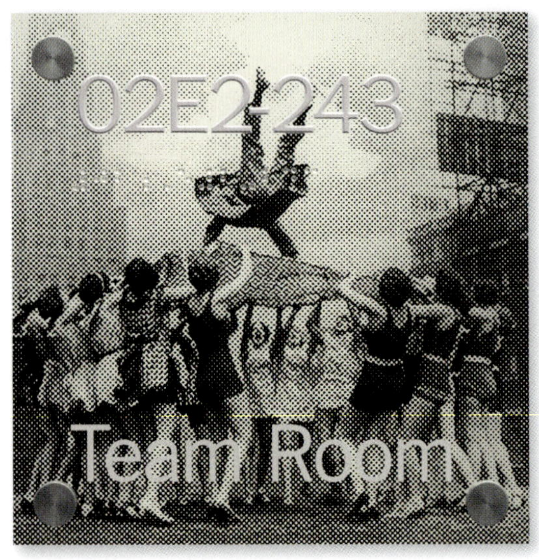
02E2-243
Team Room

21C1-007
Stat Room

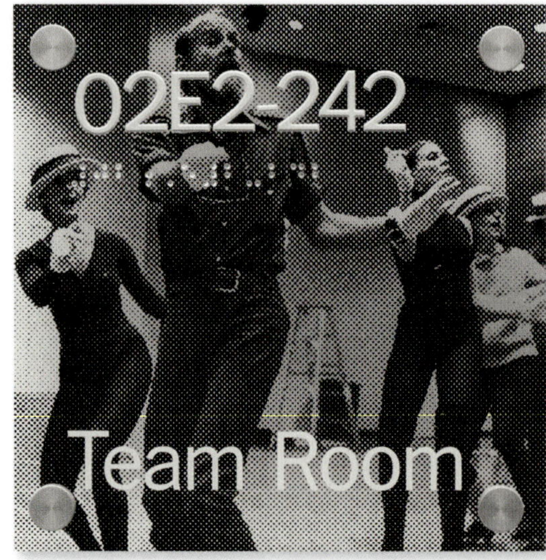
02E2-242
Team Room

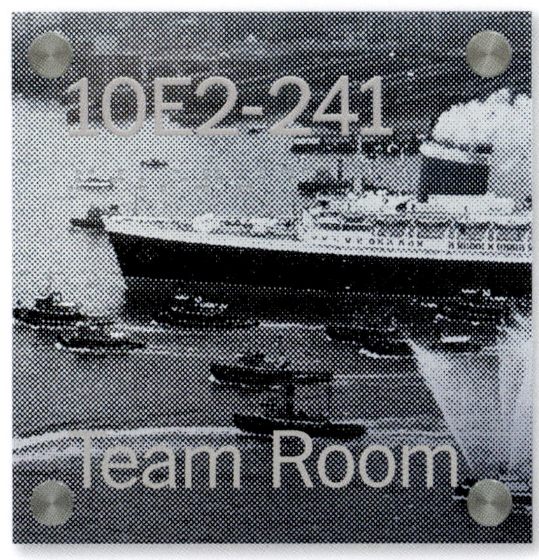
10F2-241
Team Room

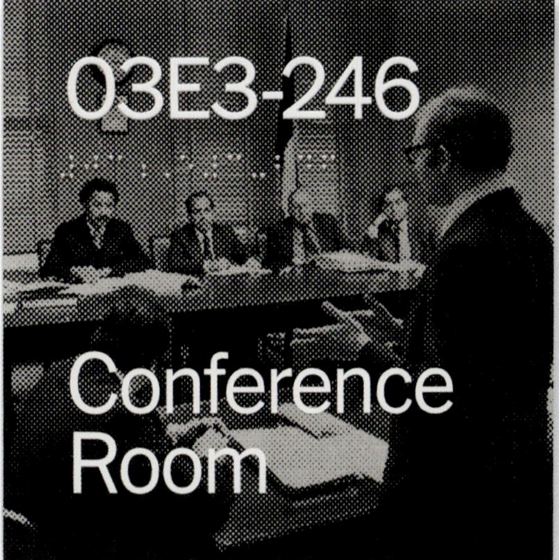
03E3-246
Conference
Room

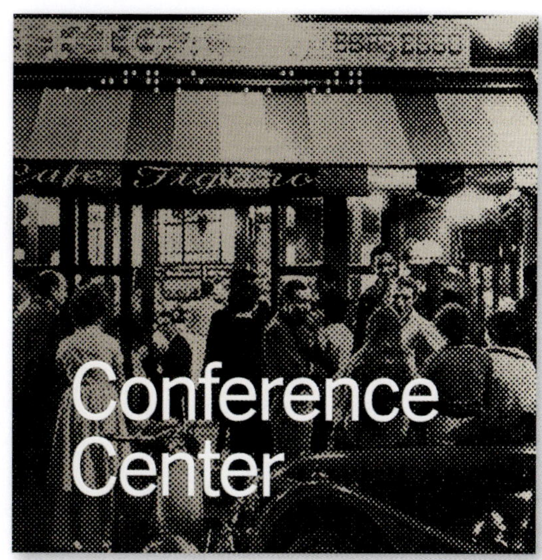
Conference
Center

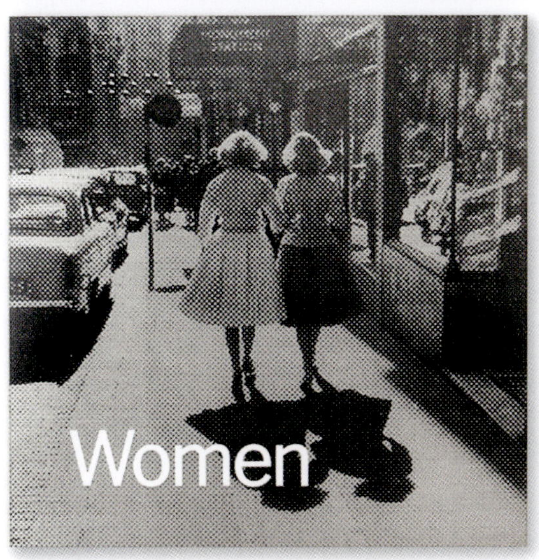
Women

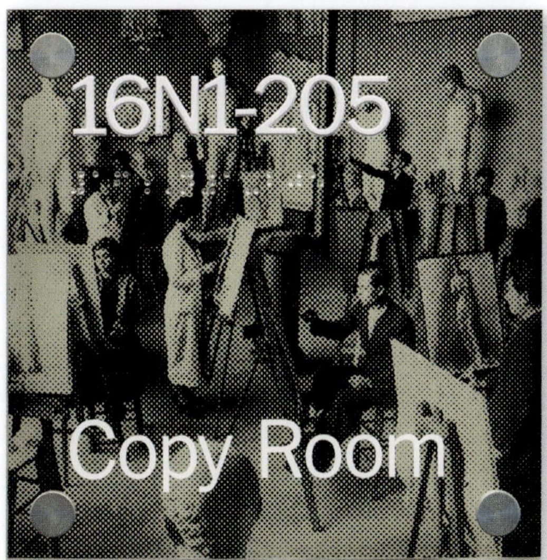
16N1-205
Copy Room

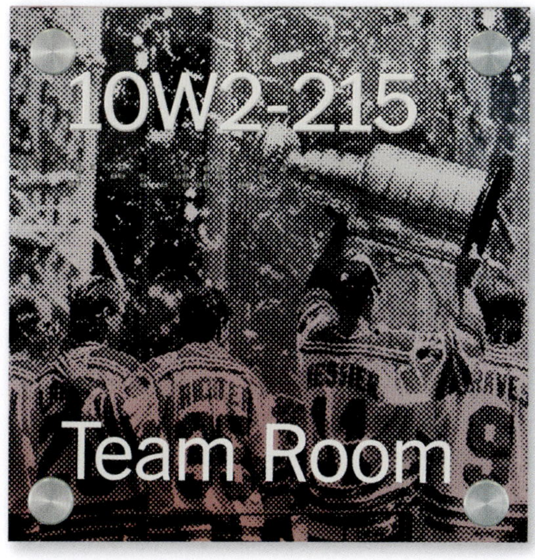
10W2-215
Team Room

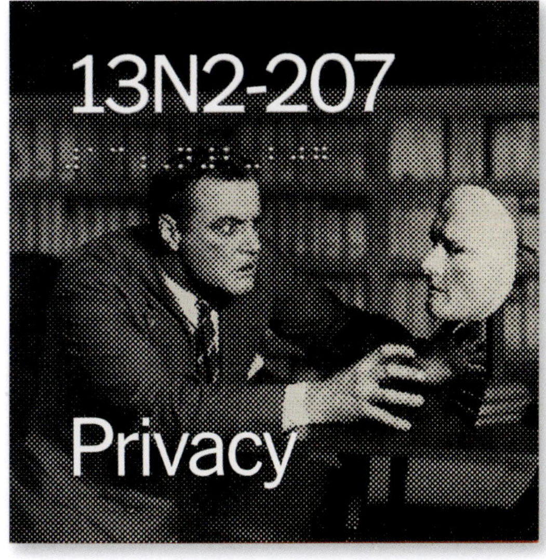
13N2-207
Privacy

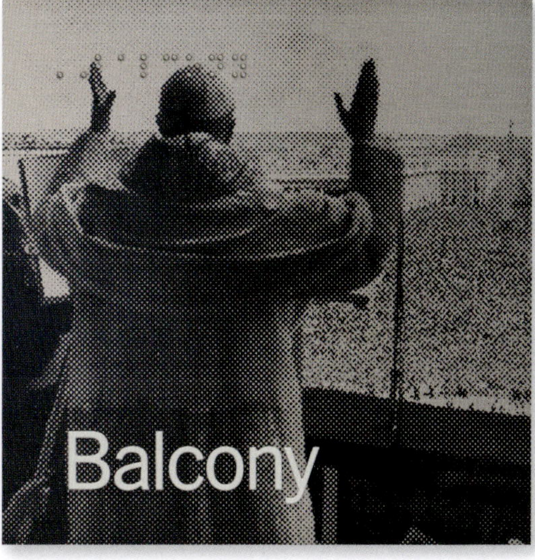
Balcony

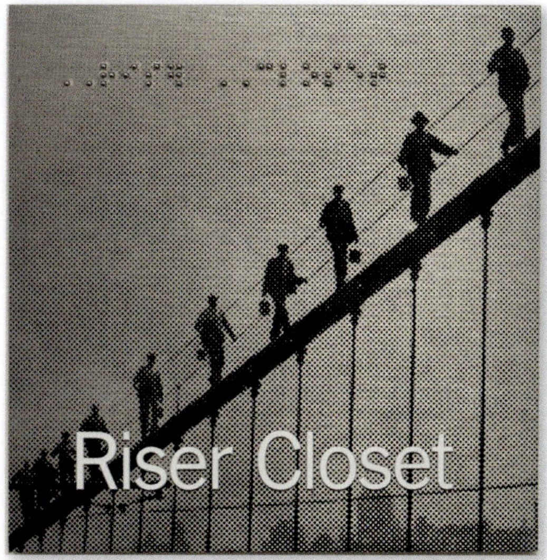
Riser Closet

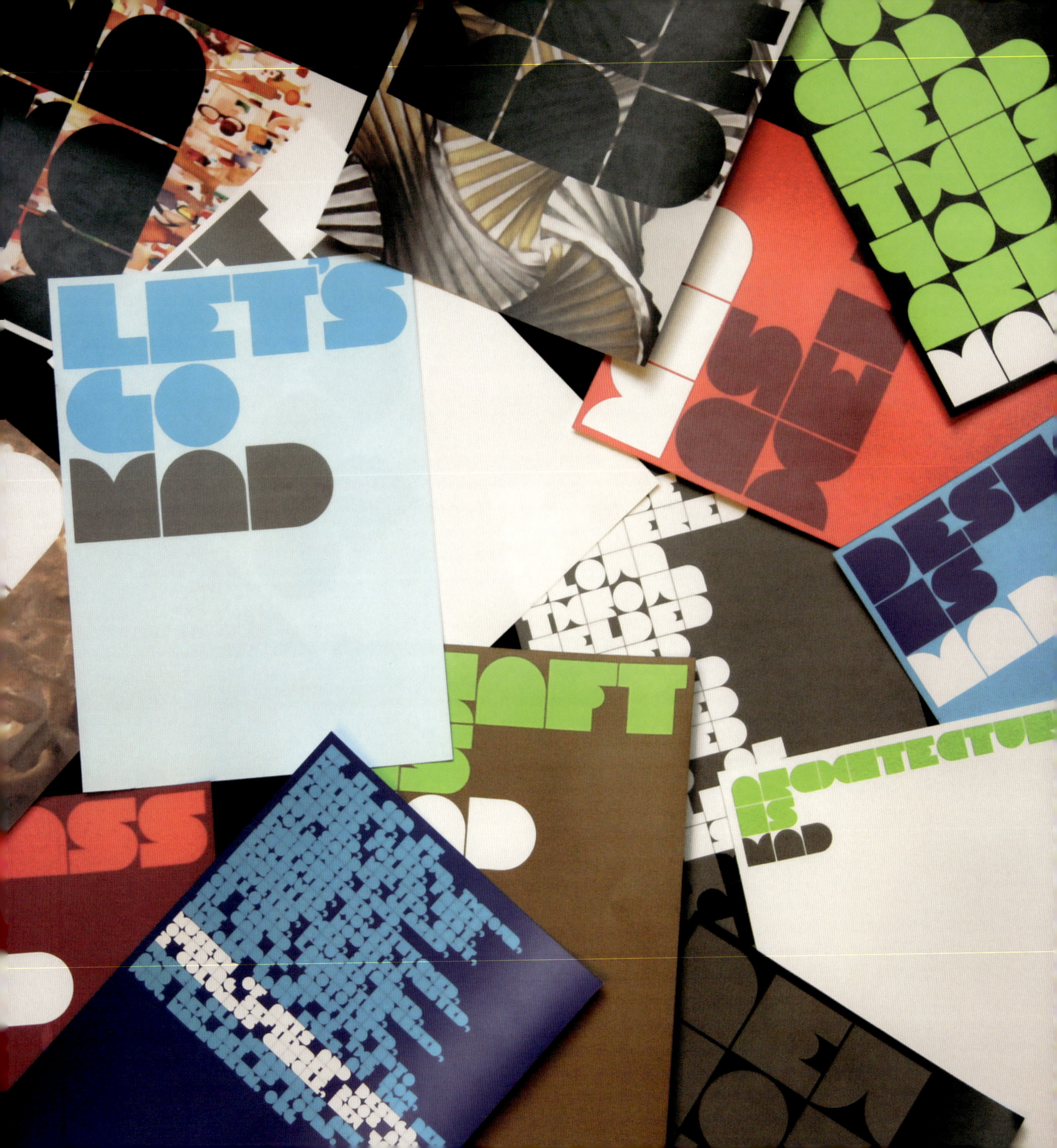
LET'S
GO
MAD

How to make a museum mad

Museum of Arts and Design

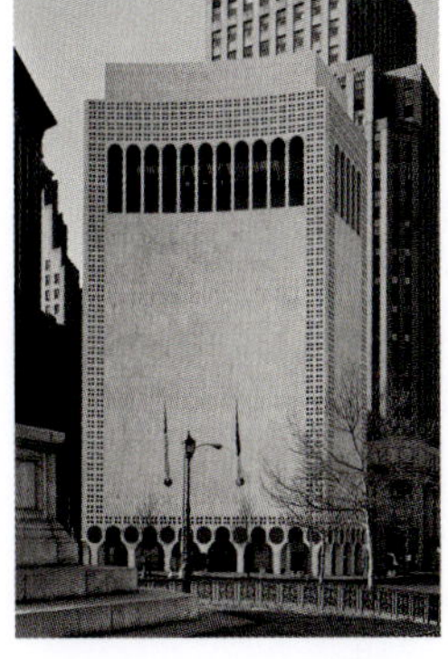

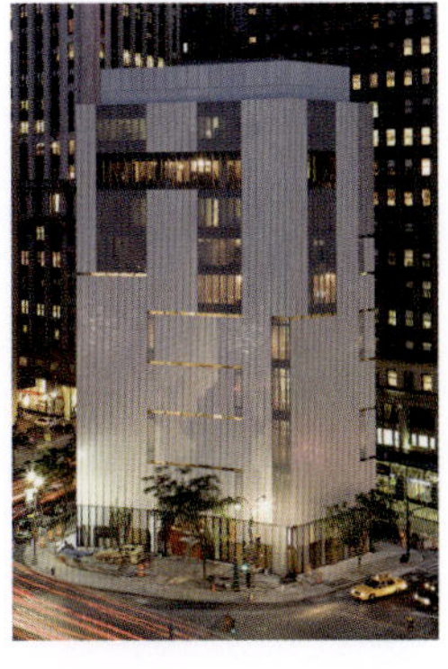

Opposite
Our identity for the Museum of Arts and Design generated a new graphic language for its new home.

Above left
Edward Durell Stone's building at 2 Columbus Circle was one of New York's most polarizing pieces of architecture.

Above right
Brad Cloepfil's controversial redesign transformed a dark warren of rooms into an interconnected series of light-filled spaces.

The Museum of Arts and Design had a long-running identity crisis. Founded in 1956 as the Museum of Contemporary Crafts, it renamed itself the American Craft Museum in 1986. In 2002, it changed its name yet again, to the Museum of Arts and Design, MAD for short. Despite the nifty acronym, five years later most people still hadn't heard of it.

But that was about to change. On Columbus Circle, where Broadway, 59th Street, and Central Park West intersect to form an awkward square, stood a peculiar structure. Completed in 1964 and designed by Edward Durell Stone as a museum for the collection of grocery-store heir Huntington Hartford, it was described by critic Ada Louise Huxtable as a "die-cut Venetian palazzo on lollipops." Hartford's museum lasted only five years. The orphaned building reverted to the city. In 2002, it was offered to the Museum of Arts and Design.

It needed work. Architect Brad Cloepfil proposed a deft transformation, cutting a continuous slot that snaked through its floors, ceilings, and walls. We were asked to create a new graphic identity to mark the rebirth. Inspired by Cloepfil's design, I proposed a logo similarly made of a single line. It was one of the best ideas I ever had.

There was only one problem: it didn't work, at least not with the name MAD. Luckily, I had heard that some people thought the acronym was undignified. I seized on this and proposed a name change to A+D, which emphasized the institution's areas of focus and, conveniently, could be made to work with my idea. I presented this in a series of meetings, armed with ever more elaborate prototypes. But I could not make the sale. If you have a great idea but can't make it work, it isn't a great idea.

That night, I stared at the site. MAD would face the only complete traffic circle in Manhattan. Squares and circles. I looked at the three letters in the name. Could squares and circles be found there as well? The answer was yes. The simplest geometry solved the problem. No longer necessary were straining machinations and feverish salesmanship. Here was that rare thing: a solution that sold itself. It was approved unanimously at the next meeting.

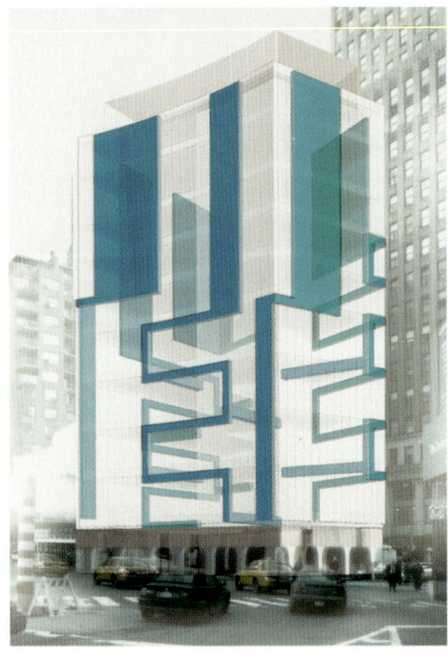

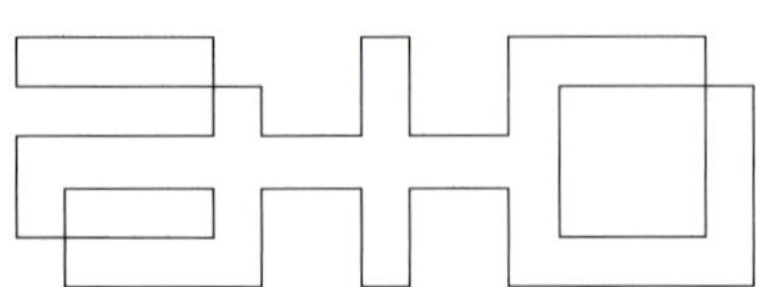

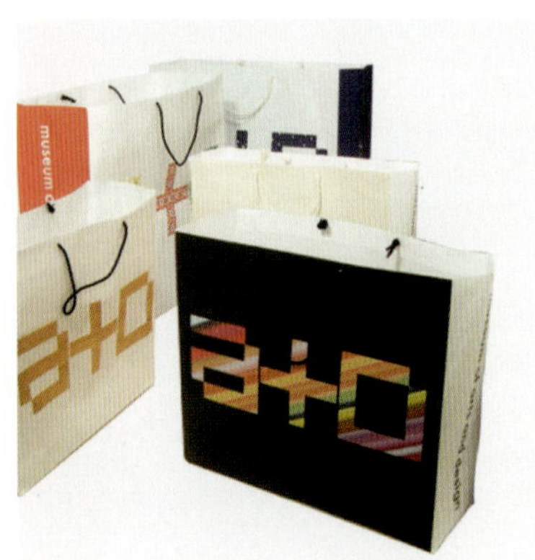

Left top
I was mesmerized by Cloepfil's diagram showing a continuous slot working its way through the building, and used it for my first design concept.

Left middle
Determined to make a logo that echoed the architecture, and finding it would not work with the letters in MAD, I proposed an unlikely name change, to A+D. The client didn't buy it.

Left bottom
Despite multiple meetings and dozens of handmade prototypes, the client was unconvinced. Deep down, so was I.

Below
My second approach abandoned intricate complexity in favor of squares and circles. Once again, simplicity wins.

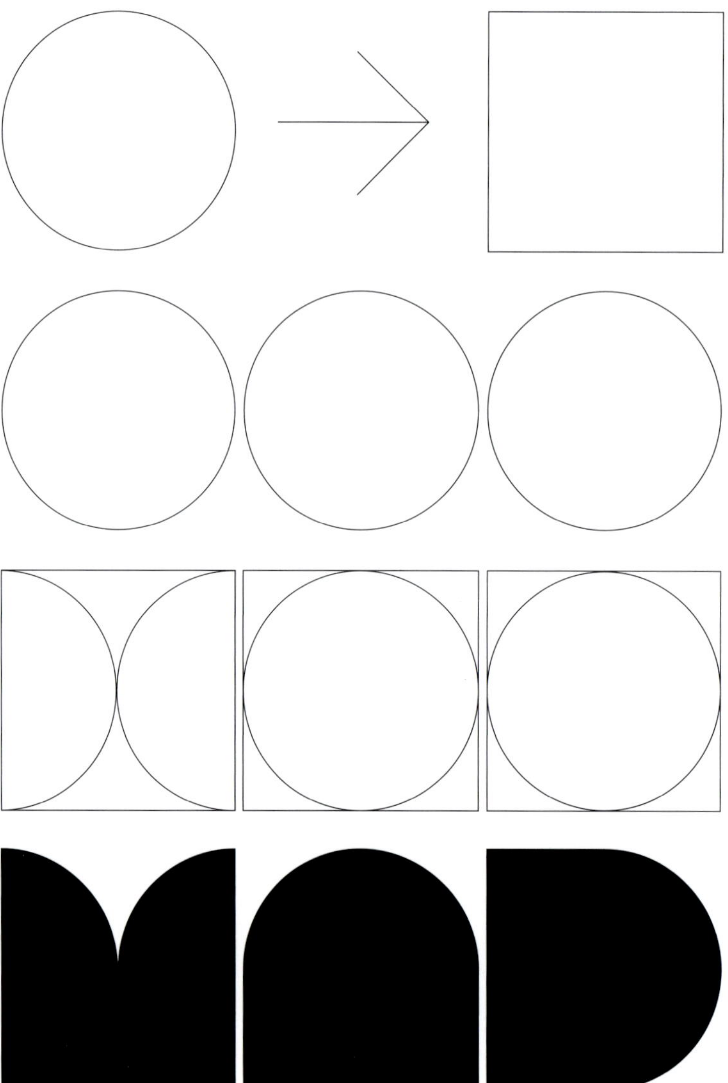

Right
As befits an institution dedicated to craft, the logo is a common form that can be rendered in many materials. Its curved tops are also a sly reference to the building's original "lollipop" columns, visible even after the redesign.

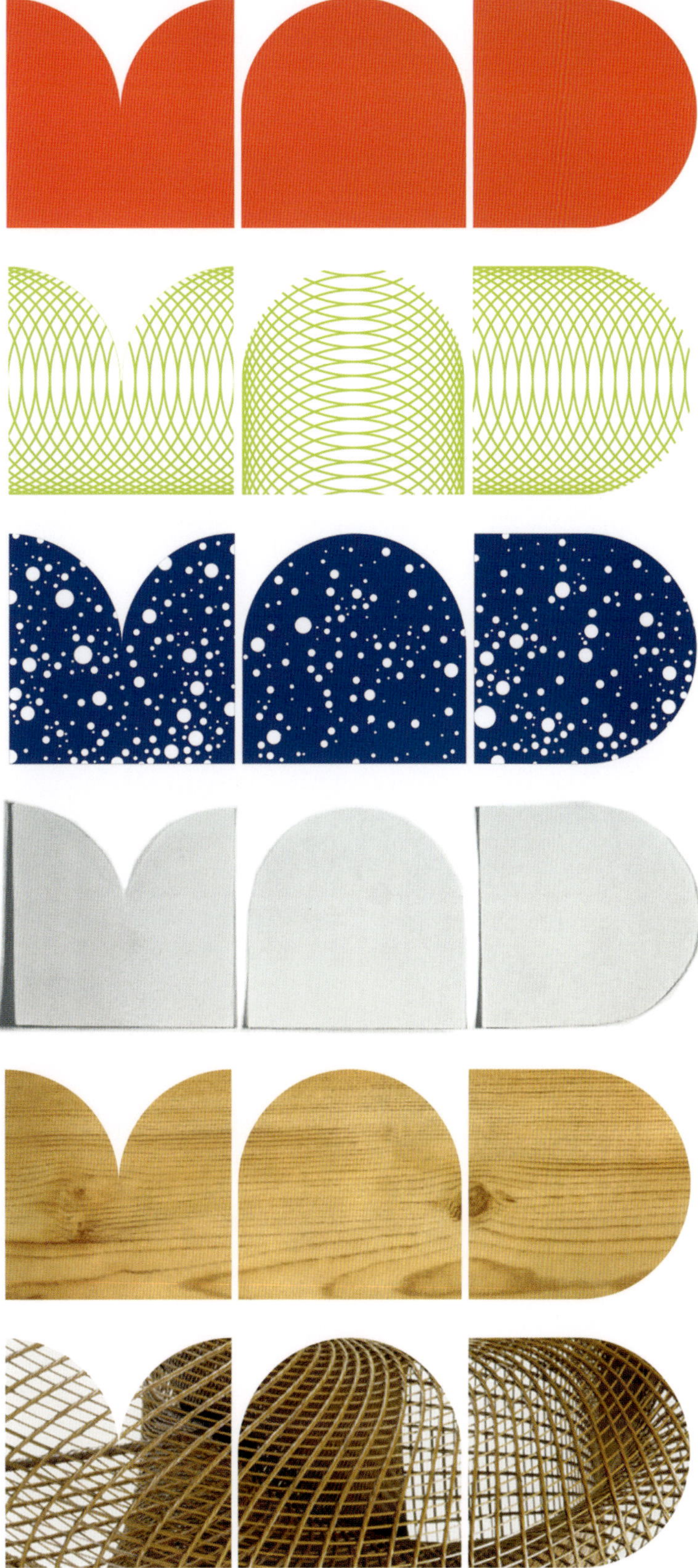

Below
Unlike the original design idea, which required special handling, the new logo was easily adapted to almost any use.

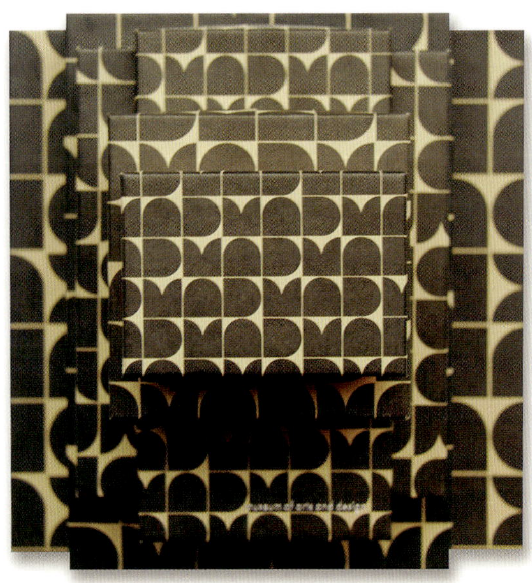

Right top
The graphic language was perfect for repeat patterns for retail shop packaging.

Right middle
Making the solid forms of the logo transparent turned it into an effective window, perfect for shopping bags.

Right bottom
Merchandise sold at MAD celebrates the new identity. Pentagram's Joe Marianek expanded the three letters of the logo into a whole alphabet: MADface. A T-shirt reading "If you can read this, you are MAD" provides commentary on the custom typeface's dubious legibility.

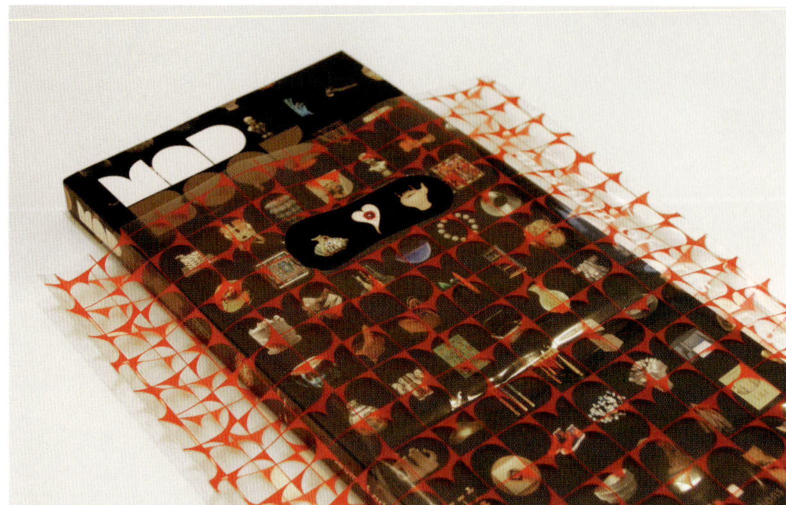

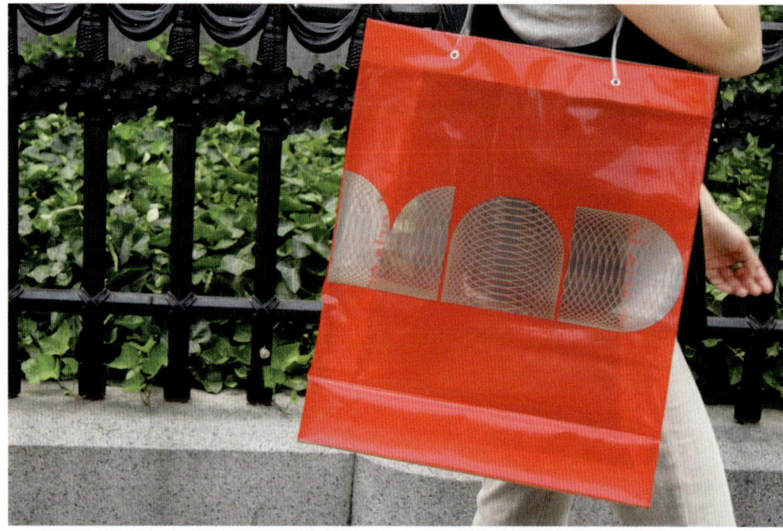

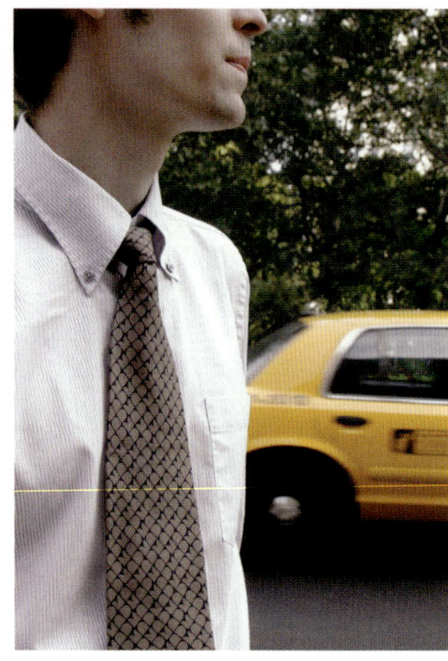

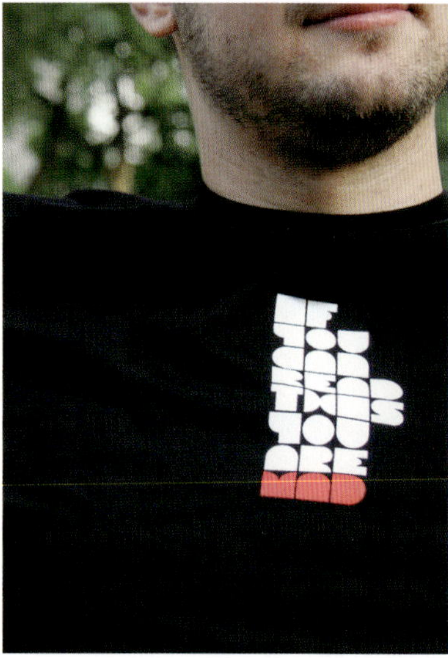

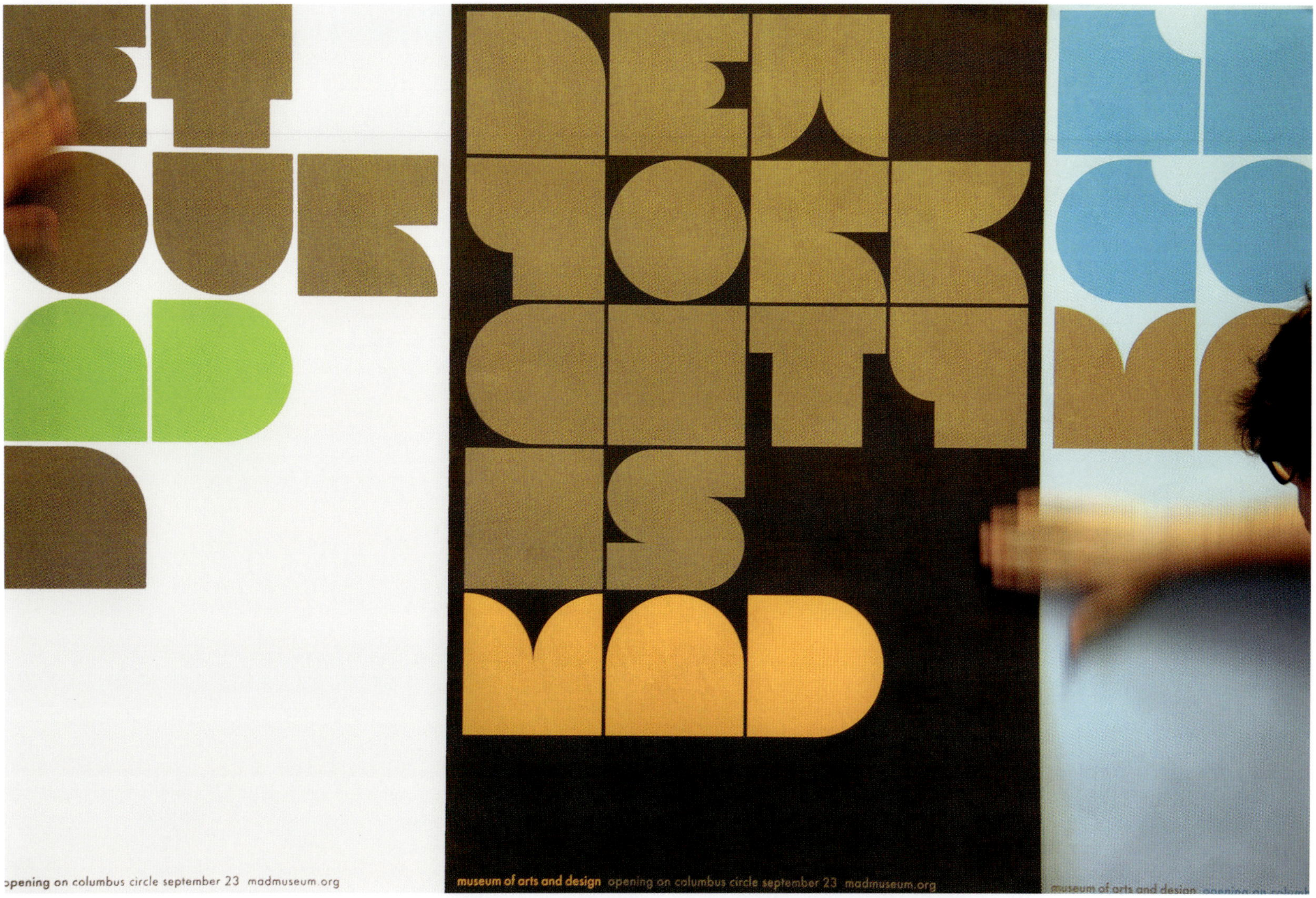

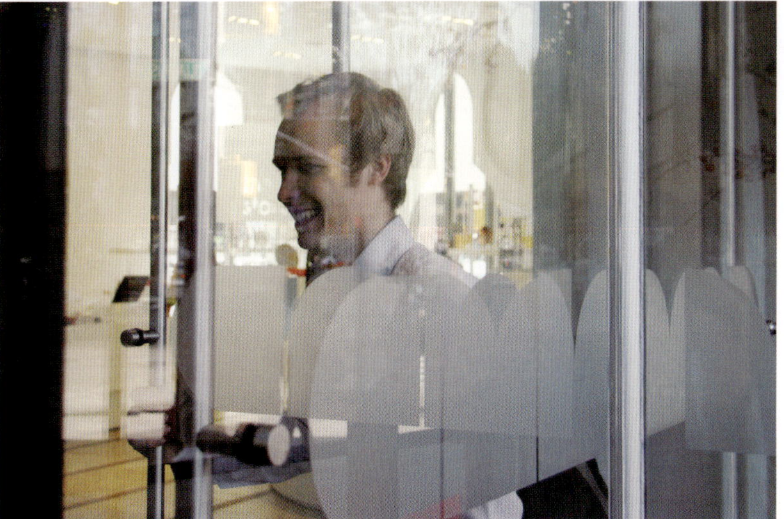

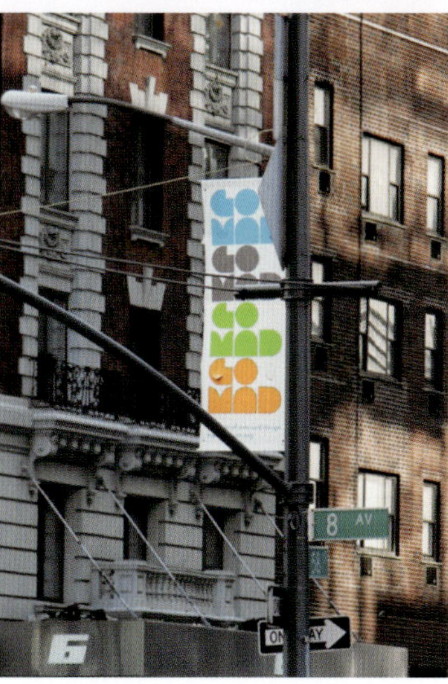

Above
By using MADface, we created a brand that merged logo and message.

Far left
The identity extends into the building both physically and digitally.

Left and next spread
The identity was ubiquitous in New York City when MAD opened in its new home in September 2008.

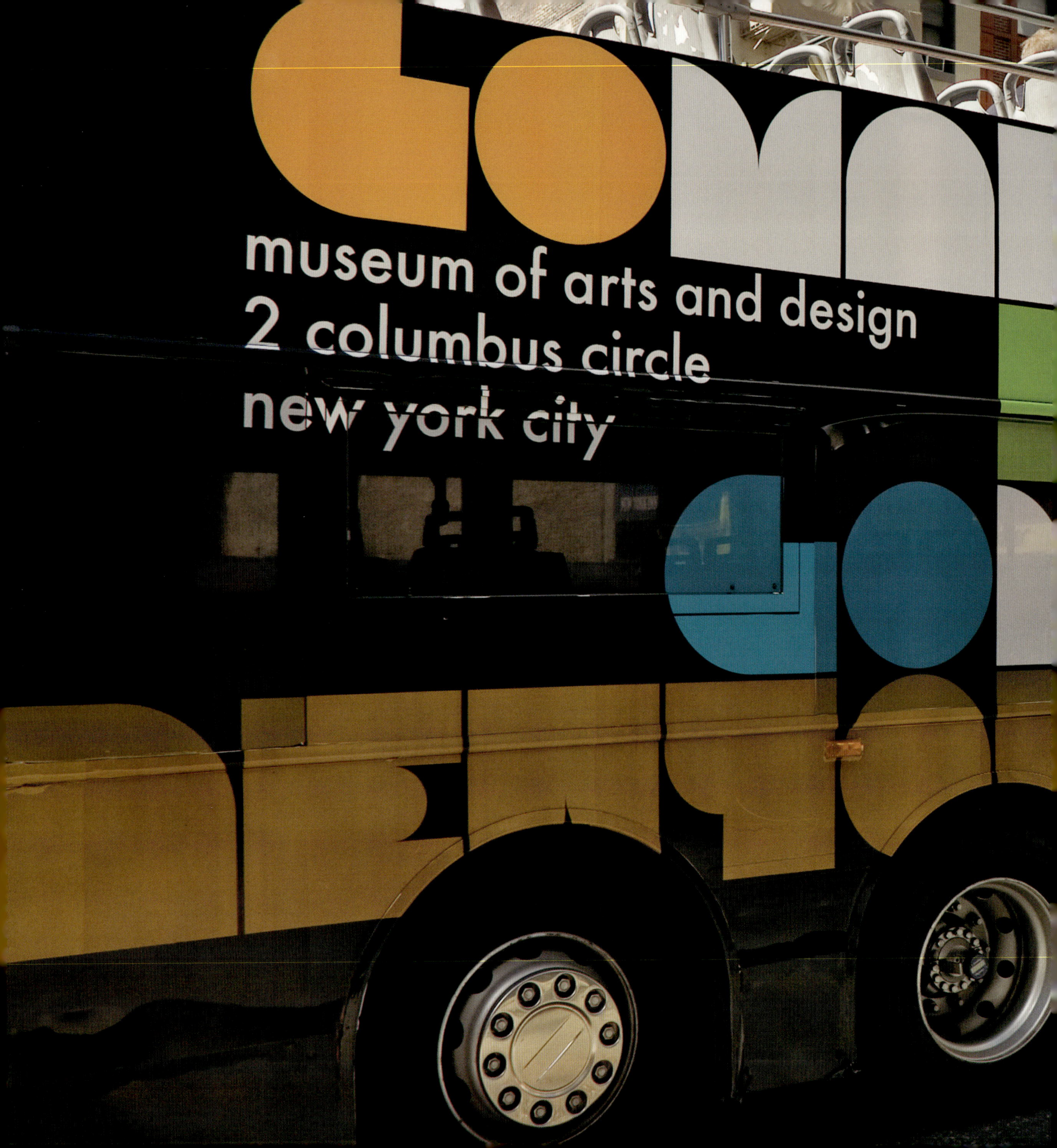
museum of arts and design
2 columbus circle
new york city

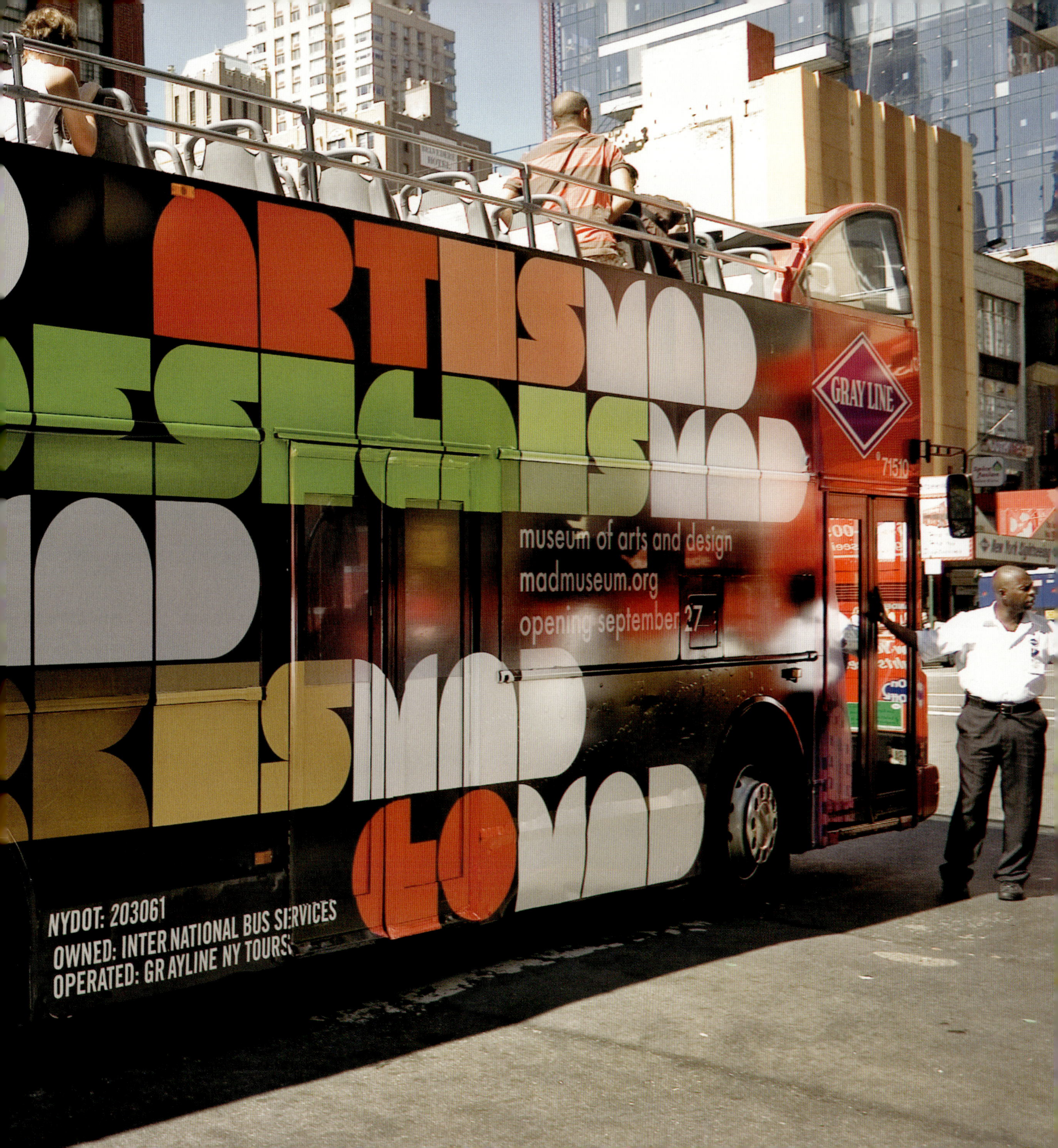
GRAY LINE
71510
museum of arts and design
madmuseum.org
opening september 27
NYDOT: 203061
OWNED: INTER NATIONAL BUS SERVICES
OPERATED: GR AYLINE NY TOURS

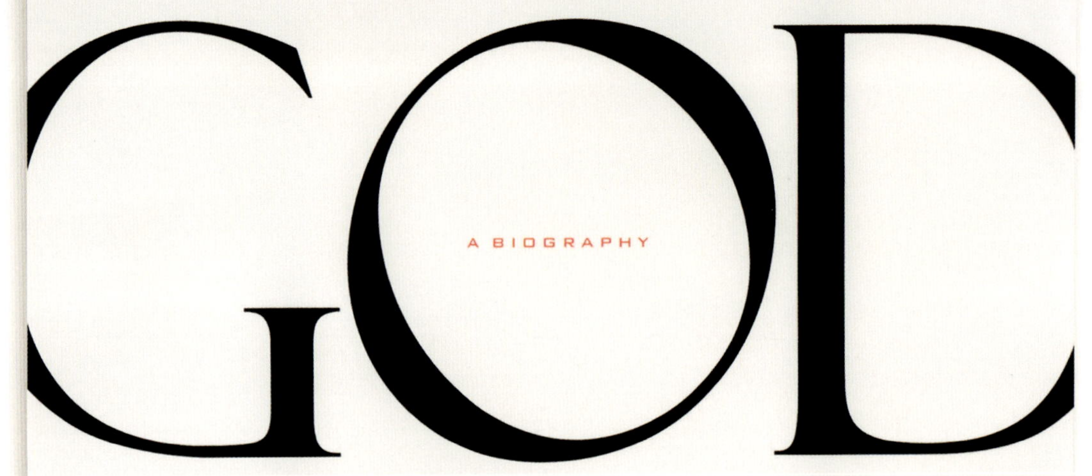

JACK MILES

How to judge a book
Covers and jackets

Opposite
This absorbing analysis by the former Jesuit seminarian Jack Miles subjects the Bible to literary criticism and, remarkably, won the 1996 Pulitzer Prize for biography. Its three-letter title, naturally too big to be contained, designed itself.

Before I took a single design class, I got my education in the aisles of bookstores. In many ways, the design of a book cover is the ultimate challenge. It is inherently, deliciously reductive: whether the book is 48 pages long or 480, it can have only one cover. And that cover, no matter how cerebral the book's contents or how complex its themes, has a single chance to make an impression. Just like a box of cereal or a can of soup, the designer's job is to package a product for sale in a competitive environment.

This is just as true today, if not more so, as both the sales of books and the books themselves move from the physical world to the digital. My goal is to make the package reflect the contents as directly as possible.

I was a bookworm as a child, and I still am today. I read compulsively. Predictably, it has always been hard for me to really enjoy a book with an ugly cover. My most hated were reissues of books newly turned into movies ("Now a Major Motion Picture!"), with covers using portraits of the featured actors to represent fictional characters I would have preferred to cast in my own head. These should really be against the law.

My favorites, naturally, were covers with only type, like the paperback editions of *The Catcher in the Rye* or *Brave New World*. They projected a sense of mystery and importance, daring me to start reading without a single hint of what kind of world I was about to enter. I learned later that many authors shared my bias; J. D. Salinger, in fact, had a clause in his contracts forbidding images of any sort on his book jackets.

It was years before I would have a chance to design a book cover myself. When I finally did, it was no surprise that my best efforts built images from barely more than the contents within: words.

Right
For the cover of this memoir of raising a child with autism, the "voice" evoked by the altered typography suggests the struggle of a mother and daughter to communicate.

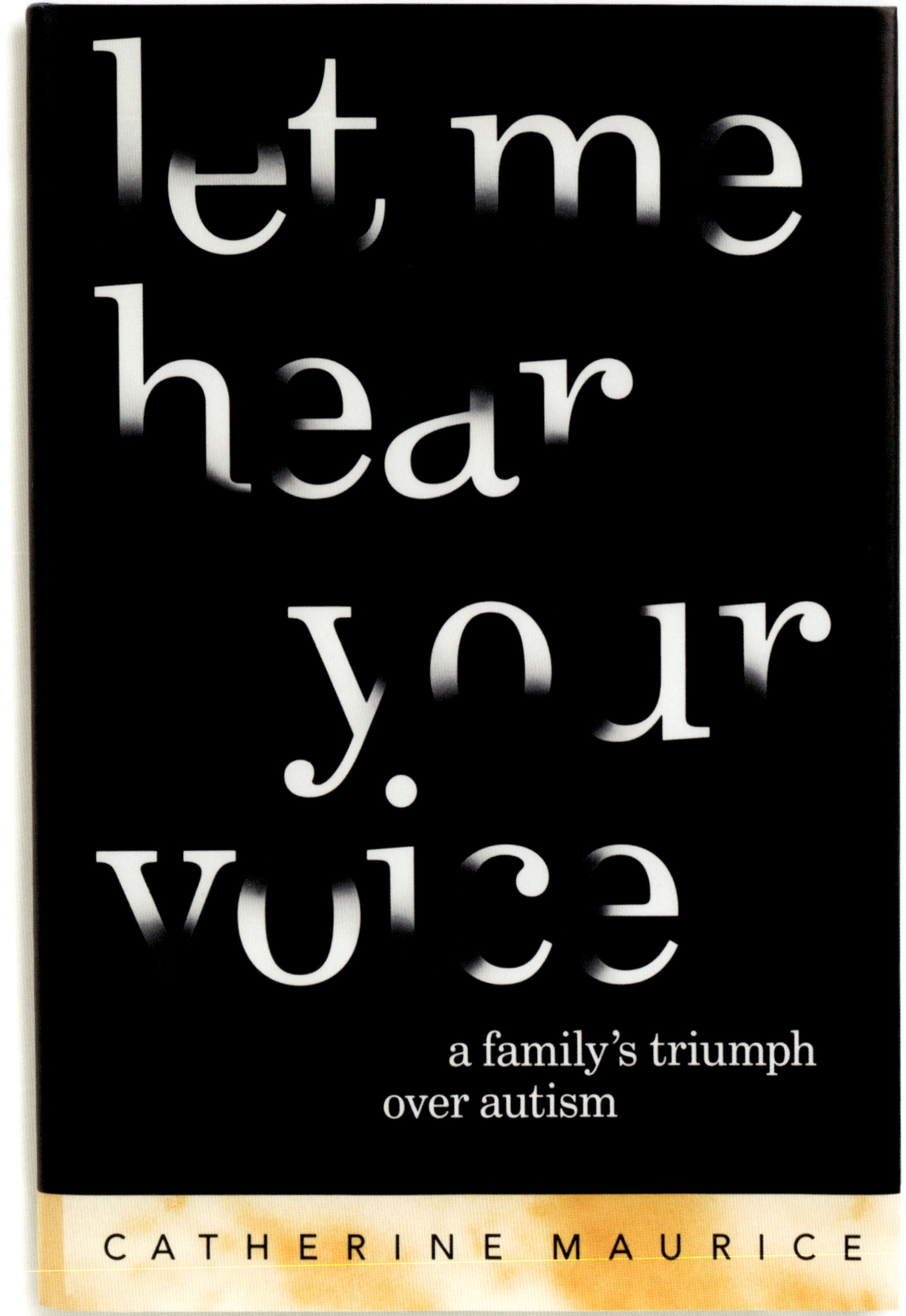

Right
The subtle colors of this memoir of growing up in the segregated South reflects at once the book's warmth, its title, and the elegance of Henry Louis Gates Jr.'s prose.

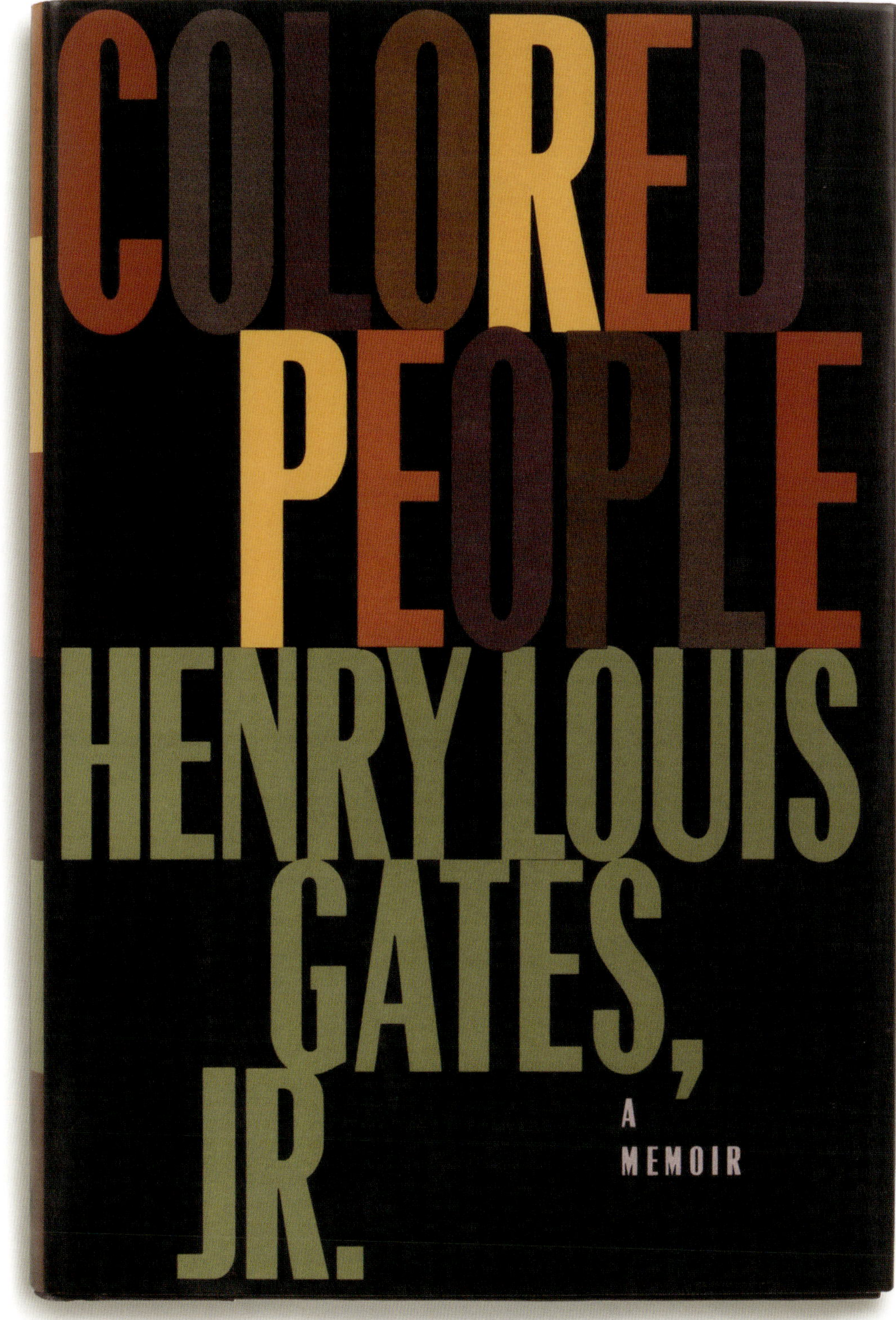

Right
Art director John Gall, facing the challenge of repackaging Vladimir Nabokov's books as paperbacks, had an inspired idea: pick a dozen designers, assign each a title, and hand out specimen boxes, the kind that butterfly collectors (like Nabokov was) use to display their finds. Each designer would fill the box with objects that evoked the book's theme. Gall would get the box photographed, add the author's name, and that would be the finished cover.

My assignment was Nabokov's beautiful memoir *Speak, Memory*. My original design filled the box with vintage photographs pinned under a piece of translucent vellum. What was I thinking? Designer Katie Barcelona, preparing the assembly for shipping, suggested (correctly) that the cover was more evocative without the images.

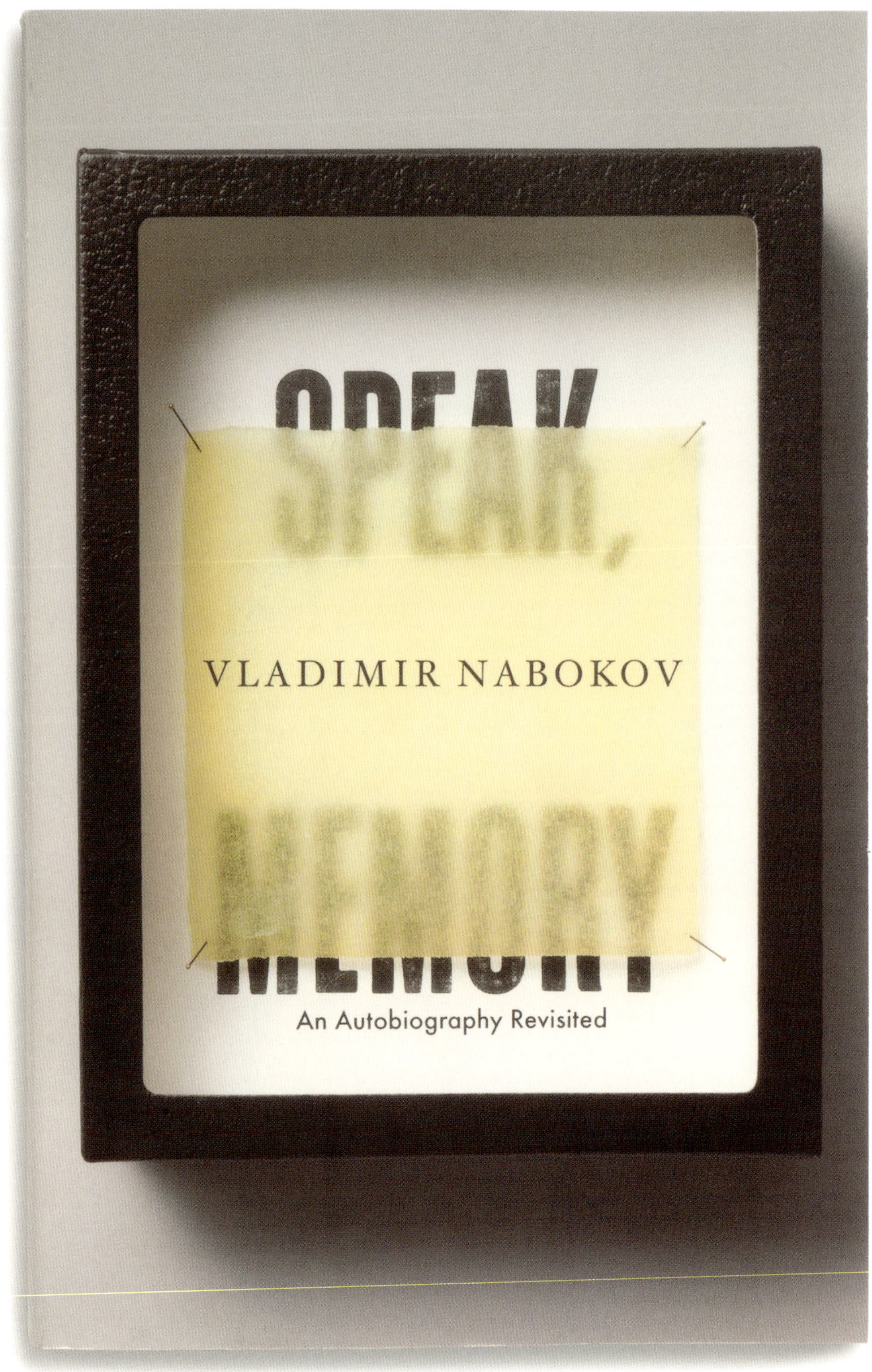

Right
For his wonderful book *Lolita: The Story of a Cover Girl*, John Bertram and Yuri Leving enlisted 80 designers to imagine covers for Nabokov's most uncover-able book. Our raw material was a vintage copy of the Mann Act, the 1910 law that prohibits transporting "any woman or girl for the purpose of prostitution or debauchery, or for any other immoral purpose." I like to think of the book's protagonist consulting the law in some small-town library, impulsively tearing the page out, and turning it into a perverse valentine.

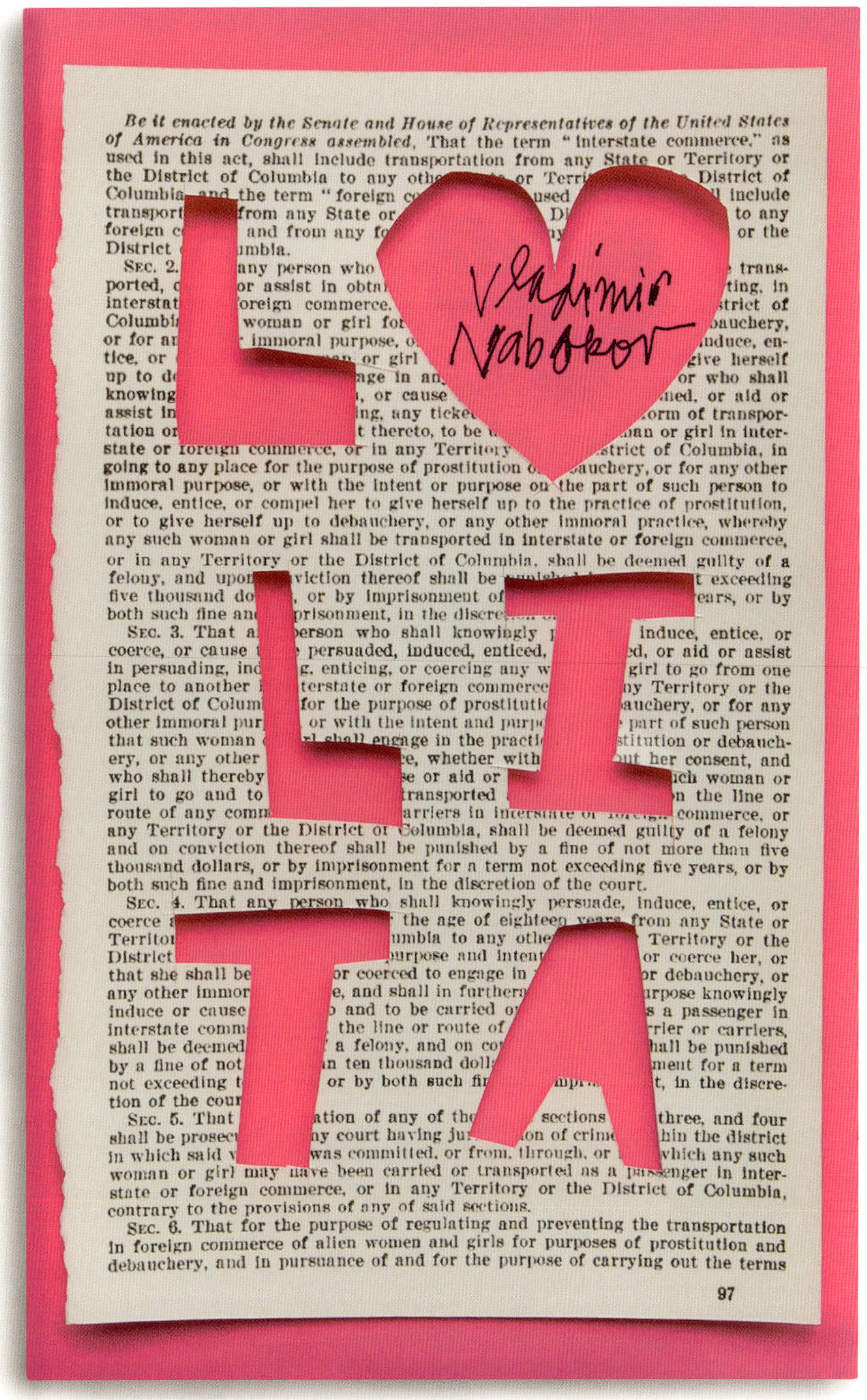

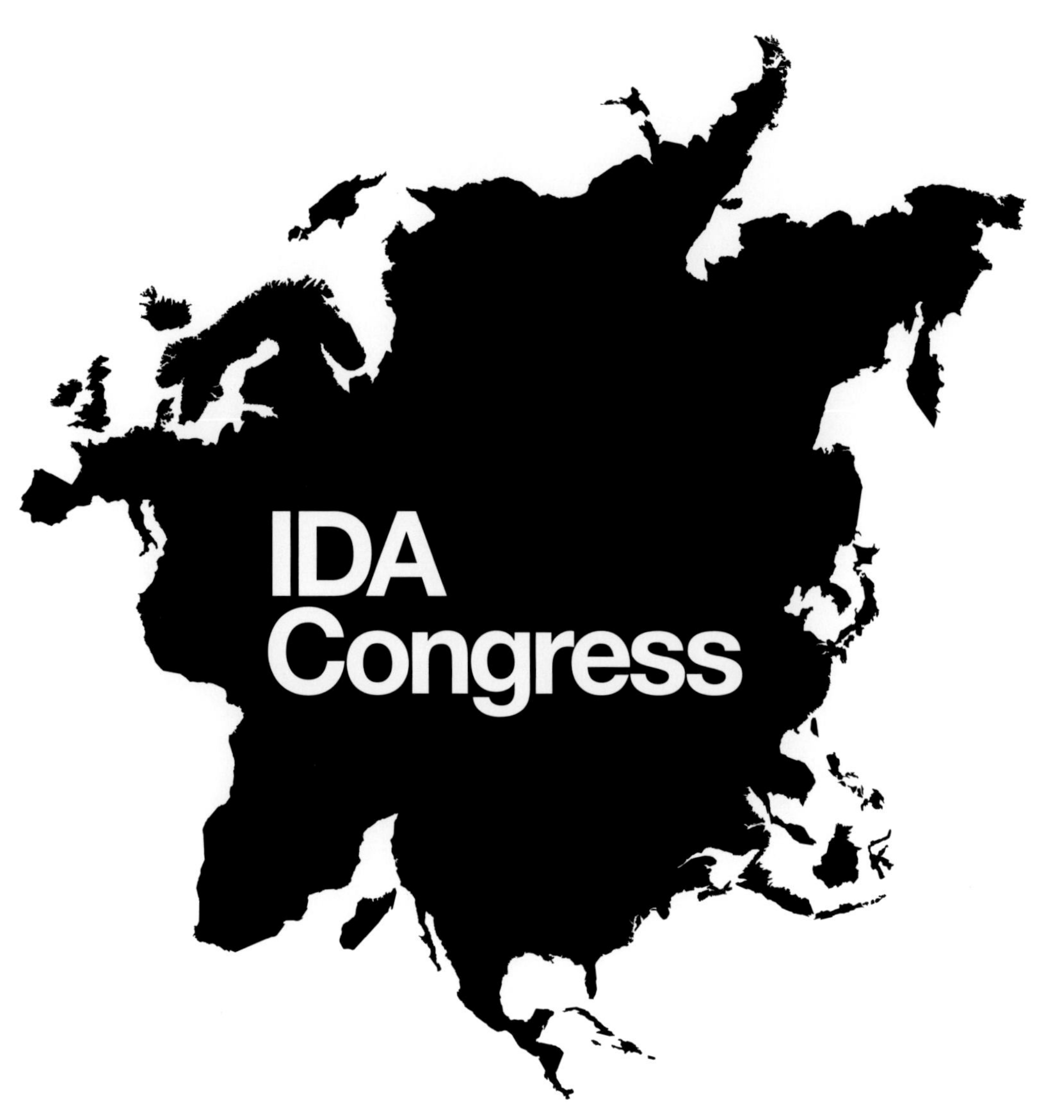
IDA
Congress

How to make a mark
Logotypes and symbols

The logo is the simplest form of graphic communication. In essence, it is a signature, a way to say, "This is me." The illiterate's scrawled X is a kind of logo, just as much as the calligraphic flourishes we associate with Queen Elizabeth or John Hancock. So are the peace sign and the swastika. And so, of course, are the graphic marks that represent Coca-Cola, Nike, McDonald's, and Apple.

The words we use to describe these things can be confusing. Some logos are essentially typographic, like Microsoft's. I call these logotypes or wordmarks. Others are shapes or images, which I call symbols. Sometimes these can be literal: the symbol for Apple is an apple; the symbol for Target is a target. Sometimes they depict real things but those things may have only an indirect association to what they symbolize. The Lacoste crocodile is derived from founder René Lacoste's nickname; the three stripes of Adidas began as no more than decoration. And sometimes they're utterly abstract, like the Chase Bank "beveled bagel," or the Bass Ale red triangle, which dates to 1777 and is one of the oldest logos in the world.

Everyone tends to get overly excited about logos. If you're a company, communicating with honesty, taste, and intelligence is hard work, requiring constant attention day after day. Designing a logo, on the other hand, is an exercise with a beginning and an end. Clients know what to budget for it, and designers know what to charge for it. So designers and clients often substitute the easy fix of the logo for the subtler challenge of being smart.

When we look at a well-known logo, what we perceive isn't just a word or an image or an abstract form, but a world of associations that have accrued over time. As a result, people forget that a brand-new logo seldom means a thing. It is an empty vessel awaiting the meaning that will be poured into it by history and experience. The best thing a designer can do is make that vessel the right shape for what it's going to hold.

Opposite
IDA Congress, 2012. The IDA Congress is a biennial conference of professional design organizations from around the world. What appears at first to be an abstract form is actually Pangaea, the ancient landmass formed by the joining of all the continents: putting the pieces together on a global scale.

Harlequin Enterprises, 2011. Publisher of romantic literature.

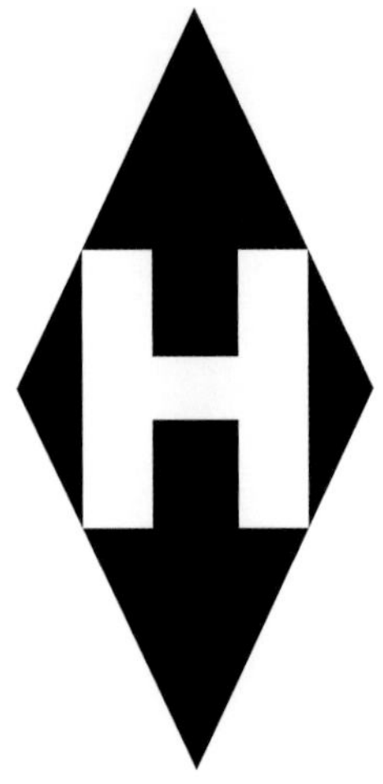

New York City Economic Development Corporation, 1992. A rising skyline.

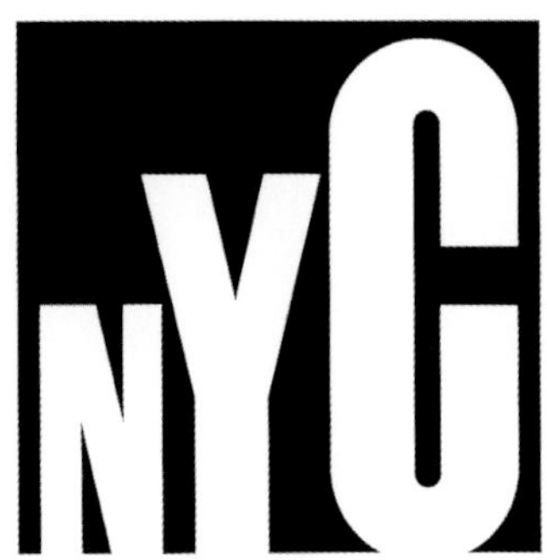

Success Academy, 2014. A coincidence of arithmetic dictates the design.

SUCCESS
ACADEMY
CHARTER
SCHOOLS

21c Hotels, 2005. Art-infused boutique hotels.

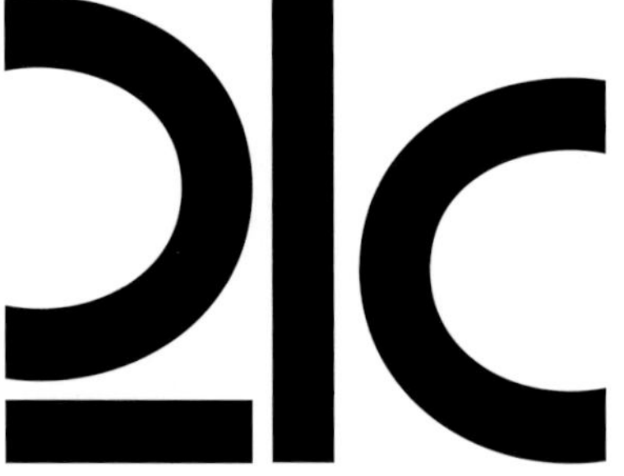

MillerCoors,
2008.
A merger of two iconic brewers, keeping the focus on the beer.

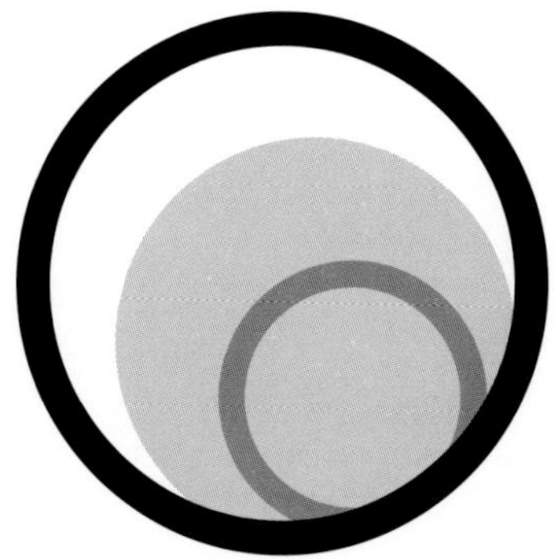

Wave Hill,
2002.
A cultural center and public gardens in the Bronx.

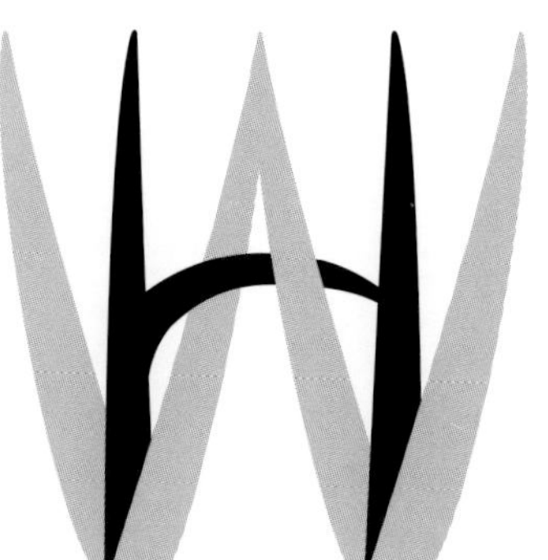

Broadway Books, 1996.
The diagonal suggests both an earmarked page and the iconic thoroughfare.

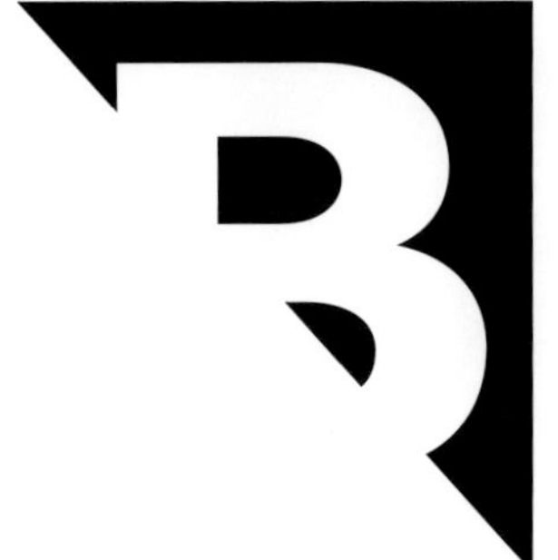

IDEO, 1997.
Refinement of the original logo by Paul Rand.

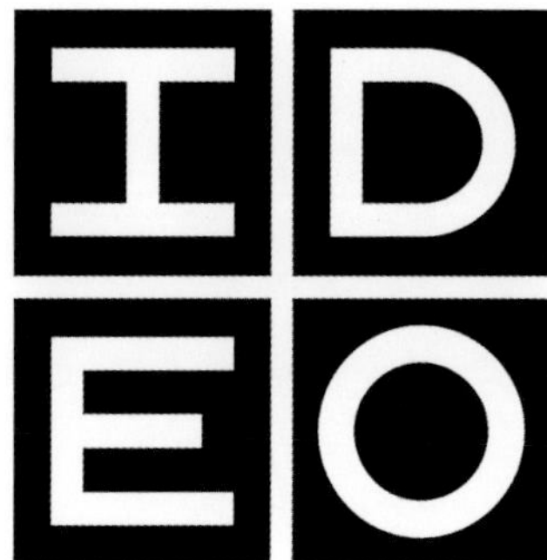

Gotham Equities, 1992. New York-based real estate developers.

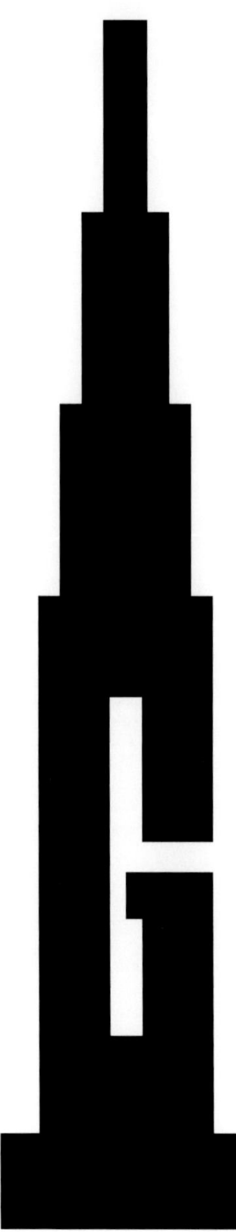

The Fashion
Center, 1993.
A big button
for the
Big Apple.

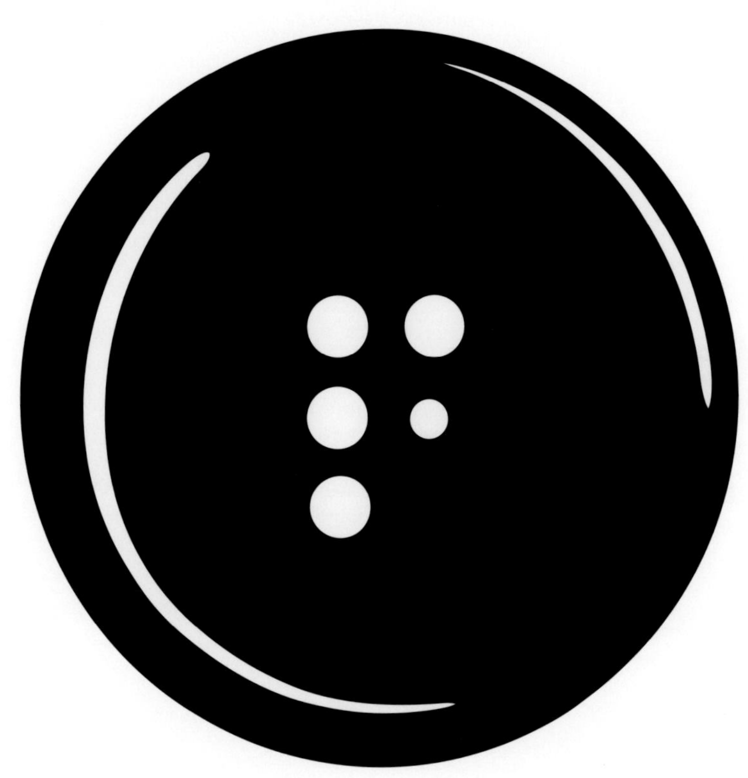

Council of Fashion Designers of America, 1991. Typography provides the emphasis.

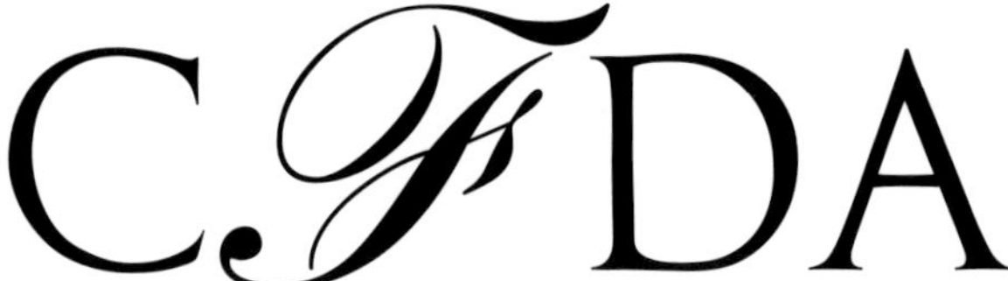

Amalgamated Bank, 2014. Founded to serve New York's garment workers, its woven acronym illustrates its name.

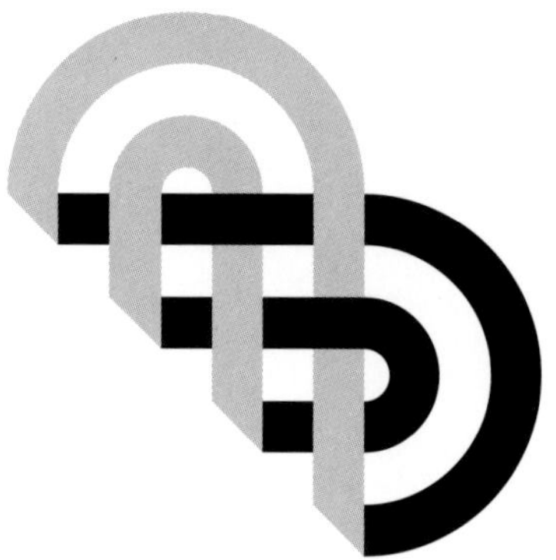

St. Petersburg/Clearwater Area Convention and Visitors Bureau, 2010. Gentle waves for America's best beaches.

Interactive Advertising Bureau, 2007. Subliminal dots for the dot-com world.

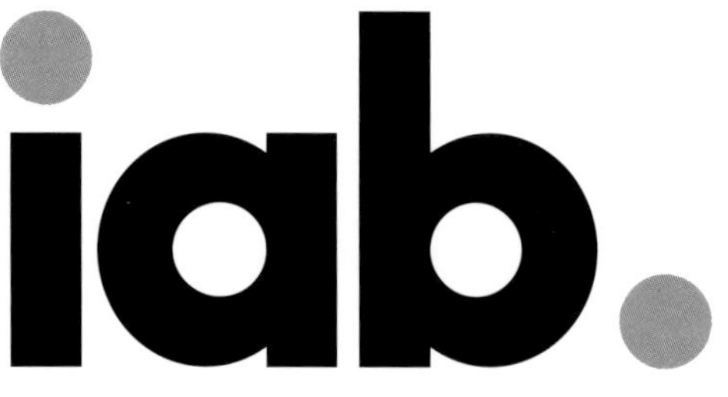

Grand Central Terminal, 2013. The clock hands hint at the landmark's birthdate: 7:13 pm, or 19:13.

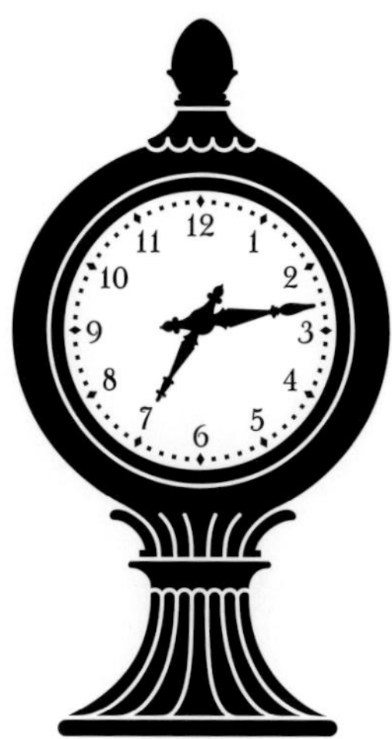

Flatiron/23rd Street Partnership Business Improvement District, 2006. The mark's form evokes both the neighborhood's street plan and the namesake building's silhouette.

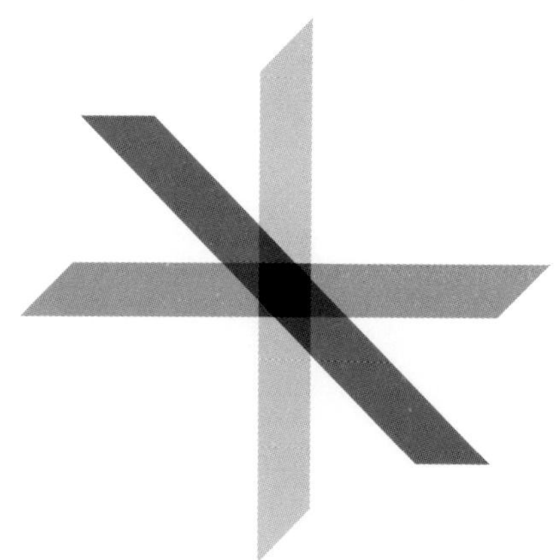

Penguin Press, 2014. Publisher's mark based on the pilcrow, the typographic designation for paragraph.

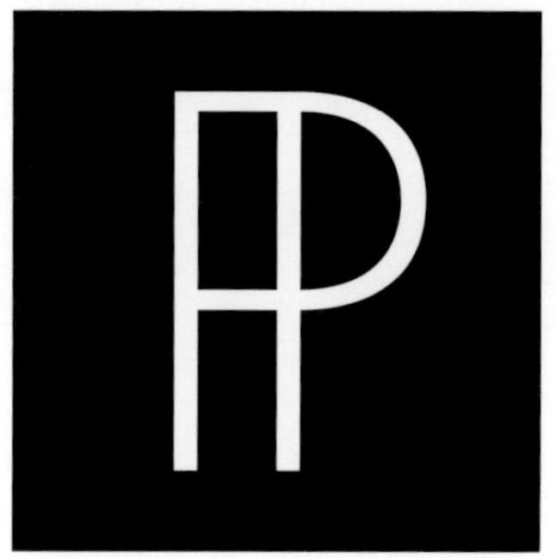

Fashion Law Institute, 2011. A classic visual pun.

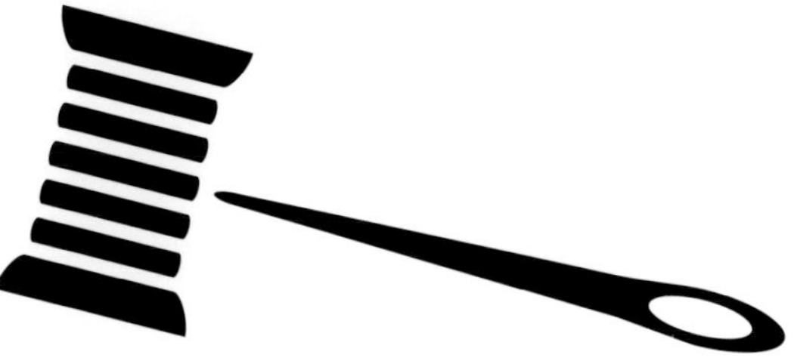

Modern Art Museum of Fort Worth, 1999. A new Tadao Ando building set on a reflecting pool.

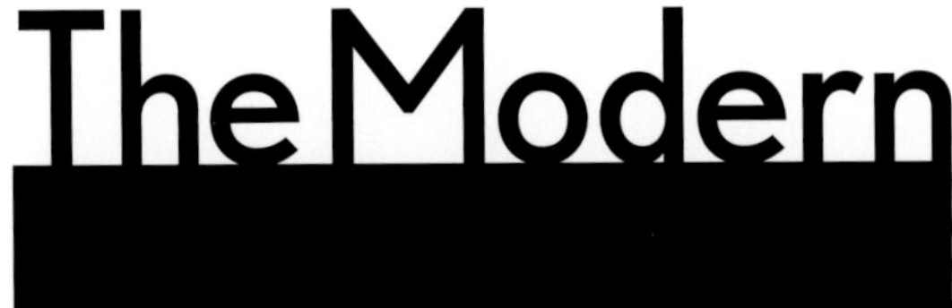

Scripps College, 2009. The investiture of the school's eighth president.

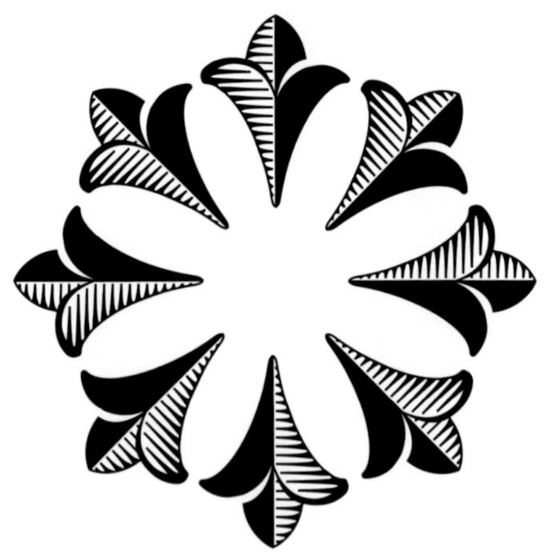

Midwood Equities, 2014. Building blocks for real estate developers.

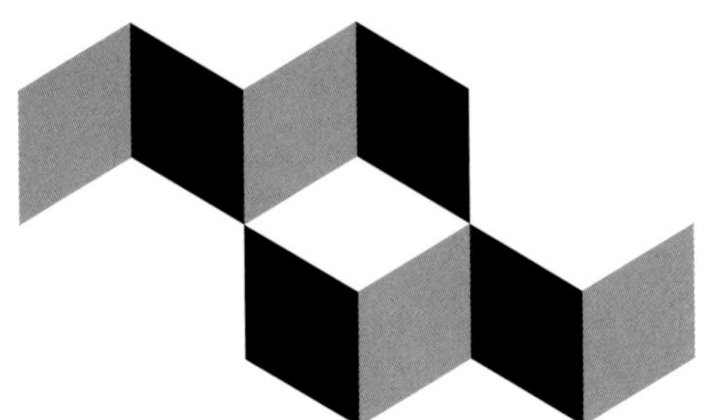

Chambers Hotel, 2001. Monogram as infographic.

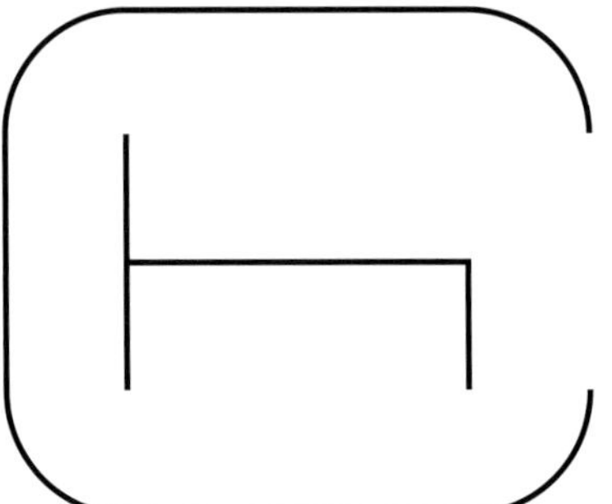

Families for Excellent Schools, 2014. Letterforms create partnership.

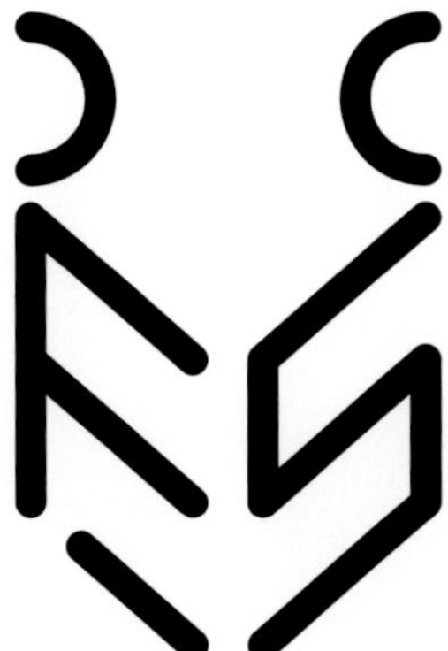

Fulton Center, 2014. Transportation hub skylit by a glass atrium.

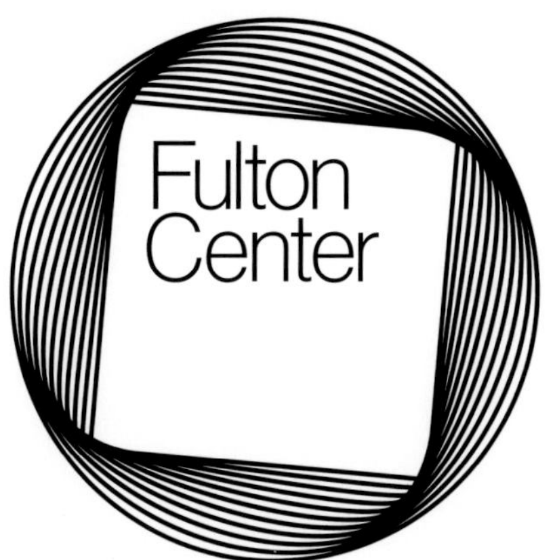

Tenement Museum, 2007. New York's most unusual, and intimate, historic site.

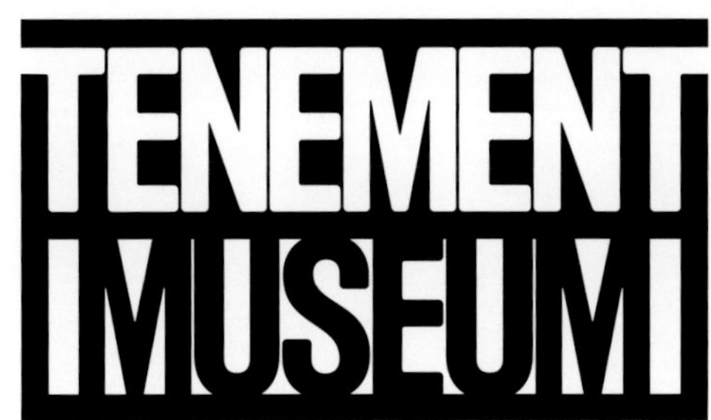

Yale School of Management, 2008. The heraldry of the conference table.

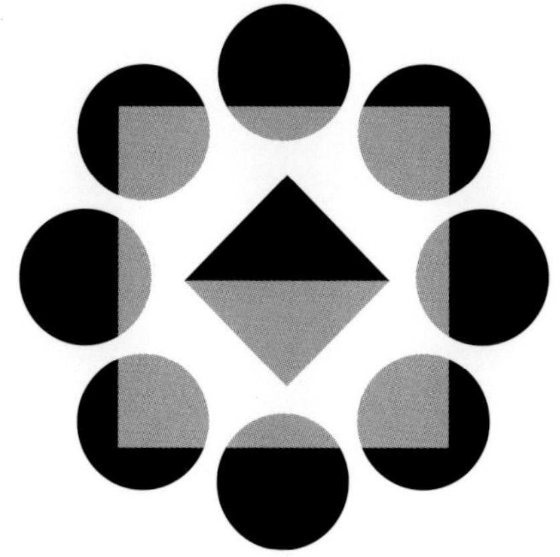

Yahoo, 2019.
Punctuating one of the online world's most enduring destinations.

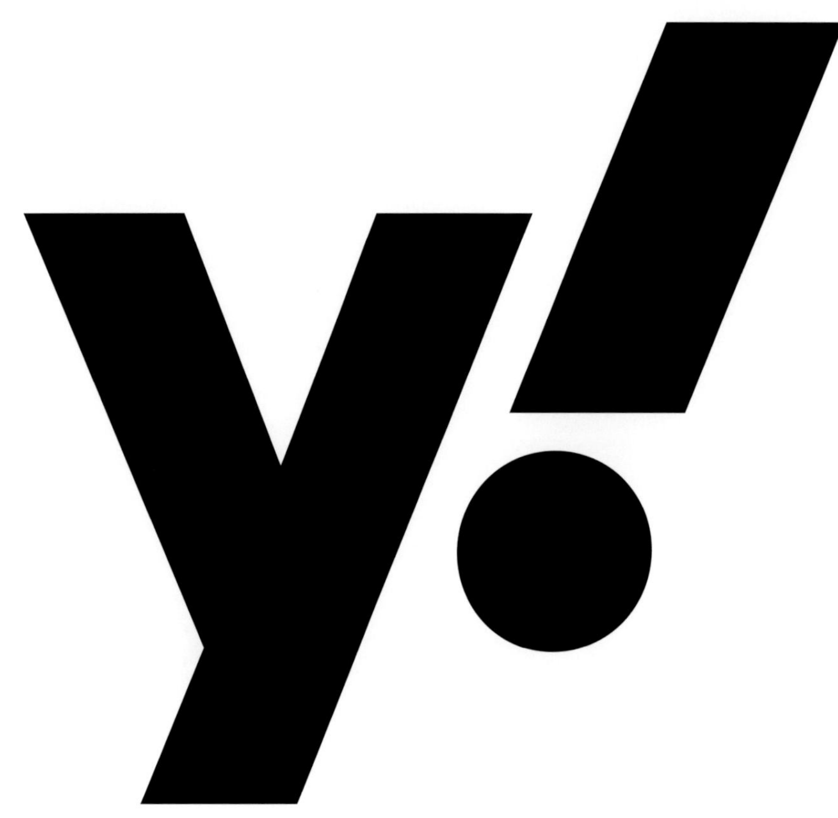

Slack, 2019. Innovative, ubiquitous, and addictive business communications software.

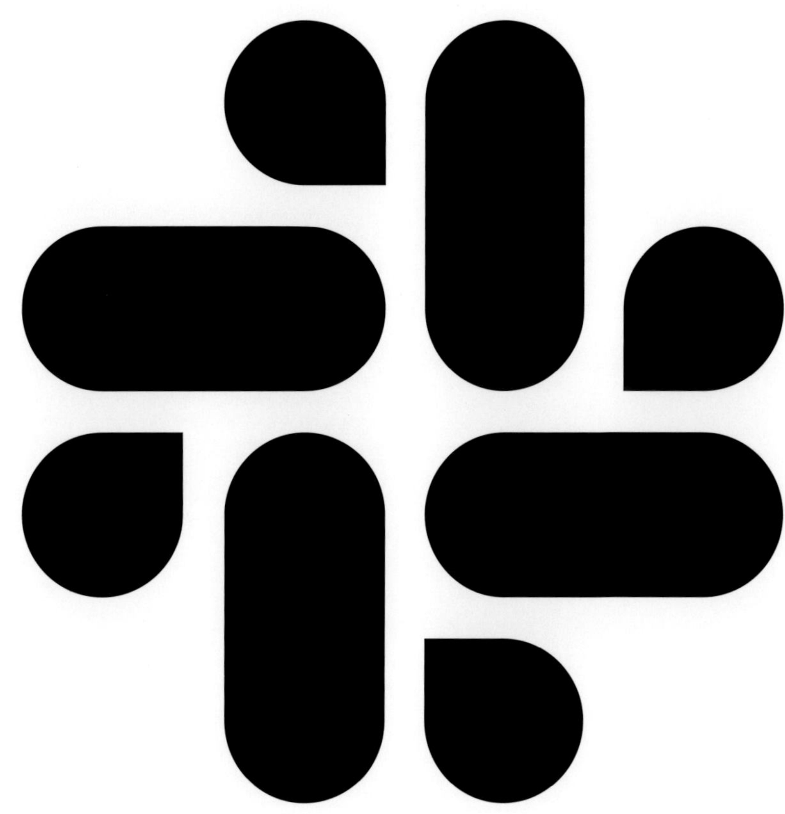

Fountain, 2019.
A double monogram for sparkling beverages infused with hemp extract.

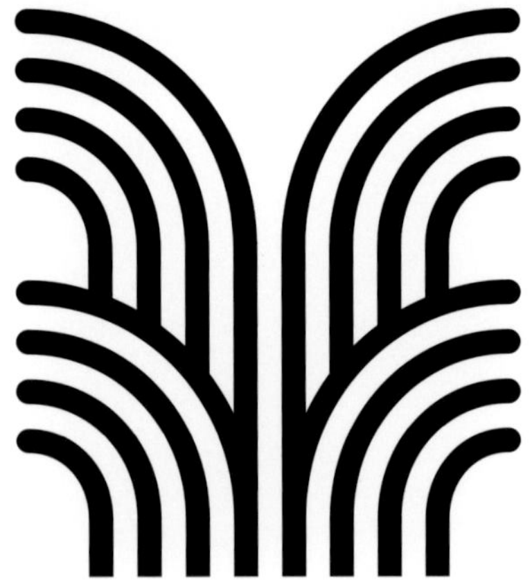

Vroom, 2018.
Speedy online car sales.

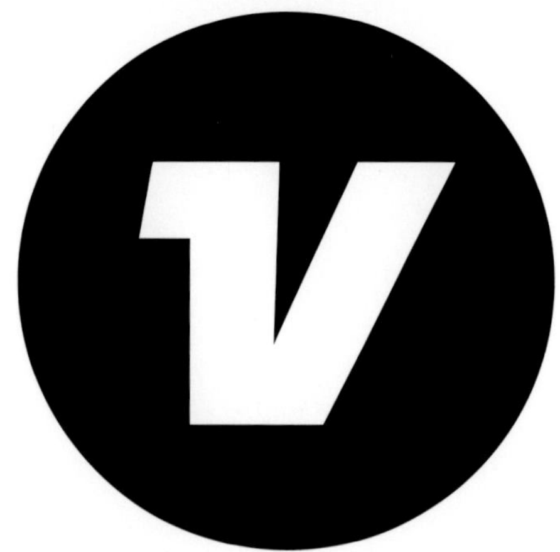

Electronic Frontier Foundation, 2018.
Defending online speech, privacy, and innovation since the dawn of the digital era.

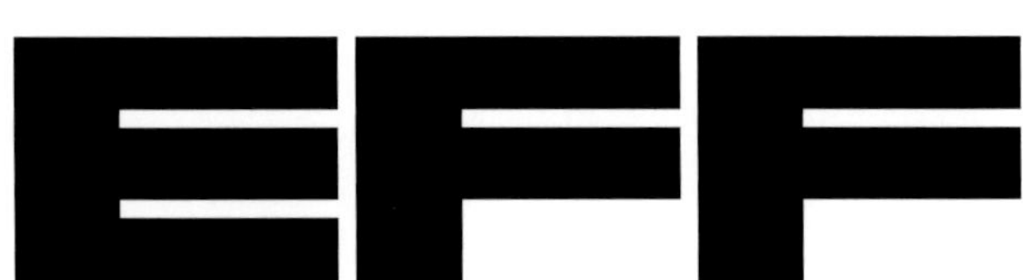

Archewell, 2020.
International nonprofit advocacy organization.

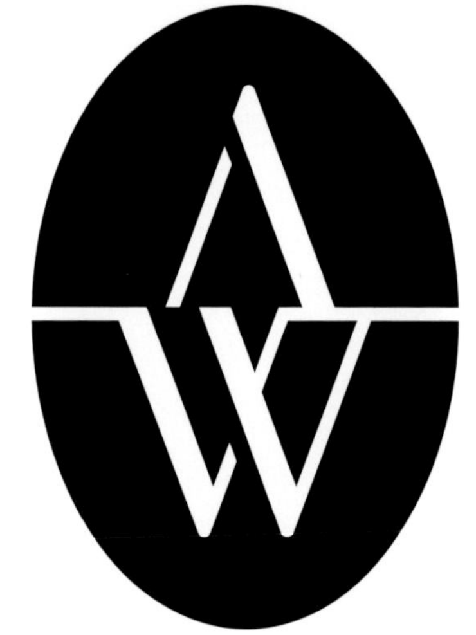

Wildlife Conservation Society, 2015. The letterform in the symbol, like the organization itself, stands for wildlife.

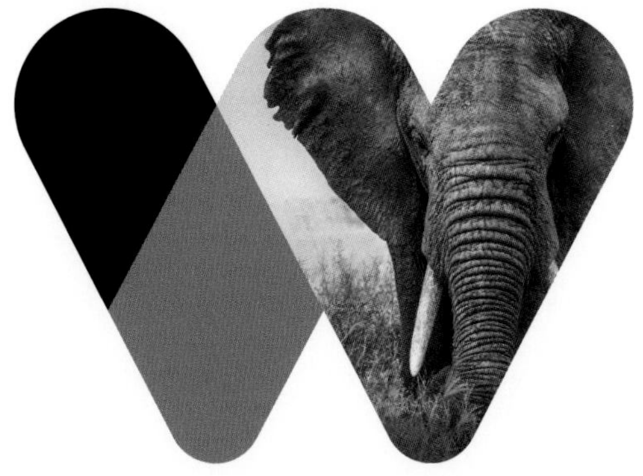

MIT Schwarzman College of Computing, 2019. Two letters connect and form a third, suggesting the transformative power of computing.

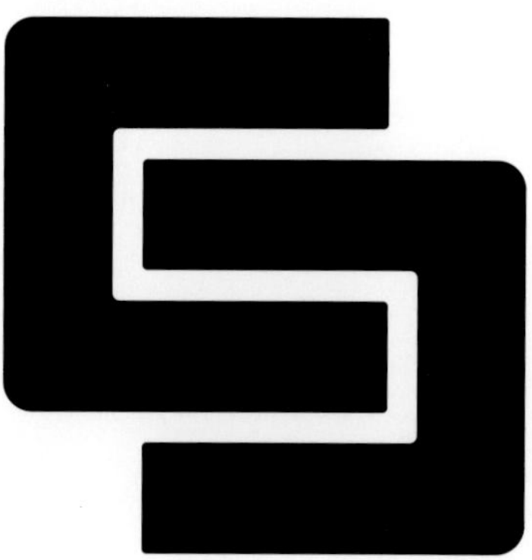

_able, 2017. Investment fund with a name that's both a versatile suffix and an anagram of the founders' initials.

_able

San Diego Zoo Wildlife Alliance, 2020. Umbrella organization for the world's most popular zoo.

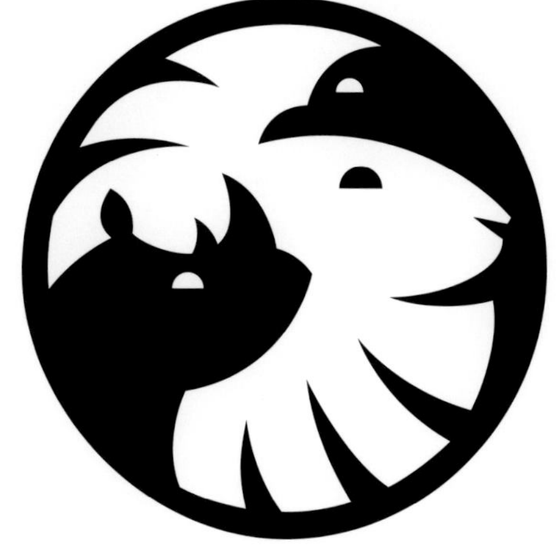

Museum of Sex, 2002. Nonprofit dedicated to human sexuality.

museumofse**x**

March of Dimes, 1998. Nonprofit dedicated to infant health.

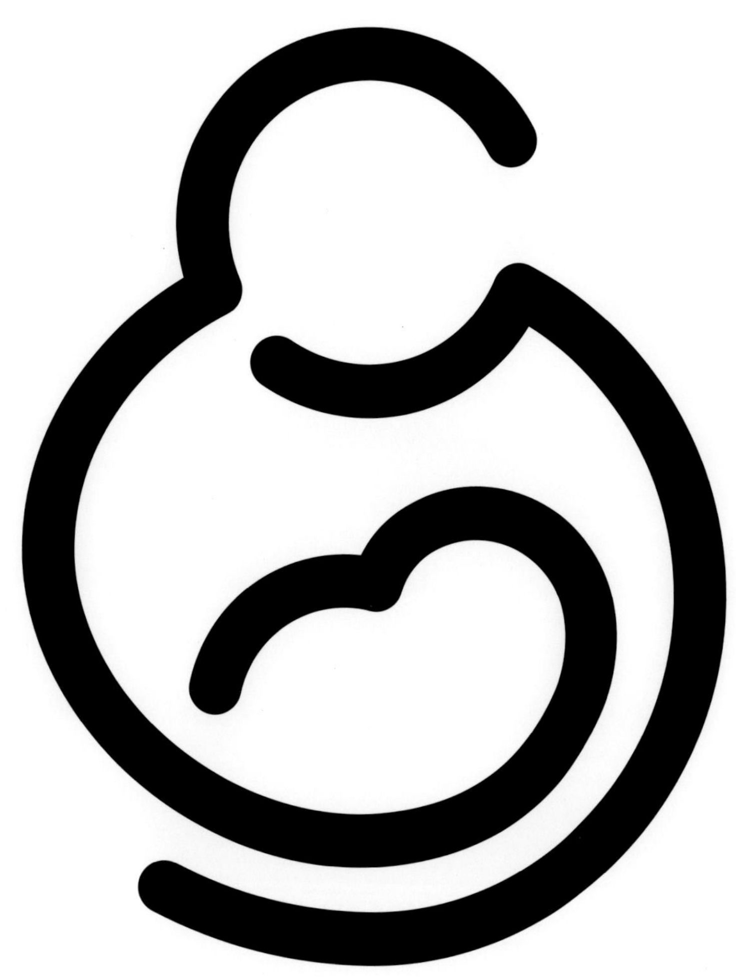

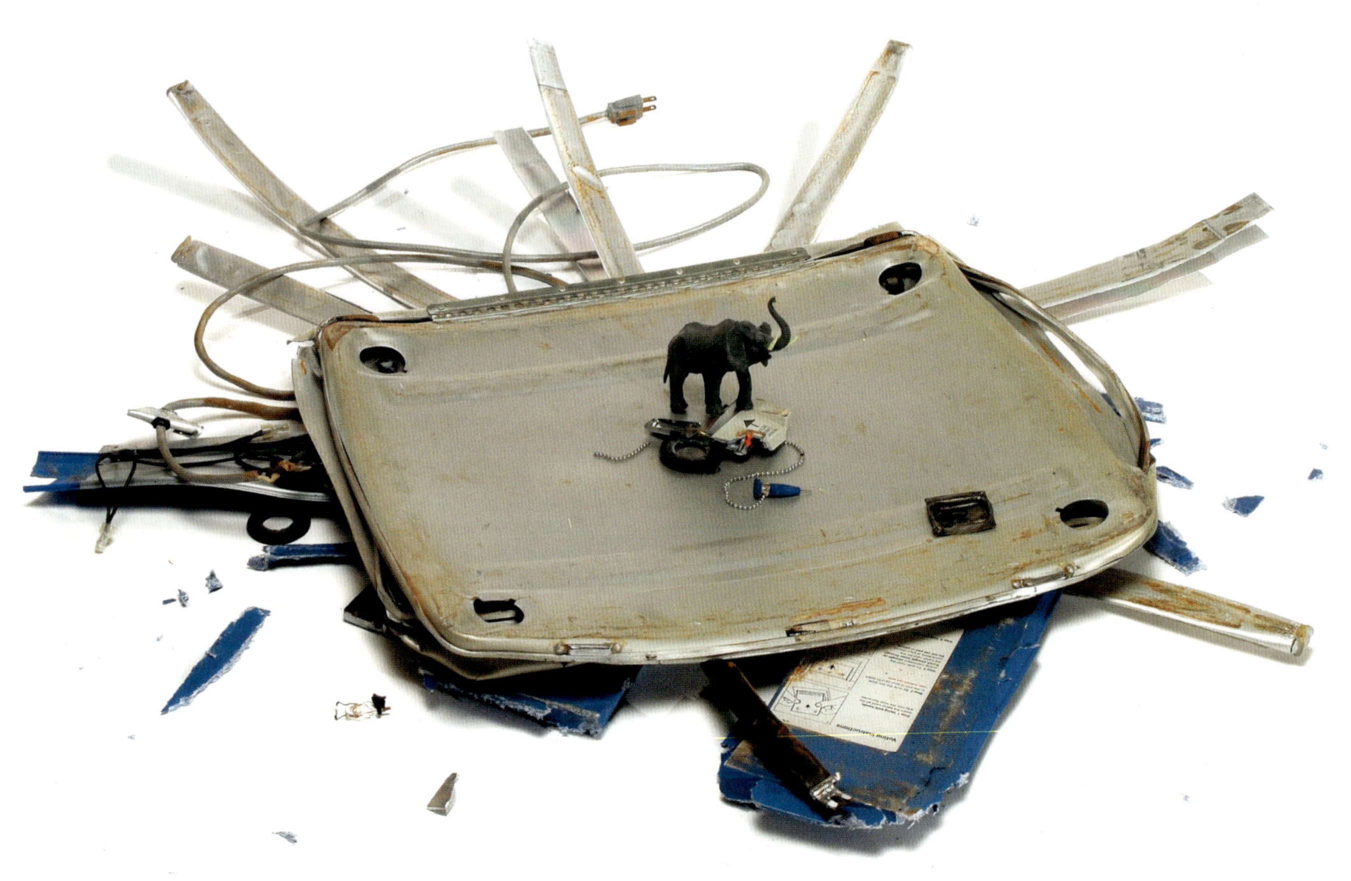

How to squash a vote

The Voting Booth Project

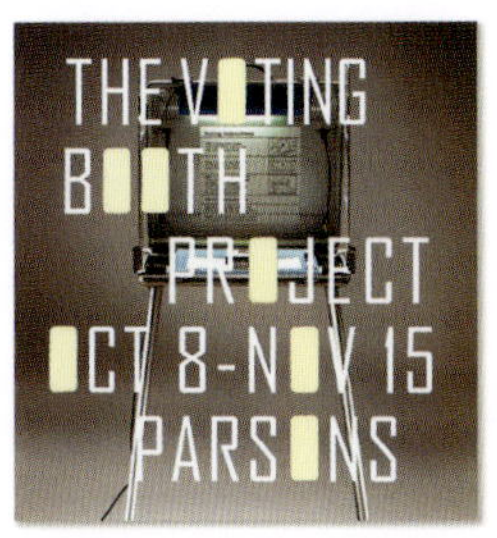

Opposite
A crushed voting booth symbolizes the messy and much-disputed outcome of the 2000 presidential election.

Above
We designed both the *Voting Booth Project* exhibition and the show's catalog. The punched-out letters on the book's die-cut cover are an obvious reference to the "hanging chads" that dominated the recount following the election.

After the debacle of the 2000 elections, when confusion over Palm Beach County's notorious "butterfly ballots" threw the outcome of the presidential election into a weeks-long limbo, the state of Florida decommissioned its Votomatic portable voting booths and put them up for sale on eBay. Seeing a chance to own a piece of history, New York City hotelier André Balazs bought 100 for $10 each and gave some away to friends. What to do with the rest? Paul Goldberger, then dean of the Parsons School of Design, suggested an exhibition in the school's gallery. Fifty designers and artists, including David Byrne, Bonnie Siegler and Emily Oberman, Milton Glaser, and Maira Kalman, were each given a booth and invited to alter it. We were asked to design the exhibition, curated by the ingenious Chee Pearlman, and to contribute a booth of our own. The show opened in October 2004, just in time for that year's presidential election.

Most of the designers transformed the booths in delightfully complex and delicate ways. My partner Jim Biber and I took a much less subtle approach: we drove over the booth with a 1.5-ton steamroller. It turns out it's remarkably easy to rent a steamroller in New York; you don't even need a driver's license to operate it. The spindly-looking Votomatic, however, proved to be surprisingly (and perhaps reassuringly) resilient. It took multiple passes to flatten it. The controlled violence of the entire process was cathartic.

The result was a handsome piece of sculpture in the style of John Chamberlain, but the blunt means seemed to demand an even blunter message. Why bother with subtlety? We bought a tiny plastic elephant—the symbol of the Republican Party—and positioned it atop the pile, leaving no doubt as to who was doing the crushing.

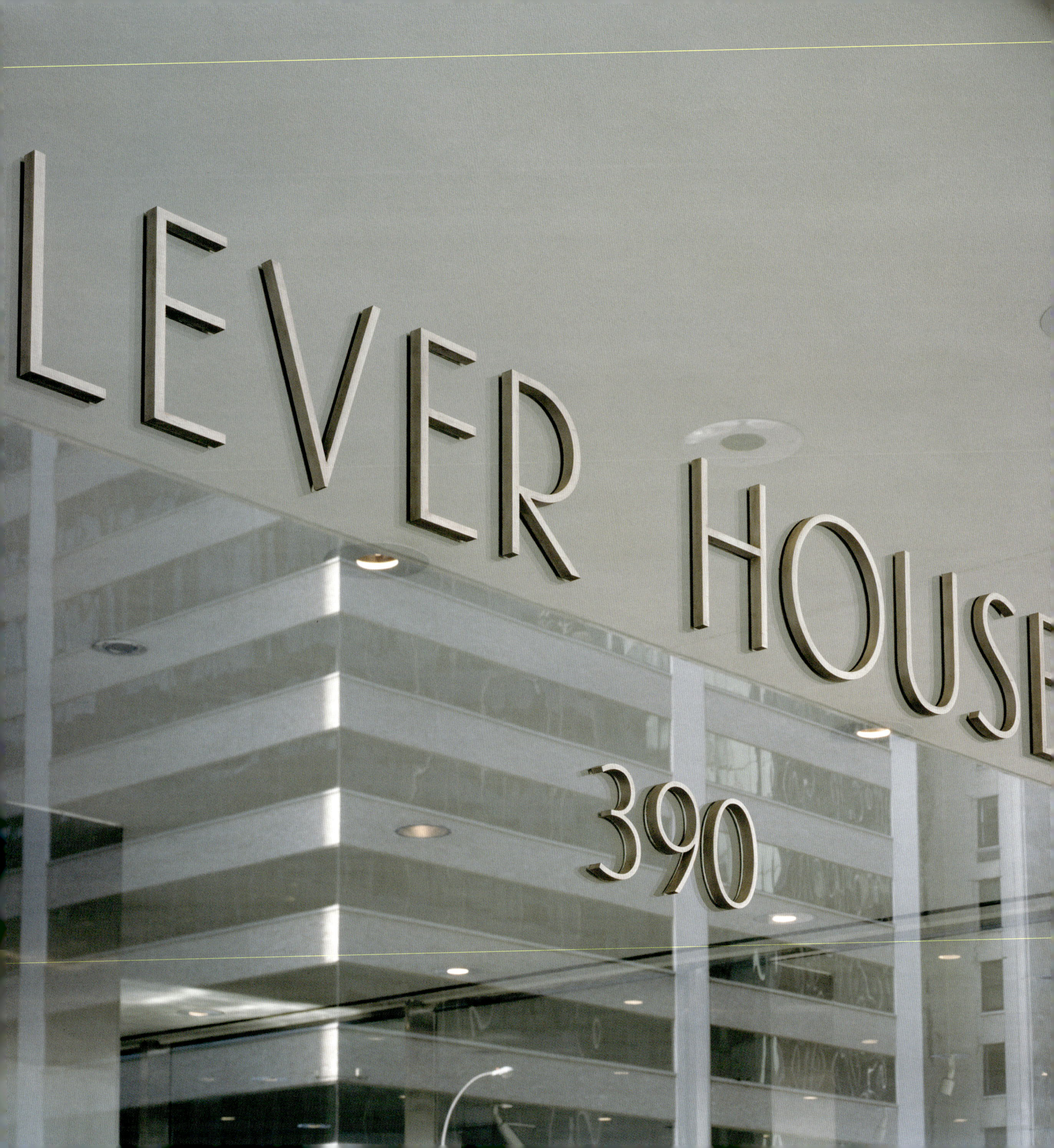

LEVER HOUSE
390

How to travel through time
Lever House

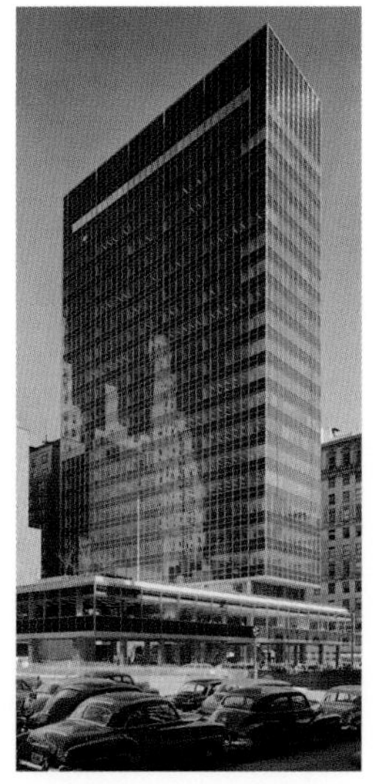

Opposite
SOM and William Georgis undertook a careful restoration of Gordon Bunshaft's 1952 Lever House for its 50th anniversary. We took the same approach to the signage.

Above
Lever House introduced the glass and steel skyscraper to midtown Manhattan and set a standard for New York office buildings for the next half century.

Architects, product designers, and fashion designers have so much to work with: steel and glass, plastics and polymers, fabrics and finishes. Graphic designers, living in a world of paper and pixels, often find our choices reduced to one: what typeface will we use? But that single choice exerts an outsized influence. "Words have meaning and type has spirit," my partner Paula Scher has said. That spirit can be contentious, elusive, and ineffable, but it is our secret weapon and most powerful tool.

In 1999, we received a call from designer William Georgis. The landmark Lever House was approaching its 50th anniversary. Georgis and the building's original architects, SOM, were working on a careful restoration. All of its old signs would need to be replaced, and new ones would be needed to satisfy 21st-century building codes. Would we join as graphic design consultants?

Lever House transformed New York when it was opened in 1952. SOM's Gordon Bunshaft conceived a glass and steel skyscraper, the first on upper Park Avenue, until then an unbroken wall of brown masonry buildings. The tower rises above a horizontal slab which itself is lifted from the street to create an open, light-filled pedestrian colonnade. The overall effect is surprisingly delicate. Hans and Florence Knoll were recruited to do the interiors, and Raymond Loewy designed public exhibitions and, it was suspected, the signs.

It took only one look at what remained of the signs to confirm that they matched no modern typeface. We decided we had no choice but to use most of our budget to extrapolate an entirely new typeface from the handful of surviving letterforms. Jonathan Hoefler and Tobias Frere-Jones were commissioned to undertake this exercise in forensic font reconstruction. The result, Lever Sans, is perfect. It evokes the *Mad Men* era without resorting to the easy tropes of cliché: typeface as time machine. It's absurd to claim that a single capital R can conjure the New York inhabited by Cary Grant in *North by Northwest*. I make that claim here.

Right
New uses, new tenants, and new regulations required new signs. In addition, all the existing signs were removed and carefully replaced with brand-new ones, each one set in Lever Sans. Our hope was that no one would notice the difference.

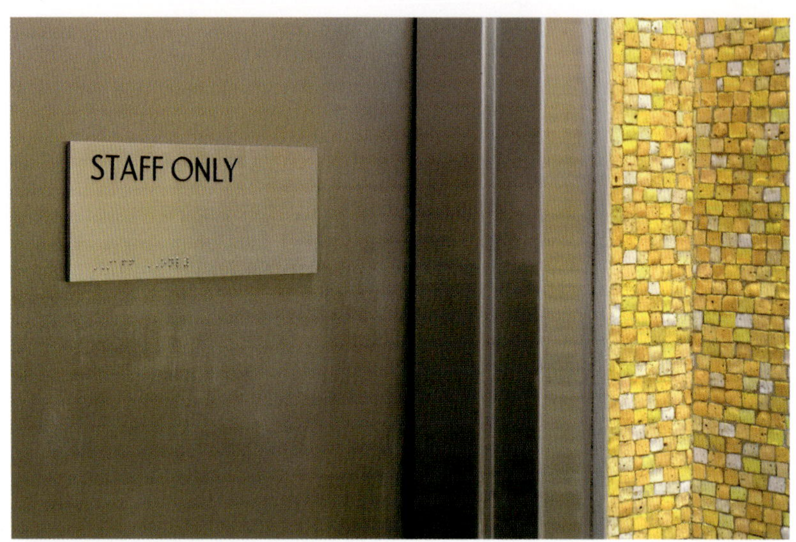

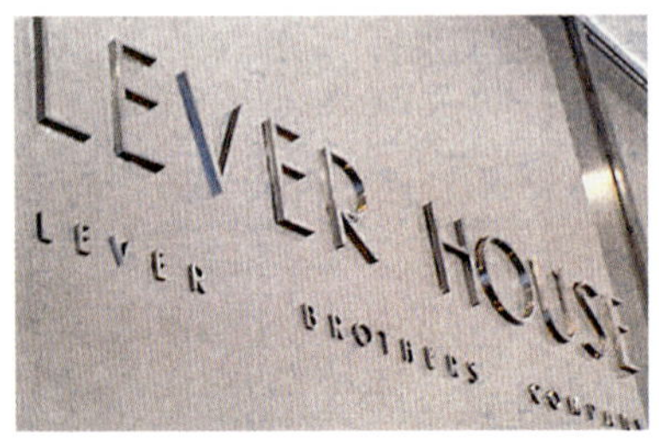

Above
It would have been easy to use an existing typeface like Futura or Neutraface for the Lever House program. But the vintage signs, even though damaged and missing letters, were too distinctive to ignore.

Opposite
Jonathan Hoefler and Tobias Frere-Jones created an entire alphabet from eight letters. Designing the numbers, for which no precedent could be found, was particularly challenging. The result was an original typeface that was as suited to its setting as every other one of the building's details.

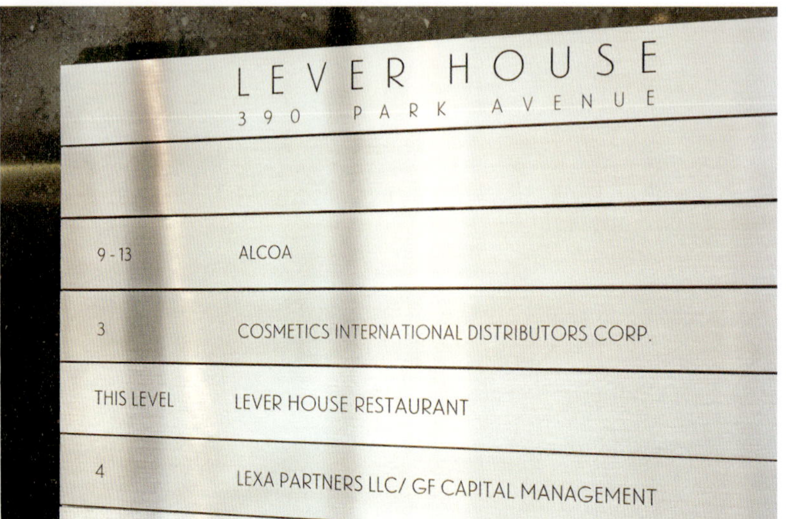

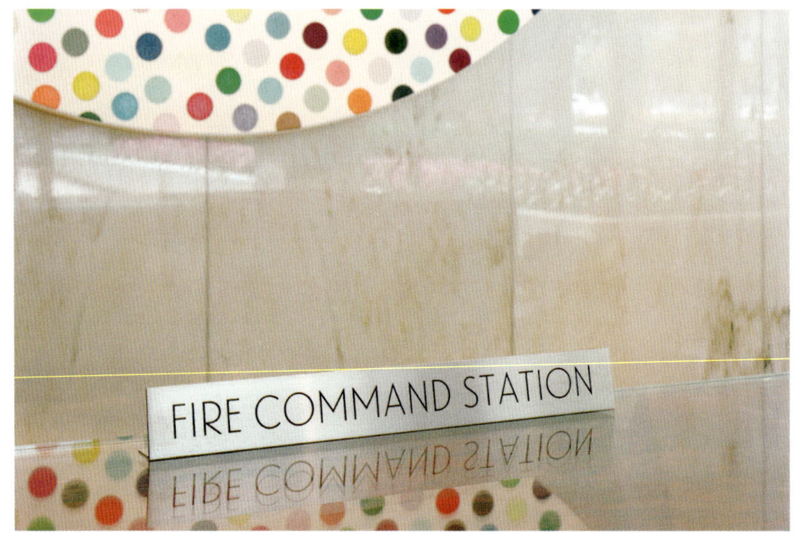

ABCDEF
GHIJKLMN
OPQRST
UVWXYZ
12345
67890

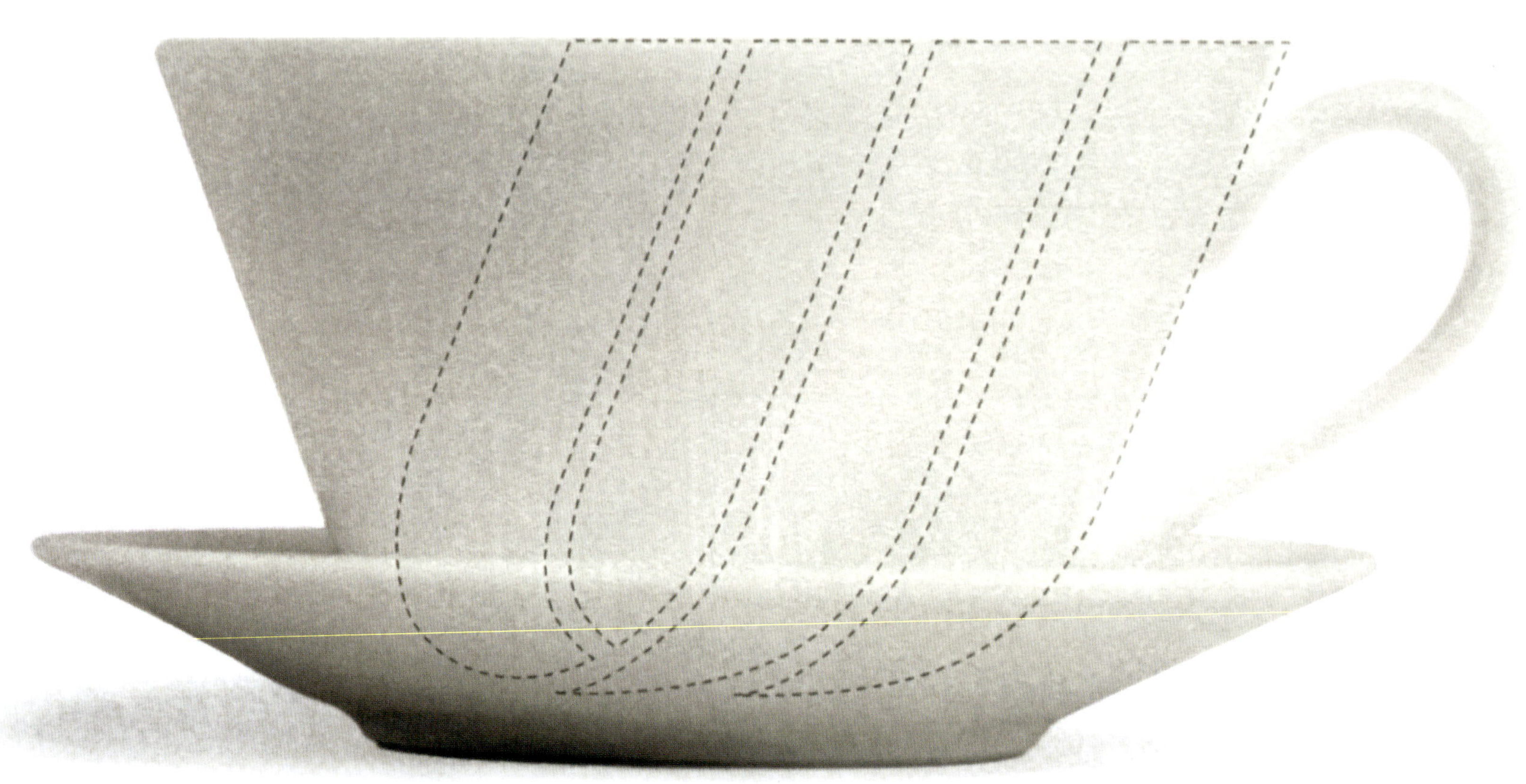

How to pack for a long flight
United Airlines

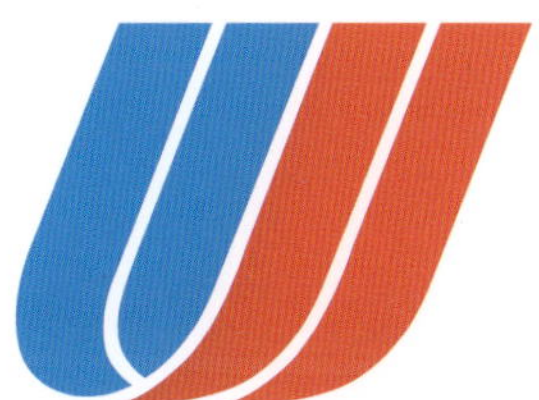

Opposite and above
The United symbol, called "the tulip" inside the company, was created in 1973 by the legendary designer Saul Bass. It had fallen into disuse before we decided to reinvigorate it. Our work with United Airlines included experiments in "branding without branding," such as Daniel Weil's use of the geometry of the symbol to generate the curve of the onboard coffee cup.

The marketing team at United Airlines was looking for a design consultant. I was told later that we were the only designers they met who seemed to express no interest in changing the way the aircraft were painted. "Passengers don't ride on the outside of the planes," I remember telling them. In truth, we had never done an airline before, and had no repainted planes in our portfolio. Instead, at our interview we talked about the things we knew how to design: restaurants, magazines, signs, coffee cups. I reasoned that what an airline really needed was not design as promotion but design as experience.

That began a 15-year relationship. At the very start, I brought in a partner from our London office, the multidisciplinary, multilingual, multitalented Daniel Weil. Danny headed up the three-dimensional projects. I focused on two dimensions. The two of us went to United's headquarters in Chicago for several days once a month, meeting with teams from all over the organization. One client is a challenge. With hundreds of clients, as we had here, the challenges mount geometrically.

Our strategy was not to design a set of abstract guidelines, but to burrow in and work guerilla-style on actual projects, large and small, methodically building a case for what a modern airline could look and feel like. We designed the housing and the user interface for one of the first automatic ticket dispensers. We designed menus, forks and spoons, concourse signage, blankets and pillows. We restored the classic logo designed by Saul Bass. And, about eight years in, we finally managed to repaint the planes.

It was not destined to last. United merged with a rival, and in a series of trade-offs motivated less by marketing theory than by the logic of the deal memo, they married their name to their new partner's symbol. A new era began, without us. It had been an amazing ride.

Below
We persuaded our client to omit the modifier "Airlines" and created a new wordmark to emphasize the suggestive power of their name, such a great descriptor for what makes air travel successful.

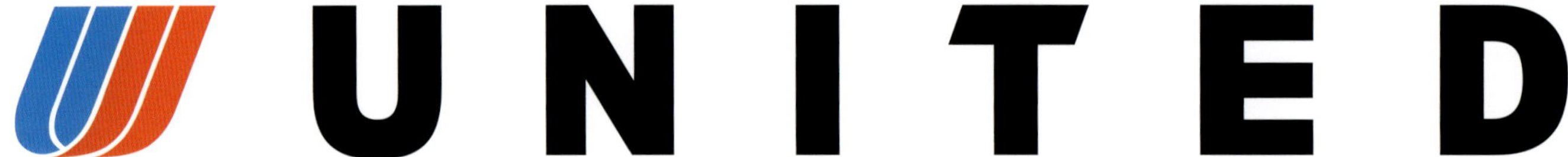

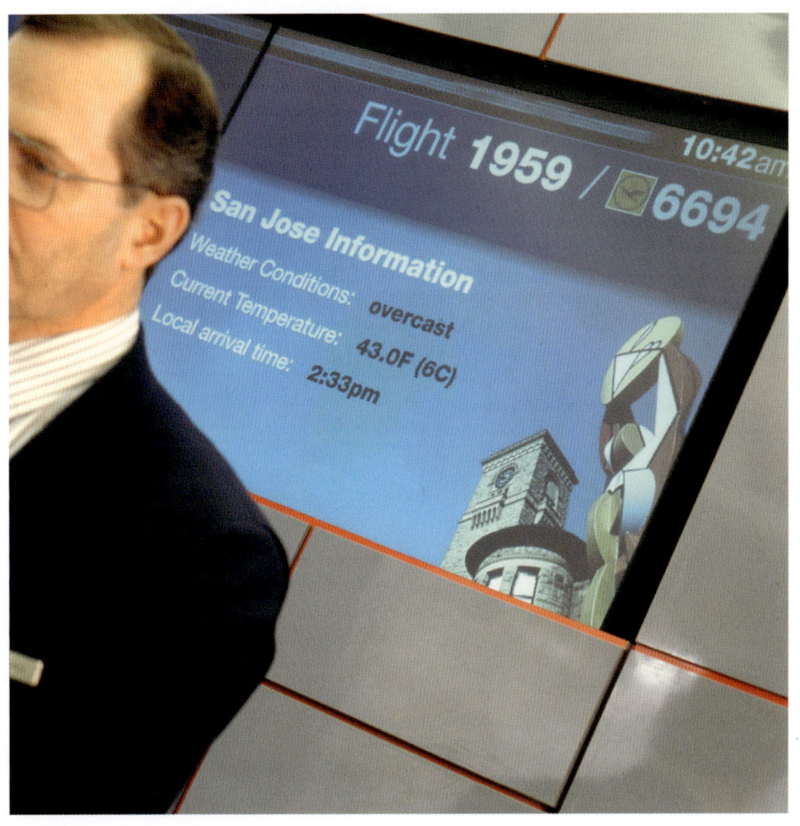

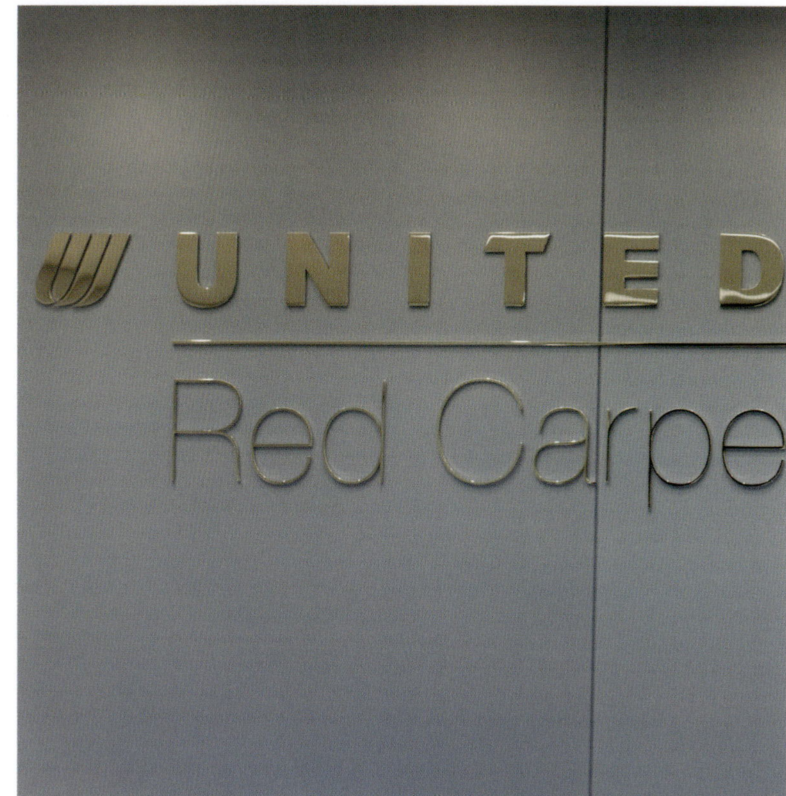

Above left
Whenever possible, we tried to improve the way passengers were given information, including at departure gates.

Above right
Our redesign of the airline's clubs included new entrance signs.

Below
We introduced a new way of using the United symbol, as a sweeping motif that suggested the drama of flight.

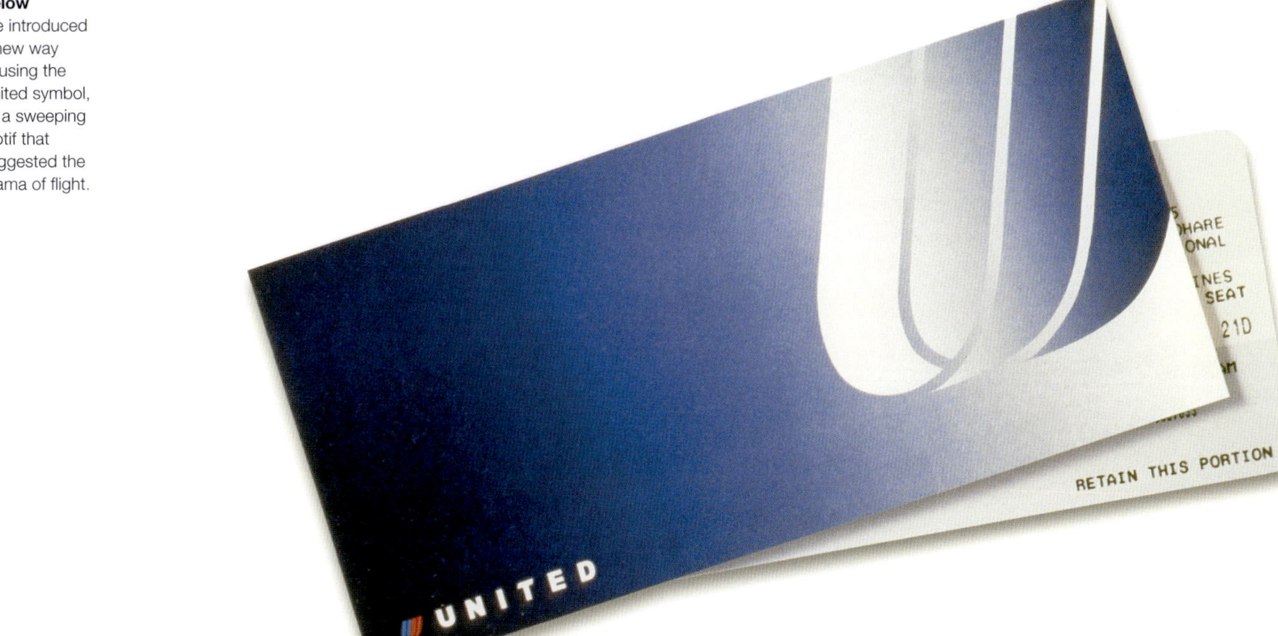

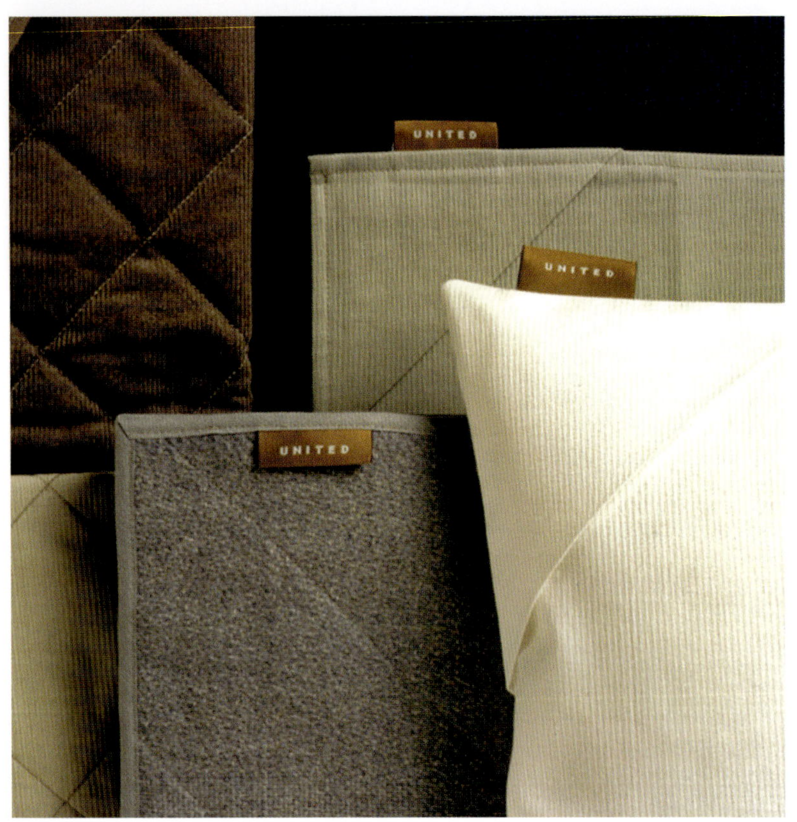

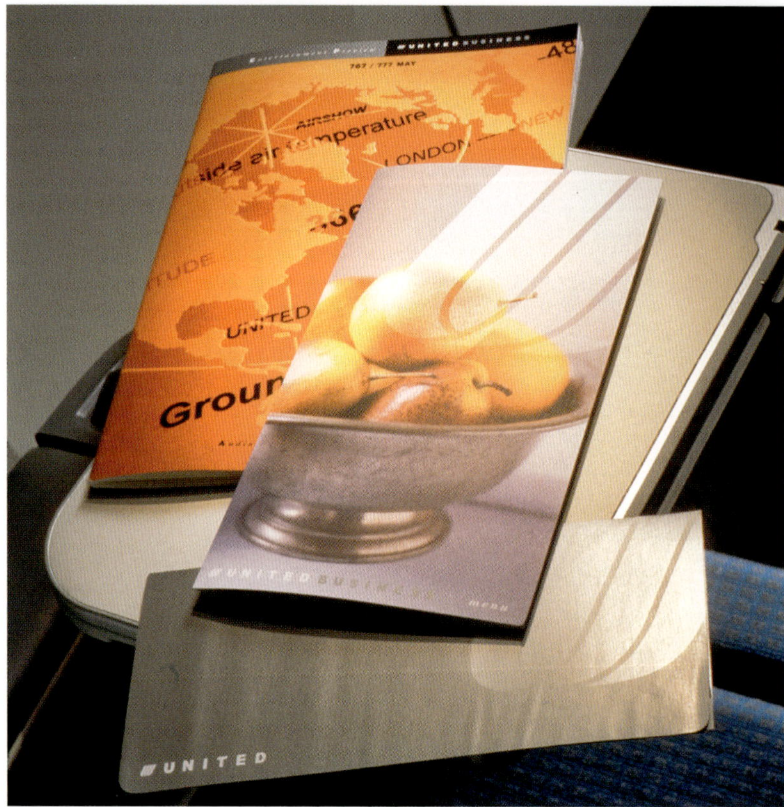

Above left
The passenger's flying experience depends less on branding and more on things to touch and feel. We proposed new blankets long before we suggested changing the logo on the outside of the plane.

Above right
Reducing waste on board meant finding efficient ways to print and recycle items like menus.

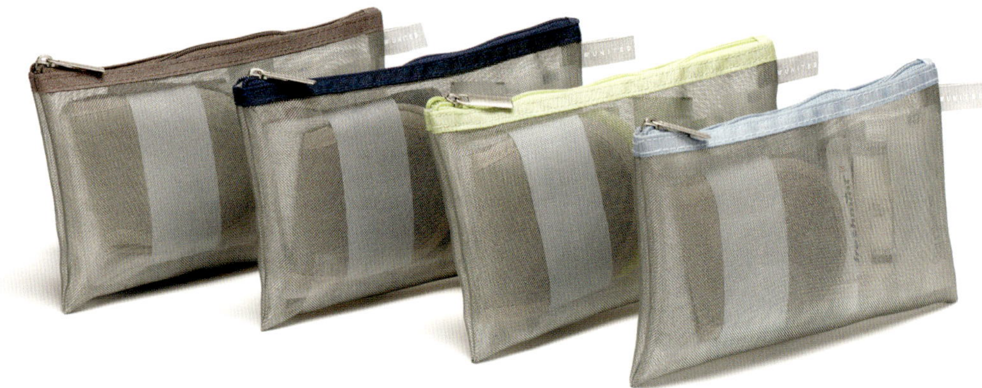

Below
Amenities kits, holding toothpaste and eyeshades, were designed to be both lightweight and reusable.

Building the United Brand

UNITED

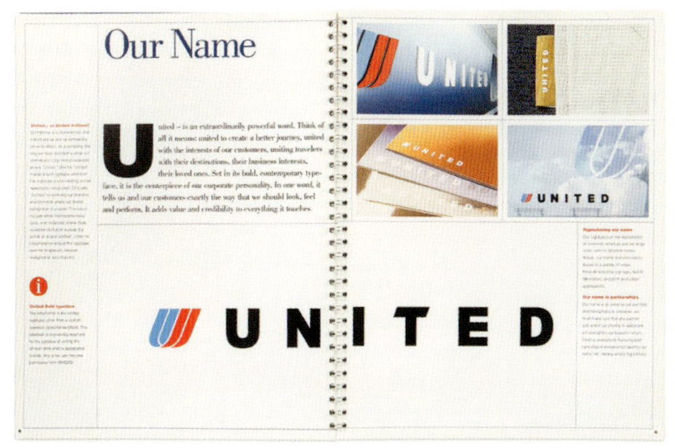

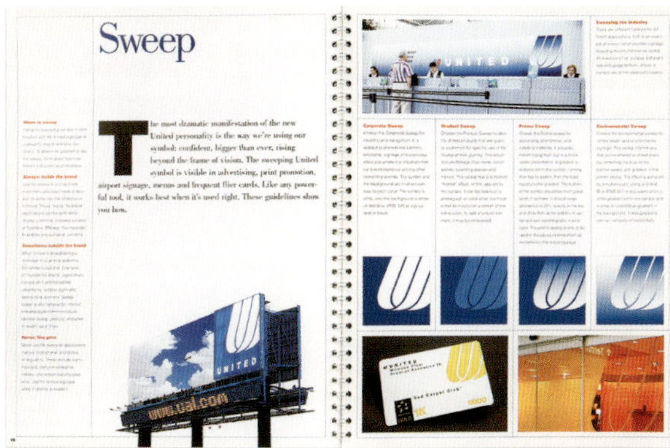

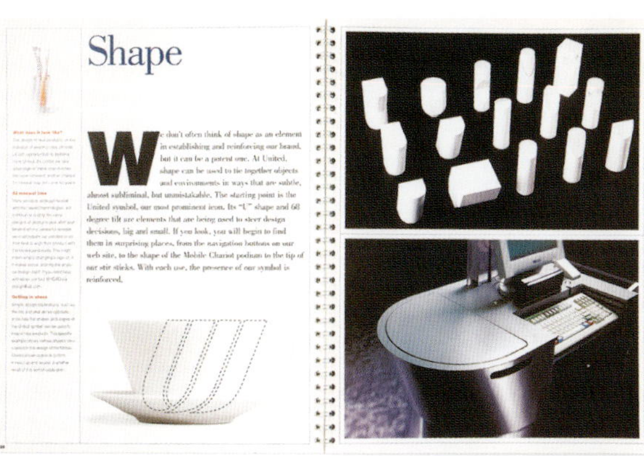

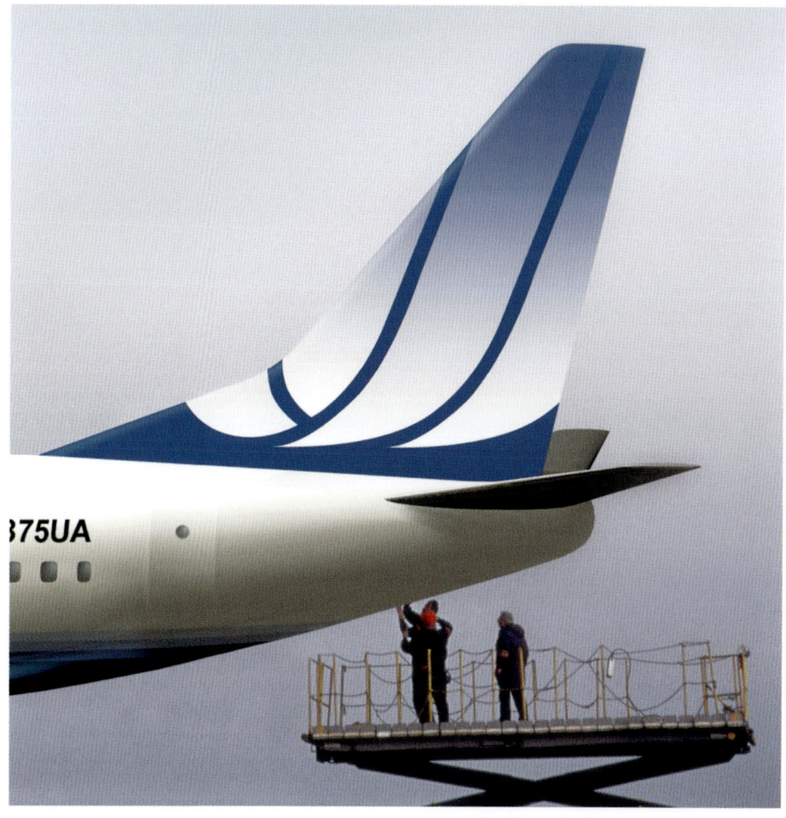

Left
Early on, we produced a guidelines document that set out a set of simple principles for designing the United way.

Above and next spread
Finally, after nearly eight years of work, the time was right to begin painting the plane exteriors to match the airline's new spirit.

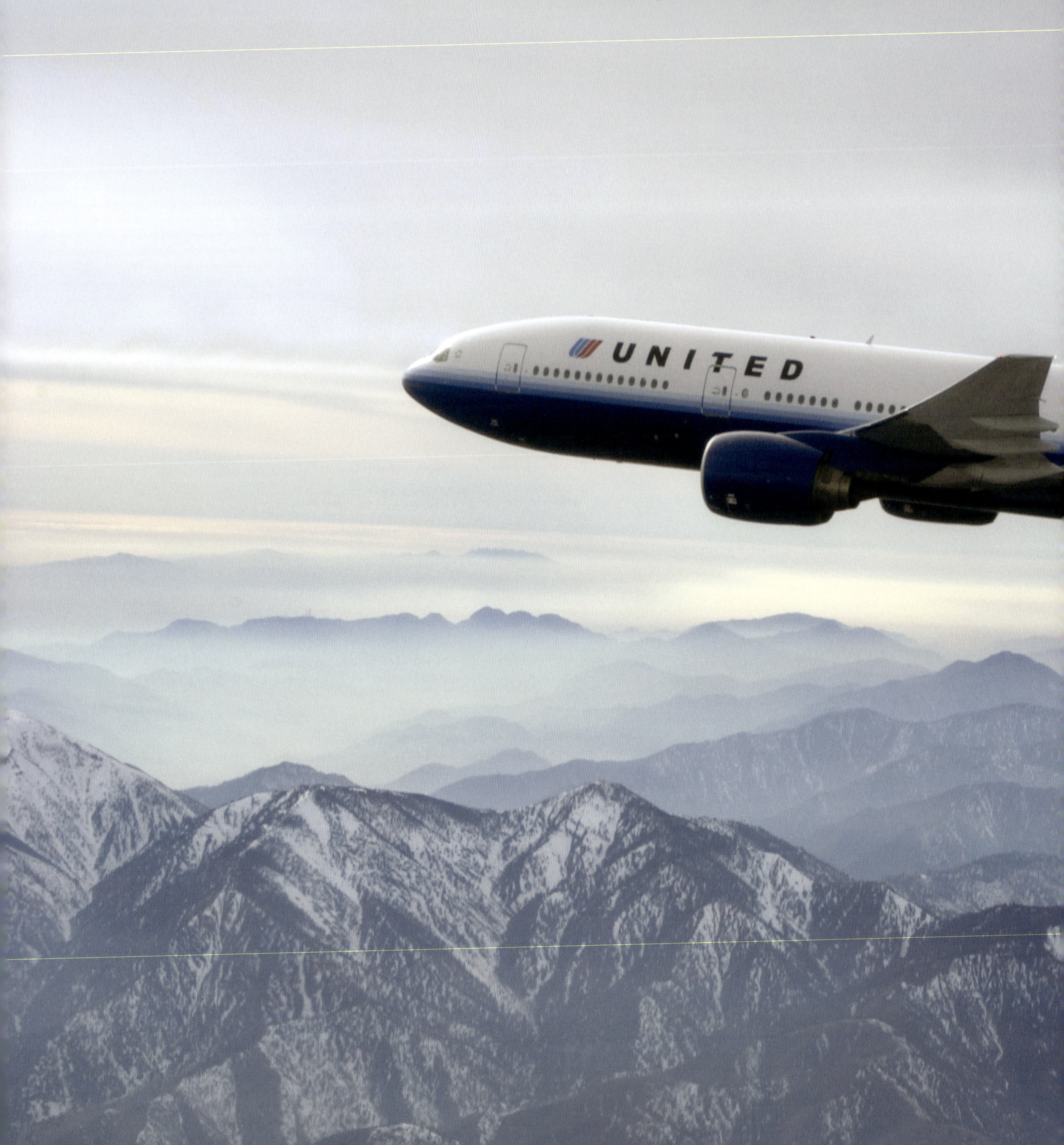
UNITED

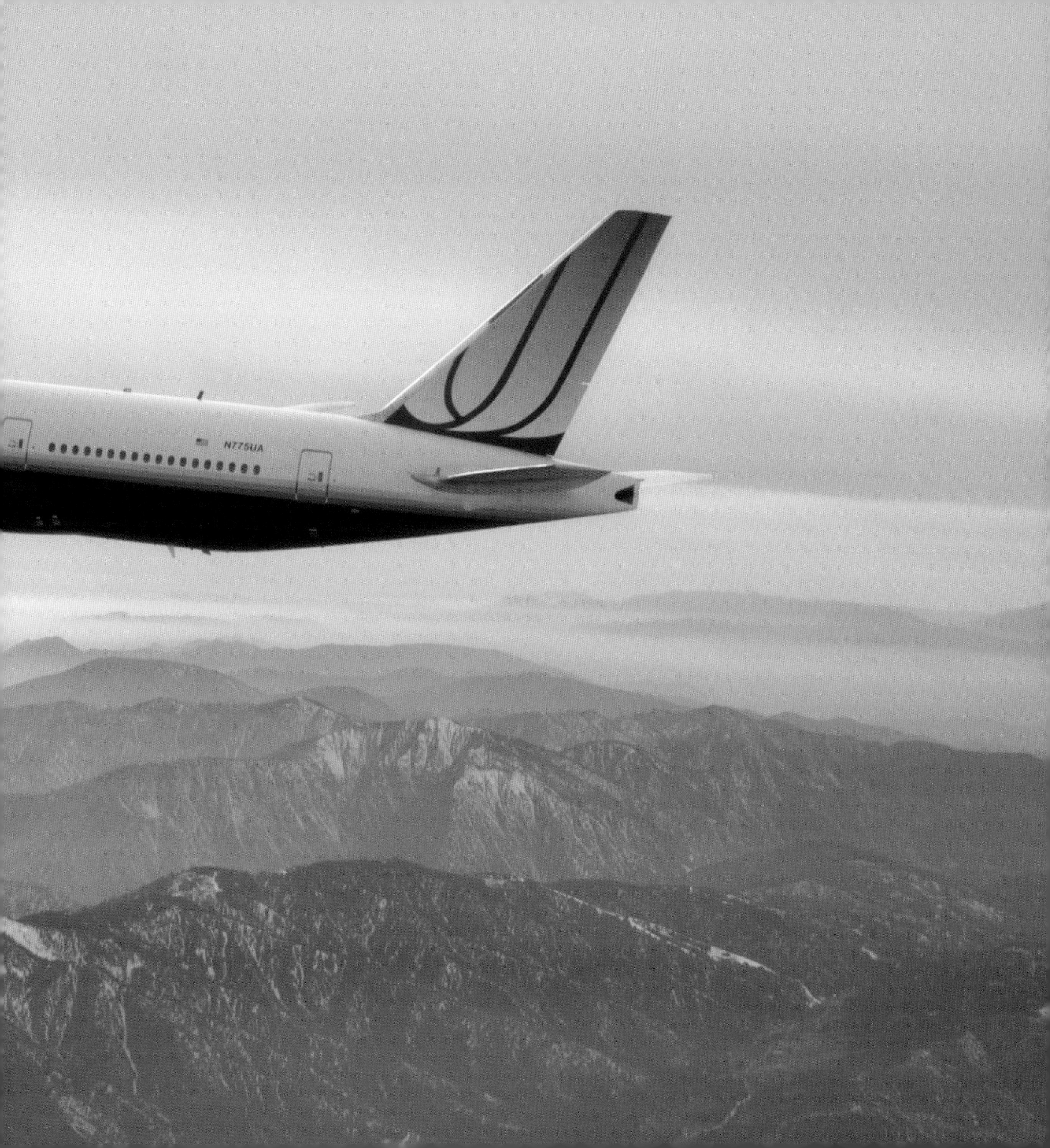
N775UA

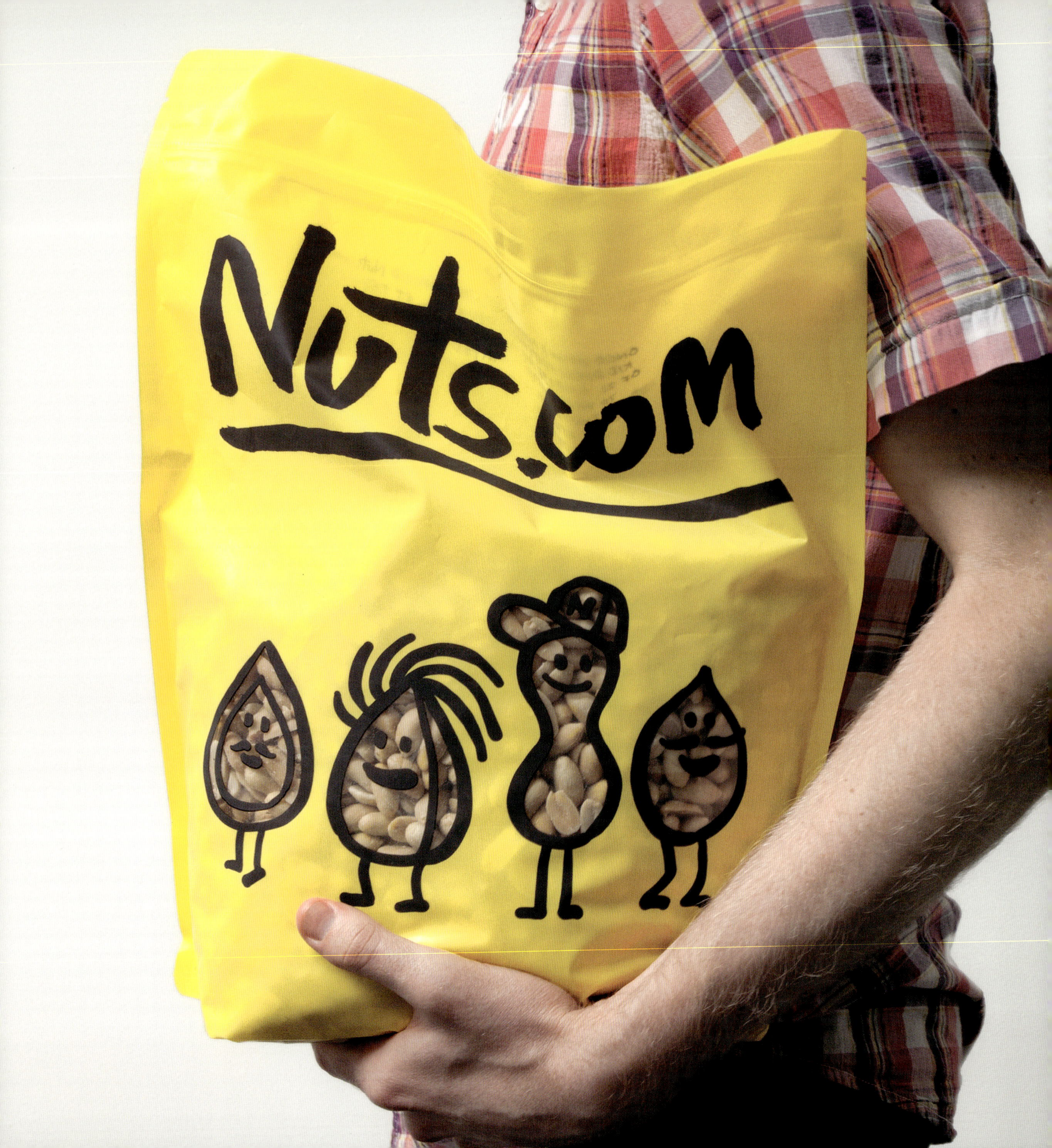
Nuts.com

How to have fun with a brown cardboard box
Nuts.com

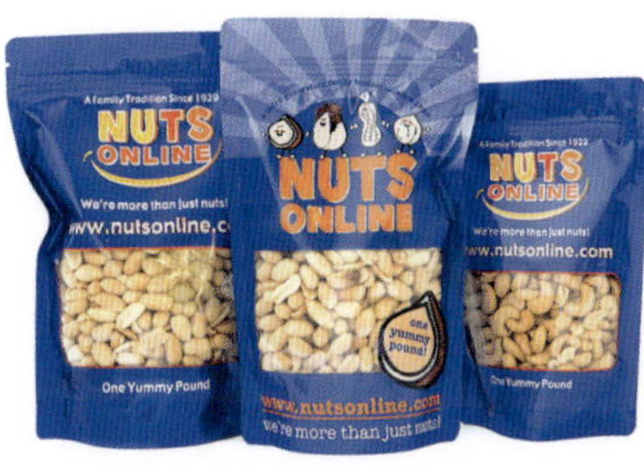

Opposite
Founded by "Poppy" Sol Braverman just before the Great Depression, Nuts.com, then the Newark Nut Company, now also sells dried fruit, snacks, chocolate, and coffee.

Above
The previous packaging featured the incongruous name "Nuts Online."

Jeff Braverman wasn't planning on going into the family business. His grandfather had founded the Newark Nut Company in 1929, selling peanuts from a single cart in the city's Mulberry Street Market. Jeff's father and uncles had turned it into a modest retail operation by the time Jeff went to Wharton School of Business in 1998. He was planning to become a banker.

But in his spare time, he set up a website with a quintessentially redundant Web 1.0 name: nutsonline.com. "My goal for the website was ten orders a day," Jeff told *Inc*. Almost immediately, the online orders overtook the retail sales. Jeff left the world of banking and took over the nut business. Within a dozen years, the site offered nearly 2,000 items and was ringing up $20 million in sales annually. And Jeff could finally get the URL he always wanted: Nuts.com. With a new name in hand, Jeff asked us to redesign the company's packaging.

Consumer packaging is a grim subset of American design. Big corporations, addicted to customer focus groups, dominate the shelves. Minimizing risk inevitably means minimizing beauty, creativity, and distinction. So Jeff's brief was refreshing. He didn't have to compete for attention in grocery stores, since customers assembled their orders online. He saw the packages as the gift wrapping his presents arrived in. "I want that arrival to be a big event," Jeff told us. Nuts.com did no advertising; instead, their shipping cartons functioned as courier-powered billboards.

We took inspiration from Jeff and his family. Sitting in a 60,000-square-foot warehouse overseeing a multimillion-dollar operation, they were as informal and funny as if they were still running a cart in the Mulberry Street Market. So, no typesetting. My hand-lettering was turned into a custom font called Nutcase, which was used to cover their packages with snack-riddled exhortations, all surrounding cartoon portraits of the Bravermans. Within two years, Nuts.com's sales had increased by 50 percent: the power of good design driven by authentic, nutty personality.

ABCDEFGHIJKL
MNOPQRSTUVW
XYZ0123456789
aBCDEFgHiJKLM
NOPQRSTUVWXyZ
0123456789ABC
deFGhIJKLMn
OPQRSTUVWXYZ

Opposite
My hand-painted letters were converted into the proprietary typeface by designer Jeremy Mickel.

Right
Nuts.com is a family business, and the brilliant illustrator (and former Pentagram intern) Christoph Niemann drew a family portrait. Client Jeff Braverman is second from the right.

Next spread
From the brown cardboard box to the individual packages, the receipt of a Nuts.com shipment is meant to be a fun occasion.

Below
The transparent forms of Niemann's characters reveal the package's nutty contents.

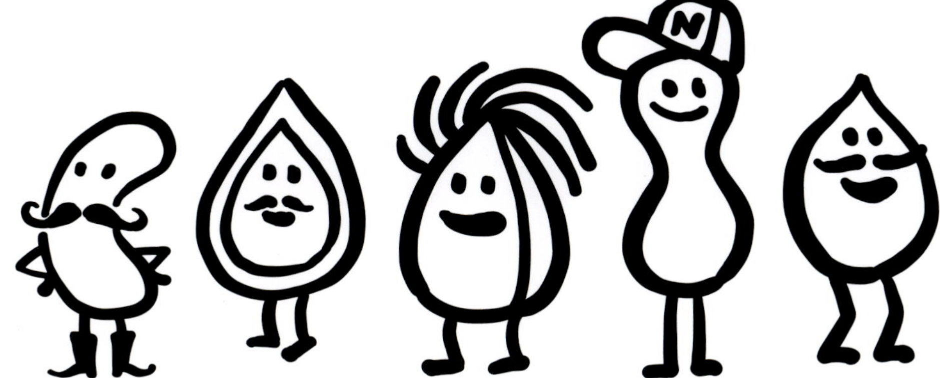

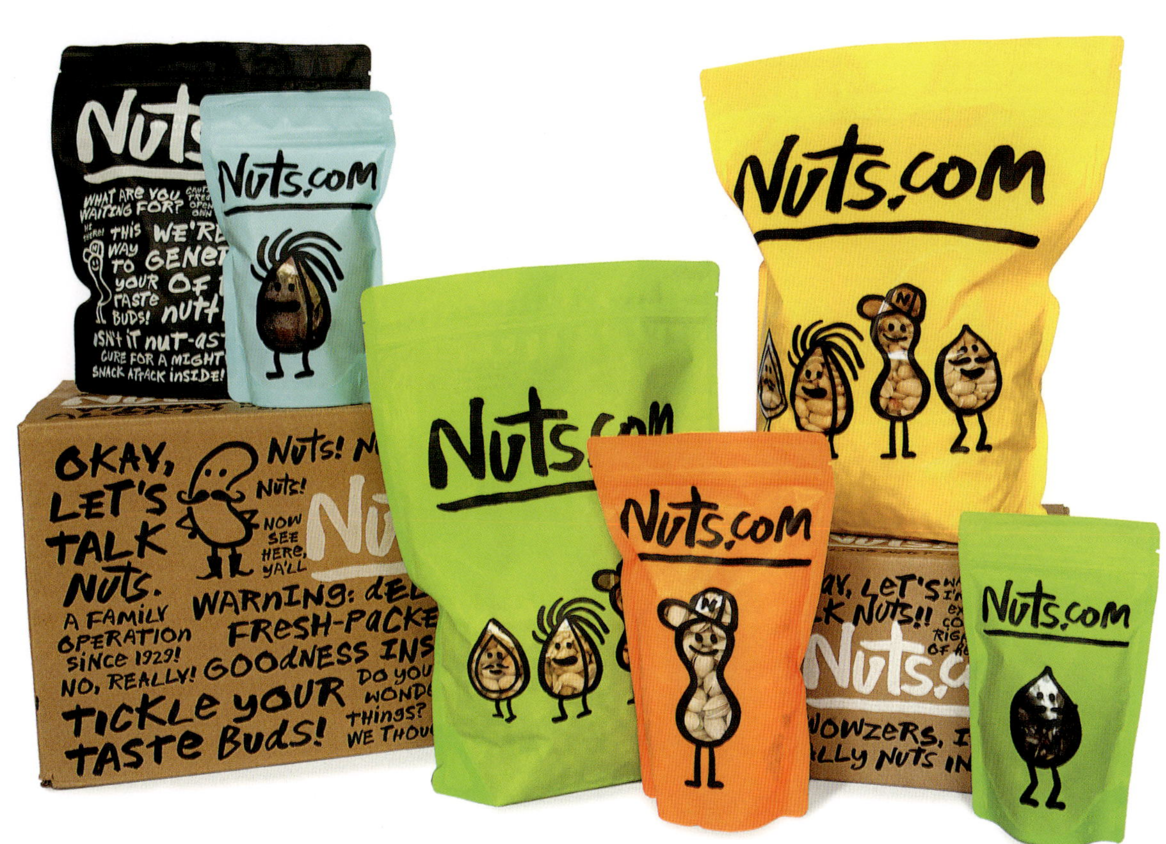

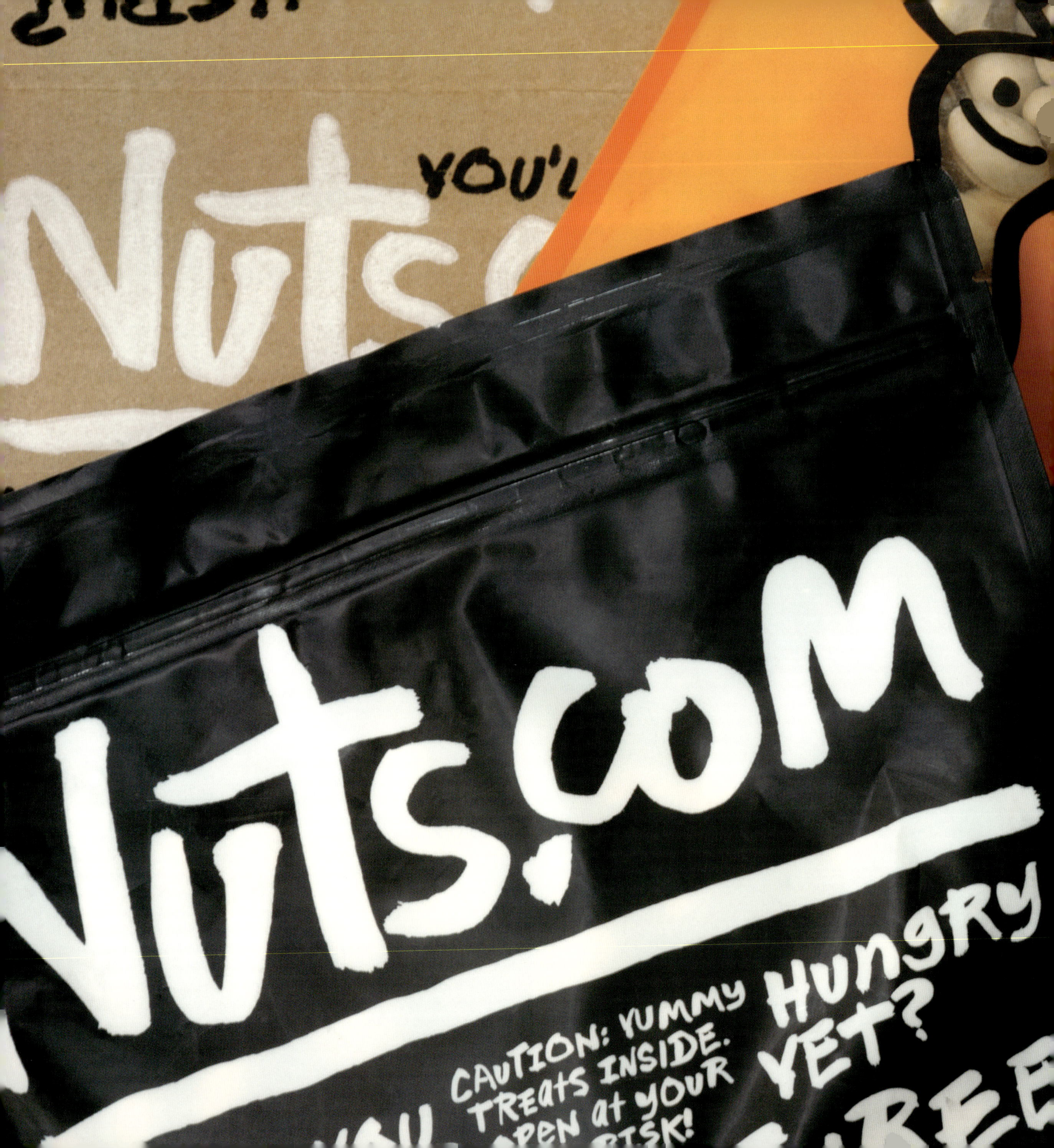
Nuts.com
CAUTION: YUMMY
TREATS INSIDE.
Hungry
YET?

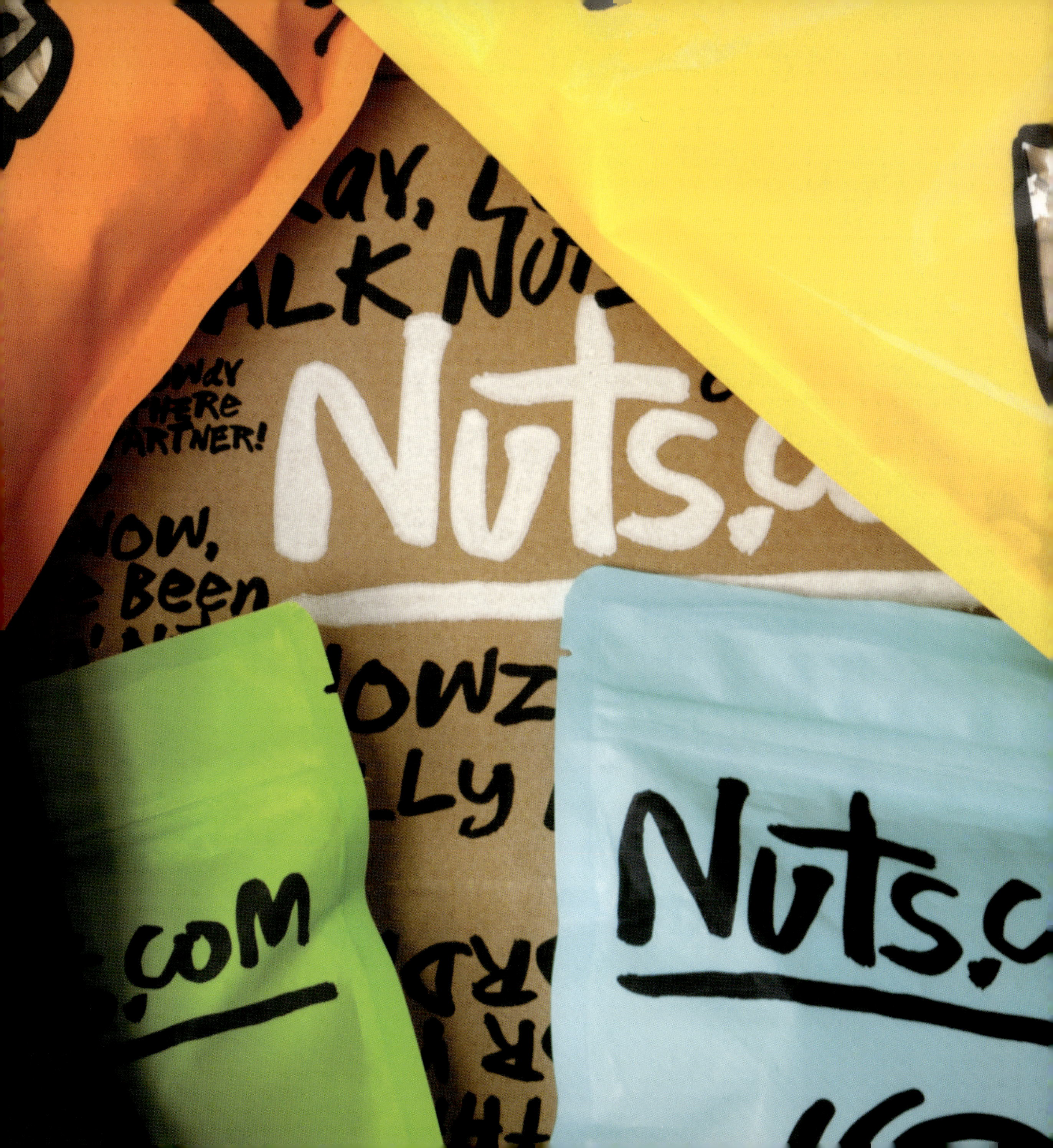

ARTNER!
Been
.COM

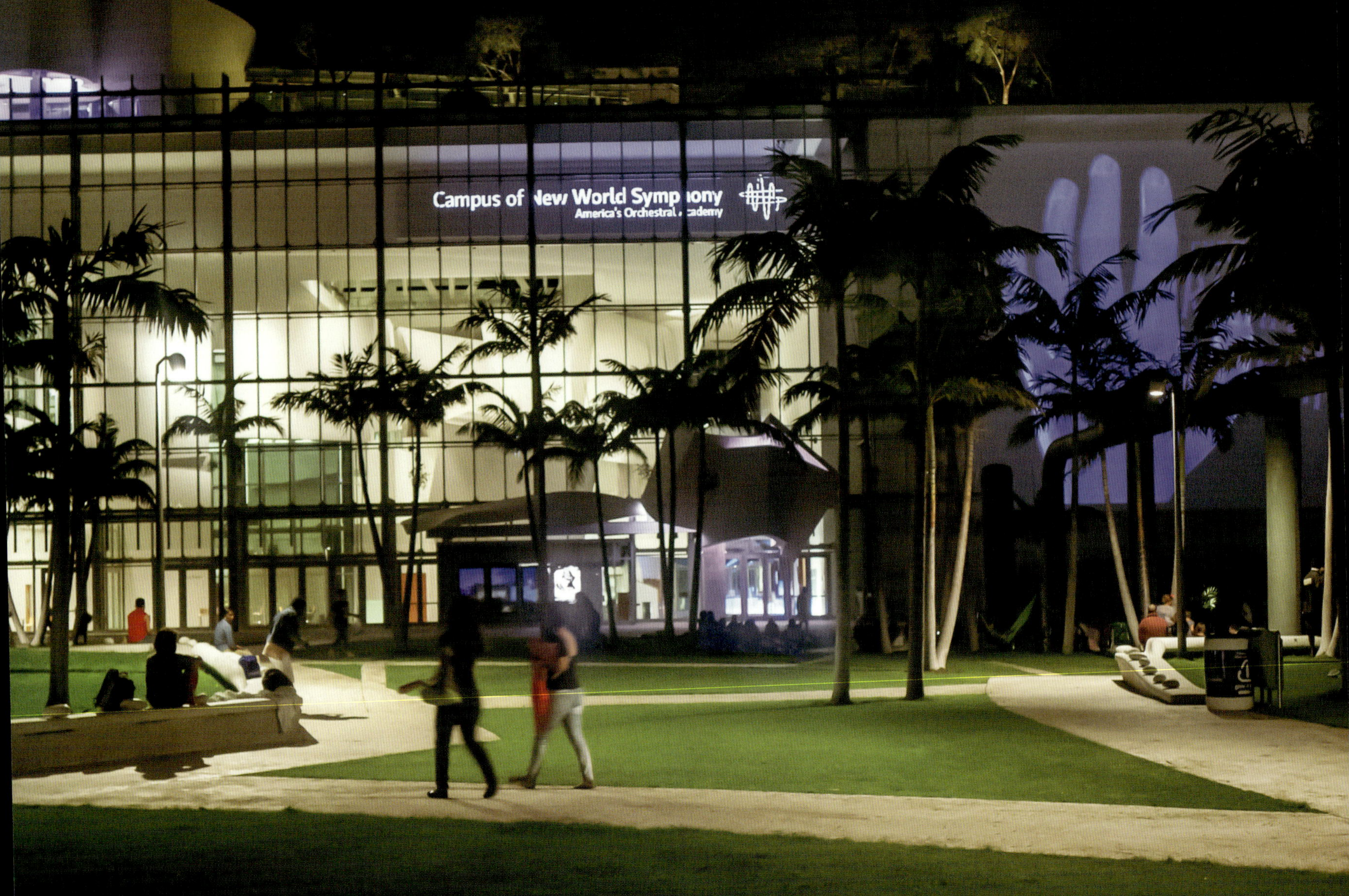
Campus of New World Symphony
America's Orchestral Academy

How to shut up and listen

New World Symphony

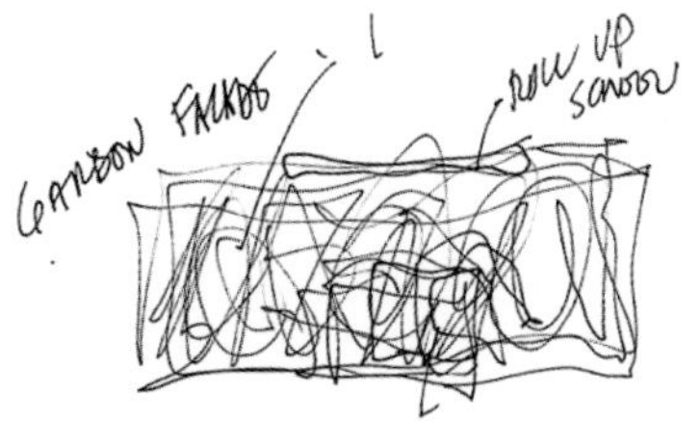

Opposite and above
Frank Gehry's gestural sketch encapsulates the energy of New World Symphony's Miami Beach home. By coincidence, Gehry had babysat NWS's artistic director, Michael Tilson Thomas, when the two were growing up in Los Angeles.

It all seemed so promising at the beginning. Michael Tilson Thomas, the charismatic and visionary conductor, pianist, and composer, was building a home for his greatest project, New World Symphony. Gifted young musicians from all over the world would come together to study in an extraordinary new building designed by Frank Gehry in the heart of Miami Beach. Music, architecture, learning: when we were asked to design the center's new logo, it seemed as though there was so much to work with. Tilson Thomas asked for something that "flowed."

Yet a solution eluded us. I was so sure I had hit the bull's-eye with my first solution, a morphing collage of curvy typography. Executive vice president Victoria Roberts told me, as politely as possible, that it made some people there feel ill. A second attempt was less idiosyncratic but perhaps too tame. I tried working with the NWS acronym, something I had resisted at first, but the result felt too stiff and corporate. Through the process, Tilson Thomas was encouraging and supportive, but I could sense his growing impatience.

Finally, I got an email with an attachment: six sketches that Tilson Thomas had done for the logo. I was despondent. It was as if he had grown tired of my frantic guesses and just decided to tell me the answer. And the sketches were incomprehensible to me. They showed the three letters of the acronym connected to form something like a swan. Was I just supposed to execute this idea? I wouldn't presume to tell my client how to conduct an orchestra. How dare anyone tell me how to design a logo!

But then I realized that I had been given a gift. Michael Tilson Thomas led a peripatetic life, jetting between engagements all over the world. In the midst of it all, he had found time to think about my problem, and put some thoughts on paper. I looked again at the sketches, and realized the single connected line—like a conductor's gesture—had one thing that all my work did not: flow. It was what he had been asking for all along, and what I had been too busy to hear. Within hours, I had the solution.

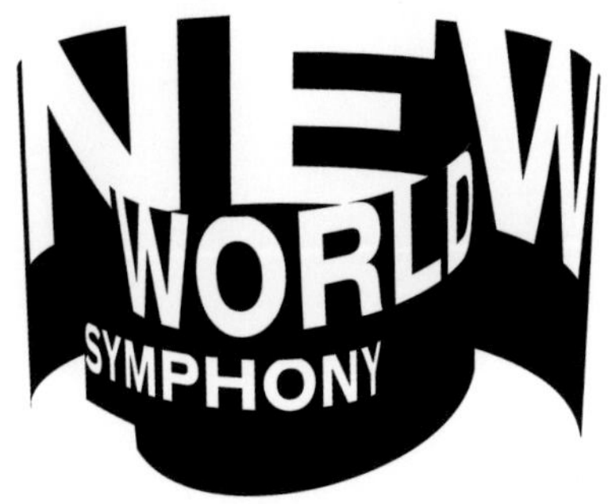

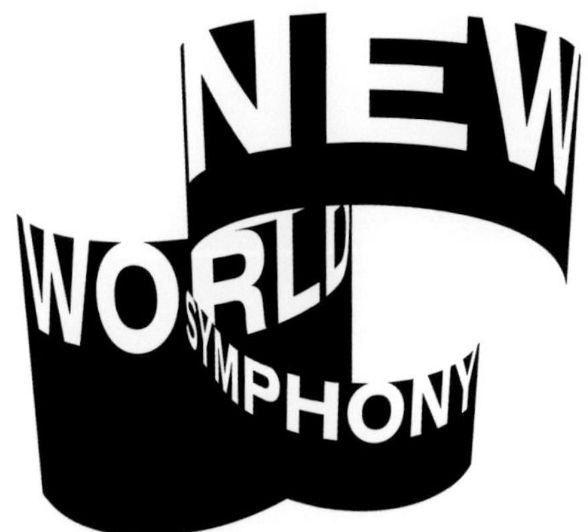

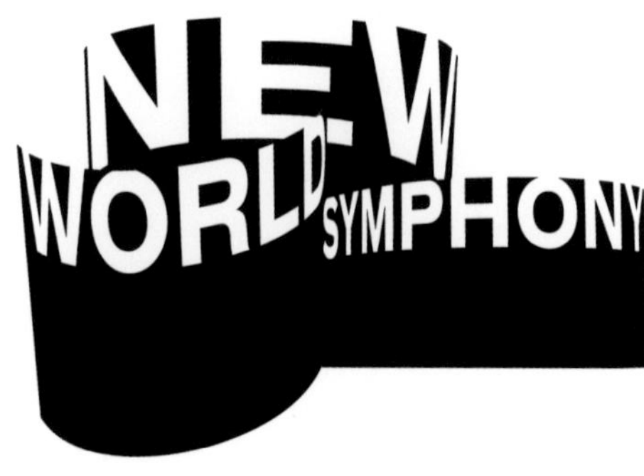

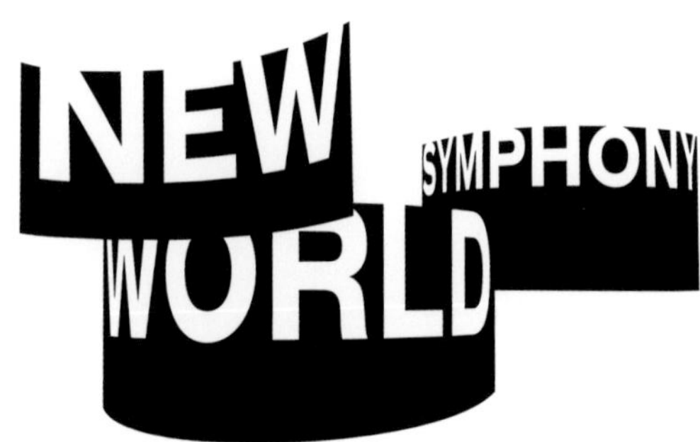

Left
I was certain that I had solved the problem with my first idea, a flexible identity. Rearranging the three words of the name in curved forms was meant to evoke Gehry's architecture. NWS's Victoria Roberts told us that this solution "made people nauseous." Not the kind of response we had hoped for.

Right
The alternating serif and sans serif letters in our next idea were meant to suggest the New World Symphony's commitment to the traditional orchestral repertory within the context of a decidedly 21st-century facility. Elegant, but too bland.

NEWWORLD
SYMPHONY

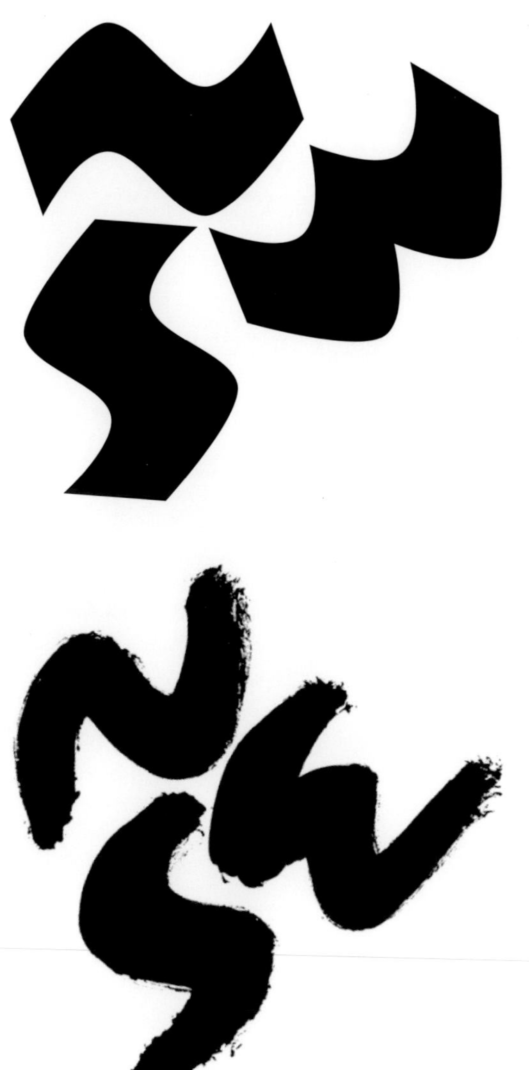

Left
I resisted using the letters NWS, reasoning that it had the same number of syllables as the full name and thus offered no economy when said aloud. I also expressed distaste for acronyms in general, despite the fact that my client himself was often called MTT. Our first try was, again, an attempt to imitate the building's architecture. To suggest more "flow" we also did a hand-drawn version. We liked neither of these.

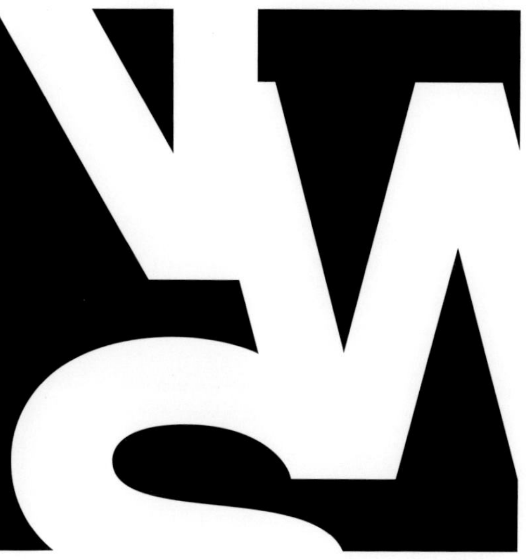

Above
The building's fragmented, episodic interior spaces suggested a positive/negative treatment of the initial letters. Our designer Yve Ludwig crafted a good solution, but one that I thought looked better suited to a chemical company than a cultural institution.

Below
Michael Tilson Thomas finally put pen to paper and sent me sketches that I initially found infuriating. Then I realized they provided the key to the answer.

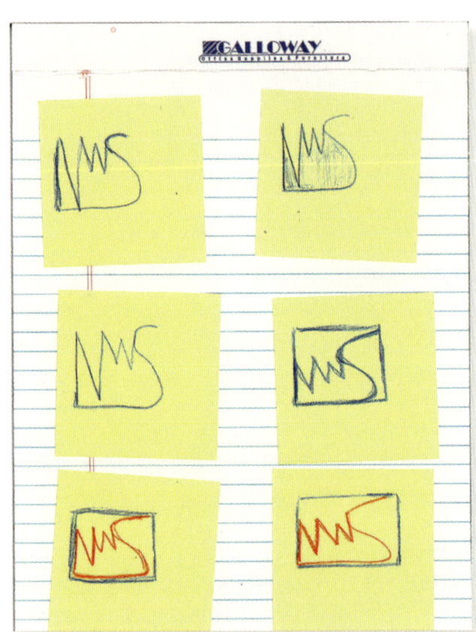

Right
Connecting the three letters in a single gesture conjured up everything from the motion of a conductor's baton to the science of sound waves to Frank Gehry's original sketch. The challenge was how to weave together N, W, and S.

The result, which emerged over a long weekend with my notebook, had a surprising sense of symmetry and coherence.

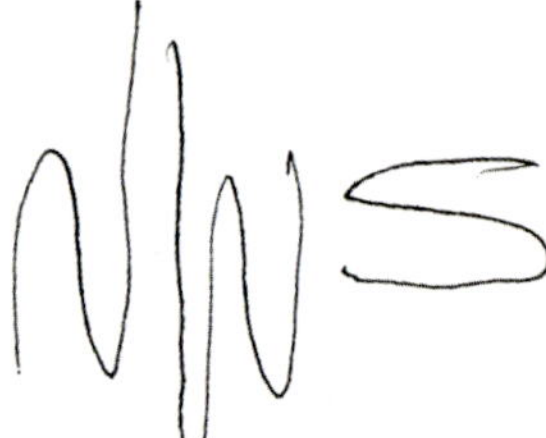

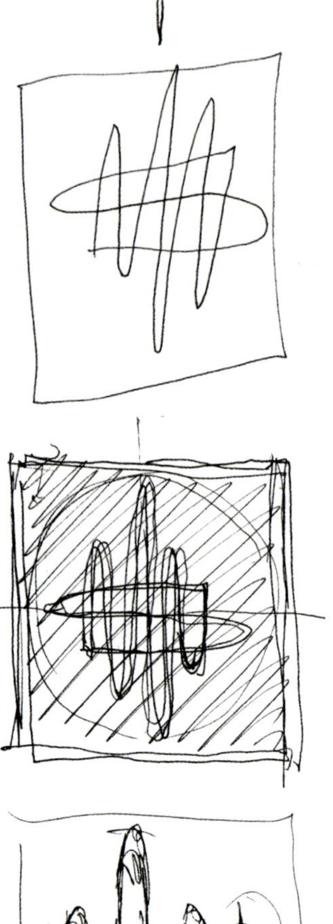

Below
For the final design, we opted to break the line selectively to make the three letters easier to read.

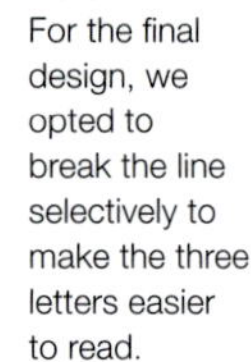

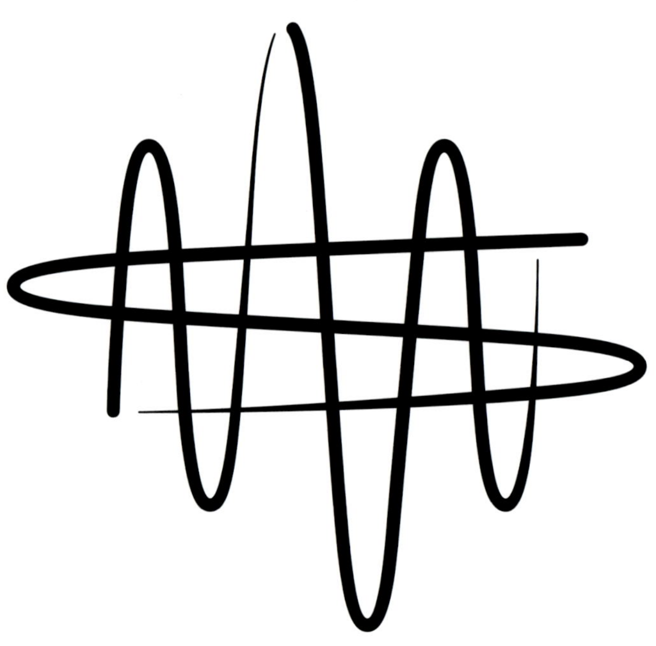

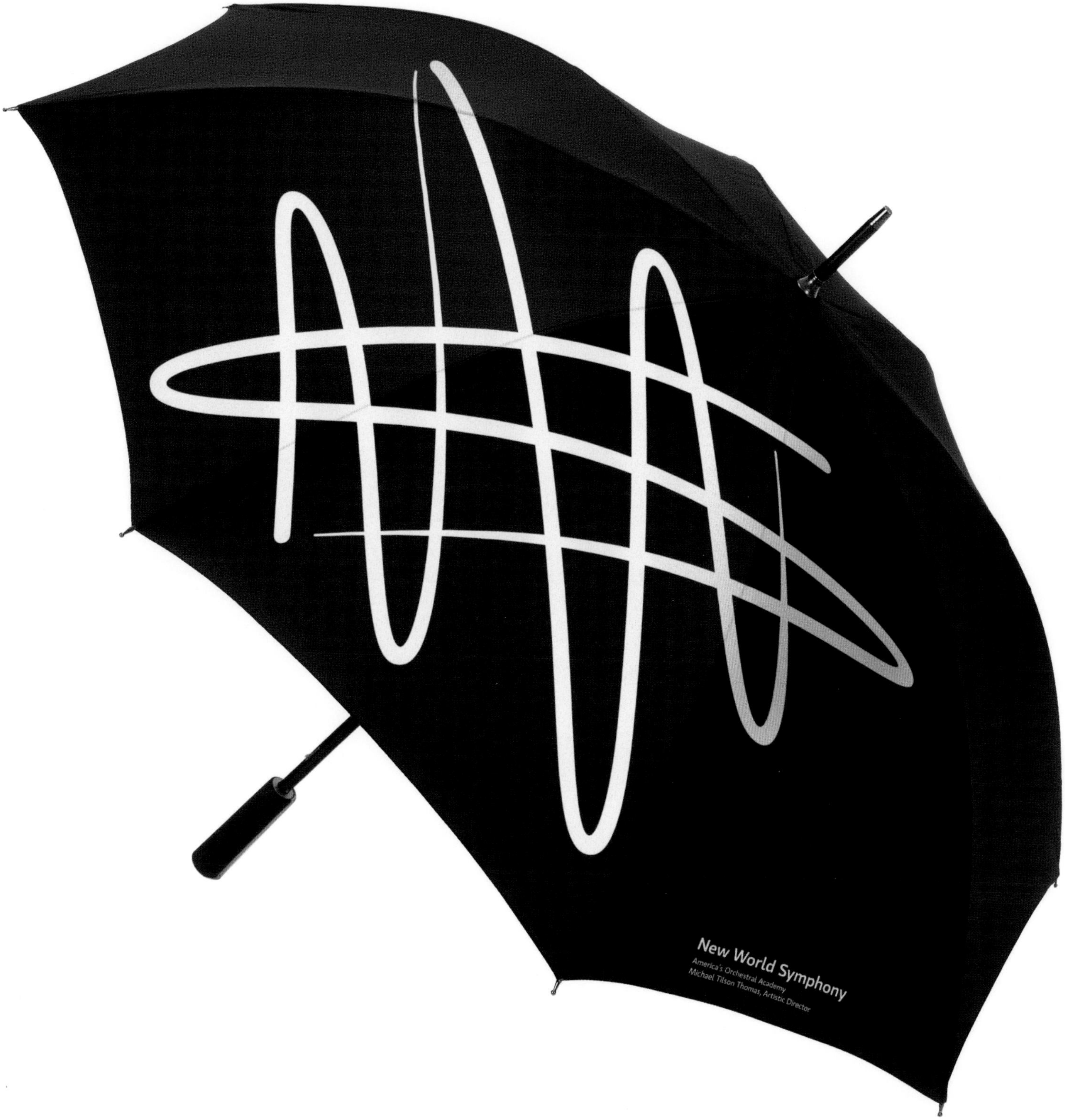

Left
The result has the expressive sense of flow that the client had asked for from the very beginning.

2 WKS. AGO	LAST WEEK	THIS WEEK	TITLE / PRODUCER (SONGWRITER)	Artist / IMPRINT/PROMOTION LABEL	CERT.	PEAK POS.	WKS. ON CHART
1	1	1	#1 6 WKS **LOCKED OUT OF HEAVEN** THE SMEEZINGTONS,J.BHASKER,E.HAYNIE,M.RONSON (BRUNO MARS,P.LAWRENCE II,A.LEVINE)	Bruno Mars ATLANTIC		1	15
0	5	2	DG SG **THRIFT SHOP** R.LEWIS (B.HAGGERTY,R.LEWIS)	Macklemore & Ryan Lewis Feat. Wanz MACKLEMORE/ADA/WARNER BROS.		2	15

The track crowns Hot Digital Songs (2-1), hiking by 18% to 279,000 downloads sold, according to Nielsen SoundScan. It rules the new Streaming Songs survey (see page 66), registering 1.5 million streams (up 17%) and charges 38-22 on Hot 100 Airplay (44 million audience impressions, up 33%), according to Nielsen BDS.

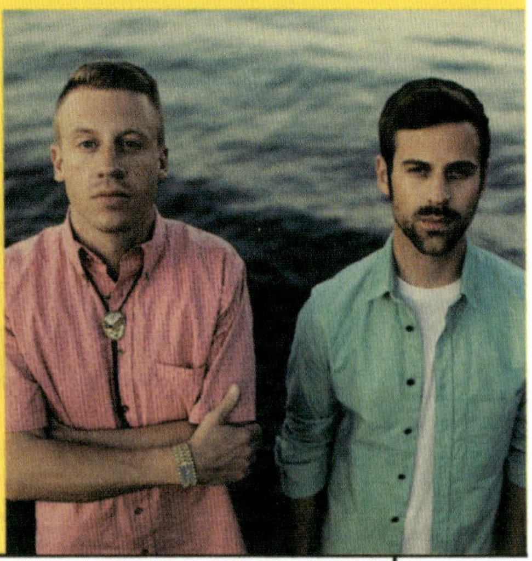

2 WKS. AGO	LAST WEEK	THIS WEEK	TITLE / PRODUCER (SONGWRITER)	Artist / IMPRINT/PROMOTION LABEL	CERT.	PEAK POS.	WKS. ON CHART
4	4	3	**HO HEY** R.HADLOCK (W.SCHULTZ,J.FRAITES)	The Lumineers DUALTONE	▲	3	32
2	3	4	AG **I KNEW YOU WERE TROUBLE.** MAX MARTIN,SHELLBACK (T.SWIFT,MAX MARTIN,SHELLBACK)	Taylor Swift BIG MACHINE/REPUBLIC	▲	2	13
3	2	5	**DIAMONDS** STARGATE,BENNY BLANCO (S.FURLER,B.LEVIN,M.S.ERIKSEN,T.E.HERMANSEN)	Rihanna SRP/DEF JAM/IDJMG	▲	1	16
2	8	6	**SCREAM & SHOUT** LAZY JAY (W.ADAMS,J.MARTENS,J.BAPTISTE)	will.i.am & Britney Spears INTERSCOPE		6	7
5	11	7	**DON'T YOU WORRY CHILD** AXWELL,S.INGROSSO,S.ANGELLO (J.MARTIN,M.ZITRON, AXWELL,S.INGROSSO,S.ANGELLO)	Swedish House Mafia Feat. John Martin ASTRALWERKS/CAPITOL		7	17

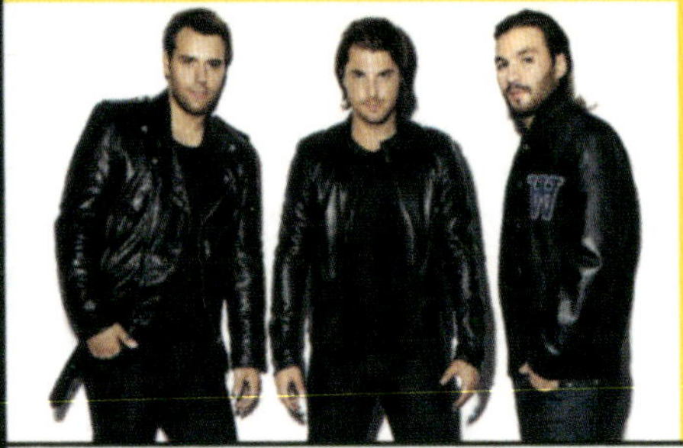

The EDM trio scores its first Hot 100 top 10 with its first chart entry. The cut ranks at No. 2 on the new Dance/Electronic Songs chart (see page 79).

2 WKS. AGO	LAST WEEK	THIS WEEK	TITLE / PRODUCER (SONGWRITER)	Artist / IMPRINT/PROMOTION LABEL	CERT.	PEAK POS.	WKS. ON CHART
5	7	8	**BEAUTY AND A BEAT** MAX MARTIN,ZEDD (MAX MARTIN,A.ZASLAVSKI,S.KOTECHA,O.T.MARAJ)	Justin Bieber Featuring Nicki Minaj SCHOOLBOY/RAYMOND BRAUN/ISLAND/IDJMG		5	14
9	6	9	**HOME** D.PEARSON (D.PEARSON,G.HOLDEN)	Phillip Phillips 19/INTERSCOPE	▲2	6	29
11	10	10	**I CRY** THE FUTURISTICS,SOFLY & NIUS,P.BAUMER,M.HOOGSTRATEN (T.DILLARD, A.SCHWARTZ,J.KHAJADOURIAN,B.JUDDIN,B.MELKI,B.RUSSELL,S.CUTLER,J.HULL,M.CAREN)	Flo Rida POE BOY/ATLANTIC		6	16

2 WKS. AGO	LAST WEEK	THIS WEEK	TITLE / PRODUCER (SONGWRITER)	IM
22	21	24	**LET ME LOVE YOU (UNTIL YOU LEARN TO LOVE** STARGATE,REEVA,BLACK (S.C.SMITH,S.FURLER, T. E.HERMANSEN,M.HADFIELD,M.DIS CALA)	
42	34	25	**DAYLIGHT** A.LEVINE,MDL,MAX MARTIN (A.LEVINE,MAX MARTIN,SAMM,M.LEVY)	
28	32	26	**HALL OF FAME** D.O'DONOGHUE,M.SHEEHAN,J.BARRY (D.O'DONOGHUE, M.SHEEHAN,W.ADAMS,J.BARRY)	The Script Featu
38	27	27	**LITTLE TALKS** OF MONSTERS AND MEN,A.ARNARSSON (N.B.HILMARSDOTTIR,R.T	Of Mons
30	33	28	**I'M DIFFERENT** DJ MUSTARD (T.EPPS,D.MCFARLANE)	
23	26	29	**CLIQUE** HIT-BOY,K.WEST (C.HOLLIS,S.M.ANDERSON, K.O.WEST,S.C.CARTER,J.E.FAUNTLEROY II)	Kanye West, J
19	23	30	**CRUISE** J.MOI (B.KELLEY,T.HUBBARD,J.MOI,C.RICE,J.RICE)	Florida
25	31	31	**WANTED** D.HUFF,H.HAYES (T.VERGES,H.HAYES)	ATLAN
46	35	32	**I WILL WAIT** M.DRAVS (MUMFORD & SONS)	Mu GENTLEMAN OF T
39	40	33	**BETTER DIG TWO** D.HUFF (B.CLARK,S.MCANALLY,T. ROSEN)	Th
44	36	34	**ADORN** MIGUEL (M.J.PIMENTEL)	
41	44	35	**EVERY STORM (RUNS OUT OF RAIN)** G.ALLAN,G.DROMAN (G.ALLAN,M.WARREN,H.LINDSEY)	
33	37	36	**LITTLE THINGS** J.GOSLING (E.SHEERAN,F.VEVAN)	
34	28	37	**TOO CLOSE** DIPLO,SWITCH,A.RECHTSCHAID (A.CLARE,J.DUGUID)	
29	38	38	**NO WORRIES** DETAIL (D.CARTER,N.C.FISHER,B.WILLIAMS,J.A.PREYAN,R.DIAZ)	Lil Wayne Fe YOUN
17	25	39	**WE ARE NEVER EVER GETTING BACK TOGE** MAX MARTIN,SHELLBACK,D.HUFF (T.SWIFT,MAX MARTIN,SHELLBACK)	
27	29	40	**CALL ME MAYBE** J.RAMSAY (J.RAMSAY,C.R.JEPSEN,T.CROWE)	Car 604
51	49	41	**RADIOACTIVE** ALEX DA KID (IMAGINE DRAGONS,A.GRANT,J.MOSSER)	Ima

How to top the charts

Billboard

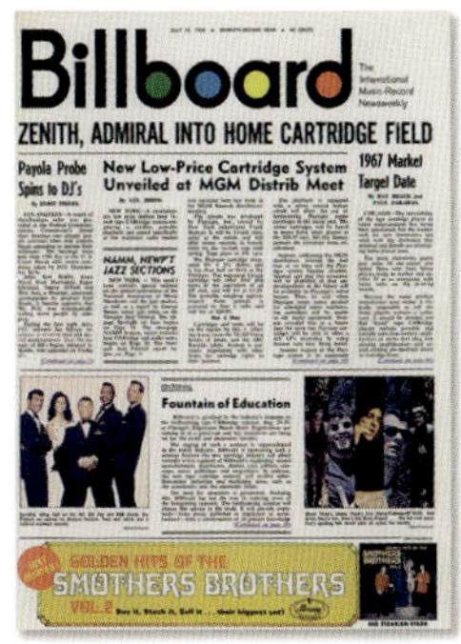

Billboard

ZENITH, ADMIRAL INTO HOME CARTRIDGE FIELD

Payola Probe Spins to DJ's

New Low-Price Cartridge System Unveiled at MGM Distrib Meet

1967 Market Target Date

NAMM, NEWP'T JAZZ SECTIONS

Fountain of Education

GOLDEN HITS OF THE SMOTHERS BROTHERS VOL. 2

Opposite
The minutely calibrated Hot 100 chart, shown here at actual size, is crammed with detail and designed to reward close scrutiny.

Above
The Bible of the music industry as I knew it as a kid in 1966.

Like many kids in the 1960s, I was obsessed with music. But, unlike most of my friends, I wasn't content with the Top 40 countdown on the radio. Instead, I went each week to the periodicals room of our local library, where I spent hours with the Bible of the music industry, *Billboard*.

Billboard is one of America's oldest publications, founded in 1894 as a trade magazine for the outdoor advertising industry. It expanded to cover circuses, vaudeville, carnivals, and—with the invention of the jukebox in the 1930s—music, which became its ultimate focus. Responding to the rise of rock and roll, it introduced the legendary Hot 100 singles chart just a few weeks before my first birthday in August 1958.

I'm not sure why I found the Hot 100 chart, and its counterpart list of the top 200 albums, so mesmerizing. Maybe I found comfort in seeing that popularity, a property that utterly confounded me in my junior high school's cafeteria, could be minutely calculated. It was a vicarious triumph every time one of my favorite groups hit number one. No matter that the charts were surrounded by baffling jargon. It was like being an insider at last.

So it was a thrill, 40 years later, to be asked to redesign *Billboard* for the new world of digital music. The logo, for instance, had barely changed since "Hanky Panky" by Tommy James and the Shondells was number one in 1966. But the number of charts had ballooned, tracking everything from regional Mexican albums to ringtones.

This was one of the more complex information design projects I've ever done. Working with *Billboard*'s art director, Andrew Horton, we created a 14-column grid to unify the publication from front to back. We strengthened the logo, focusing on its simple geometry and bright primary colors. And the charts, which had degenerated into a murky pastel-toned backwater, were restored to their former authority in bold black and white, with an emphasis on legibility.

It turns out that even in the digital era, pop artists still displayed the charts showing their first appearance at number one. We created information design that was suitable for framing.

Right
The magazine's name, almost every letter of which is made of either circles, vertical lines, or both, is a designer's dream. Even when we completely deconstructed it, it was still legible. The logo before the redesign is at the top. The final is at the bottom. Some of the dozens of versions we considered are in between.

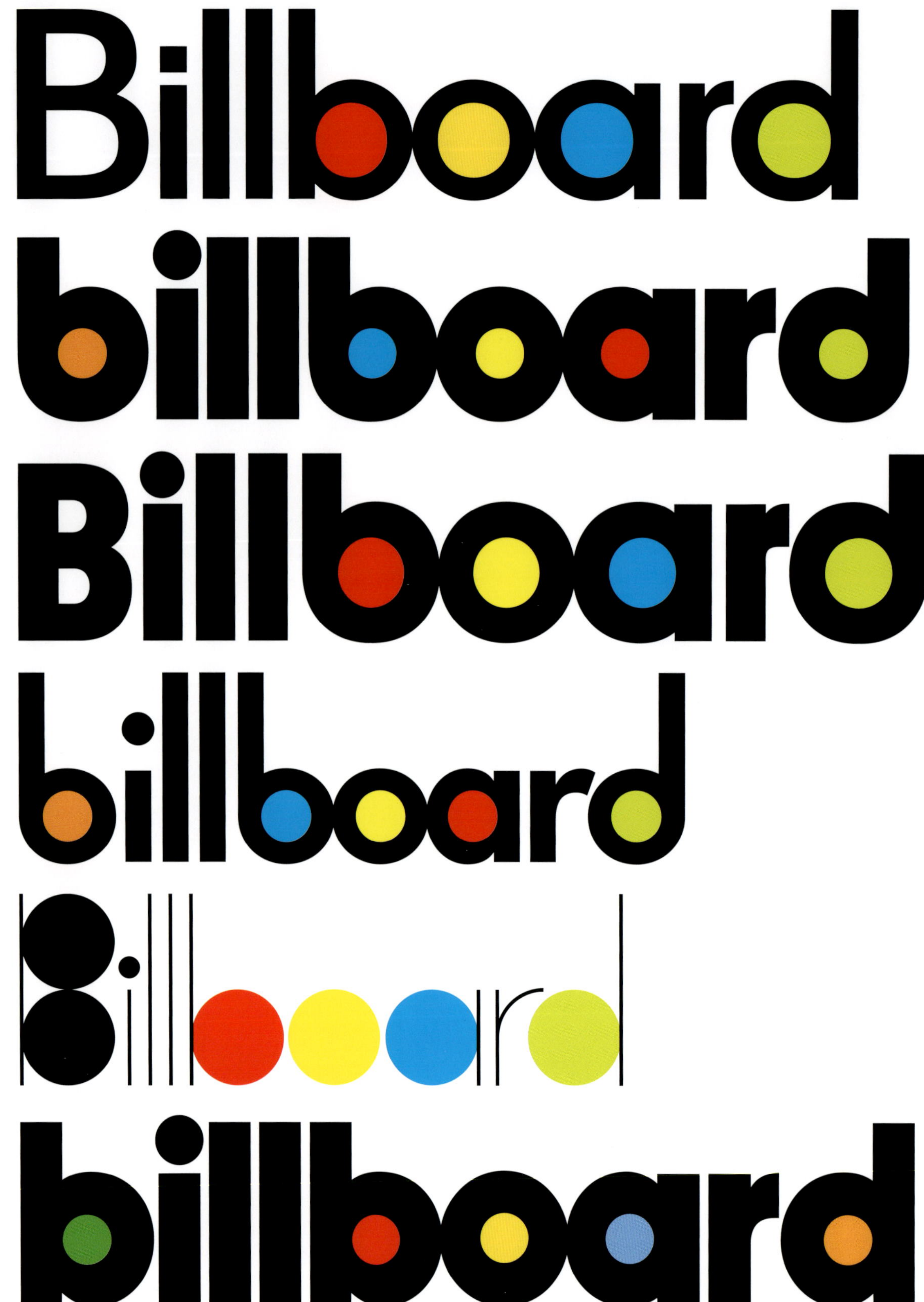

Right
The new consumer-style cover approach signaled that the magazine that was indispensible to industry insiders could also be accessible to enthusiastic fans.

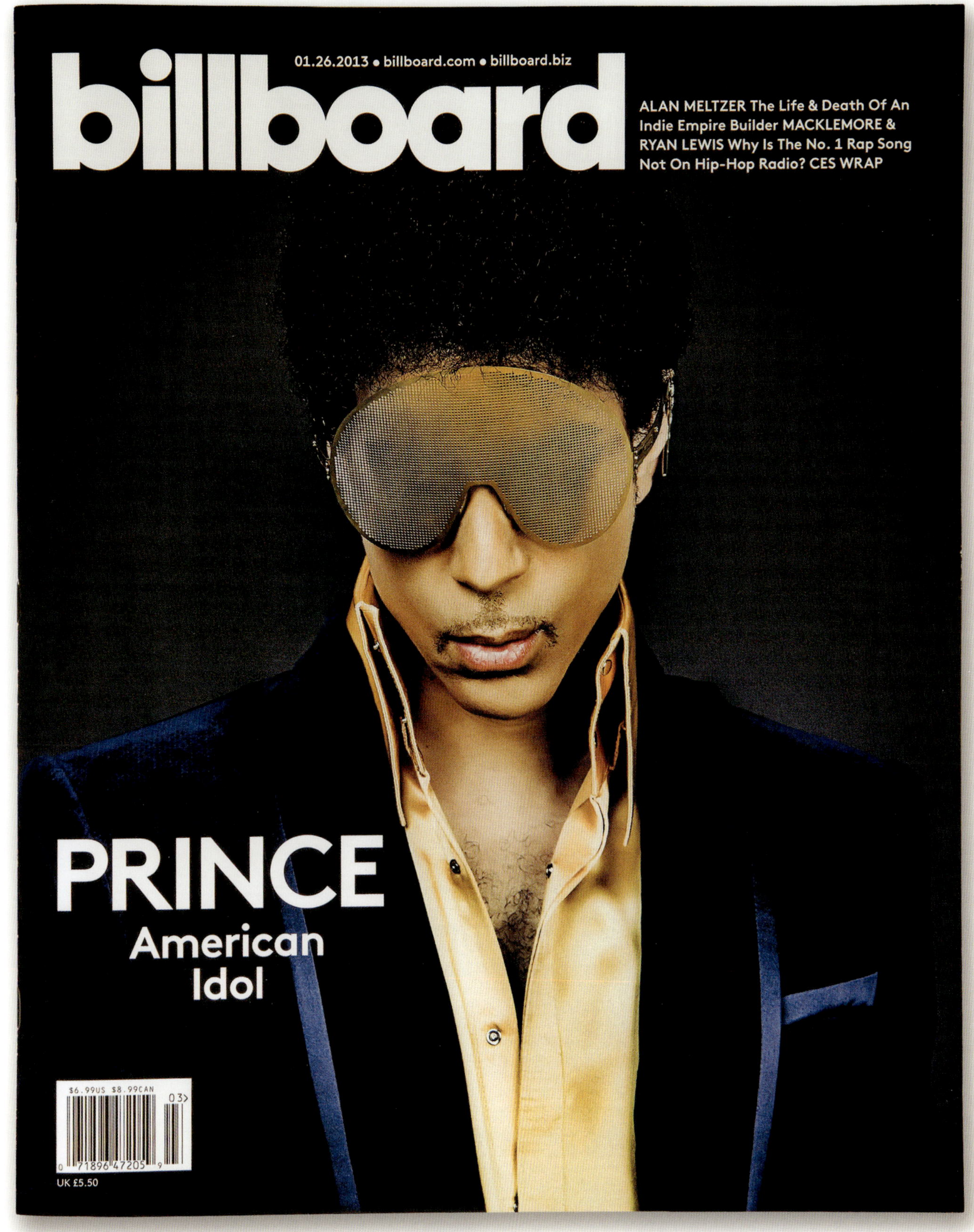

Right
The bold black-and-white geometry of the logo suggested a similarly constructed headline typeface, as well as an emphasis on high-contrast layout elements.

Opposite
The charts, which had become a cluttered afterthought, were restored to their former iconic glory, thanks to the hard work of Pentagram's Laitsz Ho and Michael Deal.

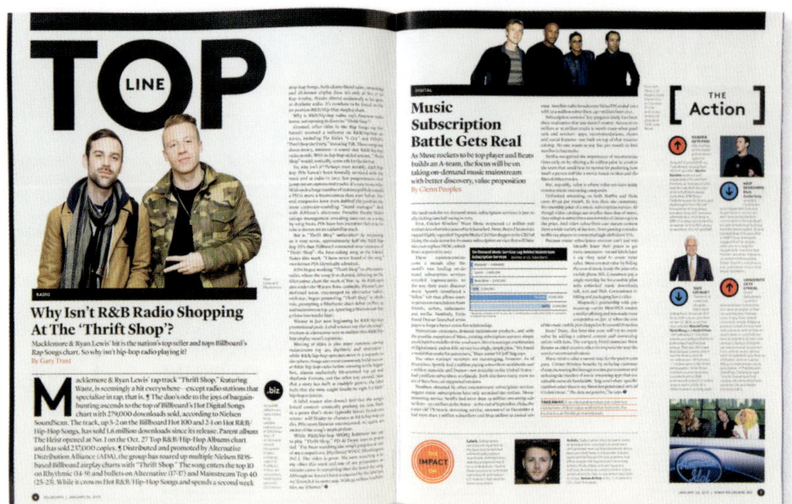

TOP LINE

RADIO

Why Isn't R&B Radio Shopping At The 'Thrift Shop'?

Macklemore & Ryan Lewis' hit is the nation's top seller and tops Billboard's Rap Songs chart. So why isn't hip-hop radio playing it?

By Gary Trust

Macklemore & Ryan Lewis' rap track "Thrift Shop," featuring Wanz, is seemingly a hit everywhere—except radio stations that specialize in rap, that is. ¶ The duo's ode to the joys of bargain-hunting ascends to the top of Billboard's Hot Digital Songs chart with 279,000 downloads sold, according to Nielsen SoundScan. The track, up 3-2 on the Billboard Hot 100 and 2-1 on Hot R&B/Hip-Hop Songs, has sold 1.6 million downloads since its release. Parent album The Heist opened at No. 1 on the Oct. 27 Top R&B/Hip-Hop Albums chart and has sold 237,000 copies. ¶ Distributed and promoted by Alternative Distribution Alliance (ADA), the group has soared up multiple Nielsen BDS-based Billboard airplay charts with "Thrift Shop." The song enters the top 10 on Rhythmic (14-9) and bullets on Alternative (17-17) and Mainstream Top 40 (25-23). While it crowns Hot R&B/Hip-Hop Songs and spends a second week

DIGITAL

Music Subscription Battle Gets Real

As Muve rockets to be top player and Beats builds an A-team, the focus will be on taking on-demand music mainstream with better discovery, value proposition

By Glenn Peoples

[THE Action]

IMPACT

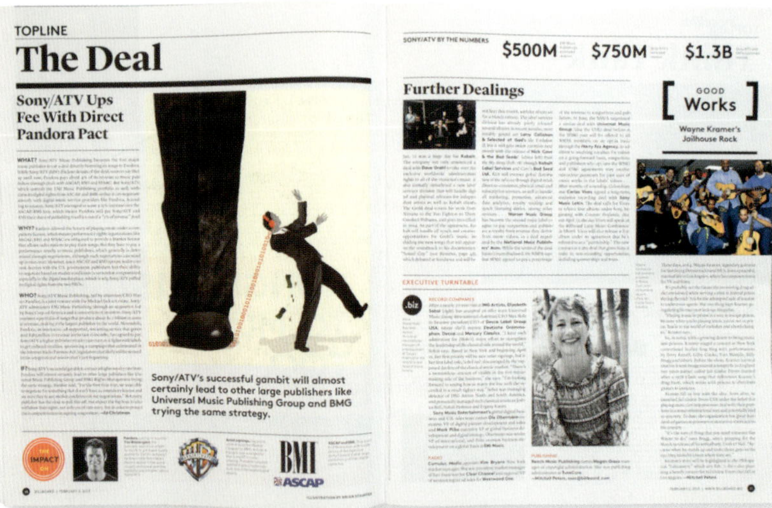

TOPLINE

The Deal

Sony/ATV Ups Fee With Direct Pandora Pact

Sony/ATV's successful gambit will almost certainly lead to other large publishers like Universal Music Publishing Group and BMG trying the same strategy.

IMPACT

BMI

ASCAP

SONY/ATV BY THE NUMBERS

$500M $750M $1.3B

Further Dealings

EXECUTIVE TURNTABLE

[GOOD Works]

Wayne Kramer's Jailhouse Rock

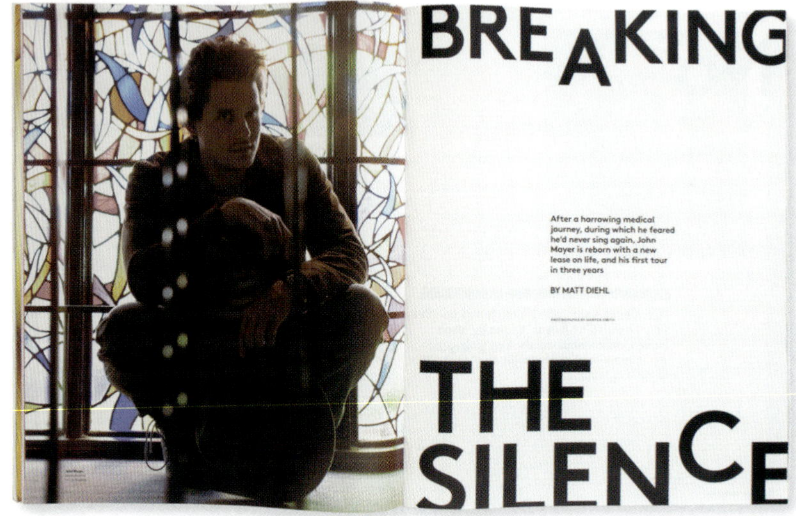

BREAKING THE SILENCE

After a harrowing medical journey, during which he feared he'd never sing again, John Mayer is reborn with a new lease on life, and his first tour in three years

BY MATT DIEHL

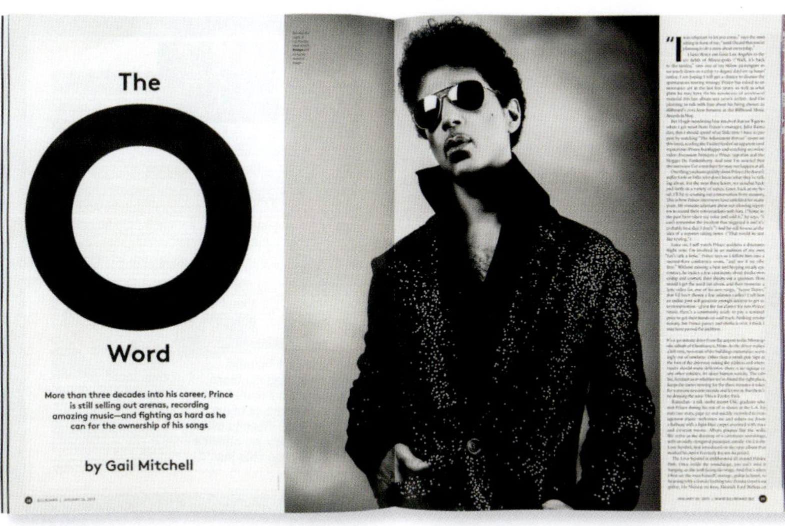
The
O
Word
More than three decades into his career, Prince is still selling out arenas, recording amazing music—and fighting as hard as he can for the ownership of his songs
by Gail Mitchell

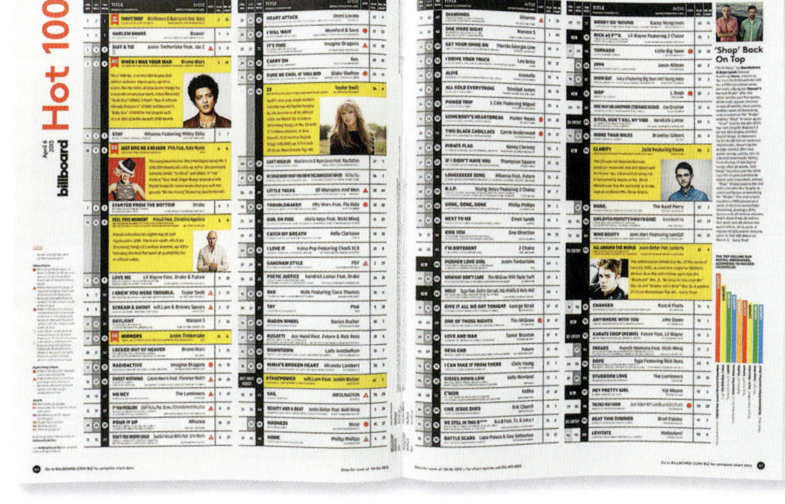
billboard
Hot 100

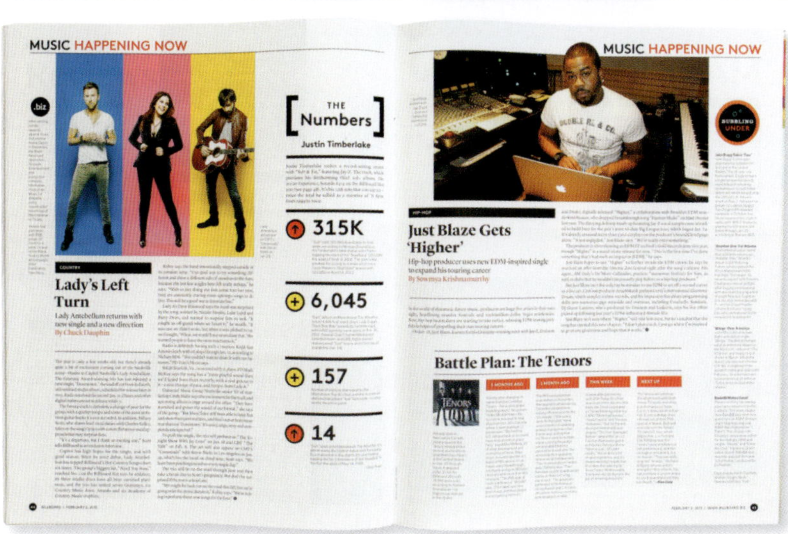
MUSIC HAPPENING NOW
Lady's Left Turn
THE Numbers
Justin Timberlake
315K
6,045
157
14
Just Blaze Gets 'Higher'
Battle Plan: The Tenors

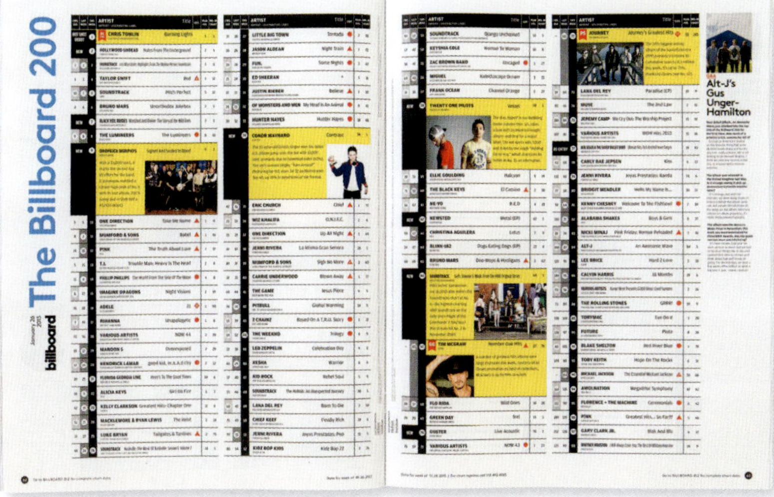
billboard
The Billboard 200
Alt-J's Gus Unger-Hamilton

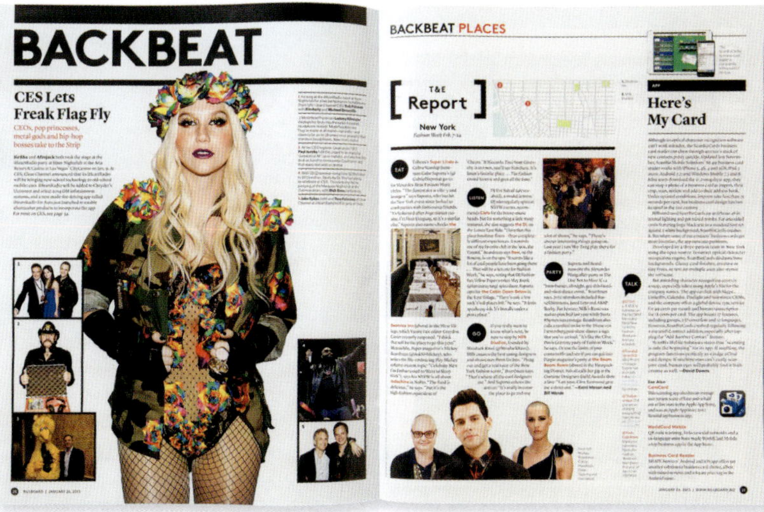
BACKBEAT
CES Lets Freak Flag Fly
BACKBEAT PLACES
T&E Report
New York
Here's My Card

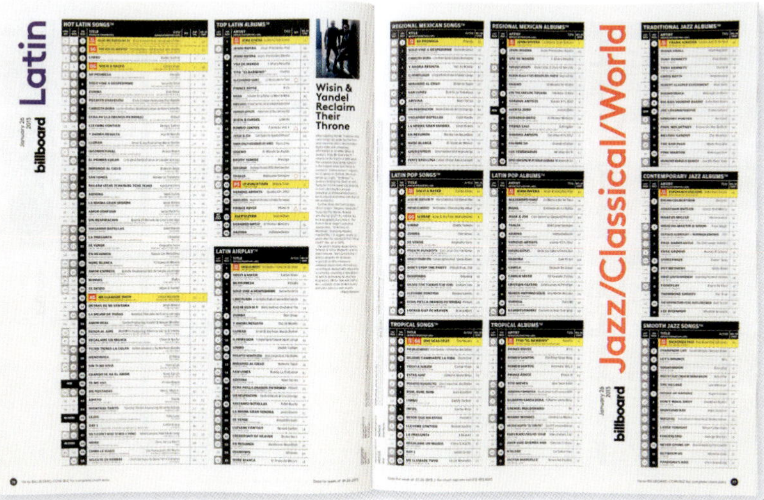
billboard
Latin
Wisin & Yandel Reclaim Their Throne
Jazz/Classical/World

Right
The Billboard Hot 100 chart is an icon of pop culture. In our redesign, readers can easily follow the progression of each song up the chart. Fast-rising hits appear as white "bullets," and weekly awards for biggest gains are marked with red banner icons. Each track's peak position and weeks on the chart appear to the right of the title. The data is set in Christian Schwartz's easy-to-read Amplitude, and chart names, like headlines throughout the magazine, appear in Aurèle Sack's round-as-a-record LL Brown.

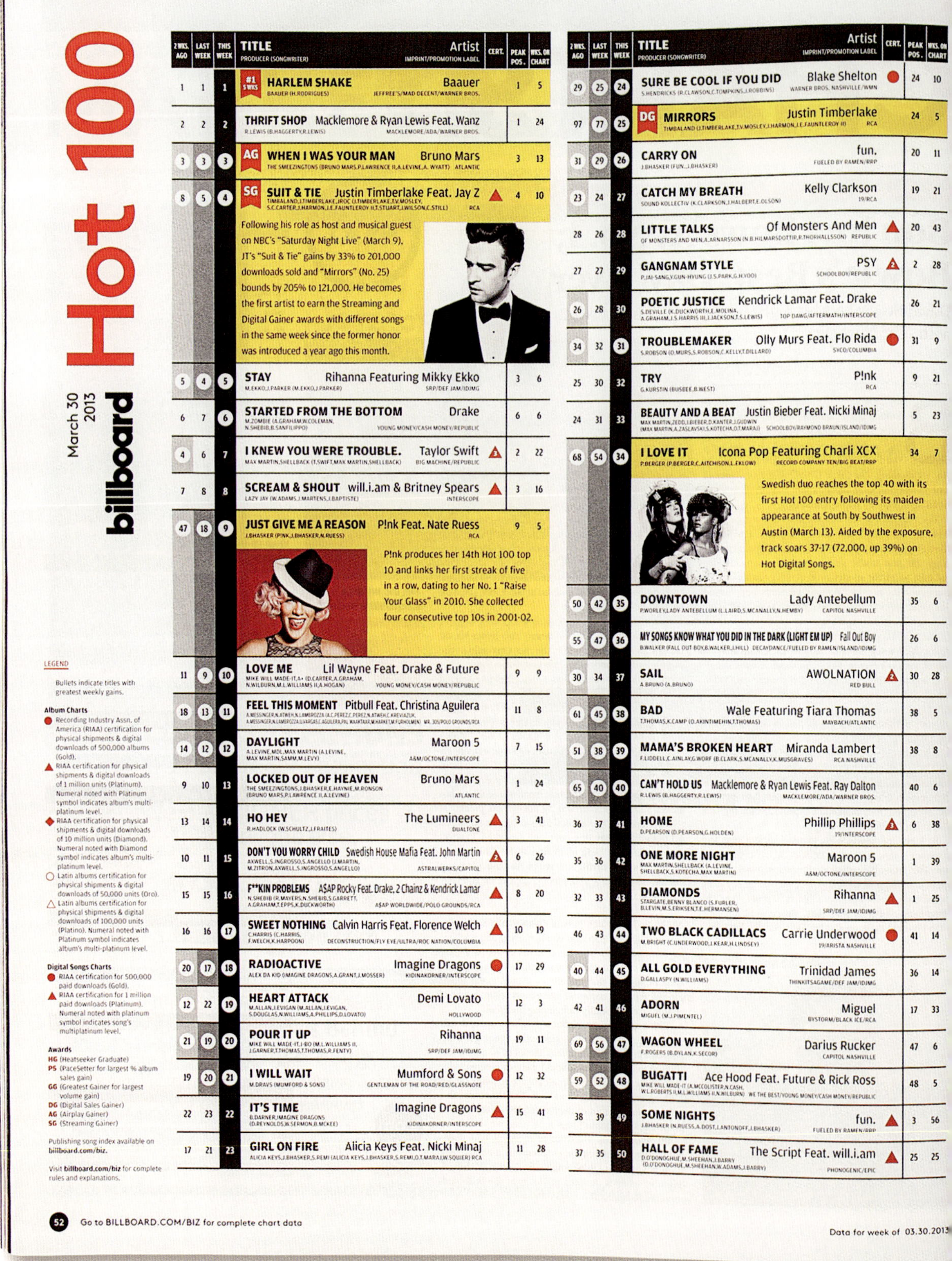

billboard March 30 2013 Hot 100

2 Wks. Ago	Last Week	This Week	Title / Producer (Songwriter)	Artist / Imprint/Promotion Label	Cert.	Peak Pos.	Wks. on Chart
1	1	1	#1 5 WKS **HARLEM SHAKE** BAAUER (H.RODRIGUES)	Baauer JEFFREE'S/MAD DECENT/WARNER BROS.		1	5
2	2	2	**THRIFT SHOP** R.LEWIS (B.HAGGERTY,R.LEWIS)	Macklemore & Ryan Lewis Feat. Wanz MACKLEMORE/ADA/WARNER BROS.		1	24
3	3	3	AG **WHEN I WAS YOUR MAN** THE SMEEZINGTONS (BRUNO MARS,P.LAWRENCE II,A.LEVINE,A. WYATT)	Bruno Mars ATLANTIC		3	13
8	5	4	SG **SUIT & TIE** TIMBALAND,J.TIMBERLAKE,JROC (J.TIMBERLAKE,T.V.MOSLEY, S.C.CARTER,J.HARMON,J.E.FAUNTLEROY II,T.STUART,J.WILSON,C.STILL)	Justin Timberlake Feat. Jay Z RCA	▲	4	10
5	4	5	**STAY** M.EKKO,J.PARKER (M.EKKO,J.PARKER)	Rihanna Featuring Mikky Ekko SRP/DEF JAM/IDJMG		3	6
6	7	6	**STARTED FROM THE BOTTOM** M.ZOMBIE (A.GRAHAM,W.COLEMAN, N.SHEBIB,B.SANFILIPPO)	Drake YOUNG MONEY/CASH MONEY/REPUBLIC		6	6
4	6	7	**I KNEW YOU WERE TROUBLE.** MAX MARTIN,SHELLBACK (T.SWIFT,MAX MARTIN,SHELLBACK)	Taylor Swift BIG MACHINE/REPUBLIC	▲3	2	22
7	8	8	**SCREAM & SHOUT** LAZY JAY (W.ADAMS,J.MARTENS,J.BAPTISTE)	will.i.am & Britney Spears INTERSCOPE	▲	3	16
47	18	9	**JUST GIVE ME A REASON** J.BHASKER (P!NK,J.BHASKER,N.RUESS)	P!nk Feat. Nate Ruess RCA		9	5
11	9	10	**LOVE ME** MIKE WILL MADE-IT,A+ (D.CARTER,A.GRAHAM, N.WILBURN,M.L.WILLIAMS II,A.HOGAN)	Lil Wayne Feat. Drake & Future YOUNG MONEY/CASH MONEY/REPUBLIC		9	9
18	13	11	**FEEL THIS MOMENT** A.MESSINGER,N.ATWEH,N.LAMBROZZA (A.C.PEREZ,C.PEREZ,N.ATWEH,C.KREVIAZUK, A.MESSINGER,N.LAMBROZZA,U.VARGAS,C.AGUILERA,PAL WAAKTAAR,M.HARKET,M.FURHOLMEN)	Pitbull Feat. Christina Aguilera MR. 305/POLO GROUNDS/RCA		11	8
14	12	12	**DAYLIGHT** A.LEVINE,MDL,MAX MARTIN (A.LEVINE, MAX MARTIN,SAMM,M.LEVY)	Maroon 5 A&M/OCTONE/INTERSCOPE		7	15
9	10	13	**LOCKED OUT OF HEAVEN** THE SMEEZINGTONS,J.BHASKER,E.HAYNIE,M.RONSON (BRUNO MARS,P.LAWRENCE II,A.LEVINE)	Bruno Mars ATLANTIC		1	24
13	14	14	**HO HEY** R.HADLOCK (W.SCHULTZ,J.FRAITES)	The Lumineers DUALTONE	▲	3	41
10	11	15	**DON'T YOU WORRY CHILD** AXWELL,S.INGROSSO,S.ANGELLO (J.MARTIN, M.ZITRON,AXWELL,S.INGROSSO,S.ANGELLO)	Swedish House Mafia Feat. John Martin ASTRALWERKS/CAPITOL	▲2	6	26
15	15	16	**F**KIN PROBLEMS** N.SHEBIB (R.MAYERS,N.SHEBIB,S.GARRETT, A.GRAHAM,T.EPPS,K.DUCKWORTH)	A$AP Rocky Feat. Drake, 2 Chainz & Kendrick Lamar A$AP WORLDWIDE/POLO GROUNDS/RCA	▲	8	20
16	16	17	**SWEET NOTHING** C.HARRIS (C.HARRIS, F.WELCH,K.HARPOON)	Calvin Harris Feat. Florence Welch DECONSTRUCTION/FLY EYE/ULTRA/ROC NATION/COLUMBIA	▲	10	19
20	17	18	**RADIOACTIVE** ALEX DA KID (IMAGINE DRAGONS,A.GRANT,J.MOSSER)	Imagine Dragons KIDINAKORNER/INTERSCOPE	●	17	29
12	22	19	**HEART ATTACK** M.ALLAN,J.EVIGAN (M.ALLAN,J.EVIGAN, S.DOUGLAS,N.WILLIAMS,A.PHILLIPS,D.LOVATO)	Demi Lovato HOLLYWOOD		12	3
21	19	20	**POUR IT UP** MIKE WILL MADE-IT,J-BO (M.L.WILLIAMS II, J.GARNER,T.THOMAS,T.THOMAS,R.FENTY)	Rihanna SRP/DEF JAM/IDJMG		19	11
19	20	21	**I WILL WAIT** M.DRAVS (MUMFORD & SONS)	Mumford & Sons GENTLEMAN OF THE ROAD/RED/GLASSNOTE	●	12	32
22	23	22	**IT'S TIME** B.DARNER,IMAGINE DRAGONS (D.REYNOLDS,W.SERMON,B.MCKEE)	Imagine Dragons KIDINAKORNER/INTERSCOPE	▲	15	41
17	21	23	**GIRL ON FIRE** ALICIA KEYS,J.BHASKER,S.REMI (ALICIA KEYS,J.BHASKER,S.REMI,O.T.MARAJ,W.SQUIER)	Alicia Keys Feat. Nicki Minaj RCA		11	28
29	25	24	**SURE BE COOL IF YOU DID** S.HENDRICKS (R.CLAWSON,C.TOMPKINS,J.ROBBINS)	Blake Shelton WARNER BROS. NASHVILLE/WMN	●	24	10
97	77	25	DG **MIRRORS** TIMBALAND (J.TIMBERLAKE,T.V.MOSLEY,J.HARMON,J.E.FAUNTLEROY II)	Justin Timberlake RCA		24	5
31	29	26	**CARRY ON** J.BHASKER (FUN.,J.BHASKER)	fun. FUELED BY RAMEN/RRP		20	11
23	24	27	**CATCH MY BREATH** SOUND KOLLECTIV (K.CLARKSON,J.HALBERT,E.OLSON)	Kelly Clarkson 19/RCA		19	21
28	26	28	**LITTLE TALKS** OF MONSTERS AND MEN,A.ARNARSSON (N.B.HILMARSDOTTIR,R.THORHALLSSON)	Of Monsters And Men REPUBLIC	▲	20	43
27	27	29	**GANGNAM STYLE** P.JAI-SANG,Y.GUN-HYUNG (J.S.PARK,G.H.YOO)	PSY SCHOOLBOY/REPUBLIC	▲2	2	28
26	28	30	**POETIC JUSTICE** S.DEVILLE (K.DUCKWORTH,E.MOLINA, A.GRAHAM,J.S.HARRIS III,J.JACKSON,T.S.LEWIS)	Kendrick Lamar Feat. Drake TOP DAWG/AFTERMATH/INTERSCOPE		26	21
34	32	31	**TROUBLEMAKER** S.ROBSON (O.MURS,S.ROBSON,C.KELLY,T.DILLARD)	Olly Murs Feat. Flo Rida SYCO/COLUMBIA	●	31	9
25	30	32	**TRY** G.KURSTIN (BUSBEE,B.WEST)	P!nk RCA		9	21
24	31	33	**BEAUTY AND A BEAT** MAX MARTIN,ZEDD,J.BIEBER,D.KANTER,J.GUDWIN (MAX MARTIN,A.ZASLAVSKI,S.KOTECHA,O.T.MARAJ)	Justin Bieber Feat. Nicki Minaj SCHOOLBOY/RAYMOND BRAUN/ISLAND/IDJMG		5	23
68	54	34	**I LOVE IT** P.BERGER (P.BERGER,C.AITCHISON,L.EKLOW)	Icona Pop Featuring Charli XCX RECORD COMPANY TEN/BIG BEAT/RRP		34	7
50	42	35	**DOWNTOWN** P.WORLEY,LADY ANTEBELLUM (L.LAIRD,S.MCANALLY,N.HEMBY)	Lady Antebellum CAPITOL NASHVILLE		35	6
55	47	36	**MY SONGS KNOW WHAT YOU DID IN THE DARK (LIGHT EM UP)** B.WALKER (FALL OUT BOY,B.WALKER,J.HILL)	Fall Out Boy DECAYDANCE/FUELED BY RAMEN/ISLAND/IDJMG		26	6
30	34	37	**SAIL** A.BRUNO (A.BRUNO)	AWOLNATION RED BULL	▲2	30	28
61	45	38	**BAD** T.THOMAS,K.CAMP (O.AKINTIMEHIN,T.THOMAS)	Wale Featuring Tiara Thomas MAYBACH/ATLANTIC		38	5
51	38	39	**MAMA'S BROKEN HEART** F.LIDDELL,C.AINLAY,G.WORF (B.CLARK,S.MCANALLY,K.MUSGRAVES)	Miranda Lambert RCA NASHVILLE		38	8
65	40	40	**CAN'T HOLD US** R.LEWIS (B.HAGGERTY,R.LEWIS)	Macklemore & Ryan Lewis Feat. Ray Dalton MACKLEMORE/ADA/WARNER BROS.		40	6
36	37	41	**HOME** D.PEARSON (D.PEARSON,G.HOLDEN)	Phillip Phillips 19/INTERSCOPE	▲3	6	38
35	36	42	**ONE MORE NIGHT** MAX MARTIN,SHELLBACK (A.LEVINE, SHELLBACK,S.KOTECHA,MAX MARTIN)	Maroon 5 A&M/OCTONE/INTERSCOPE		1	39
32	33	43	**DIAMONDS** STARGATE,BENNY BLANCO (S.FURLER, B.LEVIN,M.S.ERIKSEN,T.E.HERMANSEN)	Rihanna SRP/DEF JAM/IDJMG	▲	1	25
46	43	44	**TWO BLACK CADILLACS** M.BRIGHT (C.UNDERWOOD,J.KEAR,H.LINDSEY)	Carrie Underwood 19/ARISTA NASHVILLE	●	41	14
40	44	45	**ALL GOLD EVERYTHING** D.GALLASPY (N.WILLIAMS)	Trinidad James THINKITSAGAME/DEF JAM/IDJMG		36	14
42	41	46	**ADORN** MIGUEL (M.J.PIMENTEL)	Miguel BYSTORM/BLACK ICE/RCA		17	33
69	56	47	**WAGON WHEEL** F.ROGERS (B.DYLAN,K.SECOR)	Darius Rucker CAPITOL NASHVILLE		47	6
59	52	48	**BUGATTI** MIKE WILL MADE-IT (A.MCCOLISTER,N.CASH, W.L.ROBERTS II,M.L.WILLIAMS II,N.WILBURN)	Ace Hood Feat. Future & Rick Ross WE THE BEST/YOUNG MONEY/CASH MONEY/REPUBLIC		48	5
38	39	49	**SOME NIGHTS** J.BHASKER (N.RUESS,A.DOST,J.ANTONOFF,J.BHASKER)	fun. FUELED BY RAMEN/RRP	▲	3	56
37	35	50	**HALL OF FAME** D.O'DONOGHUE,M.SHEEHAN,J.BARRY (D.O'DONOGHUE,M.SHEEHAN,W.ADAMS,J.BARRY)	The Script Feat. will.i.am PHONOGENIC/EPIC	▲	25	25

Following his role as host and musical guest on NBC's "Saturday Night Live" (March 9), JT's "Suit & Tie" gains by 33% to 201,000 downloads sold and "Mirrors" (No. 25) bounds by 205% to 121,000. He becomes the first artist to earn the Streaming and Digital Gainer awards with different songs in the same week since the former honor was introduced a year ago this month.

P!nk produces her 14th Hot 100 top 10 and links her first streak of five in a row, dating to her No. 1 "Raise Your Glass" in 2010. She collected four consecutive top 10s in 2001-02.

Swedish duo reaches the top 40 with its first Hot 100 entry following its maiden appearance at South by Southwest in Austin (March 13). Aided by the exposure, track soars 37-17 (72,000, up 39%) on Hot Digital Songs.

LEGEND

Bullets indicate titles with greatest weekly gains.

Album Charts
- ● Recording Industry Assn. of America (RIAA) certification for physical shipments & digital downloads of 500,000 albums (Gold).
- ▲ RIAA certification for physical shipments & digital downloads of 1 million units (Platinum). Numeral noted with Platinum symbol indicates album's multi-platinum level.
- ◆ RIAA certification for physical shipments & digital downloads of 10 million units (Diamond). Numeral noted with Diamond symbol indicates album's multi-platinum level.
- ○ Latin albums certification for physical shipments & digital downloads of 50,000 units (Oro).
- △ Latin albums certification for physical shipments & digital downloads of 100,000 units (Platino). Numeral noted with Platinum symbol indicates album's multi-platinum level.

Digital Songs Charts
- ● RIAA certification for 500,000 paid downloads (Gold).
- ▲ RIAA certification for 1 million paid downloads (Platinum). Numeral noted with platinum symbol indicates song's multiplatinum level.

Awards
- **HG** (Heatseeker Graduate)
- **PS** (PaceSetter for largest % album sales gain)
- **GG** (Greatest Gainer for largest volume gain)
- **DG** (Digital Sales Gainer)
- **AG** (Airplay Gainer)
- **SG** (Streaming Gainer)

Publishing song index available on **billboard.com/biz.**

Visit **billboard.com/biz** for complete rules and explanations.

52 Go to BILLBOARD.COM/BIZ for complete chart data

Data for week of 03.30.2013

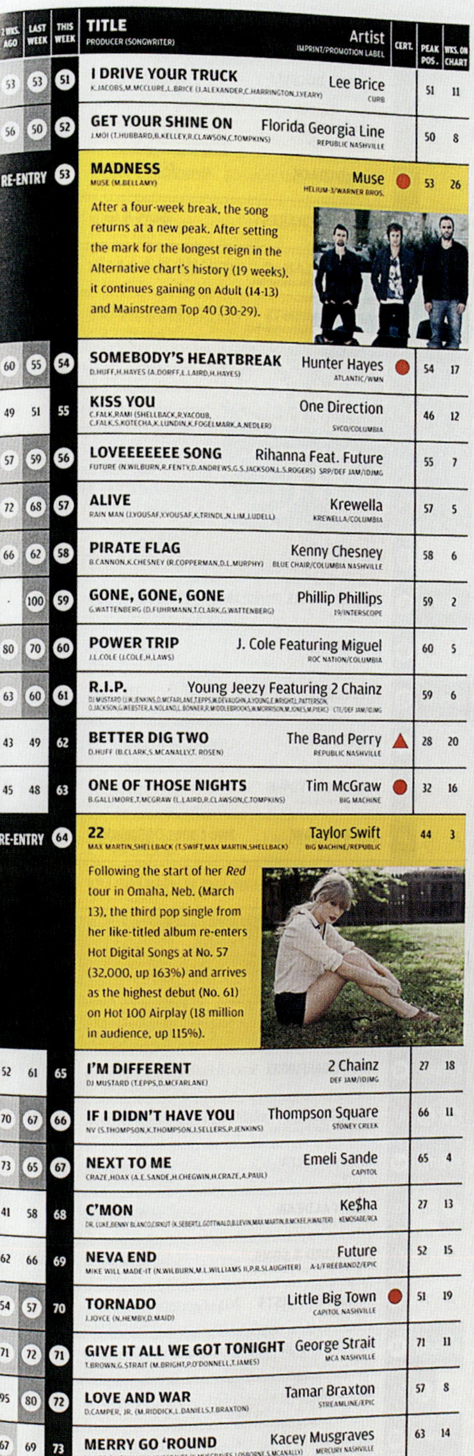

2 Wks. Ago	Last Week	This Week	Title / Producer (Songwriter)	Artist / Imprint/Promotion Label	Cert.	Peak Pos.	Wks. on Chart
53	53	51	**I DRIVE YOUR TRUCK** K.JACOBS,M.MCCLURE,L.BRICE (J.ALEXANDER,C.HARRINGTON,J.YEARY)	Lee Brice CURB		51	11
56	50	52	**GET YOUR SHINE ON** J.MOI (T.HUBBARD,B.KELLEY,R.CLAWSON,C.TOMPKINS)	Florida Georgia Line REPUBLIC NASHVILLE		50	8
RE-ENTRY		53	**MADNESS** MUSE (M.BELLAMY)	Muse HELIUM-3/WARNER BROS.	●	53	26

After a four-week break, the song returns at a new peak. After setting the mark for the longest reign in the Alternative chart's history (19 weeks), it continues gaining on Adult (14-13) and Mainstream Top 40 (30-29).

2 Wks. Ago	Last Week	This Week	Title / Producer (Songwriter)	Artist / Imprint/Promotion Label	Cert.	Peak Pos.	Wks. on Chart
60	55	54	**SOMEBODY'S HEARTBREAK** D.HUFF,H.HAYES (A.DORFF,L.LAIRD,H.HAYES)	Hunter Hayes ATLANTIC/WMN	●	54	17
49	51	55	**KISS YOU** C.FALK,RAMI (SHELLBACK,R.YACOUB, C.FALK,S.KOTECHA,K.LUNDIN,K.FOGELMARK,A.NEDLER)	One Direction SYCO/COLUMBIA		46	12
57	59	56	**LOVEEEEEEE SONG** FUTURE (N.WILBURN,R.FENTY,D.ANDREWS,G.S.JACKSON,L.S.ROGERS)	Rihanna Feat. Future SRP/DEF JAM/IDJMG		55	7
72	68	57	**ALIVE** RAIN MAN (J.YOUSAF,Y.YOUSAF,K.TRINDL,N.LIM,J.UDELL)	Krewella KREWELLA/COLUMBIA		57	5
66	62	58	**PIRATE FLAG** B.CANNON,K.CHESNEY (R.COPPERMAN,D.L.MURPHY)	Kenny Chesney BLUE CHAIR/COLUMBIA NASHVILLE		58	6
-	100	59	**GONE, GONE, GONE** G.WATTENBERG (D.FUHRMANN,T.CLARK,G.WATTENBERG)	Phillip Phillips 19/INTERSCOPE		59	2
80	70	60	**POWER TRIP** J.L.COLE (J.COLE,H.LAWS)	J. Cole Featuring Miguel ROC NATION/COLUMBIA		60	5
63	60	61	**R.I.P.** DJ MUSTARD (J.W.JENKINS,D.MCFARLANE,T.EPPS,W.DEVAUGHN,A.YOUNG,E.WRIGHT,L.PATTERSON, O.JACKSON,G.WEBSTER,A.NOLAND,L.BONNER,R.MIDDLEBROOKS,W.MORRISON,M.JONES,M.PIERC)	Young Jeezy Featuring 2 Chainz CTE/DEF JAM/IDJMG		59	6
43	49	62	**BETTER DIG TWO** D.HUFF (B.CLARK,S.MCANALLY,T. ROSEN)	The Band Perry REPUBLIC NASHVILLE	▲	28	20
45	48	63	**ONE OF THOSE NIGHTS** B.GALLIMORE,T.MCGRAW (L.LAIRD,R.CLAWSON,C.TOMPKINS)	Tim McGraw BIG MACHINE	●	32	16
RE-ENTRY		64	**22** MAX MARTIN,SHELLBACK (T.SWIFT,MAX MARTIN,SHELLBACK)	Taylor Swift BIG MACHINE/REPUBLIC		44	3

Following the start of her *Red* tour in Omaha, Neb. (March 13), the third pop single from her like-titled album re-enters Hot Digital Songs at No. 57 (32,000, up 163%) and arrives as the highest debut (No. 61) on Hot 100 Airplay (18 million in audience, up 115%).

2 Wks. Ago	Last Week	This Week	Title / Producer (Songwriter)	Artist / Imprint/Promotion Label	Cert.	Peak Pos.	Wks. on Chart
52	61	65	**I'M DIFFERENT** DJ MUSTARD (T.EPPS,D.MCFARLANE)	2 Chainz DEF JAM/IDJMG		27	18
70	67	66	**IF I DIDN'T HAVE YOU** NV (S.THOMPSON,K.THOMPSON,J.SELLERS,P.JENKINS)	Thompson Square STONEY CREEK		66	11
73	65	67	**NEXT TO ME** CRAZE,HOAX (A.E.SANDE,H.CHEGWIN,H.CRAZE,A.PAUL)	Emeli Sande CAPITOL		65	4
41	58	68	**C'MON** DR. LUKE,BENNY BLANCO,CIRKUT (K.SEBERT,L.GOTTWALD,B.LEVIN,MAX MARTIN,B.MCKEE,H.WALTER)	Ke$ha KEMOSABE/RCA		27	13
62	66	69	**NEVA END** MIKE WILL MADE-IT (N.WILBURN,M.L.WILLIAMS II,P.R.SLAUGHTER)	Future A-1/FREEBANDZ/EPIC		52	15
54	57	70	**TORNADO** J.JOYCE (N.HEMBY,D.MAID)	Little Big Town CAPITOL NASHVILLE	●	51	19
71	72	71	**GIVE IT ALL WE GOT TONIGHT** T.BROWN,G.STRAIT (M.BRIGHT,P.O'DONNELL,T.JAMES)	George Strait MCA NASHVILLE		71	11
95	80	72	**LOVE AND WAR** D.CAMPER, JR. (M.RIDDICK,L.DANIELS,T.BRAXTON)	Tamar Braxton STREAMLINE/EPIC		57	8
67	69	73	**MERRY GO 'ROUND** L.LAIRD,S.MCANALLY,K.MUSGRAVES (K.MUSGRAVES,J.OSBORNE,S.MCANALLY)	Kacey Musgraves MERCURY NASHVILLE		63	14

2 Wks. Ago	Last Week	This Week	Title / Producer (Songwriter)	Artist / Imprint/Promotion Label	Cert.	Peak Pos.	Wks. on Chart
44	64	74	**ONE WAY OR ANOTHER (TEENAGE KICKS)** J.BUNETTA,J.RYAN (D.HARRY,N.HARRISON,J.O'NEILL)	One Direction SYCO/COLUMBIA		13	5
-	98	75	**SHOW OUT** MIKE WILL MADE-IT (J.HOUSTON,J.W.JENKINS,S.M.ANDERSON)	Juicy J Featuring Big Sean And Young Jeezy KEMOSABE/COLUMBIA		75	2
64	71	76	**WICKED GAMES** DOC,C.MONTAGNESE,THE WEEKND (A.TESFAYE,C.MONTAGNESE,D.MCKINNEY)	The Weeknd XO/REPUBLIC		53	20
HOT SHOT DEBUT		77	**FREAKS** RICO LOVE,E.THOMASON (K.KHARBOUCH,O.T.MARAJ,RICO LOVE, D.L.DAVIS,O.RILEY,E.BONNER,S.DUNBAR,J.C.TAYLOR,L.O.WILLIS)	French Montana Feat. Nicki Minaj BAD BOY/INTERSCOPE		77	1
83	76	78	**I CAN TAKE IT FROM THERE** J.STROUD (C.YOUNG,R.AKINS,B.HAYSLIP)	Chris Young RCA NASHVILLE		76	6
79	78	79	**BATTLE SCARS** PRO J (W.JACO,G.SEBASTIAN,D.R.HARRIS)	Lupe Fiasco & Guy Sebastian 1ST & 15TH/ATLANTIC		73	12
-	96	80	**KISSES DOWN LOW** MIKE WILL MADE-IT,MARZ (M.L.WILLIAMS II, M.MIDDLEBROOKS,T.THOMAS,T.THOMAS,K.ROWLAND)	Kelly Rowland REPUBLIC		80	2
-	84	81	**HIGHWAY DON'T CARE** B.GALLIMORE,T.MCGRAW (B.WARREN,B.WARREN,M.IRWIN,J.KEAR)	Tim McGraw With Taylor Swift BIG MACHINE		59	3
82	75	82	**WE STILL IN THIS B****** MIKE WILL MADE-IT,MARZ (B.R.SIMMONS, JR.,M.L.WILLIAMS II, M.MIDDLEBROOKS,C.J.HARRIS, JR.,J.HOUSTON)	B.o.B Feat. T.I. & Juicy J REBELROCK/GRAND HUSTLE/ATLANTIC		75	5
58	63	83	**HEY PORSCHE** DJ FRANK E,D.GLASS,M.FREESH,T.MAZUR,H.KIPNER (D.E.GLASS,H.KIPNER,B.S.ISAAC,J.FRANKS,C.HAYNES, JR.)	Nelly REPUBLIC		42	4
86	81	84	**LIKE JESUS DOES** J.JOYCE (C.BEATHARD,M.CRISWELL)	Eric Church EMI NASHVILLE		81	4
74	73	85	**WHO BOOTY** RAW SMOOV (D.J.GRIZZELL,S.A.WILLIAMS,K.KHARBOUCH)	Jonn Hart Featuring IamSU! COOL KID CARTEL/EPIC		66	14
78	82	86	**DON'T JUDGE ME** THE MESSENGERS (C.M.BROWN,N.ATWEH,A.MESSINGER,M.PELLIZZER)	Chris Brown RCA		67	20
NEW		87	**DONE.** D.HUFF (R.PERRY,N.PERRY,J.DAVIDSON,J.BRYANT)	The Band Perry REPUBLIC NASHVILLE		87	1
75	79	88	**THE ONLY WAY I KNOW** M.KNOX (D.L.MURPHY,B.HAYSLIP)	Jason Aldean With Luke Bryan & Eric Church BROKEN BOW	●	40	19
84	87	89	**STUBBORN LOVE** R.HADLOCK (W.SCHULTZ,J.FRAITES)	The Lumineers DUALTONE		70	14
NEW		90	**SO MANY GIRLS** NOT LISTED (NOT LISTED)	DJ Drama Feat. Wale, Tyga & Roscoe Dash APHILLIATES/EONE		90	1
90	83	91	**GOLD** D.MUCKALA (B.NICOLE,D.MUCKALA,J.CATES)	Britt Nicole SPARROW/CAPITOL CMG/CAPITOL		83	3
98	93	92	**MORE THAN MILES** D.HUFF (J.EDDIE,B.GILBERT)	Brantley Gilbert VALORY		92	3
NEW		93	**1994** M.KNOX (THOMAS RHETT,L.LAIRD,B.DEAN)	Jason Aldean BROKEN BOW		93	1

Aldean's ode to the year that Joe Diffie ruled Hot Country Songs with two No. 1s becomes the eighth Hot 100 hit whose title is a year. Others include Phoenix's "1901," Bowling for Soup's "1985" and Prince's "1999." See the full list in Billboard.com's Chart Beat column. *—Gary Trust*

2 Wks. Ago	Last Week	This Week	Title / Producer (Songwriter)	Artist / Imprint/Promotion Label	Cert.	Peak Pos.	Wks. on Chart
99	90	94	**LEVITATE** LOADSTAR (HADOUKEN,A.SMITH,N.HILL,G.HARRIS)	Hadouken! SURFACE NOISE		90	3
85	85	95	**CUPS** C.BECK,M.KILIAN (A.P.CARTER,L.GERSTEIN,D.BLACKETT,H.TUNSTALL-BEHRENS,J.FREEMAN)	Anna Kendrick UME		64	12
87	86	96	**DOPE** M.ROBERTS (M.NGUYEN-STEVENSON,W.L.ROBERTS II, M.ROBERTS,J.JACKSON,C.C.BROADUS JR.,C.WOLFE,A.YOUNG)	Tyga Featuring Rick Ross YOUNG MONEY/CASH MONEY/REPUBLIC		68	8
91	88	97	**LOVE SOSA** YOUNG CHOP (K.COZART,T.PITTMAN)	Chief Keef GLORY BOYZ/INTERSCOPE		56	14
93	92	98	**CHANGED** D.HUFF,RASCAL FLATTS (G.LEVOX,N.THRASHER,W.MOBLEY)	Rascal Flatts BIG MACHINE		73	4
-	74	99	**BUZZKILL** J.STEVENS (L.BRYAN,R.THIBODEAU,J.SEVER)	Luke Bryan CAPITOL NASHVILLE		74	2
89	94	100	**LITTLE THINGS** J.GOSLING (E.SHEERAN,F.BEVAN)	One Direction SYCO/COLUMBIA	●	33	18

I'M NOT 'BOUT TO JUDGE YOU, DON'T JUDGE ME. YOU AIN'T GOTTA REALLY SING ABOUT YOUR RAP SHEET.

"BAD"—WALE FEATURING TIARA THOMAS

Q&A

Tiara Thomas

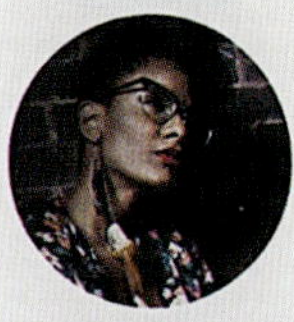

You co-wrote and sang on Wale's "Bad," which jumps 45-38 on the Billboard Hot 100 this week. You're signed to his Board Administration management/label. How did you first link with him?
[A friend] was like, "Hey, let's go to Atlanta for spring break." We went and I had a fake ID; I was under 21 at the time. We wanted to go to the club. It was like, "There's Wale, let's take a picture with him." Afterward, I sent him some YouTube videos I had online. Three months later, he hits me up: "Yo, I'm gonna fly you out to New York."

How did you come up with "Bad"?
There was this rap song called "Some Cut" by Trillville. It used to be one of my favorite songs when I was younger. It's really vulgar; I wanted to find a way to cover the song and make it sound pretty. Seven months after I dropped it on YouTube, Wale listened to it, and he really liked it. He put his verses on it and took the song to a whole new level.

So it started as your YouTube clip, and now it's the lead single on his new album?
It was just a cover at first. I just had other lyrics on there on top of the hook. Wale kind of created a story out of it—it's like a girl anthem. That's crazy. That's what I like so much about it: A rapper puts out a girl anthem. *—Chris Payne*

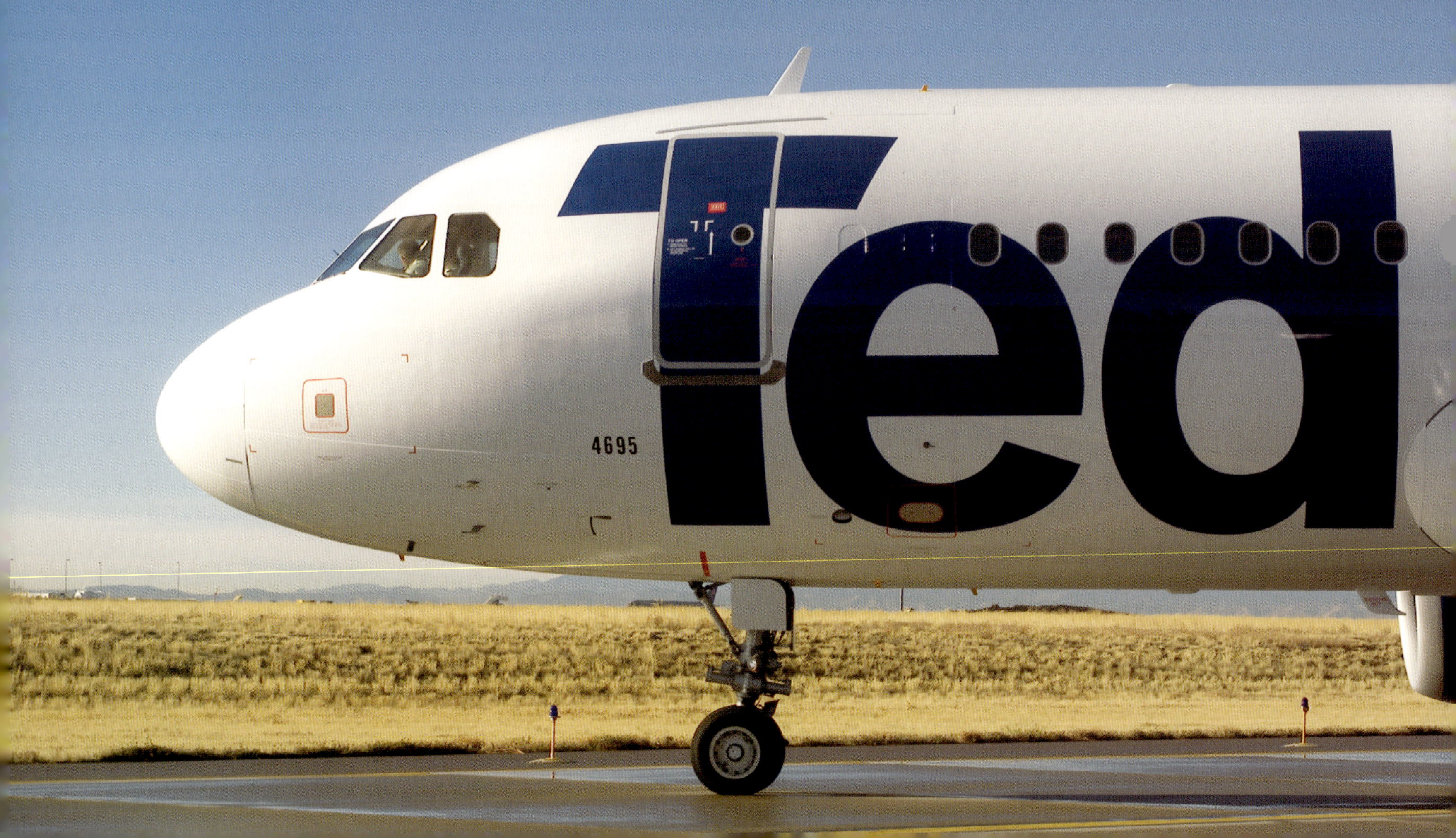
Ted
4695

How to convince people
Ted

When I graduated from design school, I thought that a great idea should sell itself. Not true. It turns out coming up with the right solution to a design problem is only the first step. The next, crucial step is convincing other people that your solution is the right one. Why is this so hard?

First, while sometimes we're fortunate enough to have a single strong-minded client, often we have to persuade a group. And the more important the project, the bigger (and more unruly) the group. Second, the correctness of a design decision can seldom be checked with a calculator. Rather, it relies on ambiguous things like intuition and taste. Finally, any good design decision requires, in the end, a leap of faith. To bring our risk-adverse congregations to salvation, we often have to transform boardrooms into revival tents.

In 2003, our client United Airlines decided to launch a low-cost operation to compete with JetBlue and Southwest, as well as newcomers like Delta's Song and Air Canada's Tango. They asked us to design the new carrier and, to make the challenge even harder, to come up with a name. (Not everyone thinks they're a designer, but anyone who's ever had a pet goldfish is a naming expert.)

After several months of work, the review of 100-plus names, and a few abortive presentations, my partner Daniel Weil and our colleague David Gibbs came up with a perfect moniker for a carrier that would be United's personable, friendly, more casual little sibling: Ted, a name that actually was a nickname, derived from the last three letters in its big brother's well-established brandmark.

We were convinced. But we knew that convincing our client would be a delicate process involving people from all over the company, up to and including marketing head John Teague and chairman Glenn Tilton. We assembled a 65-slide presentation that made the decision seem not just inevitable but fun. To this day, of all the presentations I've ever given, this is my favorite.

Opposite
We had a simple premise for the Ted brand: white plane, simple name, really big. As I told the *New York Times* when the brand launched, "When we hit on it, we realized we were on to something… It was a modest miracle that there inside the United name is that nickname, ready-made."

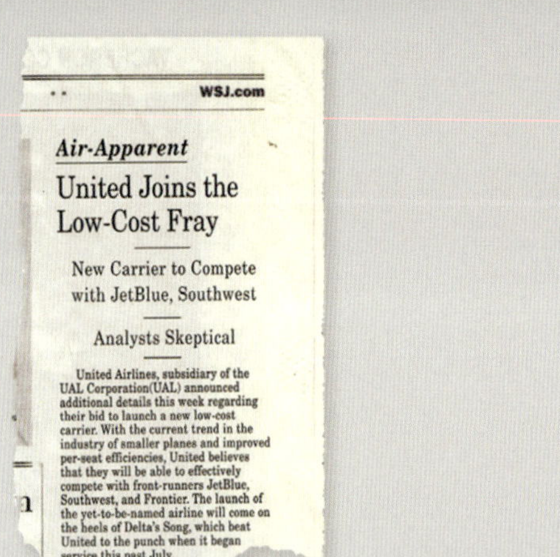

WSJ.com

Air-Apparent

United Joins the Low-Cost Fray

New Carrier to Compete with JetBlue, Southwest

Analysts Skeptical

United Airlines, subsidiary of the UAL Corporation(UAL) announced additional details this week regarding their bid to launch a new low-cost carrier. With the current trend in the industry of smaller planes and improved per-seat efficiencies, United believes that they will be able to effectively compete with front-runners JetBlue, Southwest, and Frontier. The launch of the yet-to-be-named airline will come on the heels of Delta's Song, which beat United to the punch when it began service this past July.

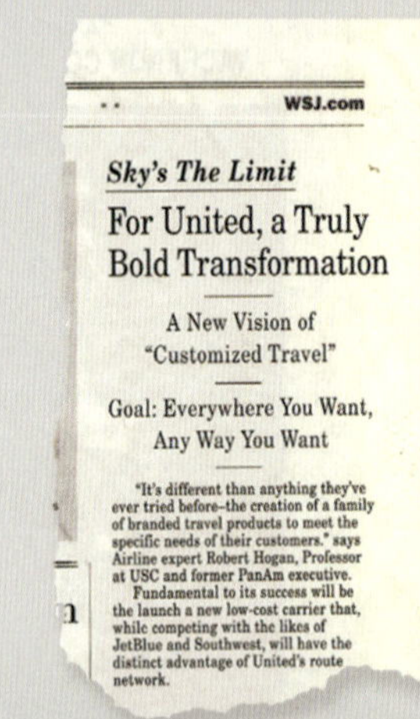

WSJ.com

Sky's The Limit

For United, a Truly Bold Transformation

A New Vision of "Customized Travel"

Goal: Everywhere You Want, Any Way You Want

"It's different than anything they've ever tried before–the creation of a family of branded travel products to meet the specific needs of their customers." says Airline expert Robert Hogan, Professor at USC and former PanAm executive.

Fundamental to its success will be the launch a new low-cost carrier that, while competing with the likes of JetBlue and Southwest, will have the distinct advantage of United's route network.

Left
We wanted to position the new carrier as a natural addition to United's portfolio of offerings, rather than a late entry to a game everyone else was already playing. To make the difference as vivid as possible, we started the presentation with two imaginary *Wall Street Journal* stories.

As everyone knows, a good presentation tells a story with a beginning, middle, and end. By the time we got involved, our clients had been working on the business case for United's low-cost carrier for nearly a year. It was important to remind them that the outside world didn't know anything about their strategy, and didn't necessarily care if they succeeded.

A point of distinction for United was that the new airline would be integrated into their huge network. This meant that its design would have to be coordinated with all the work we were doing for the rest of United, including the way the airplanes were painted. We deliberately decided to separate the decision about the design of the new carrier from the choice of name; combining the two tended to muddle the discussion because people inevitably liked one name but another design.

I gave this presentation over and over again to various teams at the company. This was one of the few presentations I've ever prepared that worked every time. It helped that we had a great solution.

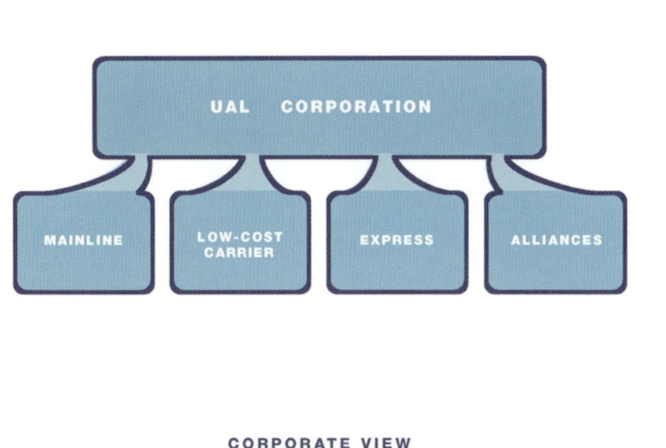

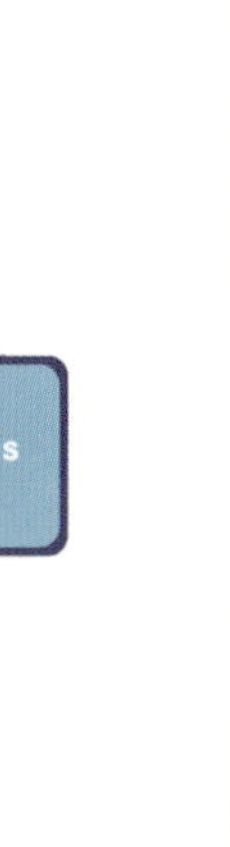

Two tools

The look and feel of the LCO identity
The LCO name

LCO brand profile

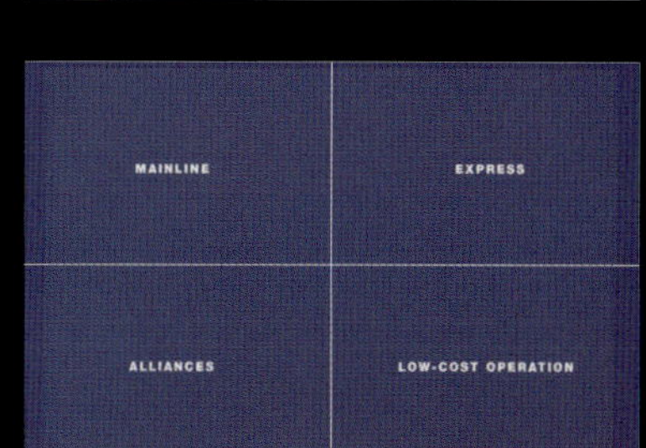

Brand advantages

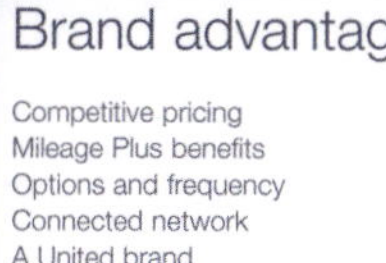

Competitive pricing
Mileage Plus benefits
Options and frequency
Connected network
A United brand

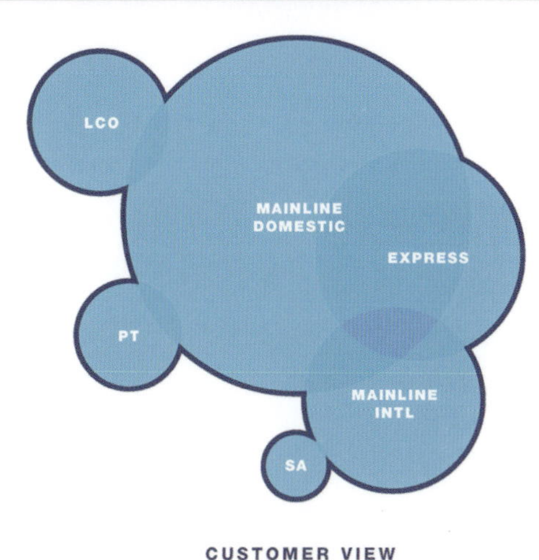

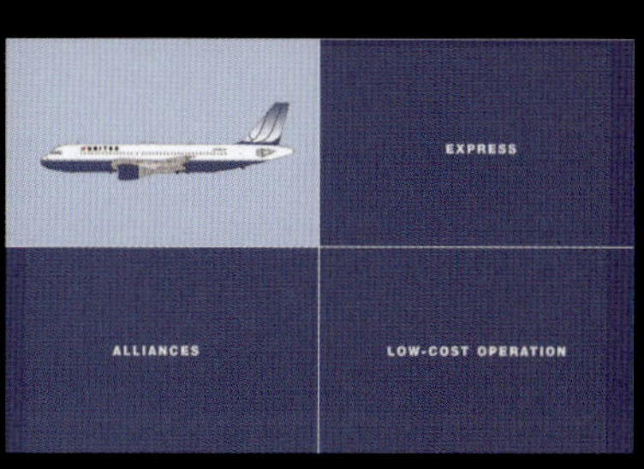

Brand attributes

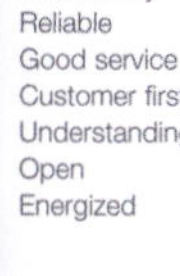

Trustworthy
Reliable
Good service
Customer first
Understanding
Open
Energized

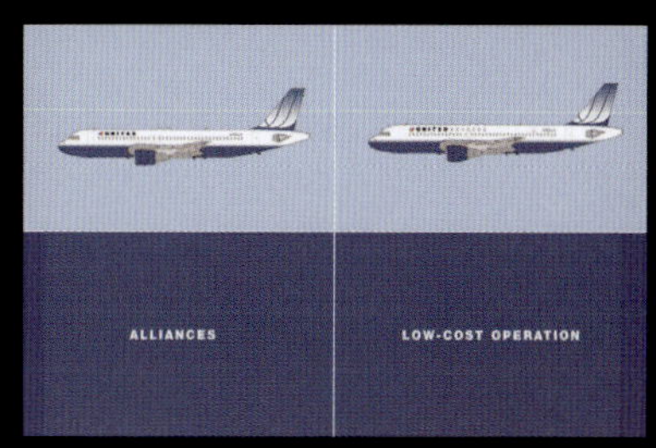

Brand experience

Retail
Friendly
Active
Engaging
Entertaining
Attractive
Simple
Changing
Social

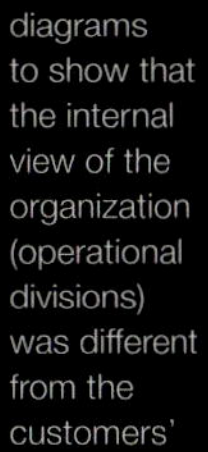

Above
We used two diagrams to show that the internal view of the organization (operational divisions) was different from the customers' view (an interconnected network).

Right
Each existing operational division had an established design appearance. How would the new carrier fit in?

Above
I usually prefer images to lists of words in presentations, but with this audience the words would resonate.

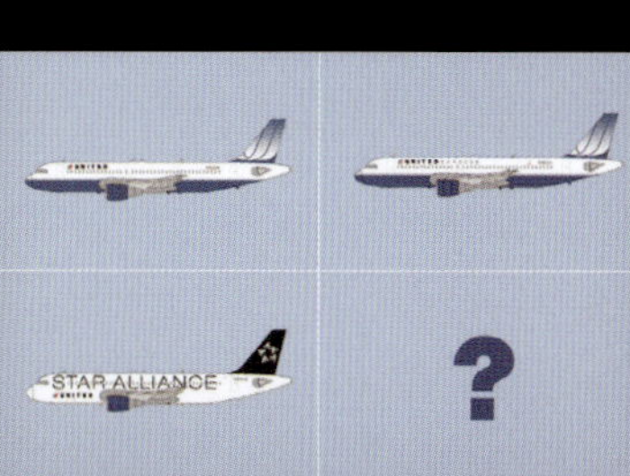

Close-in vs. further out

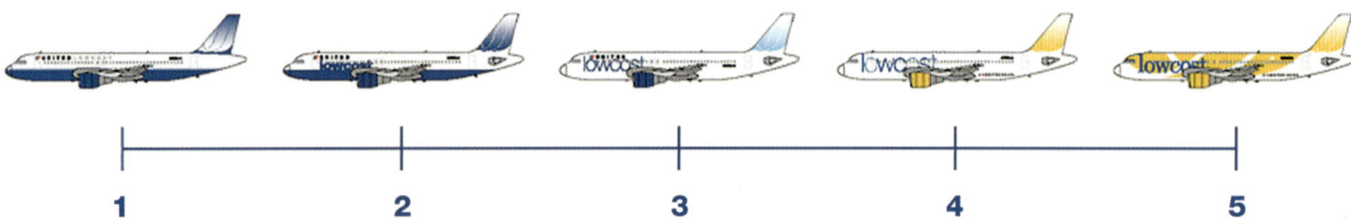

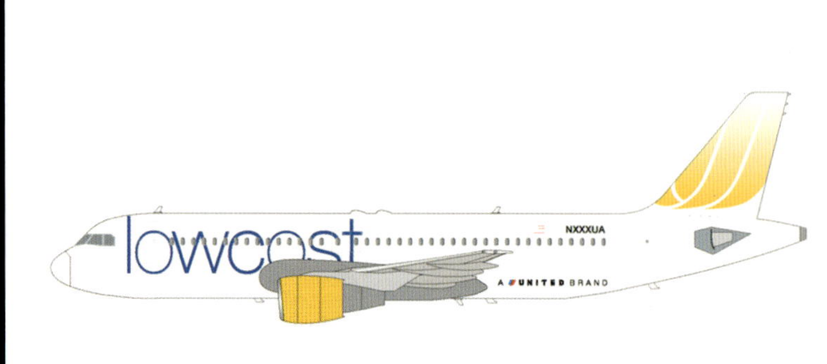

Above
Picking the name and picking the design were treated as related, but separate, decisions. Using a placeholder name, we demonstrated the critical choice: should the new carrier look like United, or look different?

Right
Our recommendation—close enough to reassure, different enough to surprise—used United's typography and retained its "tulip" symbol, but introduced a new color, orange-yellow, the opposite of their corporate blue.

Approach

No invented words (Allegis, Avolar)
Be energetic and inspiring
A clear relationship with United
Avoid "me too" options
Manage expectations

Expected vs. Unexpected

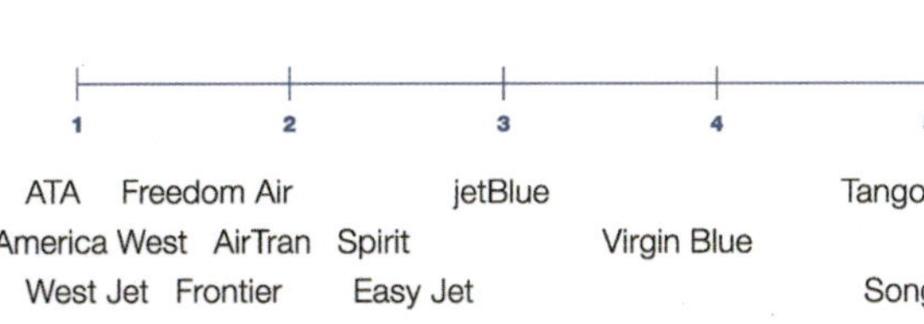

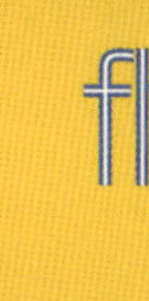

Indigo!
A UNITED BRAND

DEFINITION:
One who flies
PROS:
Passenger-focused
Simple and familiar, but hip
Participatory, energetic
Comfortable fit with current culture
FlyerFares, I'm a Flyer, Be a Flyer
CONS:
Vaguely retro

flyer

DEFINITION:
A variable color averaging a dark, silvery blue
PROS:
Indi (as in independent) + go
A shade of (United) blue
Sounds modern
Direct spanish translation
CONS:
Unfamiliar word to most

Indigo!

UNITED RED

LOOP
A UNITED BRAND

DEFINITION:
The color at the long-wave extreme of the visible spectrum
PROS:
The energetic "other half" of United
Clear implications for visual rollout
Takes on Virgin Blue and jetBlue
Easy to say, remember, pronounce
Means "network" in spanish
CONS:
In the red, seeing red

UNITED RED

DEFINITION:
A curved line forming a closed or partly open curve; a circuit
PROS:
Describes the flight network
Sounds fun
Additional meaning in Chicago area
Easy to say, remember, pronounce
CONS:
Whimsical, "loopy"

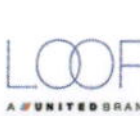

Above
Presentations happen in windowless rooms, so it's important to keep letting the outside world in. Here we lay

Above
We considered five names in all, showing pros and cons for each. All were viable, but we saved our favorite for last.

U N I T E D

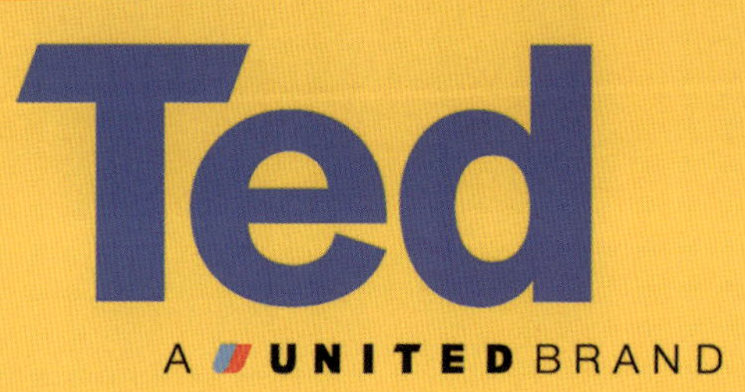

T E D

DEFINITION:

Short for Theodore (Greek, "Divine Gift")
A literal "part of United"

PROS:

Friendly, "first name basis"
Unique to the industry
Easy to say, remember, pronounce
Trus**ted**, exci**ted**, libera**ted**, res**ted**
"Ted E-fares", I'm with Ted

CONS:

Unorthodox, riskier

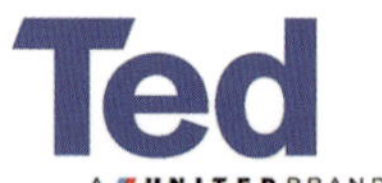

Above
Revealing our recommended name was my favorite part of the presentation. How much have you invested in promoting this name over the past 75 years?" I would ask. "A billion dollars? What if I told you we could give you a name that already had $500 million behind it?" The audience would always laugh at the answer (and the specious math behind it) but the point was made: the new name had been hiding in plain sight all along.

Right
People immediately understood the advantages of having a human name (and a nickname at that) to signal a more personal style of service; it made the other choices seem contrived. The treatment of the logo we presented borrowed the capital T from the United logotype. We later changed the tagline to "Part of United," which was direct, simple, and true in more ways than one.

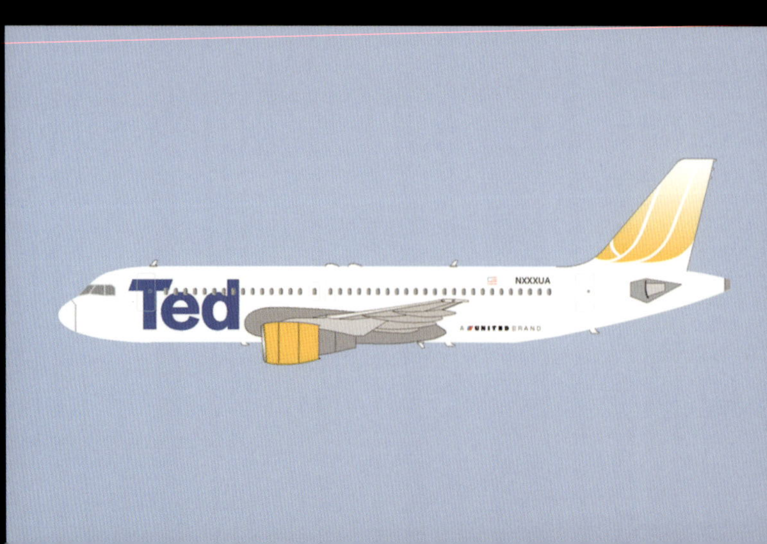

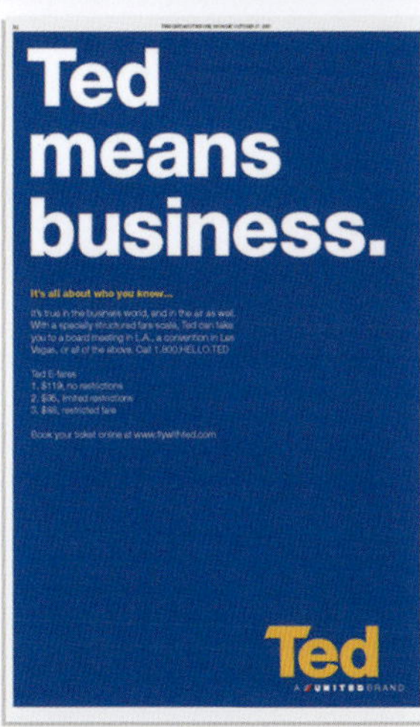

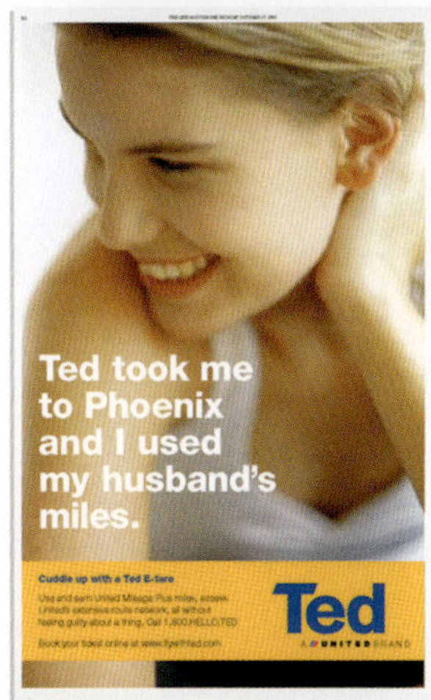

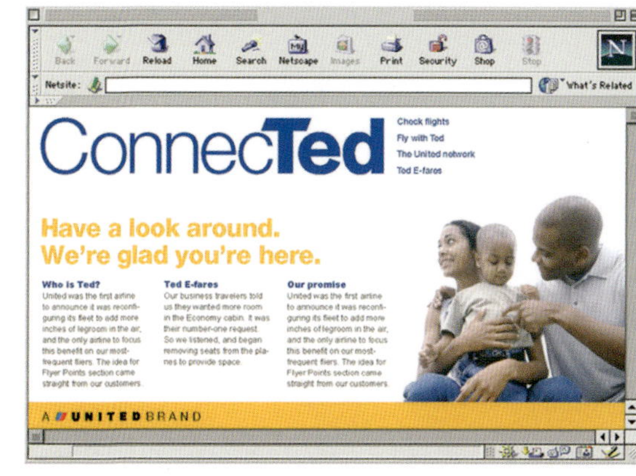

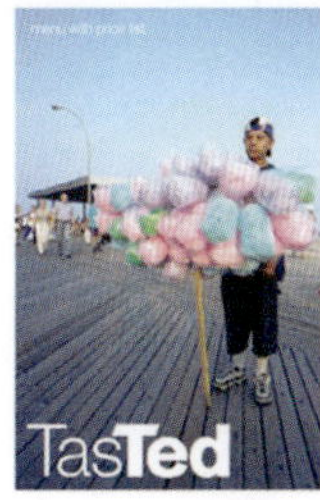

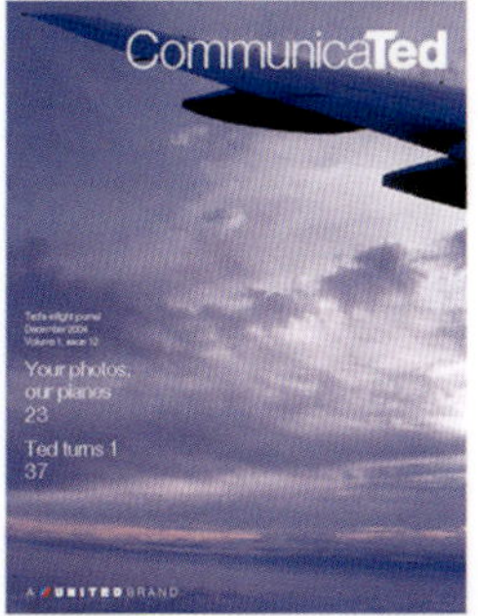

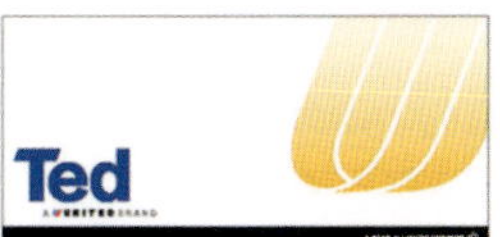

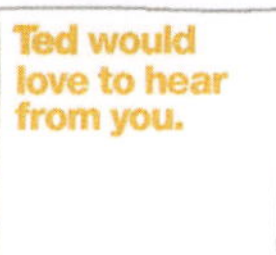

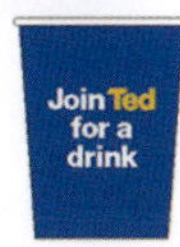

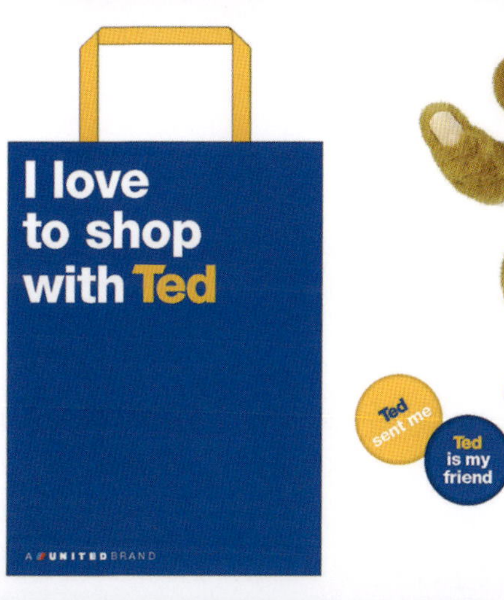

Above
Applying the new name and logotype to imaginary prototypes helped the client see how the proposal

Right
Ted's debut was preceded by an ingenious teaser campaign devised by Stuart D'Rozario and Bob Barrie at their ad agency Fallon Worldwide. Over 100 different stunts built mystery about the identity of Ted for months before its launch: buying coffee for everyone in a downtown diner, making donations to local charities, sponsoring runners in marathons, with all the credit going to the mysterious Ted. The mystery was solved when Ted was launched in Denver in February 2004. The experiment lasted only four years before the carrier's operations were folded back into United's main business. But Ted was consistently profitable, and many of the innovations it pioneered contributed to United's renaissance as it recovered from bankruptcy. Moreover, the team of United people associated with the project had the galvanizing experience of creating something from scratch, and went on to apply that thinking to projects throughout their careers.

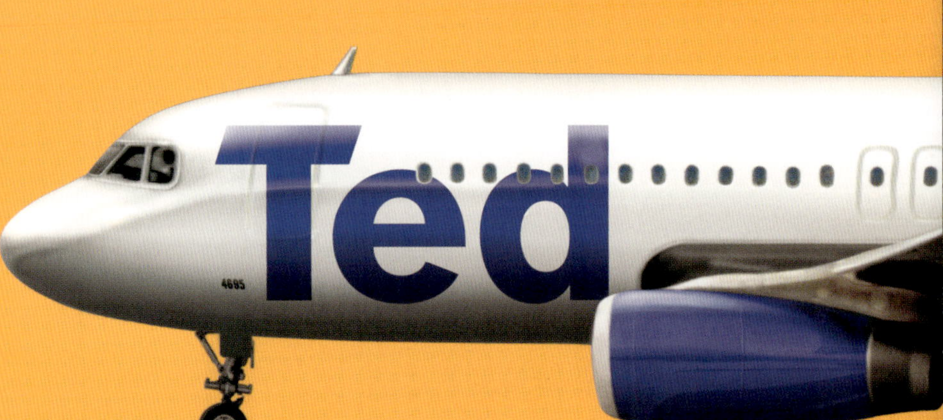

Be on a first-

Meet Ted. A new, low-fare service that flies to fun de

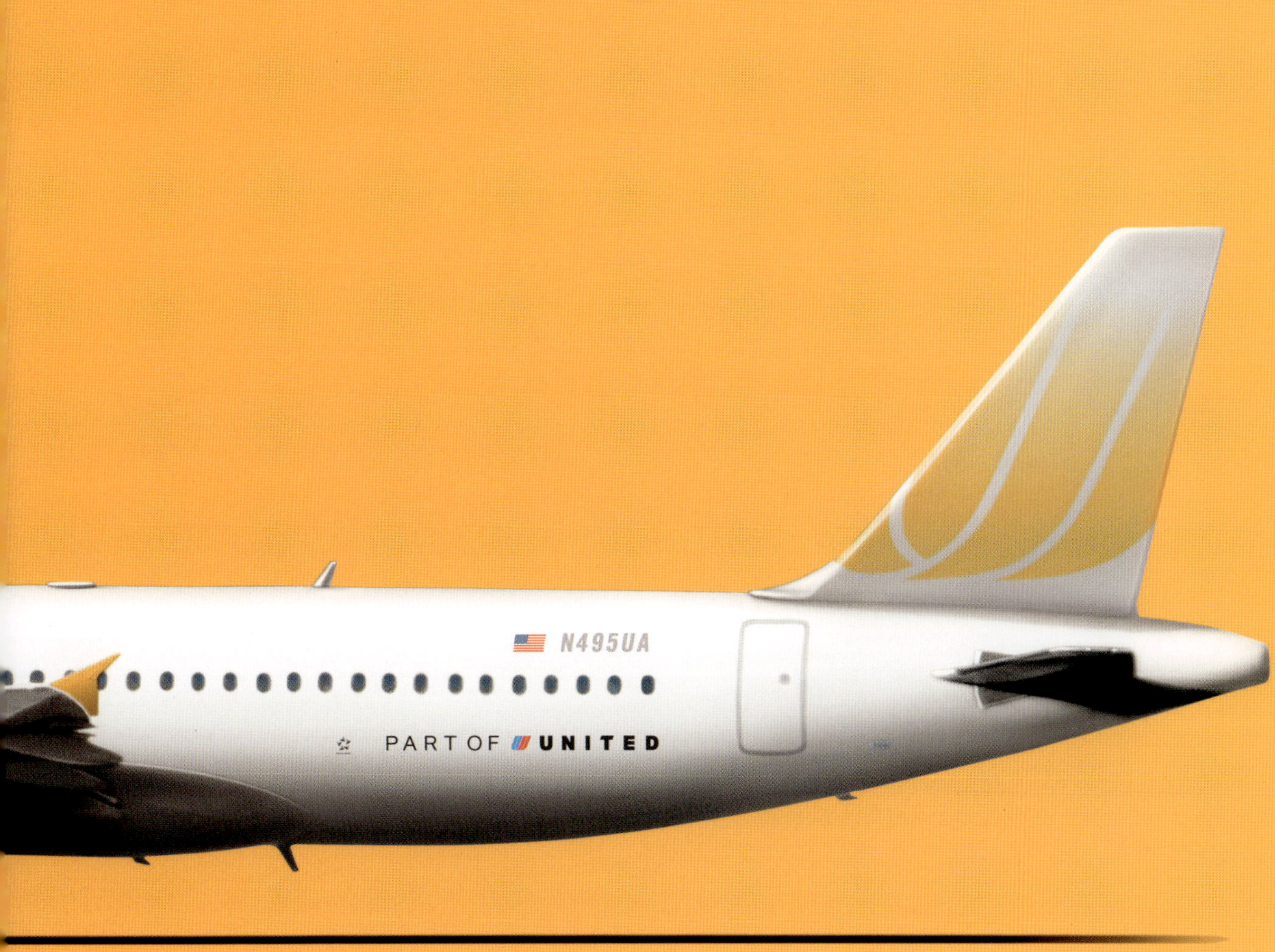

N495UA
PART OF UNITED

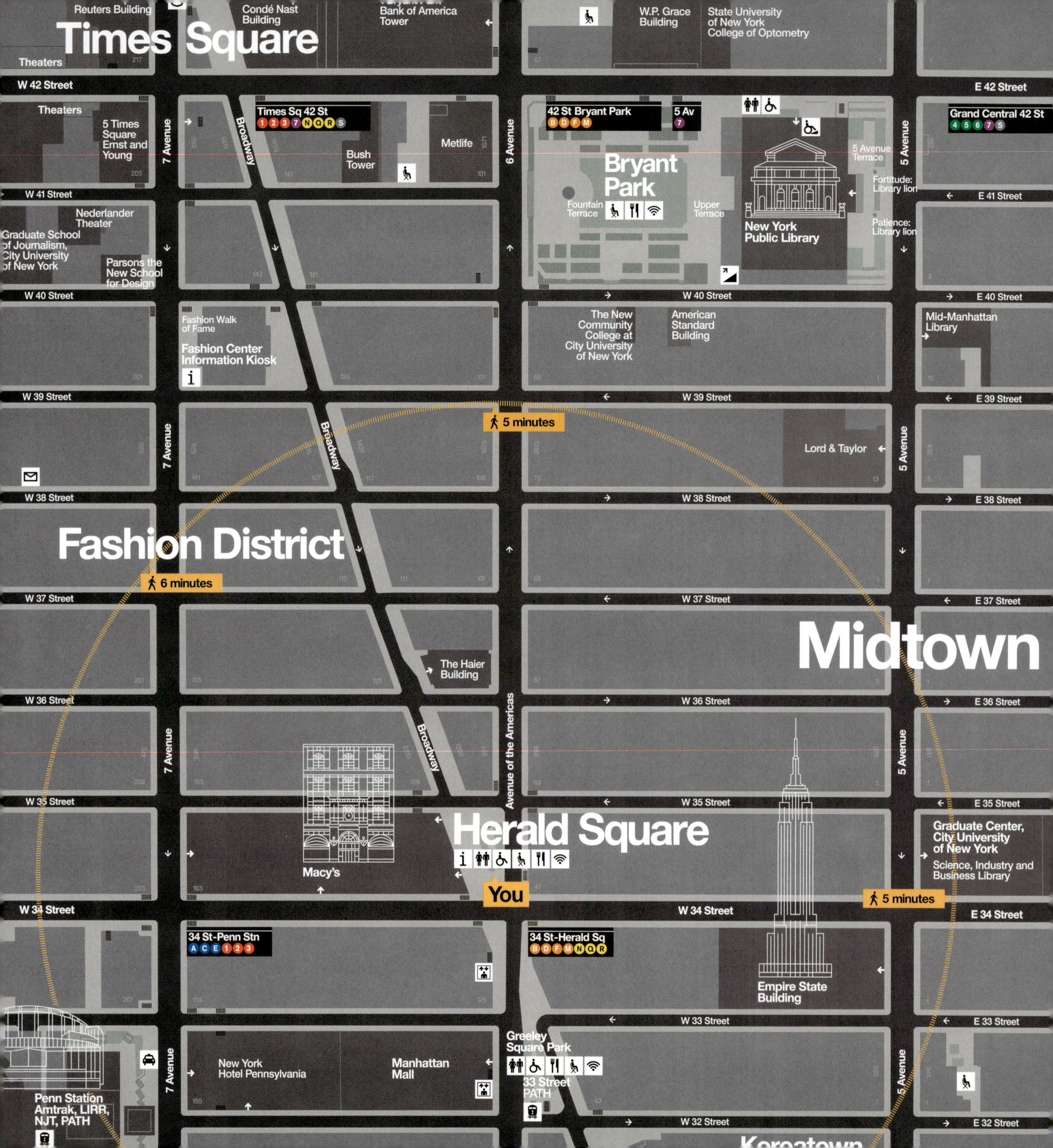

Times Square
Reuters Building
Condé Nast Building
Bank of America Tower
W.P. Grace Building
State University of New York College of Optometry
Theaters
W 42 Street
E 42 Street
5 Times Square Ernst and Young
Times Sq 42 St
Bush Tower
Metlife
42 St Bryant Park
5 Av
Grand Central 42 St
Bryant Park
5 Avenue Terrace
Fortitude: Library lion
Patience: Library lion
Fountain Terrace
Upper Terrace
New York Public Library
W 41 Street
E 41 Street
Nederlander Theater
Graduate School of Journalism, City University of New York
Parsons the New School for Design
W 40 Street
E 40 Street
Fashion Walk of Fame
Fashion Center Information Kiosk
The New Community College at City University of New York
American Standard Building
Mid-Manhattan Library
W 39 Street
E 39 Street
5 minutes
Lord & Taylor
W 38 Street
E 38 Street
Fashion District
6 minutes
W 37 Street
E 37 Street
The Haier Building
Midtown
W 36 Street
E 36 Street
Avenue of the Americas
W 35 Street
E 35 Street
Herald Square
Macy's
You
Graduate Center, City University of New York
Science, Industry and Business Library
5 minutes
W 34 Street
E 34 Street
34 St-Penn Stn
34 St-Herald Sq
Empire State Building
W 33 Street
E 33 Street
Greeley Square Park
33 Street PATH
New York Hotel Pennsylvania
Manhattan Mall
Penn Station Amtrak, LIRR, NJT, PATH
W 32 Street
E 32 Street
Koreatown
7 Avenue
Broadway
6 Avenue
5 Avenue

How to get where you want to be
New York City Department of Transportation

Opposite For this project, we joined a team led by planning consultants City ID, which was responsible for determining the basic wayfinding strategy. T-Kartor developed the cartographic database, industrial designers Billings Jackson created the structures for the signs and maps, and RBA Group provided the civil engineering expertise required to install this intricate system in a demanding urban environment.

New York City is a complicated place. Manhattan is dominated by an orderly grid, its numbered streets and avenues dictated by the Commissioners' Plan of 1811. But downtown, before the grid takes hold, you'll find West 4th Street intersecting West 11th Street. Meanwhile, in Queens, another 11th Street crosses, in order, 44th Drive, 44th Road, and 44th Avenue. New York's layout is logical except when it's not. As for Brooklyn, like they say: forget about it.

For years individual neighborhoods sought to guide confused pedestrians by creating their own signs and maps. In the 1990s, we created one such system for the crowded and confusing Financial District, inventing a unique graphic style that worked within the district but had nothing to do with the dozens of other such systems around town. Finally, in 2011, the New York City Department of Transportation decided to create a citywide system called WalkNYC that would unify wayfinding in all five boroughs. We joined a multidisciplinary team that would create maps and signs for five pilot neighborhoods.

We quickly found ourselves in a new world where people's navigating habits had been turned upside down—literally. For years, urban wayfinding often started with a single piece of artwork: a big static map, everything fixed in place, north at the top. But GPS-savvy travelers today expect a map to orient itself in the position of travel and have the ability to zoom in for more detail. Could our system's printed maps, deployed throughout the city, satisfy these expectations? Using a nimble, infinitely modifiable database capable of multiple orientations and dense detail, our team created analog maps that provide a remarkably digital experience.

Handsome, urbane wayfinding fixtures introduced the new system throughout the city in 2013. The maps now appear at bike-share locations, in subway stations, and on express-bus kiosks. Despite the ubiquity of handheld devices, the sidewalks around our wayfinding kiosks are always crowded with people figuring out how to get where they want to be in this beautifully confusing city.

Urban wayfinding is an extraordinarily complicated enterprise that requires the collaboration of a wide range of experts. How do people actually find their way in a complex city? What information do they need? How and where should it be provided? Answering these questions meant conducting dozens of workshops and interviews, stopping pedestrians on the sidewalk to find out where they were going and how they were getting there.

The NYC Department of Transportation told us that WalkNYC would affect not just wayfinding, but everything from public health (by encouraging people to walk) to economic development (more sidewalk activity means more shopping). Simplicity was the key, but achieving it was anything but simple. Our task was to translate the cartographic data into maps that we hoped would not only work well, but would become as distinctive a part of New York's graphic language as Massimo Vignelli's subway signage or Milton Glaser's "I Love NY" logo.

Right top
Consultants City ID led our team in a series of neighborhood tours with local residents and business owners to help determine the location and content of our wayfinding kiosks.

Right middle
Understanding how people find their way is complicated enough in someplace like an airport, where everyone comes through the same front door and has the same goal. In a city, where people may be starting anywhere and going anywhere, new in town or lifelong residents, in a hurry or ready to get lost, addressing the complexity means making deliberate choices.

Right bottom
Would we refer to north as uptown? How would we determine walking distances? Which landmarks qualified to appear on the maps? What colors were the most legible at day and at night? The details were seemingly endless.

Opposite
We considered many different typefaces for the system, but none conveyed the same authority as Helvetica. No surprise there: users of the New York Subway system have been trusting it since the 1970s, so why not continue the same graphic language above ground? We made one modification I've secretly wanted for years: all the square dots are round, a not-so-subtle customization for our client DOT.

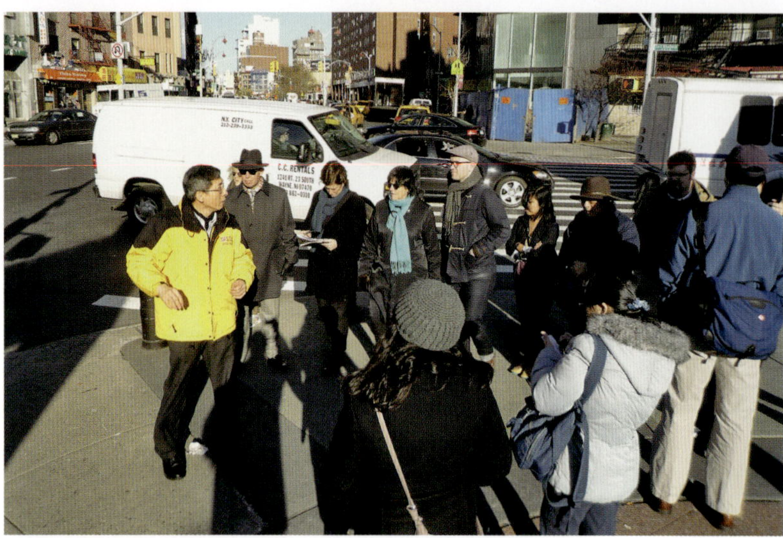

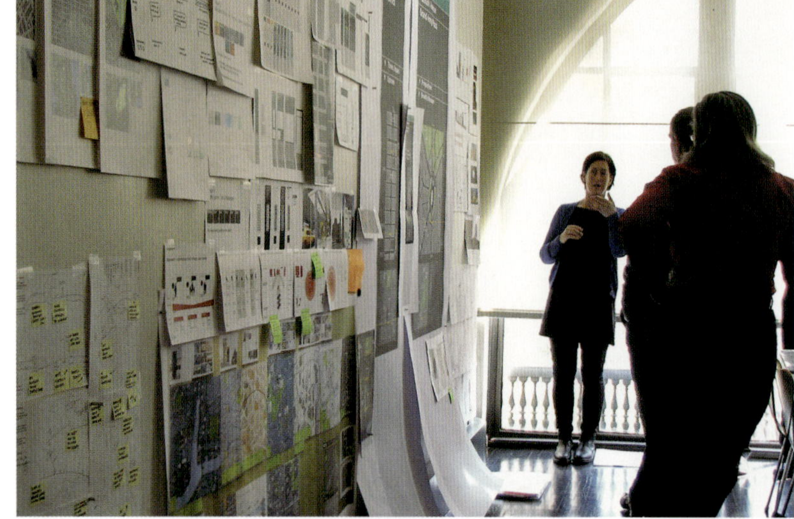

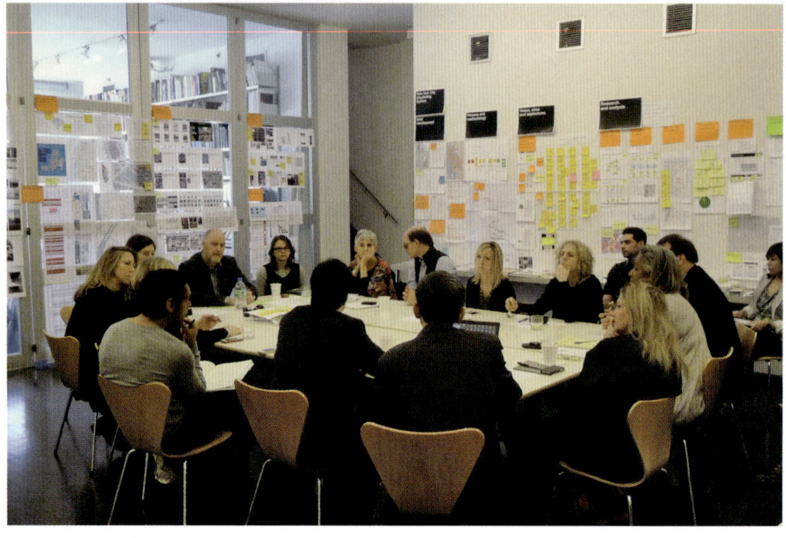

Midtown
Tribeca
Chinatown
Flatiron
You are here
ij!?:;.

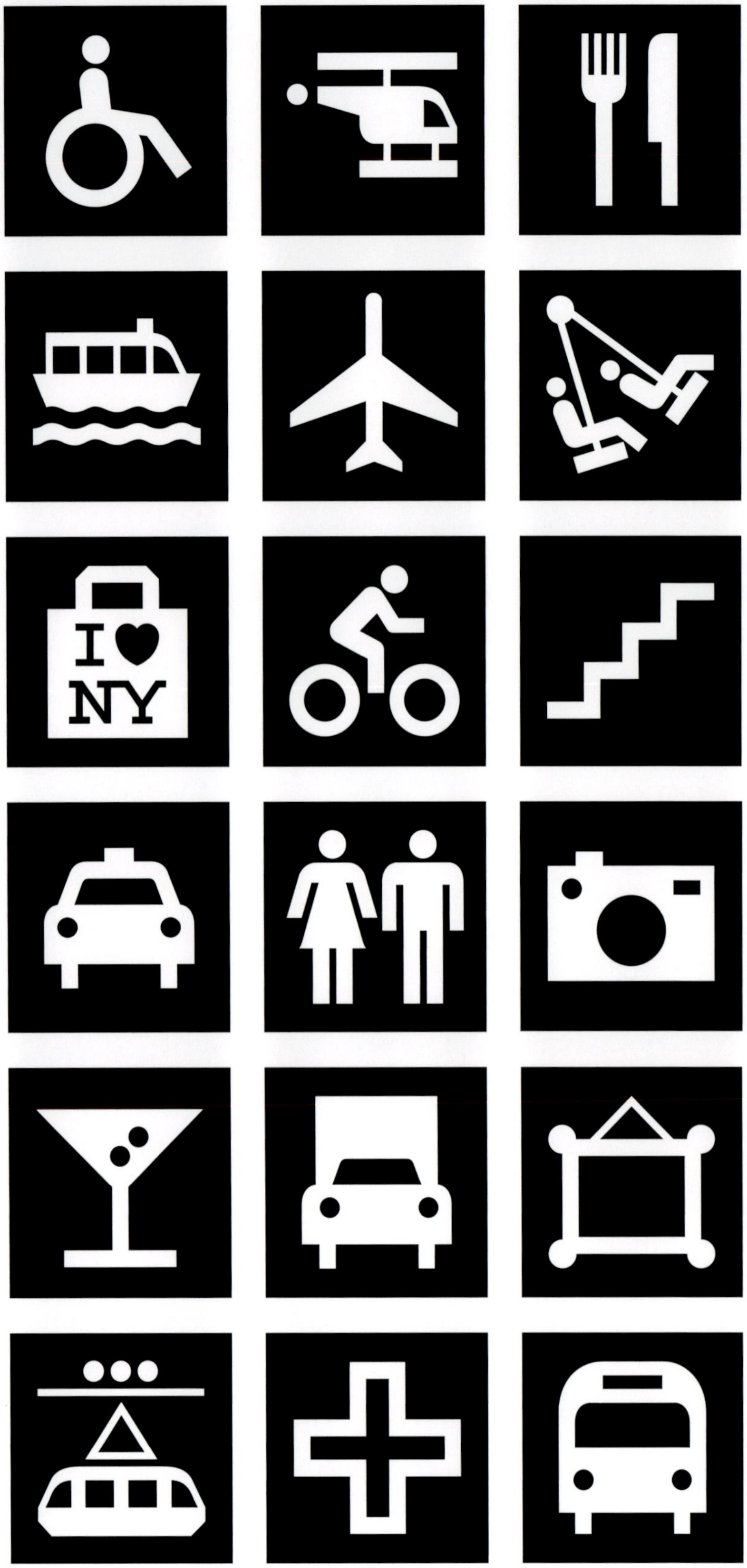

Left
Because we were managing a dense jungle of information, we knew every graphic element needed to be perfectly engineered. For instance, the symbol system developed for the US Department of Transportation by Roger Cook and Don Shanosky at the American Institute of Graphic Arts in 1974 provided some, but not all, of the icons we'd need. We customized some (changing the bike symbol to match the designs used in the city's new bike share program) and invented others (a shopping bag bearing New York's familiar slogan).

Below
We wanted the information icons to seem like an extension of the typography. This meant hundreds of small modifications, masterminded by designer Jesse Reed.

Opposite
Designer Hamish Smyth led our work for the WalkNYC program, including the design of the architectural icons that punctuate each map. Despite technology, some things can't be automated. It took an army of interns to draw over 100 of them by hand. Each one is a gem.

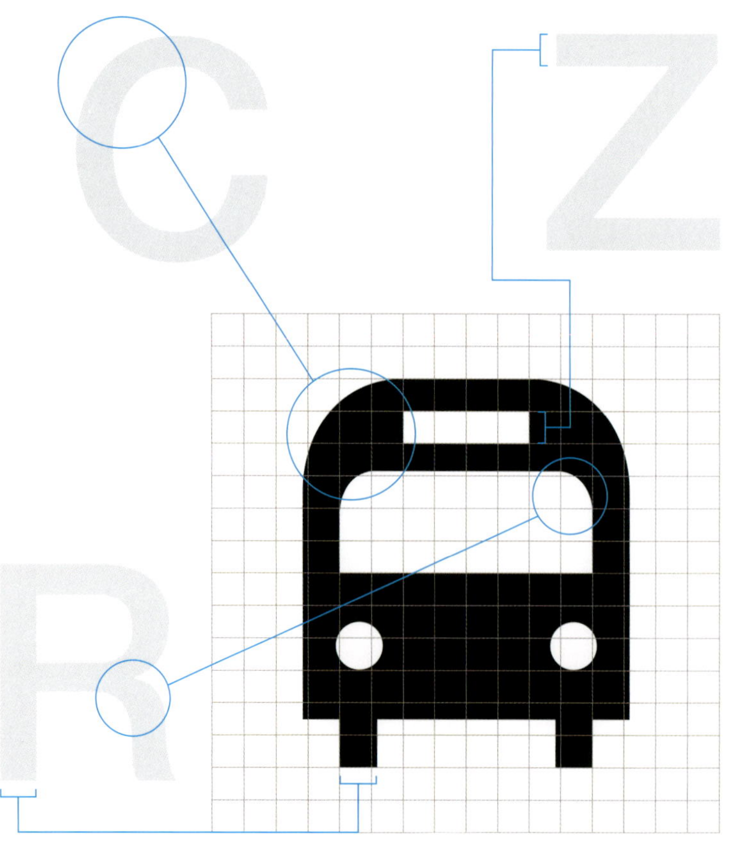

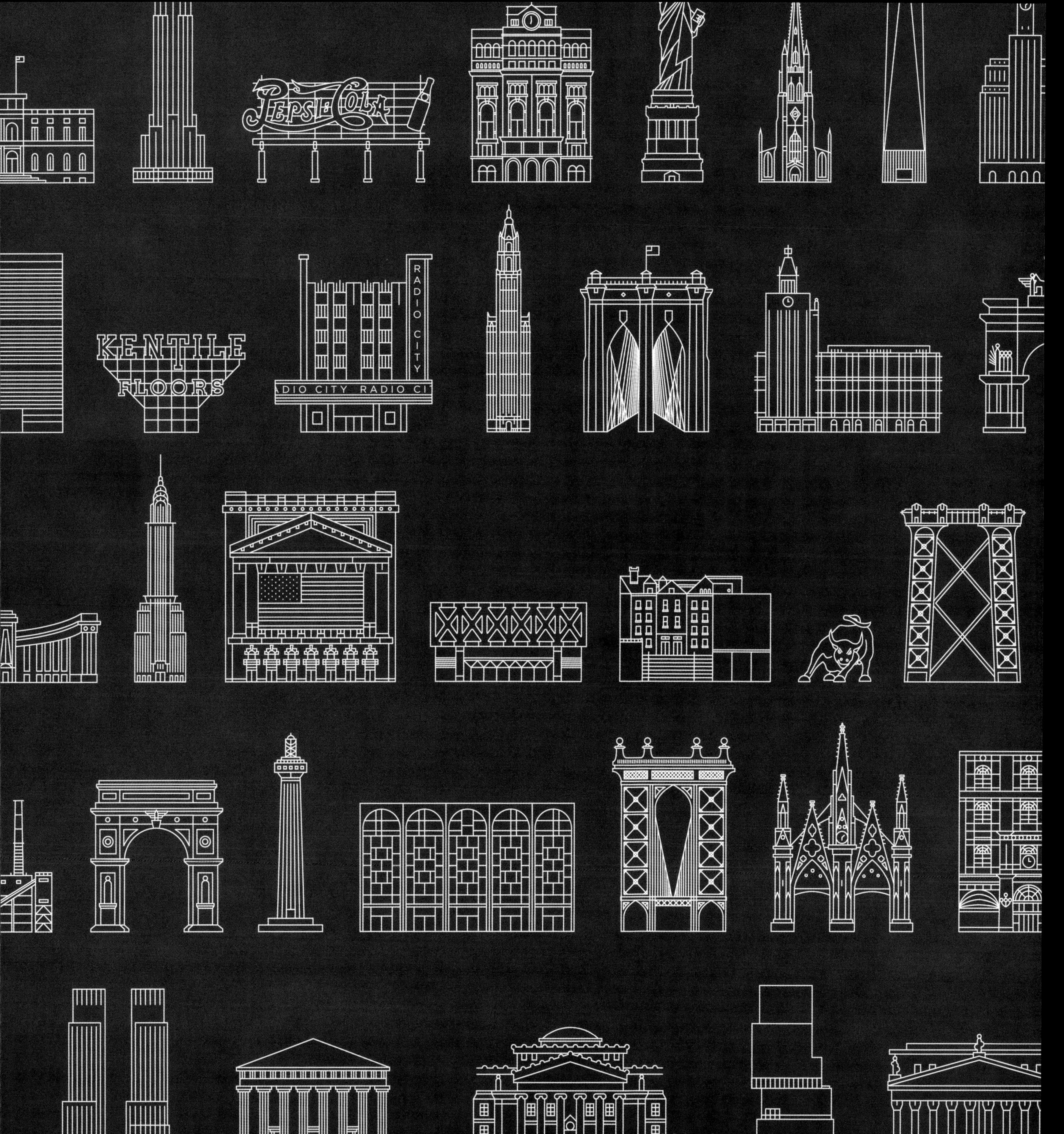
Pepsi-Cola
KENTILE
FLOORS
RADIO CITY
DIO CITY RADIO CI

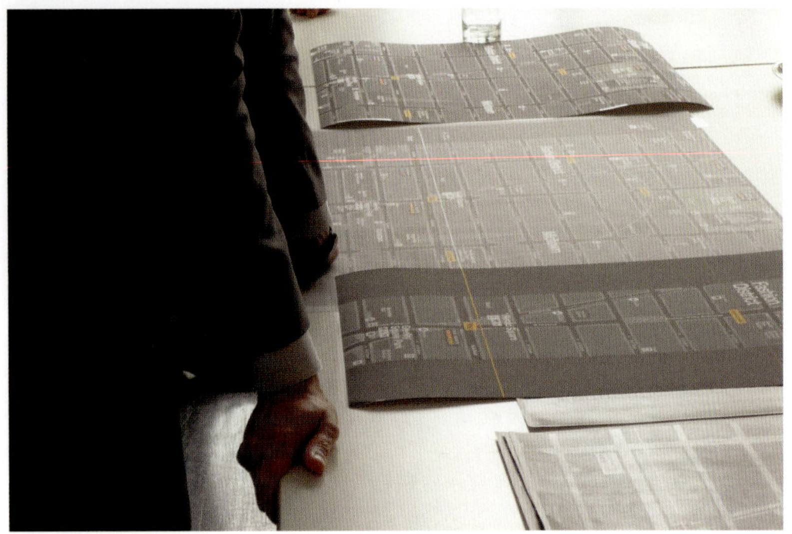

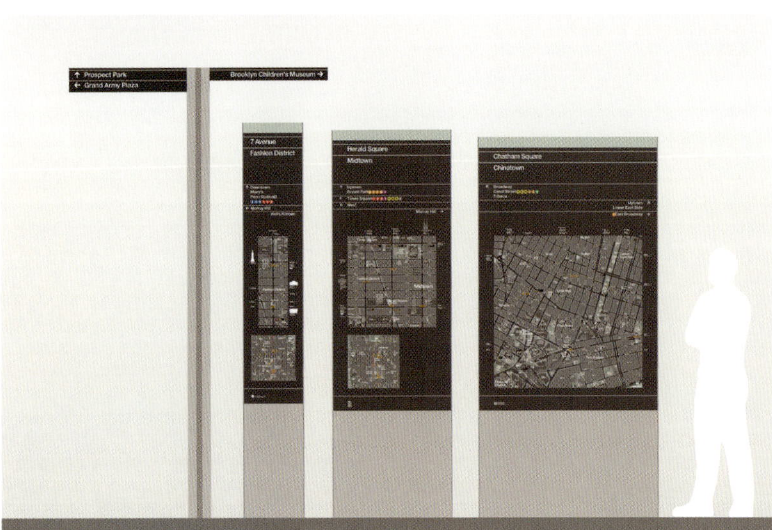

Left top
The color scheme of the maps was much debated. We recommended a subdued palette of muted grays that matched the city itself.

Left bottom
A family of kiosks of different shapes and sizes were deployed throughout the city; large kiosks were installed at major decision points; the smallest serve as guideposts in busy areas where space is at a premium. In effect, signs' sizes respond to their surroundings.

Opposite
Each sign conveys an astonishing amount of information. Maps are printed on vinyl and installed behind glass panels that can be easily dismantled when updates are required.

Next spread
The maps achieved instant ubiquity when they were deployed throughout Manhattan and Brooklyn as part of the city's first bike-share program. Thousands of people use the bikes; millions use the maps.

"Heads-up mapping" is the cartographic convention where the orientation of the map depends on the direction the viewer is facing. With traditional maps, north is always up. With heads-up maps, if the viewer is facing south, the map is turned so that south is at the top. Many were dubious—including me—that such a system would work in a city where, so it's said, "the Bronx is up and the Battery's down."

But I was persuaded by early tests that showed the new method was favored by an astounding 84 percent of users. Clearly, digital maps and global positioning systems have changed the way we navigate. Later, the *New York Times*, reporting on the system, conducted a more informal poll and discovered six out of ten New Yorkers on the street couldn't point north. Heads-up mapping is here to stay.

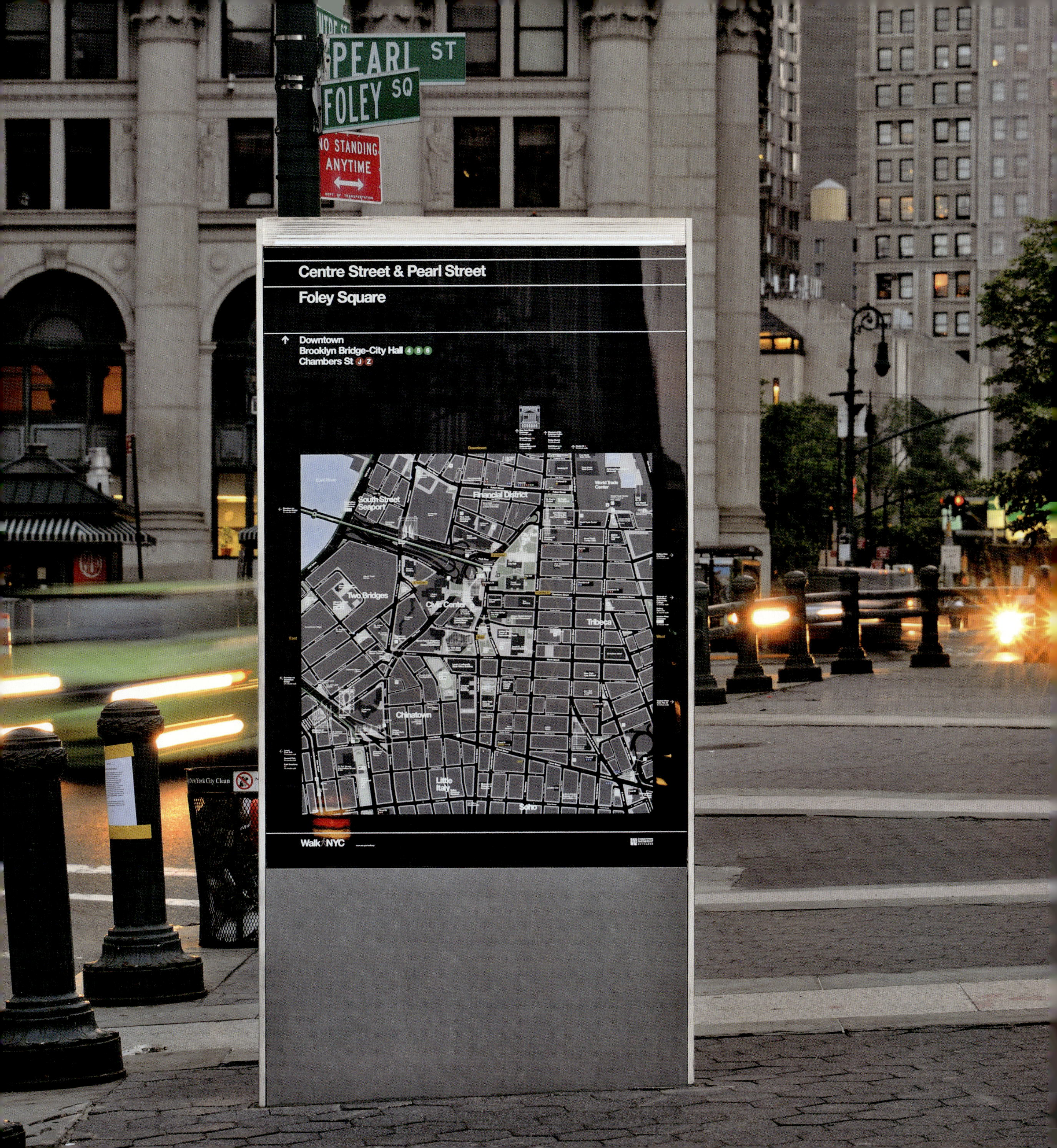
PEARL ST
FOLEY SQ
NO STANDING
ANYTIME
Centre Street & Pearl Street
Foley Square
Downtown
Brooklyn Bridge-City Hall 4 5 6
Chambers St J Z
South Street Seaport
Financial District
Two Bridges
Civic Center
Tribeca
Chinatown
Little Italy
Soho
Walk NYC

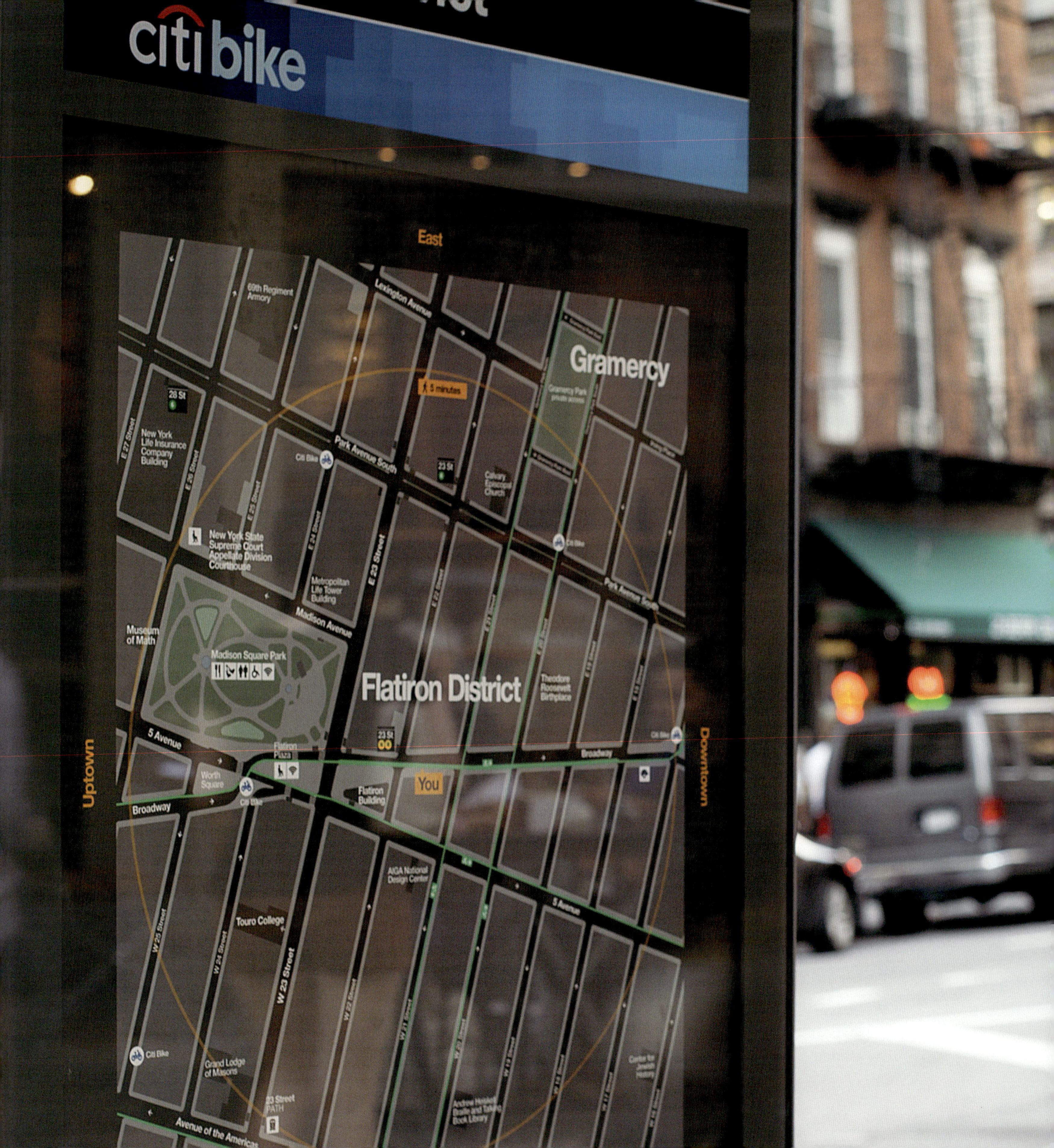
citi bike
East
Uptown
Downtown
Lexington Avenue
69th Regiment Armory
Gramercy
5 minutes
28 St
E 27 Street
New York Life Insurance Company Building
E 26 Street
Citi Bike
Park Avenue South
23 St
Calvary Episcopal Church
E 25 Street
New York State Supreme Court Appellate Division Courthouse
E 24 Street
E 23 Street
Metropolitan Life Tower Building
Madison Avenue
Museum of Math
Madison Square Park
Flatiron District
Theodore Roosevelt Birthplace
5 Avenue
Flatiron Plaza
Broadway
Worth Square
Flatiron Building
You
AIGA National Design Center
Touro College
W 25 Street
W 24 Street
W 23 Street
Grand Lodge of Masons
23 Street PATH
Avenue of the Americas

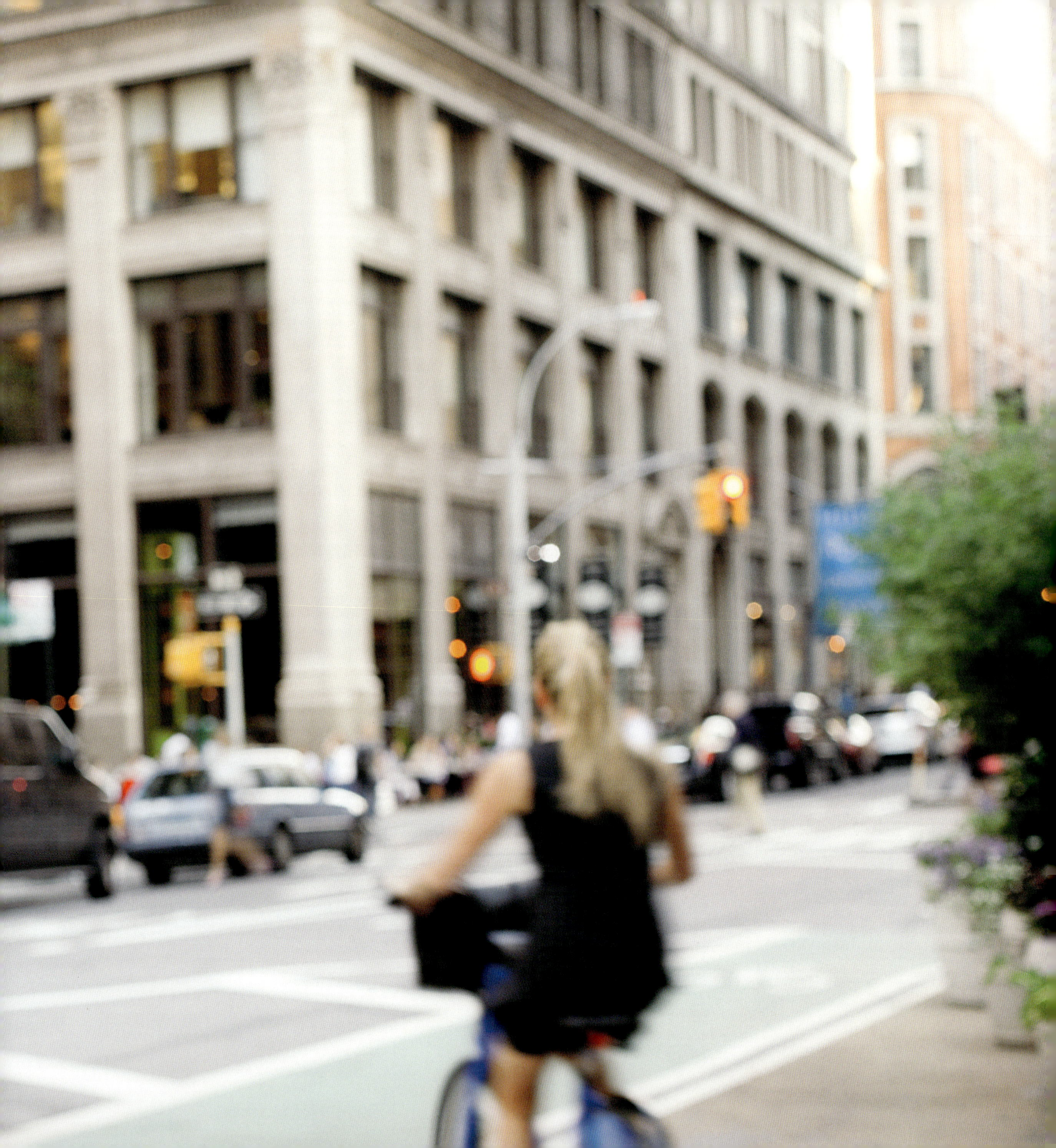

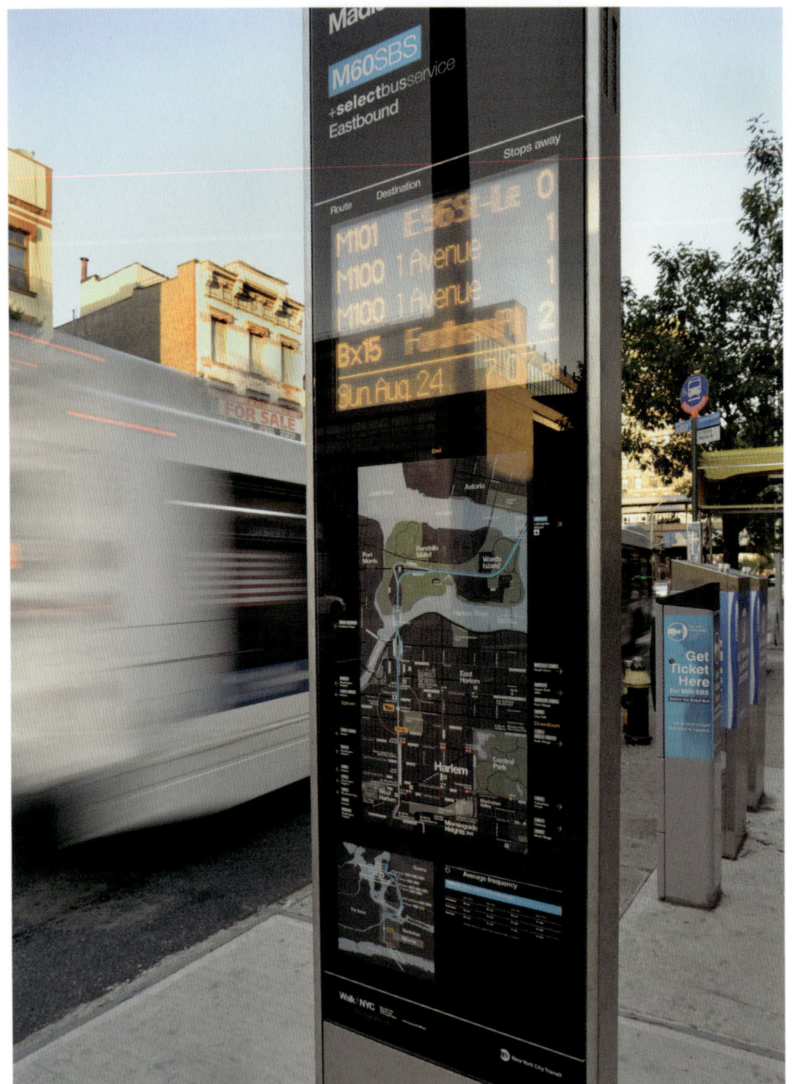

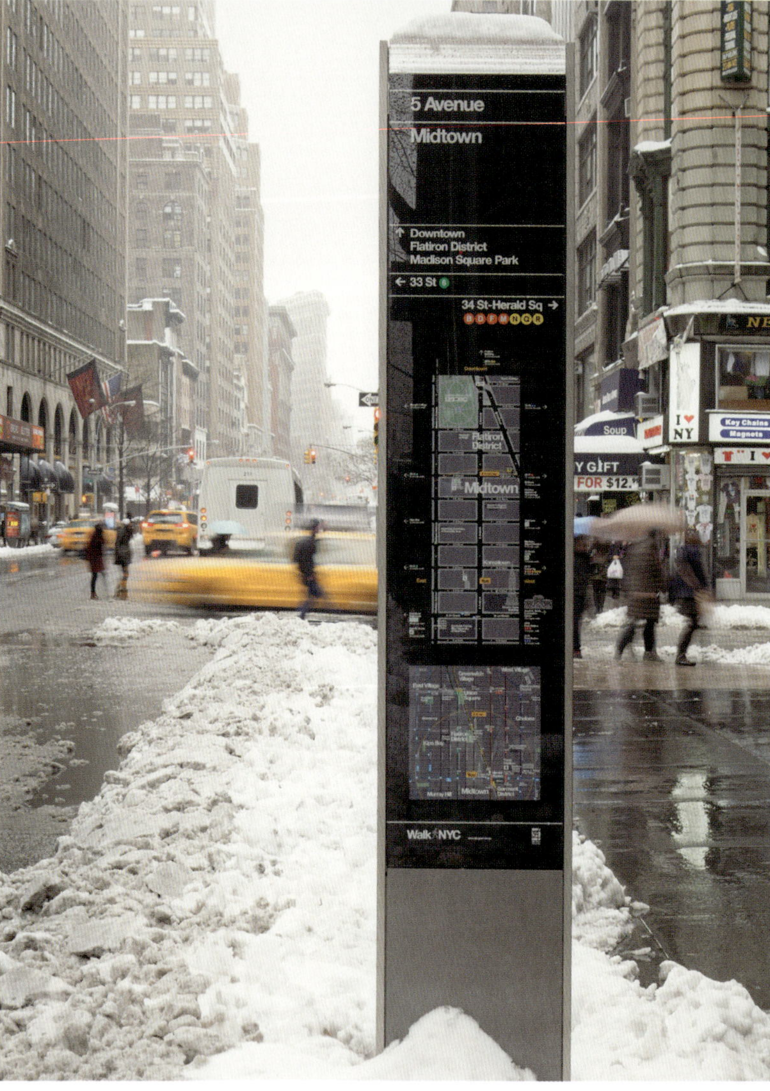

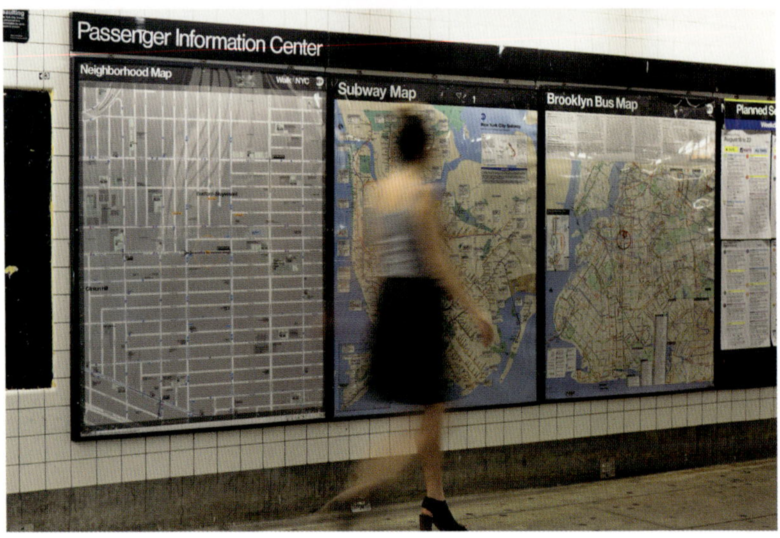

Above left
We believe that signs should be digital only when they have to be. The kiosks that support New York's Select Bus Service feature real-time schedule information.

Above right
The signs have been engineered to withstand collision, vandalism, and tough New York winters.

Left
The wayfinding maps, with their color scheme adjusted for 24-hour artificial light, have been installed in all of New York's subway stations.

Opposite
The structures that house the maps were designed to echo New York's modernist architecture.

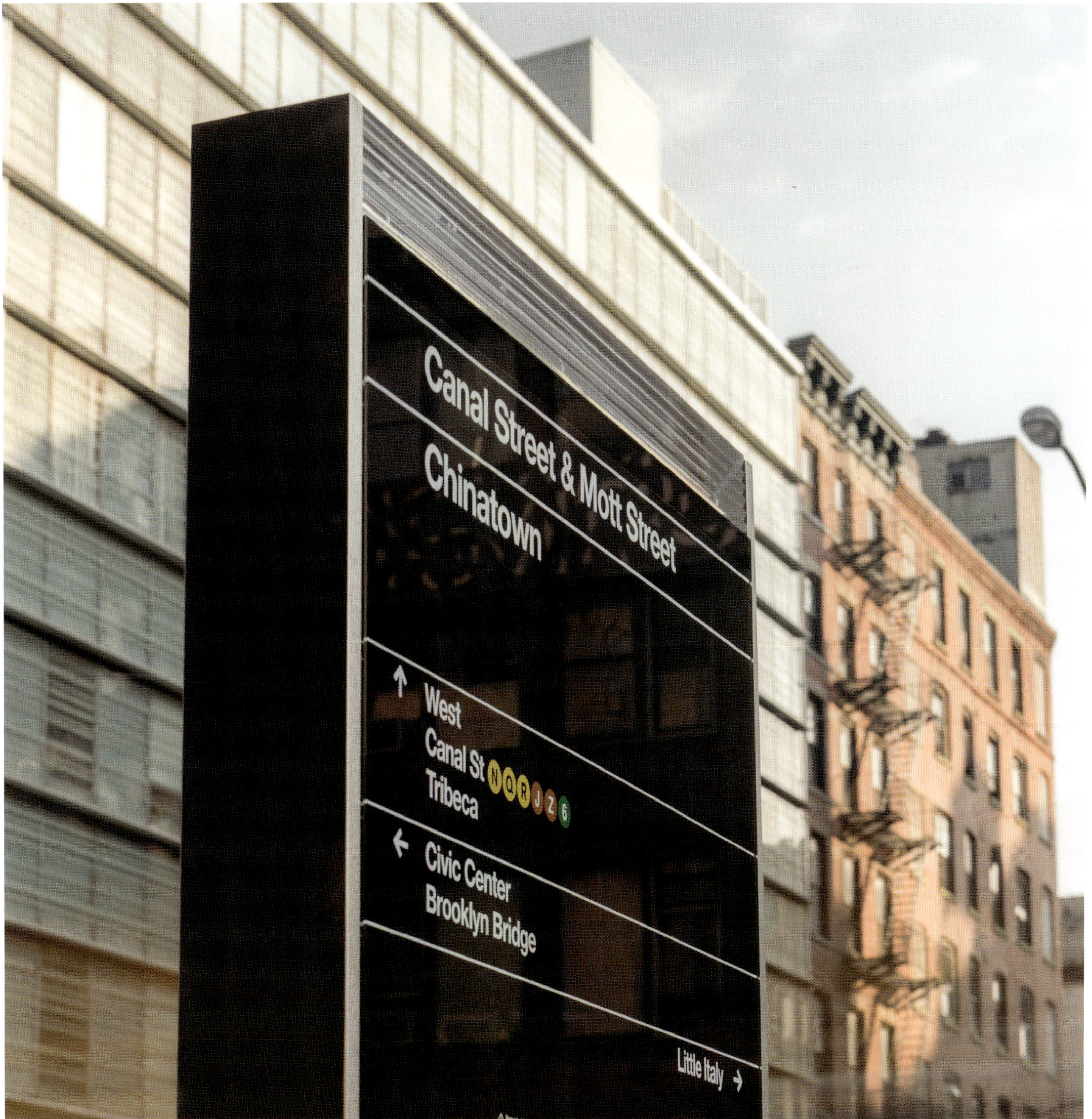
Canal Street & Mott Street
Chinatown
West
Canal St N Q R J Z 6
Tribeca
Civic Center
Brooklyn Bridge
Little Italy

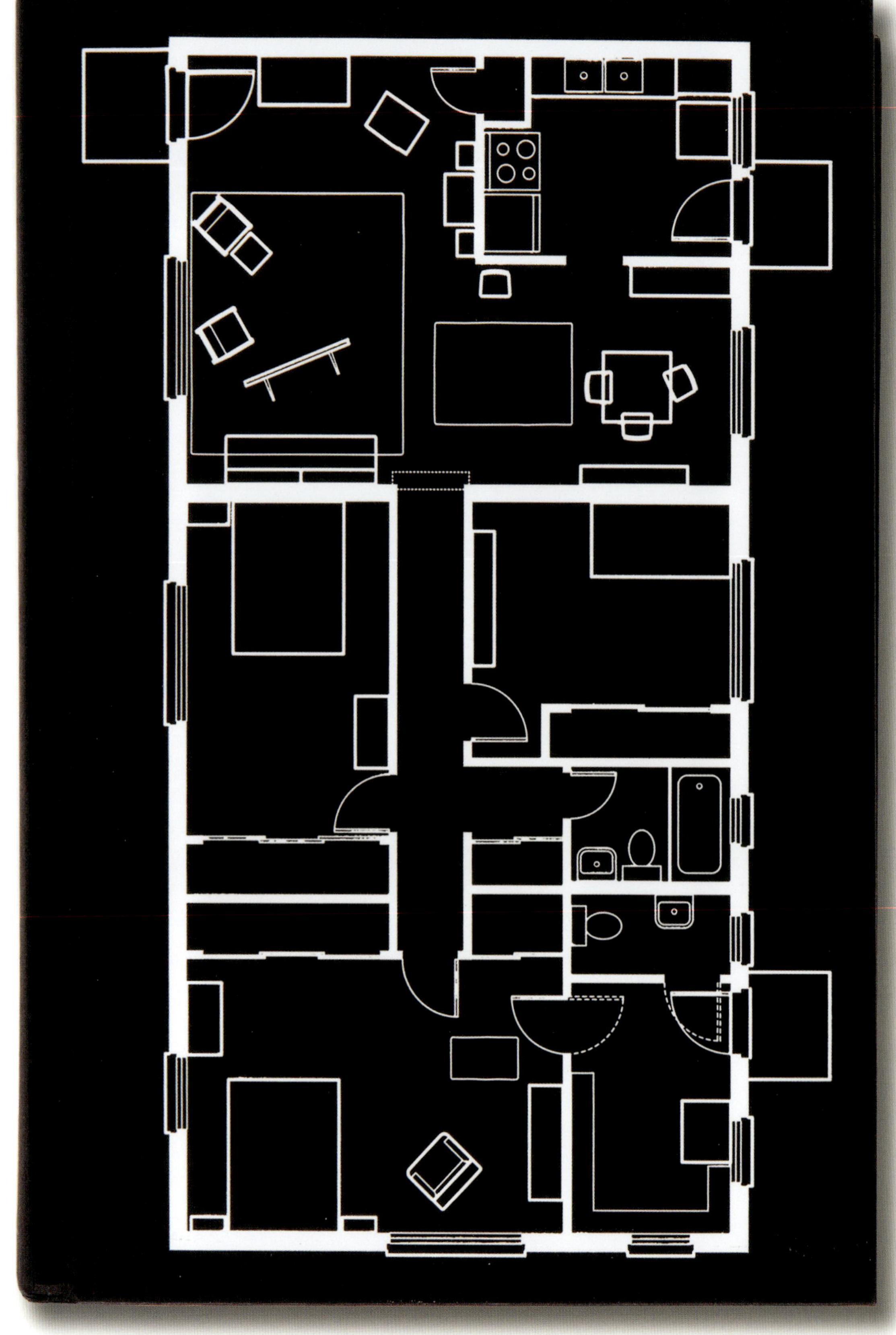

How to investigate a murder
A Wilderness of Error

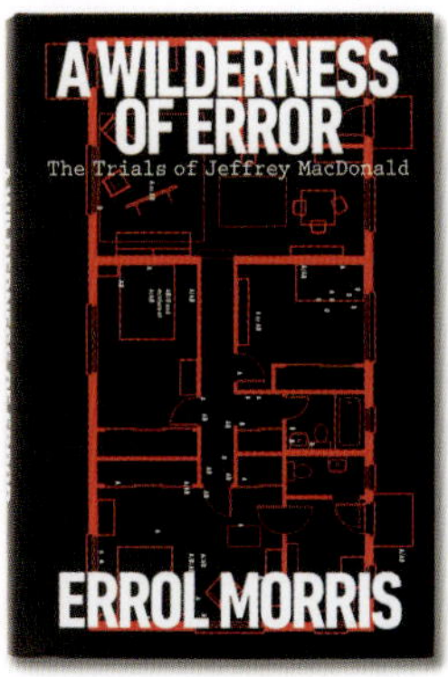

Opposite and above
The cover and dust jacket of *A Wilderness of Error*, an investigation of the murder of a wife and two children, depict, respectively, the floor plan of the MacDonald family home, and the pattern of blood types that investigators found on the scene the morning after the murders. Unusually, each of the four family members had a different blood type. This made the crime no easier to solve.

Filmmaker Errol Morris is obsessed with truth. All of his films have at their centers people who know the truth, don't want to know the truth, want to stop other people from learning the truth, or want to uncover the truth. As a former private investigator, Morris knows well how physical evidence can support or challenge conflicting testimony. So often the inanimate objects in his movies acquire an outsized significance: documents, photographs, an umbrella, a teacup. Morris's breakthrough in 1988, *The Thin Blue Line*, used interviews and reenactments to investigate the colliding stories behind an obscure shooting of a police officer in Dallas. The mesmerizing film exonerated a man on death row who had been unjustly convicted of the crime.

Brilliant and inexhaustible, Errol Morris also writes books. In 2012, he decided to examine another decades-old crime, this one anything but obscure. On February 17, 1970, army physician Jeffrey MacDonald's wife and children were brutally murdered in their home in Fort Bragg, North Carolina. Although MacDonald maintained that they were killed by intruders, he was convicted of the crime. He has been in prison since 1982, consistently maintaining his innocence. Since then, the case has been the subject of several previous books as well as two television movies. Morris was convinced there was more to be discovered.

The book he wrote about the case, *A Wilderness of Error*, is a study in black and white of a case that is anything but. For the book's design, we decided to avoid the clichés of true-crime books. Instead, we focused on the eerie collection of physical evidence that survived from that evening: a coffee table, a flower pot, a child's doll, a rocking horse, a pajama top. Mute witnesses to a crime that has defied resolution, they have been examined and reexamined so many times they have acquired an iconic status to people who know the case. We reduced each of them to a simple black-and-white line drawing. Morris realized that their stark, deadpan quality could provide the book's central visual motif; we ended up doing nearly fifty of them. The cover, the floor plan of the tiny MacDonald apartment, represents the claustrophobic "wilderness" where this mystery unfolded, and where, somewhere, the truth resides.

Right and next spread
Errol Morris is the recipient of an Academy Award for *The Fog of War* and a MacArthur Foundation "genius grant." *The Thin Blue Line*, my first exposure to his work, was like no other movie I had ever seen. The blunt, awkward interviews of criminals, cops, lawyers, and witnesses; the surreal reenactments illustrating a crime that no one described the same way; the peculiar digressions; the haunting Philip Glass score: it all added up to a revolution in documentary filmmaking. By now I have seen it many times. My favorite moment is a staged sequence where a chocolate milkshake flies through the air in slow motion, landing with a plop on the ground, a banal punctuation to a nightmarish crime.

The MacDonald case was full of these kinds of quotidian objects elevated to iconic status, each implicated in a horrific crime. Morris encouraged us to use stark images of these objects to structure the book and organize its complex themes of truth and justice. Pentagram's Yve Ludwig led the design of the book and Niko Skourtis organized the team that created the drawings.

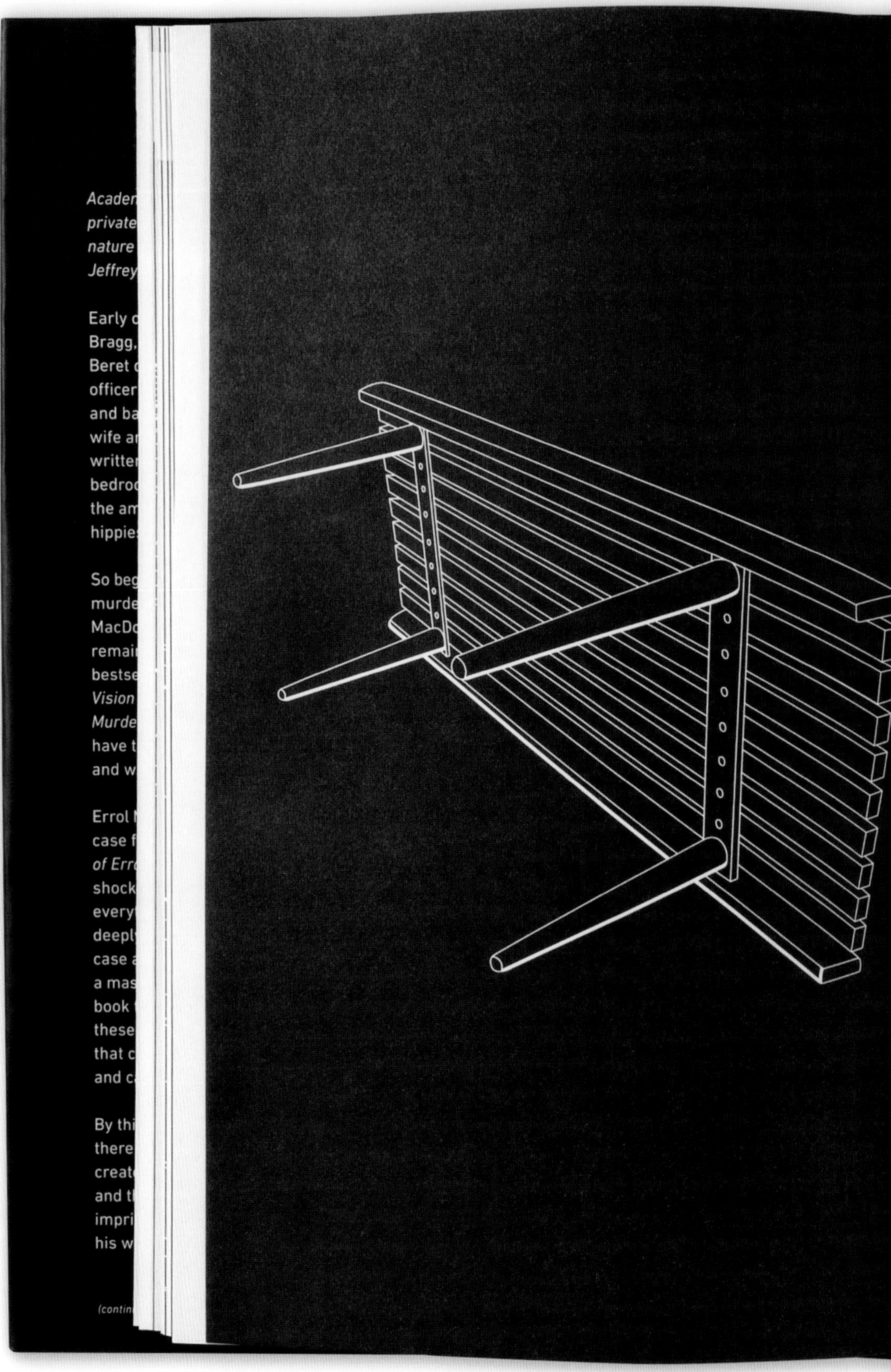

A Wilderness of Error

THE IMPOSSIBLE COFFEE TABLE

You'd better think less about us and what's going to happen to you, and think a bit more about yourself. And stop making all this fuss about your sense of innocence; you don't make such a bad impression, but with all this fuss you're damaging it.
—Franz Kafka, *The Trial*

When Jeffrey MacDonald was brought in for questioning on April 6, 1970, less than two months after the murders, he was read his rights, declined to have an attorney present, and a tape recorder was turned on. The interview was conducted by CID chief investigator Franz Grebner, Agent William Ivory, and Agent Robert Shaw. Grebner first asked for MacDonald's account of the events of February 17.

> And I went to bed about—somewheres around two o'clock. I really don't know; I was reading on the couch, and my little girl Kristy had gone into bed with my wife.
>
> And I went in to go to bed, and the bed was wet. She had wet the bed on my side, so I brought her in her own room. And I don't remember if I changed her or not, gave her a bottle and went out to the couch 'cause my bed was wet. And I went to sleep on the couch.
>
> And then the next thing I know I heard some screaming, at least my wife; but I thought I heard Kimmie, my older daughter, screaming also. And I sat up. The kitchen light was on, and I saw some people at the foot of the bed.

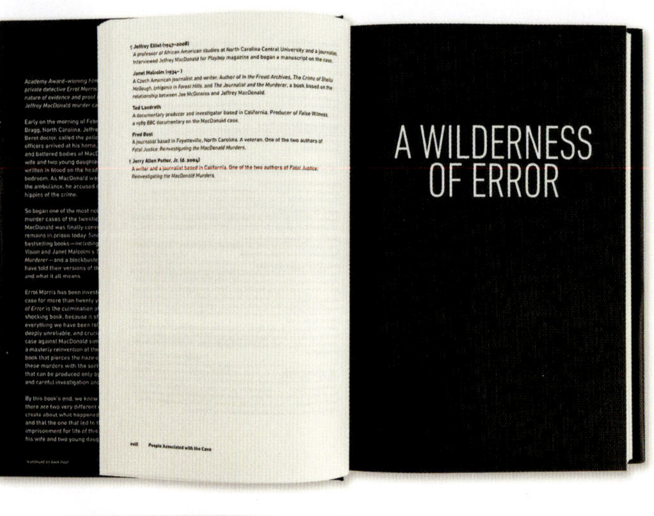

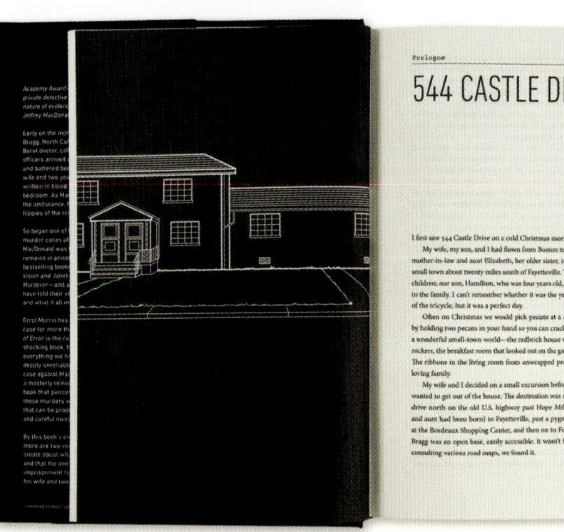

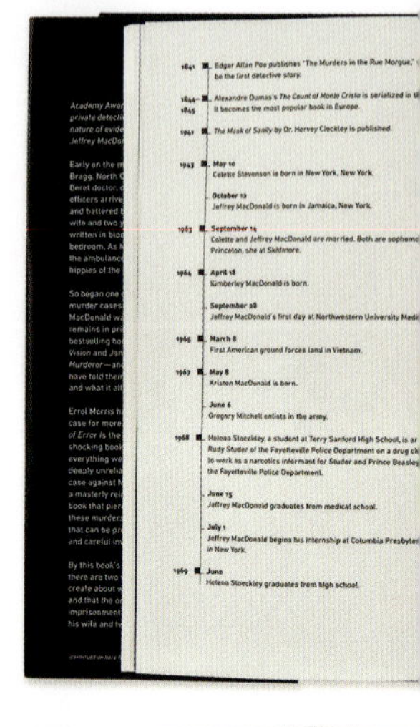

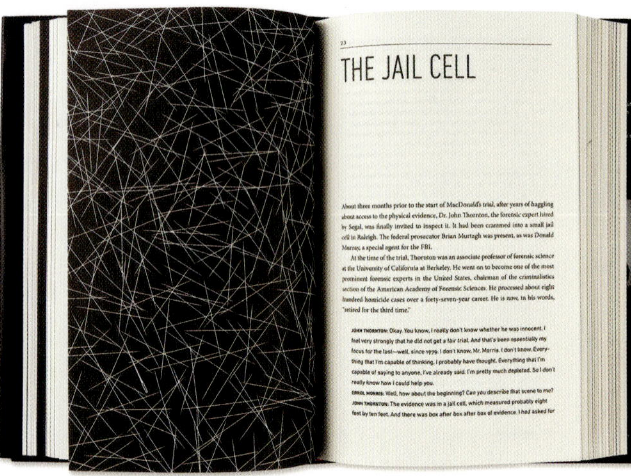

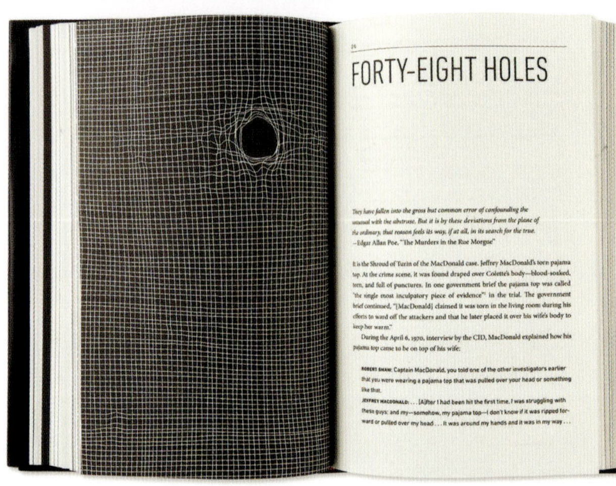

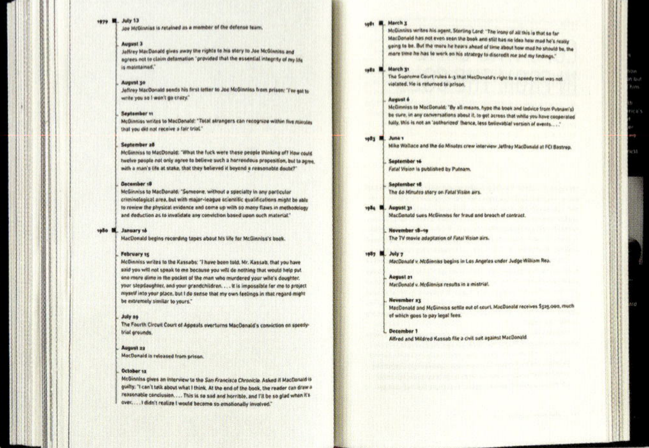

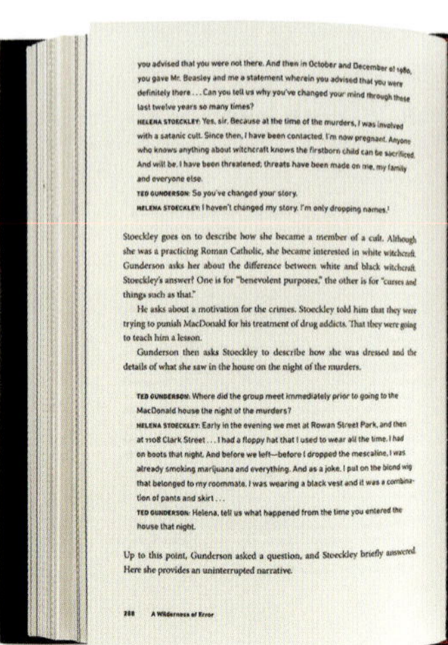

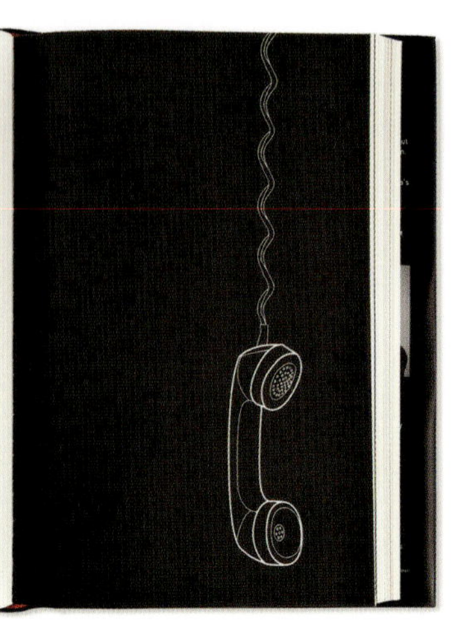

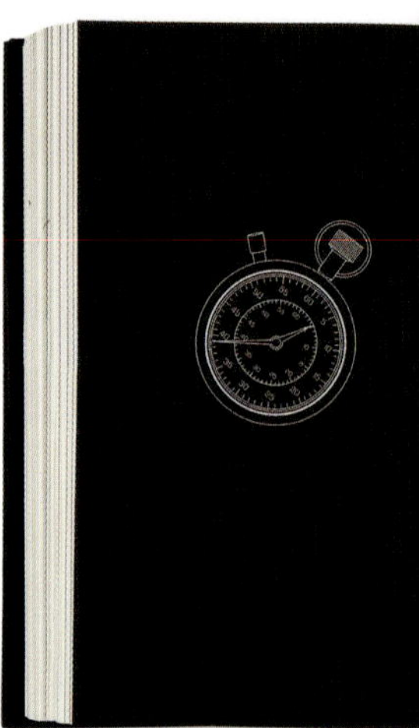

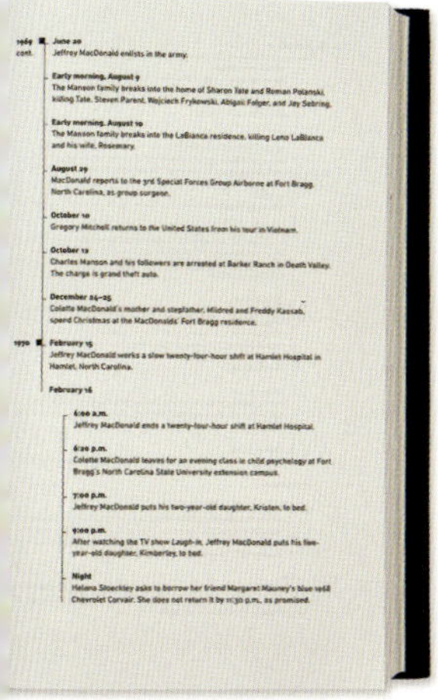

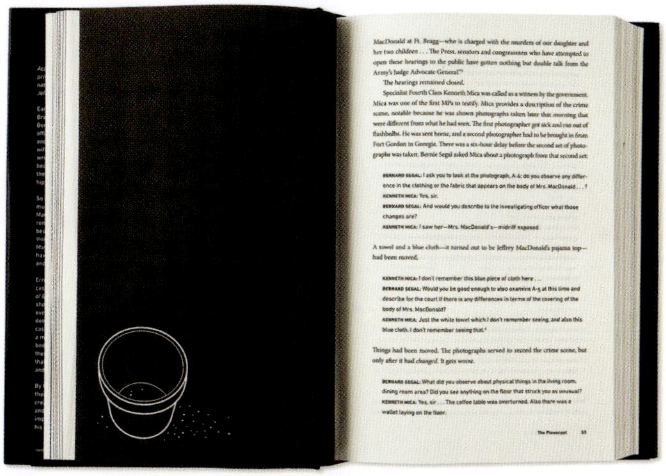

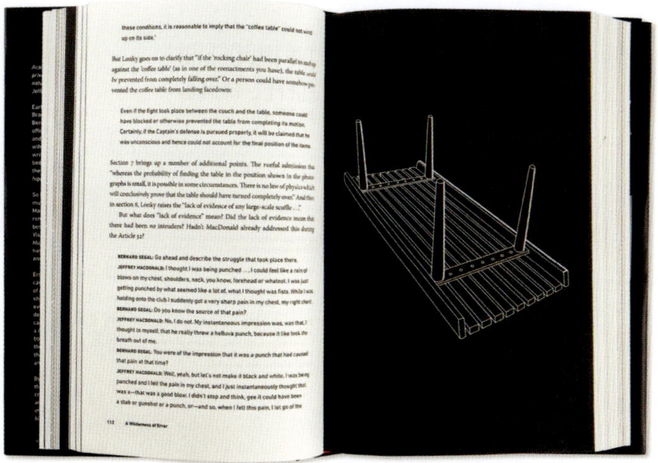

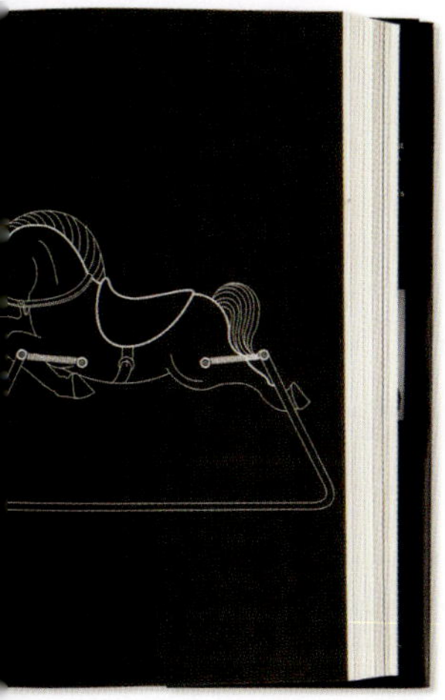

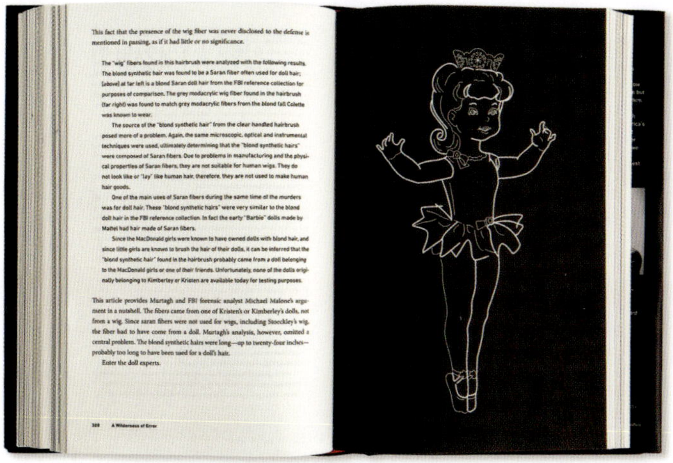

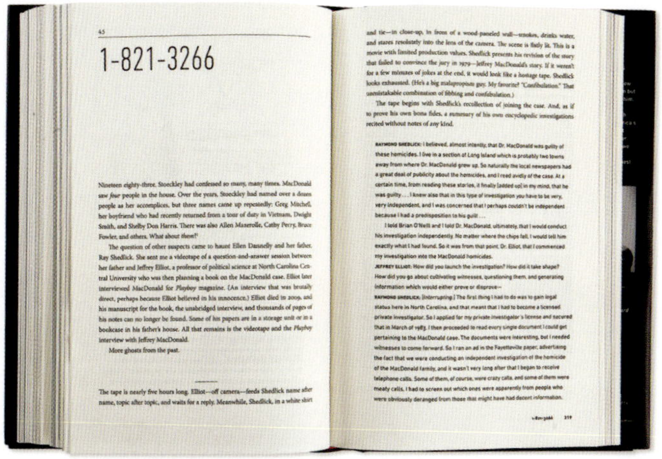

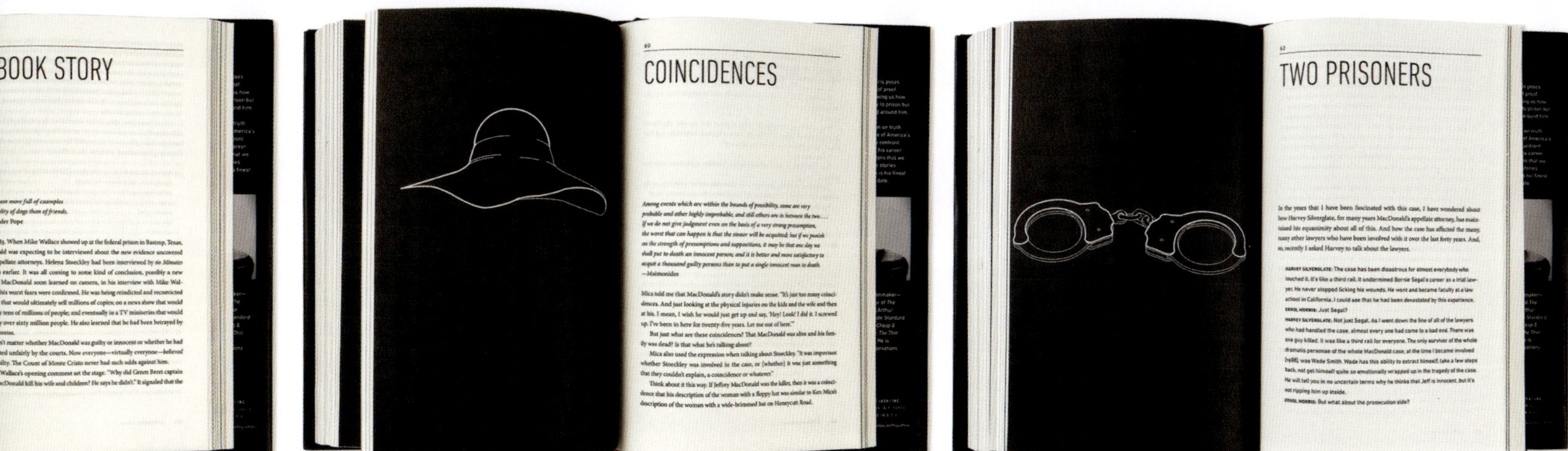
BOOK STORY
COINCIDENCES
TWO PRISONERS

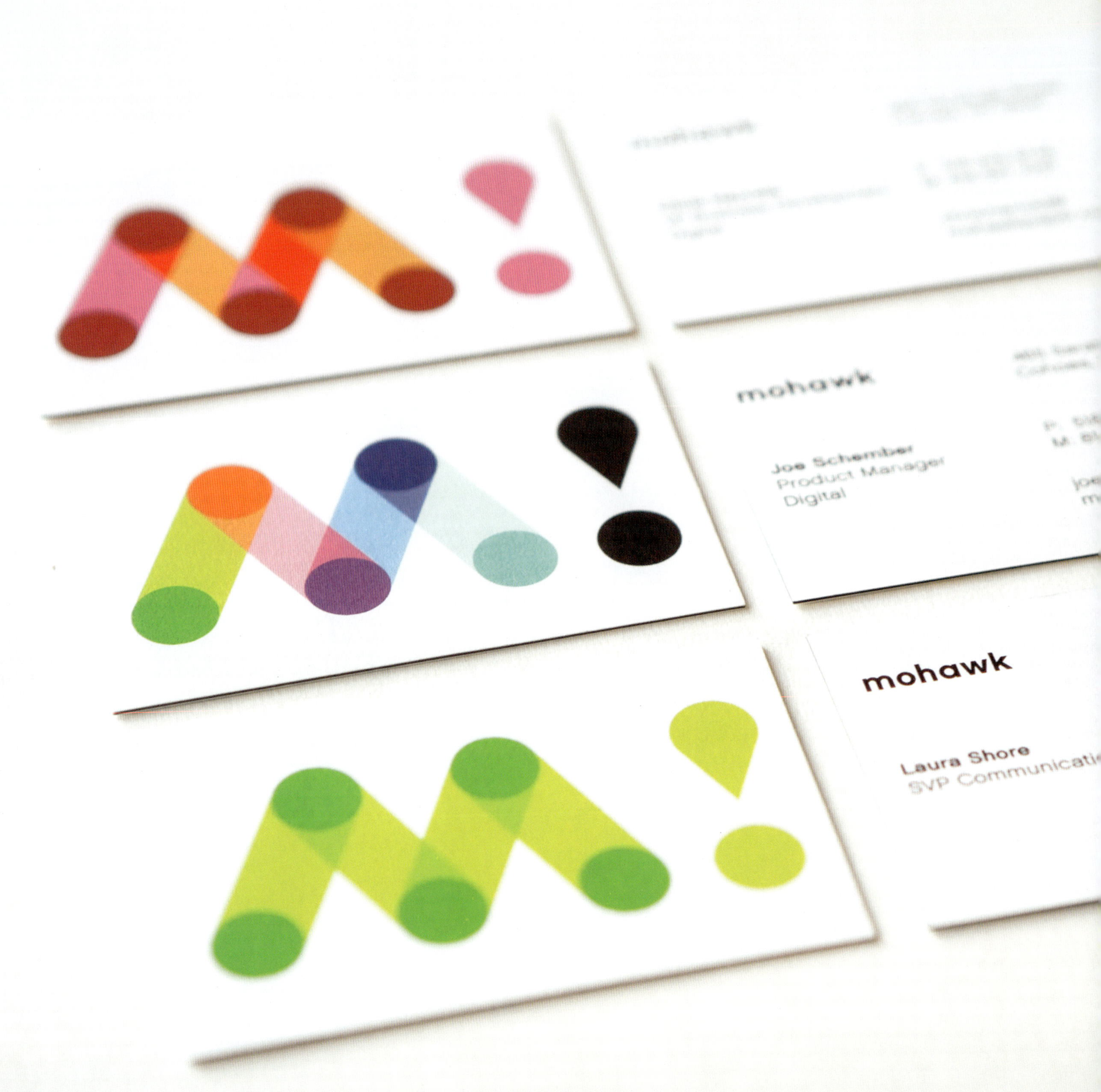

mohawk
Joe Schember
Product Manager
Digital
mohawk
Laura Shore

How to be who you are
Mohawk Fine Papers

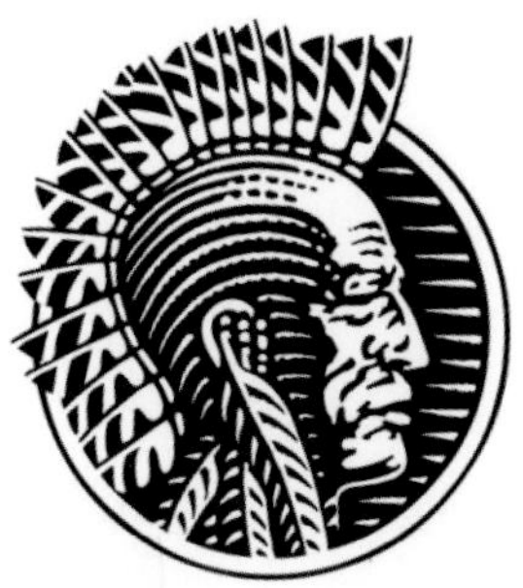

Opposite
The company's new identity introduces a dynamic initial letter that is meant to work at every size and in every medium, changing to suit the occasion while retaining its basic geometry.

Above
Throughout the 20th century, Mohawk was represented by various renditions of a Mohawk Indian tribesman, always dignified but increasingly anachronistic. Starting in the early 1990s, I began working with Mohawk's marketing head Laura Shore to craft an image for the company that matched its reality.

Once, a logo was meant to last forever. Some still do, and should. But at a time when organizations must change rapidly to meet new challenges or risk oblivion, what worked yesterday may not work tomorrow. A company's identity must be authentic and consistent, but never frozen in time.

Founded in 1931 in upstate New York at the confluence of the Mohawk and Hudson Rivers, Mohawk Fine Papers has been owned by the O'Connor family for three generations. In a digital world, papermaking remains a frankly industrial process: anyone who has toured a paper mill and seen a giant vat of swirling pulp transformed into smooth stacks of paper is unlikely to forget it. Among practitioners of this ancient art, few paper companies have been as innovative as Mohawk. From dominating the world of print with textured and colored papers in the 1940s and 1950s, to inventing processes to ensure good offset (and later digital) reproduction in the 1980s and 1990s, to becoming the first paper company in America to offset carbon emissions with wind-farm credits, this little company has met each challenge with imagination and aplomb.

Marketing paper is complicated. For years, companies like Mohawk sold it to distributors, who in turn sold it to printers, who placed orders based on the specifications of designers and art directors. The 21st century added more complexity. Large-scale orders for corporate literature like annual reports evaporated as companies went online. In the meantime, small-batch and do-it-yourself operations opened markets directly to consumers.

In response, we've redesigned the brand identity of Mohawk three times, or once every ten years. The newest identity—centered on a stylized letter M that can take many different forms—positions the company at the center of the digital world, while confirming its commitment to craft and connectivity.

The best graphic identity will fail if it doesn't connect with the authentic core of the organization it represents. Dolly Parton's advice to young singers is also the best branding philosophy I've ever heard: "Find out who you are, and do it on purpose." How lucky to have a client who knows who they are.

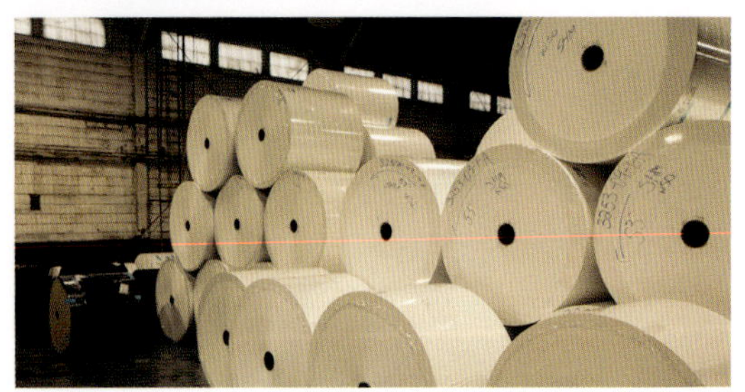

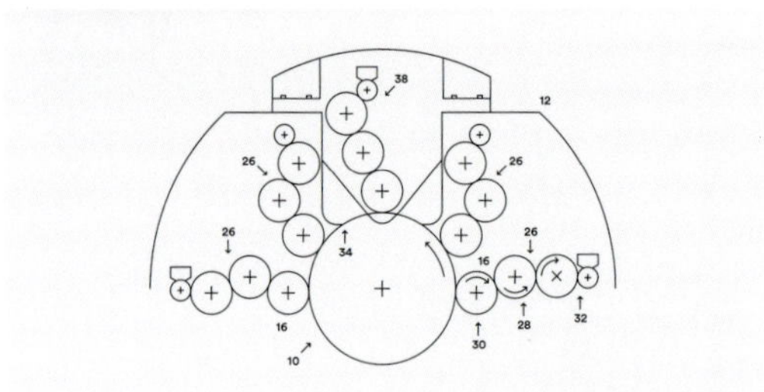

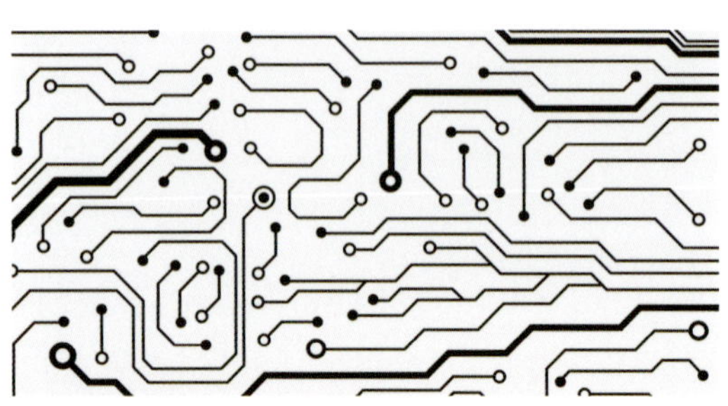

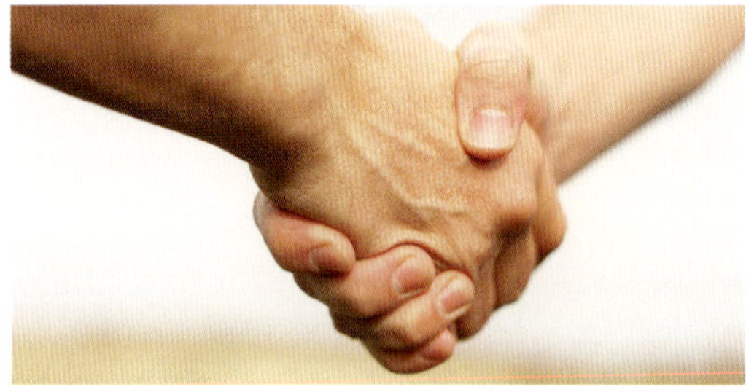

Right
The symbol can be reproduced as a line drawing as well as in a wide variety of monochromatic and multicolor combinations.

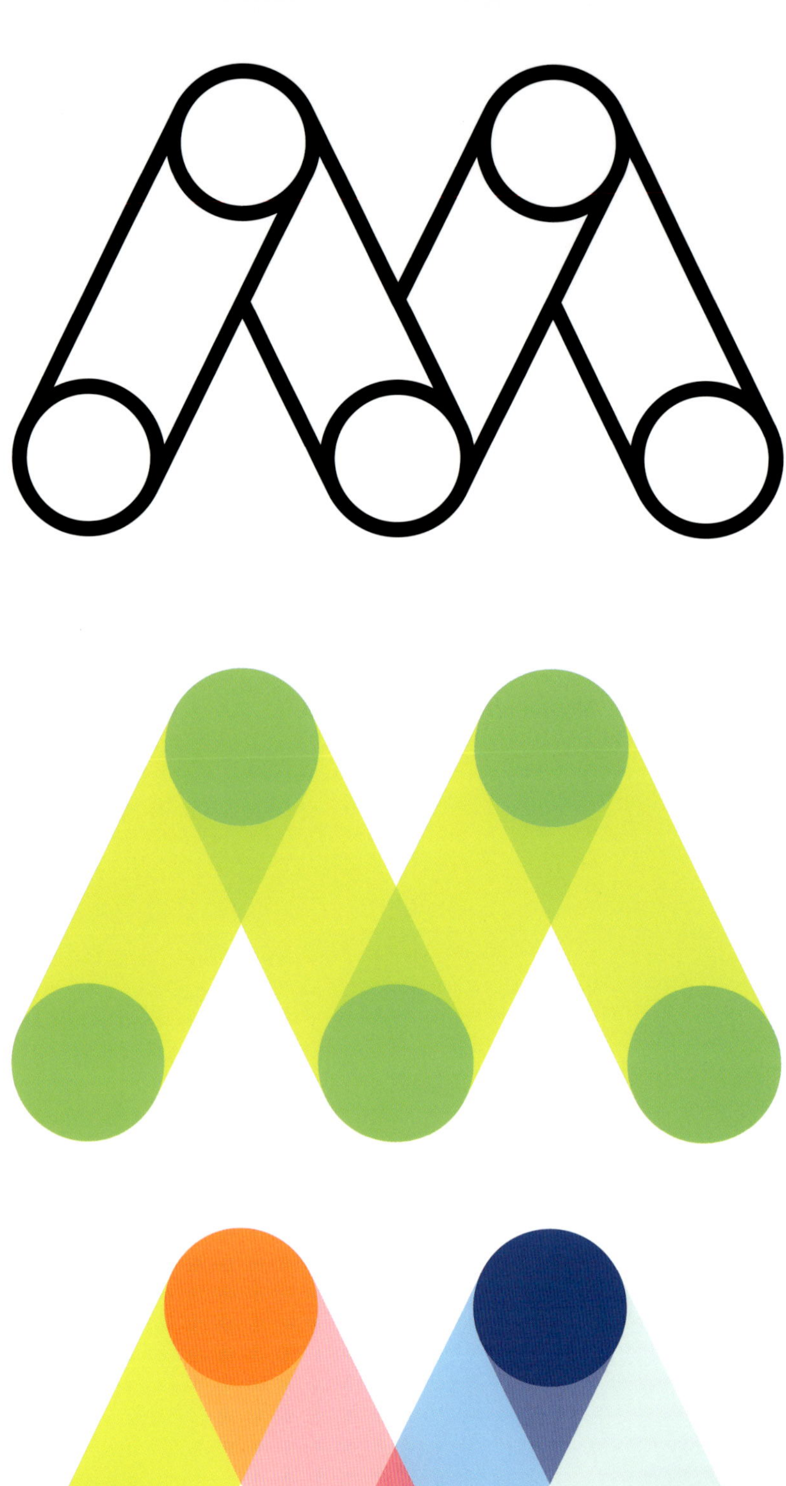

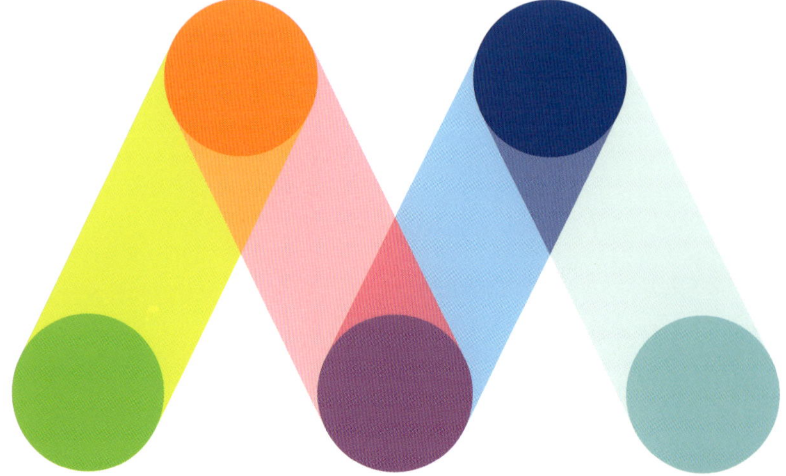

Above
The drawing of the M is meant to simultaneously evoke four things: rolls of uncut paper on the mill floor, the mechanics of offset printing, digital circuitry, and the idea of connection.

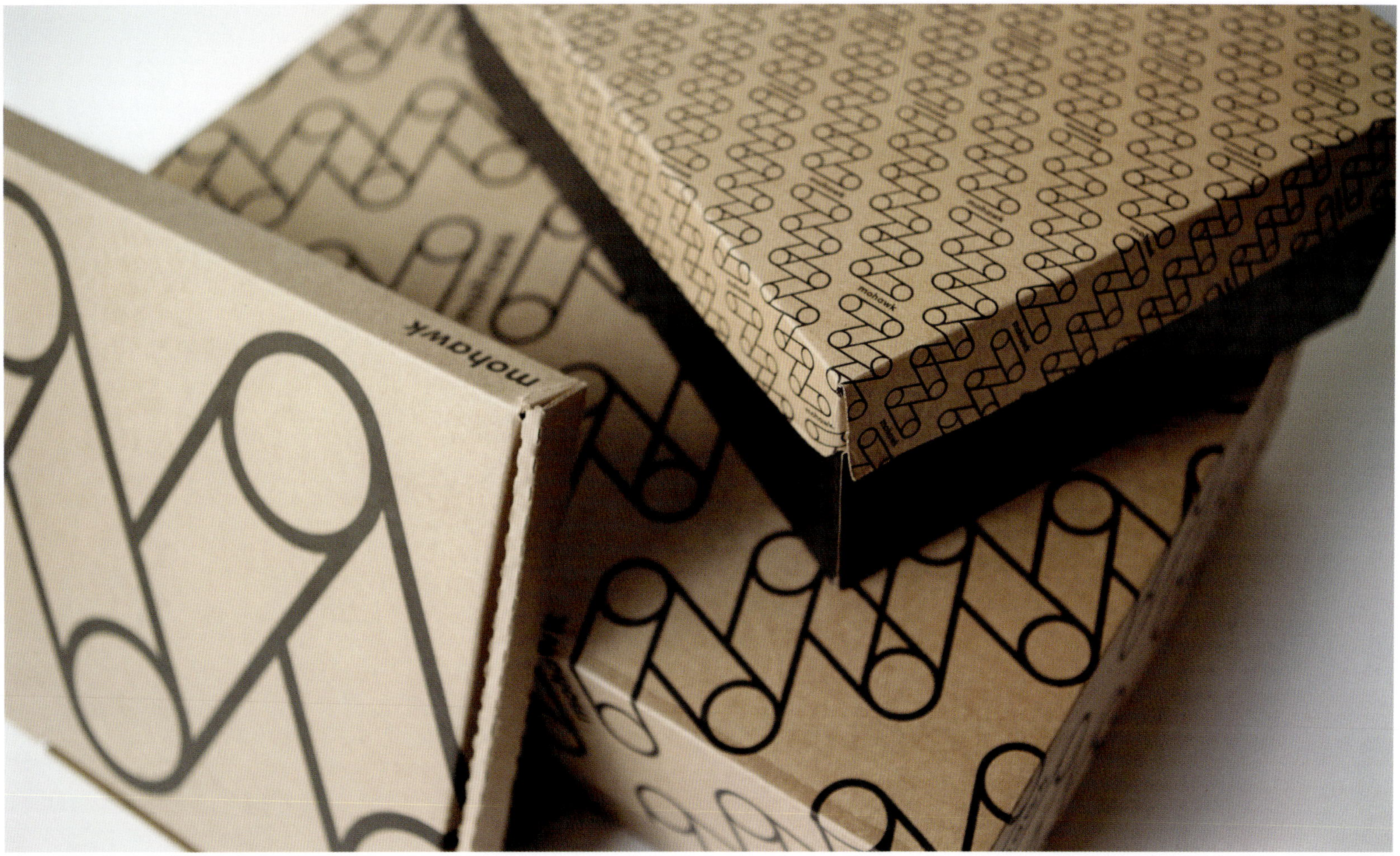

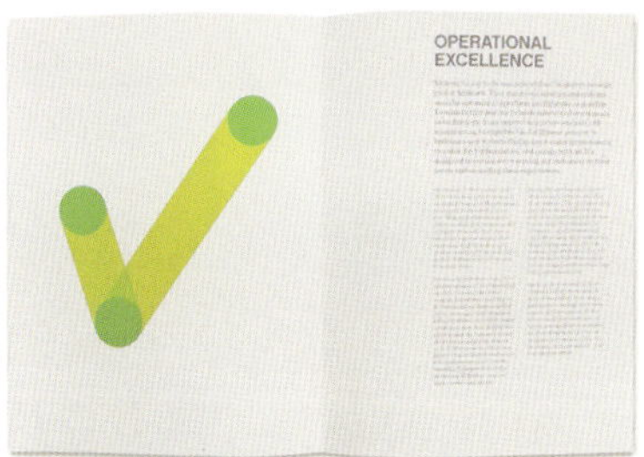

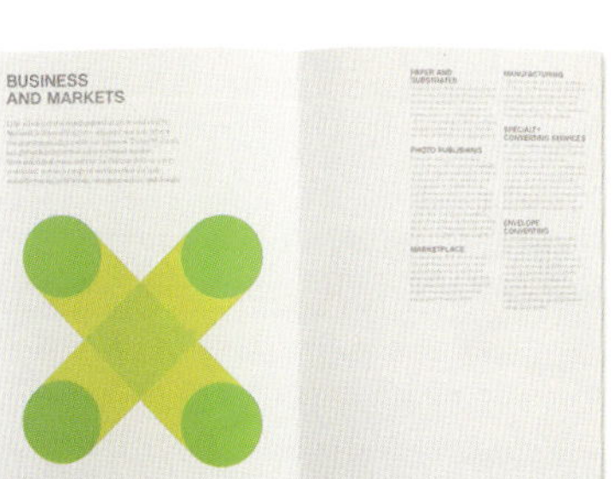

Left
The forms of the M symbol can be rearranged to form a wide variety of symbols, from exclamation marks to arithmetic notation.

Above
A simple black-on-craft-paper pattern identifies Mohawk's rugged shipping boxes.

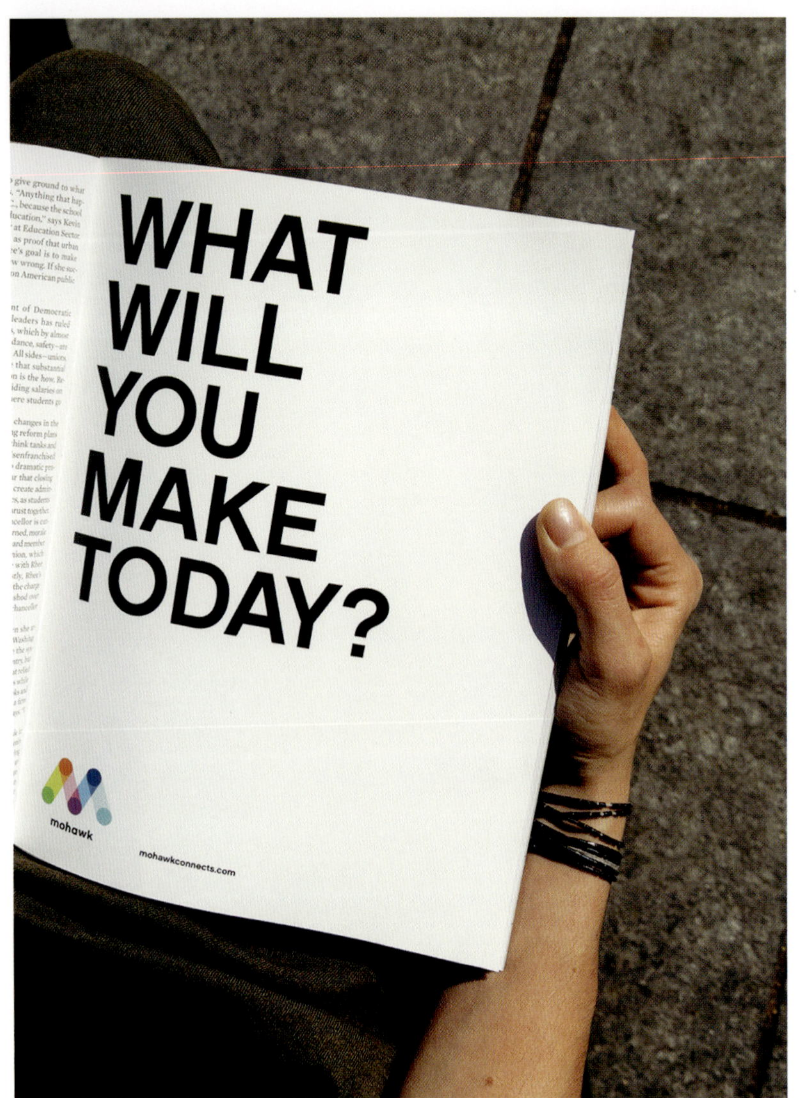

Left
With the launch of the identity, we introduced a new theme, "What will you make today?" This aligned Mohawk's products with the process of communicating ideas and transforming them into reality.

Opposite
Vivid wrapping papers help make Mohawk products stand out in stores and warehouses.

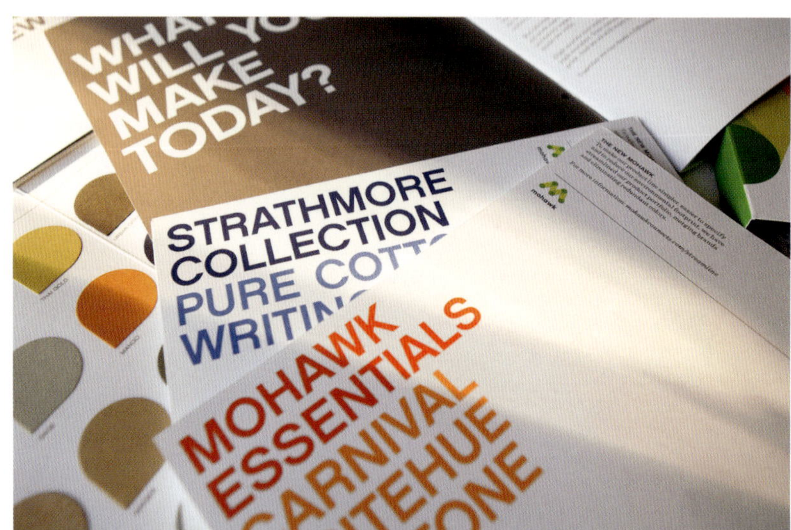

Right top
The company's new sales literature advances the theme and expands the visual identity.

Right bottom
Mohawk's delivery trucks are a common sight in upstate New York.

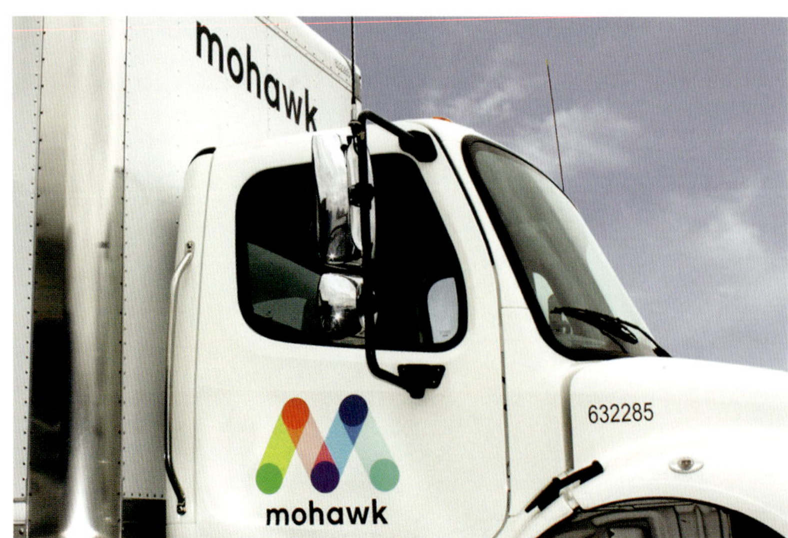

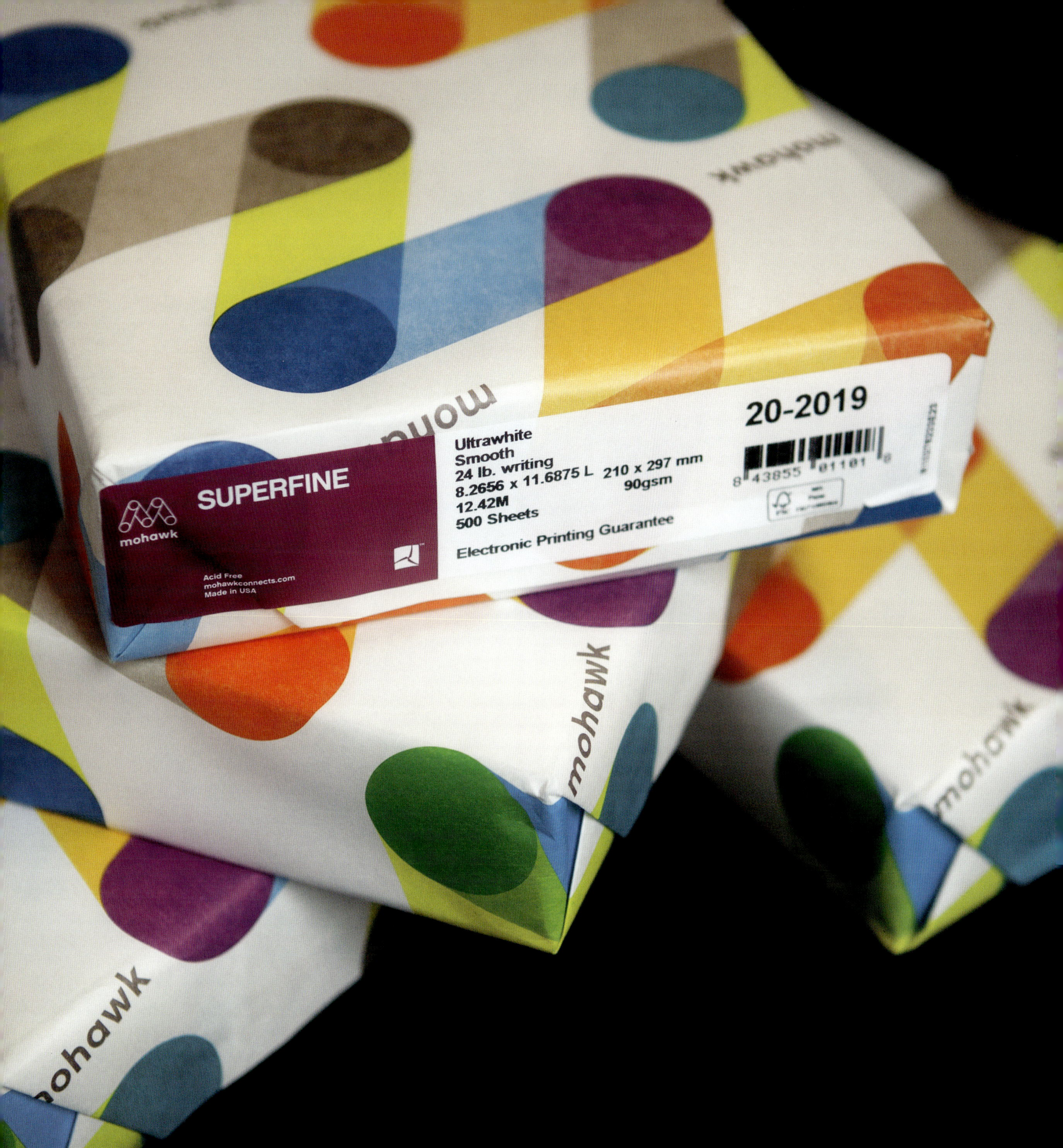

mohawk
SUPERFINE
Acid Free
mohawkconnects.com
Made in USA
Ultrawhite
Smooth
24 lb. writing
8.2656 x 11.6875 L 210 x 297 mm
90gsm
12.42M
500 Sheets
Electronic Printing Guarantee
20-2019

AIA

A[]A

A[WE]A

How to get the passion back

American Institute of Architects

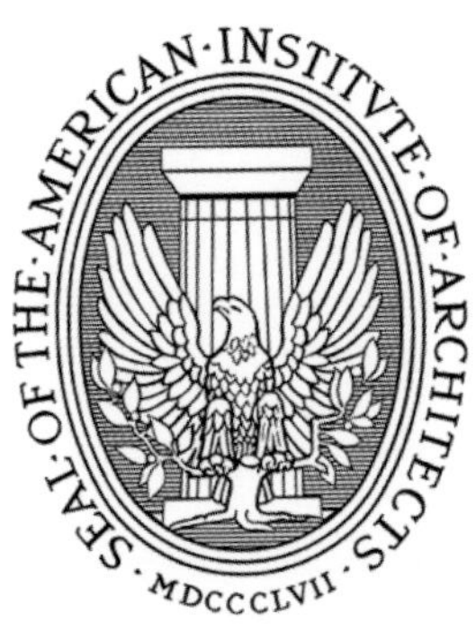

Opposite
Our animated logo for the new AIA emphasizes the collective power that supports each individual member.

Above
The AIA's original logo was meant to convey authority and reinforce the idea of architecture as a protected guild.

Founded in 1857, with more than 80,000 members today, the American Institute of Architects is the oldest and largest design organization in the United States. The 13 original members, bearded white men all, would not recognize the profession as it approaches its 160th birthday. In recent years the AIA has faced unprecedented challenges: the global economic downturn, the revolutionary effect of technology, an ever-more-diverse potential membership base. In response, the organization, led by the deliberate and determined Robert Ivy, undertook a sweeping repositioning process. We were asked to help imagine what this new AIA might look like.

Reinventing an organization this old and this big is a difficult and potentially traumatic process. As is often the case, part of the challenge was figuring out exactly what the challenge was. The AIA hoped to improve the general public's opinion of architects. But that wasn't really the problem: as we learned from an analysis conducted by my colleague Arthur Cohen, people like architects. The problem was that architects didn't like architects. Frequently demoralized by the multiple stresses on their profession, many could only dimly recall the passion that led them into architecture in the first place. They looked to the AIA for education, affirmation, and support. We wanted to restore the passion as well.

Our work, then, had multiple audiences, but at the center sat the architects, who inevitably were the best advocates for their own value. We began to unify the communications issued by AIA and its network of chapters and components, creating a new tone of voice suited to their new initiatives. We invented a proprietary typeface based on the simple Doric column-like character of the capital I that sits at the center of their acronym. And I got personal with a heartfelt 193-word manifesto that addressed what motivates individual designers, and why we're all stronger together. The first time it was presented at an AIA board meeting, a few members confessed they were moved to tears. The passion was back.

Below
An ad conceived by our colleagues at LaPlaca Cohen focuses not on architecture but on the people that architecture serves.

Opposite
A new typeface, AIArchitype, unifies the organization's communications. Drawn by Jeremy Mickel, it is based loosely on a post-and-lintel system, with strong verticals supporting narrower horizontals.

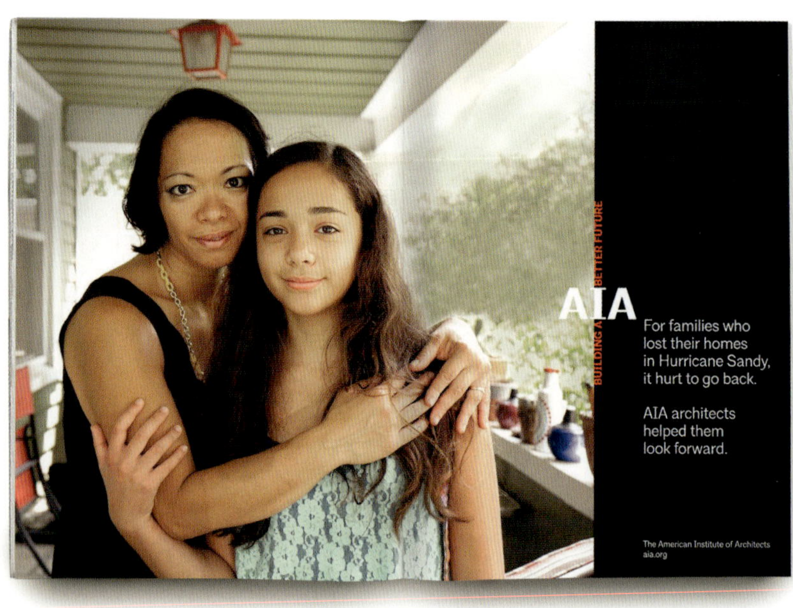

TECTONIC STRENGTH

God is in the Details

BUILDING COMMUNITIES

Cantilevered Support Structure

2419 Design Iterations

One Corbusier Lamp

Mister Wright

PRESERVING LANDMARKS

Computer Aided Design

Right and opposite
The AIA's annual convention in 2014 was held in Chicago, America's greatest architectural city. It was a perfect place to launch the organization's new voice. Pentagram's Hamish Smyth worked with the AIA's in-house marketing team on a coordinated program, all anchored by an energetic wordmark that literally embedded the AIA into the destination. Ads and merchandise paraphrase a famous quote by Chicago's master planner Daniel Burnham: "Make no little plans. They have no magic to stir men's souls."

Next spread
We conducted months of research on what motivated architects and what they wanted from their professional organization, and reduced it to a simple 200-word manifesto.

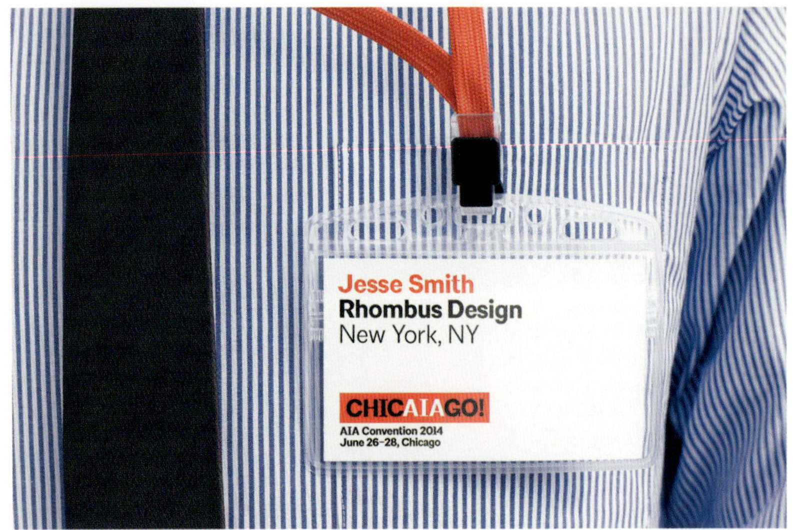

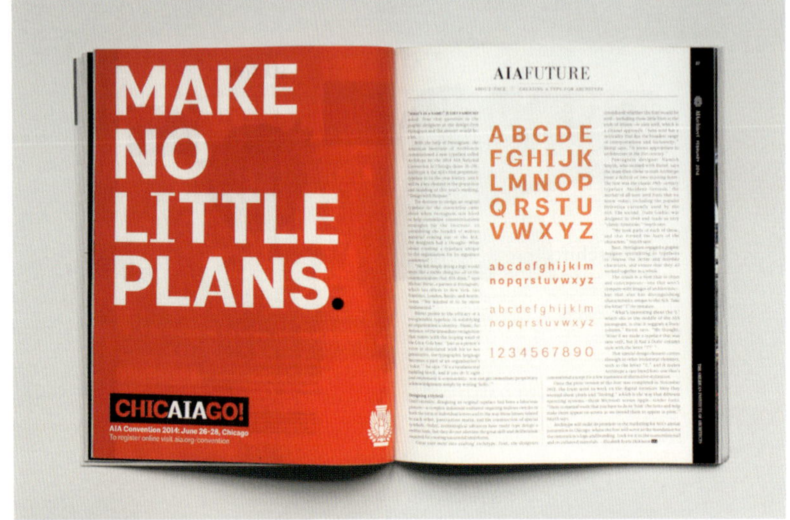

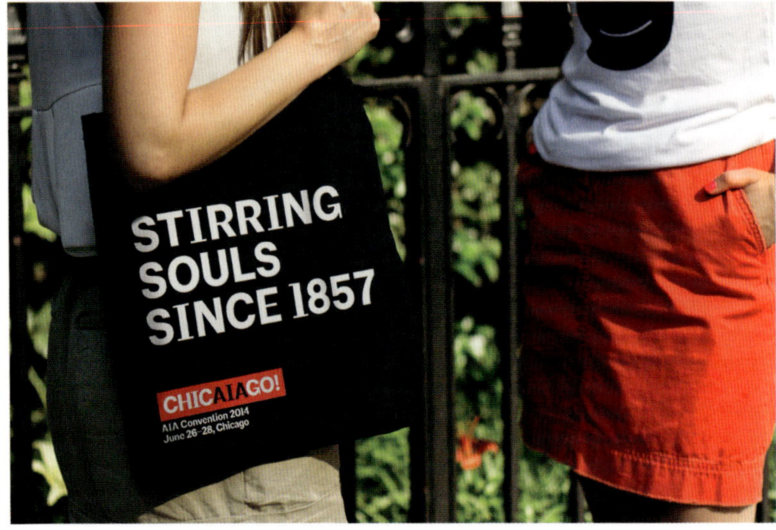

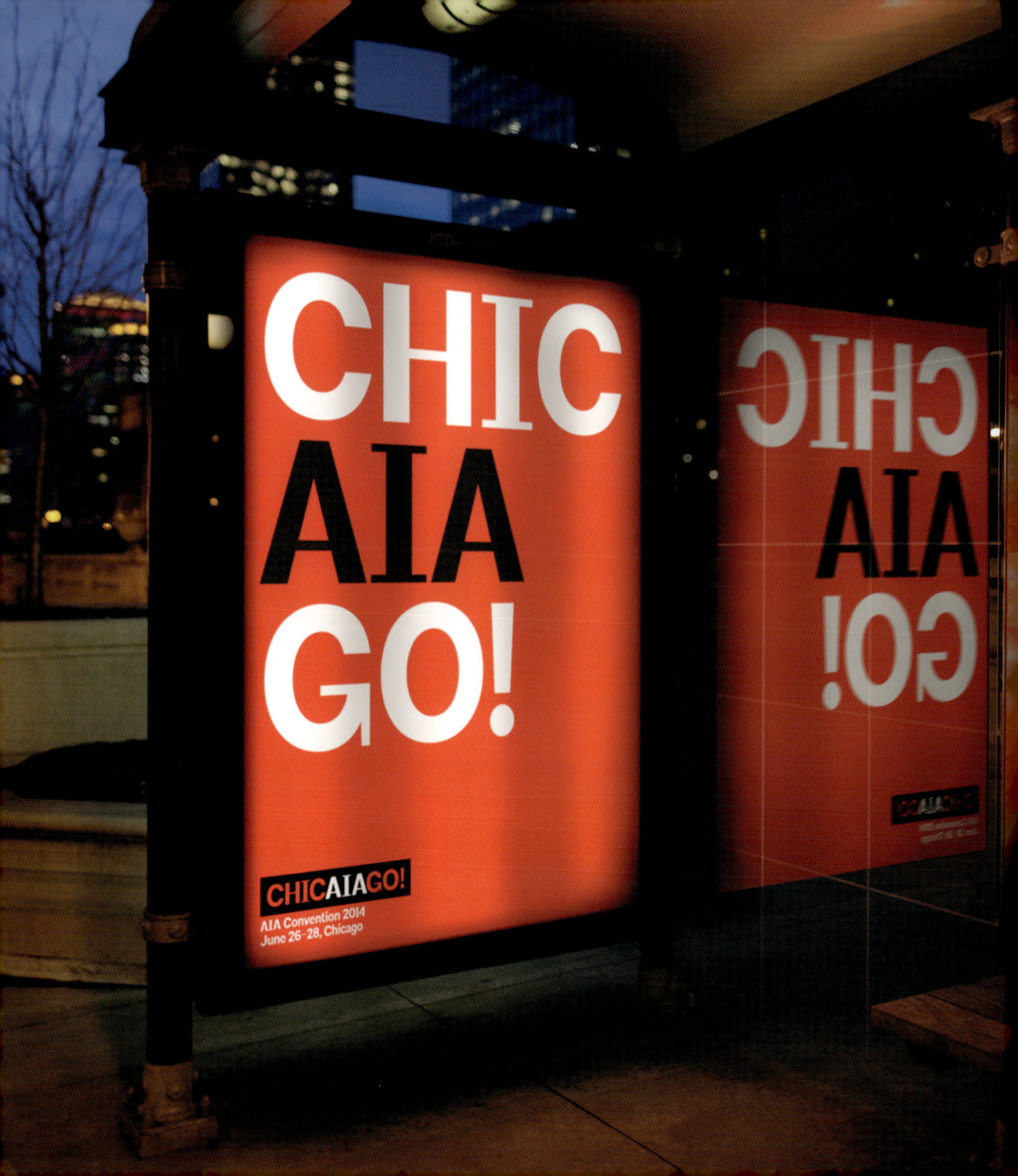

CHIC
AIA
GO!

CHICAIAGO!
AIA Convention 2014
June 26–28, Chicago

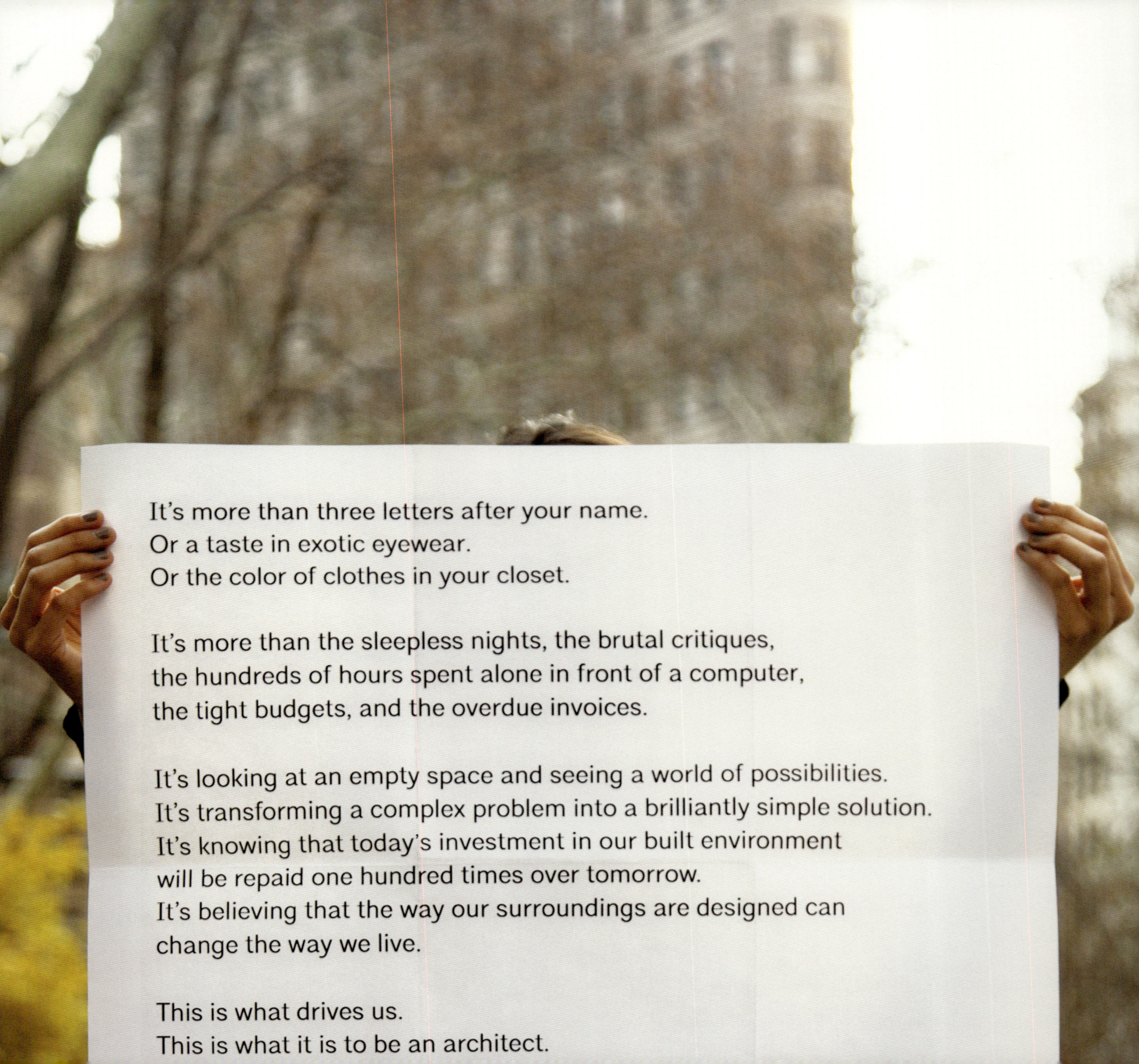
It's more than three letters after your name.
Or a taste in exotic eyewear.
Or the color of clothes in your closet.
It's more than the sleepless nights, the brutal critiques,
the hundreds of hours spent alone in front of a computer,
the tight budgets, and the overdue invoices.
It's looking at an empty space and seeing a world of possibilities.
It's transforming a complex problem into a brilliantly simple solution.
It's knowing that today's investment in our built environment
will be repaid one hundred times over tomorrow.
It's believing that the way our surroundings are designed can
change the way we live.
This is what drives us.
This is what it is to be an architect.

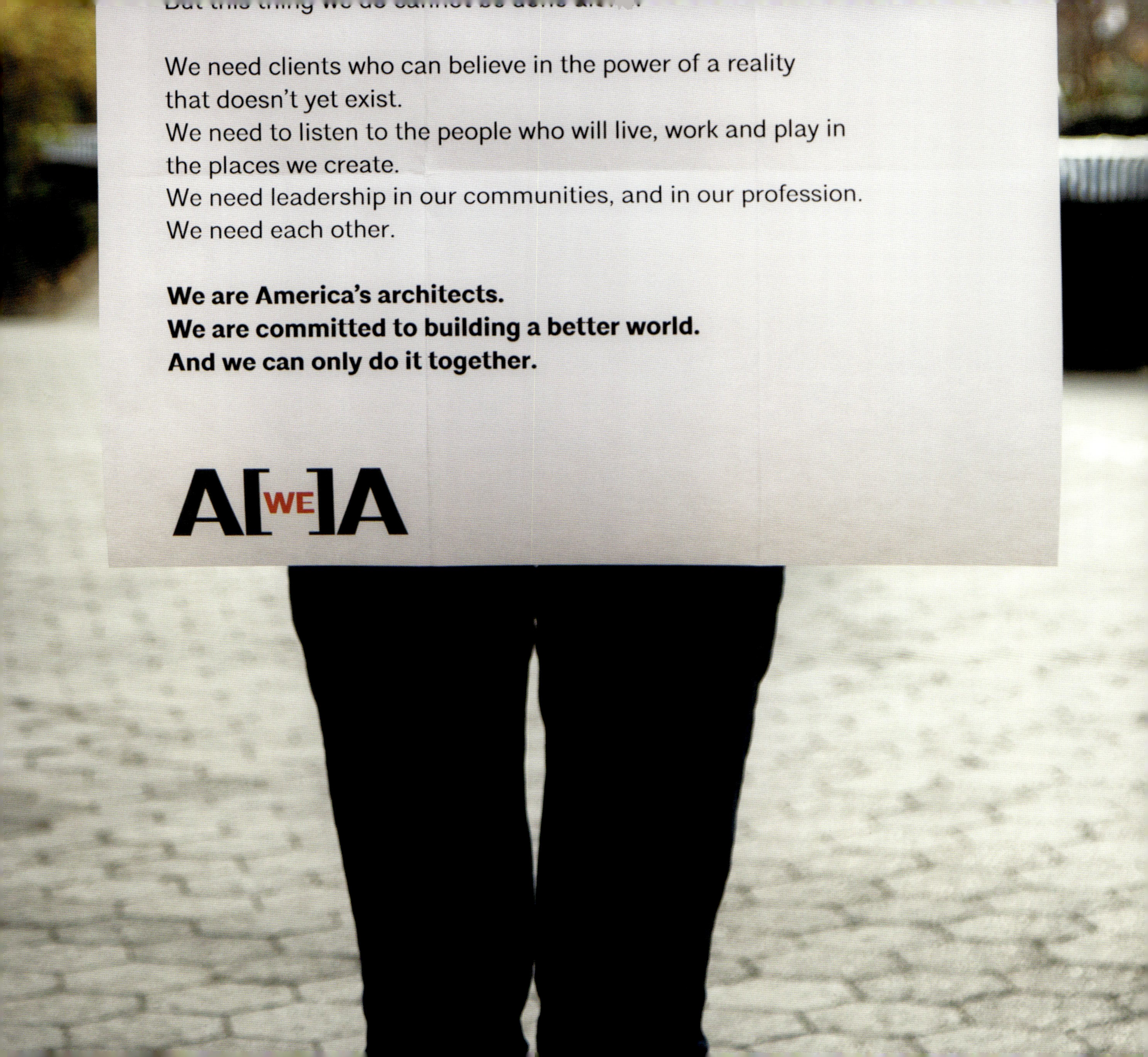

We need clients who can believe in the power of a reality
that doesn't yet exist.
We need to listen to the people who will live, work and play in
the places we create.
We need leadership in our communities, and in our profession.
We need each other.

We are America's architects.
We are committed to building a better world.
And we can only do it together.

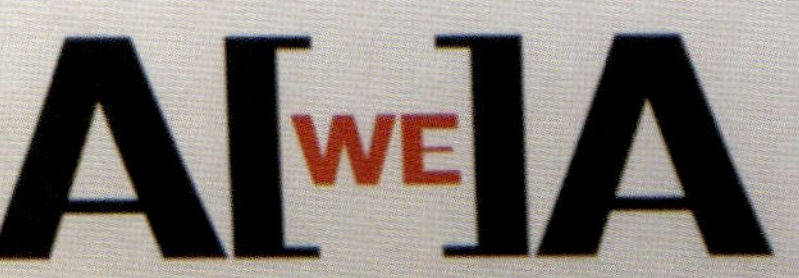

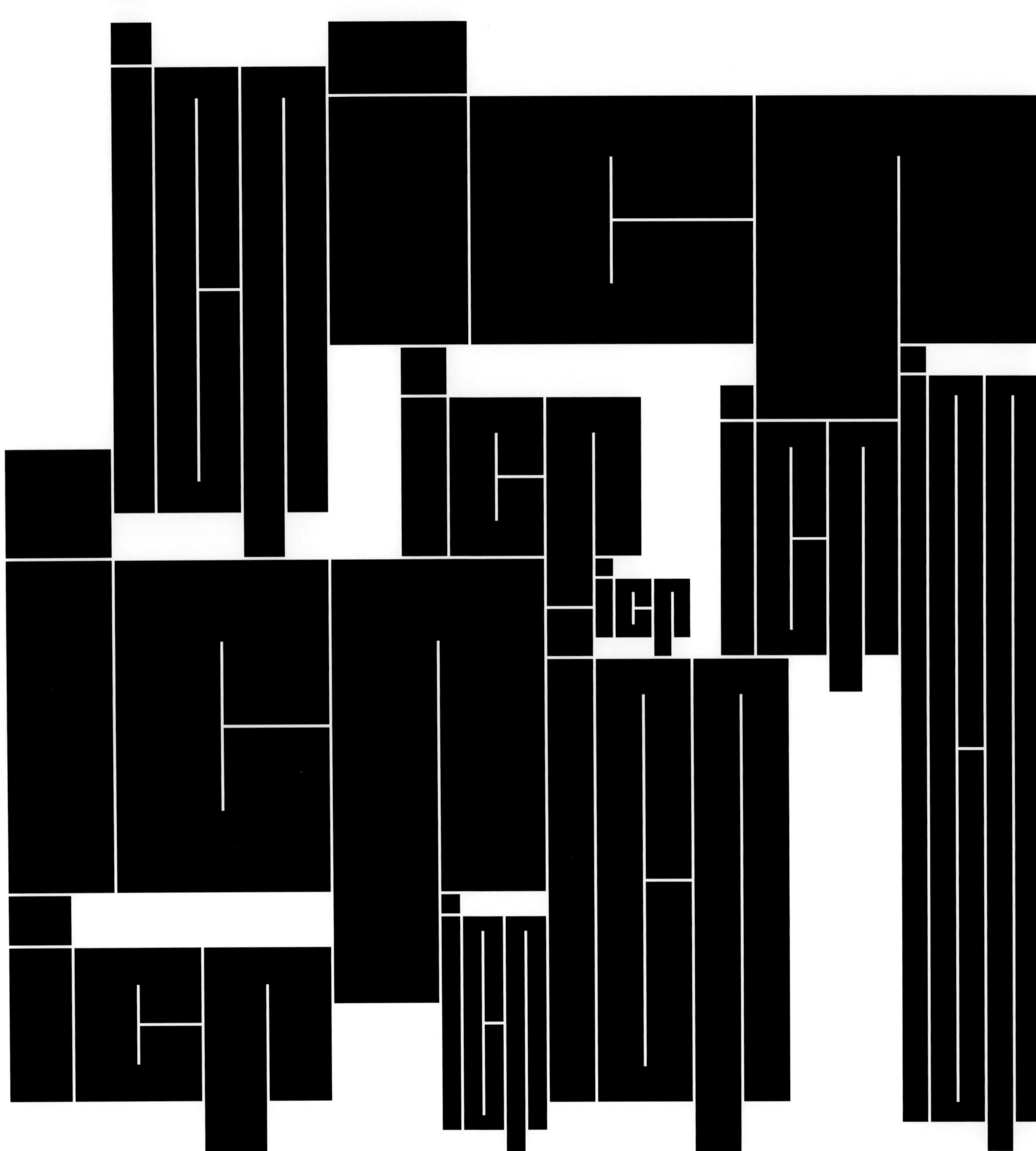

How to frame a picture

International Center of Photography

When I began my career, I liked words more than pictures. I was mesmerized by typefaces and the way they work beneath the surface, triggering subconscious responses through ambiguous means. Photographs, promising truth, faithfully recorded and efficiently communicated, left me with little to do but place them on the page and move on. It took me years to appreciate the profound judgment that photographers exercise in that simple search for truth, and the role that designers can play in making that search dramatic.

Cornell Capa spent his life on that quest. In the mid-20th century, he and a group of other passionate photojournalists defined an ethos described in his 1968 book, *The Concerned Photographer*, as a commitment to “images in which genuine human feeling predominates over commercial cynicism or disinterested formalism.” Like his late brother Robert Capa, the legendary war photographer, he saw photography as a way to not only frame the world but to change it. It was in that spirit that Cornell Capa founded the International Center of Photography in 1974. Combining a museum, school, and archive, ICP champions the idea of photography as both an art form and an agent of social change. Over the next 40-plus years, ICP would have many logos and a confusing variety of locations, but that mission would never change.

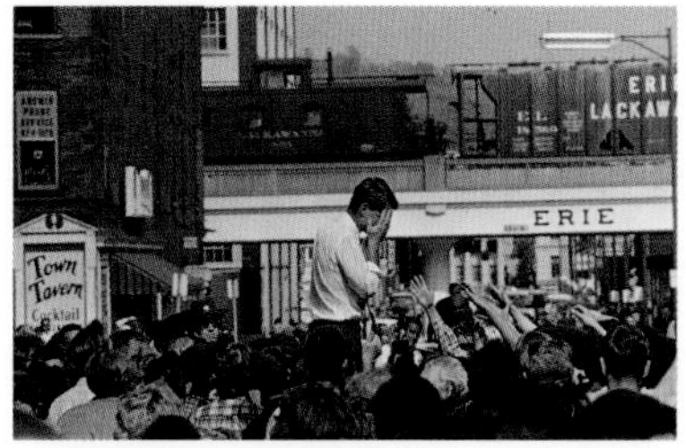

Opposite
The new ICP logo, adapted from a monogram created by Arnold Saks for the announcement of ICP’s opening, can assume an infinite number of formats, reflecting the vastness of today’s image culture.

Above
Cornell Capa’s photographs helped shape our understanding of the 20th-century world. “Images at their passionate and truthful best,” he once said, “are as powerful as words can ever be.” He established the International Center of Photography in 1974.

When, in 2020, ICP finally consolidated its activities at a new home on New York’s Lower East Side, we were asked to mark the occasion with a new graphic identity. The world of photography, in the meantime, had undergone a revolution. No longer the exclusive enclave of artists, image making was now in the hands of anyone with a mobile phone; influential pictures could be created by amateurs as well as professionals. But this democratization of the medium confirmed Cornell Capa’s thesis: anyone who creates a record of the world has a chance to transform it.

For ICP’s new identity, we adapted the geometric monogram that Capa commissioned in 1974. No longer just a square, it can now be reframed into any proportion, acknowledging the choice of focus that any photographer makes when creating an image, and the seemingly infinite number of such choices that together define today’s dazzling image culture.

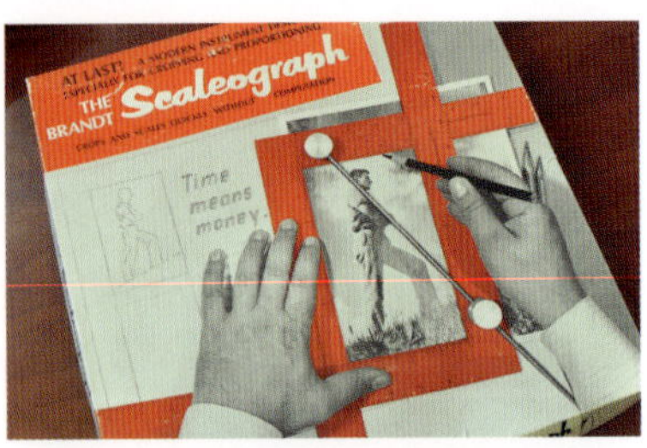

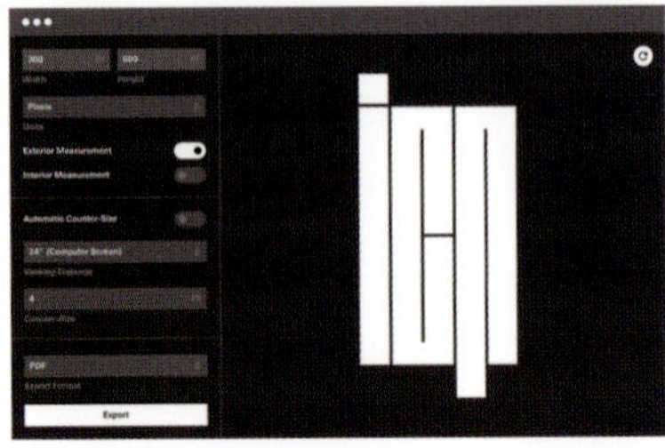

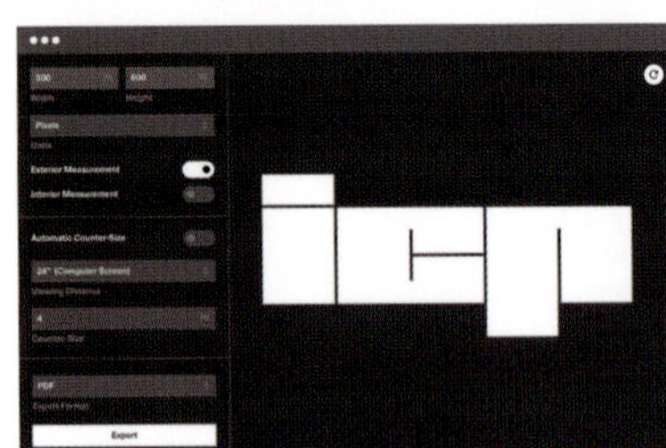

Left
The fundamental choice for both the photographer and the layout artist is the crop. What is included and what is excluded? The mechanical premise of yesterday's analog tools lives on in the digital interface of today's photo apps. We created a program that pushed cropping to its limit: the logo can assume any width and any height without internal distortion.

Right
The monogram, created with designer Jonny Sikov, takes many forms in ICP's environmental graphics, by Delta Murphy and Susan May, as well as ICP's print materials.

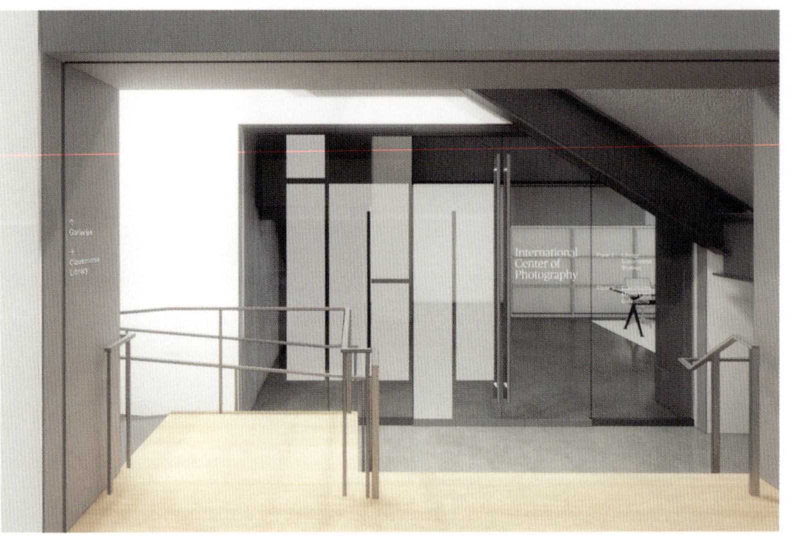

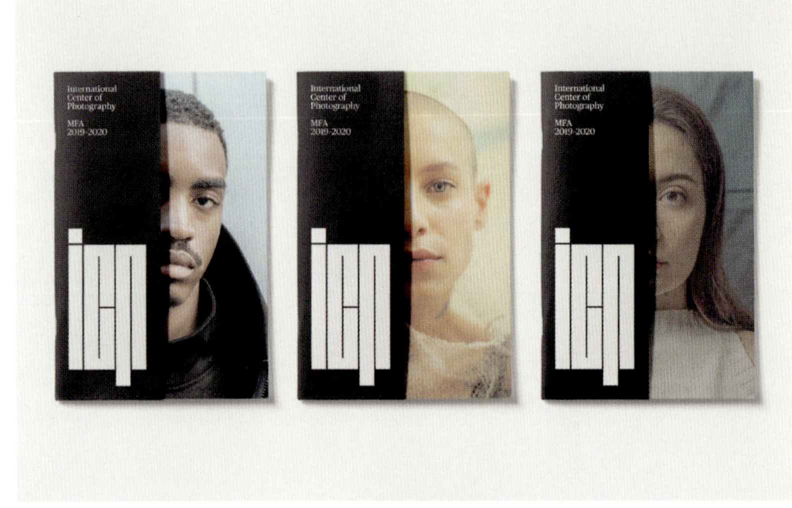

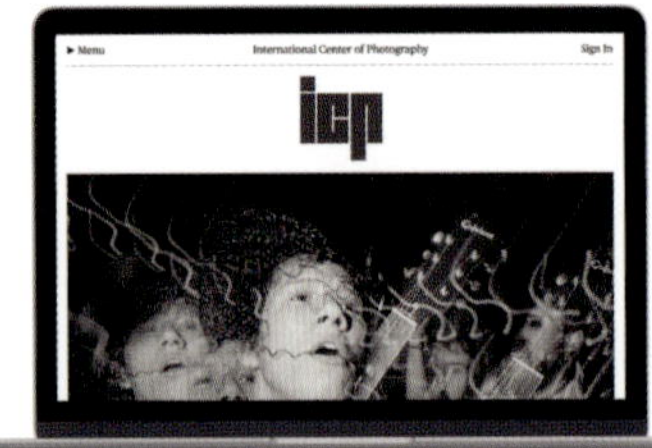

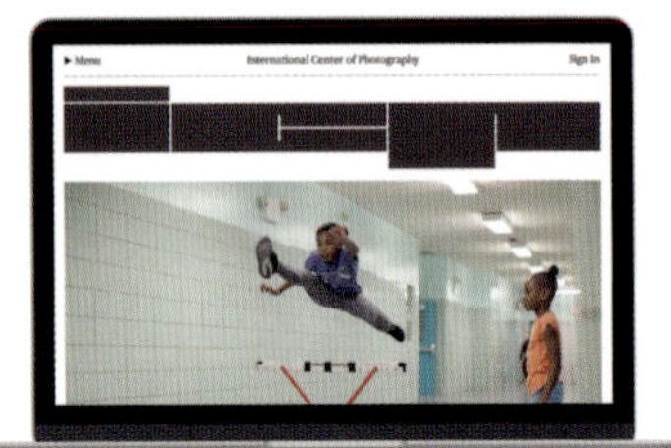

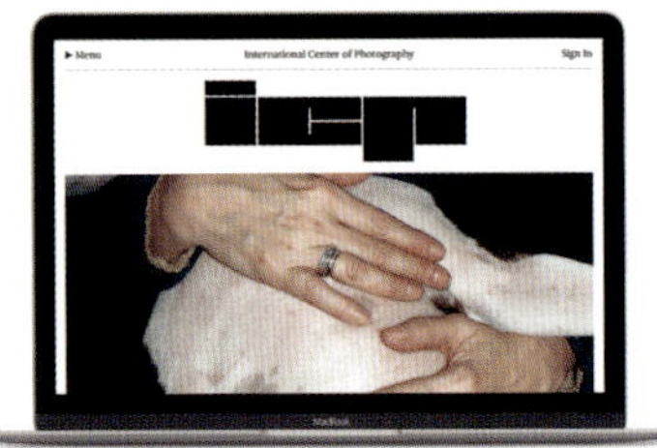

Left
A scalable logo adapts easily to the changing formats of various digital platforms.

Above and right
Serif typography from the world of newspapers and magazines reconfirms the relationship of photography and journalism.

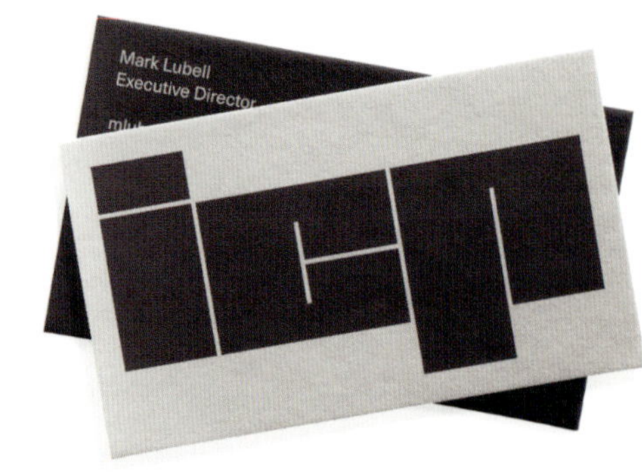

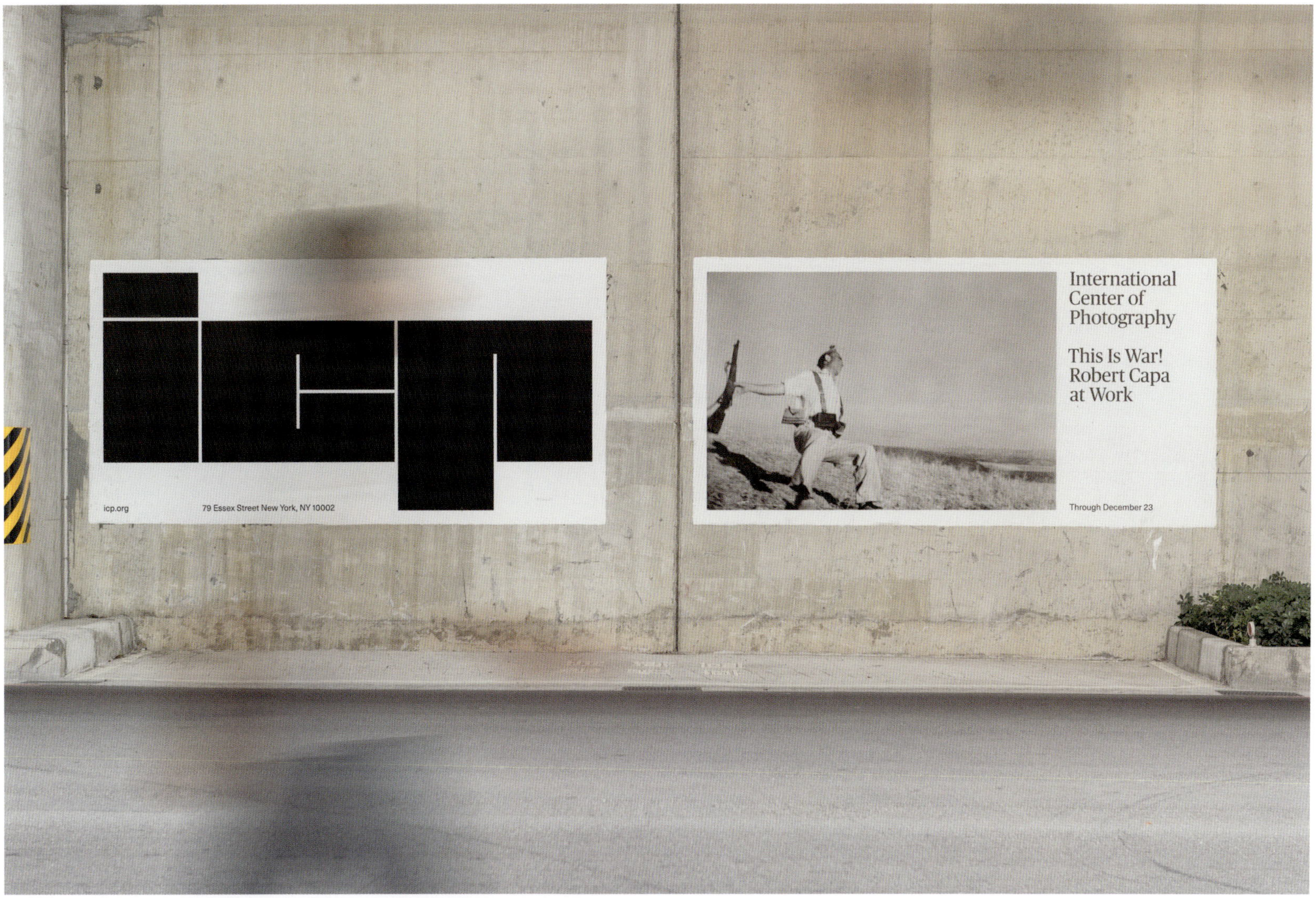

Left
Its new headquarters on Essex Street on Manhattan's Lower East Side reunites ICP's gallery and school, making it a true center for photography in one of New York's busiest and most vibrant neighborhoods.

Above
ICP's museum exhibitions explore the history and future of image making.

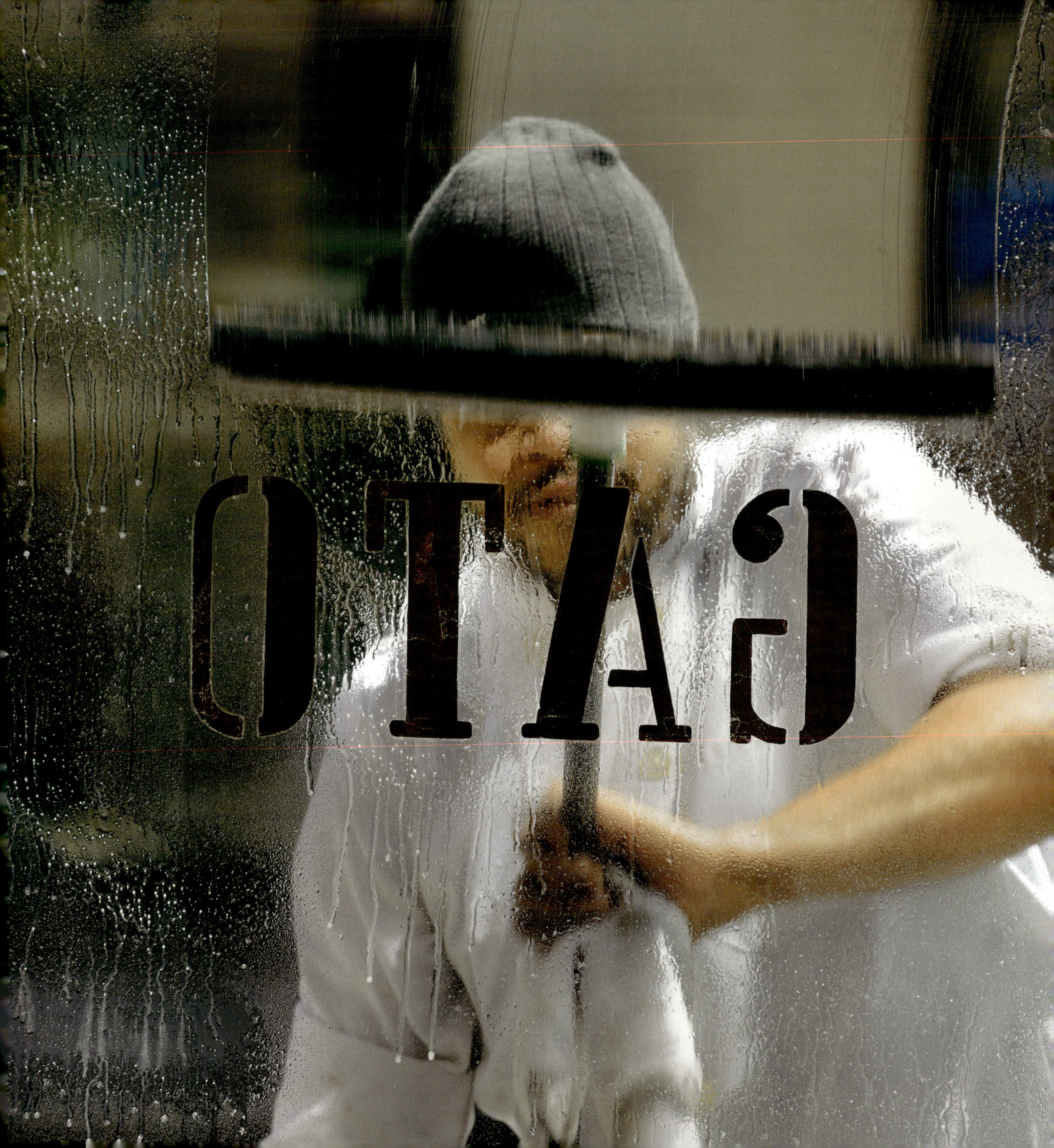

How to set a table

The restaurants of Bobby Flay

Opposite
My partners and I have worked with chef Bobby Flay on almost all of his restaurants. His latest is Gato, in downtown Manhattan.

A few years back, "experience design" was all the rage. Designers, advertisers, and marketers suddenly seemed to realize that consumers didn't form their impressions of brands based solely on logos and advertisements. Instead, their opinion of a product or company emerges from a broad range of "touchpoints" based on a "360-degree view" of human experience. Or, as normal people might call it, real life. This was evidently a surprise to self-obsessed communications professionals. But it wouldn't have been a surprise to anyone who's ever run a restaurant.

Great restaurateurs understand that a restaurant experience must engage all five senses; that the way you're greeted at the door is just as important (maybe more) as the way the food tastes; and that the dining experience is fundamentally theatrical, with guests who are both audience and performer.

Bobby Flay is one of the best-known chefs in the world. A culinary wunderkind born and bred in New York, he mastered the art of southwestern cuisine at Mesa Grill, and reinvented the midtown dining experience at Bar Americain. He and his partner Laurence Kretchmer know exactly what it takes to run a deliriously successful restaurant.

We discovered the key is communicating with absolute precision to the target audience. What should they expect and how can you exceed those expectations? Bobby's Burger Palace is a "fast casual" experience: great burgers, fries, and shakes delivered to your seat with efficient finesse. Everything about the design of the space supports this idea: the counters that snake around the room, the horizontal lines that reinforce the idea of speed. Our logo borrows those forms to make a hamburger out of the name itself: bun, burger, and lettuce in perfect equipoise.

Bobby's upscale restaurant, Gato, in Manhattan's Noho district, is the opposite: inventive, customized dishes, each created to order, with every detail implying the attention of the passionate chef behind the scenes. The graphics are tailored and understated. Two restaurants, two graphic languages, two experiences: working on Gato and Bobby's Burger Palace reminded us that what ends up on the plate is only the beginning.

Bobby's Burger Palace is Flay's tribute to the hamburger joints of his youth. Painstakingly researched on trips back and forth across the United States, the menu features everything from the Philadelphia Burger (provolone cheese, griddled onions, hot peppers) to the Dallas Burger (spice-crusted patty, coleslaw, Monterey Jack cheese, BBQ sauce, pickles) to the LA Burger (avocado relish, watercress, cheddar cheese, tomato). Starting with a single location in suburban New Jersey in 2008, there are now 18 BBPs around the United States.

Right and opposite
Everything about the graphic program for BBP is bright and lively. We based our graphic motifs and color scheme on Rockwell Group's energetic interior design, which can be reconfigured for spaces of all sizes and shapes. Bobby offers to "crunchify" each burger (by adding a layer of potato chips); designer Joe Marianek and I tried to keep the graphic program just as brazen.

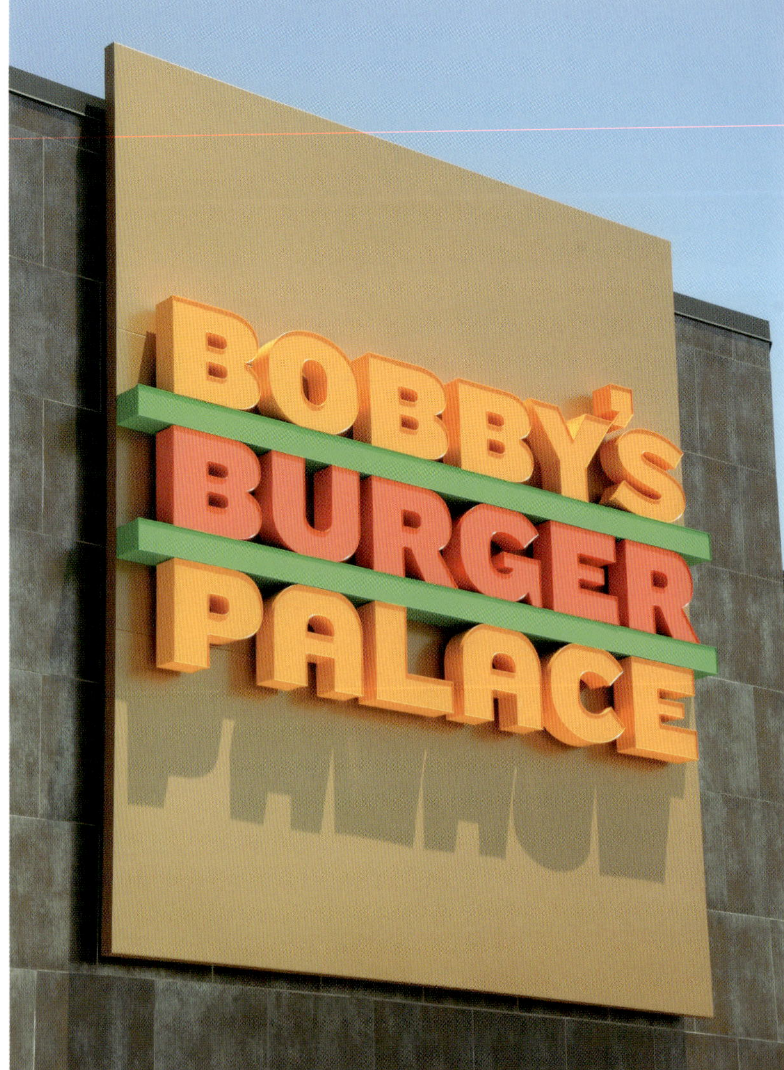

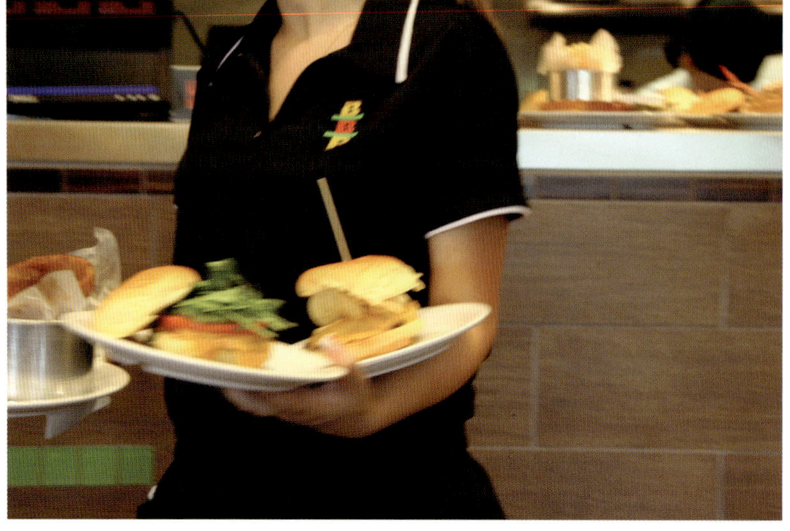

BOBBY'S
BURGER
PALACE

Above
The typography for the Bobby's Burger Palace logo is stacked like the joint's signature product. It can also reduce to a vertical initials-only acronymic "slider."

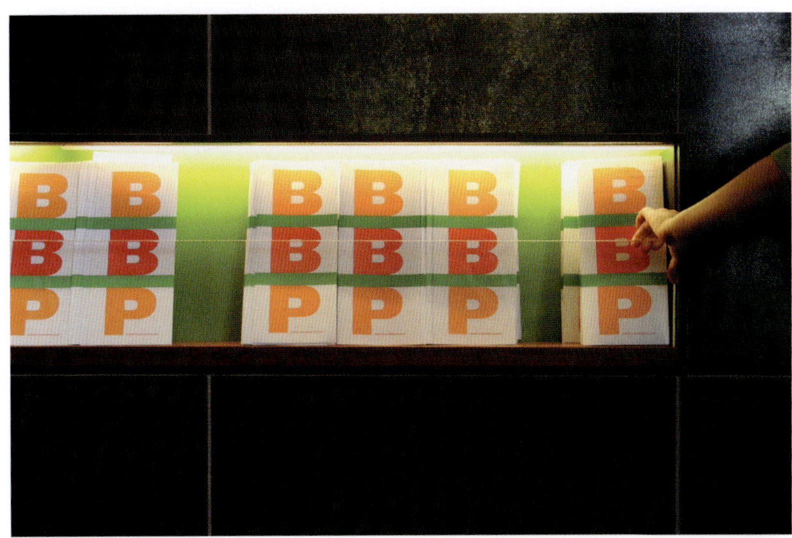

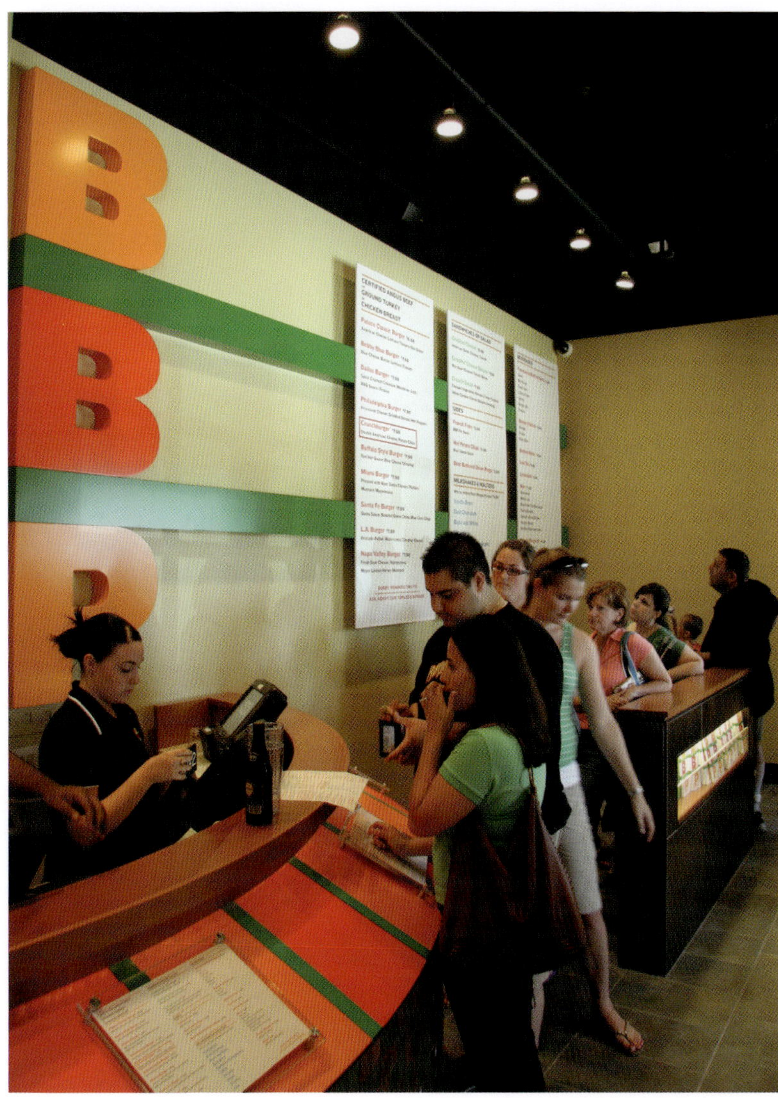

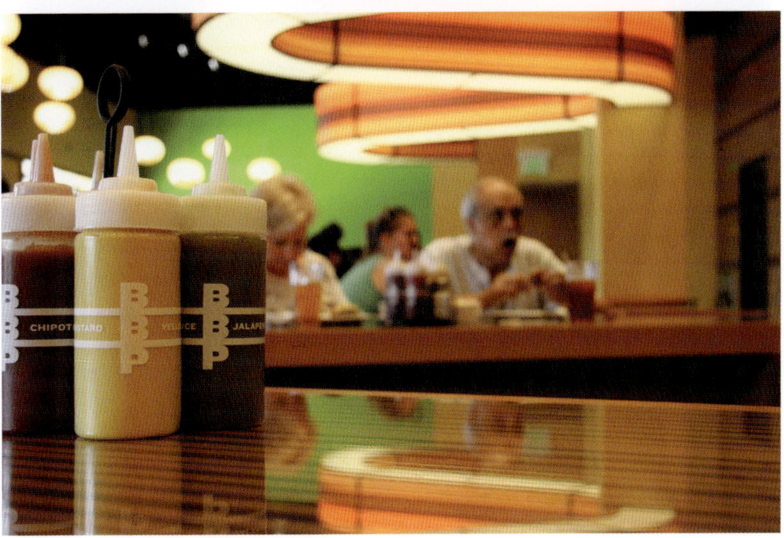

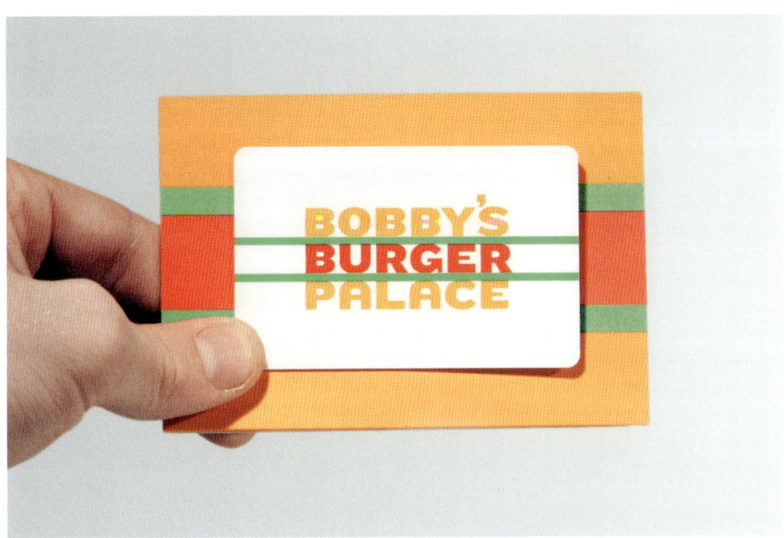
BOBBY'S
BURGER
PALACE

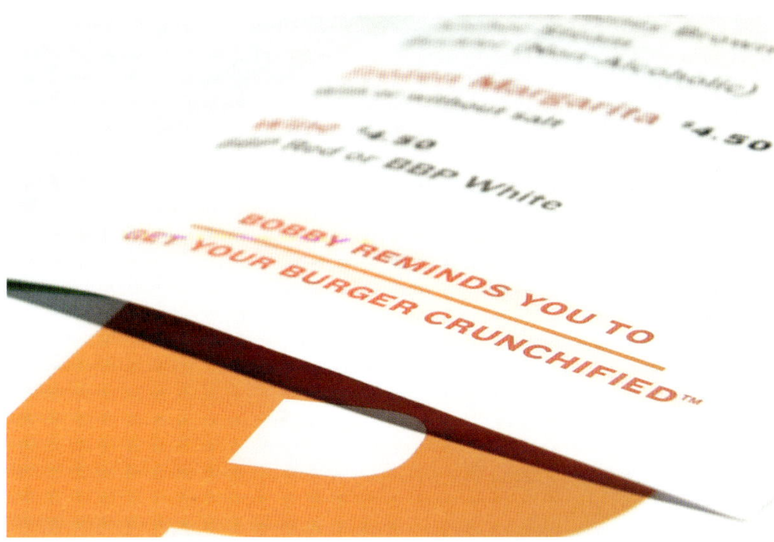
BOBBY REMINDS YOU TO
GET YOUR BURGER CRUNCHIFIED™

Gato opened on Lafayette Street in lower Manhattan in 2014, Bobby Flay's first new restaurant in nearly ten years. Located in a renovated 1897 warehouse, it celebrates the flavors of the Mediterranean, with dishes and ingredients from Spain, Italy, France, and Greece. The space's renovation, again by Rockwell Group, balances cosmopolitan luxury with downtown grit. Our goal with the graphic program was to do the same.

Right and opposite
The balance of tough and luxe is maintained in every detail. The secondary typeface Pitch, a refinement of monospaced typewriter fonts, is paired with deep blues from the hand-set tile work on Gato's floors. Pentagram's Jesse Reed supervised details from the gold leaf logos on the windows to the hand-painted "Employees must wash hands" notice in the WC.

Next spread
The exterior of Gato on Lafayette Street. The chef is visible through the window on the right.

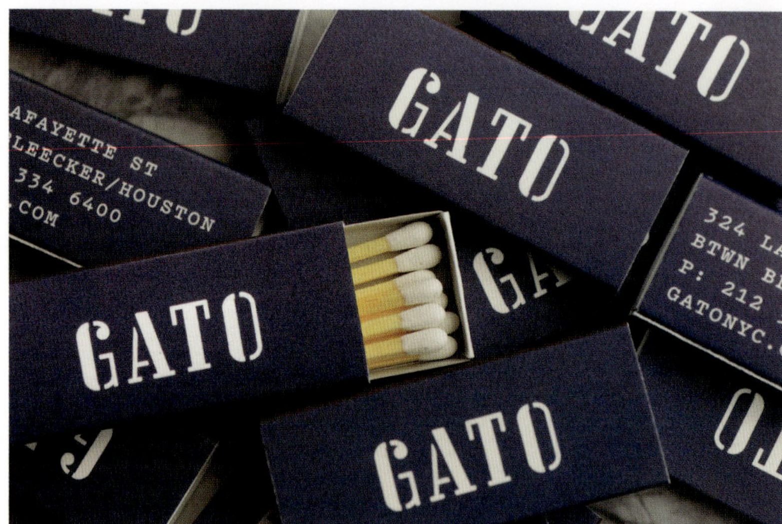

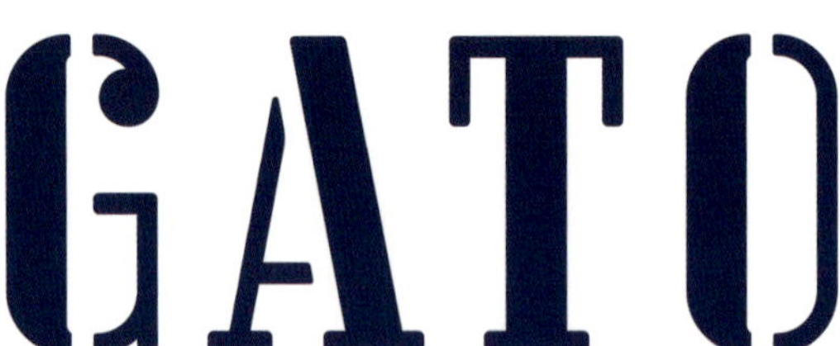

Above
Gato's logo is based on Anthony Burrill's stylish-but-tough typeface Lisbon, itself inspired by the street addresses of its namesake city and other Mediterranean locales.

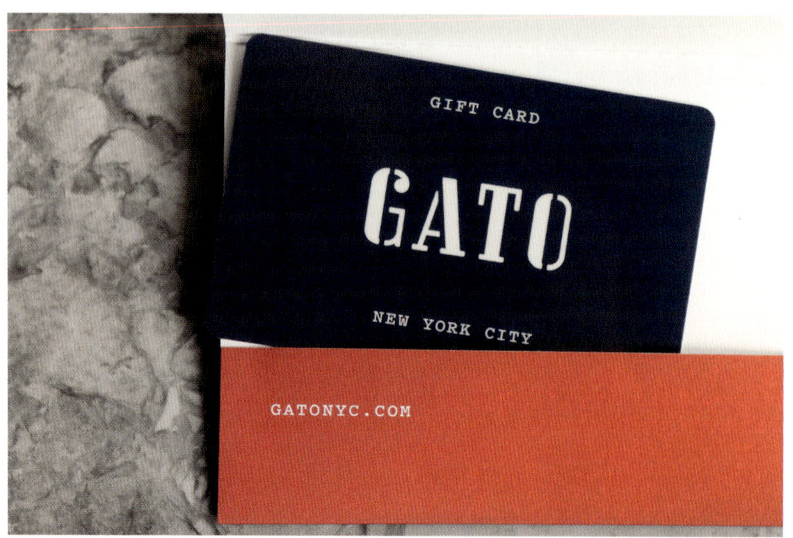

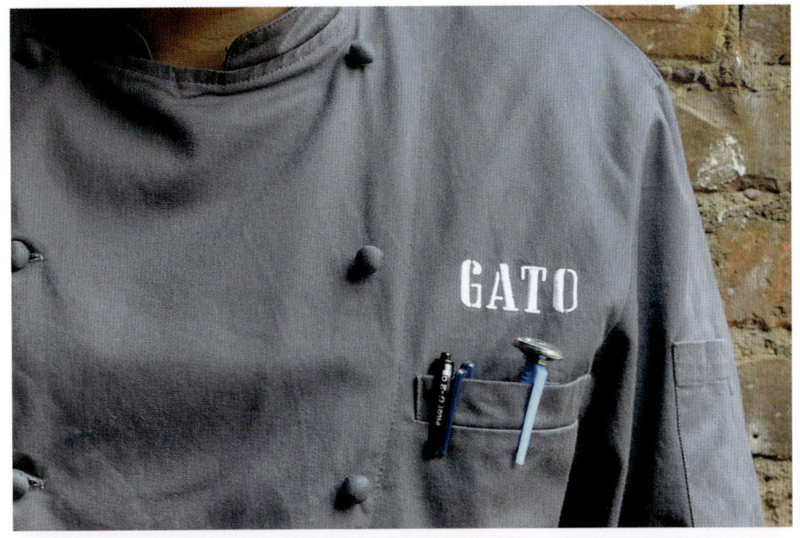
GATO

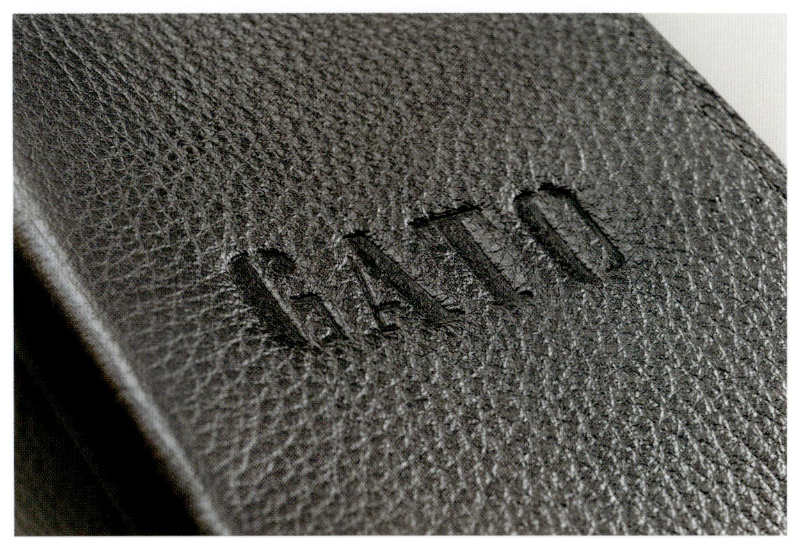
GATO

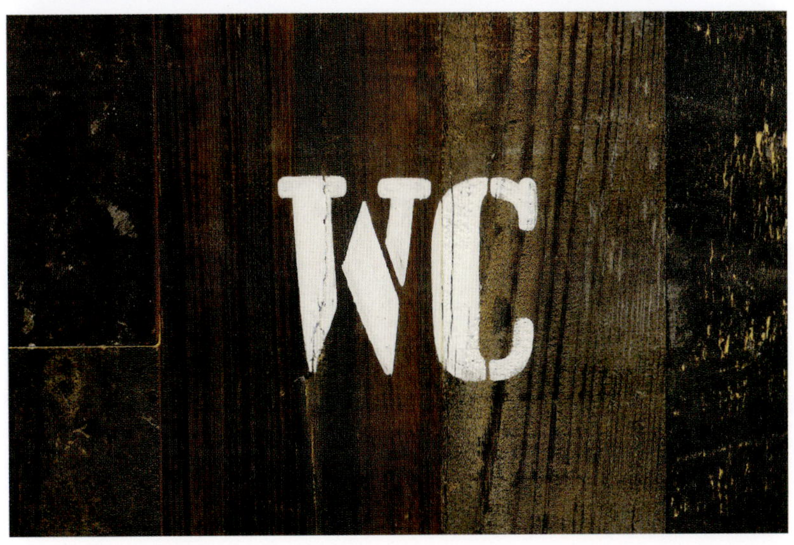
WC

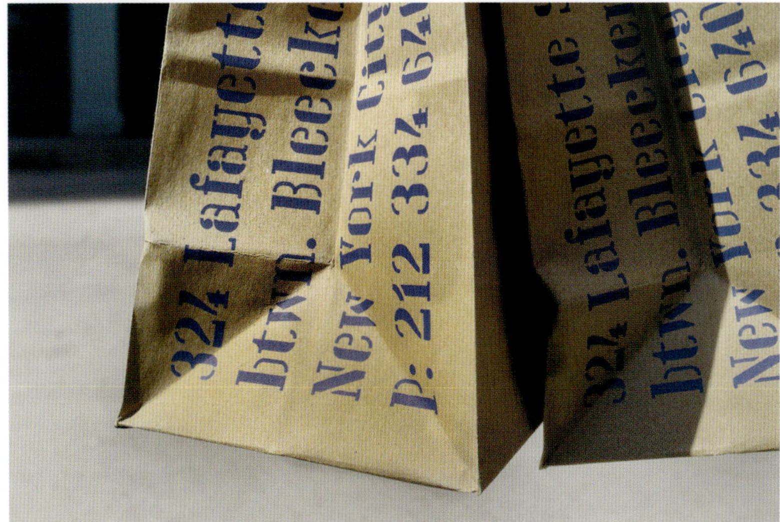
324 Lafayett
btwn. Bleeck
New York City
P: 212 334 64

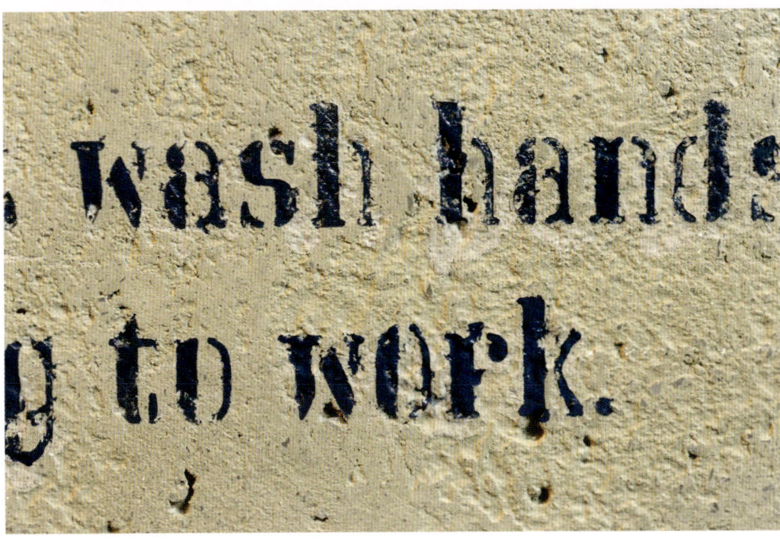
wash hands
to work.

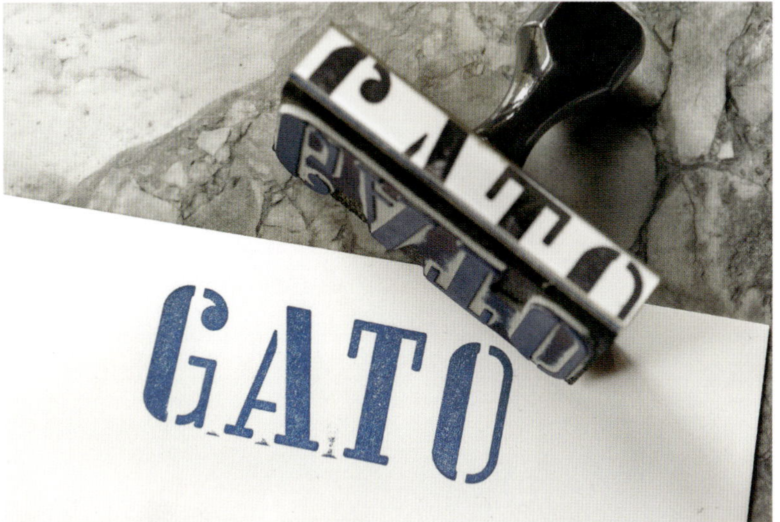
GATO

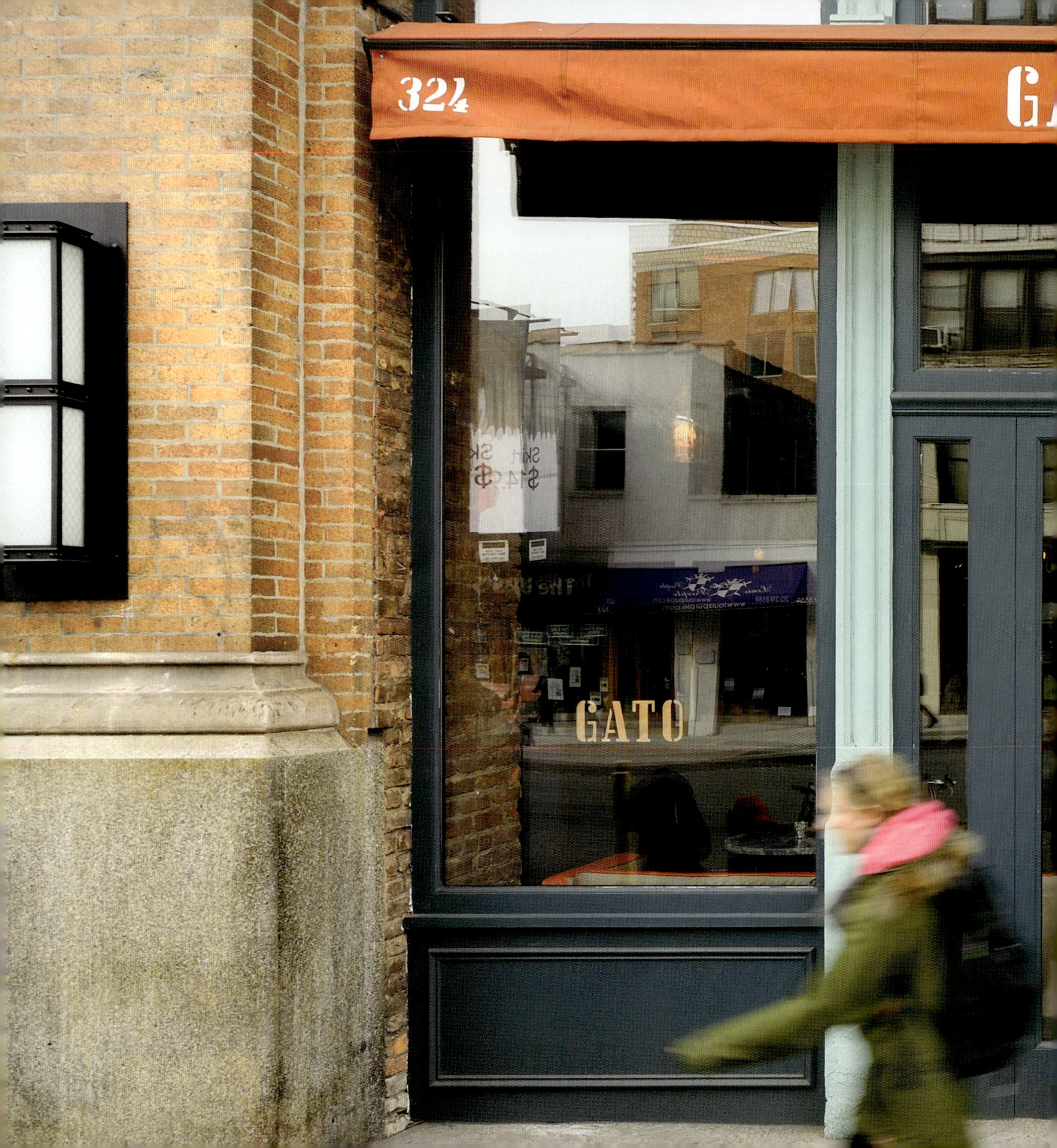
324
GATO

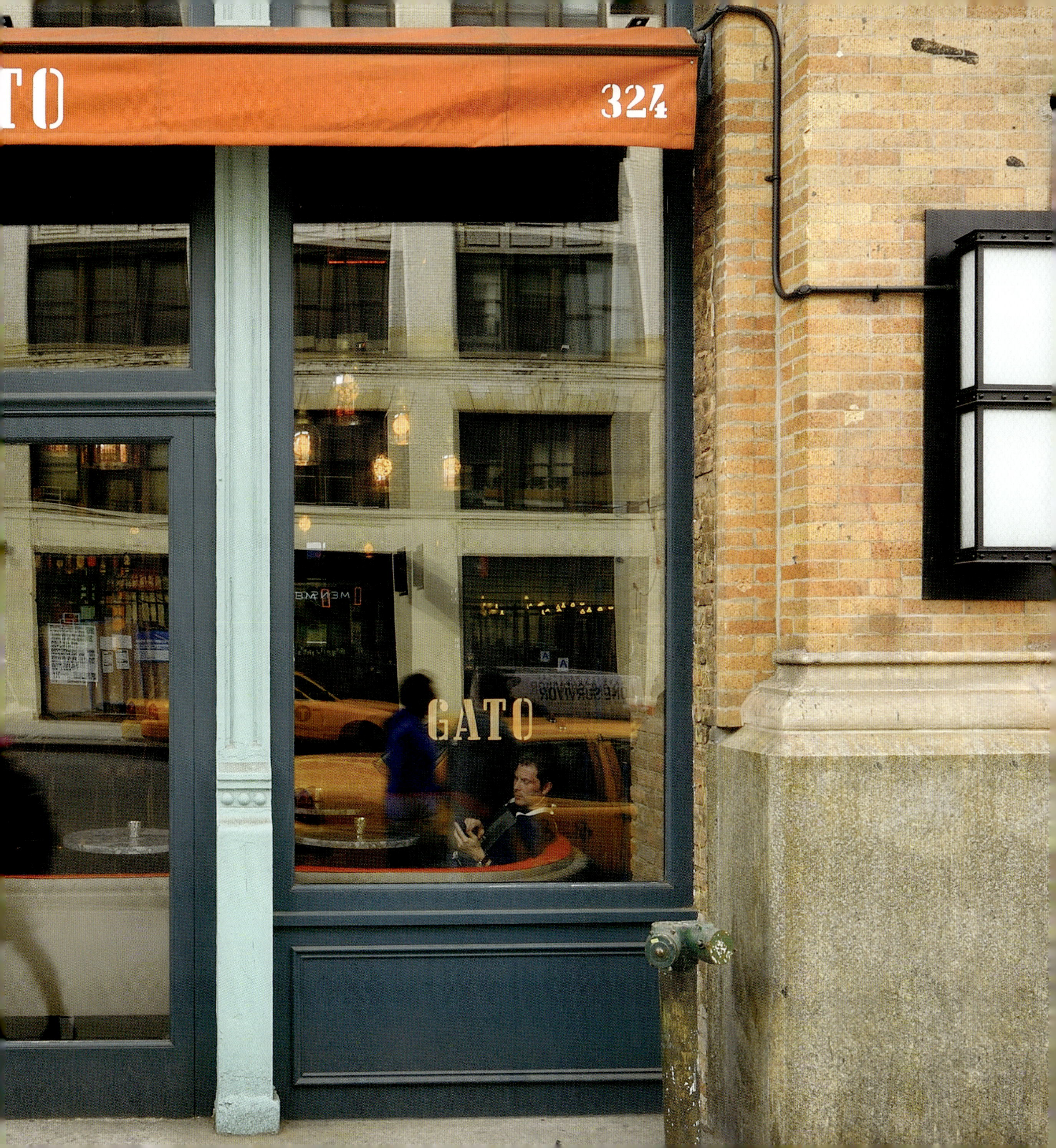
TO
324
GATO

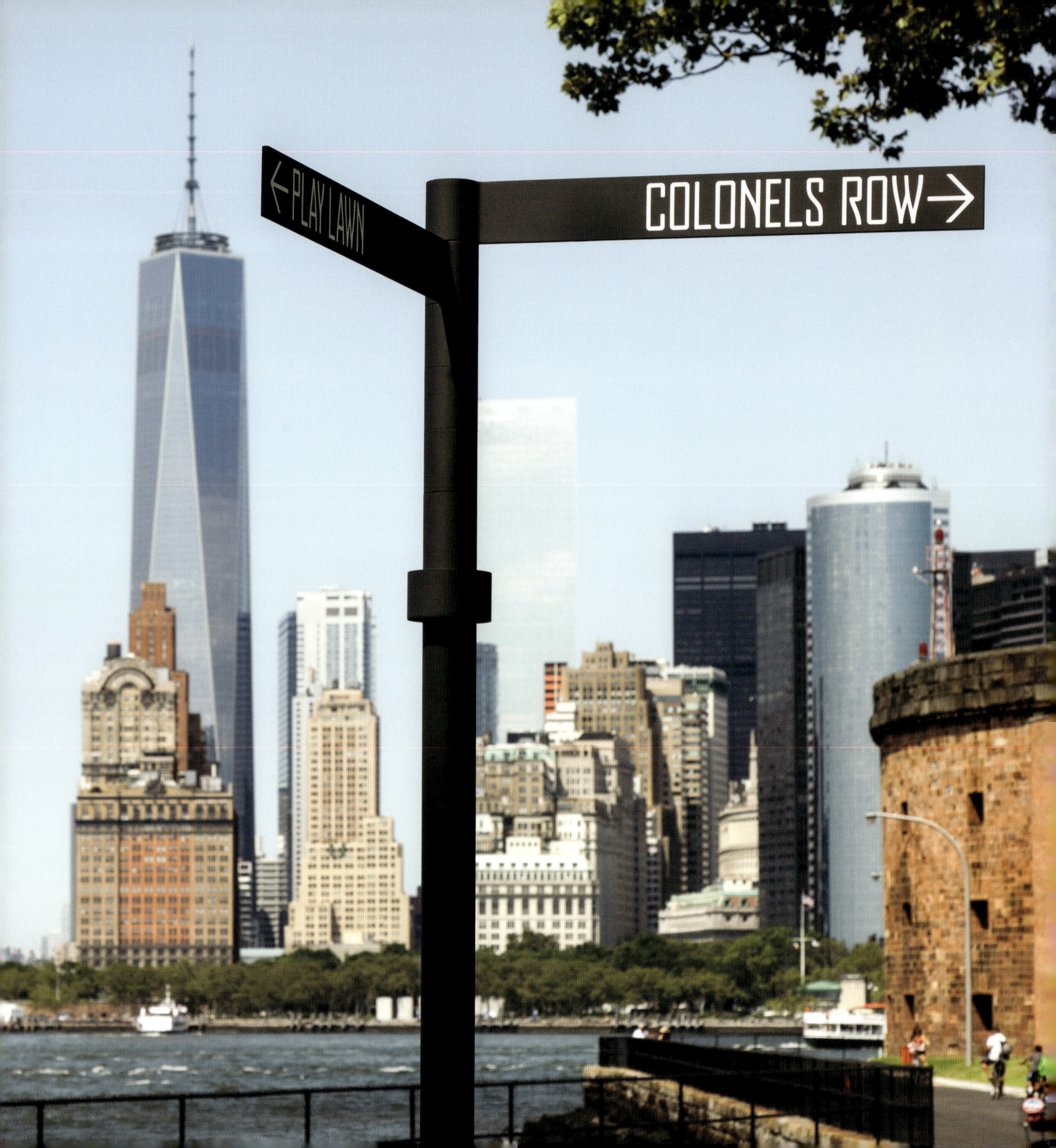
PLAY LAWN
COLONELS ROW

How to survive on an island

Governors Island

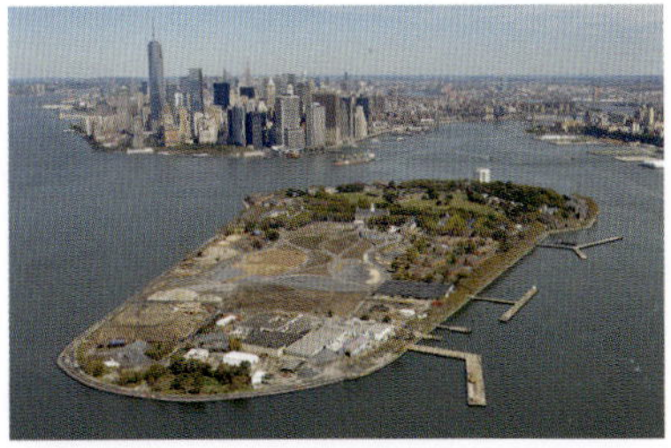

Opposite and above
For most of its history, Governors Island had very few visitors. It was a secret destination hiding in plain sight less than half a mile from the coast of Lower Manhattan. Today, it is open to the public all summer and accessible only by ferry. The island has astounding views that serve to orient visitors as they move about its periphery.

Next spread
The enormous gantries at the island's docks serve as gateways upon arrival and as frames upon departure. Their structure provided the key to our approach to the island's signs.

Governors Island sits 800 yards off the shore of lower Manhattan, reachable only by ferry, a ride that takes a little more than seven minutes. But the contrast with the city is positively surreal. There are no cars. There are no crowds. Instead, to the north, just an abandoned military base, elegant and eerie, built over a century ago. And to the south, stretches of featureless landfill, overlooking astonishing views of Manhattan, Brooklyn, New York Harbor, and the Statue of Liberty.

Our client Leslie Koch, appointed by the mayor to shape Governors Island's 172 acres of undeveloped landfill, devised a competition to create the city's newest public park. Dutch landscape architects West 8, led by the brilliant Adriaan Geuze, won. Our job was to create the signs that would help the island's visitors find their way around.

The island has just two "front doors," the docks for ferries from Manhattan and Brooklyn. It wasn't really so big you could get lost. And the glorious views provided constant orientation. It seemed easy.

Yet we were struggling. I had become fixated on a single approach: bulky, cylindrical signs that worked in 360 degrees, just like the island itself. I presented ever-more-developed versions in meeting after meeting. The more I developed them, the less I liked them. Neither, I sensed, did anyone else. Finally I admitted defeat.

"Can I show you something?" I asked my partner Paula Scher. I laid out months of work, alongside pictures from our many visits to Governors Island. Paula had never been there. She pointed at a picture we had taken of a gantry, one of the giant, skeletal superstructures at the island's docks. "This is what the signs should look like. It's all about the views, right? So why not make signs you can see through?"

That took three minutes. I visited our colleagues at West 8 and asked for permission to throw everything out and start over. I thought they would be alarmed. Instead they were relieved. The new approach worked perfectly, and from the first moment we showed it to Leslie Koch, I could tell we had the answer. Today she calls them "the most beautiful signs in New York."

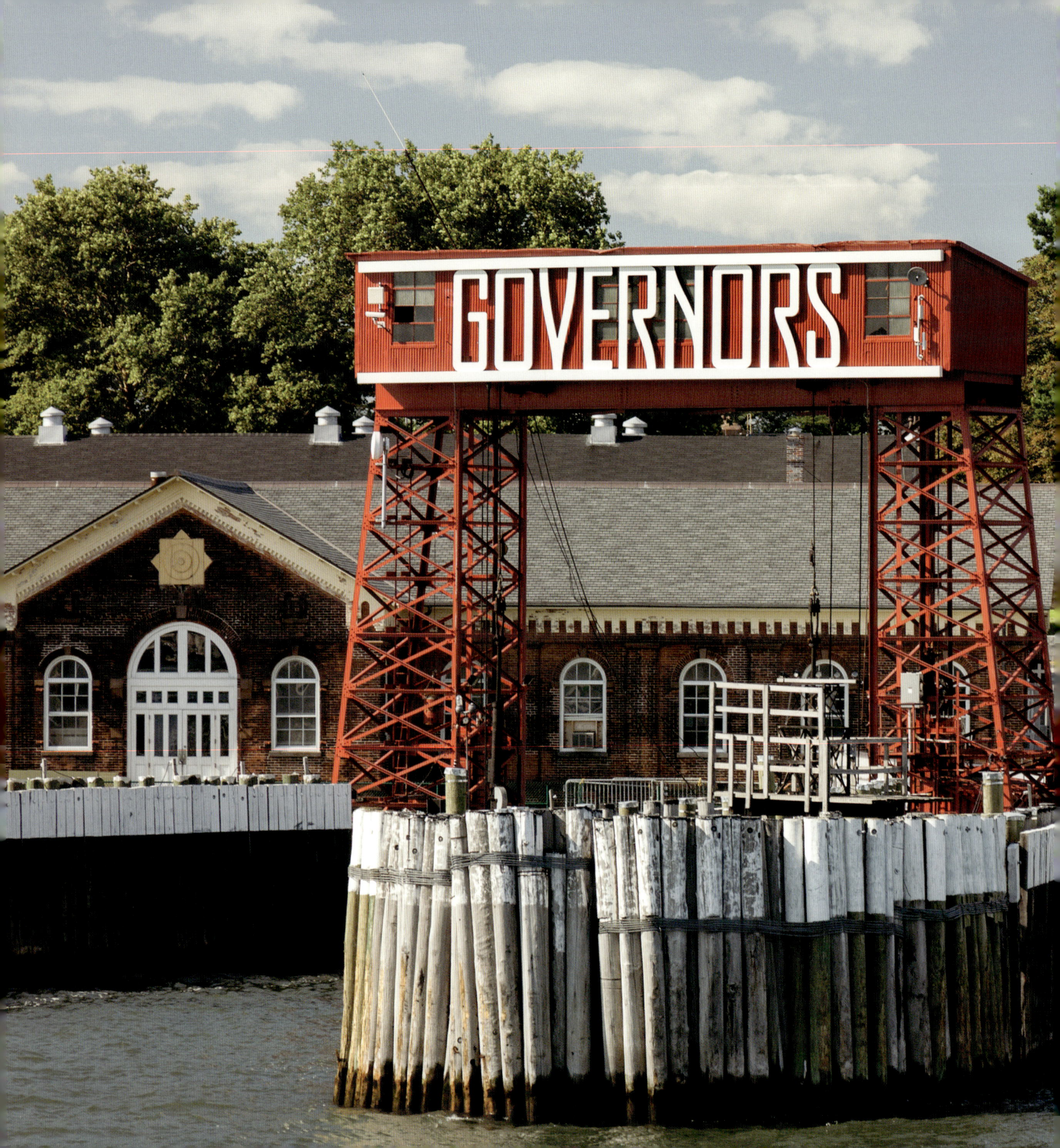
GOVERNORS

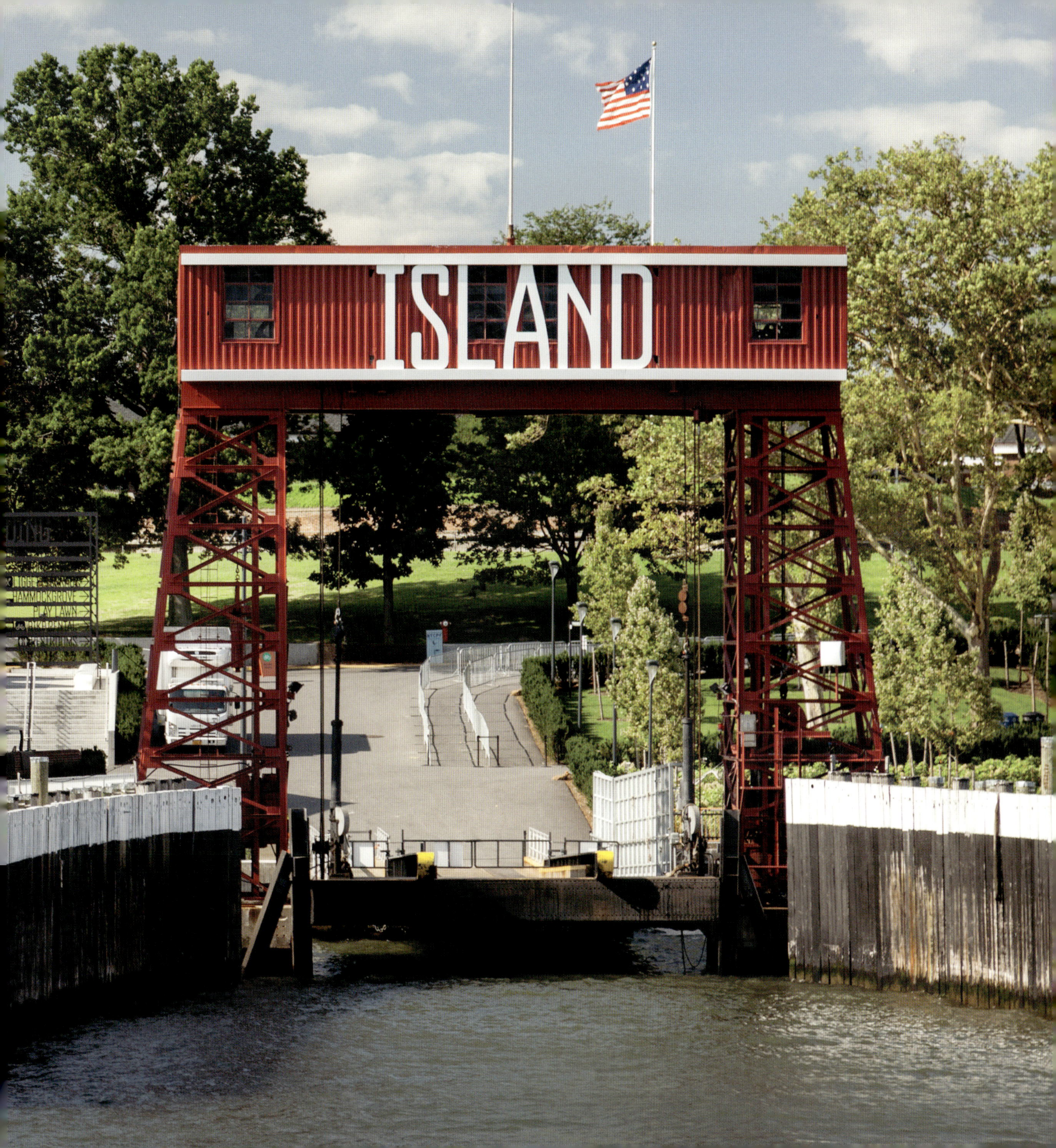
ISLAND
HAMMOCK GROVE
PLAY LAWN

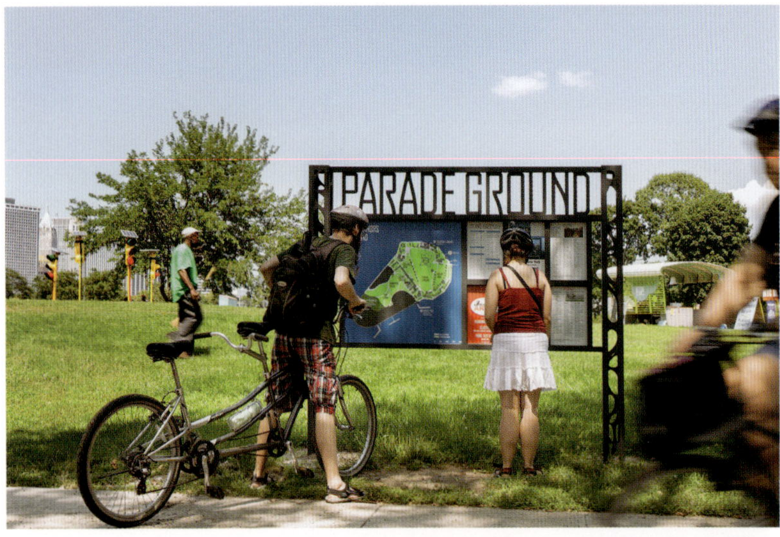

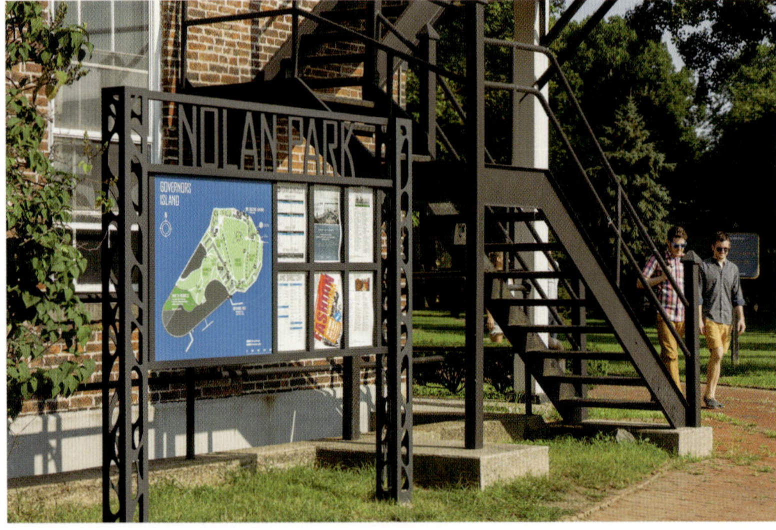

ABCDE
FGHIJK
LMNOP
QRSTU
VWXYZ

Above
The signs had to look robust but playful, big enough to stand out in the environment but capable of fading into the background. Adriaan Geuze, Jamie Maslyn Larson, and their team at West 8 helped create the signs' structures, including supports that incorporate the curvy, organic patterns that can be found throughout their designs for public spaces.

Above
We designed a custom typeface for Governors Island called Guppy Sans, a cross between a rugged sans serif (to reflect the island's utilitarian past) and an ornamental display font (to suggest the lush parkland to come). Pentagram's Britt Cobb and Hamish Smyth masterminded the design's deployment and spent many hours walking and biking the island's paths.

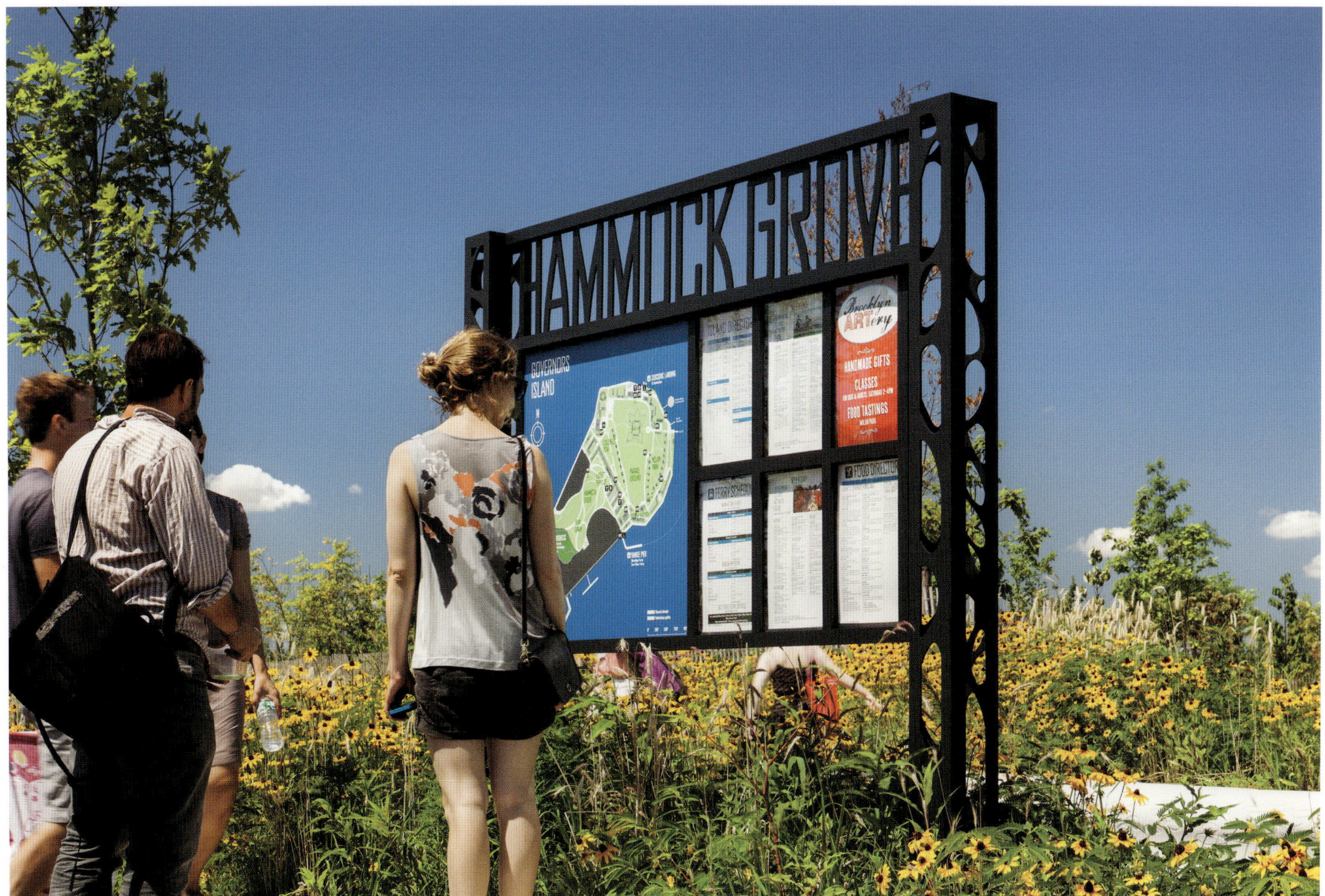

Above
A key challenge for the island's signage program was anticipating change. The signs had to look permanent, but needed to be updated weekly to accommodate temporary events, and seasonally to incorporate new destinations. As a result, the signs are built from modular elements that can be easily updated.

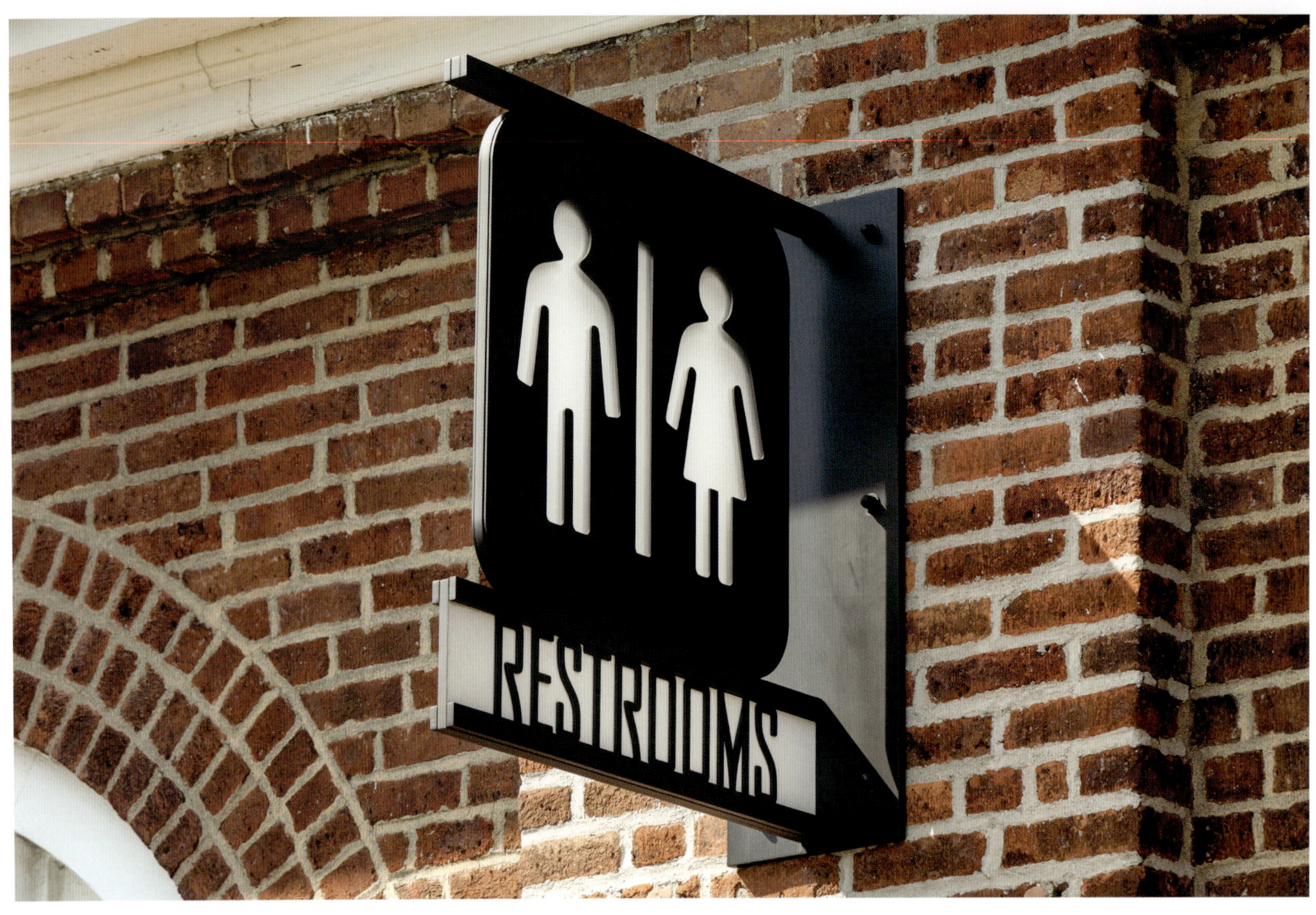

Above
No matter how complicated the signage system, one sign is inevitably the most important.

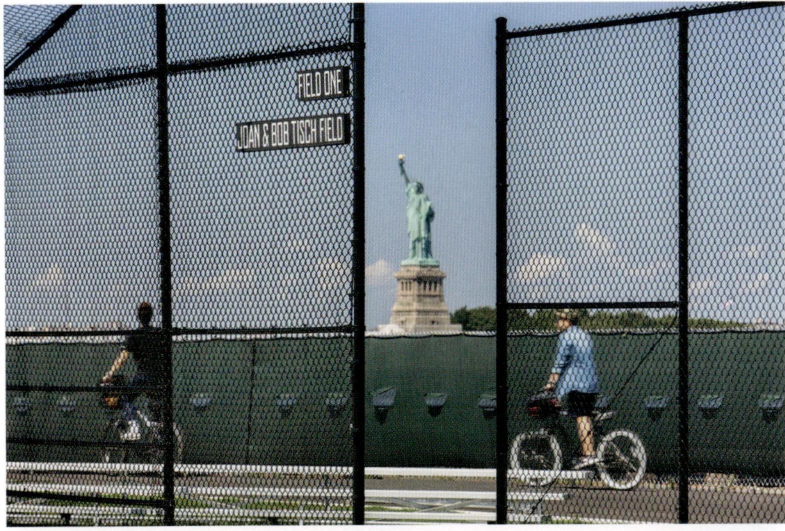

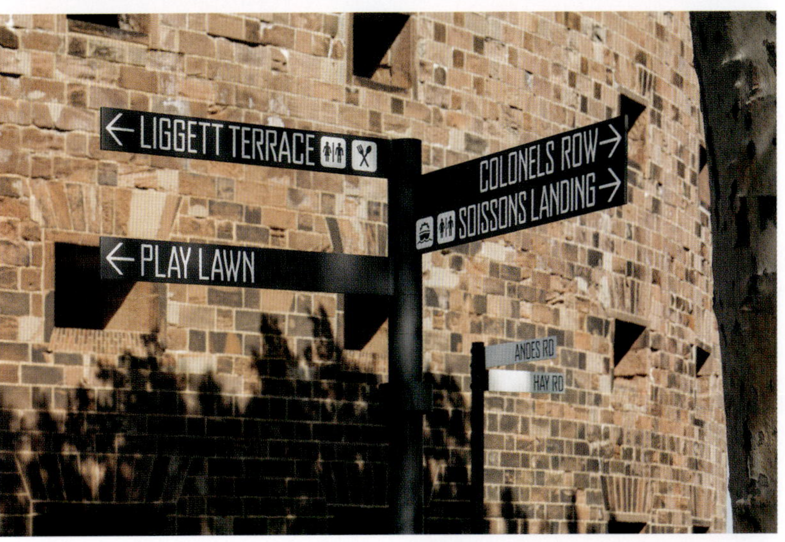

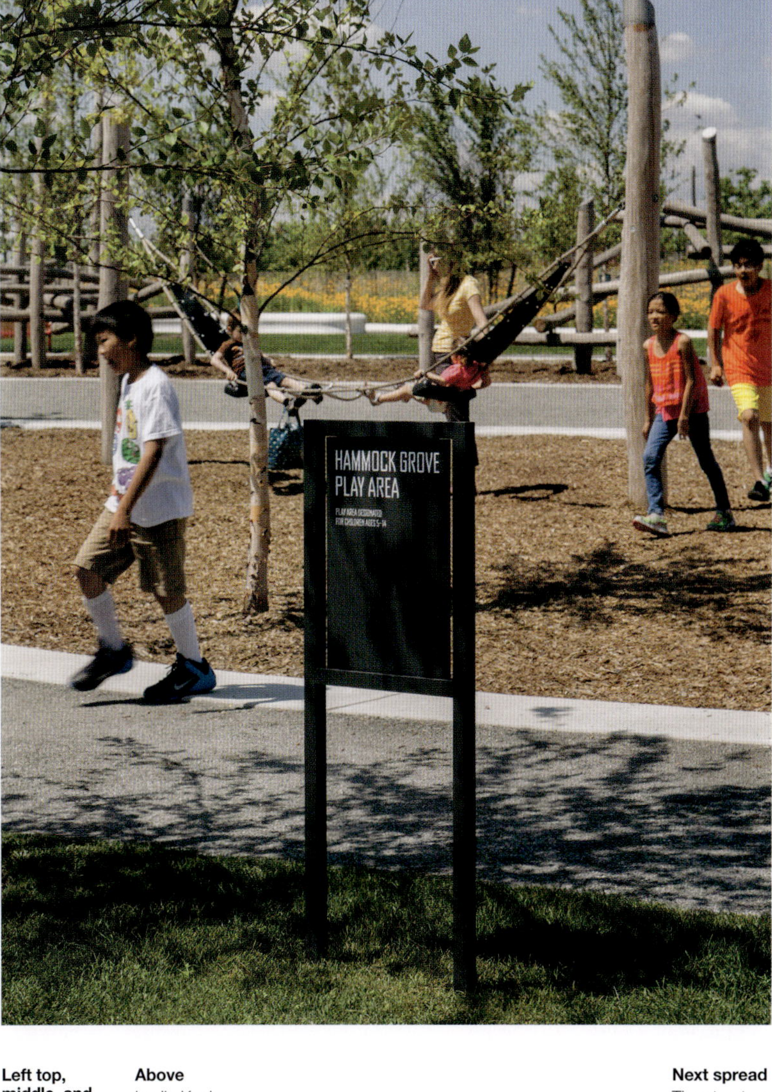

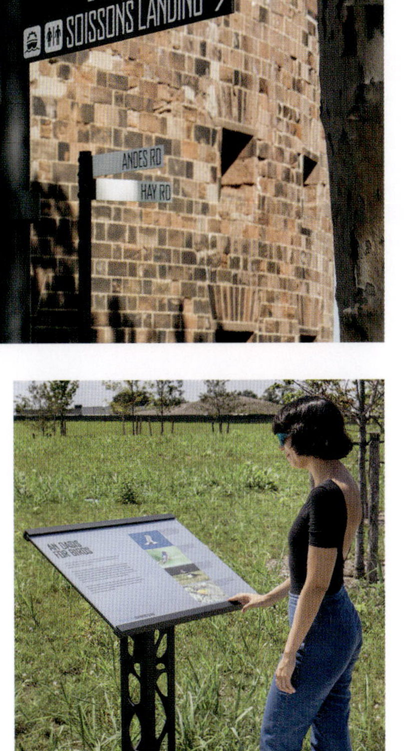

Left top, middle, and bottom
By using the same custom typeface on every sign, including street signs, informational signs, and interpretive signs, we hoped to create a distinct sense of place that would set the island apart from other New York destinations.

Above
Leslie Koch believes strongly that memorable place names are key to wayfinding. On the island, some are historic (Colonels Row) and others are brand-new (Hammock Grove); they build anticipation even as words on a map.

Next spread
The structure of the signs, and their location in the lush landscape of the island's park and open spaces, suggest they might be excellent trellises. My private fantasy is to see them smothered in vines, achieving the perfect synthesis of design and nature.

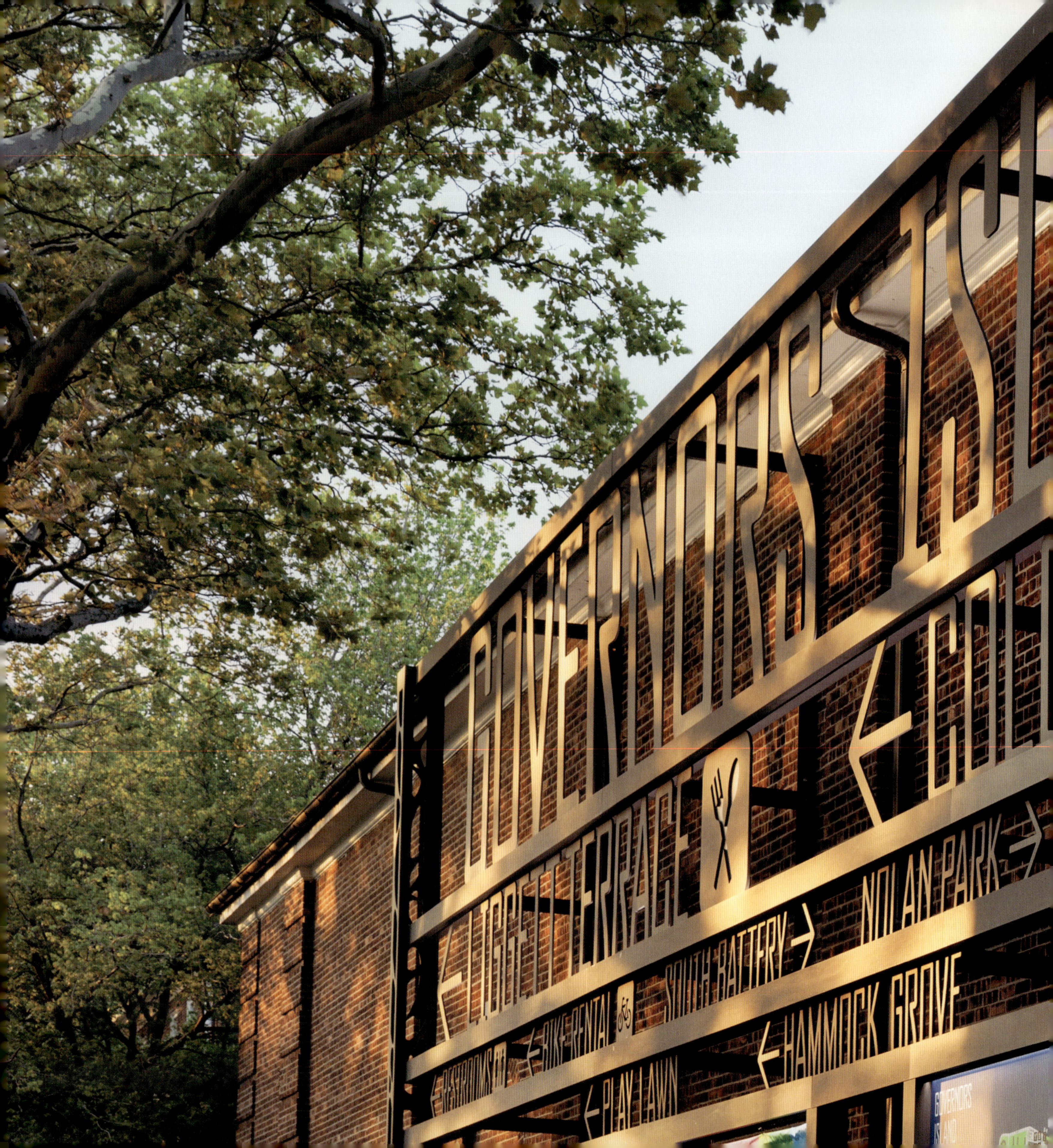

GOVERNORS
LIGGETT TERRACE
NOLAN PARK
SOUTH BATTERY
BIKE RENTAL
RESTROOMS
HAMMOCK GROVE
PLAY LAWN
GOVERNORS ISLAND

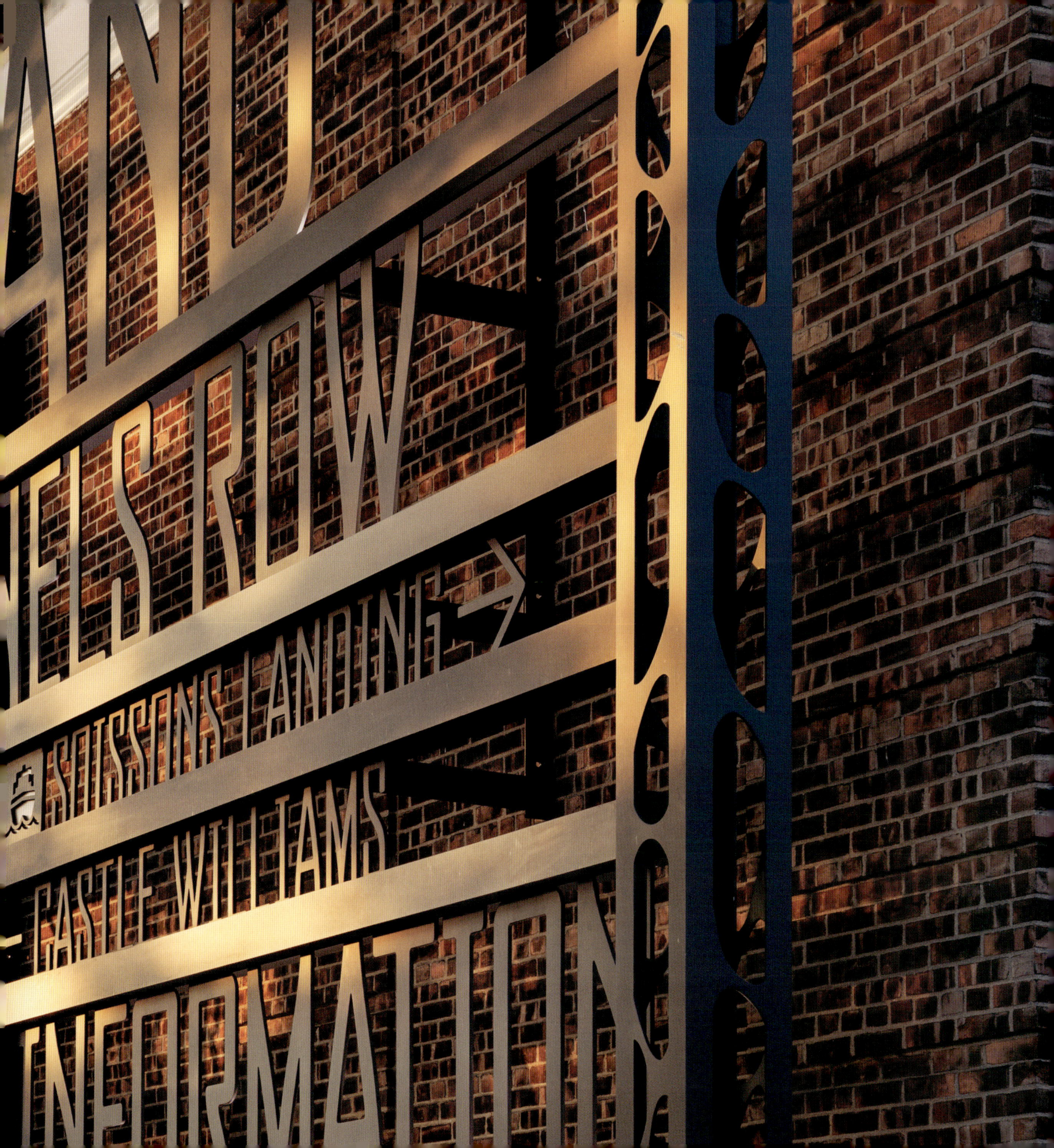
SOISSONS LANDING
CASTLE WILLIAMS
INFORMATION

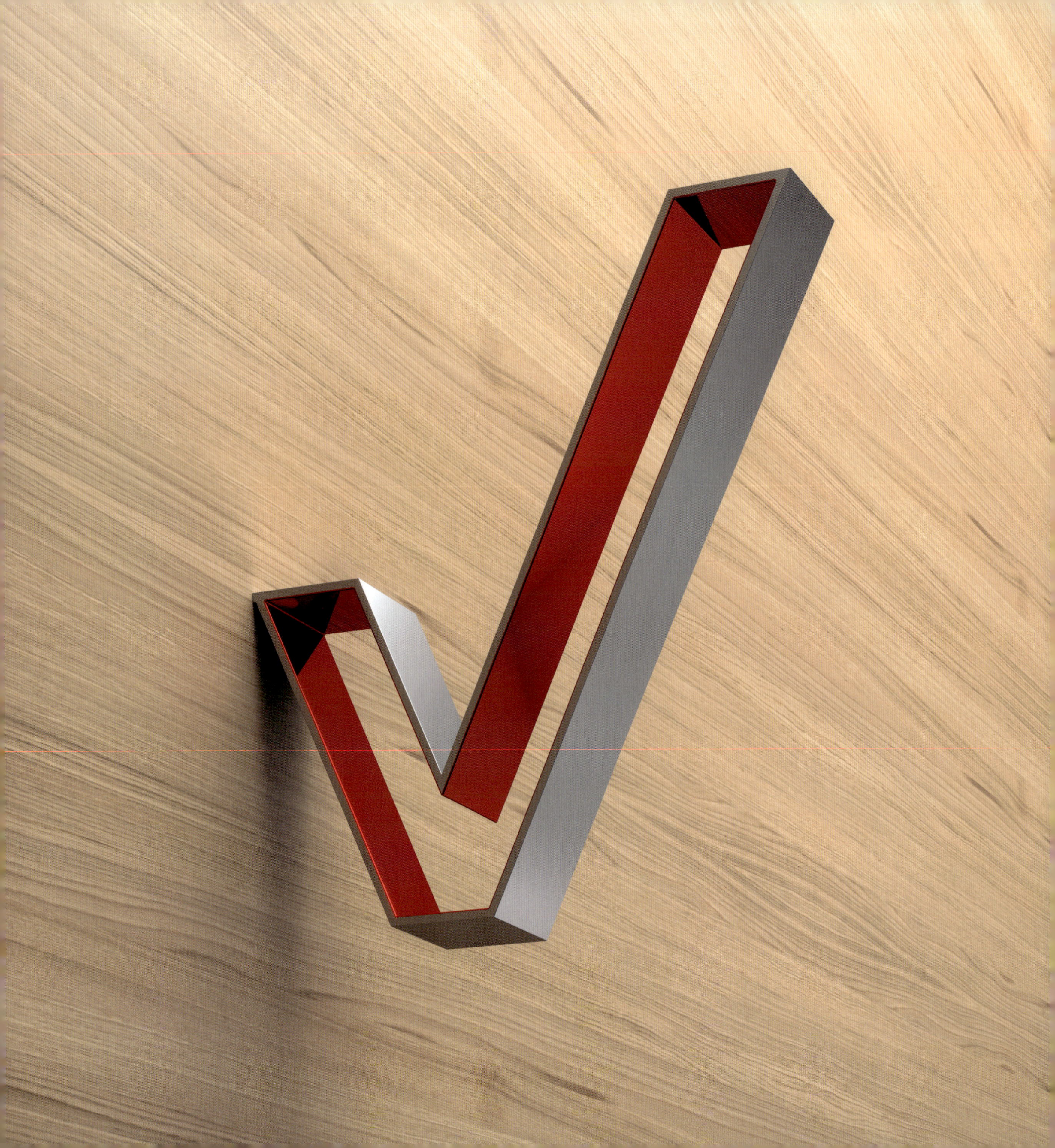

How to network
Verizon

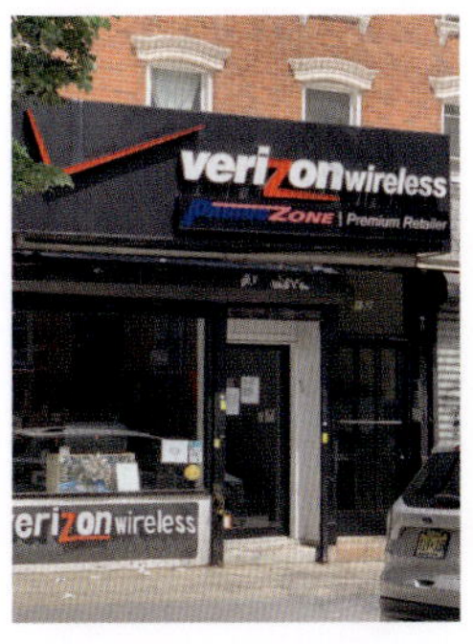

Opposite
Instead of inventing a new symbol, we adapted an existing one. The checkmark works as pixels on a mobile device or built in three dimensions at a retail store, as in this version by my partner Daniel Weil.

Above
Meant to represent a company that was simple, reliable, and user-friendly, the original Verizon logo was complicated, inconsistent, and confusing: not a good match.

In 1969, when I was a sixth grader in suburban Cleveland, the Bell Telephone System introduced a new corporate identity program. Our local subsidiary, Ohio Bell, had previously used an old-fashioned logo that had barely changed for 80 years. Now, trucks and telephone booths, ads and directories, began to sport a sleek new logo and a modern sans serif typeface. It was then, and probably still is today, the most extensive rebrand in American history.

I don't remember noticing. The new identity, by the legendary Saul Bass, was clean and consistent, but there was nothing clever about it. The old symbol was a clunky-looking bell in a circle; the new symbol was a slick-looking bell in a circle. At 12, I was excited by album covers and movie posters. A phone company logo didn't excite me.

But it wasn't meant to. Bell's job was to provide seamless, ubiquitous, flawless telephone service to every household in the country. Its public face matched its mission: calm, confident, and consistent, built to last forever. It didn't. In 1984, after years of antitrust actions, Bell parent company AT&T was forced to divest itself of its operating companies. One of them, New York Telephone, was merged with New England Telephone to create NYNEX. Eventually it merged with Bell Atlantic and then with GTE to create an entirely new company, Verizon. It was hard to keep track.

Their logo was everywhere. I wasn't a fan. It combined an aggressive bold italic, an odd, oversized "Z," and a confusing angled shape that vaguely suggested a checkmark. So I was excited to get a call in 2015 from their new head of marketing, Diego Scotti, to talk about a possible redesign. The challenge was unique. How can you create a brand that will be encountered everywhere, at scales large and small? How do you design something that can acquire meaning, even change meanings, over time? We needed something like Bass's Bell logo, modest and powerful, built from simple, resilient ingredients. We reduced the complicated logo to its essence, punctuating the Verizon name with an immediately understandable accent: a bright red checkmark, the universal symbol for a task completed. As communications, technology, and culture change over the years, the new symbol will serve both as a reassuring constant and as a canvas for invention as it adapts to continuous change.

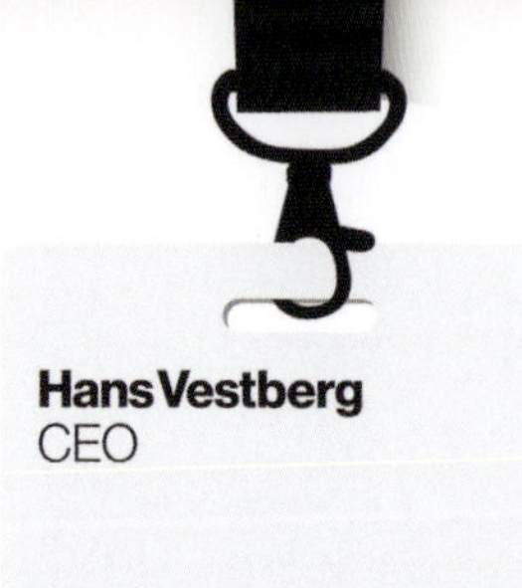

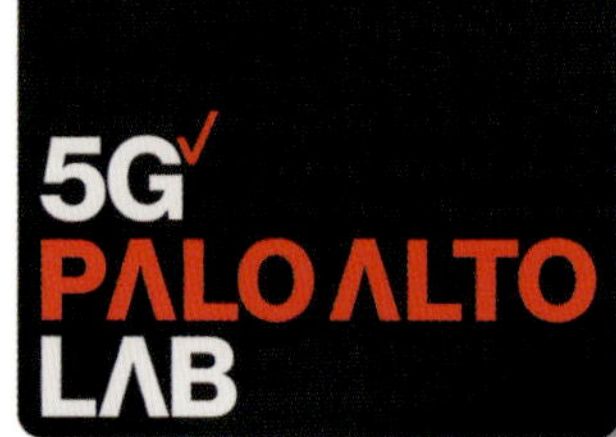

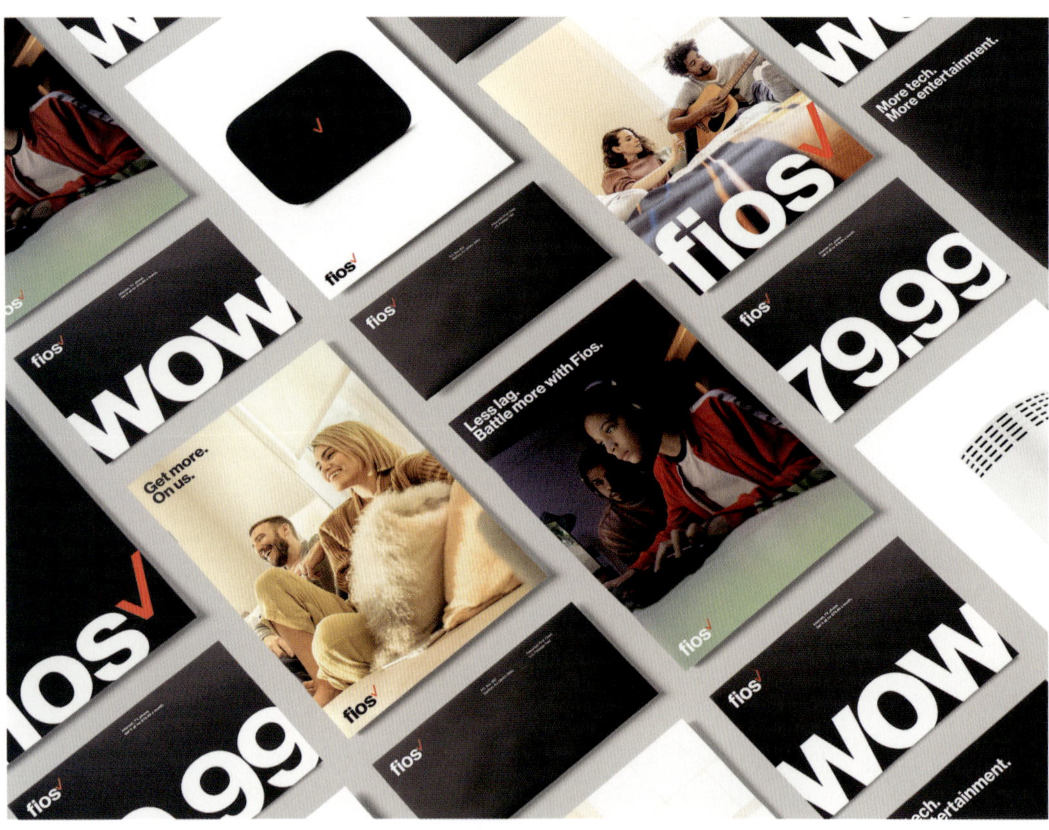

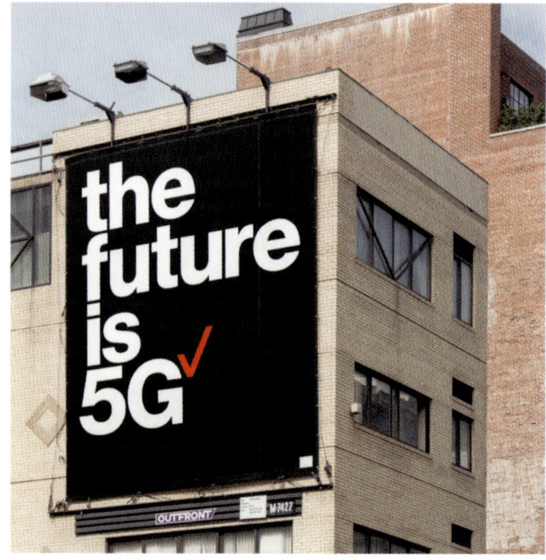

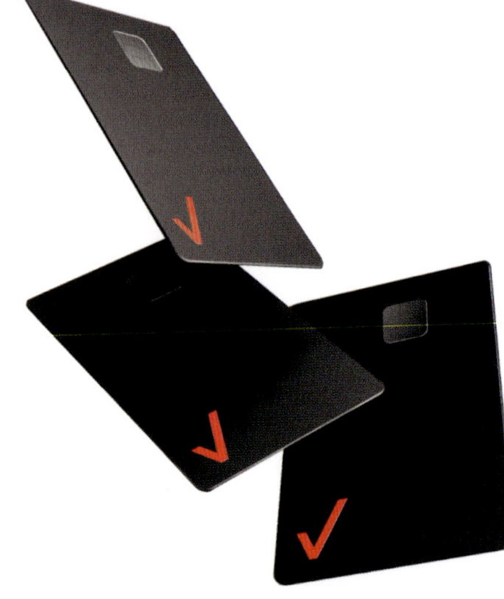

Above
The logotype is adapted from Neue Haas Grotesk, Christian Schwartz's loving restoration of Helvetica, used in Saul Bass's Bell System identity 40 years before. Neue Haas Grotesk is Verizon's primary typeface family.

Right top
Sub-brands like Verizon's 5G Labs are differentiated with customized versions of the brand typeface.

Right middle
The checkmark signals the parentage of products, features, and services even when the brand name doesn't appear.

Right bottom
On the Verizon credit card, the checkmark stands alone.

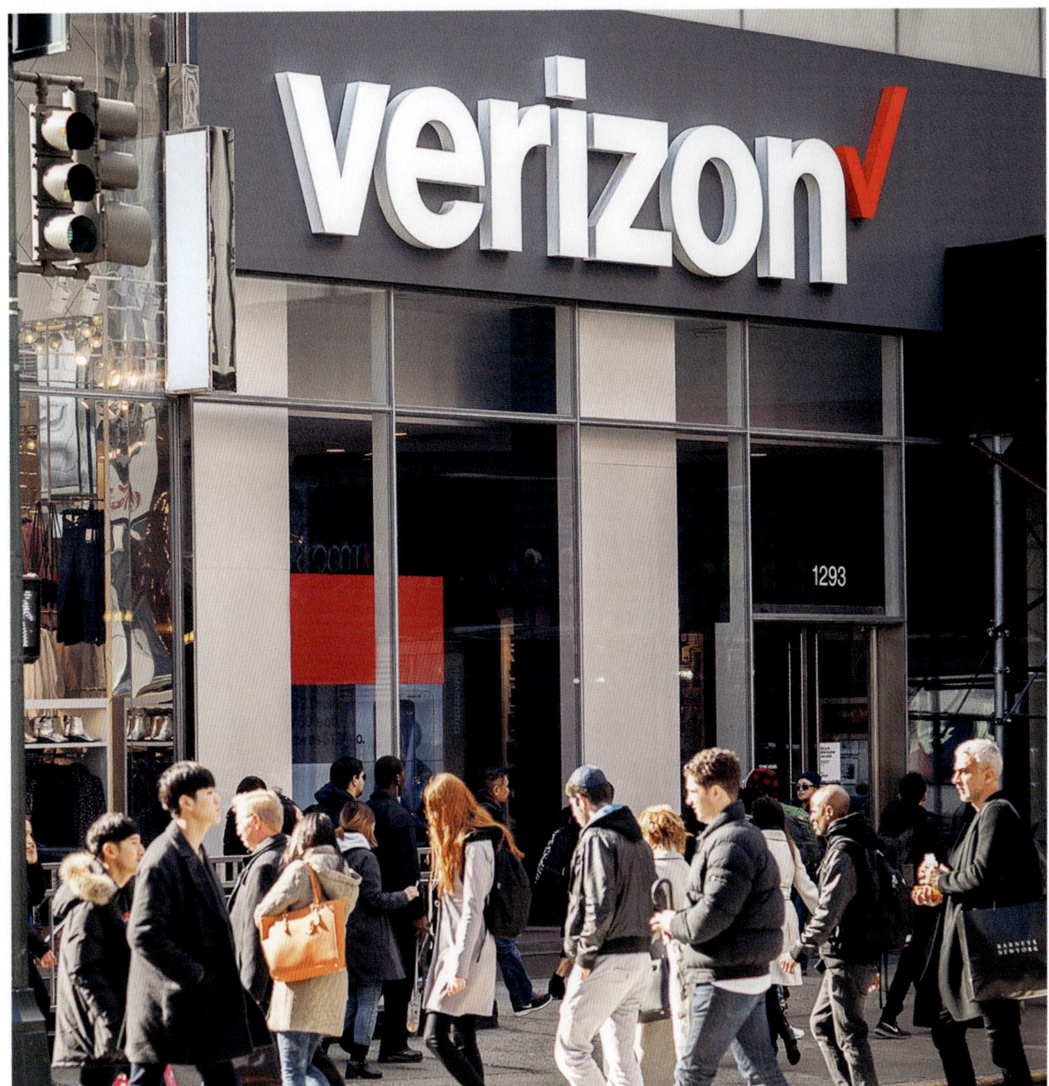

Left
The logotype identifies over 2,000 stores across America.

Next spread
Over five years, we've worked with the company and our colleagues at other agencies to build out a comprehensive set of online graphic standards. These pages offer just a small sample.

Following spread
Helping to shape the brand identity of Verizon, a company that touches almost every part of daily life in America, has been one of my favorite challenges. I could not have done it without the help of Sonsoles Alvarez, Sachi Chandiramani, Britt Cobb, Aron Fay, Chris Guerrero, Jon Luehmann, and Jonny Sikov, and the brilliant project management of Abby Matousek.

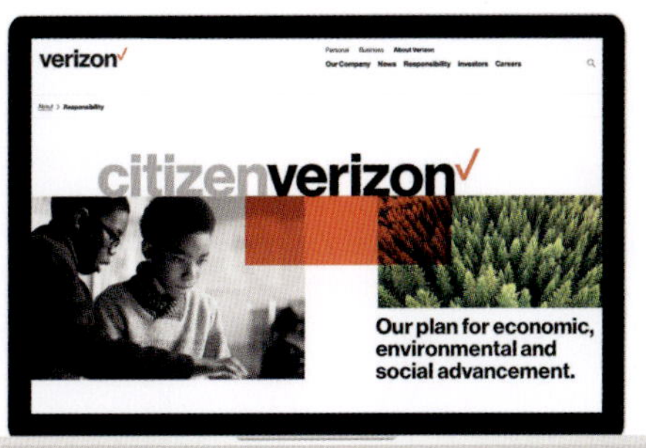

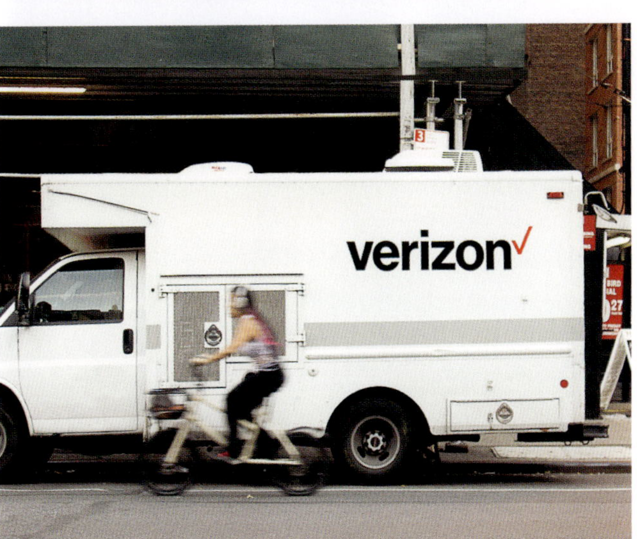

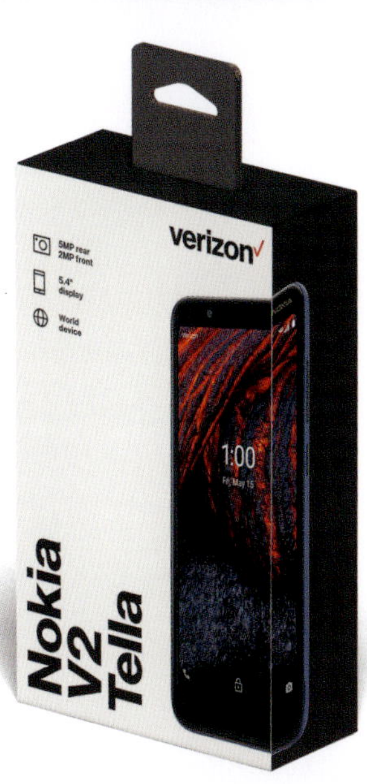

Far left
Nearly 25,000 vehicles serve as rolling billboards for the brand and are ubiquitous sights on America's streets.

Left
The same brand ingredients are used on packaging and products.

Above
Citizen Verizon is the company's channel for its wide range of social responsibility initiatives.

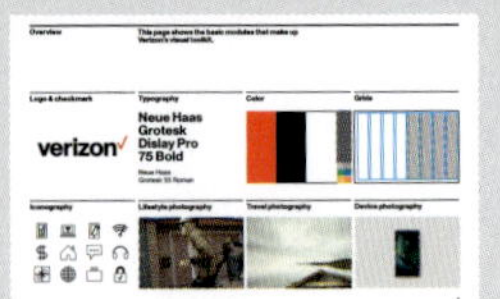
verizon
Neue Haas Grotesk Display Pro 75 Bold
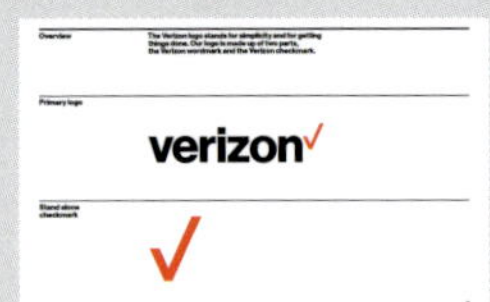
verizon
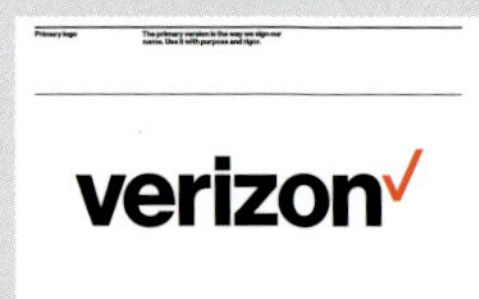
verizon
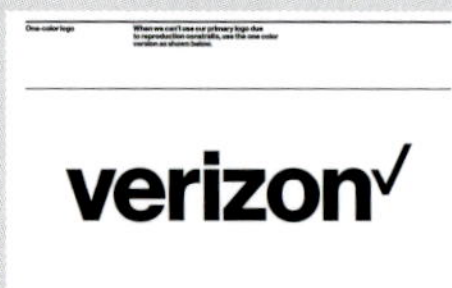
verizon
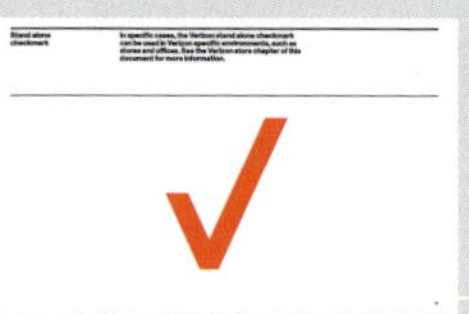
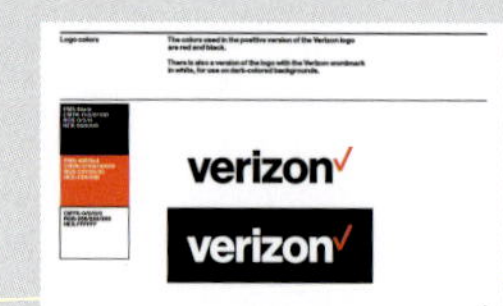
verizon
verizon
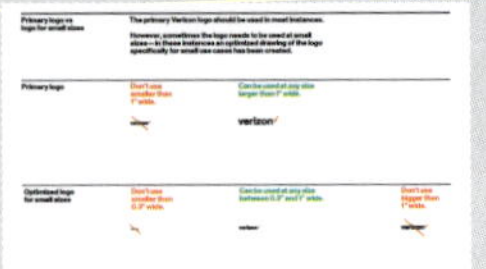
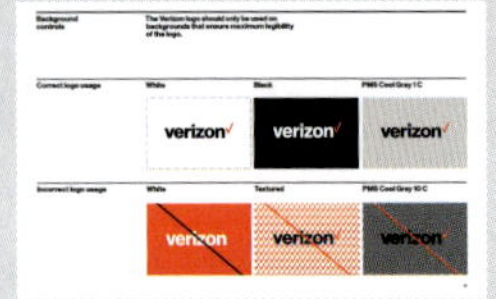
verizon
verizon
verizon
verizon
verizon
verizon
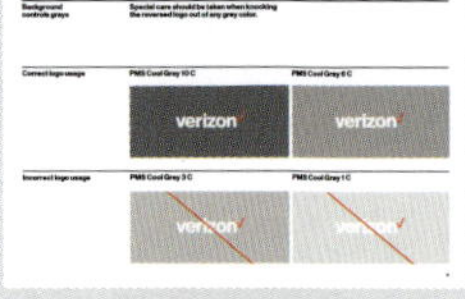
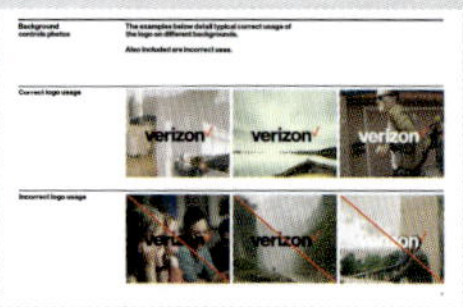
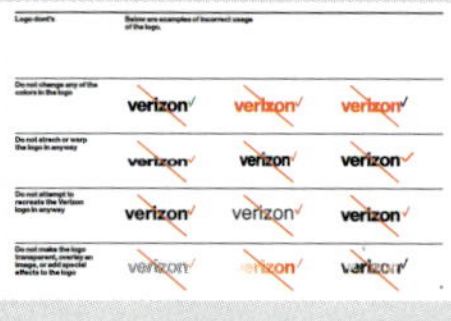
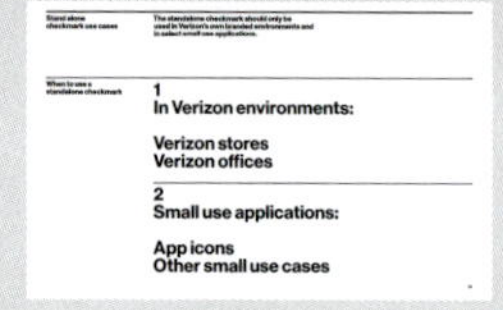
1
In Verizon environments:
Verizon stores
Verizon offices
2
Small use applications:
App icons
Other small use cases
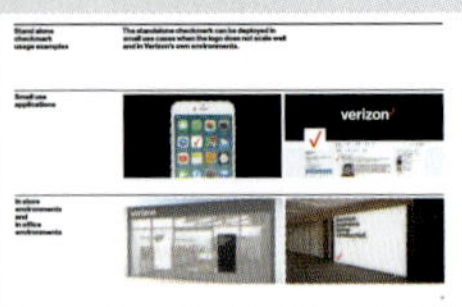
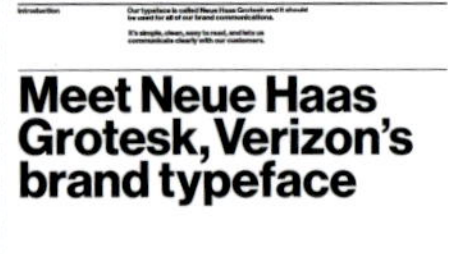
Meet Neue Haas Grotesk, Verizon's brand typeface
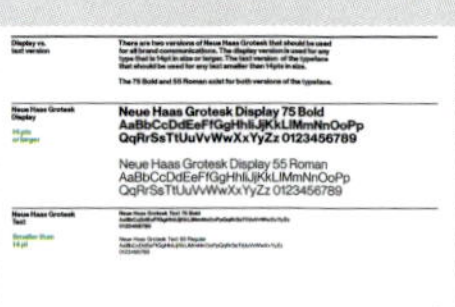
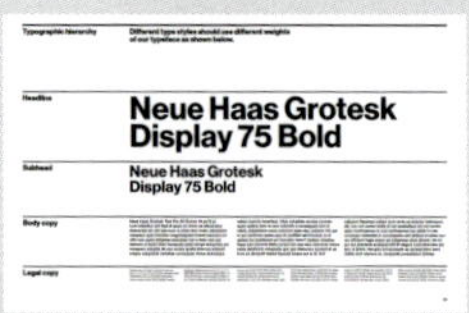
Neue Haas Grotesk Display 75 Bold
Neue Haas Grotesk Display 75 Bold
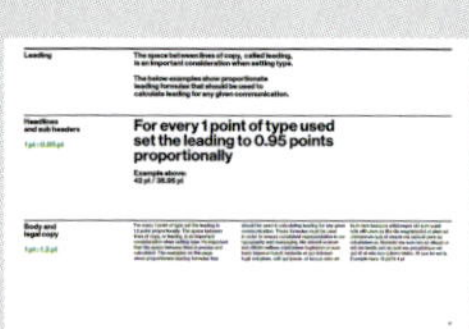
For every 1 point of type used set the leading to 0.95 points proportionally
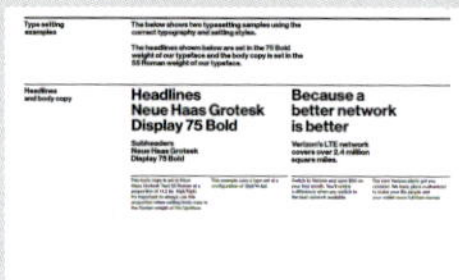
Headlines
Neue Haas Grotesk Display 75 Bold
Because a better network is better
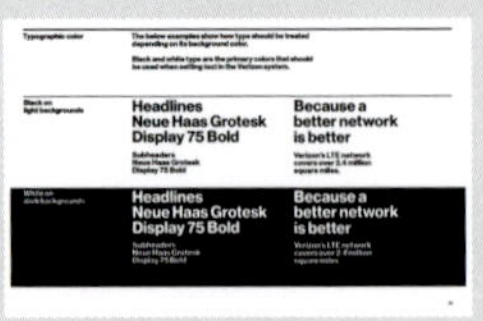
Headlines
Neue Haas Grotesk Display 75 Bold
Because a better network is better
Headlines
Neue Haas Grotesk Display 75 Bold
Because a better network is better
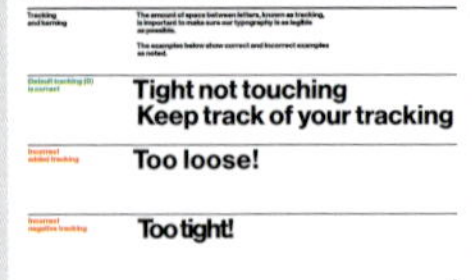
Tight not touching
Keep track of your tracking
Too loose!
Too tight!
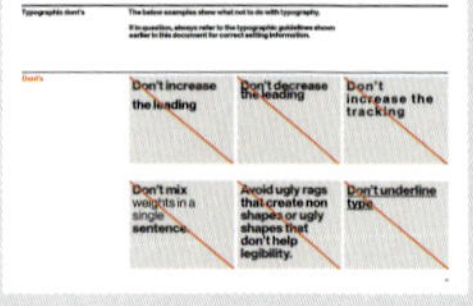
Don't increase the leading
Don't decrease the leading
Don't increase the tracking
Don't mix weights in a single sentence.
Avoid ugly rags that create non shapes or ugly shapes that don't help legibility.
Don't underline type
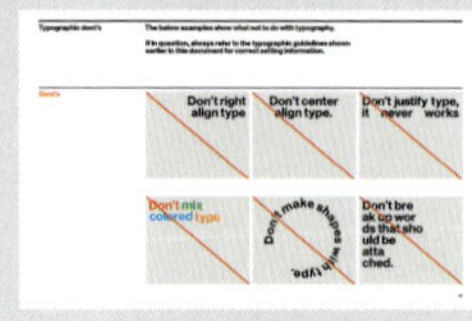
Don't right align type
Don't center align type.
Don't justify type, it never works
Don't mix colored type
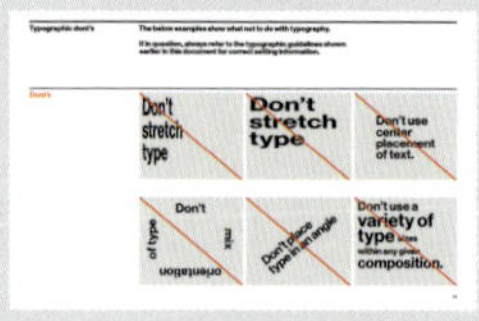
Don't stretch type
Don't stretch type
Don't use center placement of text.
Don't use a variety of type sizes within any given composition.
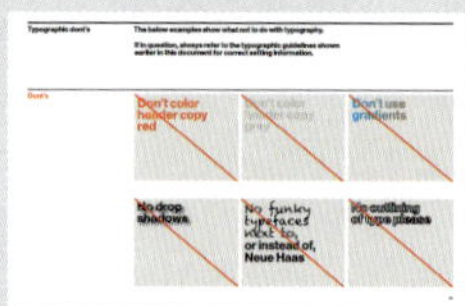
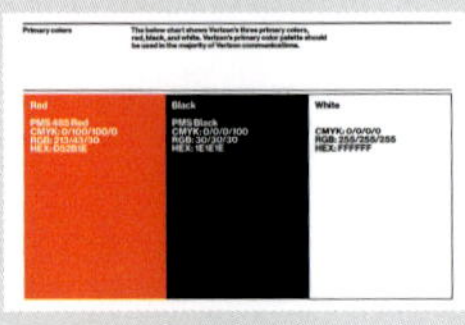
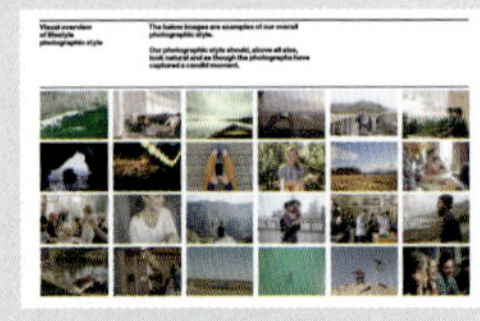
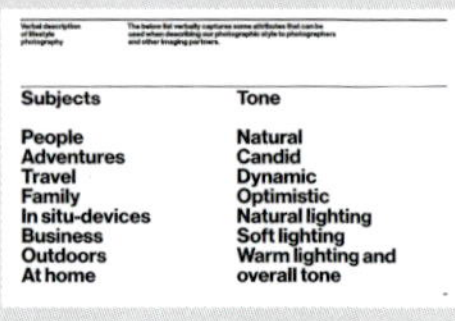
Subjects
People
Adventures
Travel
Family
In situ-devices
Business
Outdoors
At home
Tone
Natural
Candid
Dynamic
Optimistic
Natural lighting
Soft lighting
Warm lighting and overall tone
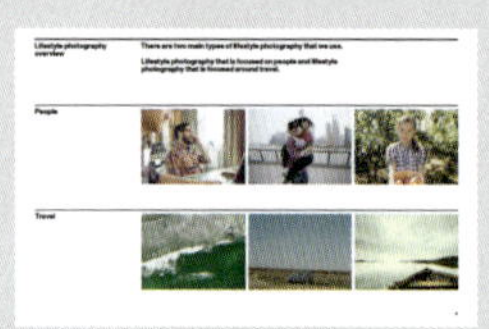
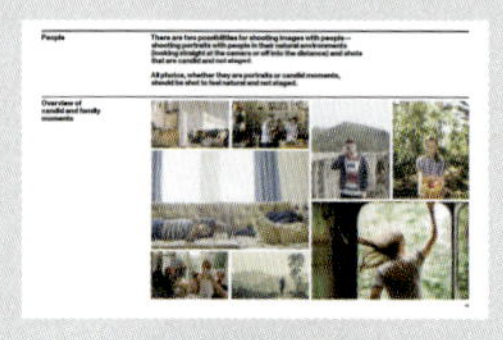
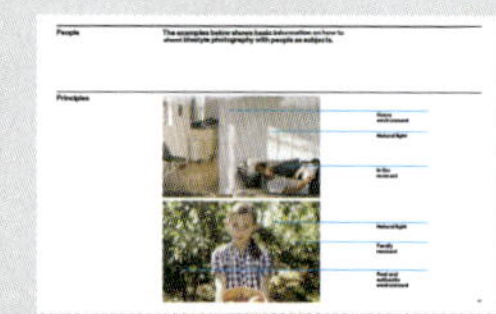
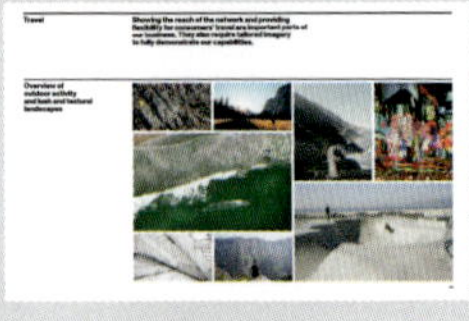
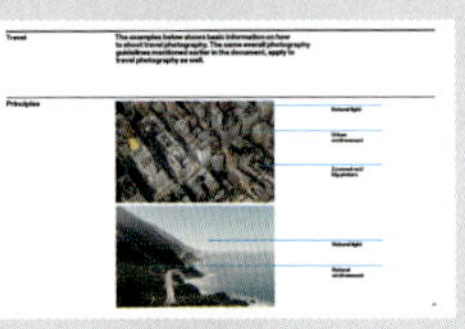
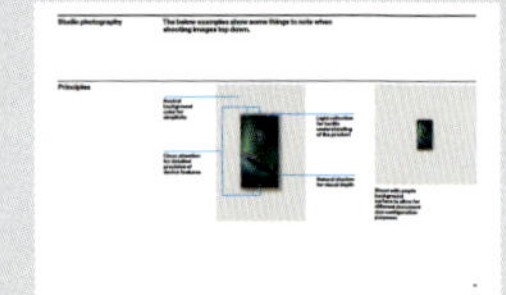
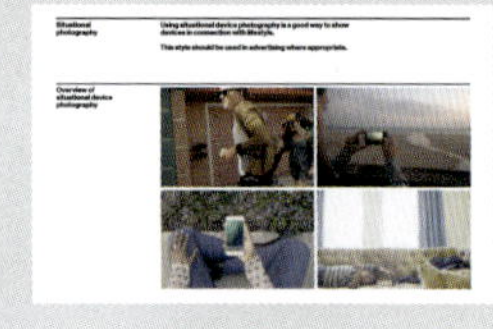
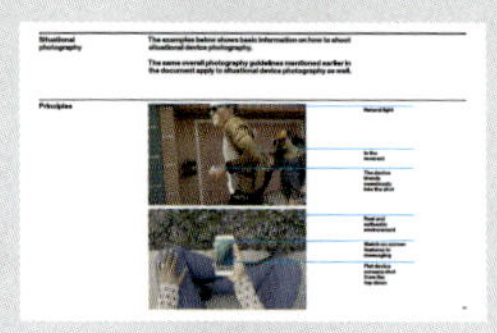
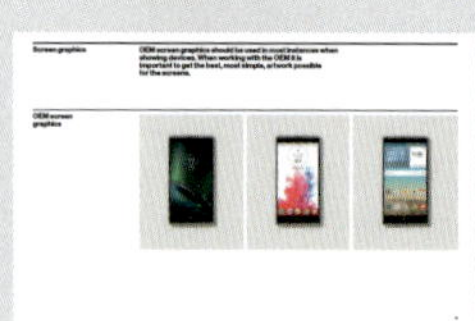
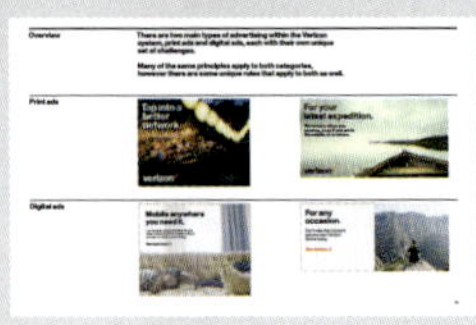
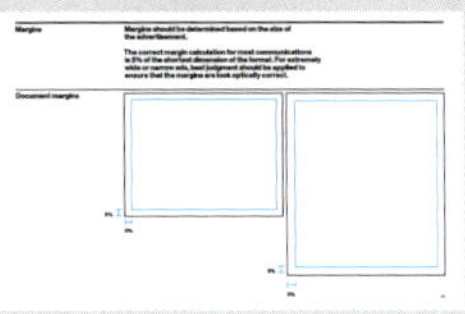
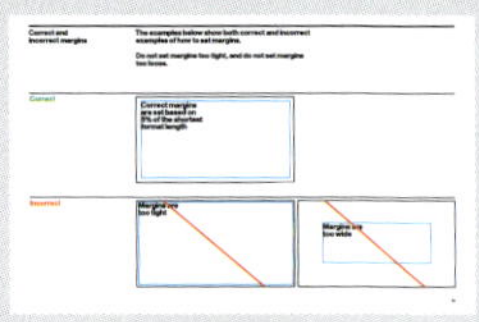
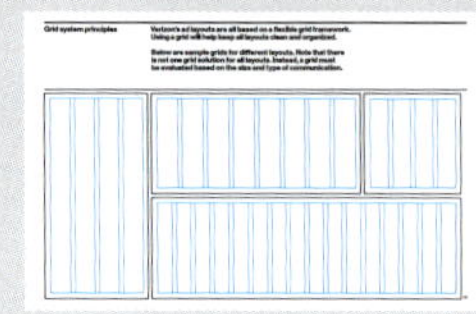
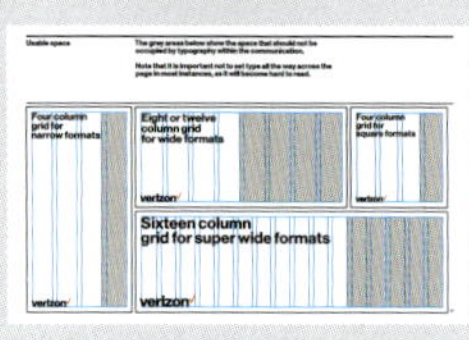
Sixteen column grid for super wide formats
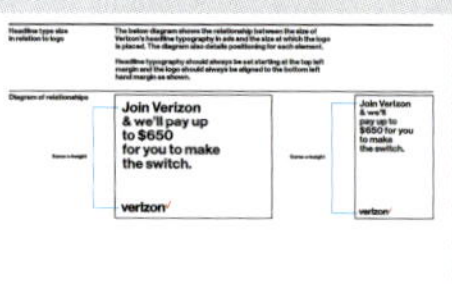
Join Verizon & we'll pay up to $650 for you to make the switch.
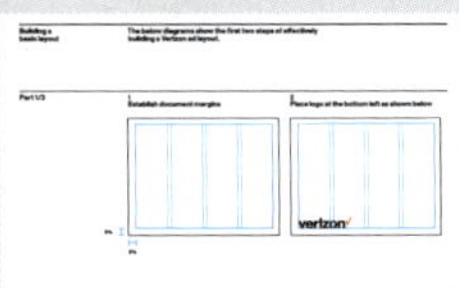
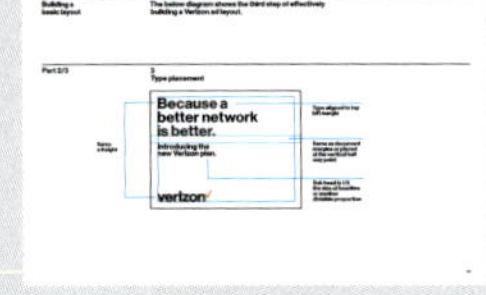
Because a better network is better.
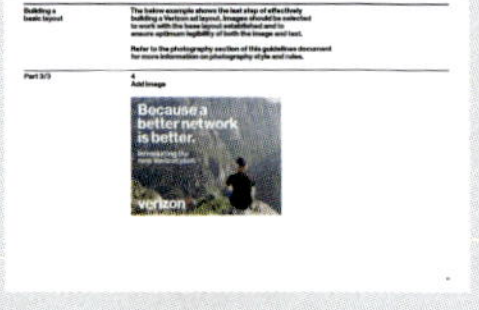
Because a better network is better.
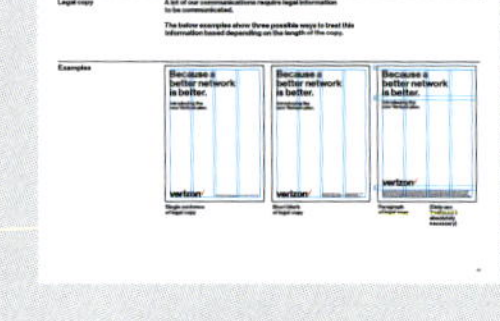
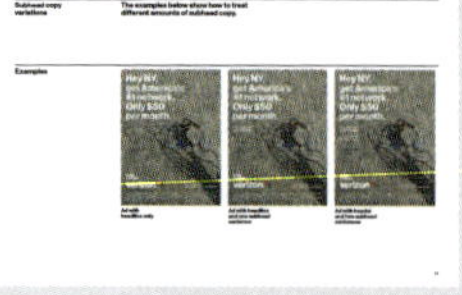
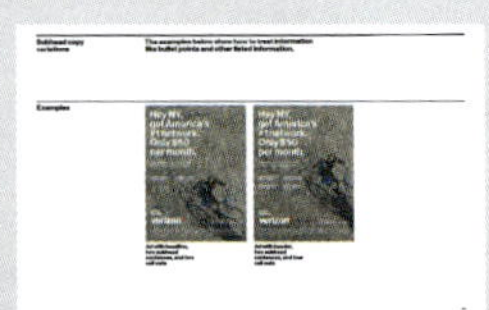
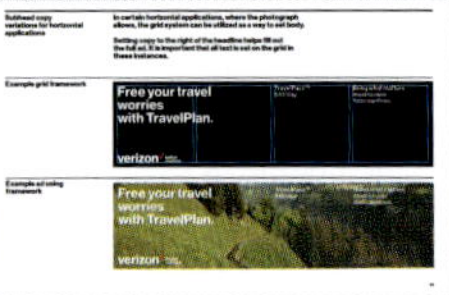
Free your travel worries with TravelPlan.
Free your travel worries with TravelPlan.
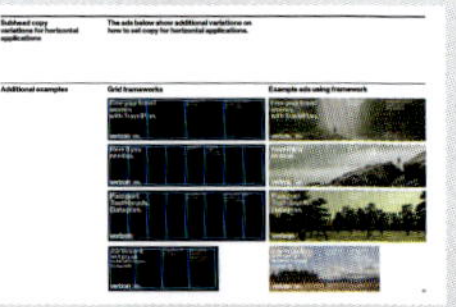
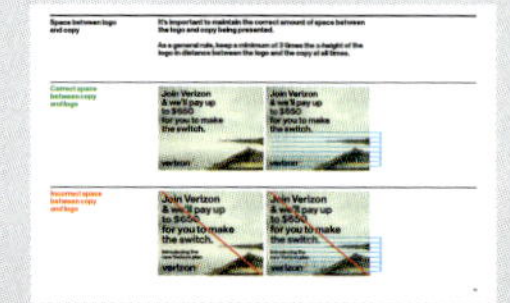
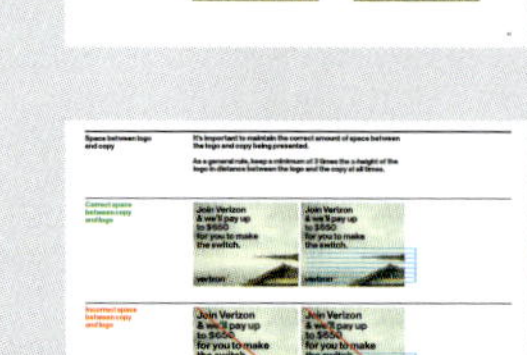
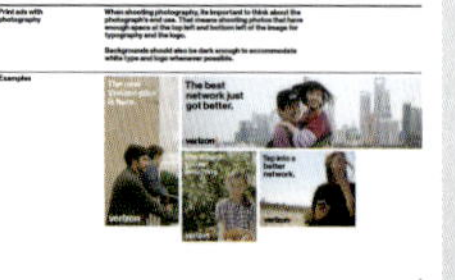

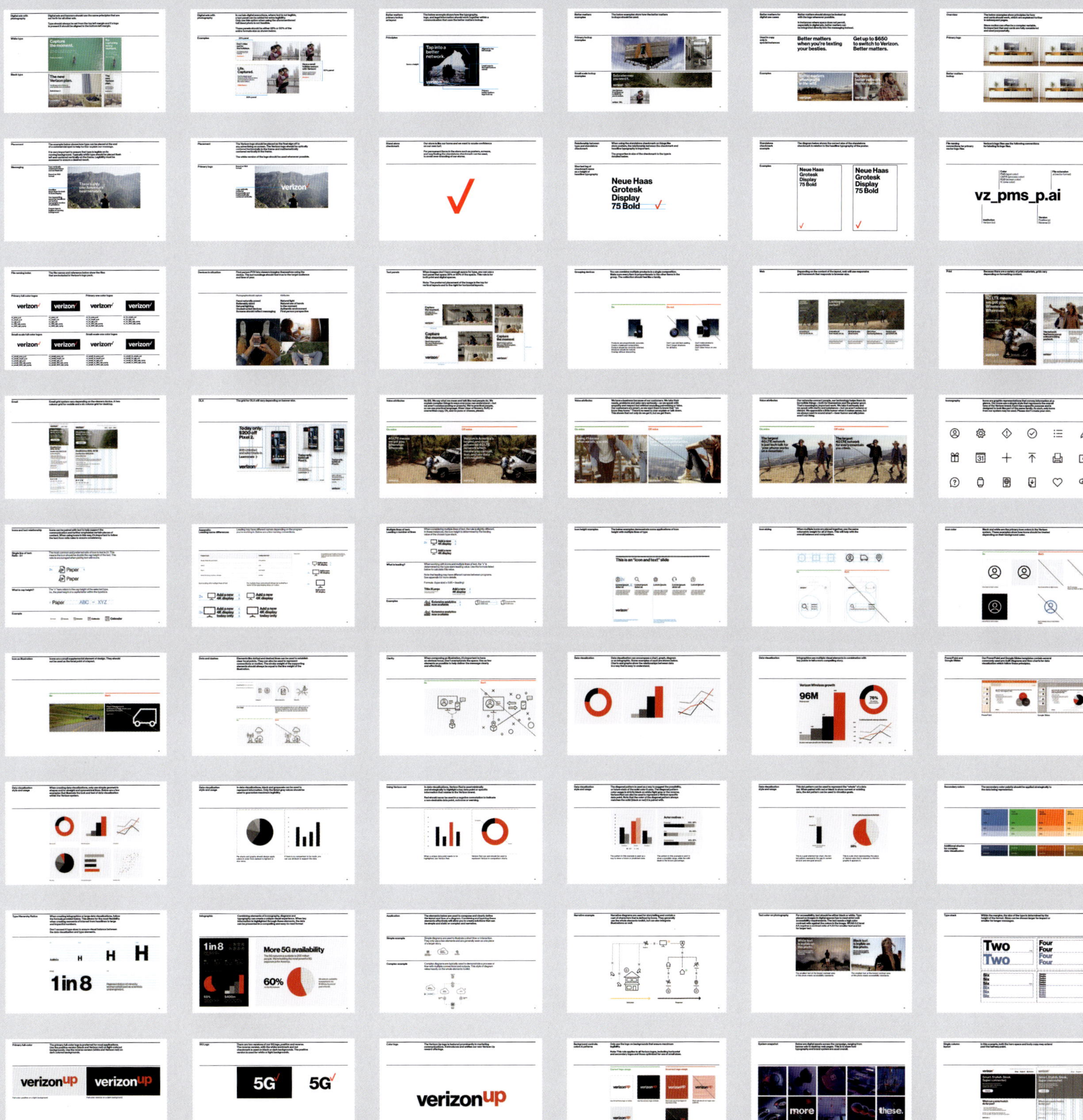

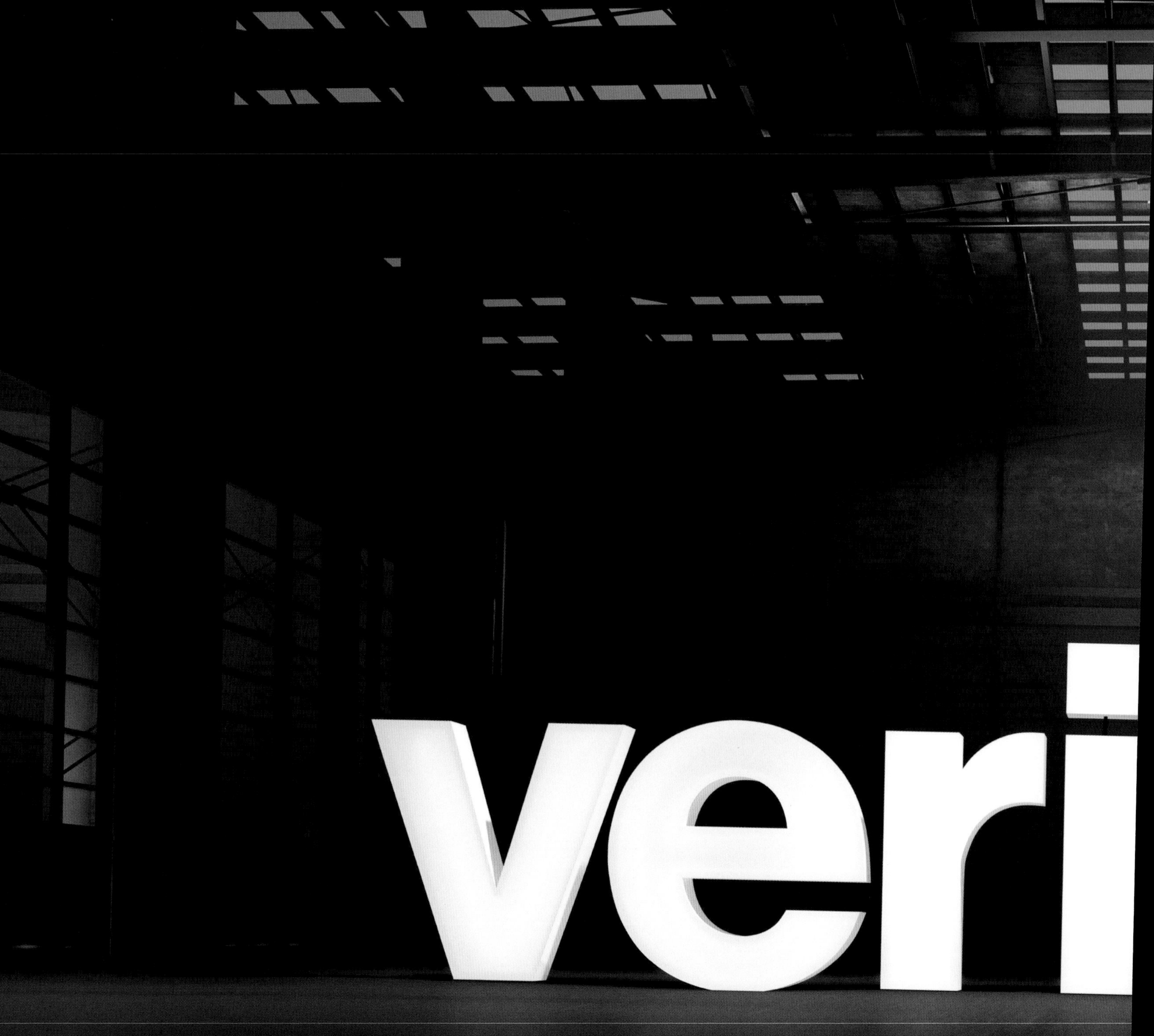

veri

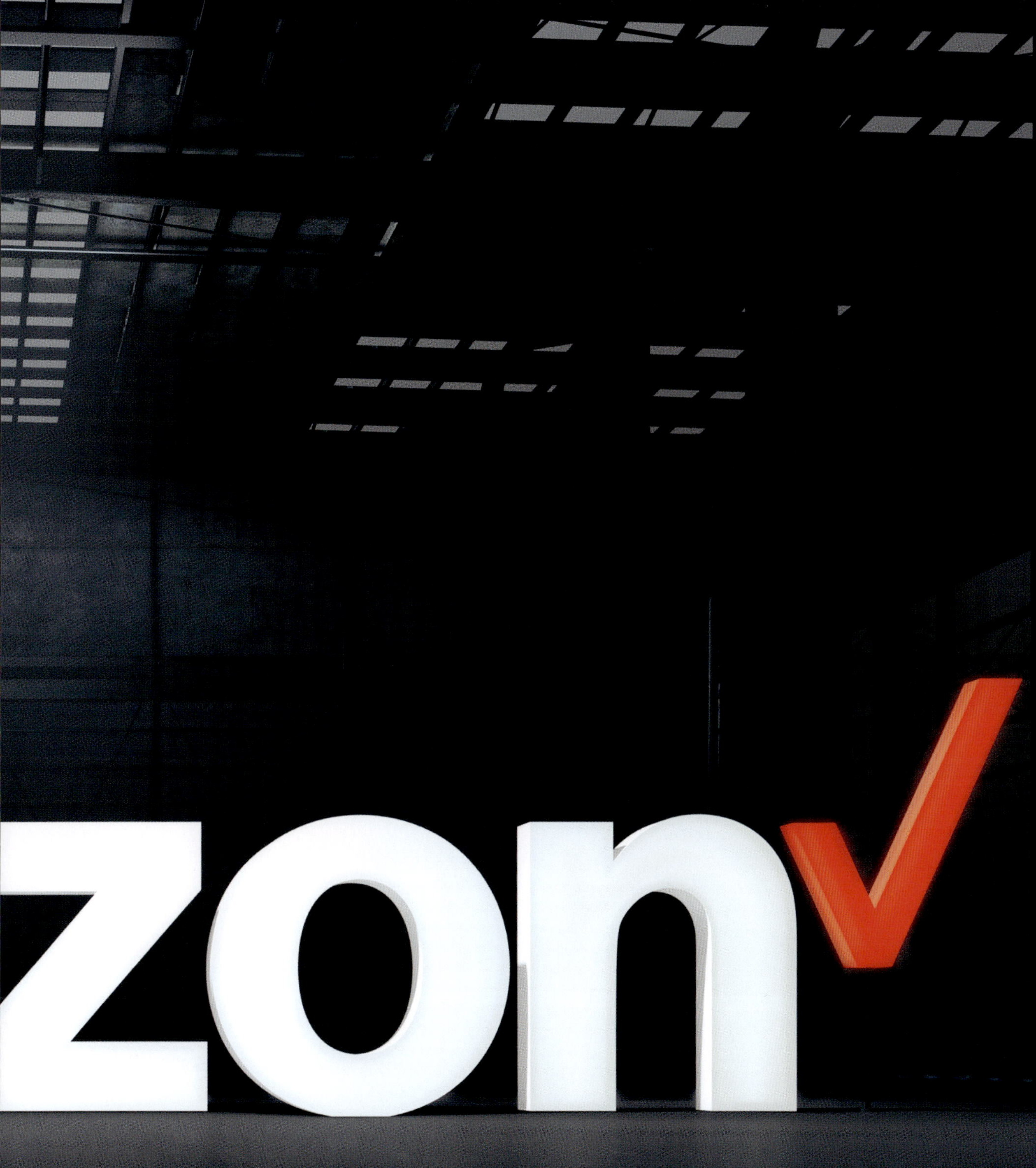
zon

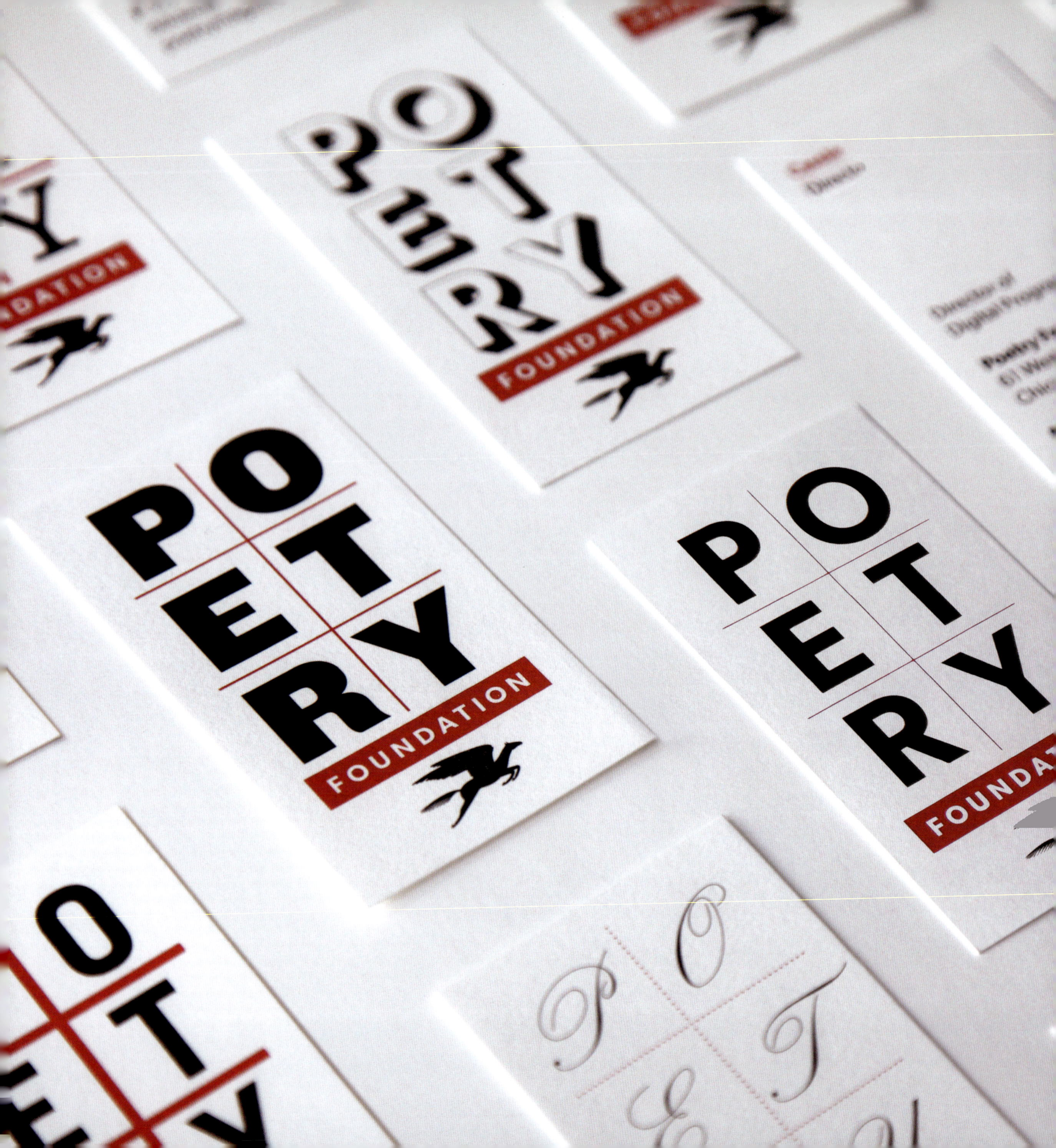
P O
E T
R Y
FOUNDATION

How to write a sonnet

Poetry Foundation

Rather than any of the visual arts, I am more likely to turn to music for inspiration. The finite number of notes on the scale can be arranged in an infinite number of ways, and the result can prepare you to charge into battle or make you remember a lost love. Yet music—Western music's diatonic scale, at least—is shaped by underlying mathematical principles that apply equally to Beethoven and Chuck Berry. These twin challenges of limited means and strict parameters should be familiar to any designer.

My favorite piece of music was written by Johann Sebastian Bach. Published in 1741, the *Goldberg Variations* are thirty variations on a theme, a deceptively simple aria that Bach transforms into an astonishing range of expressions without ever completely diverging from the harmonic structure of the original. This idea of theme and variations is familiar to everyone. Even if you don't care for Bach, you've probably heard *The Star-Spangled Banner* rendered by both Jimi Hendrix and Whitney Houston. Same song, completely different performances. R&B legend Wilson Pickett once said his philosophy was "You harmonize; then you customize," describing the need to respect the practical requirements of a song form and the challenge to express a unique point of view.

The idea of theme and variations is fundamental to graphic design. The pages of a book can demonstrate this idea: an underlying grid provides the structure for layouts that can surprise with every turn of the page. The same is true for poetry. Poems as simple as limericks and as sophisticated as sonnets are governed by structural rules that are at once non-negotiable and open to endless interpretation.

I was thinking of themes and variations when we were asked to create a new identity for the Poetry Foundation and their magazine, now in its second century of publication. Typography is fundamental to poetry, and the medium has inspired radical experiments for centuries. We started by arranging the six-letter word "poetry" in a two-by-three letter configuration. Then we sought every possible variation of this theme: formal and informal, conventional and radical, bold and delicate. The result is a public face for a storied institution that is both timeless and endlessly changing, just like poetry itself.

Opposite
The graphic identity of the Poetry Foundation is derived from a tradition of typographic experimentation as old as the medium itself. Laitsz Ho created the system and applied it to the Foundation's communications materials, including business cards that were customized for each staff member.

Next spread
Rather than designing a logo for its flagship magazine, we created a framework for invention. The two-by-three typographic arrangement functions as logo, mission statement, and cover illustration, and changes with every issue. I asked designers Elizabeth Goodspeed and Mariah Xu to create five years' worth of covers in one sitting to prove not only that it could be done, but that one could have fun doing it.

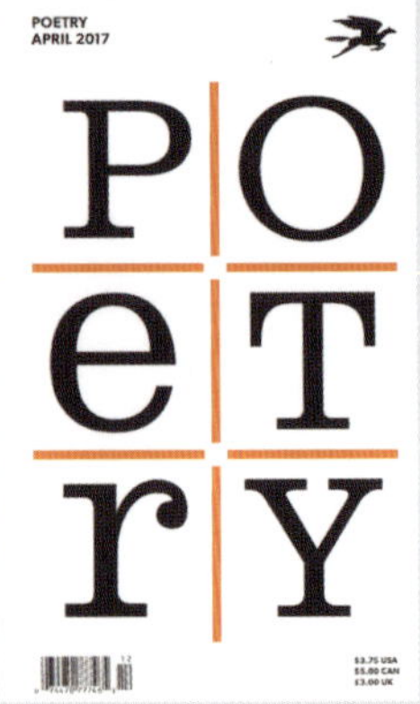
POETRY
APRIL 2017
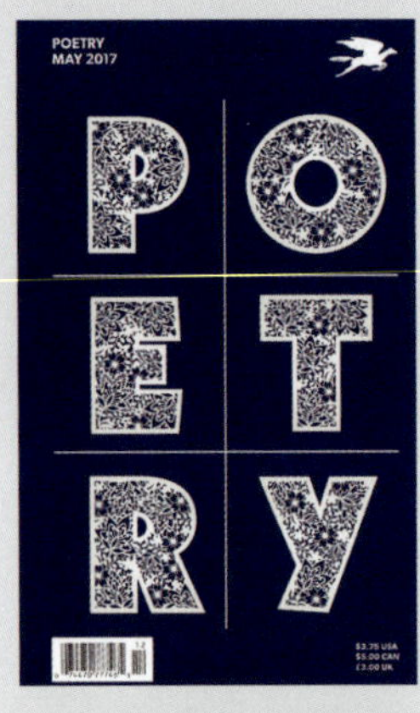
POETRY
MAY 2017
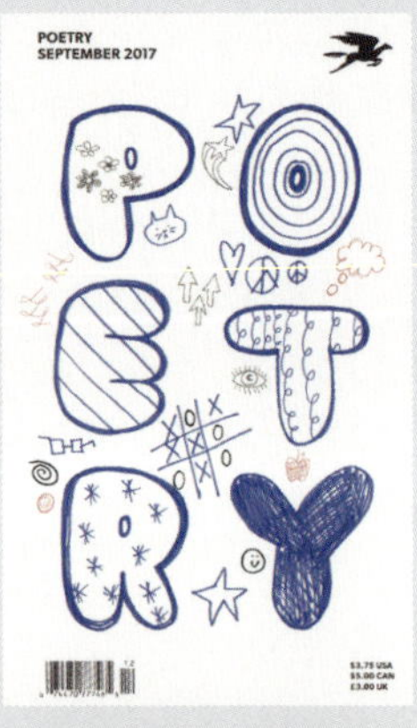
POETRY
SEPTEMBER 2017
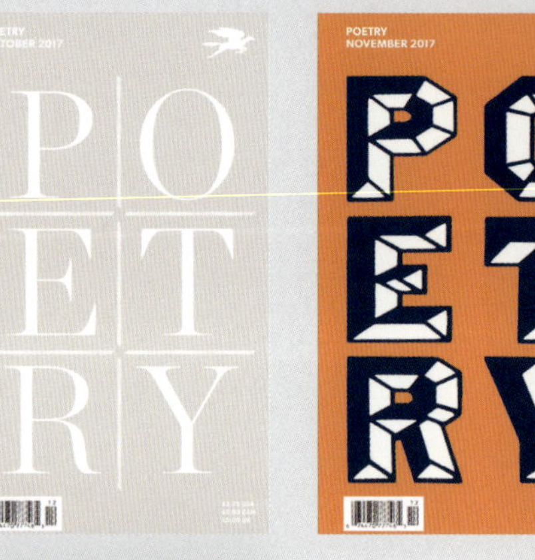
POETRY
OCTOBER 2017
POETRY
NOVEMBER 2017
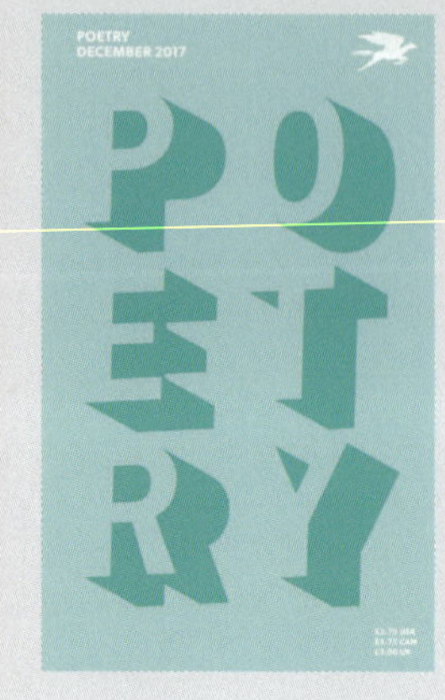
POETRY
DECEMBER 2017
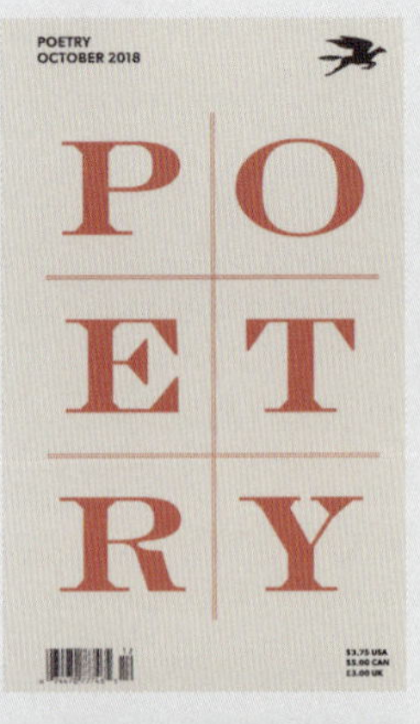
POETRY
OCTOBER 2018
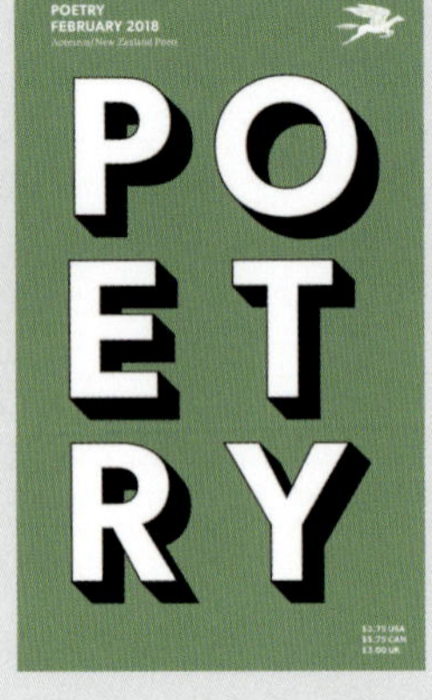
POETRY
FEBRUARY 2018
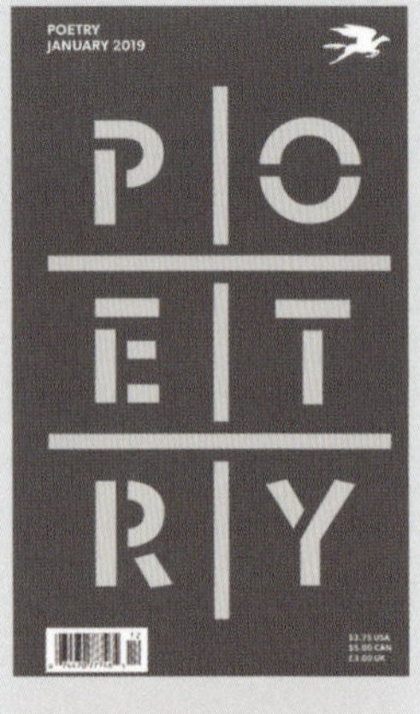
POETRY
JANUARY 2019
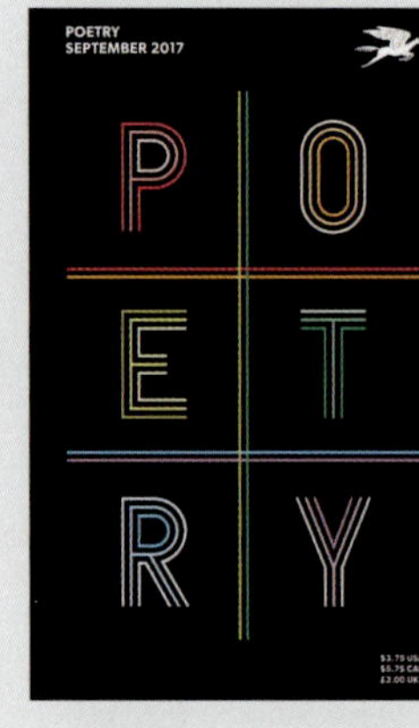
POETRY
SEPTEMBER 2017
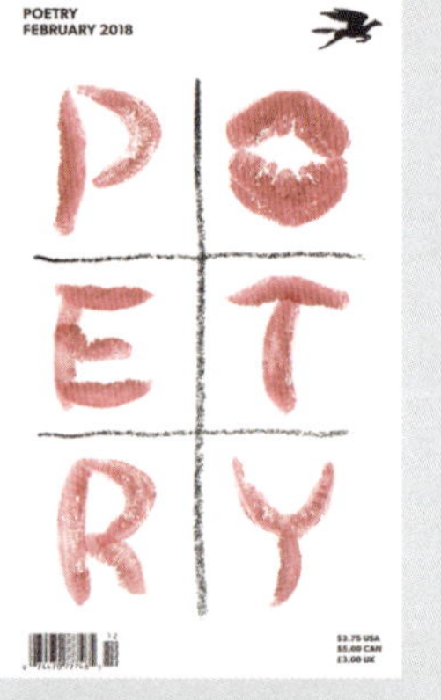
POETRY
FEBRUARY 2018
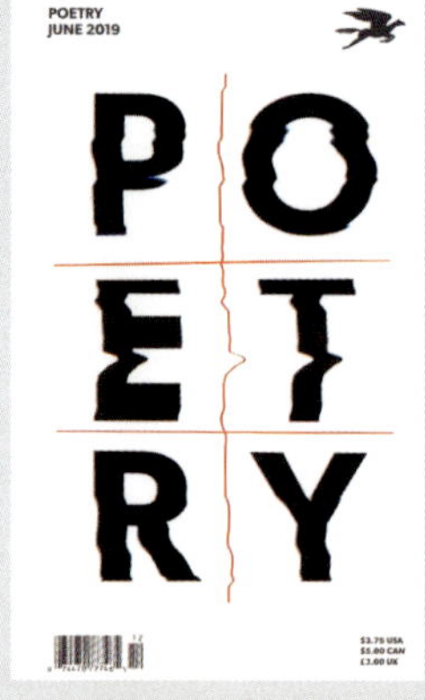
POETRY
JUNE 2019
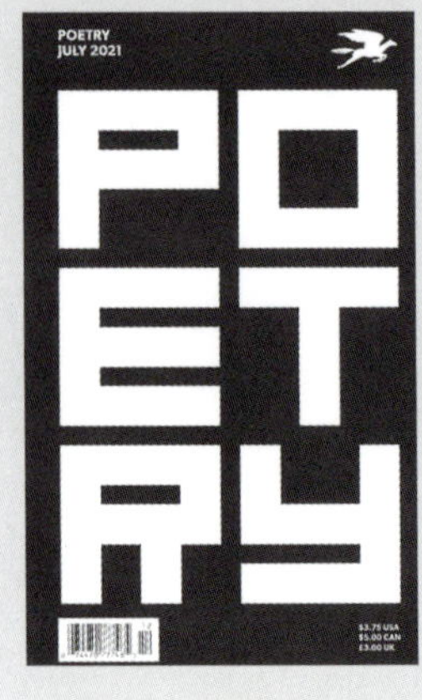
POETRY
JULY 2021

POETRY
OCTOBER 2017
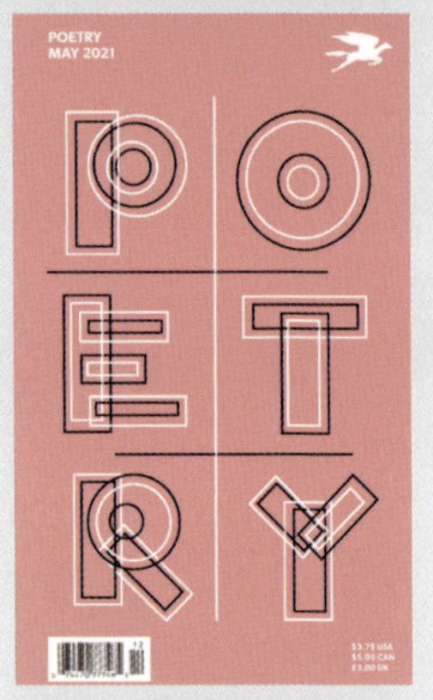
POETRY
MAY 2021
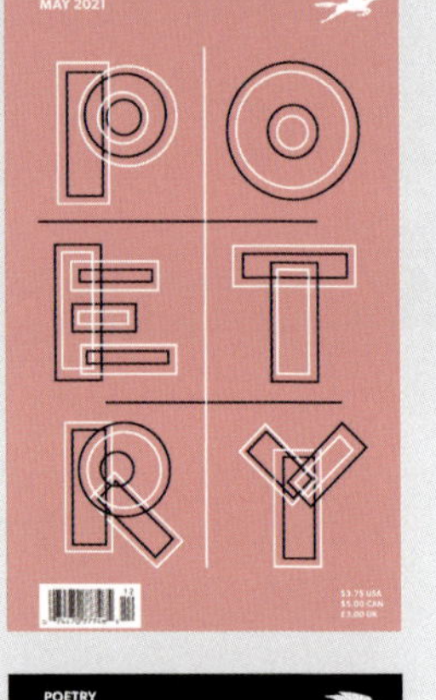
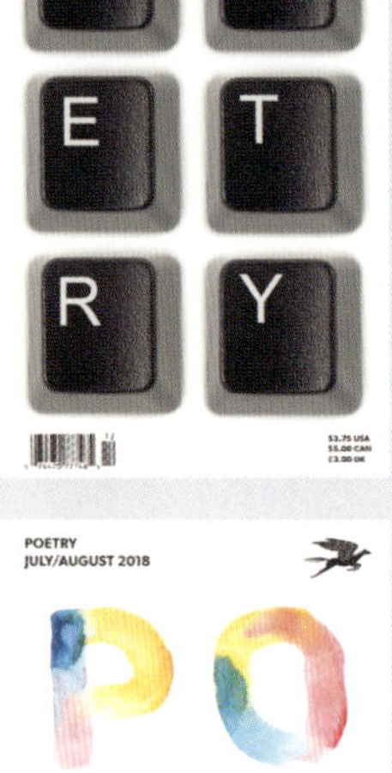
POETRY
APRIL 2021
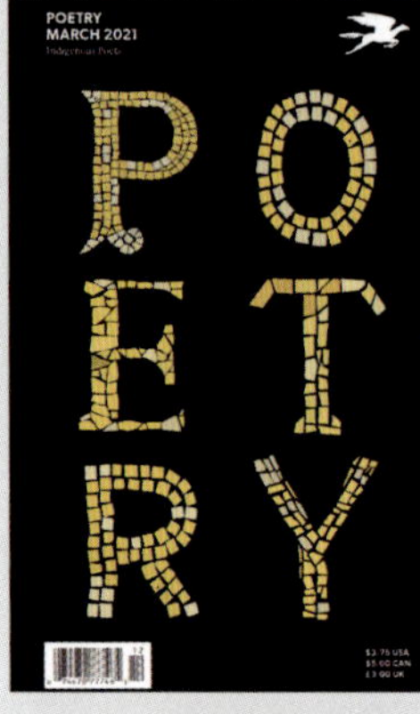
POETRY
MARCH 2021
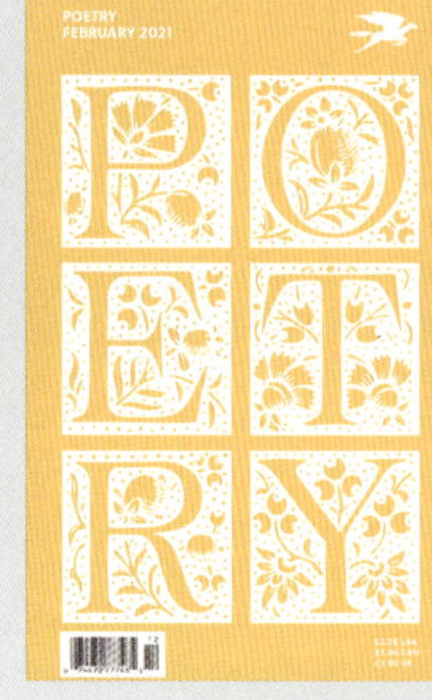
POETRY
FEBRUARY 2021
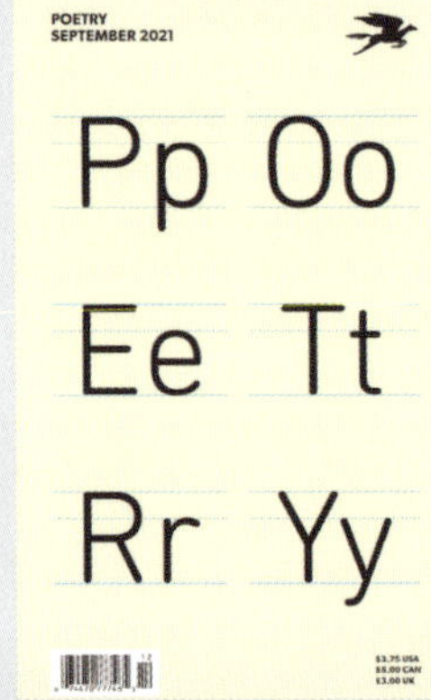
POETRY
SEPTEMBER 2021
Pp Oo
Ee Tt
Rr Yy
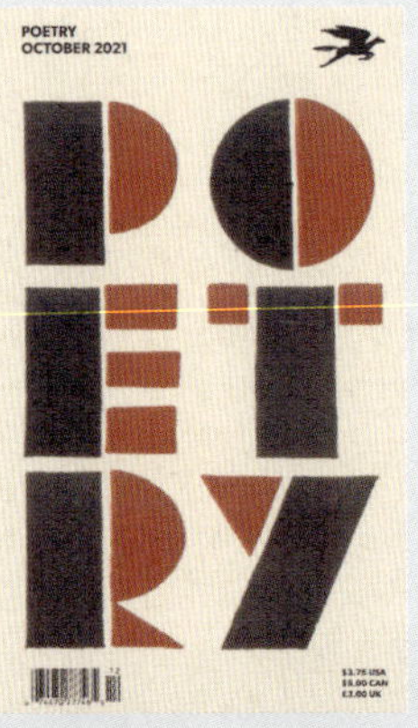
POETRY
OCTOBER 2021
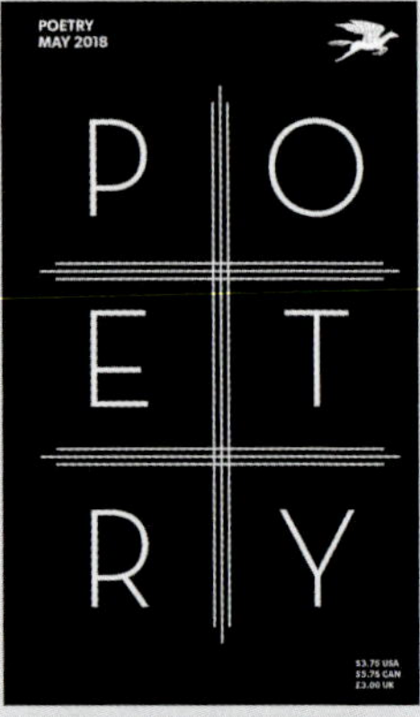
POETRY
MAY 2018
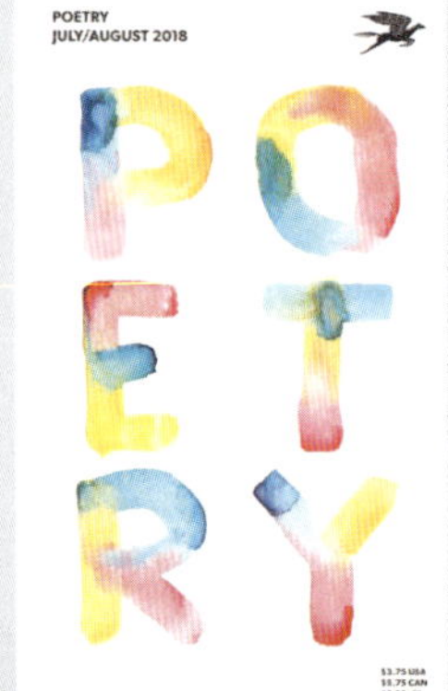
POETRY
JULY/AUGUST 2018
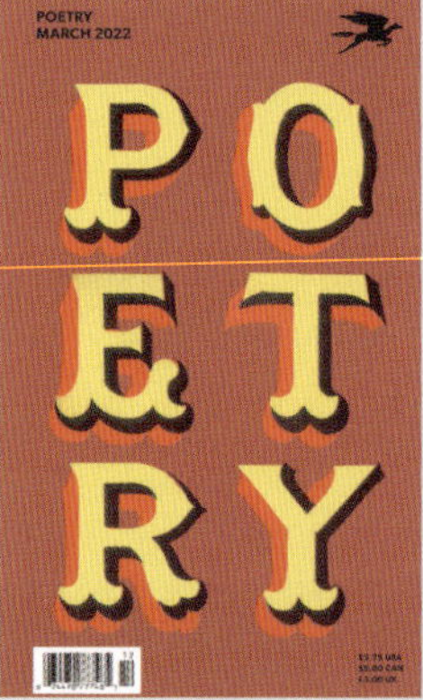
POETRY
MARCH 2022
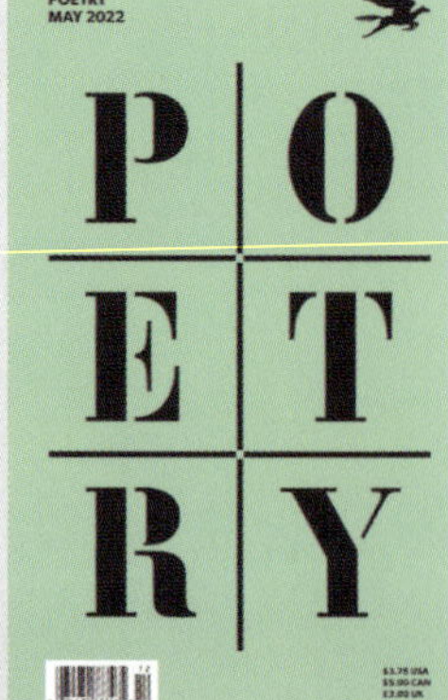
POETRY
MAY 2022

POETRY
FEBRUARY 2019

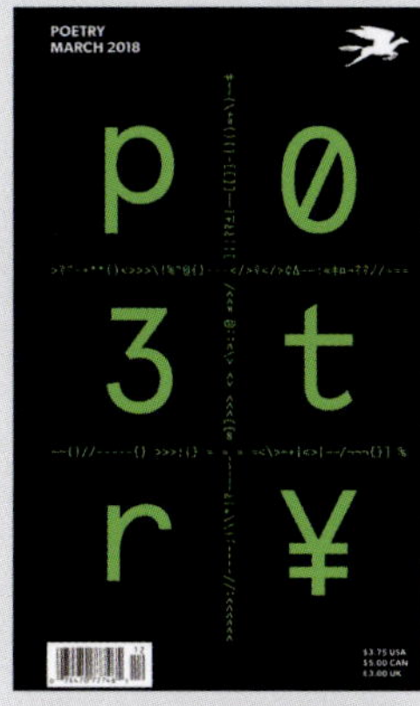
POETRY
MARCH 2018

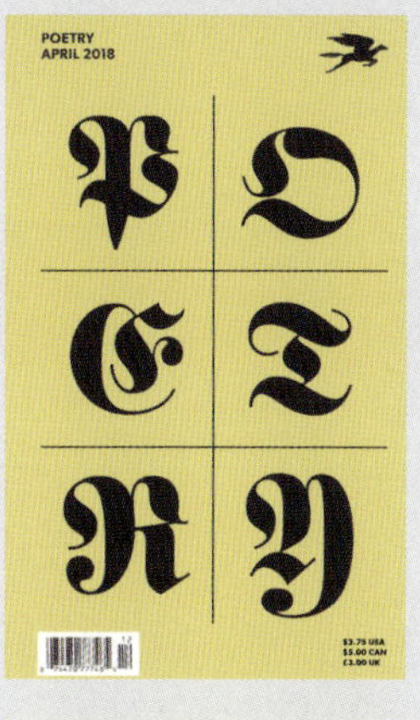
POETRY
APRIL 2018

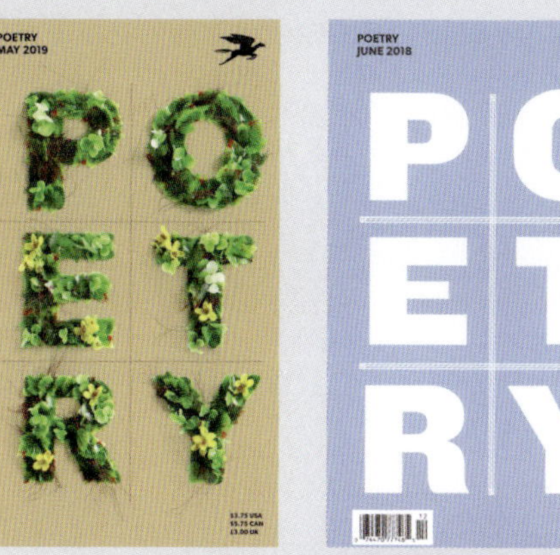
POETRY
MAY 2019
POETRY
JUNE 2018

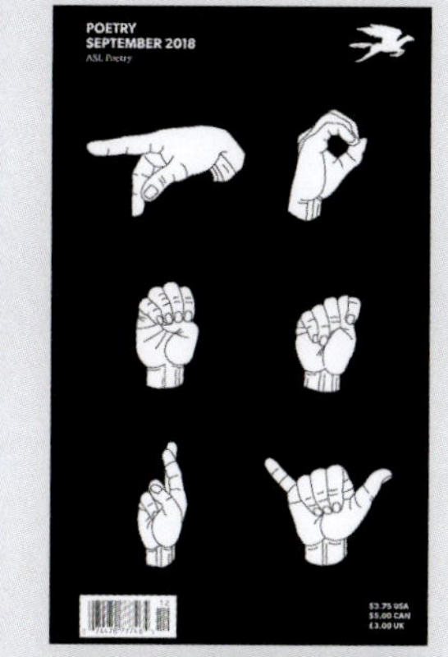
POETRY
SEPTEMBER 2018

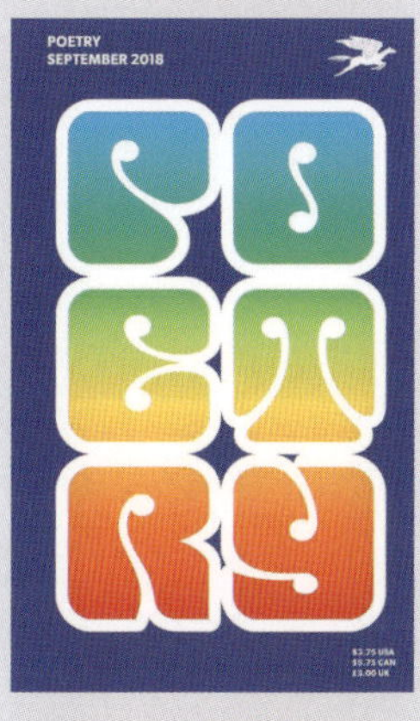
POETRY
SEPTEMBER 2018

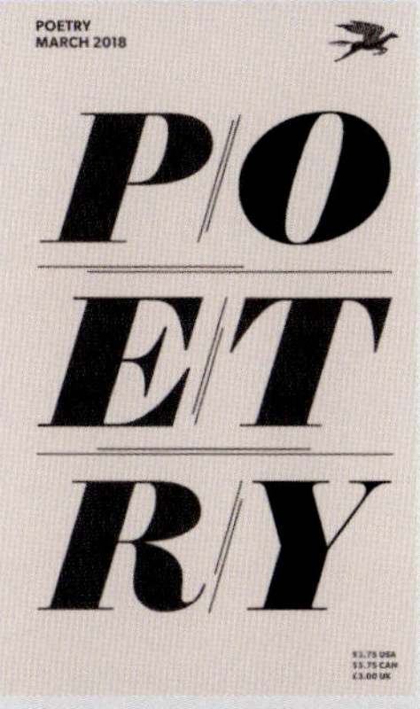
POETRY
MARCH 2018

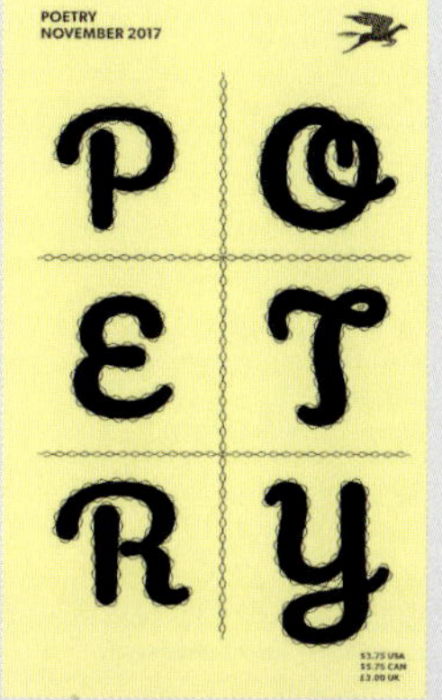
POETRY
NOVEMBER 2017

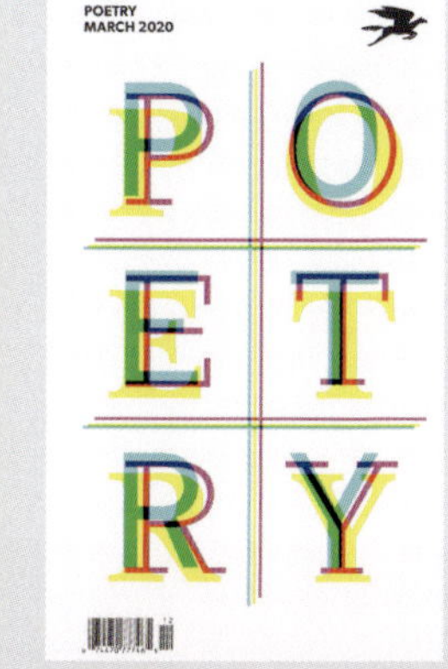
POETRY
MARCH 2020

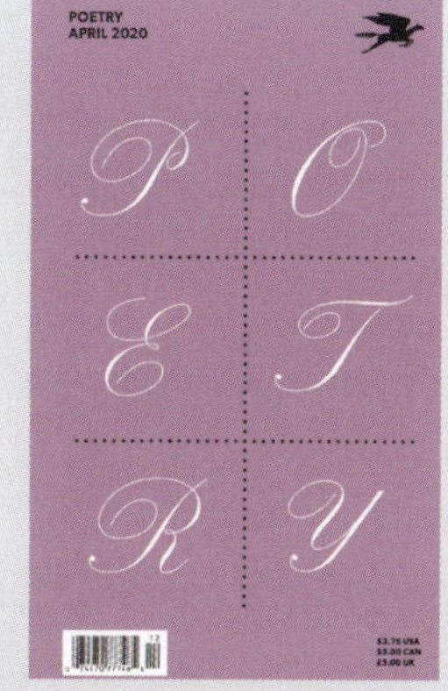
POETRY
APRIL 2020

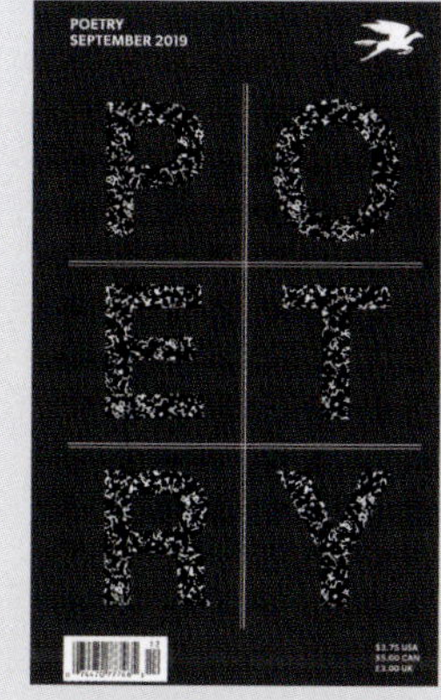
POETRY
SEPTEMBER 2019

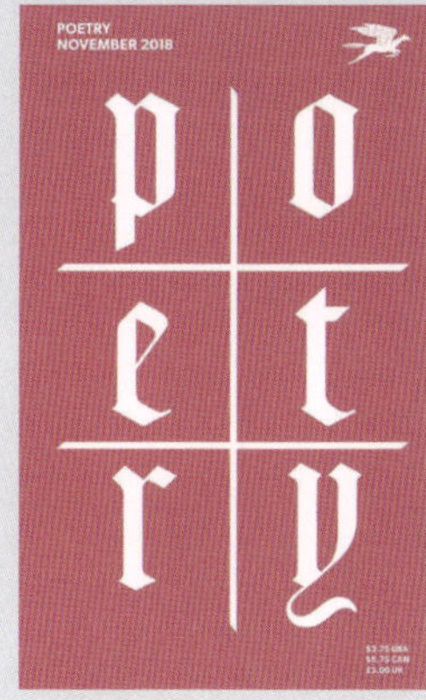
POETRY
NOVEMBER 2018

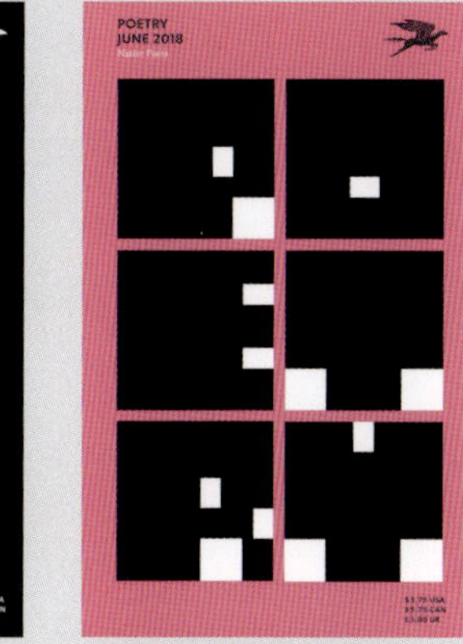
POETRY
JUNE 2018

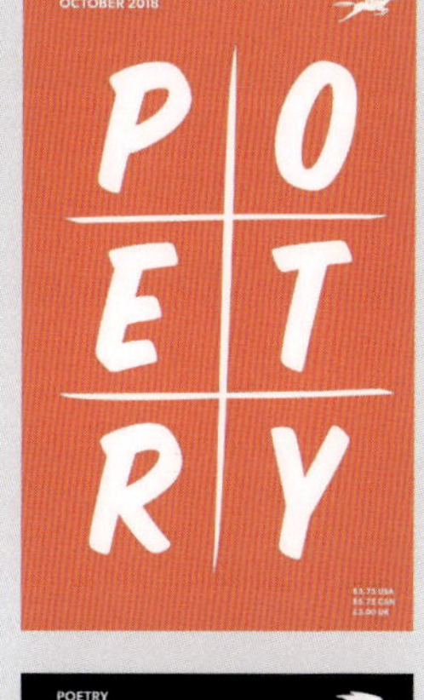
POETRY
OCTOBER 2018

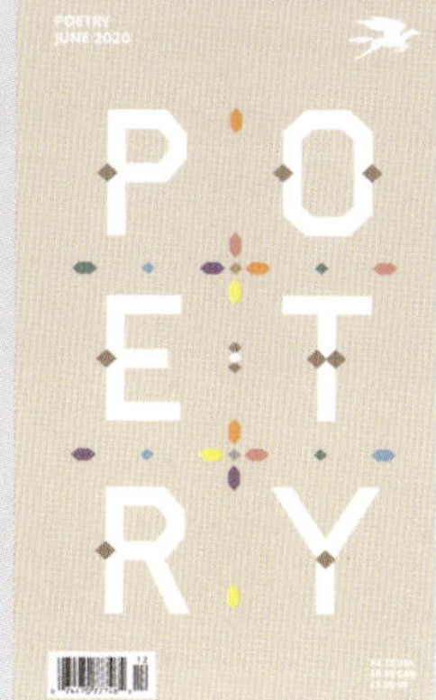
POETRY
JUNE 2020

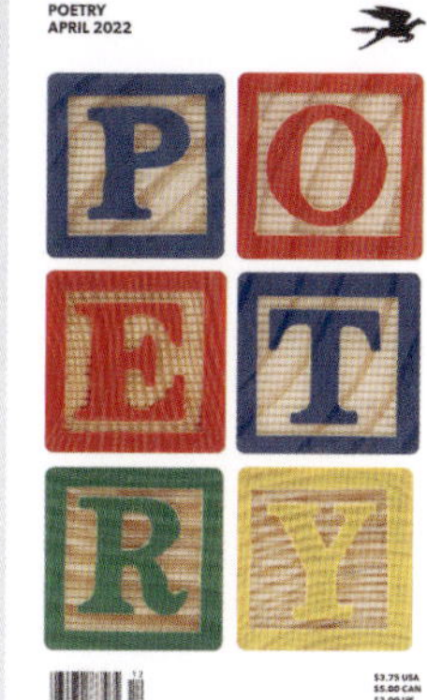
POETRY
APRIL 2022

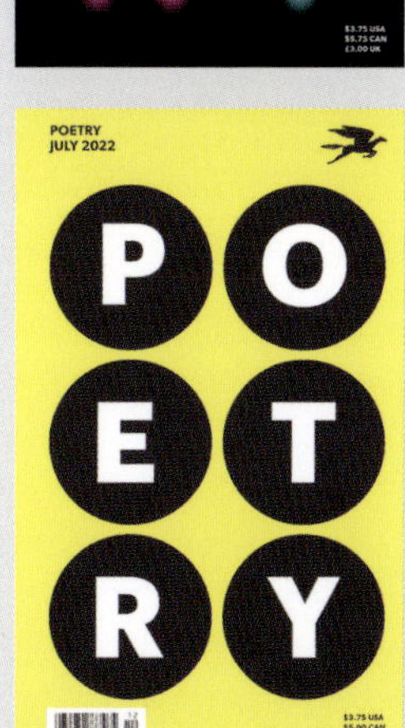
POETRY
JULY 2022

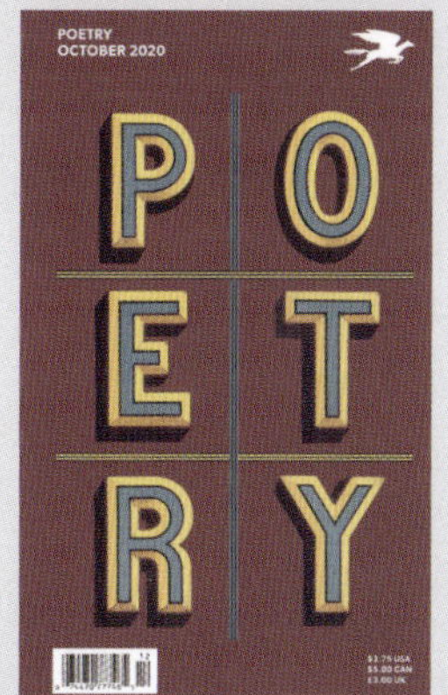
POETRY
OCTOBER 2020

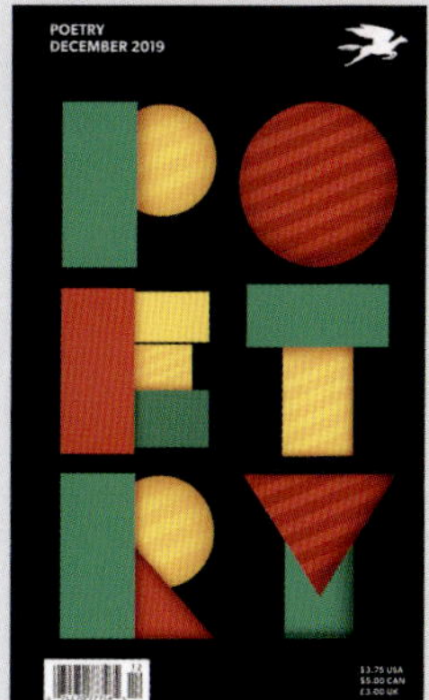
POETRY
DECEMBER 2019

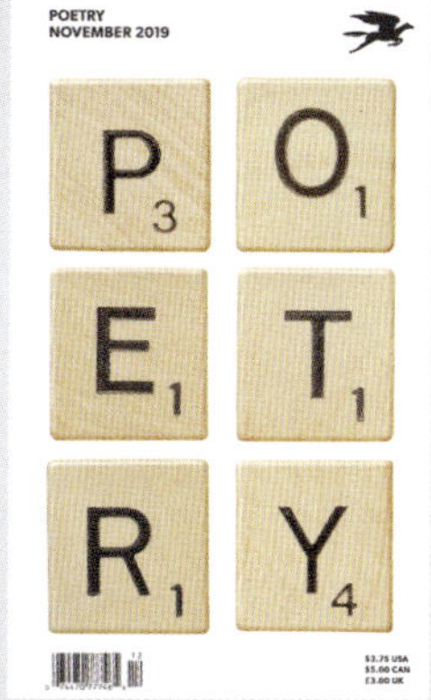
POETRY
NOVEMBER 2019

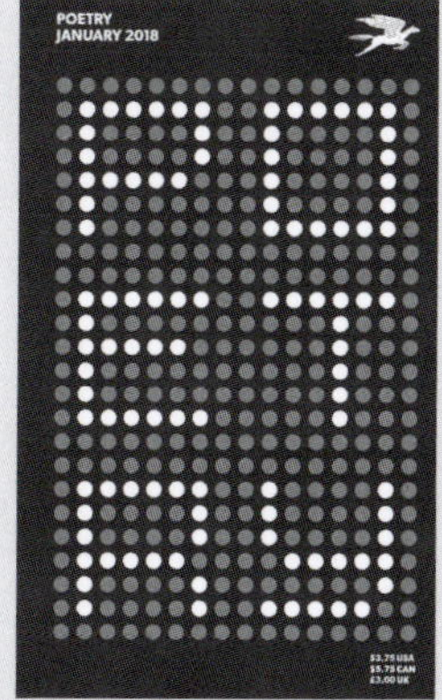
POETRY
JANUARY 2018

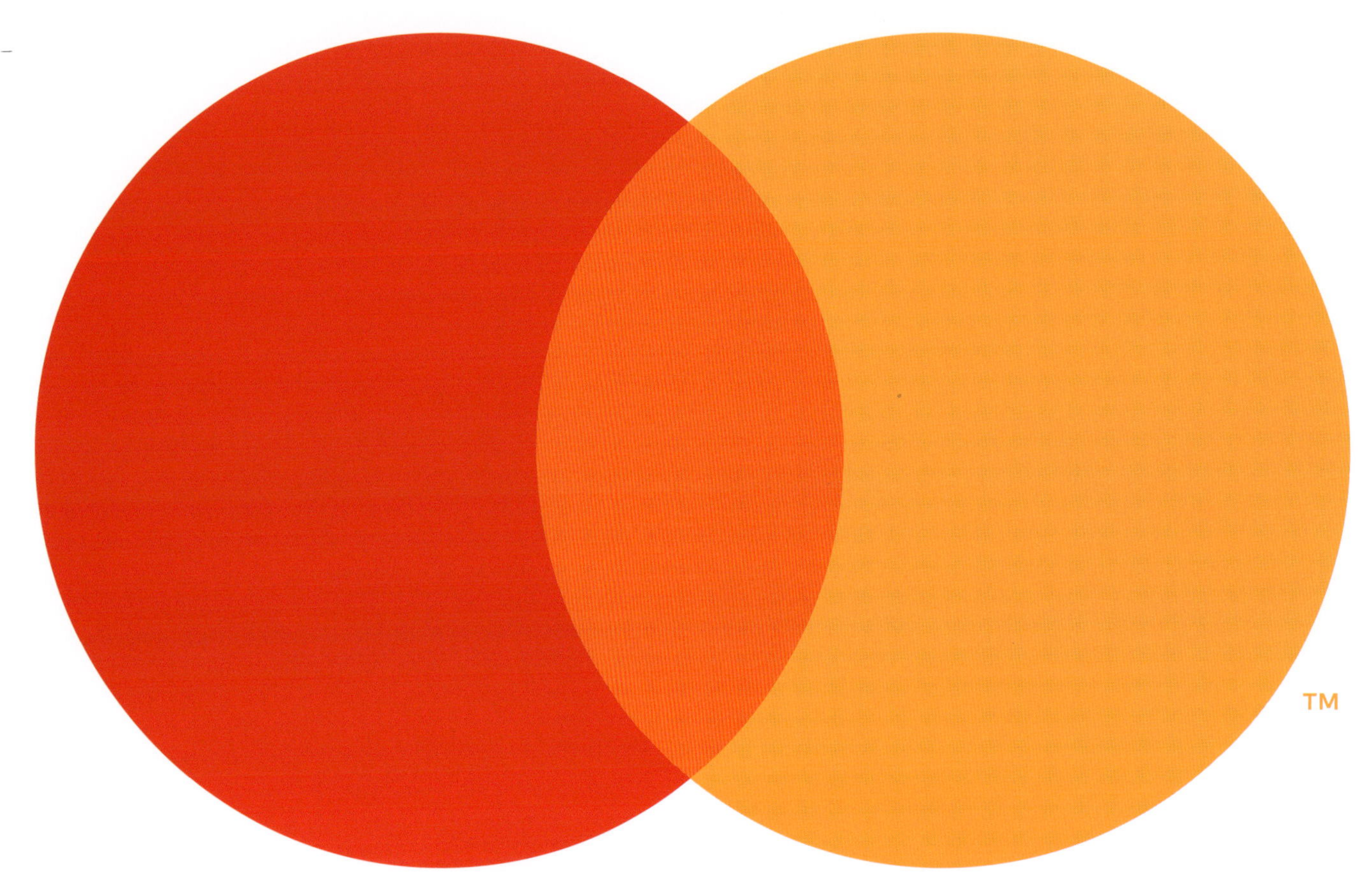
TM

How to keep it simple

Mastercard

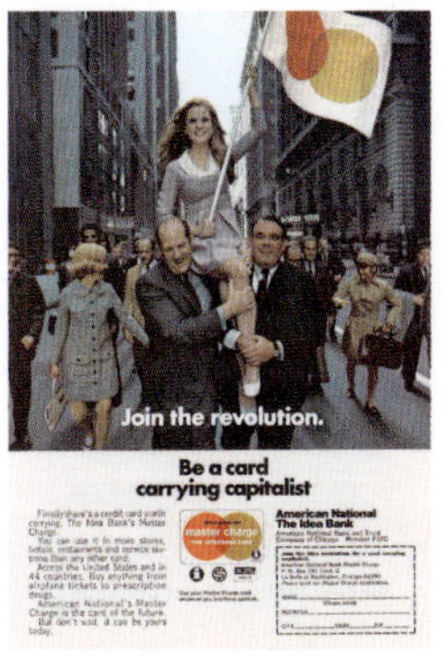

Opposite
Two circles, three colors, one brand.

Above
Styles changed over Mastercard's history, but its commitment to a basic visual language was reliably constant.

I am mystified by the power of simplicity. Why do certain shapes and colors provoke a strong emotional response? Nobel Prize–winning neuroscientist Eric Kandel has observed that abstract images activate our brains in a fundamentally different way than figurative images do. In his 2016 book, *Reductionism in Art and Brain Science*, Kandel writes that abstraction "requires the beholder to substitute primary process thinking—the language of the unconscious, which easily forms connections between different objects and ideas and has no need of time or space—for secondary process thinking—the language of the conscious ego, which is logical and requires time and space coordinates." Figurative images communicate immediately, but the connection we make with abstraction is more profound. I was thinking of that difference when we met with Mastercard.

For over fifty years, Mastercard's symbol had been two overlapping circles, one red, one deep yellow. No one I spoke to seemed to know why. Some thought it was an allusion to the two hemispheres on a world map. I preferred to think it had to do with mutual interests of two parties coming together. Over the years, the company had transformed itself from a pioneer in providing credit in the form of plastic cards to a global financial entity serving over 2.3 billion consumers, operating in more than 200 countries and 150 currencies, and processing 70,000 transactions a minute. Their business was digital, and the brand was as likely to appear on a mobile screen as a merchant's front door. To reflect this transformation, we were asked to redesign the Mastercard symbol with a completely blank slate.

As we began our design exploration, one fact in our research stood out. More than four out of five people could identify the company's red and yellow interlocking circles even without the Mastercard name—an astonishing level of recognition too precious to squander. The conclusion was inescapable: Mastercard, thanks to half a century of relentless investment, had come to own two primary colors and the world's most fundamental geometric shape. The solution was not to change the symbol, but to reduce it to its essence. We built an entire design system out of carefully calibrated colors and circular geometry, from layouts to icons to typography. And today it is the symbol alone—utterly abstract, undeniably powerful—that represents Mastercard around the world.

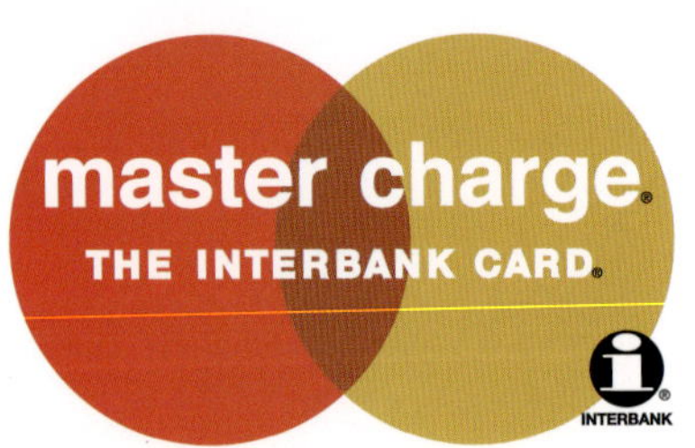

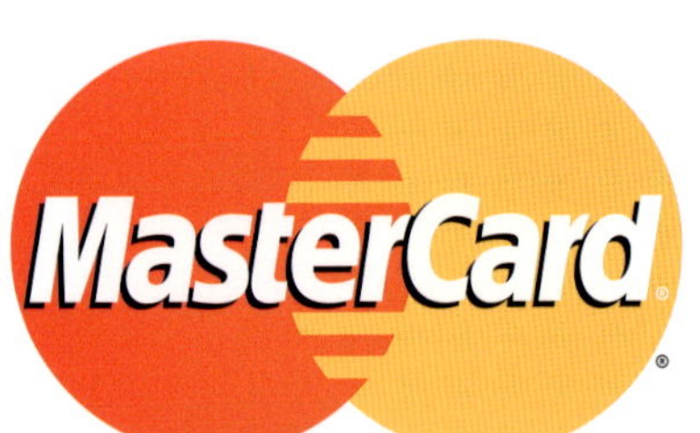

Left
Here are Mastercard logos from 1968 and 1996. As the company responded to ever-more complex business challenges, its logo had grown more and more complicated too, incorporating stripes, shadows, and colors.

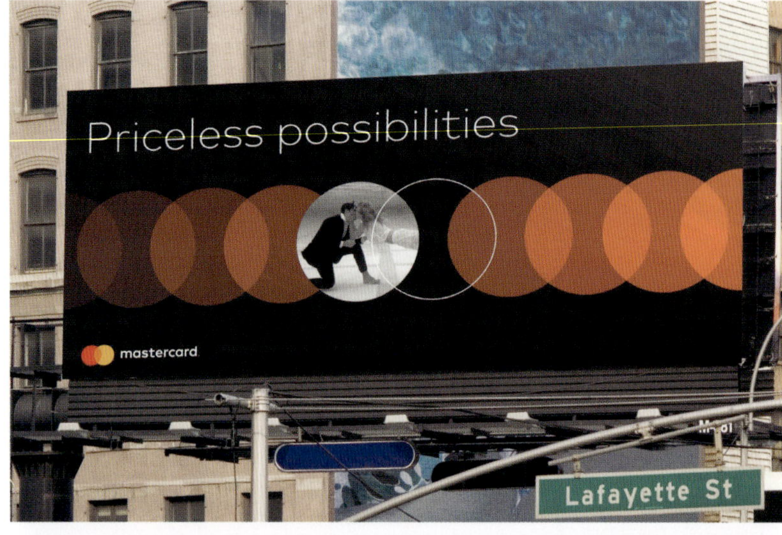

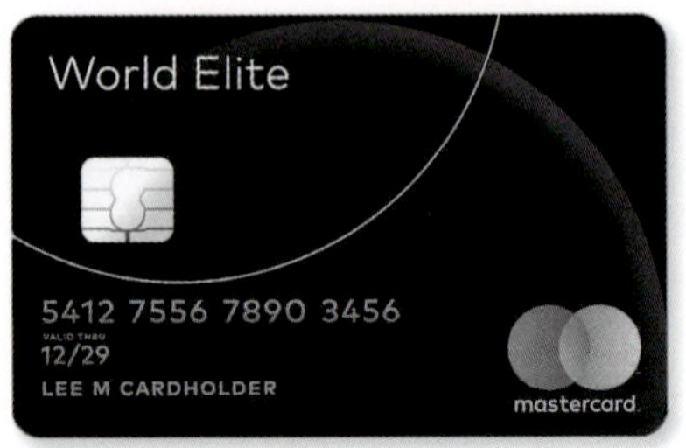

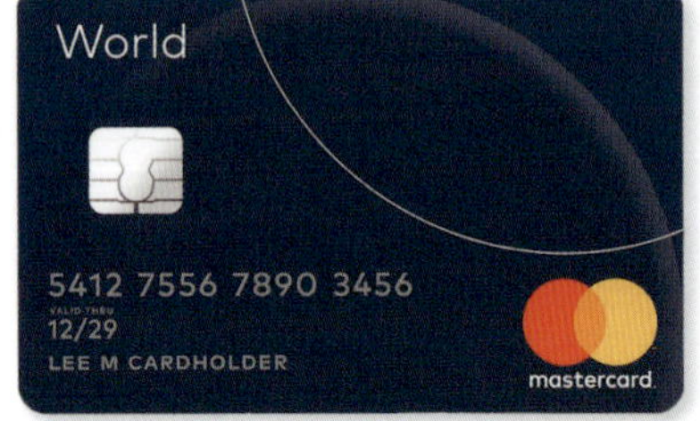

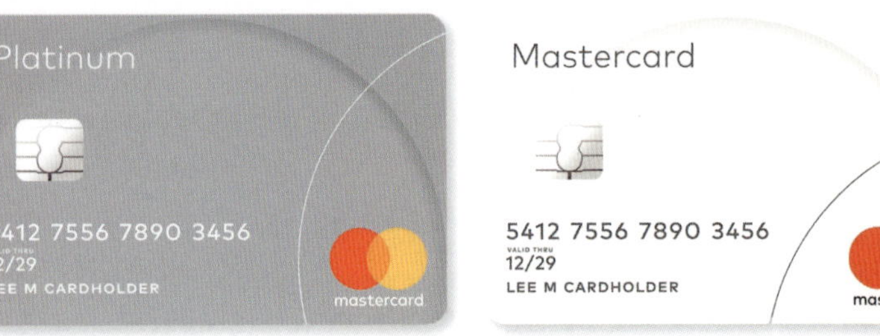

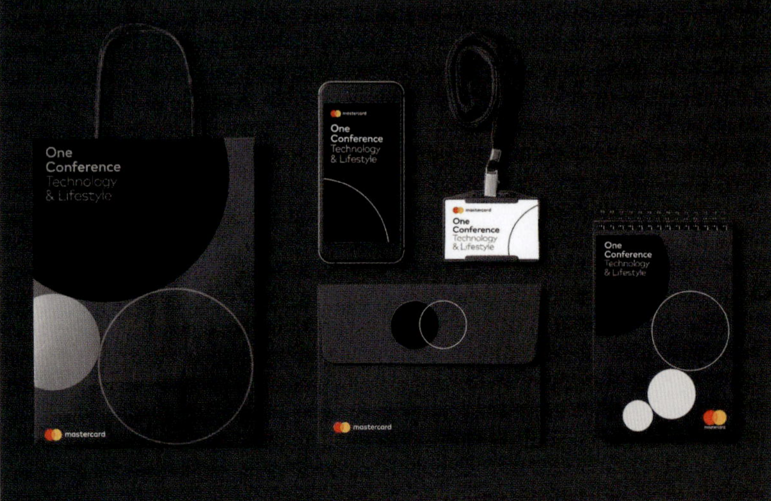

Above
In developing the new symbol, we shifted the overlap of the red and yellow to a brighter orange. Hamish Smyth led the exploration of hundreds of different variations of the three colors as we searched for the perfect combination.

Right top, middle, and bottom
The simplicity of the new symbol was designed to work at any scale, from mobile devices to billboards.

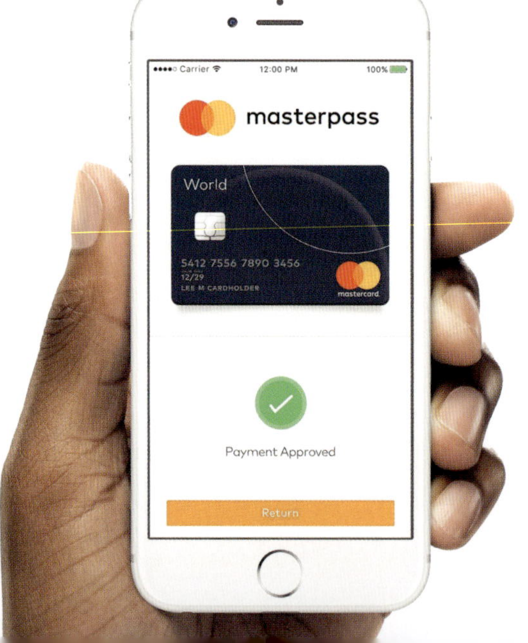

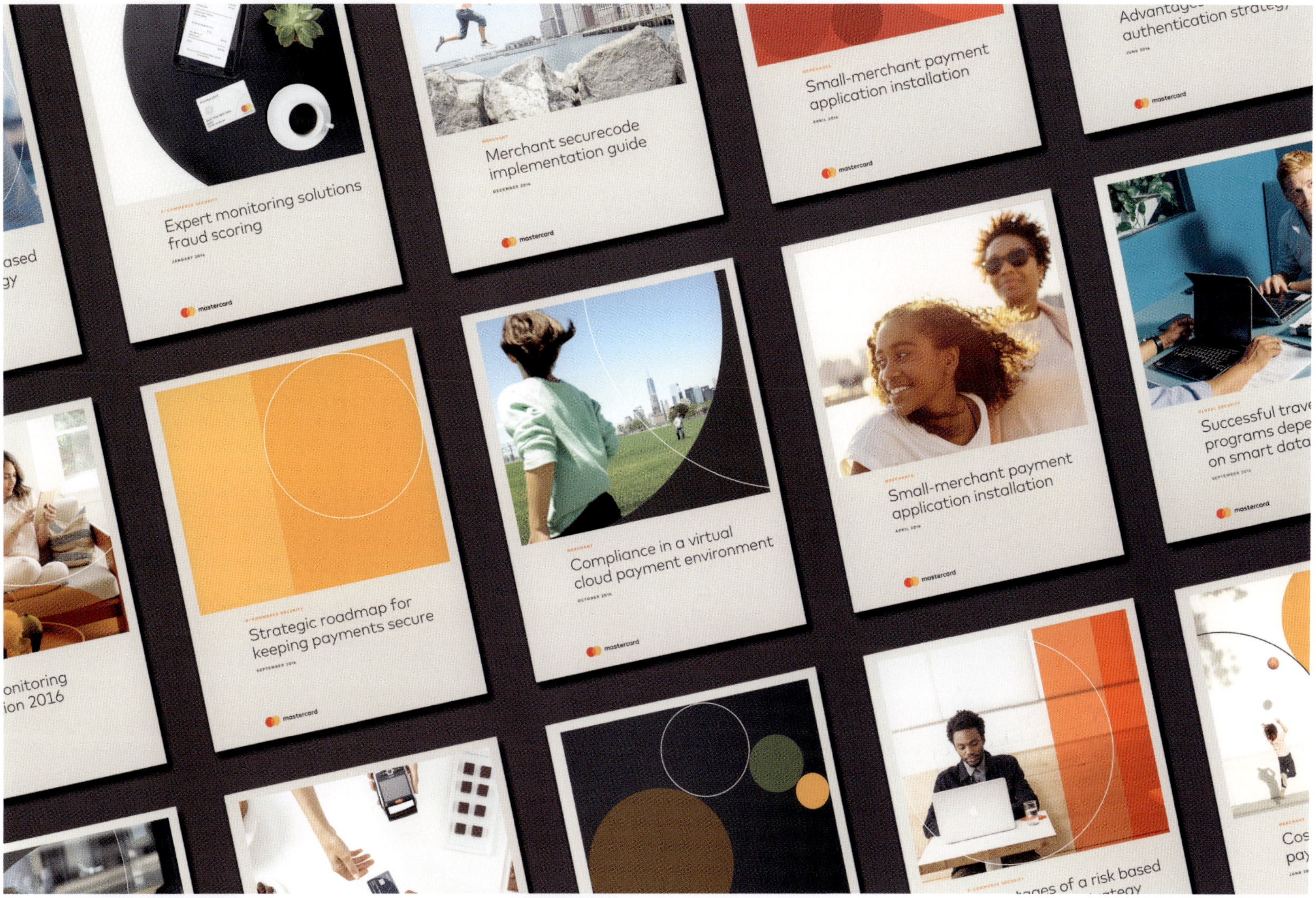

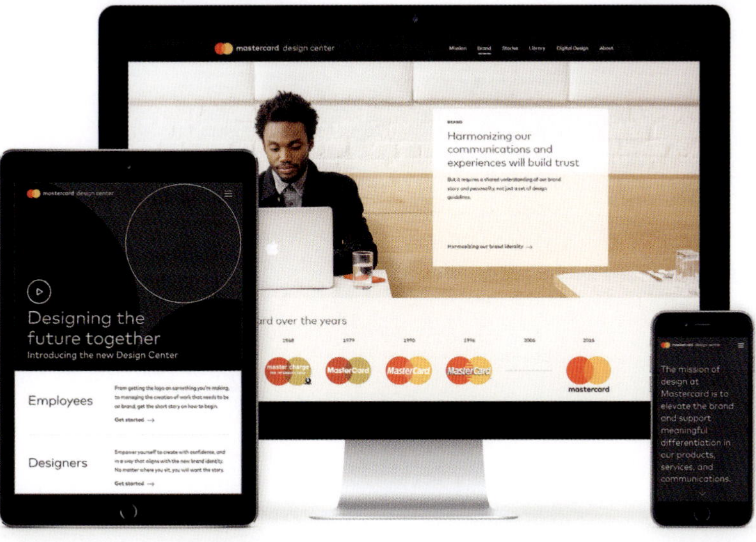

Left
My partner Luke Hayman and designer Andrea Trabucco-Campos led the brand identity's worldwide rollout. Online brand guidelines ensured consistency across Mastercard's network of worldwide agencies.

Above
Inspired by the parametric work of artists like Sol LeWitt, we used the symbol's basic geometry to establish sets of rules that could generate a wide range of flexible layouts. The circular theme was reinforced by Mastercard's brand typeface, FF Mark by Hannes von Döhren and Christoph Koeberlin.

Next spread
Even in crowded visual environments, the minimalist elements of the Mastercard logo stand out.

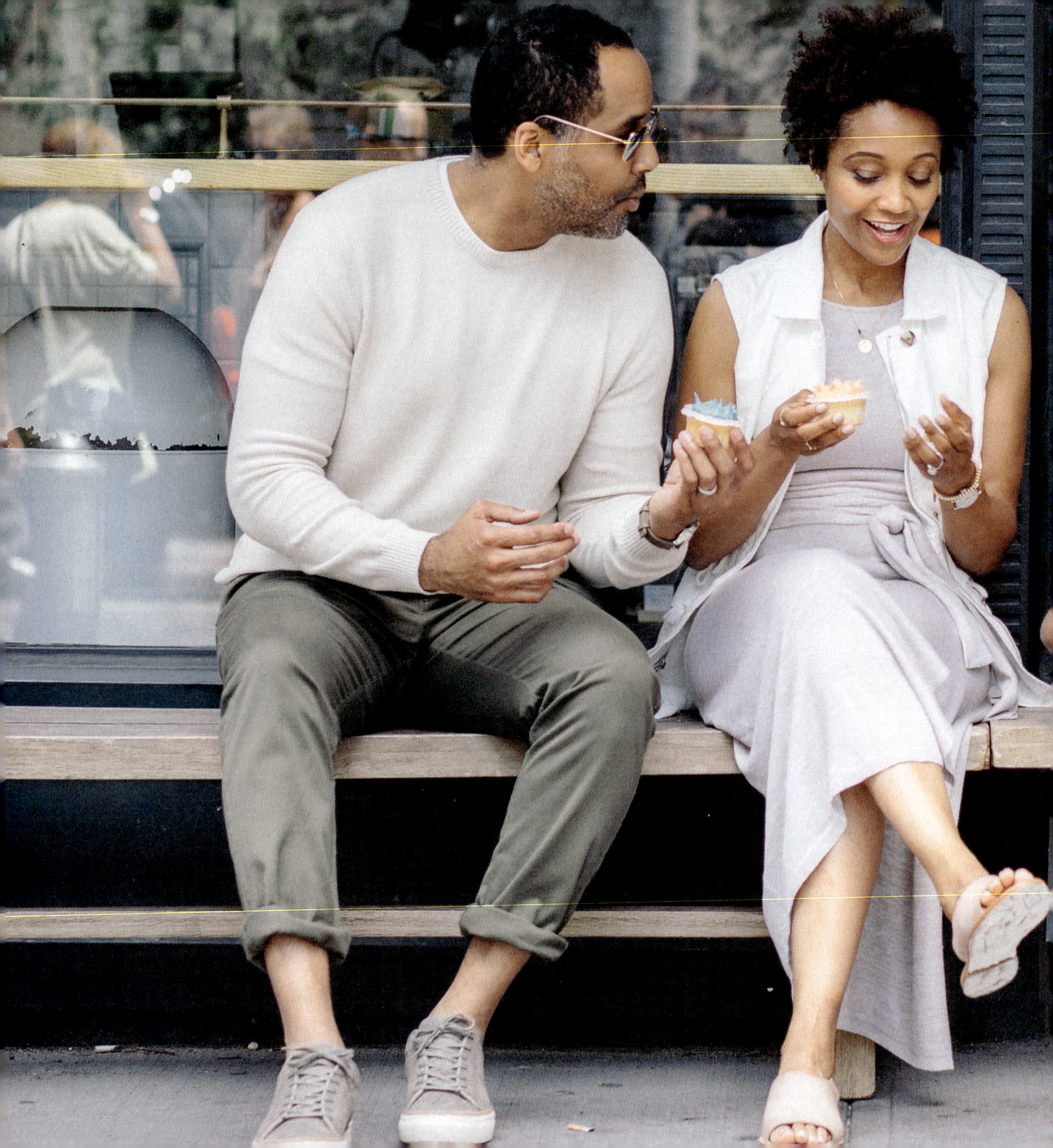

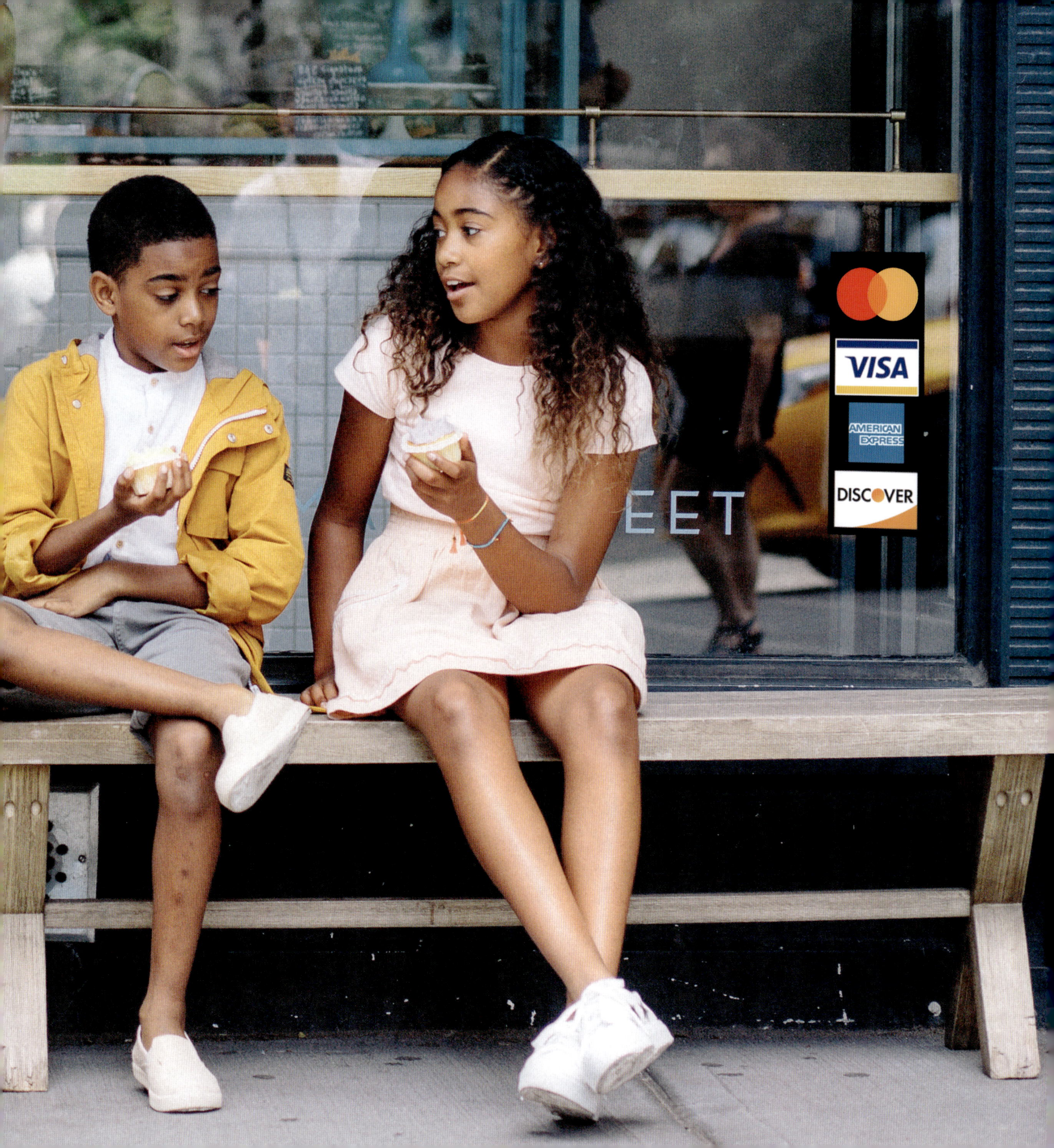
VISA
AMERICAN EXPRESS
DISCOVER
EET

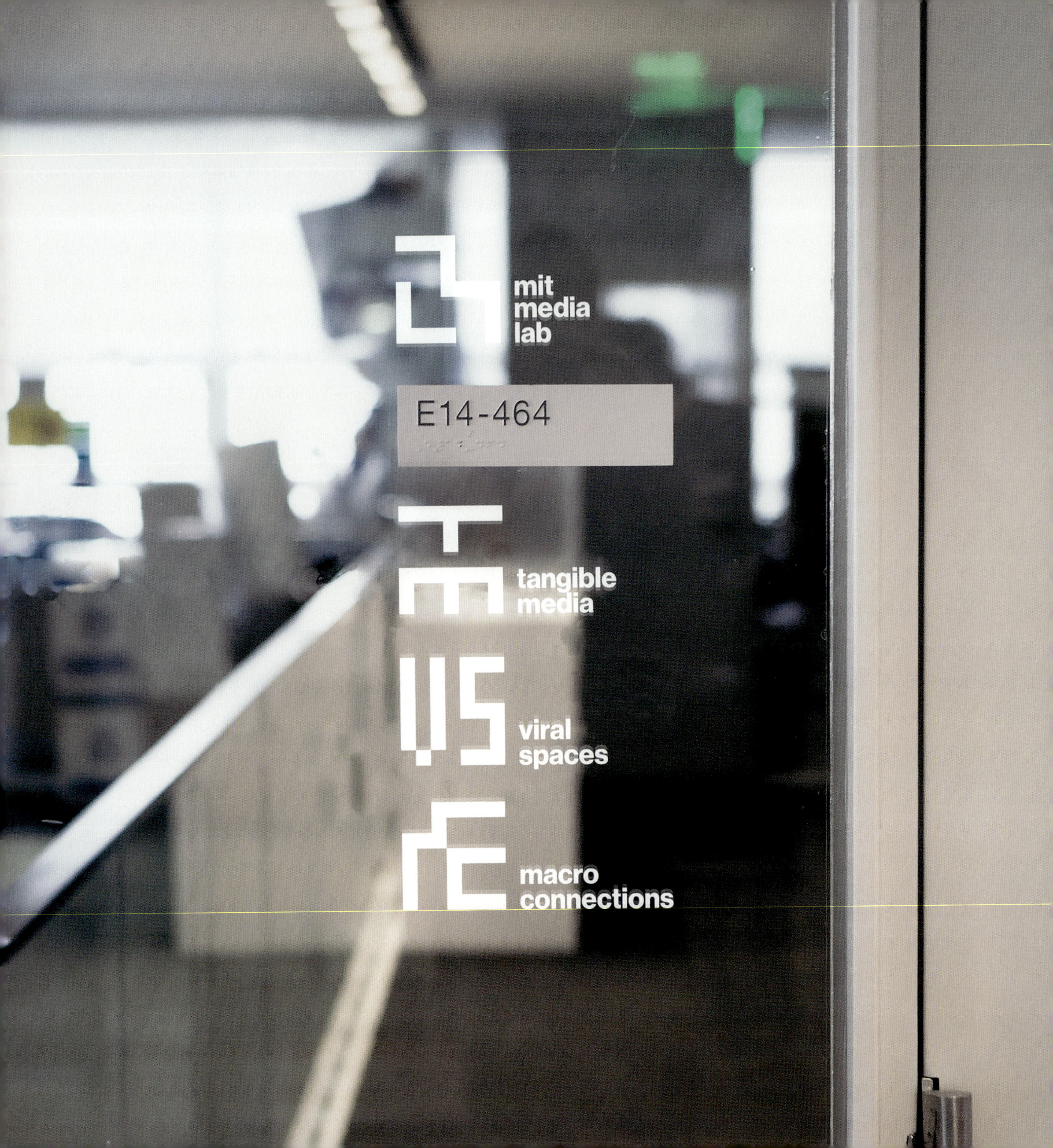

mit
media
lab

E14-464

tangible
media

viral
spaces

macro
connections

How to design two dozen logos at once

MIT Media Lab

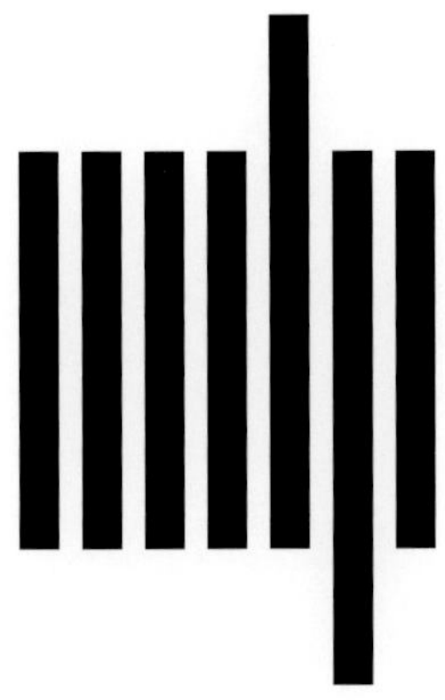

Opposite
The MIT Media Lab logo, created with a team at MIT led by Nicholas Negroponte, Neri Oxman, Hiroshi Ishii, and Ellen Hoffman, is intended to combine timelessness and flexibility.

Above
Designer Muriel Cooper, head of MIT's pioneering Visual Language Workshop, was critical in the formation of the Media Lab. Her 1962 symbol for the MIT Press looks contemporary and was held up as a model for our identity work.

Digital technology forever transformed the way we communicate. It also overturned the way we decide what makes a good logo. Then came the rise of digital media. The old tests (can you fax it?) were replaced by new ones (can you animate it?). Complexity and dynamism were not only made possible by new technology, but inescapably came to symbolize it.

Since 1985, the global epicenter of digital innovation has been the research groups at the Massachusetts Institute of Technology Media Lab. The Lab's first identity, by Jacqueline Casey, was a malleable motif of colored bars inspired by an installation that artist Kenneth Noland had created for the original Media Lab building. It lasted two dozen years. For the Lab's 25th anniversary, designer Richard The created a dazzling algorithmic system capable of generating over 40,000 permutations. Both programs were models of dynamic identity, capable of infinite change. But looming large at MIT was another model: the classic logo designed by Media Lab legend Muriel Cooper for MIT Press. A minimalistic configuration of seven vertical lines, it has remained unchanged since 1962. The team at MIT Media Lab came to us with a question: could a single logo combine these two traditions of timelessness and flexibility?

I was already thinking about this question. Having designed more than my share of dynamic identities and non-logo logos, I had begun to doubt their power. All that variability had come to seem entropic, projecting difference without meaning. The symbols designed by Cooper and her peers during the golden age of American corporate identity, by comparison, were striking in their clarity and confidence.

Our solution came after many false starts. Using a seven-by-seven grid, we generated a simple ML monogram. This would serve as the logo for the Media Lab. Then, using that grid, we extended the same graphic language to each of the 23 research groups that lie at the heart of the Lab's activities. The result is an interrelated family of logos that at once establishes a fixed identity for the Media Lab, and celebrates the diverse activities that make the Lab great.

Right
Our logo for MIT Media Lab was created by constructing a simple ML monogram on a seven-by-seven square grid.

Opposite
The symbol for the Media Lab does not vary, but the relationship between type and symbol does.

Next spread
The same seven-by-seven grid was used to create logos for the Lab's research groups, from Affective Computing to Viral Communications. Each logo uses the group's initial letters to generate a unique configuration.

Following spread
Because all the logos in the system share the same underlying geometry, they are perceived as a family, a whole that exceeds the sum of its parts.

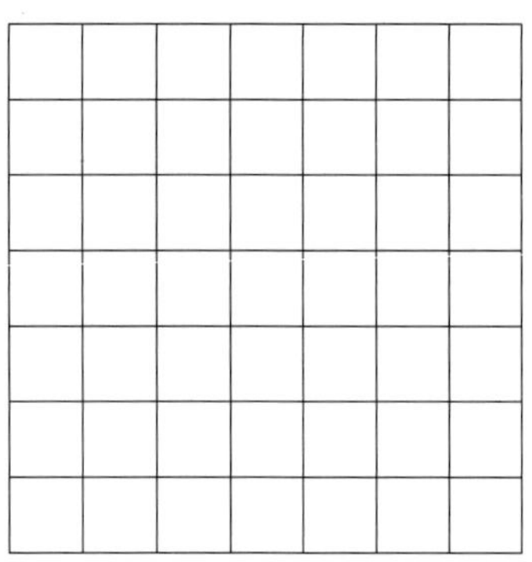

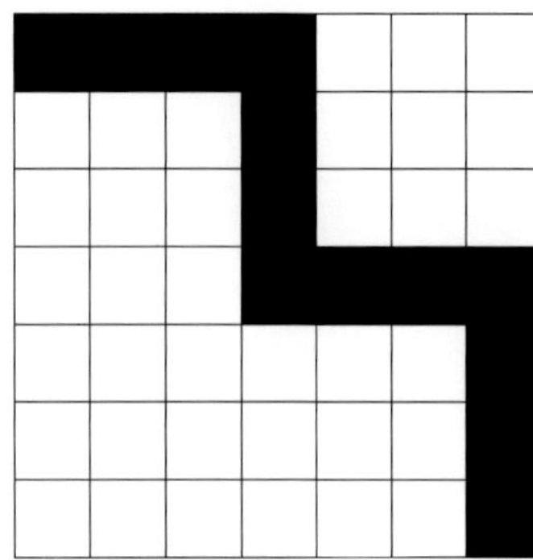

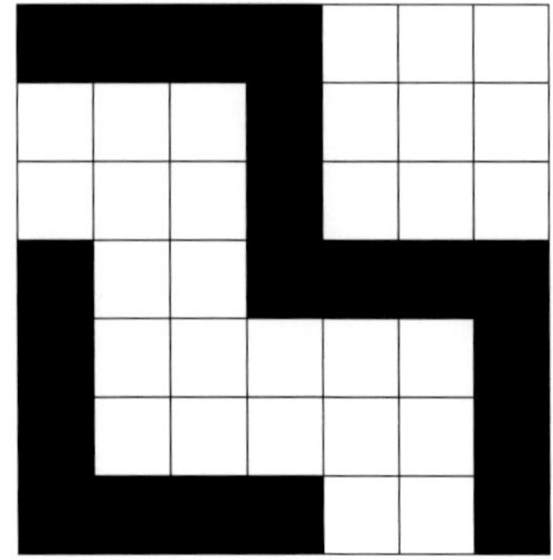

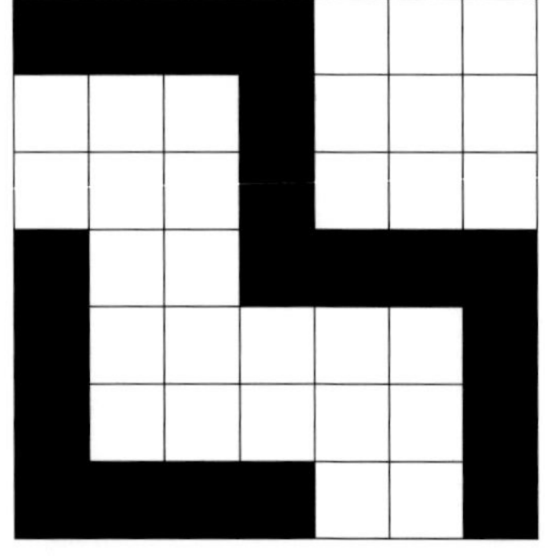

mit
media
lab

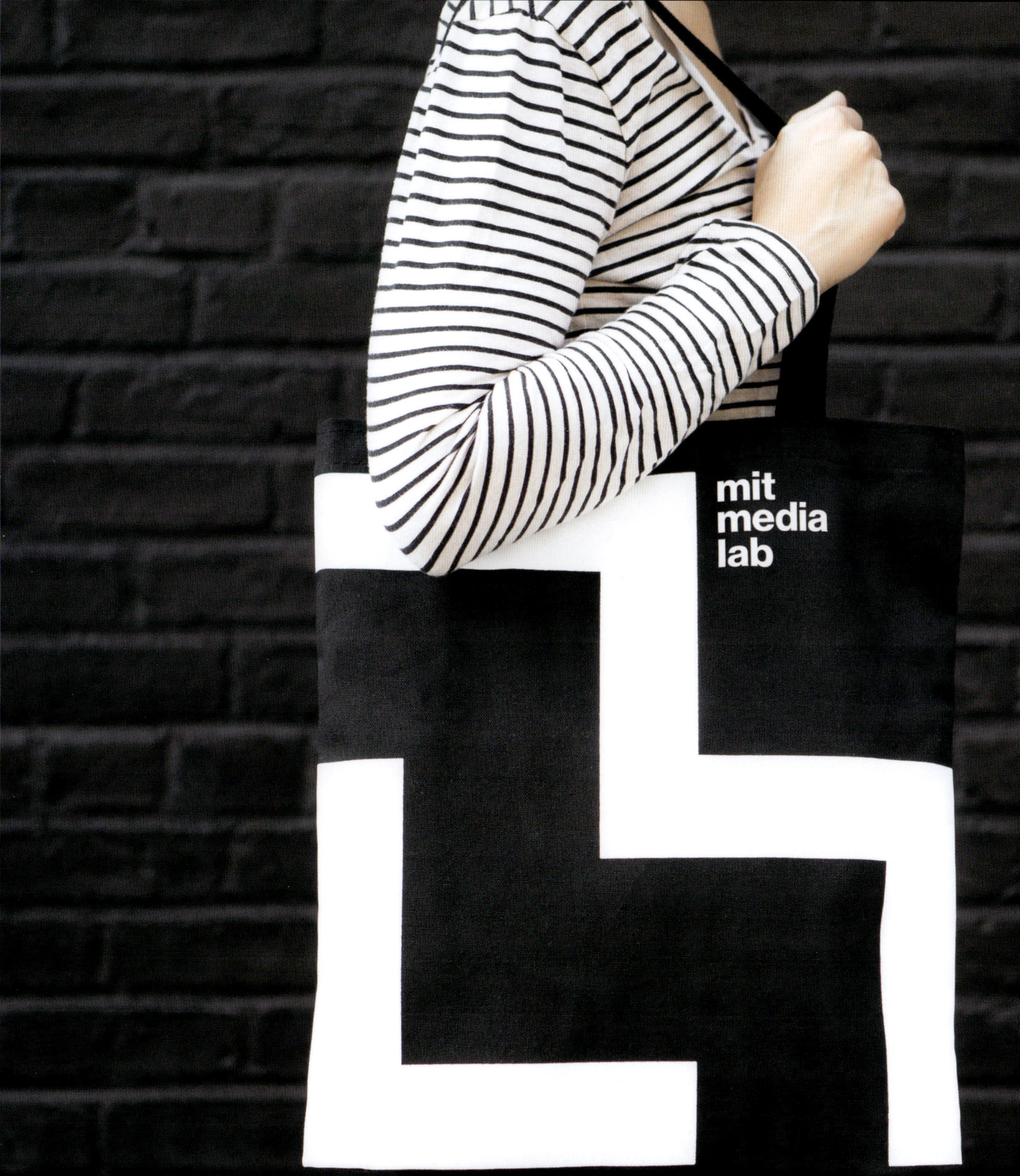
mit
media
lab

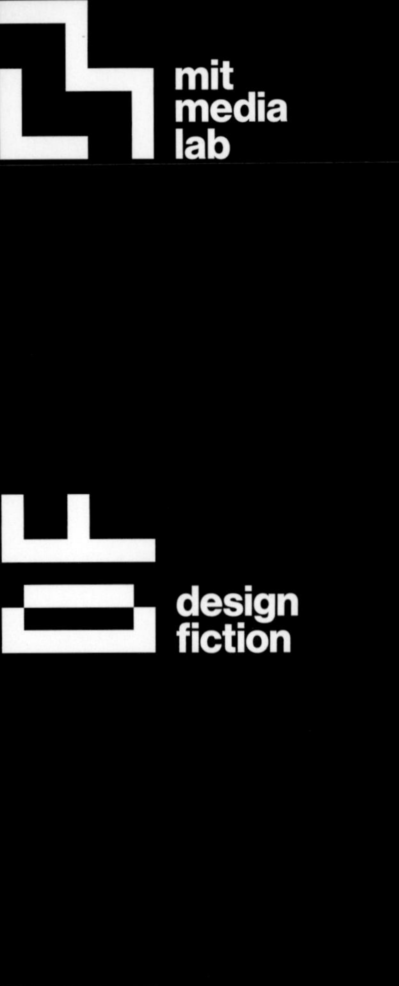

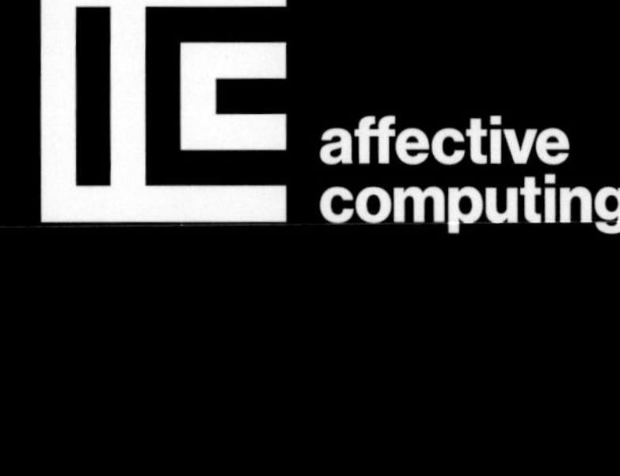

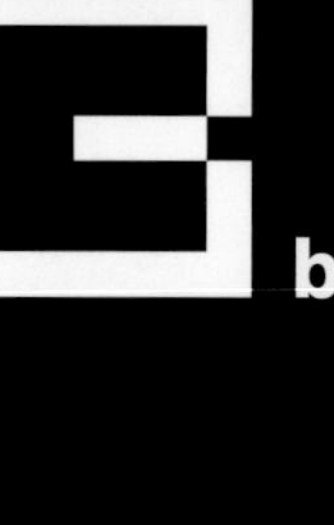

biomechatronics

fluid
interfaces

human
dynamics

molecular
machines

object-based
media

opera of
the future

social
computing

social
machines

speech +
mobility

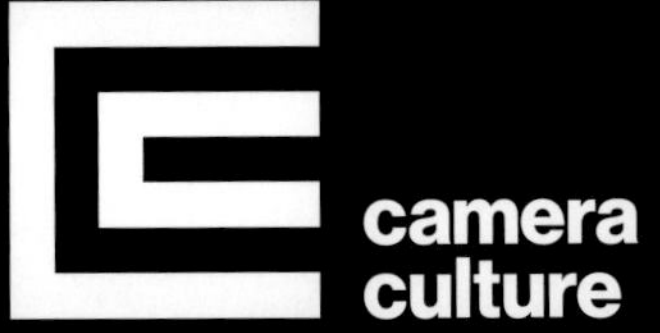
camera
culture

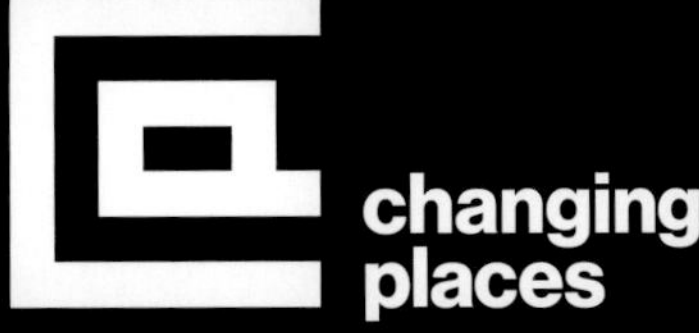
changing
places

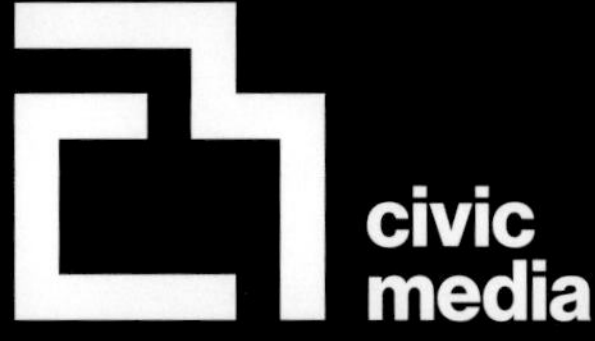
civic
media

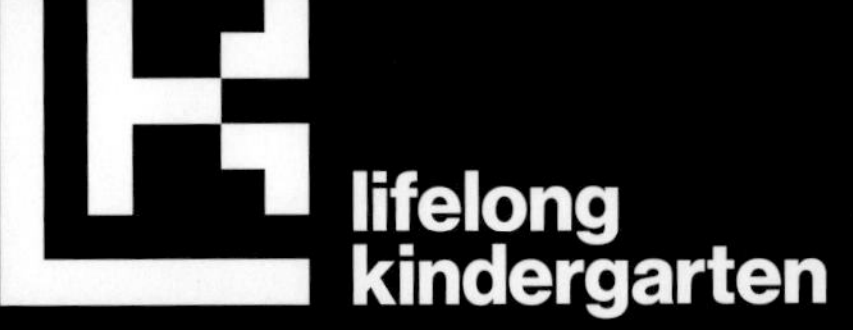
lifelong
kindergarten

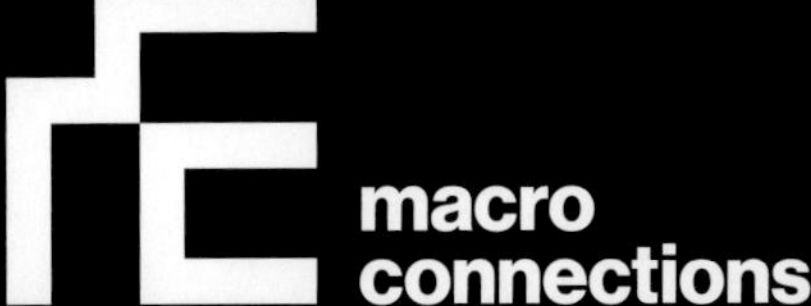
macro
connections

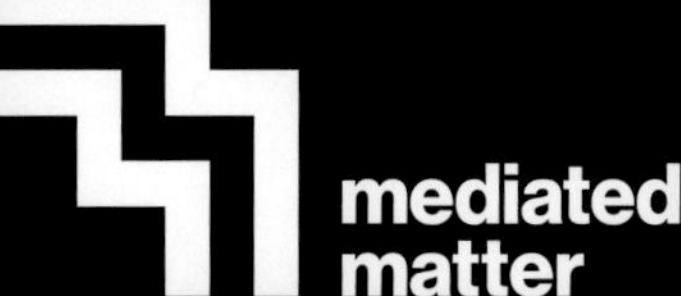
mediated
matter

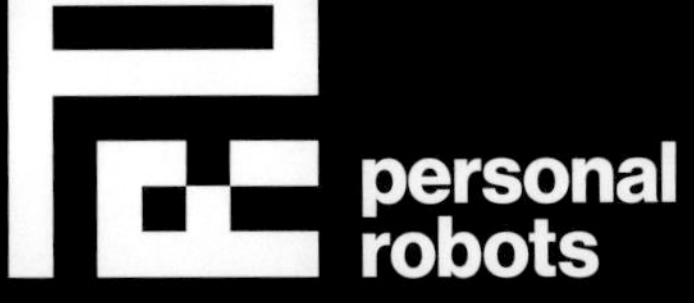
personal
robots

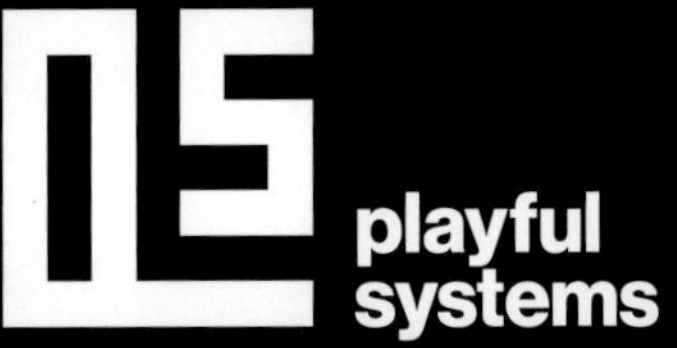
playful
systems

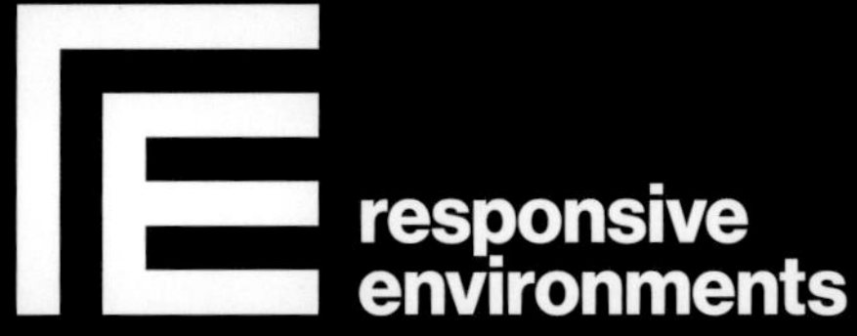
responsive
environments

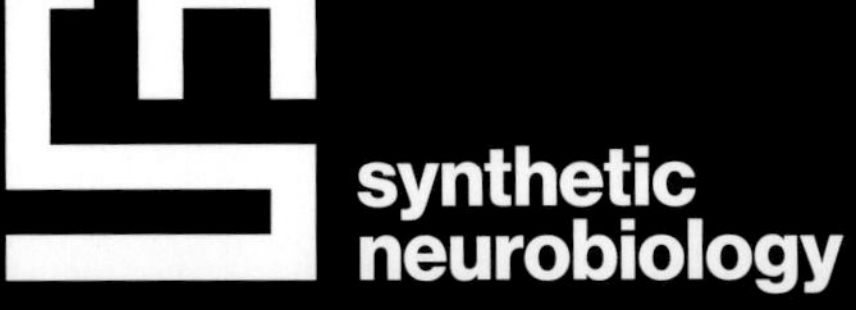
synthetic
neurobiology

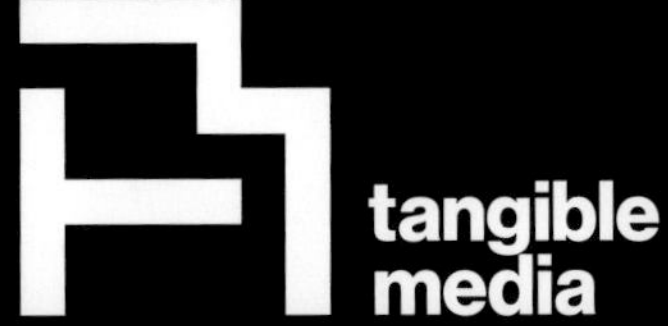
tangible
media

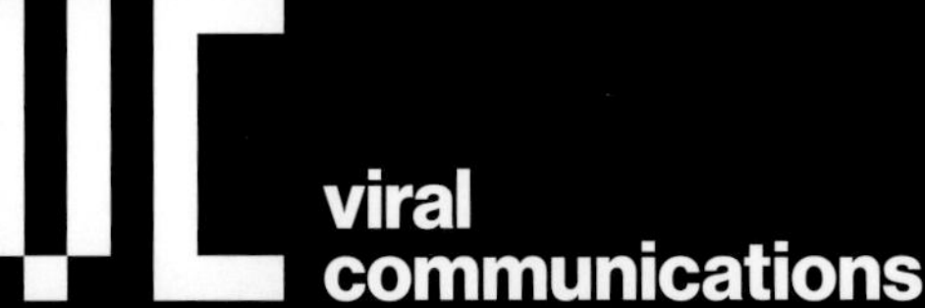
viral
communications

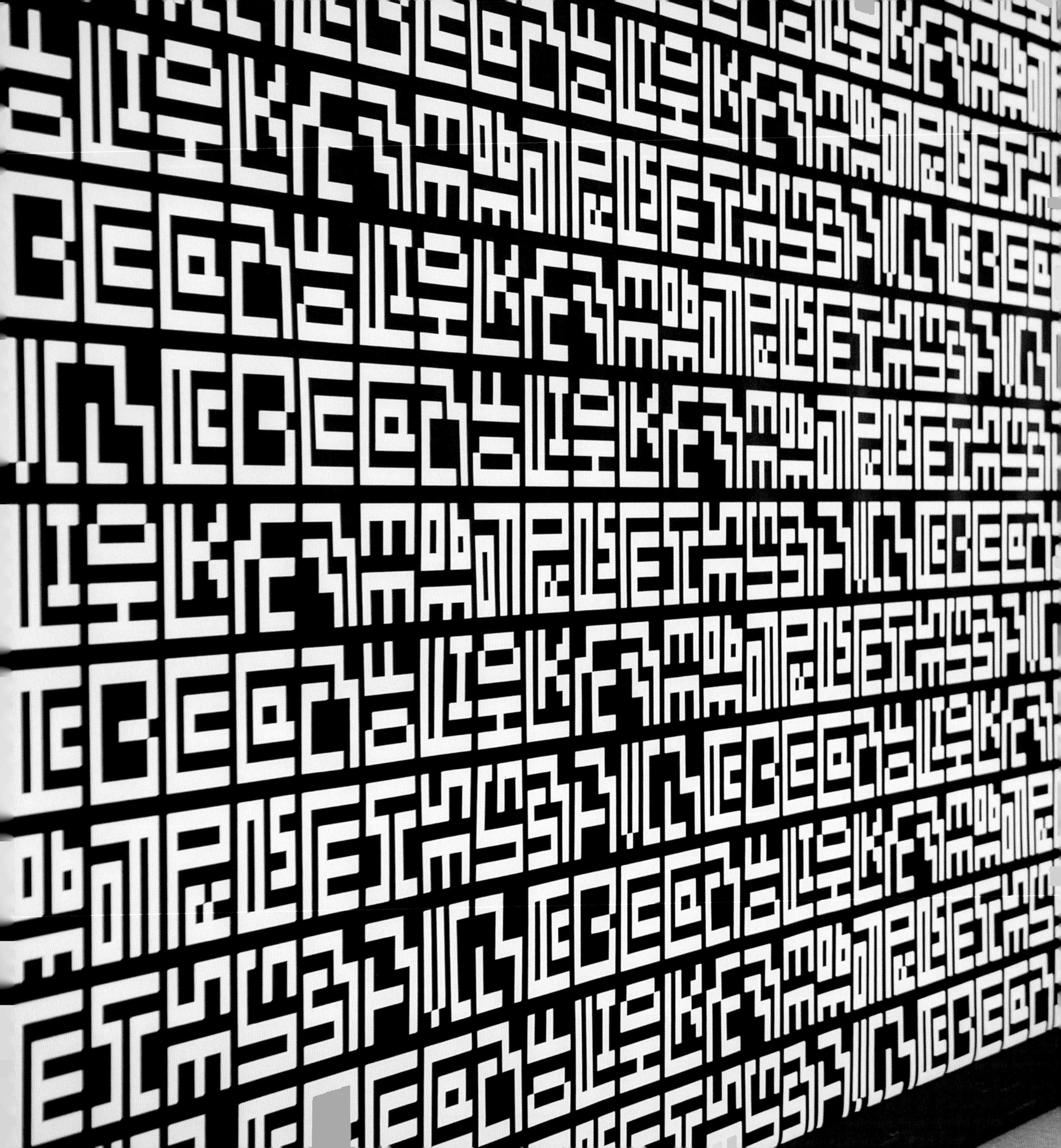

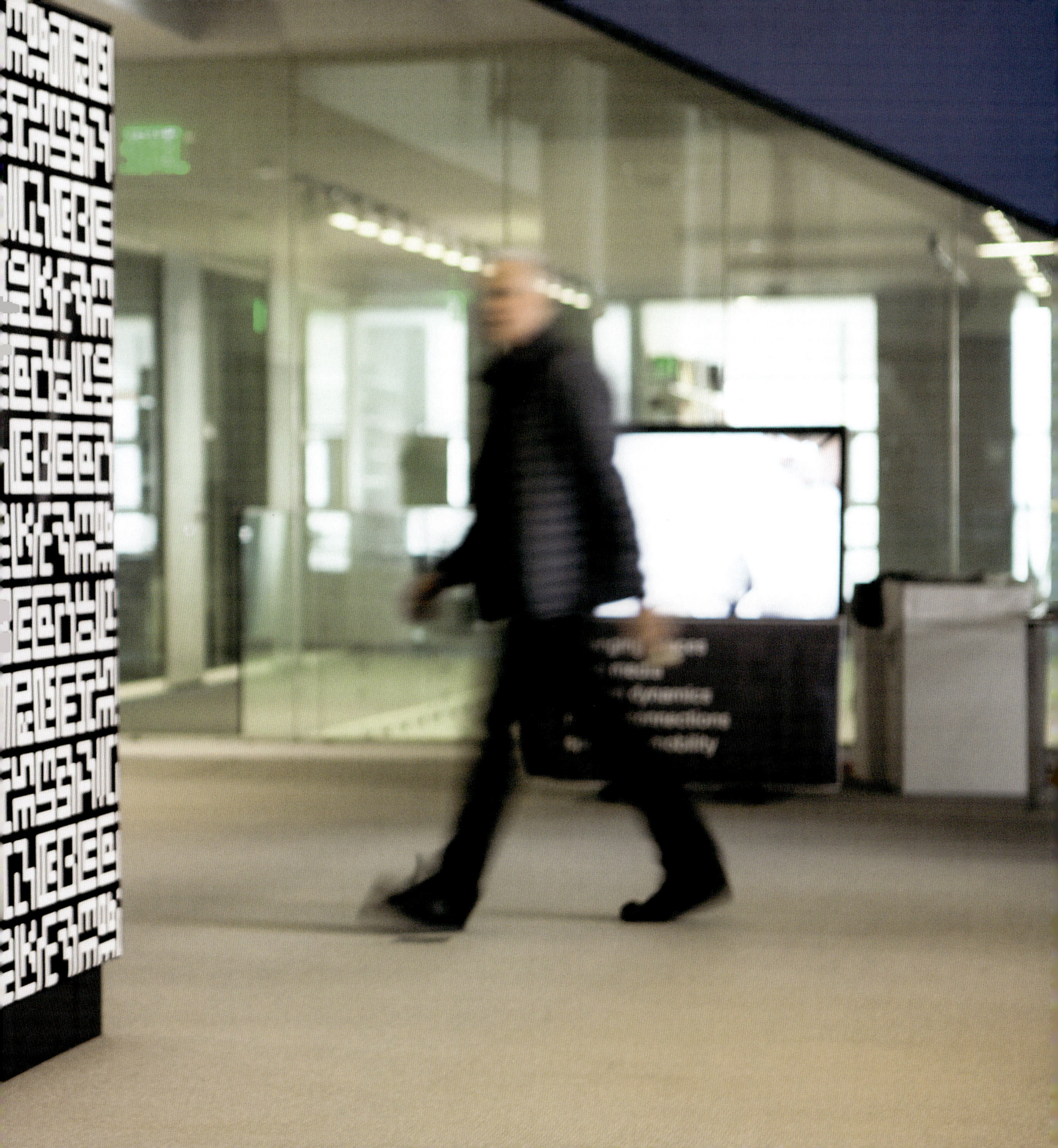

Right top
The typeface Helvetica has been associated with MIT's graphics since the 1960s, when designers like Jacqueline Casey, Muriel Cooper, Ralph Coburn, and Dietmar Winkler were among the first to introduce the Swiss-based "international style" of design to the United States. We used it throughout the identity program, and extended it to the Lab's wayfinding.

Right bottom
The logo, rearranged, becomes a playful arrow pointing to the Media Lab's upper floors.

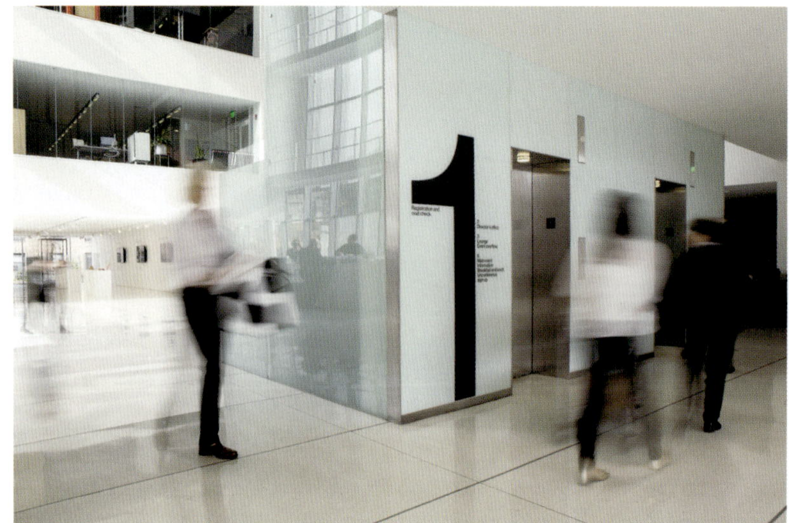

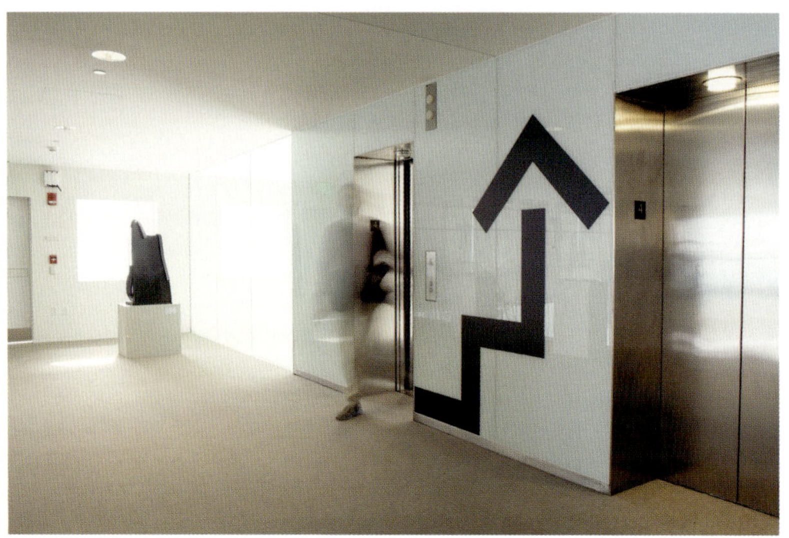

Right top and bottom
Interactive touchscreens help visitors find their way throughout the Lab complex and announce current programs and coming events.

Next spread
The new identity was launched at the Media Lab's Fall 2014 Member Event, which appropriately had the theme "Deploy."

Following spread
Designer Aron Fay masterminded the implementation of this intricate program, including the application of the same graphic language to posters celebrating the Deploy Member Event.

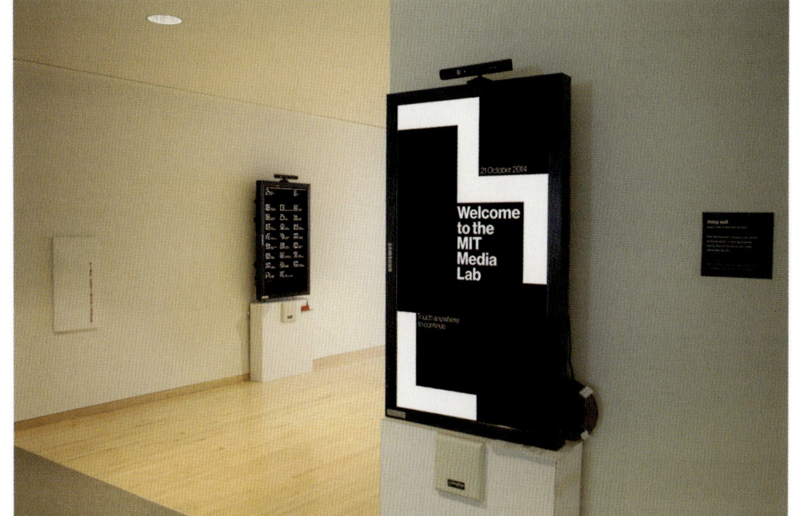

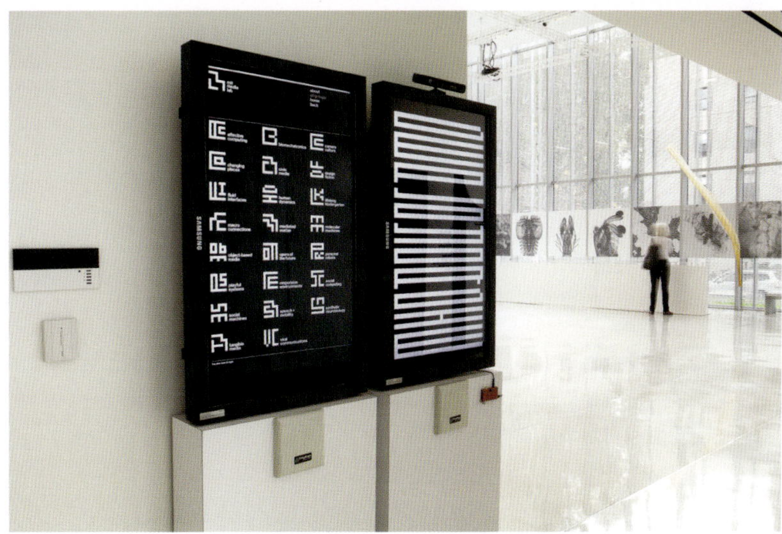

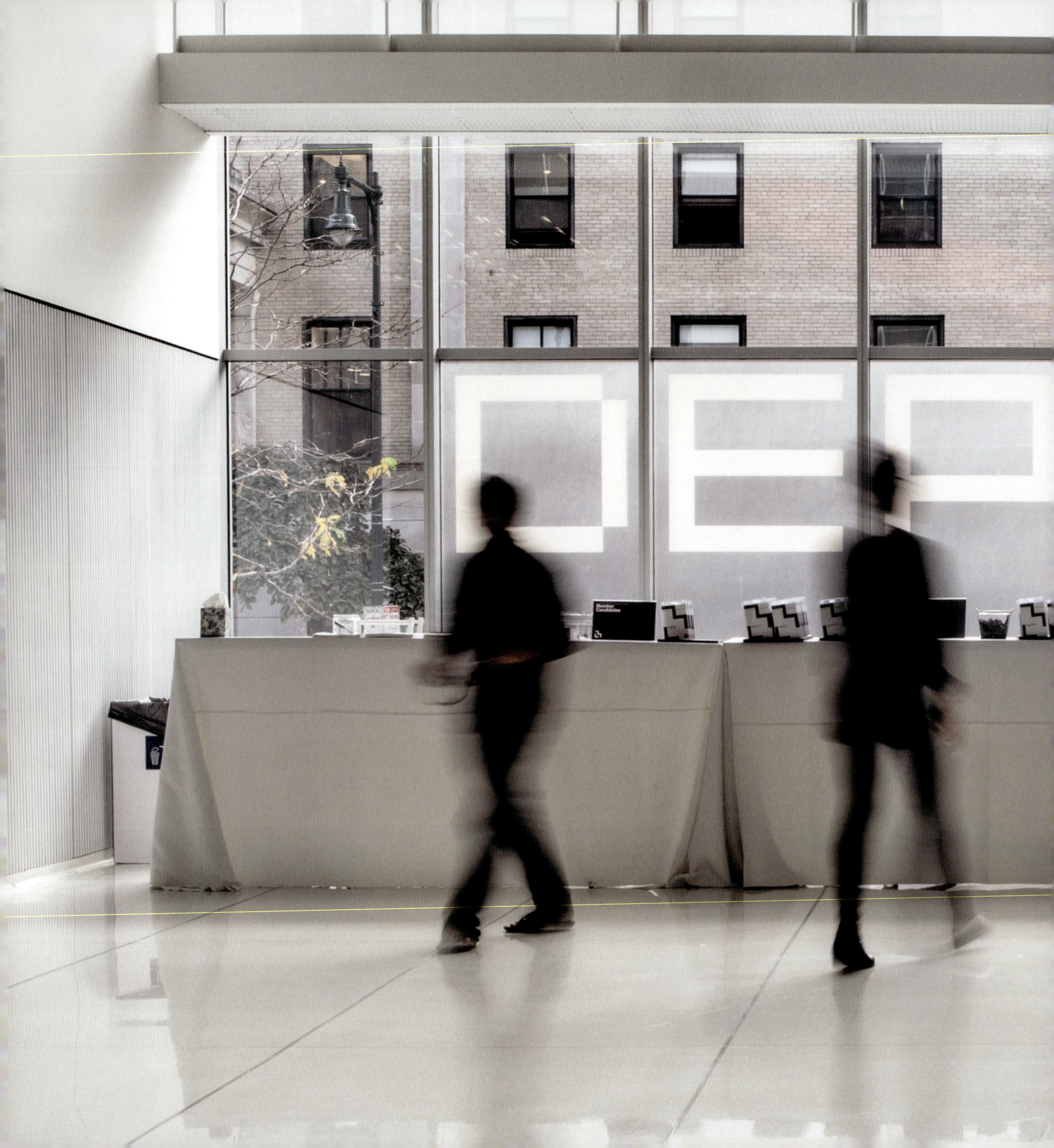

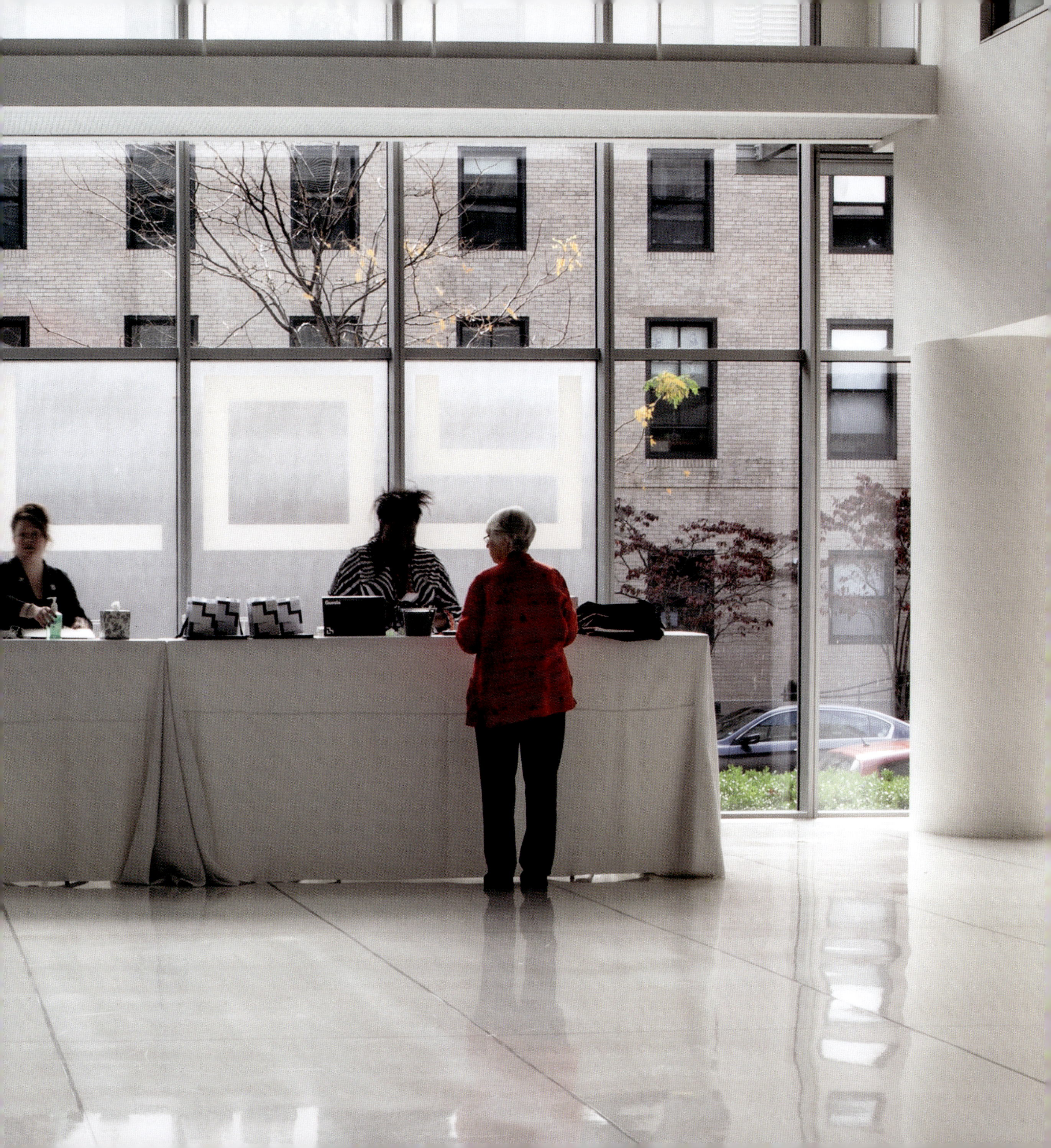

DEPLOY
DEPLOY
DEPLOY
DEPLOY
DEPLOY
12:30pm
Lunch and Unconference
Sign Up
1:20
Special Presentation
Bob Langer, MIT
2:05
Open House
4:30
Unconference
Sign Up
5:00
Unconference
Session
6:00
Reception and Dinner at
McDermott Court
9:05
Special Presentation:
10:55
Morning Break
12:05
Lunch and Unconference
Sign Up
2:00
Open House
4:30
Unconference Sign Up
5:00
Unconference Sessions
6:30
Reception and Dinner at
McDermott Court
Deploy
MIT Media Lab
October 21-23
Thursday
October 23 Agenda

Deploy
MIT Media Lab
October 21–23
Tuesday October 21
Agenda
8:00am
Registration and Breakfast
Member Candidate Breakfast
9:00
Welcome
9:20
Special Presentation: New Media Lab Identity
10:05
Deploy: Introduction
10:15
Session One: Participating
Andy Lippman
Mitch Resnick
Ethan Zuckerman
Michael Bove
Deb Roy
Ramesh Raskar
11:15
Break
11:30
Session Two: Living
Cesar Hidalgo
Kent Larson
Roz Picard
Pattie Maes
Kevin Slavin
Goren Gordon
12:30pm
Lunch and Unconference Sign Up
1:20
Special Presentation: Bob Langer, MIT
2:05
Open House
4:30
Unconference Sign Up
5:00
Unconference Sessions
6:00
Reception and Dinner at McDermott Court
Featuring Boston's Best Food Trucks
Breakfast
Workshops
Lunch and adjourn
Registration and Breakfast
Member Candidate Breakfast
Welcome
Special Presentation: New Media Lab Identity
10:05
Deploy: Introduction

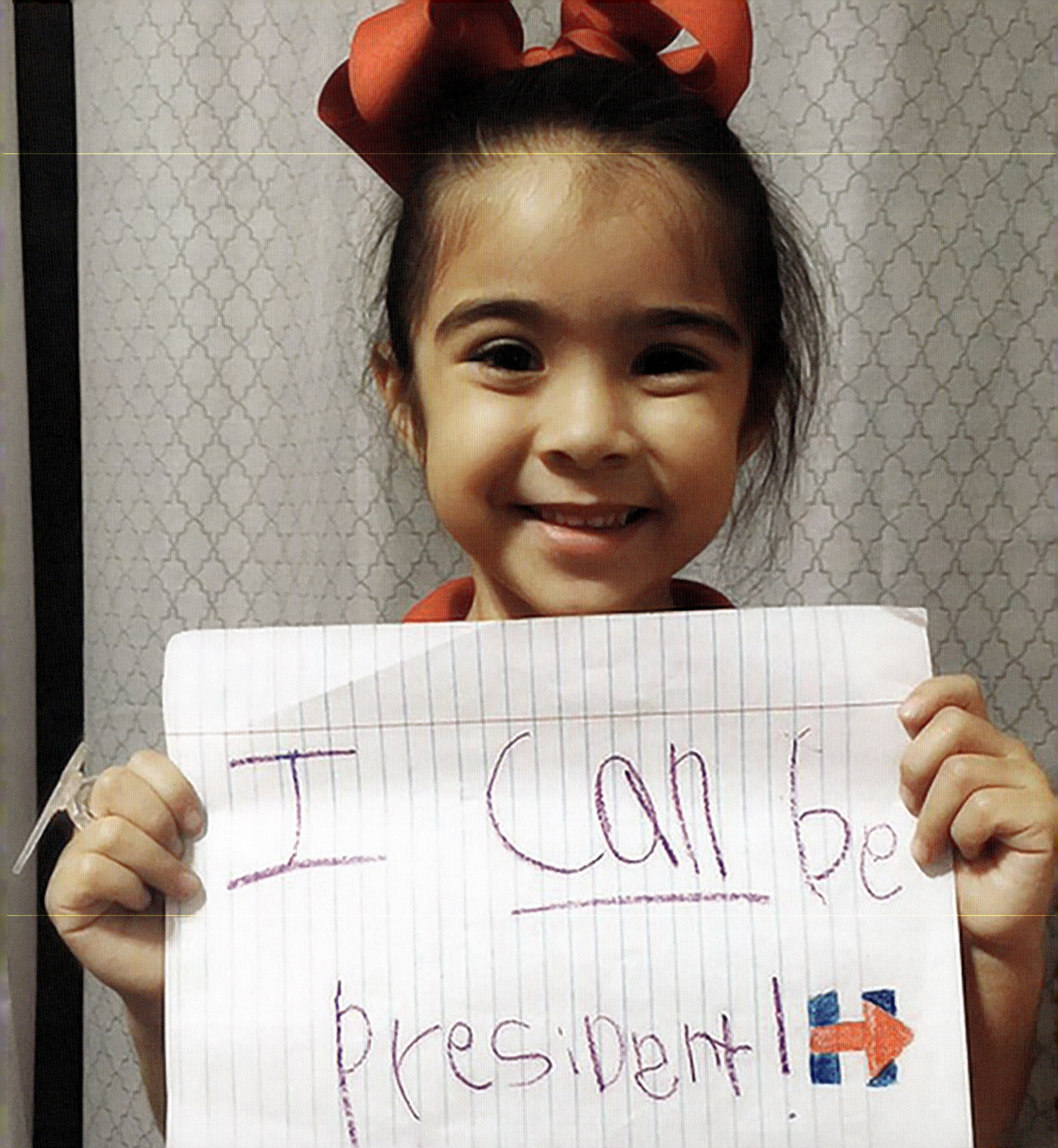
I Can be
President!

How to play politics

Hillary for America

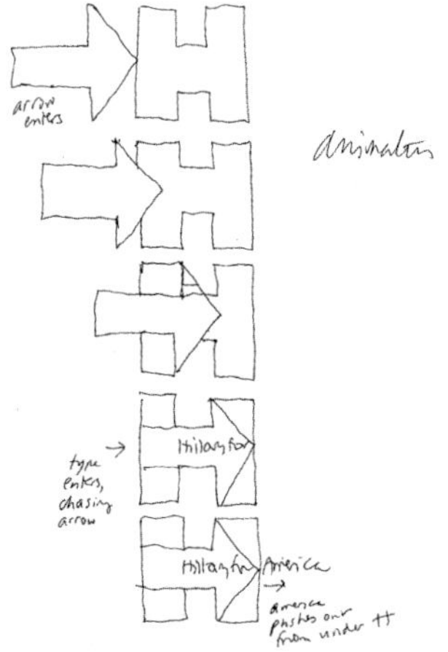

Opposite
Our goal was a logo so simple it could be made with colored construction paper and kindergarten scissors. It was thrilling to see it rendered by so many different hands.

Above
My first sketches explored the ways a letter and an arrow could come together.

"Our candidate has 100 percent name recognition." That's how my first meeting began. It was January 2015, and I was getting briefed on a secret project: to design a symbol for a presidential bid by former Senator and Secretary of State Hillary Clinton.

There's a theory that people are torn between two opposing impulses, a yearning for reassurance on the one hand and excitement on the other. Design can mediate between those poles, making new things seem comforting and finding surprise in the familiar. Hillary Clinton, a figure in public life for three decades, was seeking a logo that would, in effect, reintroduce her to the American public.

In contrast to Barack Obama's circular logo, our candidate's initial "H" could be drawn in a perfect square. To counter that shape's stability, we introduced a sense of dynamism by simply crossing the H with a forward-facing arrow. Obama's symbol was beautiful but complicated. We wanted something like a peace sign or a smiley face, something anyone could draw and reinvent. Hillary Clinton was one of the best listeners I've ever met. She asked great questions, made useful suggestions, approved the work, and within weeks her campaign—and the logo—was launched.

We got a lot of criticism from people who thought the logo wasn't simple, but crude. "My three-year-old could have done that," they said. But that was the point. Over the next 18 months, those simple forms took on an inexhaustible number of expressions. It was thrilling to see something that began as a scribbled sketch in my notebook fill my television screen the evening of the nominating convention; even better were the images sent by friends showing it decorating a sandcastle or an apple pie. It was what we had hoped: a device that was at once familiar and surprising. What no one knew when we began the work was that a candidate with near-universal name recognition would, implausibly enough, face one with even more. Hillary Clinton's team had spent a year and a half establishing a logo; Donald Trump had devoted his entire life to building a brand. I wouldn't expect graphic design to be credited for a victory. I'm not sure it's rightfully blamed for the loss. But that loss was devastating all the same.

I worked on the Hillary for America logo in secret alongside designer Jesse Reed and project manager Julia Lemle, all of us unpaid volunteers to the campaign. We were guided by the brilliant Wendy Clark, on leave from the world of advertising, and the whip-smart campaign consultant Teddy Goff. I met with Hillary Clinton three times and was impressed by her ability to focus on a project that others might have dismissed as a trivial bit of marketing. She was sharp, personable, warm, and funny, an ideal client. She would have made a fantastic president.

Once the campaign was underway, I suggested they hire my former colleague Jennifer Kinon to be the campaign's design director. Jennifer and her design team worked tirelessly until Election Day to create one of the most beautifully sustained communications programs I've ever seen. And the fight goes on: the team she recruited in 2016 continue to work today for a broad range of progressive causes, demonstrating how designers can engage as citizens in the issues that affect us all.

Right
The Hillary symbol was meant to evoke not the intricacies of a corporate logo, but the geometric clarity of a flag. Its construction could be described with complete accuracy in a minute-long phone call. The campaign had a complementary custom font called Unity from typeface designer Lucas Sharp. A guidelines document established the system's basic rules.

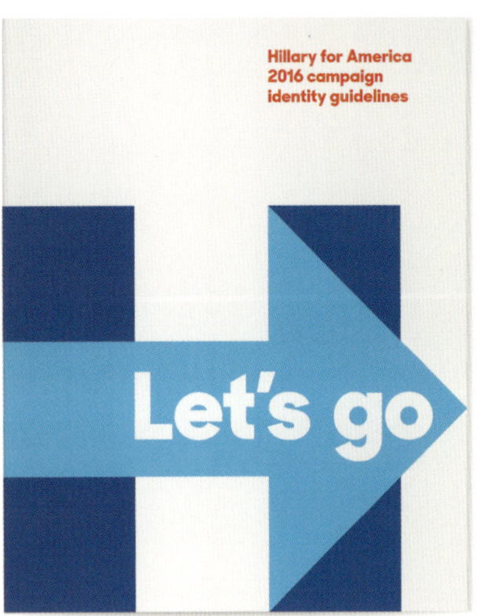

Opposite
Like any contemporary symbol, the Hillary logo was expected to be effective at any size, from a tiny icon on your iPhone's social media feed to the giant stage upon which she kicked off her campaign on New York's Roosevelt Island.

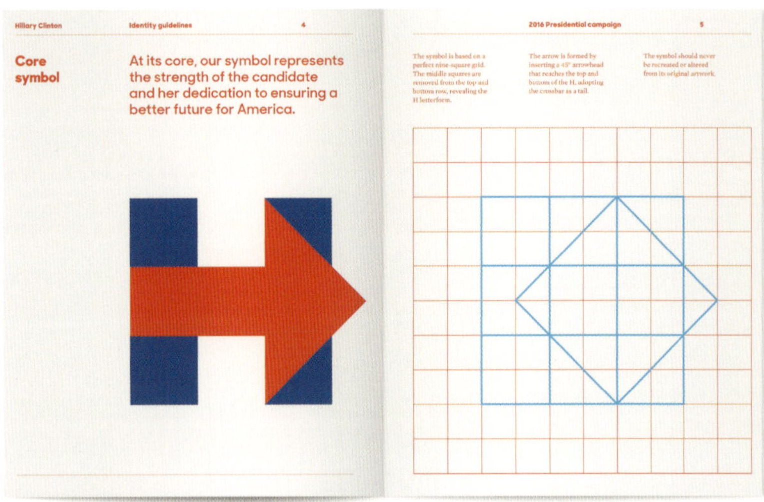

Next spread
The symbol launched in red and blue, but it was designed to work in nearly any color combination, enlivening views of the convention crowd in Philadelphia the night of Clinton's nomination.

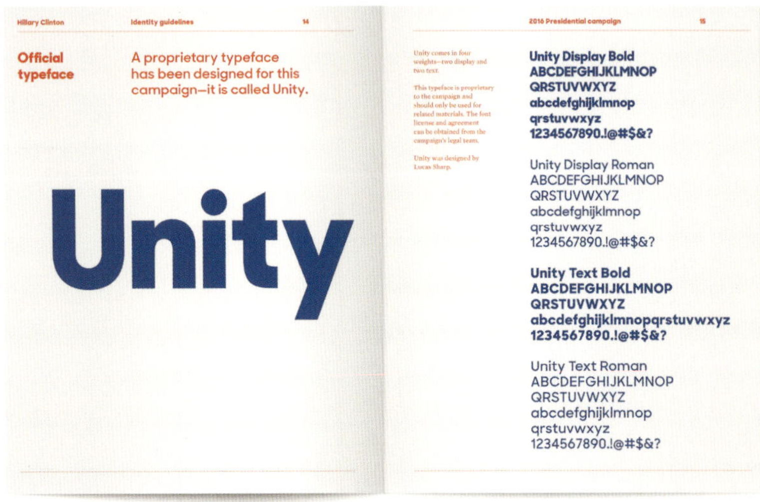

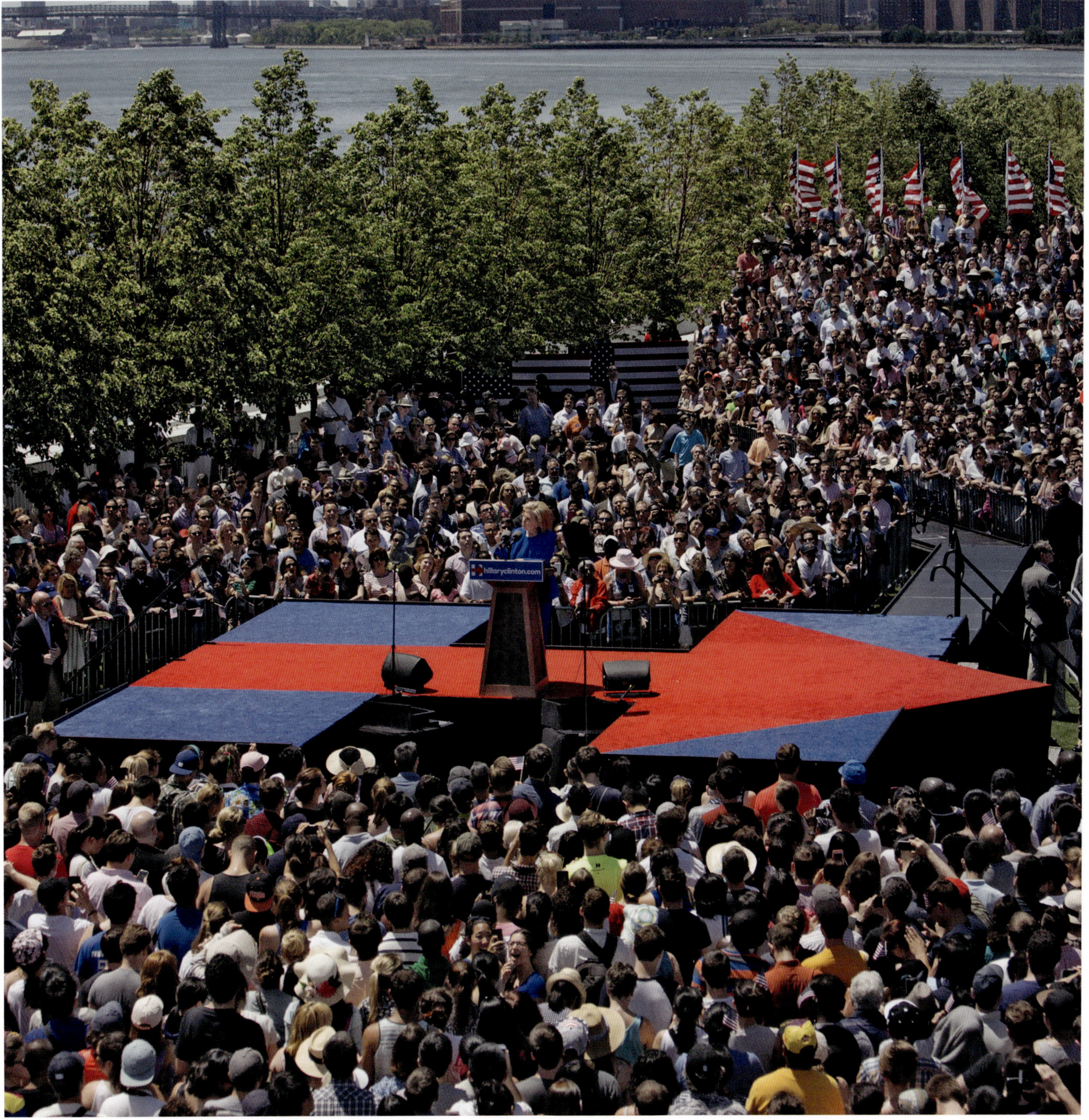
hillaryclinton.com

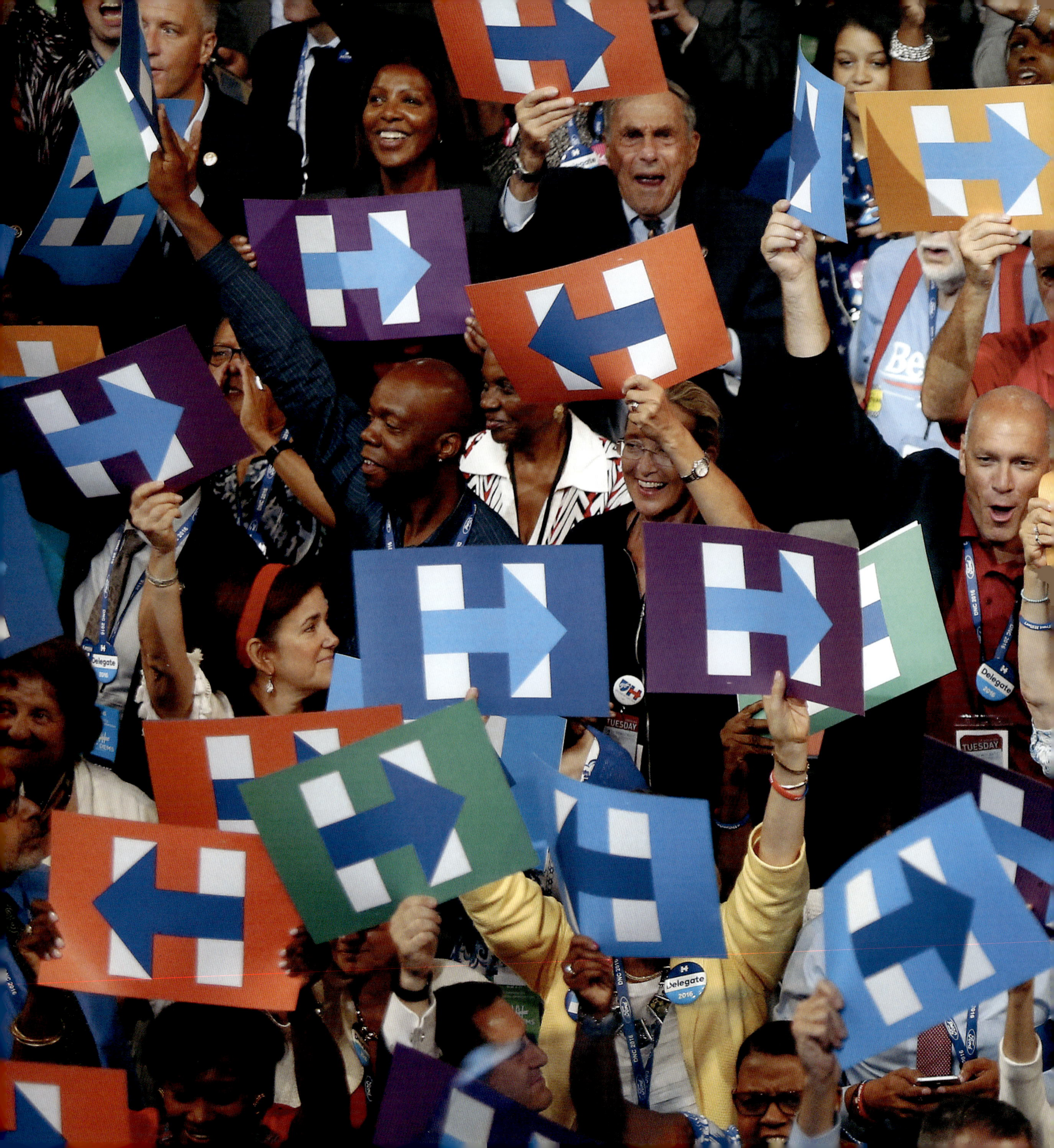
Delegate
2016
TUESDAY
DNC 2016

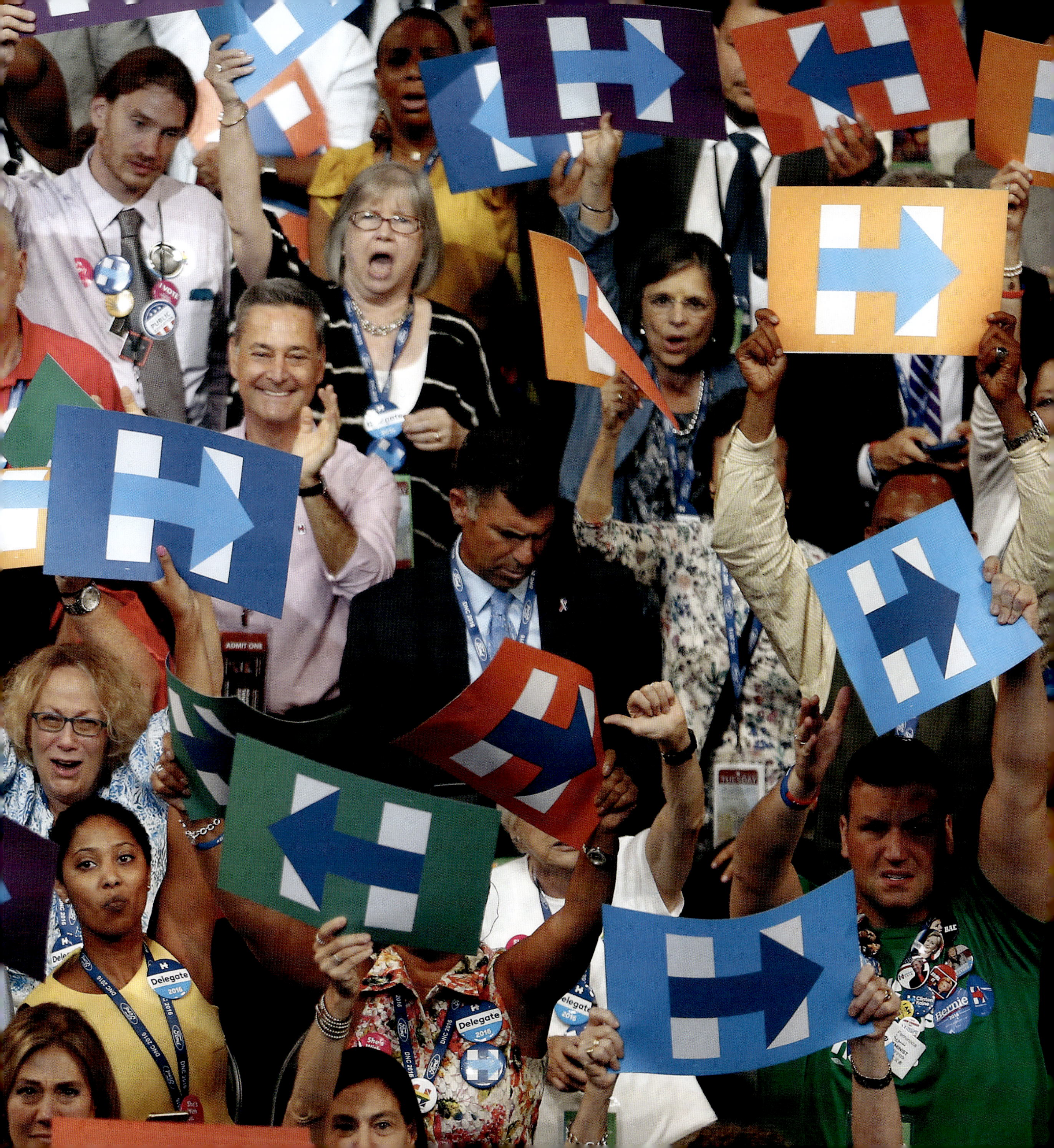
Delegate
2016
Delegate
2016
Bernie
DNC 2016

Right
Jennifer Kinon's team at campaign headquarters in Brooklyn never stopped finding ingenious and often funny ways to transform the H and arrow, celebrating holidays from Halloween to Valentine's Day.

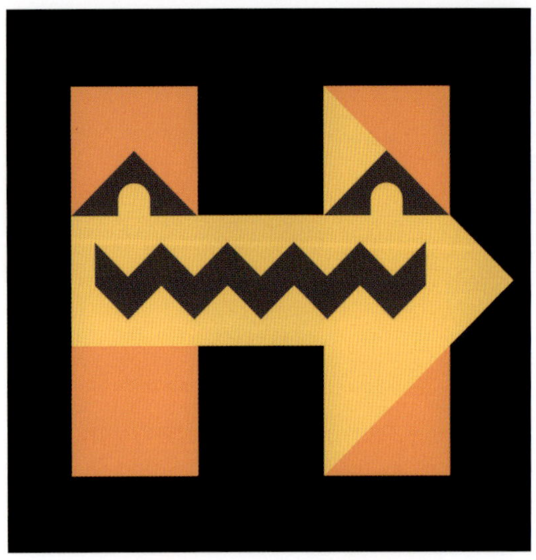

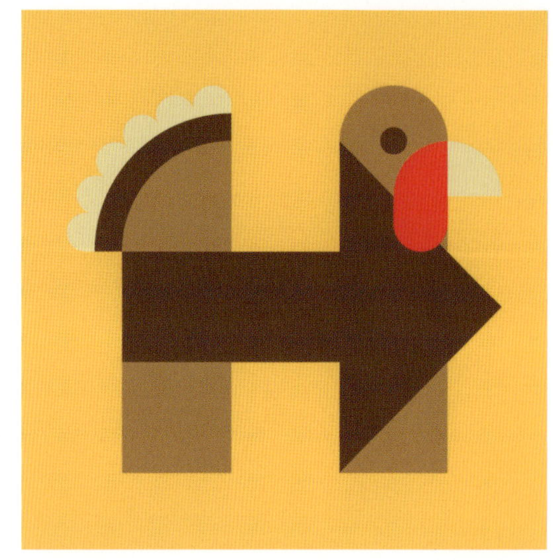

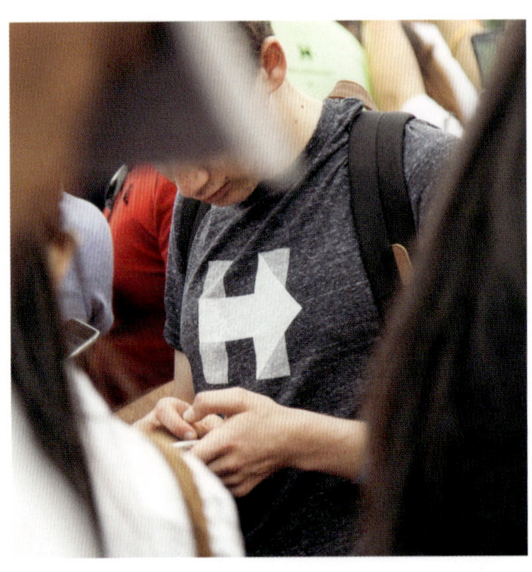

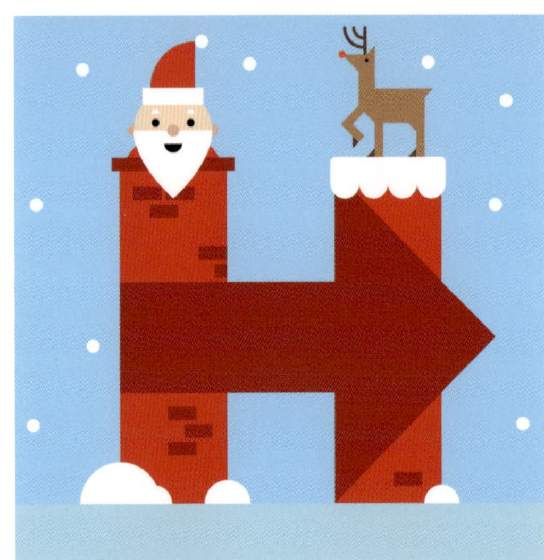

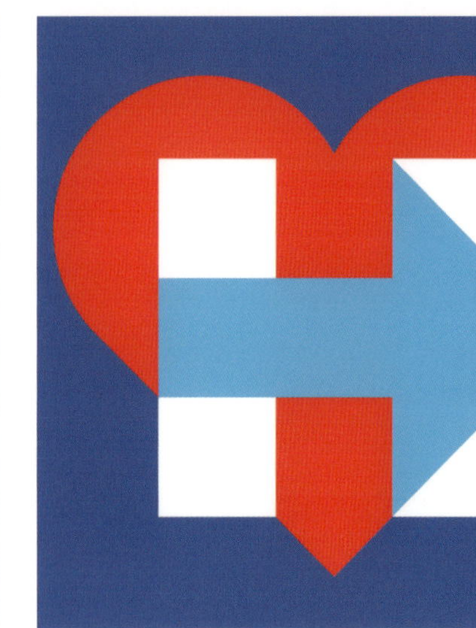

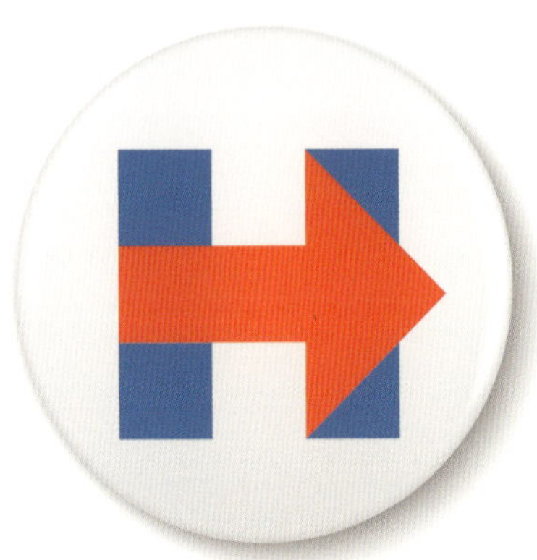

Left
I was always a little taken aback when people asked me to explain the logo's design rationale. I usually said, "It's an H because her name is Hillary, it's an arrow because she wants to move the country forward, and it's red, white, and blue because of America."

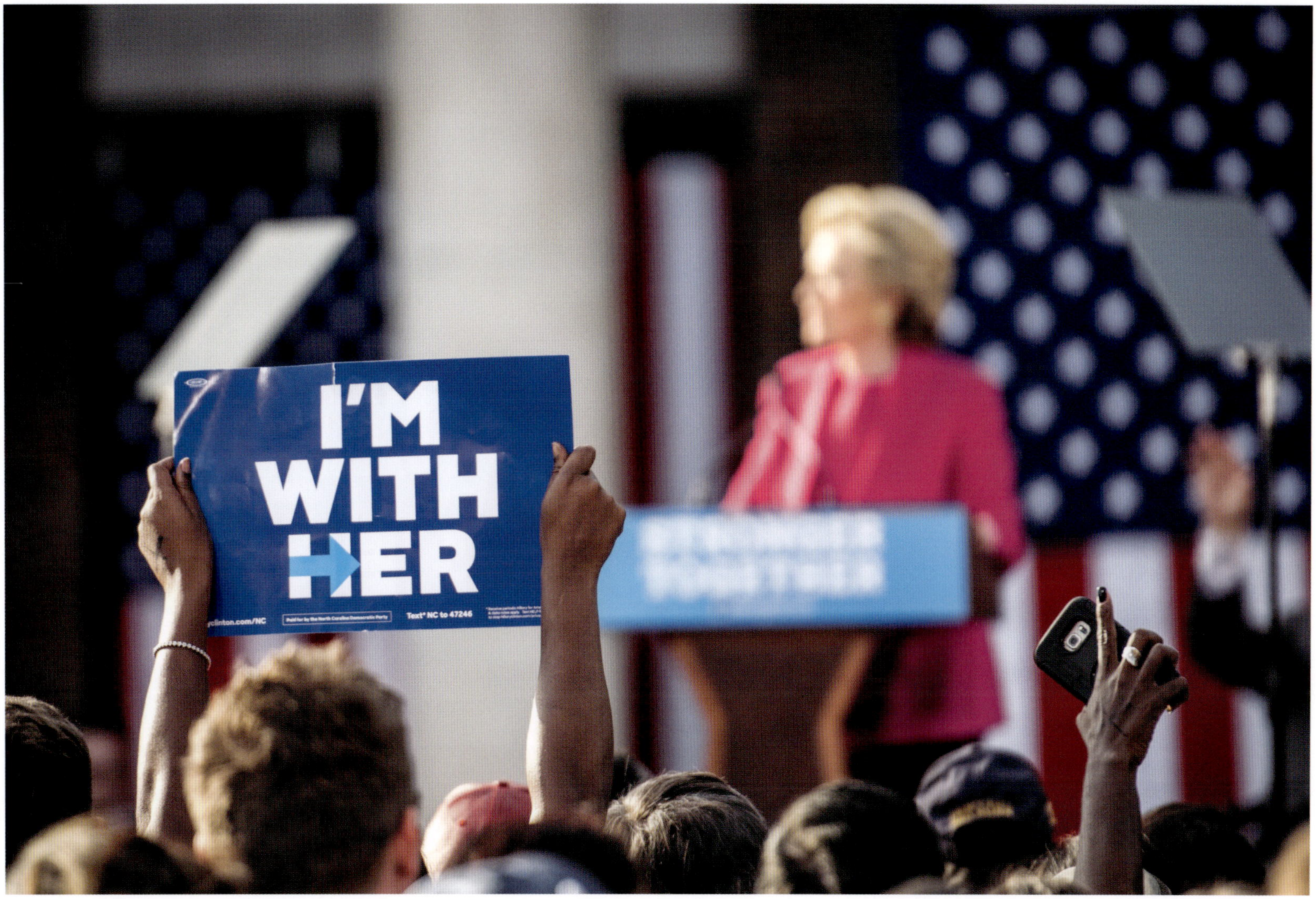

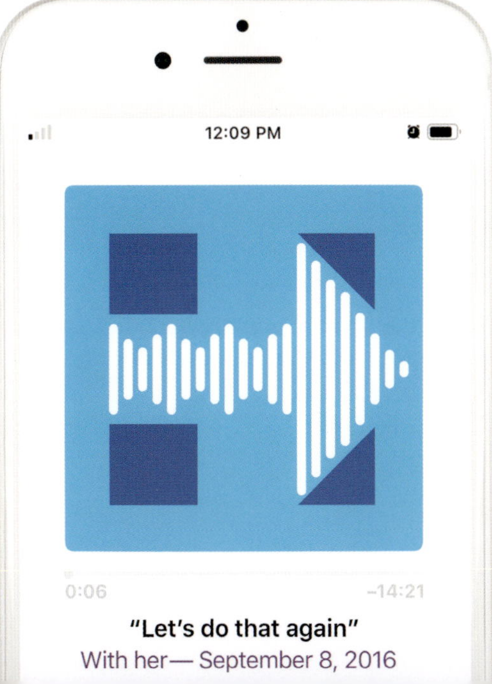

Left
By the time the campaign launched its podcast, the symbol was so ubiquitous it barely needed an explanation.

Above
Hillary for America designer Ida Woldemichael, sketching ideas for a bumper sticker, came upon a simple three-word phrase that neatly incorporated the H symbol. It became the campaign's de facto slogan.

Next spread
Late in the campaign, a client told me about a friend who was a fan of both the candidate and her graphics, and introduced me to Karen Todd. Karen had been improvising a version of the logo every day for months and posting the results on her Facebook page. Her ingenuity was joyful and inspiring.

Following spread
Despite receiving nearly three million more votes, Hillary Clinton lost because of agonizingly close races in three mid-western states and the idio-syncrasies of the Electoral College.

It was a heartbreaking outcome, but I am as proud of the work we did for her campaign as anything I've done in my life.

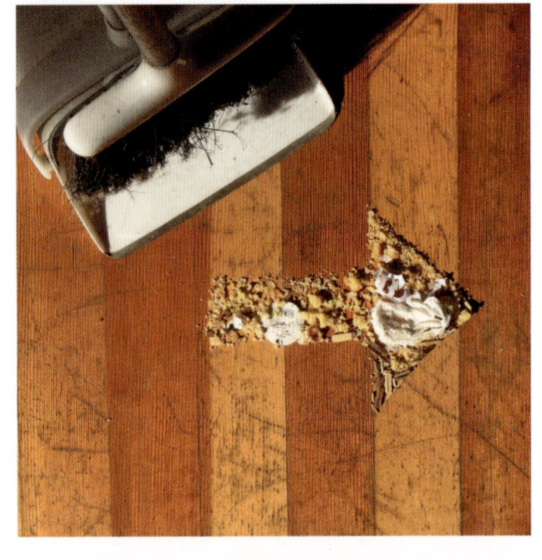

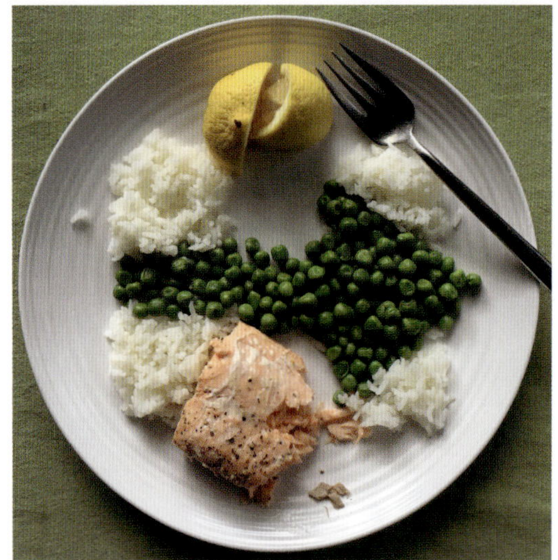

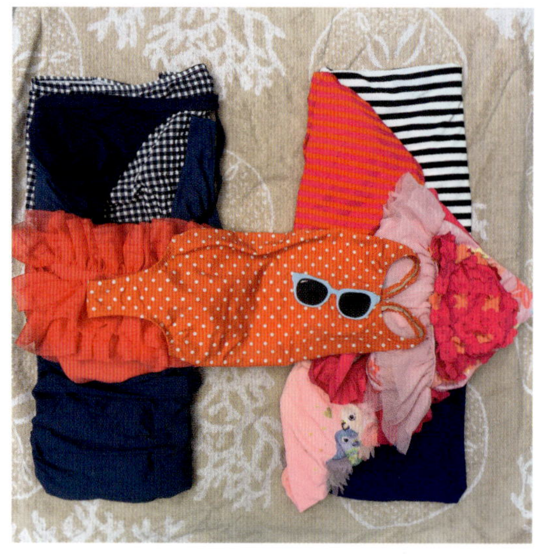

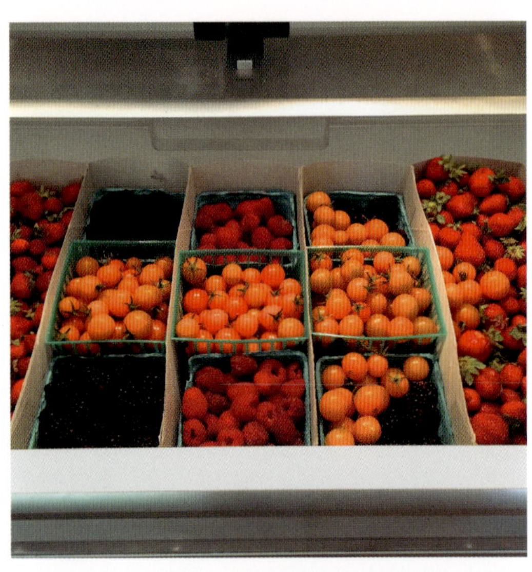

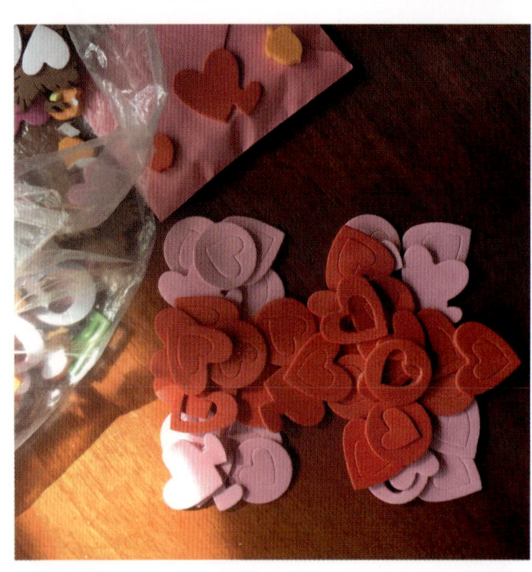

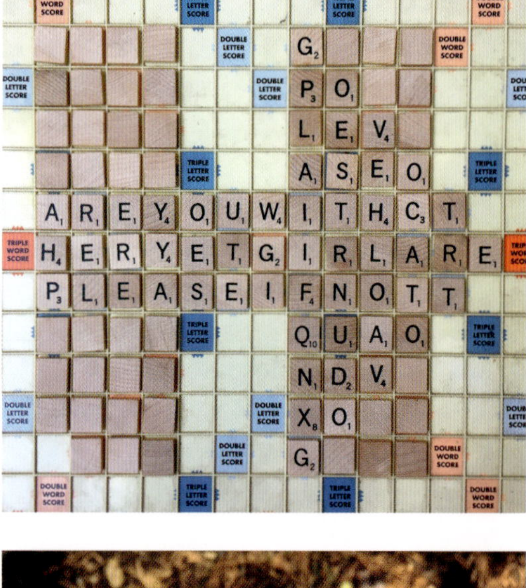
G
PO
LEV
ASEO
AREYOUWITHCT
HERYETGIRLARE
PLEASEIFNOTT
QUAO
NDV
XO
G

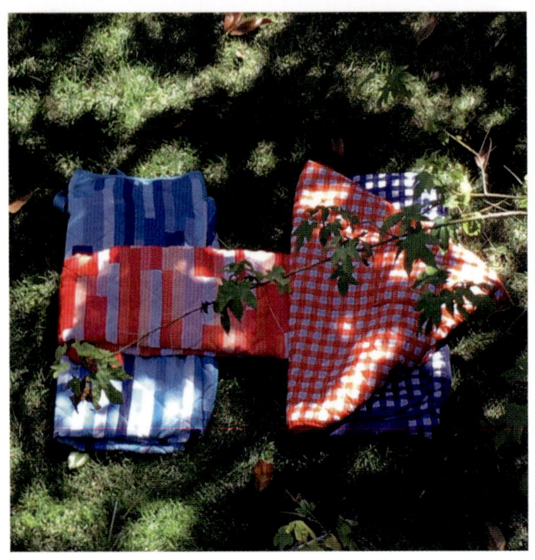

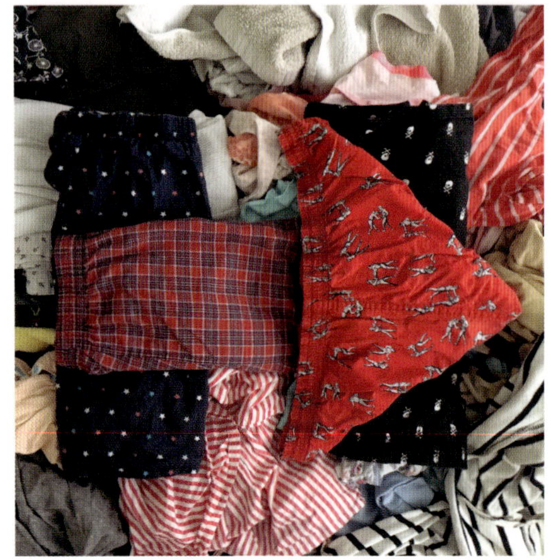

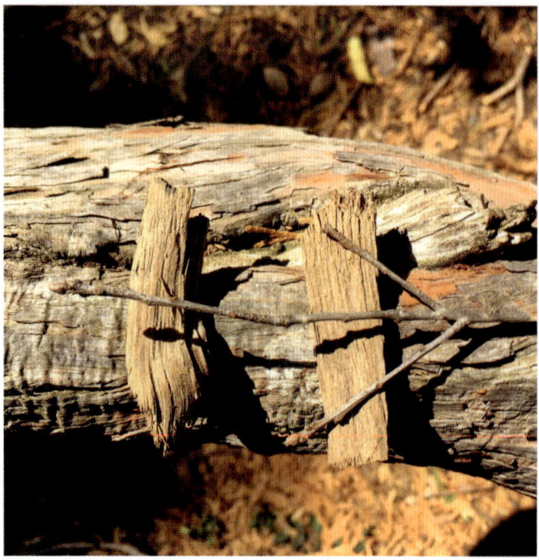

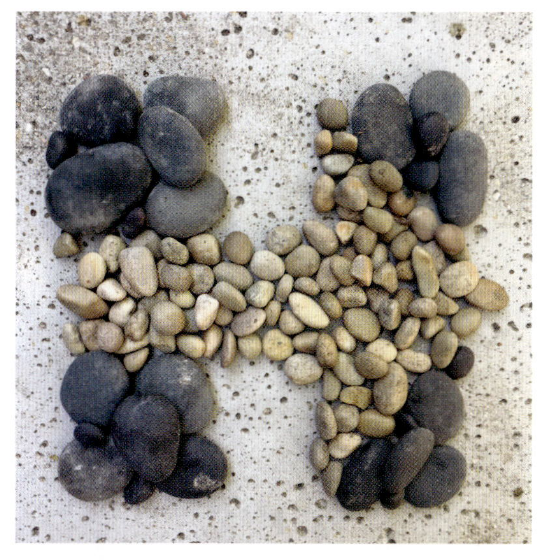

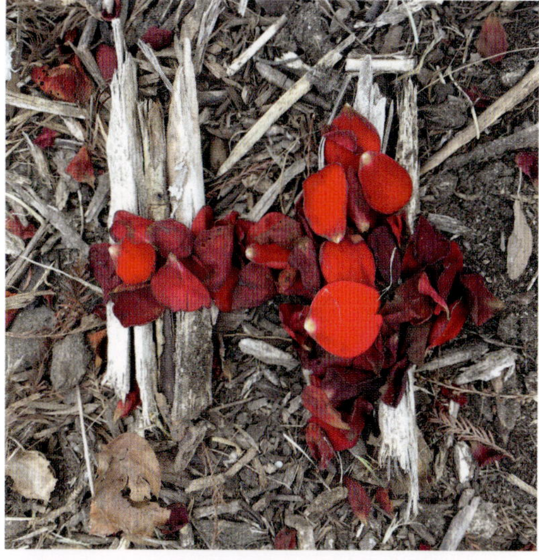

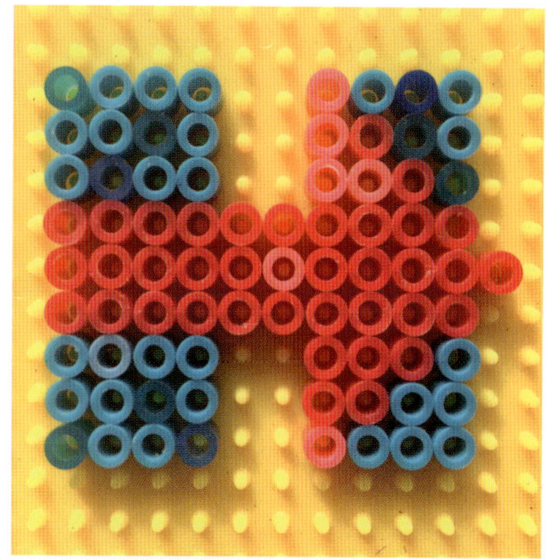

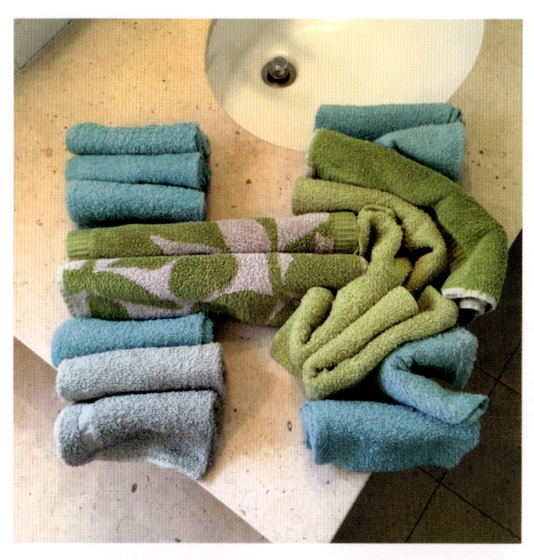

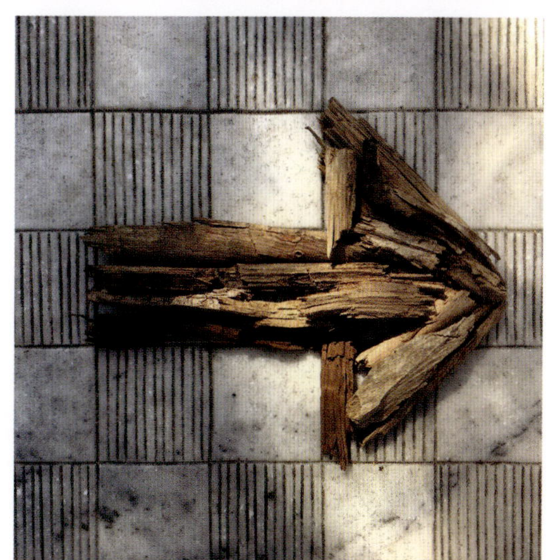

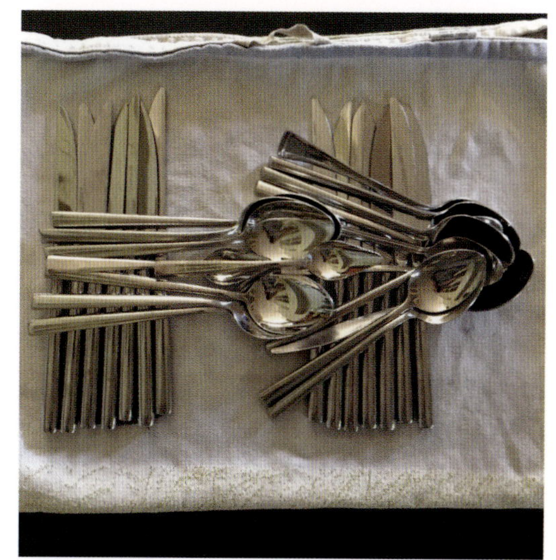

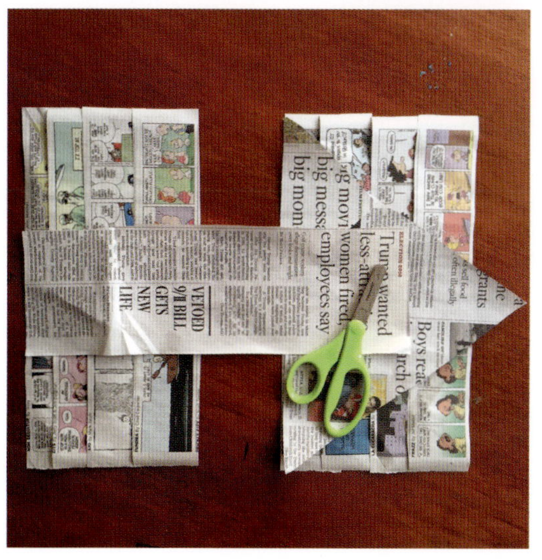
VETOED 9/11 BILL GETS NEW LIFE
Trump wanted
employees say

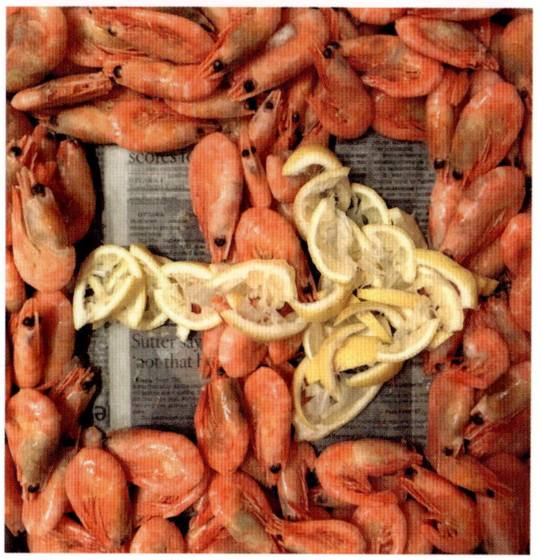

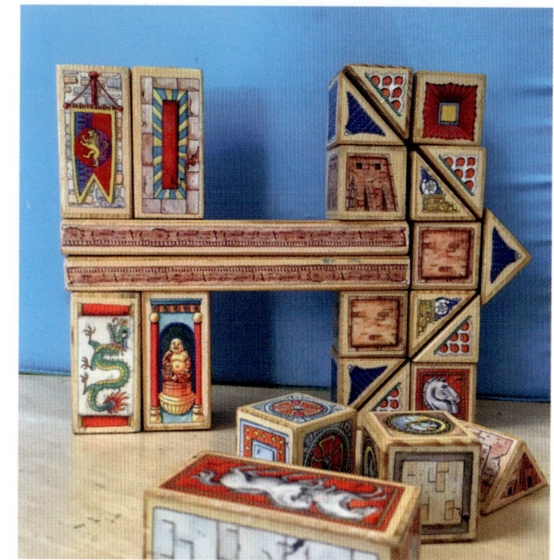

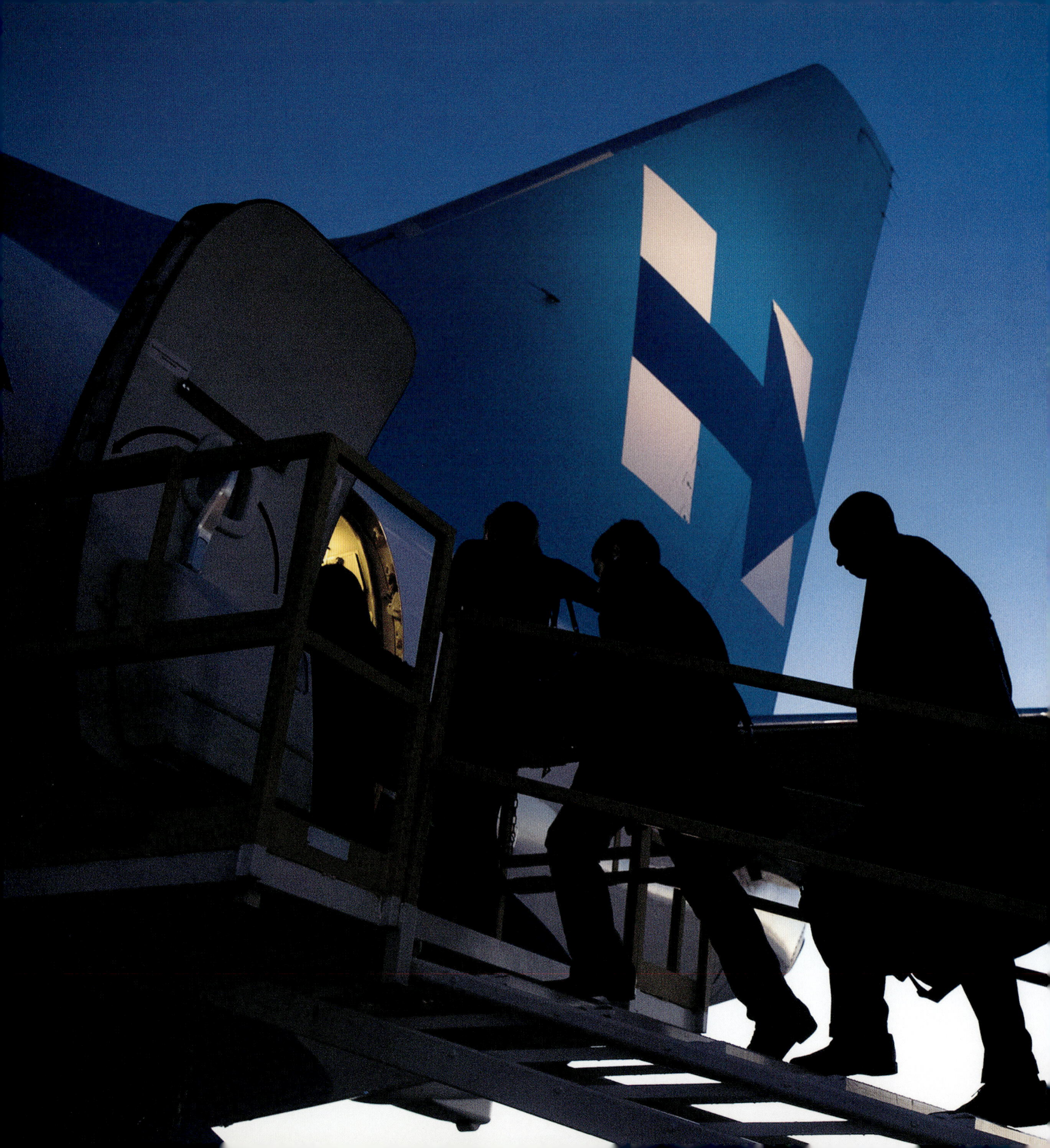

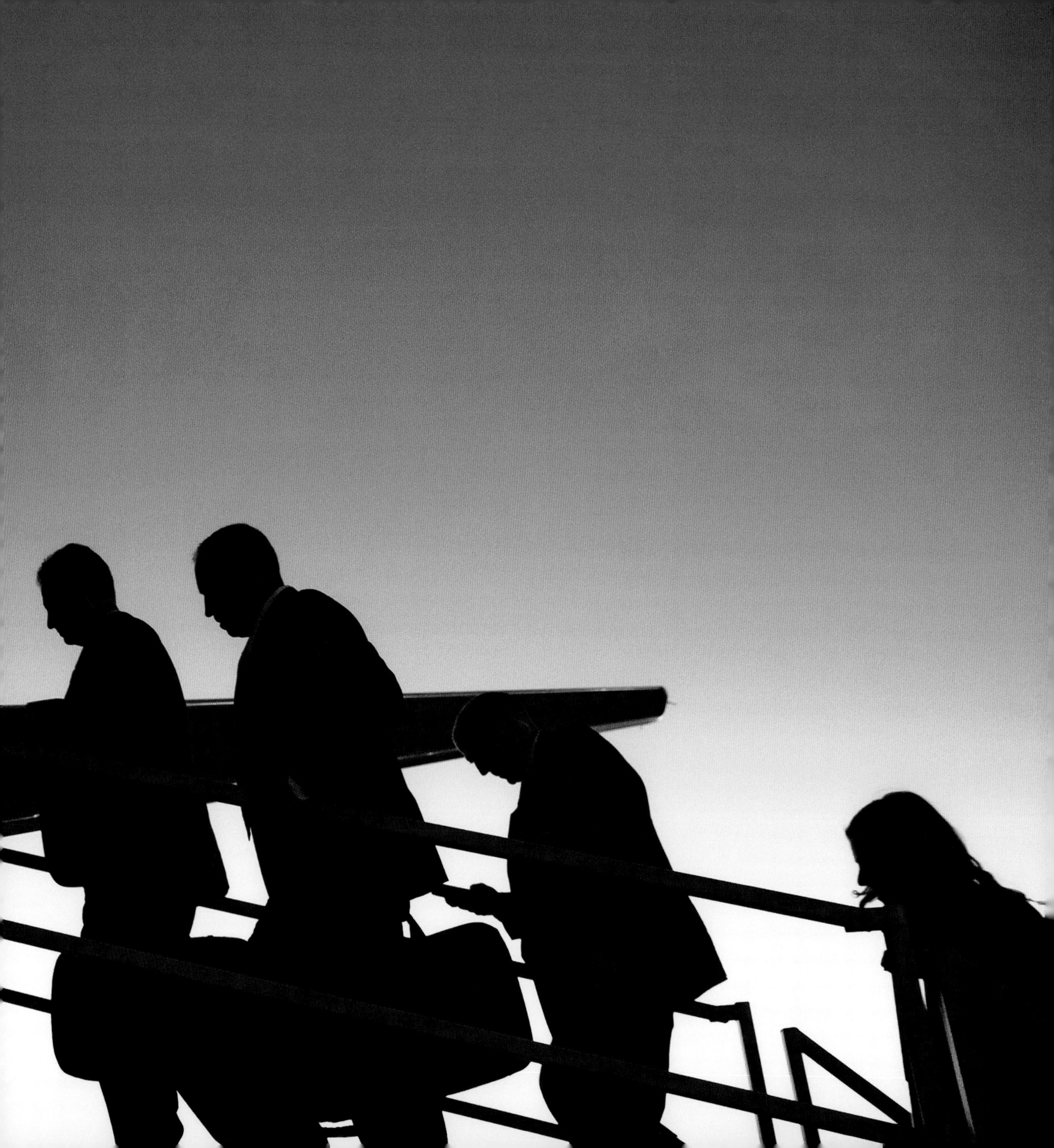

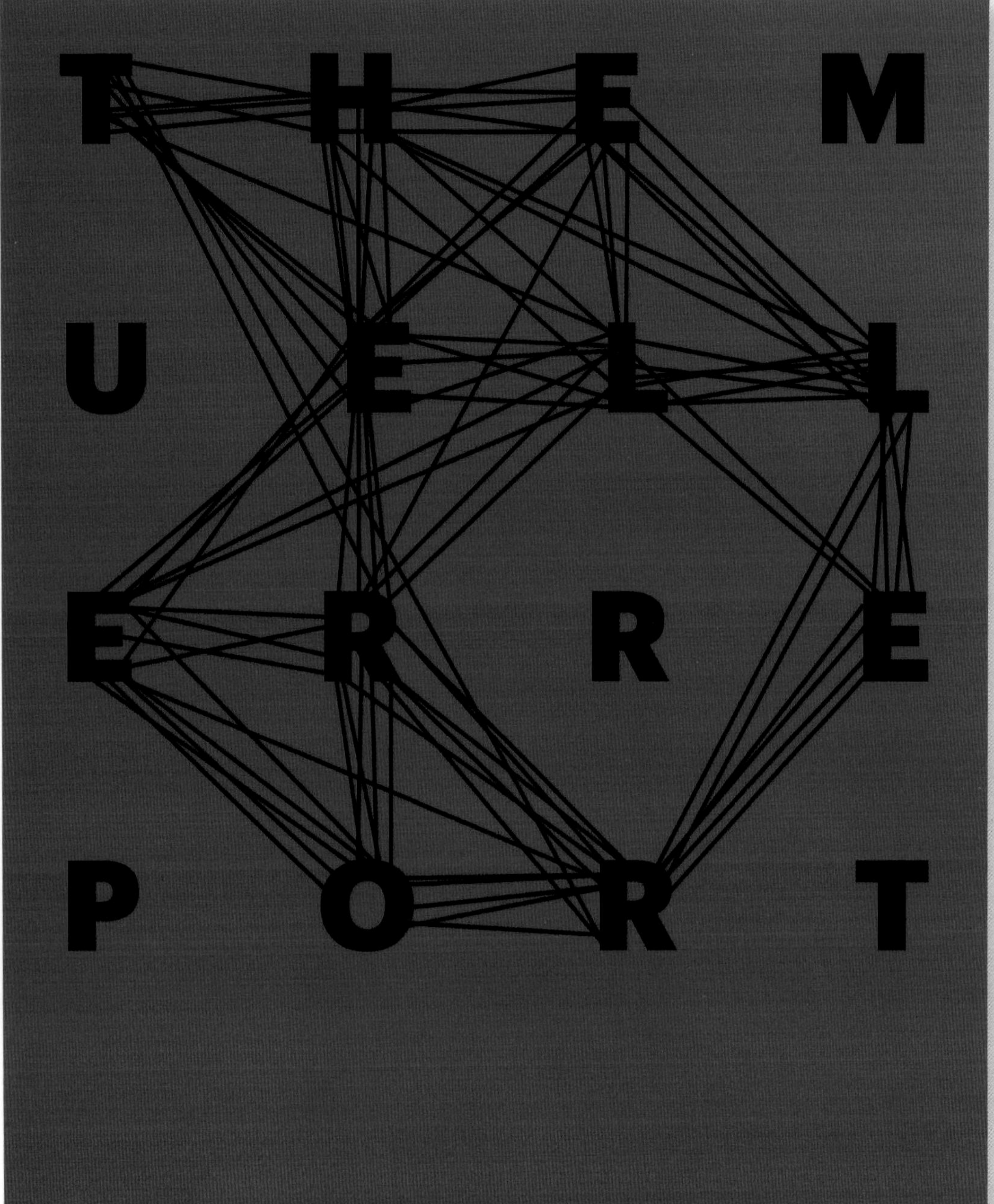

The Mueller Report

The Findings of the Office of the Special Counsel on Russian Interference in the 2016 Election

How to cover something up

The Mueller Report

The years since the 2016 election have been discouraging in so many ways. But there is cause for hope: the explosion of creativity on the part of activists at every level, addressing climate change, gun violence, racial injustice, and more. Everyday citizens have created protest signs, murals, videos, and a one-page guide to knitting a pink hat. As a result, indelible images have reached hundreds—or hundreds of thousands, even millions—of people. Social media has neutralized the authority of traditional gatekeepers. This shift can be disconcerting to professional designers, but I find it thrilling.

After the 2016 election, I wasn't sure what role design could play in politics. In many ways, I'm still not sure. I still feel that clarity is better than confusion; that intelligence is better than stupidity; and that if something is worth doing, it's worth doing well. What I still wonder, at least in the world of politics, is: Can professionalism be a substitute for passion? Will artifice, no matter how beautifully wrought, ever be as effective as authenticity? Sometimes, the best response is to amplify the most passionate and authentic voices you can find. As a result, I've declined a lot of invitations and let others do the talking.

I did take on one political assignment, cerebral but cathartic. Prior to the publication of special counsel Robert Mueller's report on Russian interference in the 2016 election, the *New Yorker* asked a handful of designers to imagine what its cover might be. Weird coincidences and too-tidy arithmetic are components of conspiracy theories, but they proved unavoidable. I arranged the report's 16-letter title in an orderly if less-than-intelligible pattern; a web of lines evoked the sinister connections between the players. I realized that it might look better if some elements lay outside the web. Five letters revealed themselves as if on a Ouija board, leaving the main protagonist frustratingly untouched. It was a depressingly prescient intellectual exercise and a reminder that the most important marks we can make are on ballots.

Opposite
Nicholas Blechman of the *New Yorker* asked Janet Hansen, Na Kim, Alex Merto, Paul Sahre, and me to create imaginary covers for the Mueller Report. Can you find the hidden patterns in my proposal?

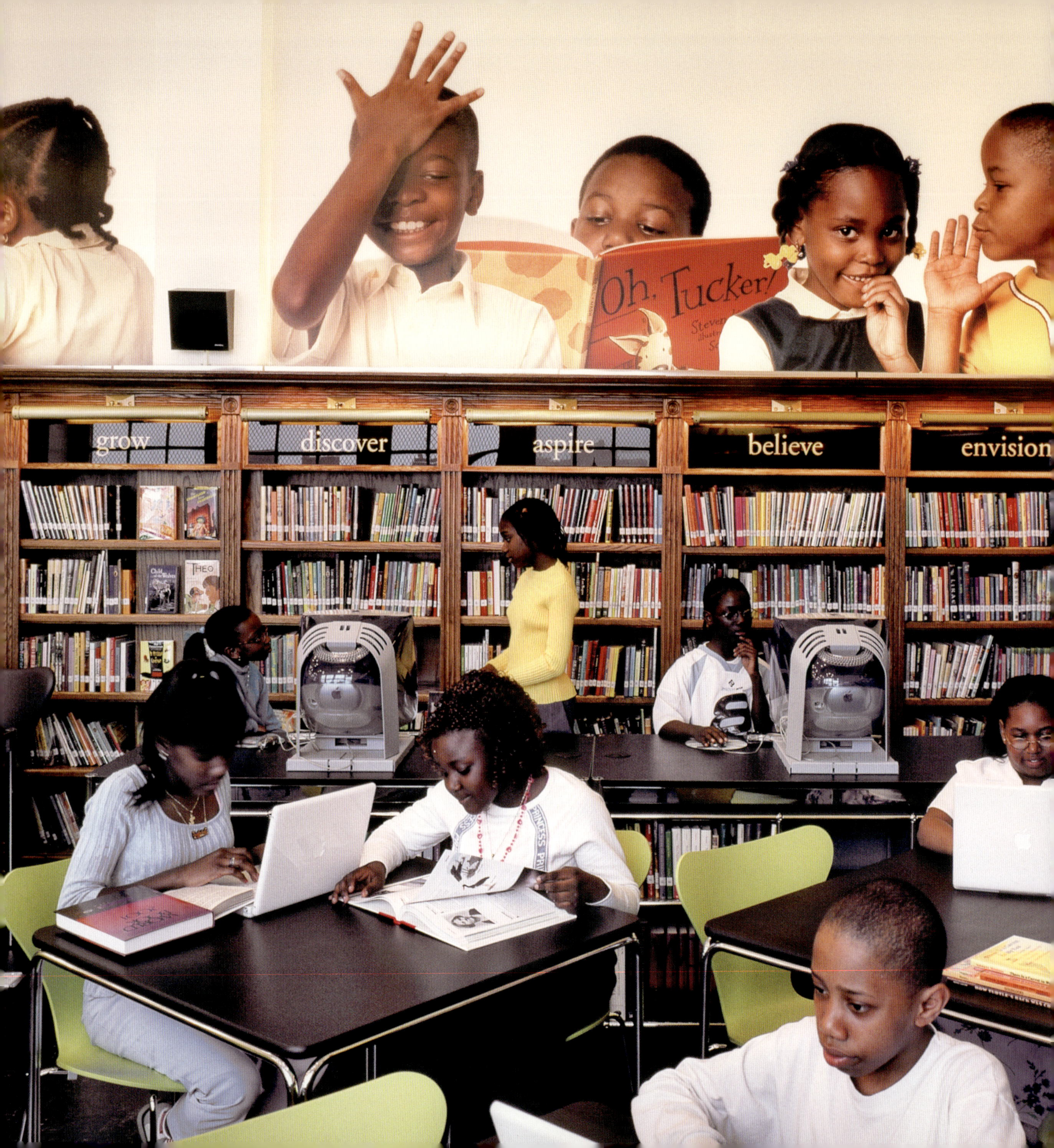
Oh, Tucker!
grow
discover
aspire
believe
envision

How to save the world with graphic design

The Robin Hood Foundation's Library Initiative

Opposite
One of my favorite projects began with a technical problem. Designing graphics for libraries in schools throughout New York City, we learned that the buildings were old and the ceilings were high. But the kids were little, so the highest shelf they could reach was only halfway up the wall. What could fill the rest of that space? At P.S. 184 in Brooklyn, the answer was oversized portraits by my wife, Dorothy Kresz.

The Robin Hood Foundation had taken on a big challenge: transforming the quality of education at public schools in some of New York's toughest neighborhoods by focusing their attention on a single room, the school library. A group of architects was asked to design the libraries, and we volunteered to be the project's graphic designers.

Our assignment seemed clear: give the program a logo, and create signs to identify the participating schools. We were almost done when one of the architects asked us to help fill the space between the kid-size shelves and the high ceiling. I pictured a modern version of a classical frieze along the top of the walls, celebrating not ancient gods but the kids themselves. My wife, Dorothy, took their portraits. It became a favorite in the system. Every school wanted a mural.

The new libraries were opening in places like Harlem, East Brooklyn, and the South Bronx, serving hundreds of children and, after school, their communities. We decided to make each mural different. We asked illustrators Lynn Pauley and Peter Arkle to do portraits. Designers like Christoph Niemann, Charles Wilkin, Rafael Esquer, Stefan Sagmeister, and Maira Kalman agreed to contribute.

One day, we took a tour of the completed libraries. It was thrilling to see them filled with kids that might discover their futures there, as I had so many years ago in my own school library. Our last stop was at the end of the school day. It was getting late. As the librarian was closing up, she asked, "Would you like to see how I turn out the lights?" Slightly baffled, I said, sure. "I always turn this light out last," she explained. It was the one that lit the mural of the faces of the school's students. "I like to remind myself why we do all this."

I understood only then the real purpose of our project: to help this librarian and the dozens like her to do their jobs better. In a way, this is the only purpose my work has ever had. For design can't save the world. Only people can do that. But design can give us the inspiration, the tools, and the means to try. We left determined to keep trying.

The Robin Hood Foundation is New York's most remarkable charity. True to its name, it takes money donated by the city's wealthiest citizens and uses 100 percent of those funds to help the city's poorest. Robin Hood's genius is finding ways to magnify the impact of those dollars, often using design as a tool. The Library Initiative, which rallied dozens of publishers, builders, and architects, is a perfect example. As the project's graphic design directors, we asked the best illustrators and designers in New York to join us in transforming the one room in a public school where students are most likely to learn in a group environment: the library.

Below
Reasoning that a new idea needed a new name, I wasted a lot of time coming up with puns like "The Red Zone" and acronyms like "OWL" (which I recall stood for Our World Library or something). The project's guiding light, Robin Hood's Lonni Tanner, hated them. I protested that kids think that libraries are boring. "Michael," she told me, "most of our kids have never seen a real library." Set straight, we did a straightforward logo, hinting that these particular libraries were something special just by tinkering with one letter.

Opposite
Because we weren't designing a franchise operation, we decided to come up with a different approach to each library's graphics. This impractical choice complicated our efforts substantially, but a customized solution made each space much more memorable, such as this grand entrance at C.S. 50 in the Bronx, designed by architect Henry Myerberg.

Next spread
We asked the best artists in New York to contribute to the library project. Illustrator Peter Arkle interviewed students and included their words in his black-and-white portraits at P.S. 287 in Brooklyn, designed by architect Richard Lewis.

L!BRARY

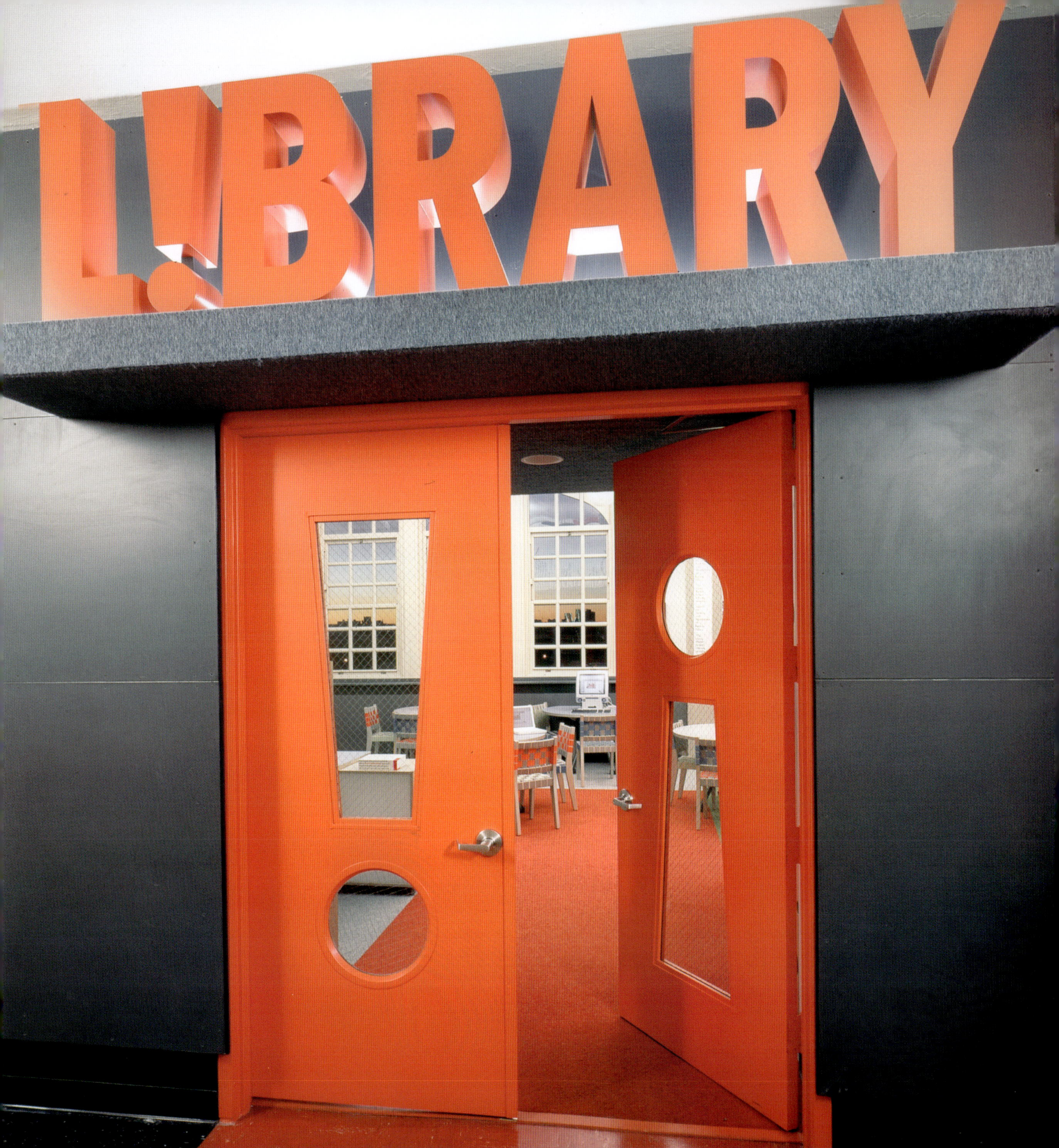
L!BRARY

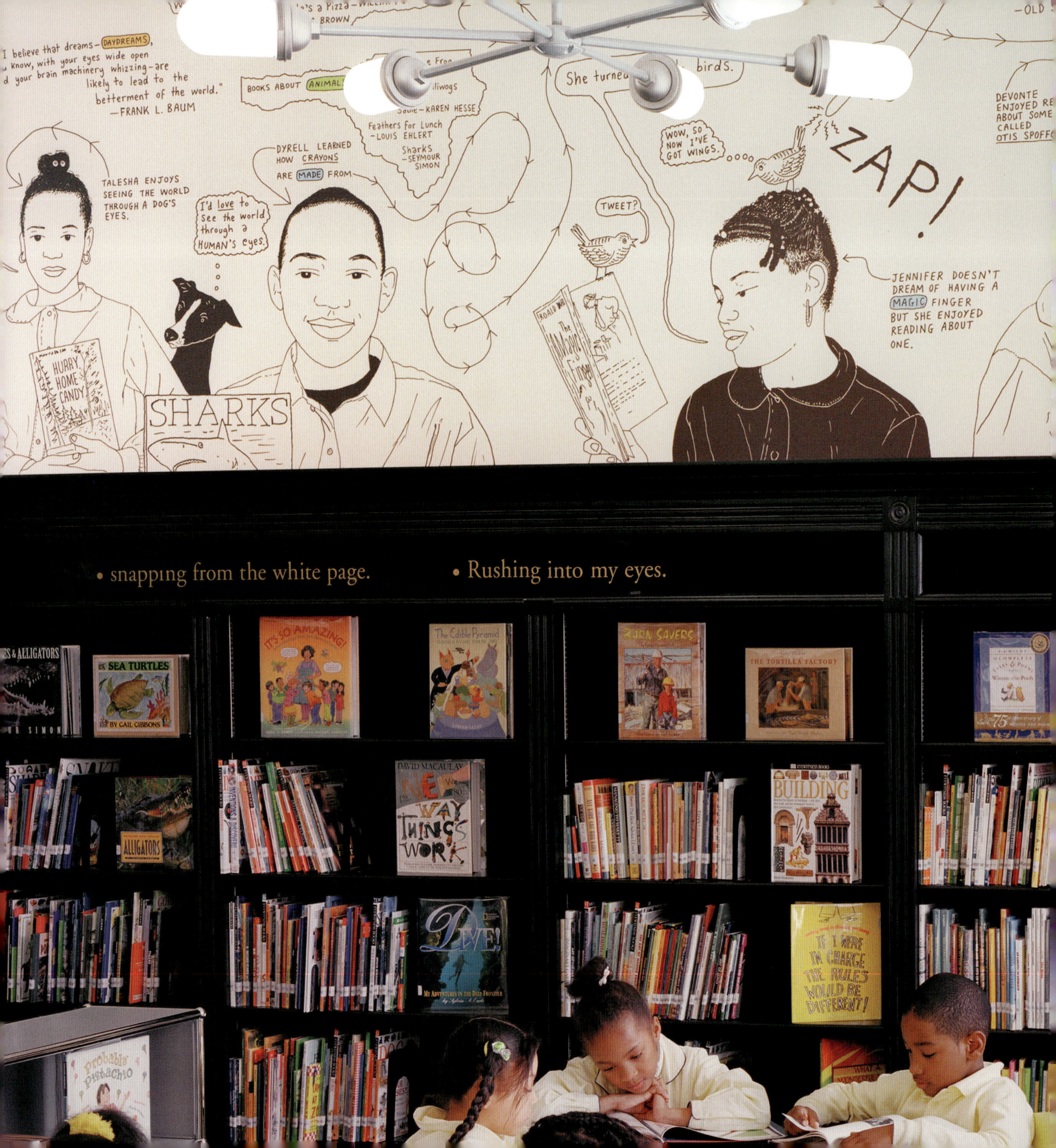

I believe that dreams—DAYDREAMS, you know, with your eyes wide open and your brain machinery whizzing—are likely to lead to the betterment of the world."
—FRANK L. BAUM
BOOKS ABOUT ANIMALS
Feathers for Lunch
—LOUIS EHLERT
Sharks
—SEYMOUR SIMON
—KAREN HESSE
She turned
birds.
WOW, SO NOW I'VE GOT WINGS.
ZAP!
DEVONTE ENJOYED READING ABOUT SOME CALLED OTIS SPOFF
TALESHA ENJOYS SEEING THE WORLD THROUGH A DOG'S EYES.
I'd love to see the world through a HUMAN'S eyes.
DYRELL LEARNED HOW CRAYONS ARE MADE FROM
TWEET?
JENNIFER DOESN'T DREAM OF HAVING A MAGIC FINGER BUT SHE ENJOYED READING ABOUT ONE.
HURRY, HOME CANDY
SHARKS
The Magic Finger
• snapping from the white page.
• Rushing into my eyes.
SEA TURTLES
BY GAIL GIBBONS
IT'S SO AMAZING!
The Edible Pyramid
BARN SAVERS
THE TORTILLA FACTORY
ALLIGATORS
THE NEW WAY THINGS WORK
DAVID MACAULAY
BUILDING
DIVE!
IF I WERE IN CHARGE THE RULES WOULD BE DIFFERENT!
Probably Pistachio

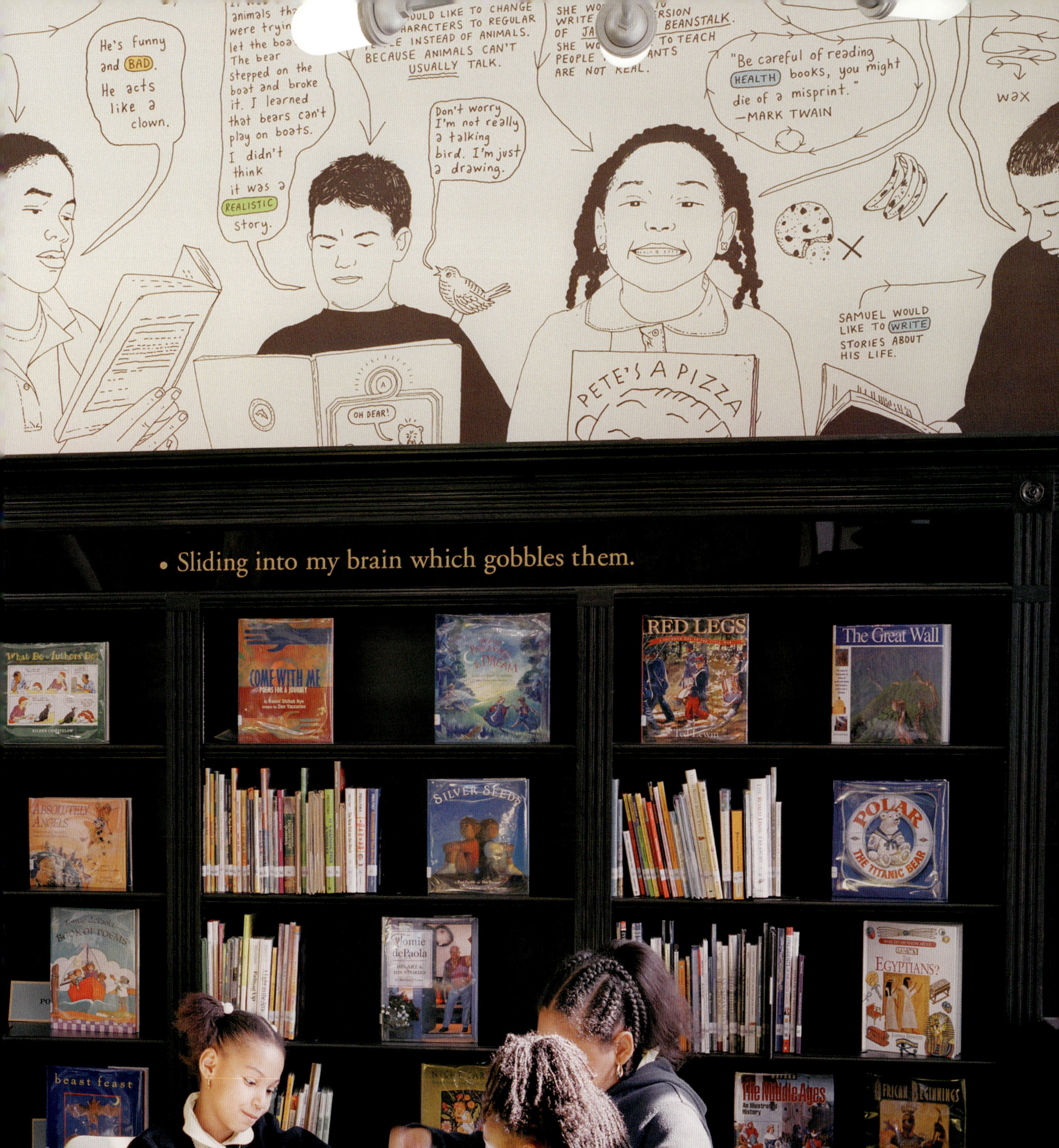

He's funny and BAD. He acts like a clown.
The bear stepped on the boat and broke it. I learned that bears can't play on boats. I didn't think it was a REALISTIC story.
BECAUSE ANIMALS CAN'T USUALLY TALK.
Don't worry I'm not really a talking bird. I'm just a drawing.
OH DEAR!
PETE'S A PIZZA
"Be careful of reading HEALTH books, you might die of a misprint." —MARK TWAIN
wax
SAMUEL WOULD LIKE TO WRITE STORIES ABOUT HIS LIFE.
• Sliding into my brain which gobbles them.
COME WITH ME
RED LEGS
Ted Lewin
The Great Wall
SILVER SEEDS
POLAR THE TITANIC BEAR
Tomie dePaola
EGYPTIANS?
beast feast
The Middle Ages

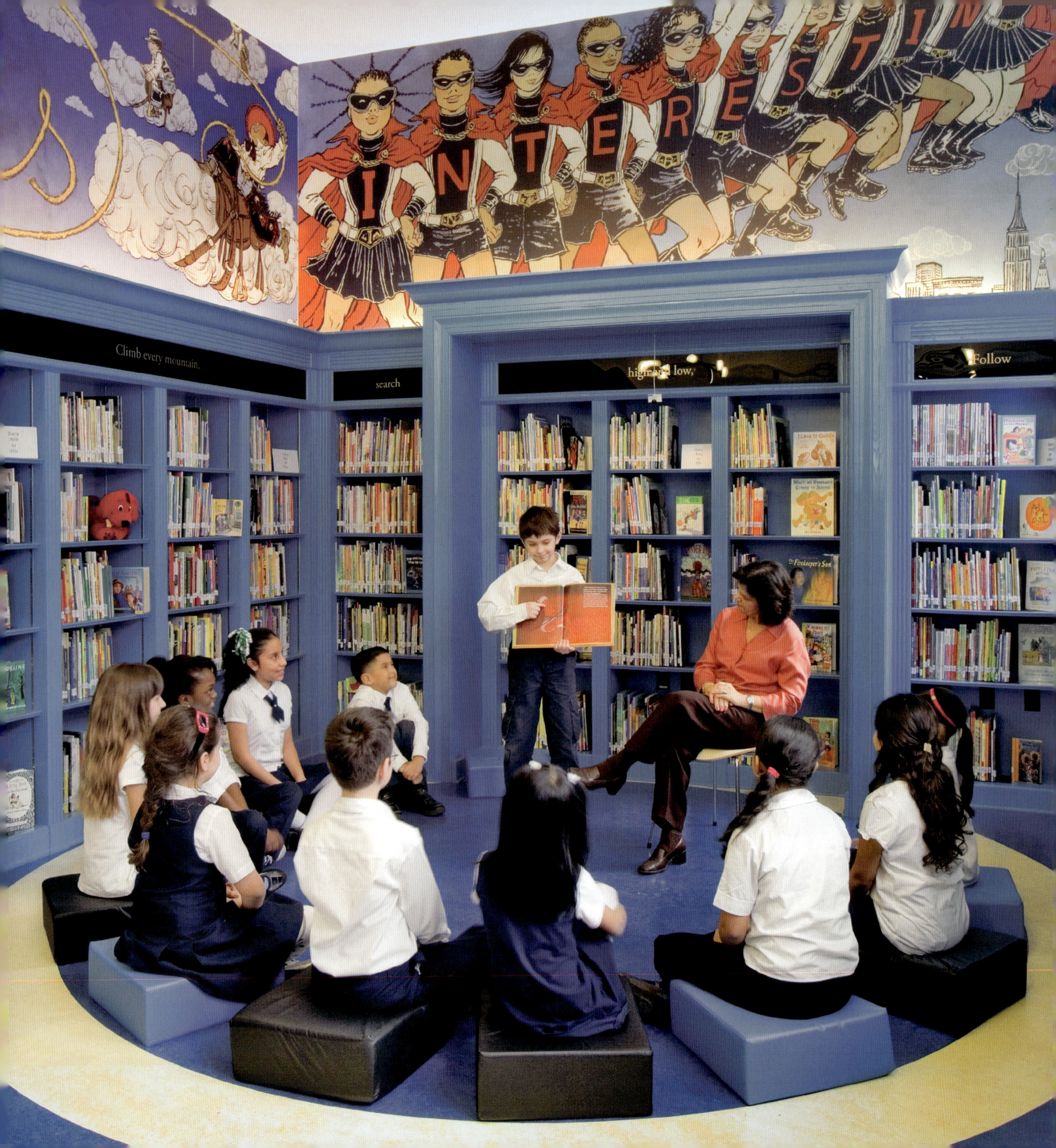
Climb every mountain.
search
Follow

Opposite
Designer Stefan Sagmeister and illustrator Yuko Shimizu bring the phrase "Everybody who is honest is interesting" to life on the walls of P.S. 96 in the Bronx.

Right top
Illustrator Lynn Pauley traveled from school to school painting portraits of students in a variety of styles for several libraries, including P.S. 36 in the Bronx.

Right bottom
At P.S. 196 in Brooklyn, designer Rafael Esquer created murals that illustrated the words of students in thousands of tiny silhouettes.

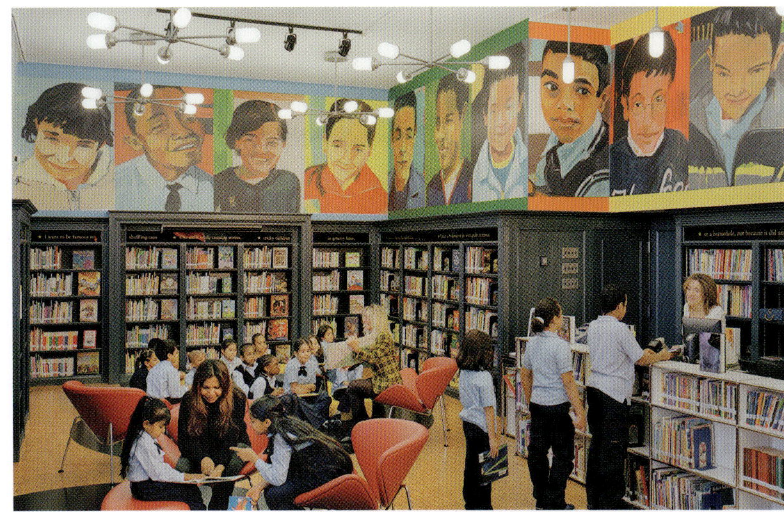

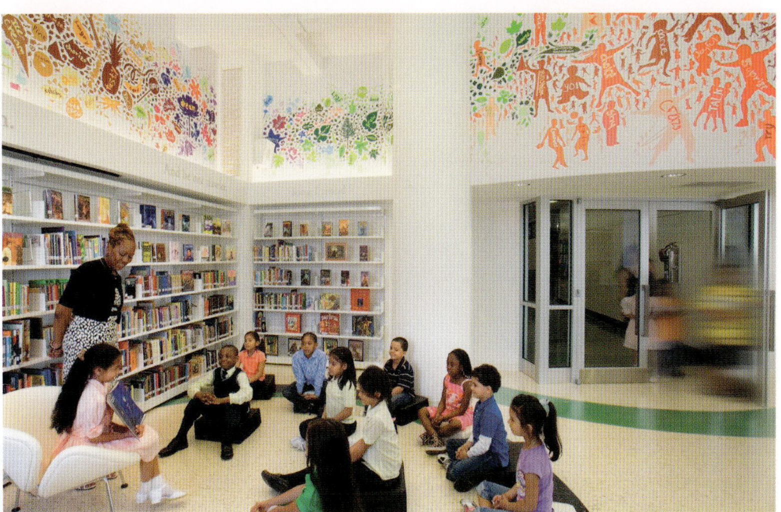

Next spread
Christoph Niemann's mural at P.S. 69 in the Bronx playfully integrated books into various images: Ahab's whale, an eagle's wings, and the American flag.

Following spread
Writer and illustrator Maira Kalman invented a three-dimensional installation that included images, objects, and her own idiosyncratic handwriting.

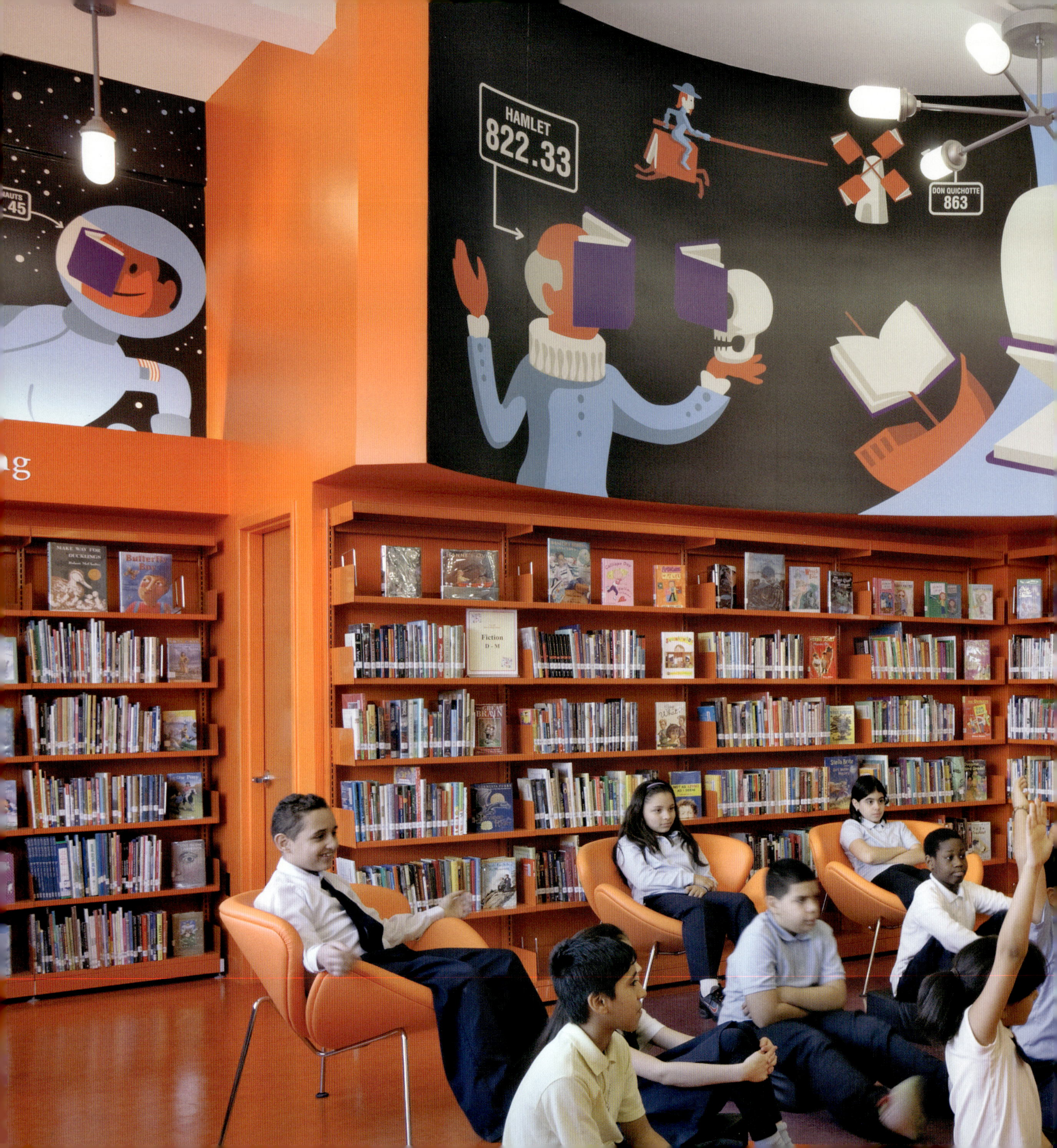
HAMLET
822.33
DON QUICHOTTE
863
Fiction
D – M

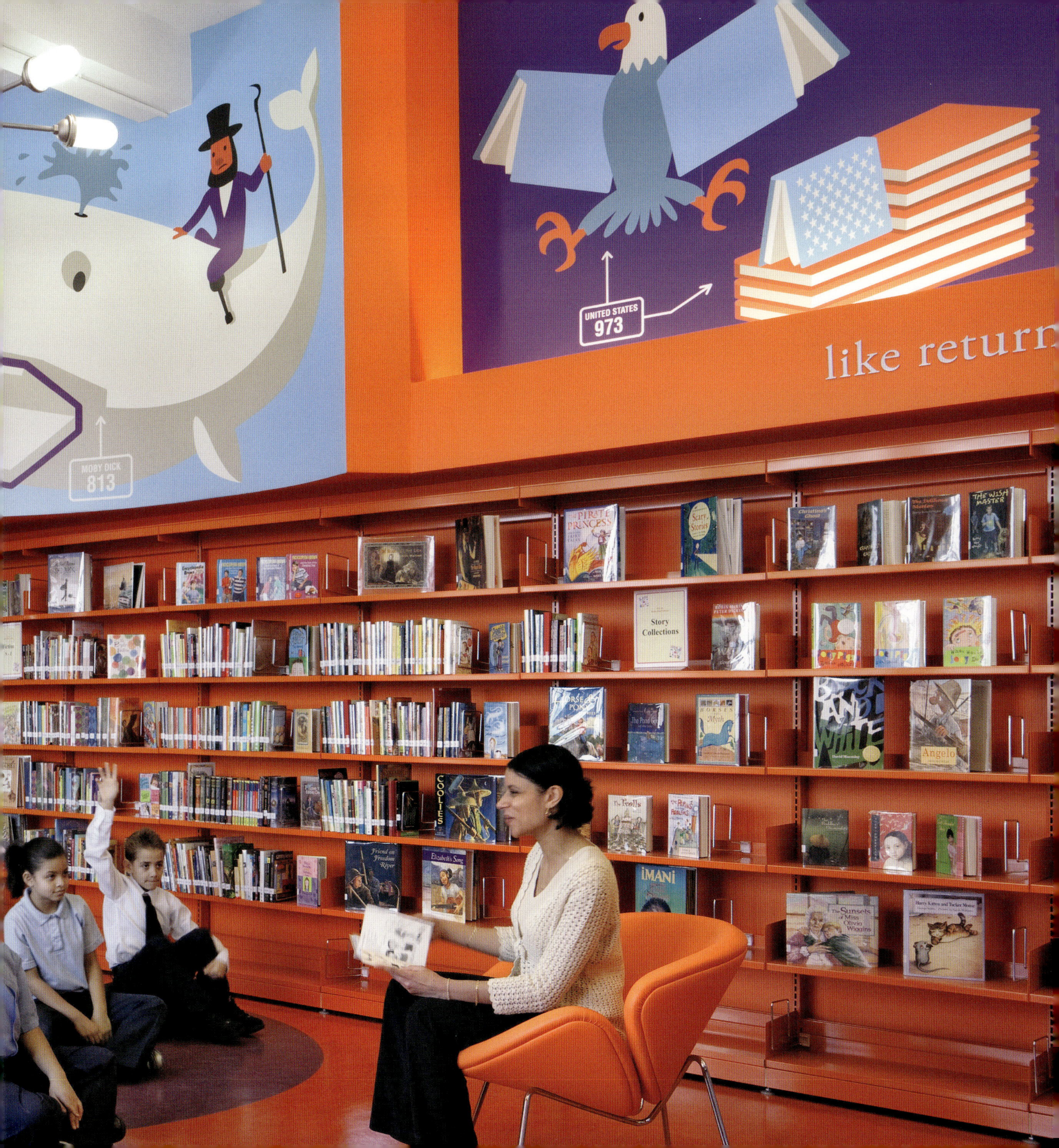
MOBY DICK
813
UNITED STATES
973
like return
Story Collections

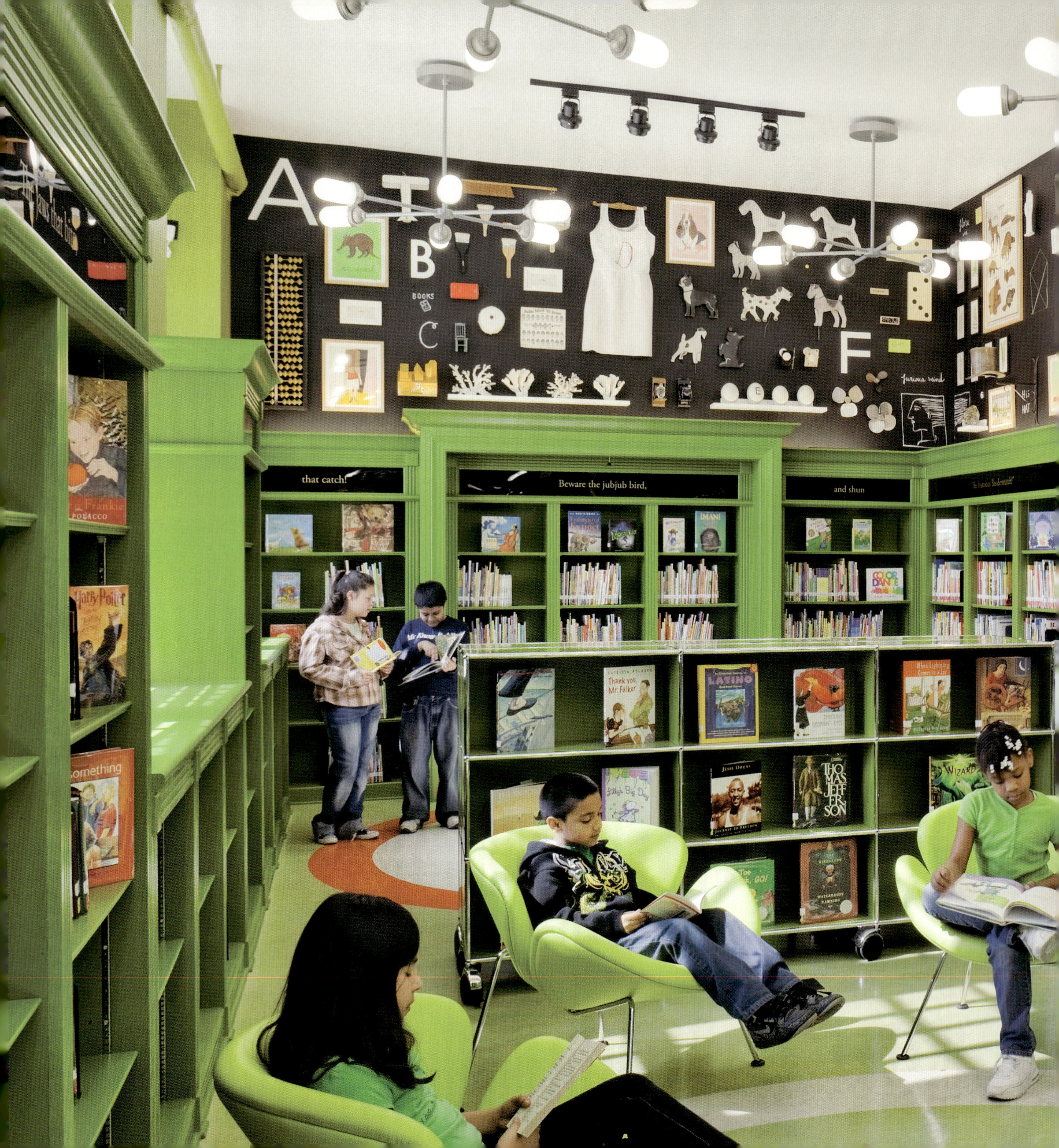

that catch!
Beware the jubjub bird,
and shun
Harry Potter
Frankie
something
Thank you, Mr. Falker
LATINO
THOMAS JEFFERSON
COLOR DANCE
IMANI
WIZARD

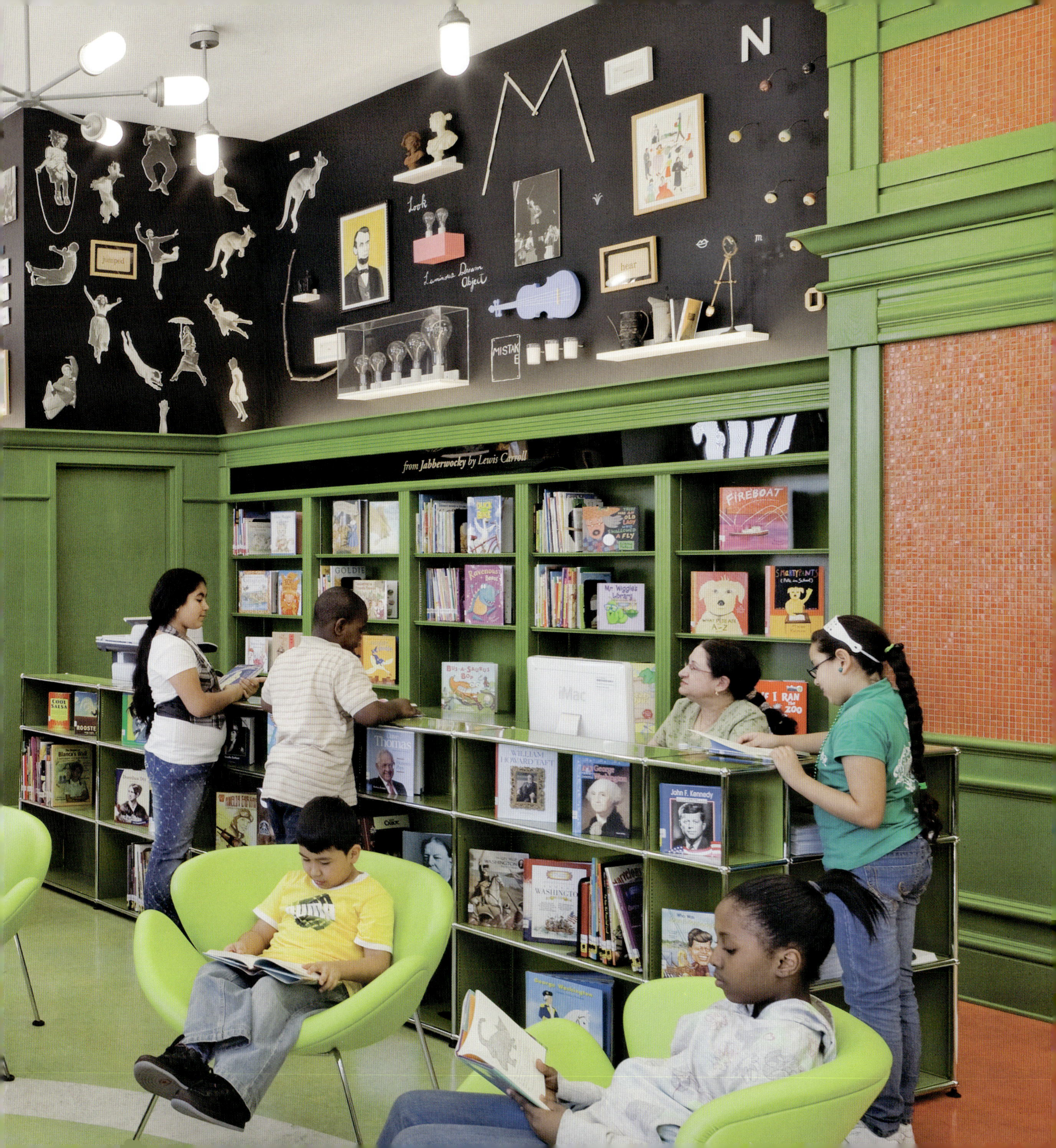

jumped
Look
hear
from Jabberwocky by Lewis Carroll
FIREBOAT
Mr Wiggles Library
iMac
WILLIAM HOWARD TAFT
John F. Kennedy
COOL SALSA

Acknowledgments

This book is dedicated to the memory of two extraordinary men: Massimo Vignelli and William Drenttel. From Massimo, I learned how to be a designer. From Bill, I learned that there were no limits to what a designer could contribute to the world. I strive to reach the standards they set.

Long before I knew what a graphic designer was, my parents, Leonard and Anne Marie Bierut, encouraged me to be an artist. My parents and my wonderful brothers, Ronald and Donald, must have found me baffling, but they usually managed to conceal it. They were the best thing about growing up in suburban Cleveland.

In junior high school, in high school, and in college, I had remarkable, dedicated teachers like Sue Ann Neroni, John Kocsis, Gordon Salchow, Joe Bottoni, Anne Ghory-Goodman, Stan Brod, Heinz Schenker, and Robert Probst. When I entered the workplace as a lowly intern, Chris Pullman and Dan Bittman were my first bosses and my earliest mentors.

My life as a designer has been shaped by the 30 years I've spent as a partner at Pentagram. I am grateful to Colin Forbes, Woody Pirtle, and Peter Harrison, who put their faith in me at the very start. I am so proud to be part of an organization that includes amazing designers like Lorenzo Apicella, Jody Hudson-Powell, Angus Hyland, Domenic Lippa, Sascha Lobe, Jon Marshall, Justus Oehler, Harry Pearce, Luke Powell, Naresh Ramchandani, John Rushworth, William Russell, Astrid Stavro, DJ Stout, Yuri Suzuki, Marina Willer, and my favorite traveling companion Daniel Weil.

Most important are my partners in New York, past and present, who inspire me every day: James Biber, Michael Gericke, Luke Hayman, Natasha Jen, Giorgia Lupi, Abbott Miller, Emily Oberman, Eddie Opara, Lisa Strausfeld, and Matt Willey. Paula Scher and I joined Pentagram together, and she is still the person I am desperately trying to impress.

The work for which I cheerfully take credit is actually the product of many hands. My team has benefited from the many brilliant designers who decided to share a few years of their careers with me, including Naomi Abel, Sonsoles Alvarez, Katie Barcelona, Josh Berta, Rion Byrd, Tracey Cameron, Emily Hayes Campbell, Lisa Cerveny, Sachi Chandiramani, Britt Cobb, Karla Coe, Talia Cotton, Elizabeth Ellis, Aron Fay, Angie Foster, Sara Frisk, Agnethe Glatved, Chris Guerrero, Sunnie Guglielmo, Daisy Dal Hae Lee, Lisa Anderson Hill, Laitsz Ho, Elizabeth Holzman, Melissa Jun, Sera Kil, Jennifer Kinon, Julia Lemle, Michelle Leong, Jon Leuhmann, Dorit Lev, Julia Lindpaintner, Yve Ludwig, Joe Marianek, Abby Matousek, Susan May, Tess McCann, Katie Meaney, Delta Murphy, Asya Palatova, Karen Parolek, Camila Pérez, Kerrie Powell, Jesse Reed, Nicole Richardson, Katie Rominger, Kai Salmela, Jena Sher, Jonny Sikov, Niko Skourtis, Hamish Smyth, Trish Solsaa, Robert ("P.M.") Stern, Jessica Svendsen, Jacqueline Thaw, Brett Traylor, Armin Vit, and especially Tamara McKenna, who is the glue that holds everything and everyone together.

Thanks to everyone who has helped me to be a better writer over the years, especially Steve Heller, Chee Pearlman, Rick Poynor, and my guiding light, Jessica Helfand.

I undertook this project at the urging of Thames & Hudson's Lucas Dietrich. Thank you, Lucas. Andrea Monfried encouraged me to say yes, and gave me all the support I was too afraid to ask for. Thank you to Liz Sullivan and her team at Harper Design.

Chloe Scheffe was instrumental in the earliest stages of the design of this book; the absolutely heroic efforts of Sonsoles Alvarez are what brought it to completion. Julia Lindpaintner worked with Kurt Koepfle and Claire Banks to track down and credit dozens of photographs. Rebecca McNamara was a superb copy editor. Joshua Sessler and Judy Scheel provided critical professional advice.

Finally, anything good I've ever accomplished, including helping to raise three incredible people named Elizabeth, Drew, and Martha, is because of the 40 years of support I've received from the love of my life, the first and only girl I ever kissed. Dorothy, thank you for always being there for me.

Note to the Second Edition
I am grateful to Thames & Hudson and Harper Design for publishing a revised and expanded edition of this book. Much has changed in five years. The alterations I've made and the new work I've added reflects these changes, as well as the evolution of my ideas about the ways that design can respond to them.

I thank Britt Cobb and Lauren Fox for their help in bringing this volume up to date, to Camila Pérez for research, and Tamara McKenna for project management. Finally, my biggest debt of gratitude is, as always, to my designers, clients, friends, and collaborators. They never fail to remind me that graphic design is a social activity, and getting the chance to work together is the very best part.

Michael Bierut

Image credits

Peter Aaron/OTTO: 54–59; Richard Bachmann: 68 (right); Bob Barrie and Scott D'Rozario/Fallon: 236–237; Benson Industries: 158; Jim Brown: 170–171; Courtesy of Bulletin of the Atomic Scientists: 107; Cornell Capa, [Robert F. Kennedy campaigning for the Senate, Elmira, New York], 1964. International Center of Photography, The Robert Capa and Cornell Capa Archive, Gift of Cornell and Edith Capa, 1994 (155.1994): 271; Robert Capa, [Death of a Loyalist Militiaman, near Espejo, Córdoba front, Spain], 1936. International Center of Photography, The Robert Capa and Cornell Capa Archive, Gift of Cornell and Edith Capa, 2010 (2010.86.629): 273 (top); Emilio Callavino: 214; Courtesy of the Cathedral of St. John the Divine: 131, 136; Kevin Chu and Jessica Paul: 344, 345 (bottom); Brad Cloepfil: 166 (left top); Commodore Construction Corp: 283; Fred R. Conrad/The New York Times/Redux: 155 (bottom); Whitney Cox: 49 (bottom), 50–51; Steve Freeman, Christopher Little, and Rita Nannini: 66–69 (Princeton University "With One Accord" photographs); Lauren Fox: 295; Michael Gericke: 15 (bottom); Mitchell Gerskup: 52; Gori910/ Shutterstock: 266 (top); Timothy Greenfield-Sanders: 44 (hand photograph); David Grimes: 46–47; Andrew Harrer/Bloomberg/Getty: 328–329; Peter Harrison: 15 (top); David Heald: 165 (right); Hillary for America: 327, 330 (top right group of illustrations), 331 (bottom); Ronnie Kaufman/ CORBIS: 235 (top left); Robert King/Getty: 36 (bottom); Barbara Kinney/Hillary for America: 331 (top); Dorothy Kresz Bierut: 100; Richard Levine/ Age Foto Stock: 295 (top left); Cocu Liu: 267; Courtesy of Mastercard: 305–309; Peter Mauss/ Esto: 115 (top & bottom left), 116–117, 154, 159–163, 196, 198 (right), 282, 284–291, 338, 341–343, 345 (top), 346–349; OK McCausland: 272 (middle bottom); Doug Mills/The New York Times/Redux: 334–335; Daniel Mirer/CORBIS: 235 (bottom right); Courtesy of Mohawk: 257, 258 (top left), 260 (right); Courtesy of PentaCityGroup: 240, 244 (top), 248 (right); Pentagram: 16, 18–35, 38–39, 40, 41 (bottom), 42, 44, 48–49, 62–65, 68 (left), 69 (left), 70, 72–79, 86, 88–99, 106, 108–111, 118, 120, 122–124, 126–129, 132, 134–135, 137, 164, 168–169, 172–177, 200, 203 (bottom), 204–205, 208–209, 211–213, 219–220, 223, 224 (middle & bottom), 225 (middle left & top right), 226–227, 230–235, 246–247, 248 (left top & bottom), 249–256, 259 (bottom left), 261, 264, 266 (middle & bottom), 268–269, 272 (left bottom, right top & bottom), 276–277, 292–297, 300, 302–303, 310, 313, 316–323, 325; Edén Ramírez: 324; Jesse Reed: 330 (left); Antonov Roman/Shutterstock: 258 (left bottom); Courtesy of Saks Fifth Avenue: 112–113, 114 (right), 115 (right), 116–117, 119, 121; Nick Sansone: 272 (middle top); Martin Seck: 245, 274, 278–281; James Shanks: 224 (top), 225 (top left, bottom left, middle right, bottom right); Boris Spremo/ Getty: 53; Ezra Stoller/Esto, 165 (left), 197, 198 (left); Takito/Shutterstock: 258 (left middle); Sean Thorenson: 272 (top left); The New York Times: 156–157; Karen Todd: 332–333; Courtesy of United Airlines: 203 (top), 206–207, 228; Courtesy of Verizon: 298–299; Massimo Vignelli: 41 (top); Lannis Waters/The Palm Beach Post/ ZUMAPRESS.com: 36 (top); Anna Watts: 272 (middle center); Stephen Welstead/LWA/CORBIS: 235 (top right); Don F. Wong: 101–105; Reven T. C. Wurman: 80–85. Special thanks to Claudia Mandlik for Pentagram project photography.